Justice Blind?

IDEALS AND REALITIES

OF AMERICAN CRIMINAL JUSTICE

Second Edition

Matthew B. Robinson

Appalachian State University

PEARSON

Prentice
Hall

Upper Saddle River, New Jersey 07458

Library of Congress Cataloging-in-Publication Data

Robinson, Matthew B.
  Justice blind? : ideals and realities of American criminal Justice /
Matthew B. Robinson.—2nd ed.
    p. cm.
  Includes bibliographical references.
  ISBN 0-13-113787-5
  1. Criminal justice, Administration of—United States.   2. Social
justice—United States.   I. Title.

  HV9950.R635 2004
  364.973—dc22

                                                    2004007095

Executive Editor: Frank Mortimer, Jr.
Assistant Editor: Korrine Dorsey
Production Editor: Penny Walker, *The GTS Companies*/York, PA Campus
Production Liaison: Barbara Marttine Cappuccio
Director of Manufacturing and Production: Bruce Johnson
Managing Editor: Mary Carnis
Manufacturing Buyer: Cathleen Petersen
Creative Director: Cheryl Asherman
Cover Design Coordinator: Miguel Ortiz
Cover Designer: Jill Little
Cover Image: Bill Burrows, SIS.Images.com
Editorial Assistant: Barbara Rosenberg
Marketing Manager: Tim Peyton
Formatting and Interior Design: *The GTS Companies*/York, PA Campus
Printing and Binding: Phoenix Book Tech Park

Pearson Education LTD.
Pearson Education Singapore, Pte. Ltd
Pearson Education, Canada, Ltd
Pearson Education–Japan
Pearson Education Australia PTY, Limited
Pearson Education North Asia Ltd
Pearson Educaçion de Mexico, S.A. de C.V.
Pearson Education Malaysia, Pte. Ltd

10 9 8 7 6 5 4 3 2 1
ISBN 0-13-113787-5

Dedication

This second edition is dedicated to the memory of E. J. Williams, former friend and faculty member at Fayetteville State University in North Carolina. Thank you for your inspiration.

CONTENTS

PART I. THE "CRIMINAL JUSTICE SYSTEM": IDEALS AND REALITIES   1

CHAPTER ONE
What Is the Criminal Justice System? Ideals   3

CHAPTER TWO
The Role of Politics and Ideology in Criminal Justice: Realities   30

LIST OF FIGURES AND TABLES

FIGURES

TABLES

FOREWORD TO THE SECOND EDITION

On September 11, 2001, our country (and citizens from at least 80 other countries) was attacked by terrorists who flew our own airliners into the World Trade Center and the Pentagon, and who would have flown another plane into a target in Washington, DC—either the White House or the U.S. Capitol, according to most sources—if not thwarted by passengers and flight attendants. Since that day, the people and government of the United States of America have been obsessed with terrorism.

Terrorism generally refers to the use of violence to instill fear in order to achieve some political purpose. For example, *Merriam–Webster's Collegiate Dictionary*, 10th ed. (1998), provides this definition of terrorism: "the systematic use of terror (a state of intense fear) especially as a means of coercion . . . violence (as bombing) committed by groups in order to intimidate a population or government into granting their demands."

America's obsession with terrorism might lead you to believe that *crime* has taken a backseat in terms of importance. To a degree, this is true. Public opinion polls, for example, show that since September 11th, fear of and concerns about terrorism have been much higher than at any other time in modern history. Fear of and concerns about ordinary street crimes (even violent crimes such as school shootings and child abductions) have plummeted.

However, most, if not all, forms of terrorism are also crimes. You probably got a sense of that by reading the preceding definition of terrorism. Indeed, many criminologists would probably argue that the attacks of September 11th ought to be counted as homicides (murders). The approximately 3,000 people who died that day would be roughly one-fifth of the 15,980 people who were murdered by "ordinary" means in 2001. The U.S. government decided that the thousands of victims killed by terrorism on September 11th would not be officially called homicide victims, and thus their deaths were not included in the Federal Bureau of Investigation's *Uniform Crime Reports* (UCR), at least not as murders.

Yet our responses to the terrorist attacks were very similar to our responses to ordinary murders. They have been remarkably similar to the American criminal justice processes of police, courts, and corrections. For example, as the police do with alleged criminals, we investigated who committed the attacks, tried to learn how they organized and successfully carried out their plans, who funded them, and who supported and encouraged them, and even (to a much lesser degree) tried to understand their motivations. Although the attackers themselves were dead, we launched military action against Afghanistan, the country that was said to have harbored the attackers and allowed terrorist training camps to be run on its soil. As a result, as the courts do with alleged criminals, we detained thousands of individuals who were suspected of having "links to" or "connections to" or being "affiliated with" individual terrorists, terrorist groups, organizations that in some way support terrorism, and/or countries that support and encourage terrorism. Many of these individuals are still being detained as "enemy combatants" (rather than "prisoners of war")—in Cuba no less—so that they are not entitled to be treated in accordance with the Geneva Conventions for prisoners of war (POWs). Some have even been tried or waived their trials in favor of guilty pleas and are now being housed in correctional facilities.

So, the terrorist attacks of September 11th have great significance for an examination of crime. And America's response to these attacks, including the war on Iraq that the United States initiated in violation of international law, has great import for understanding where we are as a nation and where we are headed. Now, in addition to our "war on crime" and our "war on drugs," we also have a "war on terrorism." Each is just a part of the larger American war on anything and everything perceived as harmful to American interests.

Throughout this book, I examine America's war mentality and discuss how it is relevant to the main thesis of the text. I show, for example, that the antiterrorism laws in the United States have swung the pendulum farther toward a *crime control model* of criminal justice by eroding the Constitutional protections that Americans enjoy in order to make it easier for police, courts, and corrections to investigate, arrest, detain, convict, and punish terrorists. Additionally, I illustrate how media coverage of September 11th (and America's subsequent wars in Afghanistan and Iraq) created fear in Americans so that they are more likely to support tougher methods of crime fighting, even if it means giving up some of their own freedoms. Americans are also less likely even to question their own government and its actions, which inevitably can lead to the types of abuses of official power (such as corruption and wrongful conviction) and erosions of Constitutional protections that I documented in the first edition of this book and discuss in this second edition.

We have been told "September 11th changed everything." While that may not be true, it has significantly changed this book.

PREFACE

Injustice anywhere is a threat to justice everywhere.

— Martin Luther King, "A Letter from the Birmingham Jail"

As eloquently written by Dr. Martin Luther King, Jr., in his letter from a jail cell in Birmingham, Alabama, when an injustice occurs anywhere, justice everywhere is threatened. King wrote this letter on April 16, 1963, after being jailed for "civil disobedience," a peaceful, nonviolent form of resistance. The letter was his response to criticisms that, as an "outsider" from Atlanta, he had no business in Birmingham.

King countered:

> I cannot sit idly by in Atlanta and not be concerned about what happens in Birmingham. . . . We are caught in an inescapable network of mutuality, tied in a single garment of destiny. Whatever affects one directly, affects all indirectly. Never again can we afford to live with the narrow, provincial "outside agitator" idea. Anyone who lives inside the United States can never be considered an outsider anywhere within its bounds.

So, injustice anywhere in America is a threat to all persons living in the United States. And injustice in America is every American's business. The injustices of American criminal justice are the motivation for this book.

As children, we grow up reciting Francis Bellamy's Pledge of Allegiance, written in 1892. It states, "I pledge allegiance to the flag of the United States of America, and to the Republic for which it stands, one nation (under God), indivisible, with liberty and justice for all." With liberty and justice for all—this is the ideal we all pledge to assure. But what are "liberty" and "justice"? And does "for all" really include all of us?

When I began my college experience as a criminology and criminal justice major, I had some ideas in my head about what agencies of criminal justice were supposed to achieve. I thought that police, courts, and corrections were supposed to protect us from harmful acts committed intentionally by other people. In my first semester, however, I learned that these agencies of criminal justice in the United States are focused on only a small portion of all harmful acts. Many other behaviors that are committed intentionally, acts that kill and injure people and result in loss of property, nevertheless are not "crimes" or are not vigorously pursued by such agencies.

Later, in graduate school, I learned about the massive criminal justice expansion of the last 30 years of the 20th century, an expansion driven not by facts about crime or increasing crime rates but by politics, fear, and the desire to be punitive—and at times downright hateful—toward certain segments of the population. To me, this incongruence between the ideals of American criminal justice and the realities of the American criminal justice didn't seem right.

How can the United States spend so much money and direct so much effort toward punishing a relatively small portion of harmful behaviors while virtually ignoring so many others? Why would we disinvest in the nation's future by overrelying on methods of crime control that we know are ineffective, while failing even to try methods that seem more promising? None of this seemed "just" to me.

If justice really meant what I had always thought it meant, how could criminal justice in the United States, of all places, be so unjust? That is the question addressed in this book. *Justice Blind? Ideals and Realities of American Criminal Justice* attempts to demonstrate how and why American criminal justice agencies fail to live up to their ideals and, thus, are unjust.

This book grew out of my experiences with teaching an introductory criminal justice course more than 30 times. Through my teaching, I realized that no introductory criminal justice text on the market exposed readers to the realities of criminal justice in the United States. This book strives to do that.

THE MAIN ASSERTION OF *JUSTICE BLIND?*

The book proceeds from the following assertions:

- Myths and stereotypes about crime, criminals, and criminal justice are created when acts are defined as crimes by the criminal law.
- These myths and stereotypes are reinforced as the mass media broadcast stories about crime, criminals, and criminal justice.
- These myths and stereotypes are also reinforced as police, courts, and corrections enforce the criminal law.
- Because the criminal law in the United States is inherently biased against certain groups (e.g., the poor, people of color, and women), the activities of police, courts, and corrections are also biased against these groups.

This does not suggest that the U.S. media, police, courts, and corrections are intentionally biased. Rather, by focusing on those acts that come to be defined as "serious" in the criminal law, each of these institutions becomes biased in an "innocent" way. The figure on page xix illustrates how this "innocent bias" is created in the United States. The arrows suggest that each step of the process affects all other stages—that is, that myths and stereotypes about crime, criminals, and criminal justice created by the criminal law are strengthened as agencies of criminal justice and the media operate. Throughout this book, I elaborate on this process and provide evidence for the main assertions listed here.

The Process of Innocent Bias

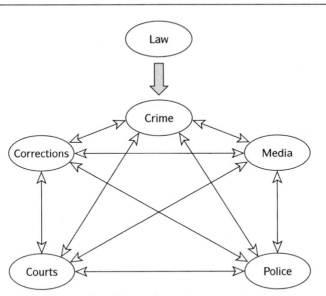

Source: Adapted from Robinson (2000: p. 136)

CHAPTER BY CHAPTER

The book is divided into four main parts. In Part I, The "Criminal Justice System": Ideals and Realities, I discuss the most important issues necessary to gaining a complete understanding of the reality of criminal justice practice in the United States. In Chapter One, I define the common term *criminal justice system* and show that there really is no such thing as a system of criminal justice in the United States. Nevertheless, I seek to identify the ideal goals of what I term the *criminal justice network*—that is, what American criminal justice is supposed to be aimed at achieving. At the end of Chapter One, in the Issue in Depth, I take a close look at Lady Justitia, whose image adorns the cover of this book.

In Chapter Two, I explore alternative goals of criminal justice, including serving limited interests and controlling the population. In this chapter, I discuss the role of politics and ideology in American criminal justice to provide a more realistic assessment of what criminal justice is really all about. These important topics were investigated briefly in Chapter One of the first edition but have been developed into a new chapter here so as to discuss them more fully. The new Issue in Depth at the end of Chapter Two examines the issue of what impact "McDonaldization" has had on American criminal justice, showing that the overriding ideology of American criminal justice clearly parallels that of our fast-food industry.

In Chapter Three, I begin my analysis of actual criminal justice practice with an examination of the lawmaking process. In this chapter, I explore American law, including types of law, purposes of criminal law, and a detailed examination of who makes the law and votes for it. I also provide a detailed satisfaction on how money shapes politics. A new section has been added that illustrates how the criminal law fails to protect Americans. A new Issue in Depth has also been added at the end of the chapter, examining laws that have been passed to fight terrorism in the United States. These laws erode basic freedoms and thus provide a good example of the struggle to balance crime prevention efforts with protections of our own rights.

In Part II of the book, Crime: Images and Realities, I discuss the most important issues necessary to gaining a complete understanding of crime in the United States. In Chapter Four, I define the term *crime* and lay out different types of crime in the United States. In this chapter, I also discuss different sources of crime data and then examine long-term crime trends. Most importantly, I identify the most dangerous forms of crime in America—white-collar deviance. A detailed examination of recent large-scale financial scandals involving companies such as Enron, WorldCom, Tyco, and many others is added in a new Issue in Depth at the end of the chapter.

In Chapter Five, I examine the role of the media in crime and criminal justice. Because no one can fully understand crime or criminal justice activity without understanding how these issues are framed in the mass media, this chapter is one of the most important in the book. I have added a new Issue in Depth to show how the tragedy of September 11, 2001, has been used for political gain and ratings by mainstream media outlets. My goal in this chapter is to illustrate how media inaccuracy drives dangerous criminal justice policies.

In Part III of the book, Components of Criminal Justice: Police, Courts, and Corrections, I discuss the basics of police, courts, and corrections (as in all introductory texts) and provide detailed, critical assessments of each component of criminal justice (unlike most introductory texts). In Chapter Six, I not only provide descriptions of who the police are, how policing is organized in the United States, and basic responsibilities of American police officers, but also carefully examine the realities of American policing. I introduce the concept of "innocent bias" to show the fundamental flaws of policing in the United States and examine differential stop rates and arrest rates and issues such as the use of force, opinion of the police, and corruption in American policing. The Issue in Depth at the end of the chapter deals with corruption in criminal justice generally and law enforcement particularly.

In Chapter Seven, I examine basic court issues such as the organization of courts in the United States, basic court functions, and responsibilities of the courtroom workgroup. I also discuss injustices in pretrial procedures such as bail and plea bargaining, as well as in trial procedures. I have added a new section on the imbalance of power in the court, demonstrating how power has been shifted from judges to prosecutors over the past 30 years. In the Issue in Depth at the end of the chapter, I examine the causes of wrongful conviction.

In Chapter Eight, I examine numerous aspects of punishment, including sentencing and justifications for punishment. In this chapter, I also examine the relative effectiveness of certain types of punishment and the issue of bias in the sentencing process. A new Issue in Depth has been added to the end of the chapter, in which I discuss the argument of a notable criminologist as to why we should expect American criminal punishment to fail to reduce crime appreciably.

In Chapter Nine, I deal with issues related to incarceration and compare America's incarceration rate with that of other countries. In this chapter, I illustrate who is in the nation's jails and prisons and what happens to inmates while in prison and after release. Finally, I explain how and why corrections reflects criminal justice bias. At the end of the chapter, I have added a new Issue in Depth that examines the emergence of the "Convict School of Criminology."

In Part IV of the book, Bad Criminal Justice Policy and How to Fix This Mess, I examine criminal justice practices that many people in criminology and criminal justice have now come to see as massive failures. In Chapter Ten, I discuss the most extreme form of punishment available, capital punishment. In this chapter, I discuss key death penalty facts and critically assess justifications for capital punishment. I also carefully examine the issue of public support for capital punishment and provide a thorough summary of alleged problems with the administration of the death penalty. The Issue in Depth is expanded to discuss findings from Parts I and II of a major death penalty report, which is a scathing indictment of the way we carry out capital punishment in the United States.

In Chapter Eleven, I discuss America's war on drugs, a significant part of America's war on crime. In this chapter, I examine the extent of drug use in the United States, harms associated with drugs, and provide a critical assessment of why some drugs are legal while others are not. Finally, using government data, I show precisely how the war on drugs causes more harm than it prevents. The Issue in Depth at the end of the chapter has been expanded and ends with a well-developed call for decriminalization of drugs.

In Chapter Twelve, I consider the implications of America's war on crime against relatively less powerful groups in the United States, including the poor, racial and ethnic minorities, and women. A new Issue in Depth has been added, one that examines the claim by a major civil rights group that American criminal justice practices pose a serious threat to civil rights.

Finally, in Chapter Thirteen, I conclude the book with a summary and a series of 50 recommendations for overcoming the problems identified in the book. I discuss the likelihood of success and end with a new Issue in Depth that documents various groups already working to overcome the problems outlined in the book and to achieve social justice.

FEATURES

Justice Blind? contains several useful features for students of criminology, criminal justice, sociology, social problems, political science, and related disciplines. Each chapter contains an Issue in Depth section that explores one issue raised in the chapter. Each chapter concludes with a series of discussion questions that deal with the important material discussed. Finally, the web site for *Justice Blind?* (www.justiceblind.com) will continue to offer various forms of activities, links, and PowerPoint slides that students, instructors, and general readers will find useful. Throughout the book, highlighted key terms appear, which are listed on the web site and can be defined by students to promote active learning.

TO THE READER

Unlike many introductory criminal justice texts, *Justice Blind?* contains a careful analysis of the role that race, class, and gender play in crime and criminal justice. The critical approach of *Justice Blind?* is also unique. Most introductory criminal justice texts start with the perspective that the American criminal justice system meets its ideal goals. They introduce and discuss main concepts and terms without offering critical assessments. I want you, the reader, to learn not only about the ideals of criminal justice in America, but also about the realities. Whereas other texts emphasize the way things are supposed to operate, this book places greater emphasis on the way agencies of American criminal justice system *really* operate.

This book focuses on injustice in criminal justice, an important topic for students and citizens alike to understand. Of course, people who study criminal justice and who work within agencies of

American criminal justice need to gain an understanding of basic, introductory-level concepts and issues to become more knowledgeable and to become better employees. Many fine texts are on the market to meet this need. But this book takes a different approach: It begins with injustice as a problem.

In fact, I suggest that injustice is a social problem that plagues the United States. Lauer and Lauer (2000), in their book, *Troubled Times*, write that social problems begin "as a sense of something wrong in society—of suffering and deprivation growing out of a situation of injustice." I hope that this book convinces you that something is very wrong with criminal justice in America. I hope that, because of this work, injustice within American criminal justice will be viewed as a significant social problem. This is why several of the topics addressed in this book (e.g., the death penalty; drug use; the role of race, class, and gender in criminal justice) also may be appropriate for social problems classes.

As you read this book, I challenge you to keep an open mind. Do not allow your deeply entrenched beliefs about crime, criminal justice, or politics interfere with your understanding of the main argument of the book. If this reading has been assigned to you, remember that you do not have to agree with the arguments I put forth in this book, but you do need to understand them. In fact, I challenge you to read the book from a critical perspective, not automatically believing everything you read. Read the book from a perspective that will allow you to discover your own truth. Your own truth, after all, is the only truth that will matter to you.

ACKNOWLEDGMENTS

This book is the product of many years of thought and study, both formal and informal. I would like to thank the faculty and staff of the Florida State University School of Criminology and Criminal Justice for the wonderful education I received there. Much of what I learned there inspired this book. Also, I want to thank my colleagues and friends at Appalachian State University, who made the transition to faculty life much easier and who gave me tremendous opportunities for personal and professional growth.

I also want to sincerely thank friends and colleagues around the country, especially within the Southern Criminal Justice Association (SCJA), many of whom have written and spoken about some of the same issues in their careers. I hope you know my work would not have been possible without yours.

I thank each of the reviewers for their hard work. I especially appreciate the feedback from David Friedrichs, Sarah Eschholz, and Ronald Iacovetta for the first edition; and Chuck Brawner, Gwen Hunnicutt, Long Le, Ray Newman, Gary Perlstein, and Gary W. Potter for the second edition; all reviewers who went above and beyond the call of duty. Thanks also to Derek Paulsen for reviewing my original chapter on the media. I offer my sincere thanks to my research assistants, Anna Sheely and Dickie Lee Brown, who helped me compile the extensive references. I also want to thank Kim Davies, who was senior acquisitions editor at Prentice Hall when she saw promise in the project, and all the fine people behind the scenes who worked very hard to make the final product come together. Thanks so much to my students at Appalachian State University, especially those who took my special topics class, Injustice in America, which led directly to this book. Finally, I must thank my loving and supportive families — the Robinsons, Andersons, Chiodos, Kings, Murphys, Clements, and Johnsons: I appreciate all of you so much more than you know.

THE "CRIMINAL JUSTICE SYSTEM": IDEALS AND REALITIES

CHAPTER ONE

WHAT IS THE CRIMINAL

JUSTICE SYSTEM? IDEALS

INTRODUCTION

What is the criminal justice system? Why do we have it? Does it achieve its goals? Are we winning the war on crime? If not, why not? This chapter introduces the ideal goals of what is called the criminal justice system, including doing justice and reducing crime. Although *justice* is difficult to define, at least two conflicting conceptions of justice emerge, consistent with two competing ideal models of justice, known as the *crime control* and *due process* models. This chapter demonstrates how criminal justice policy in the United States has shifted toward a crime control model of criminal justice over the past three decades, at the expense of individual Constitutional protections and due process. I suggest that failures of American criminal justice are explained by this shift. Finally, I examine the meaning of the Lady Justice, "Justitia," whose image adorns the cover of this book. I suggest that she should serve as a reminder of what justice is supposed to mean in terms of American criminal justice policy.

WHAT IS A SYSTEM?

According to *Merriam-Webster's Collegiate Dictionary*, 11th ed. (2003), a *system* is a

> regularly interacting or interdependent group of items forming a unified whole . . . a group of interacting bodies under the influence of related forces; an assemblage of substances that is in or tends to equilibrium; a group of body organs that together perform one or more vital functions; the body considered as a functional unit; a group of related natural objects or forces; a group of devices or artificial objects or an organization forming a network especially for distributing something or serving a common purpose; a form of social, economic, or political organization or practice; an organized set of doctrines, ideas, or principles usually intended to explain the arrangement or working of a systemic whole; a harmonious arrangement or pattern.

In this definition, the key words and phrases include *interdependent, unified whole, equilibrium, functional, common purpose, organized*, and *harmonious*. Thus, a system can be thought of as a group of parts that make up a unified whole, in balance, that depend on one another, and that serve a common purpose, in an organized and harmonious manner.

What Is the Criminal Justice System?

When people talk about the "criminal justice system," they are talking about its interdependent components—the police, courts, and correctional facilities within the federal government, as well as the agencies of criminal justice of each of the 50 states. Walker (1998, p. 26) thus claims that the United States actually has 51 criminal justice systems. Additionally, each state has scores of municipalities, each having its own law enforcement agencies and, in some cases, its own forms of courts and correctional facilities, as does the District of Colombia.

You can think of the criminal justice system as a whole made up of these three interdependent components, something like a pie with three pieces. Although each of these components has its own functions and personnel, they are expected to work together as a unified whole, in balance, to serve some common purposes in an organized and harmonious manner (Cole and Smith 2000; Schmalleger 2001). This is why scholars refer to the arrest, conviction, and punishment of criminals as the processes of the criminal justice system.

The primary responsibilities of each component of criminal justice are as follows.

- *Police:* Investigating alleged criminal offenses, apprehending suspected criminal offenders, assisting the prosecution with obtaining criminal convictions at trial, keeping the peace in the community, preventing crime, providing social services, and upholding Constitutional protections.
- *Courts:* Determining guilt or innocence of suspected offenders at trial (adjudication), sentencing the legally guilty to some form(s) of punishment, interpreting laws made by legislative bodies, setting legal precedents, and upholding Constitutional protections.

- *Corrections:* Carrying out the sentences of the courts by administering punishment, pro- viding care and custody for accused and convicted criminals, and upholding Constitu- tional protections.

Although each of these agencies of criminal justice has its own goals, ideally they will also share some larger goals. This means that personnel of police, courts, and corrections should refrain from behaving in ways that may threaten these ideal goals. One goal I discuss later in this chapter is doing justice, which means holding the guilty accountable for their criminal acts while ensuring that the criminal justice process is fair and impartial.

When police investigate criminal offenses and make arrests, their desire to reduce crime should not interfere with ensuring that the right person is caught. Additionally, their own per- sonal prejudices and animosities should not affect their behaviors when interacting with citi- zens. Furthermore, members of the courtroom workgroup, including the prosecutor and defense attorney, should always remember that they are, first and foremost, officers of the court and, therefore, are not entitled to allow their desire to win cases to interfere with their commitment to the ethics of their profession. Judges also should be fair in administering sen- tences so that justice is achieved and should ensure that prosecutors and defense attorneys fol- low the law. Finally, correctional facilities must not permit offenders to be assaulted or unduly humiliated for the sake of the enjoyment or empowerment of their employees. Punishment should be administered humanely and fairly. As you will see throughout this book, this logic has been lost on U.S. politicians, who have made criminal justice more and more punitive over the past 30 years.

Why the Criminal Justice System Is Not a System

It's easy to see why some are reluctant to refer to criminal justice in the United States as a "sys- tem." With three main components, each acting at three levels of government, the fight against crime is not an efficient, smoothly running process. Some view the three criminal justice compo- nents as a system, but many do not. As you will learn in this book, what is referred to as the crimi- nal justice system is not an "integrated system with a single, coordinated set of objectives and programs" (Gottfredson 1999, p. 8). Unlike most other systems, it is not organized, harmonious, uniform, or in equilibrium. And police, courts, and corrections have developed separately from the others. Each has "developed within different governmental structures, each has different sources of support and different budgets, and each has different objectives. Each has developed its own requirements for staffing, drawing on different resource pools for personnel and requir- ing different programs of training and education."

As explained by the National Criminal Justice Commission, "The decisions made at each level of the system can severely impact other elements. Yet there is no systematic process used in mak- ing decisions. Rather, each component is left to its own, often fighting for resources against other parts of the system" (Donziger 1996, p. 181). As noted by Arrigo (1999, p. 1), "The conditions under which the criminal justice system maintains an effective administration of law enforce- ment, criminal courts, and correctional practices can and does get bogged down in a number of competing, sometimes even conflicting, circumstances."

These are some of the reasons that many criminal justice scholars do not view criminal justice agencies as a system and that some instead call it a "network" (e.g., Cox and Wade 1998). In this book, I follow this lead and refer to the collection of agencies of police, courts, and corrections as the *criminal justice network* (except when I am quoting directly from another source). A network is a group of parts, agencies, or organizations that are interconnected and interrelated but not necessarily organized and harmonious.

All of the agencies of criminal justice are expected to work together to achieve the goals of criminal justice as a whole, and each component of criminal justice is affected by the actions of the others. Walker (1998, p. 29) says it this way: "The systems model focuses attention on the flow of cases between agencies, the interrelationships (or 'components'), and the pervasiveness of discretionary decision making in controlling the flow of cases." No one component can operate without the others. Police must solve crime by making arrests of suspects; otherwise, courts have no need to hold trials. Similarly, if courts do not convict people, then correctional facilities such as prisons have no one to punish. Finally, if correctional facilities do not effectively administer punishment in communities, then police will surely be overrun by crime. If we are to achieve our overall criminal justice goals, the three components must work together efficiently. The fact that they do not currently work this way in reality does not mean that they should not work this way ideally.

The three parts of the criminal justice network are not equal in size, as law enforcement has historically employed the most personnel and has had the largest operating budget (see Figure 1.1). The rationale for this is discussed in more depth later in this chapter. For now, keep in mind that all criminal justice cases must come into the criminal justice network through police contact, so to some degree it is logical for police to be the largest part. That is, police are the source of input for the criminal justice process. The following box illustrates how crime is typically processed through the entire criminal justice network.

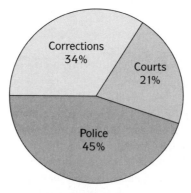

FIGURE 1.1

Relative Size of American Police, Courts, and Corrections (Percentage of All Criminal Justice Employees, 2000)

Data refer to percentage of total criminal justice employees.

SOURCE: Bureau of Justice Statistics (www.ojp.usdoj.gov/bjs).

The typical criminal justice process

The criminal justice network operates through numerous steps in a specified sequential order, although this does not necessarily mean that the criminal justice network operates like an efficient assembly line. There may be long delays between one stage and the next. For example, a crime may go unreported to the police for a long period of time, as happens when a victim does not discover his or her victimization immediately or when a murder goes unsolved for some period of time. Because murder cases have no statute of limitations, they can go to trial at any time in the future as long as a suspect has been identified and arrested. Additionally, accused offenders may sit in jail in preventive detention, awaiting trial, for more than a year.

When cases move quickly through the criminal justice process, the process can be accurately described as an assembly line. The criminal justice network moves more expeditiously for some types of cases and for some types of defendants than for others. Whether this is fair and therefore just is discussed in Chapter Seven. Typically, poor people are processed through criminal justice agencies quickly, while wealthy citizens (who rarely are processed by the system at all) can afford to tie the process up if it is to their benefit to do so.

At each stage of the criminal justice process, many cases do not pass on to the next stage because of a process called *filtering*, which allows some cases to be screened out of the criminal justice network. Cases are filtered out for dozens of reasons. Examples are provided in this section as we move through each stage of the process.

Crime

Obviously, the criminal justice process begins with the commission of a *crime*. The issue of what is crime is discussed in Chapter Four. A short definition of a crime is "an act in violation of the criminal law." For example, theft occurs when a person takes property from its owner with the intent to deprive the owner of the property permanently. Normally, when a crime is committed, it is not immediately detected by the police (Wrobleski and Hess 2000). Rather, it is typically reported to the police either by the victim or by another citizen who discovers the crime. Therefore, any law or criminal justice policy that discourages citizens from getting involved in the process will be detrimental to the operations of the criminal justice network.

Criminal offenses reported to the police by citizens are not automatically assumed to be crimes. That may sound strange, but citizens may think they have been victimized by crimes when, in fact, the act that was committed against them did not violate the criminal law. Whether reported acts violate the criminal law is determined by police when they conduct an investigation. Even when crimes have actually been committed, police do not necessarily conduct a thorough investigation; they use their *discretion* in deciding whether or not to act. Discretion is the ability of an agent to act according to his or her own professional judgment rather than some preset rules of procedures (Cole and Smith 2000; Schmalleger 2001). Using their discretion, police may determine that the crime committed is so minor that it does not warrant the expenditure of police resources or that the likelihood of solving the crime or recovering stolen property is too remote.

Think about the disadvantage the police already face when a crime has been committed. The suspect is typically long gone before the police arrive. It is estimated that 75% of all crimes are *cold crimes*, crimes in which a suspect is not caught at the scene of the crime (Wrobleski and Hess 2000). Given that policing in the United States is largely reactive and dependent on citizen reports, it is very difficult to do a good job of clearing cases by making arrests. Thus, the majority of crimes that are committed do not lead to an arrest.

Of course, the likelihood of *clearing a case by arrest* is a function of the type of crime committed. Murders are the most likely type of street crime to lead to an arrest, for several reasons. First, murder victims are almost always discovered by police. Second, the crime is heinous in nature, so police take this offense very seriously. Third, in about half of murders in the United States, the victim is killed by an acquaintance or relative. This makes it easier to locate the offender. Other crimes, such as theft, are less likely to be cleared by arrest. Thefts are not always discovered by the victims. Even when they are, they may be considered minor or not worthy of calling the police for some other reason. Also, thefts are more likely to be committed by strangers than by people known to the victim, so that locating suspects is much more difficult for the police.

The bottom line is that police do not even know about most crimes, even those committed on the street. Estimates suggest that police discover somewhere between 30% and 50% of all street crimes in any given year (Schmalleger 2001; Walker 1998). The remaining 50% to 70% of street crimes never even enter the criminal justice network because they are not discovered. The main reason that this "dark figure of crime" remains hidden to the police and thus to the criminal justice network is that many crimes are simply not reported to the police by victims or witnesses. For reasons that are not the fault of police, law enforcement is highly ineffective at apprehending suspects and therefore at reducing crime and doing justice.

Furthermore, with nearly 800,000 sworn police officers in the United States for a population of 280 million Americans, there are only 2.86 police officers on the street for every 1,000 people. If only 5% of these 1,000 persons are serious, repetitive criminals, this means that, on average, there are only 2.86 police officers on the street for every 50 career criminals (e.g., see Wolfgang, Figlio, and Sellin 1972). And this figure includes only street criminals; it does not include those who commit white-collar crimes and deviance (see Chapter Four). Imagine 2.86 police officers in your community trying to keep up with the criminal acts of 50 career criminals, plus the occasional acts of the rest of the citizens who violate the law.

Investigation

Police *investigation*, the second stage in the criminal justice process, begins when the patrol officer responds to the scene of the alleged crime. If police determine that the act was not illegal, then the case gets filtered out of the criminal justice network and thus does not lead to the next stage, arrest. If the responding officers determine that a crime was in fact committed, their primary job is to "solve the crime," which in law enforcement terms equates to making an arrest. Ideally, a criminal investigation leads the police to answer the question, "Who done it?" Patrol officers conduct a *preliminary investigation* at the crime scene; later, when the scene has been secured, trained detectives conduct a *secondary investigation*. The primary goal of the preliminary investigation is to secure the crime scene to protect the integrity of the evidence and to identify, locate, and question potential witnesses and/or victims. The secondary or follow-up investigation will lead to a more thorough collection, preservation, and presentation of evidence (Wrobleski and Hess 2000).

Arrest

Once police identify a suspect by collecting enough high-quality evidence, their goal is to remove the alleged offender from the street. This is usually accomplished through an *arrest*. An arrest occurs when the police take a suspect into custody so that prosecution of the suspect may begin. Generally, arrests must be based on *probable cause*—a reasonable belief that a particular person has committed a crime. For serious crimes such as felonies, police officers "must have knowledge of sufficient facts and circumstances that would allow a person of reasonable caution to believe that a crime has been committed" (Gottfredson 1999, p. 31).

At this point in the process, some cases are filtered out before the next stage, booking. For example, juveniles may be sent directly to the juvenile justice system. If police discover that they arrested the wrong person, the suspect may be immediately released.

At the point of arrest, police are required to read suspects their *Miranda* rights, so named because of the 1966 Supreme Court case *Miranda v. Arizona*. Since this ruling, police have been required to read suspects their Constitutional protections when an arrest occurs or is imminent. The *Miranda* warning reads:

> You have the right to remain silent. If you choose to give up this right, anything you do say can and will be used against you in a court of law. You have the right to an attorney. If you cannot afford one, one will be appointed to you.

Suspects are then asked if they understand these rights and, if so, whether they want to give up their rights and make statements or answer questions. Many claim that this requirement places an undue burden on the police and makes it harder for the criminal justice network to obtain convictions because it encourages criminals to withhold vital information from the police. As a result of such concerns, numerous exceptions to this rule have been established through case law (see Chapter Six).

Booking

After arrest, *booking* occurs. At this point, an administrative record of the suspect is made. Typically, the suspect's photograph and fingerprints are taken, and he or she may be questioned further by the police and/or placed in a lineup for witness or victim identification.

After booking, the suspect may be charged with specific criminal offenses, if the prosecutor thinks that there is a sufficient quality and quantity of evidence indicating that the suspect is indeed guilty of the offenses charged. A suspect can always be released and later rearrested if further evidence of guilt is discovered. Release is another form of filtering.

Initial Appearance

After being formally charged with a crime or crimes by the prosecution, suspects make an *initial appearance* before a judge. At this stage, suspects are notified of the charges against them and advised of their rights. The judge determines whether *bail* is necessary; if not, suspects are released on their promise to reappear for trial (called *release on own recognizance*). When a flight risk exists, that is, the judge fears that the suspect may flee the jurisdiction to avoid trial, suspects may be required to post bail or may even be held in *preventive detention* in cases where the judge determines that there is a flight risk and some danger to the community (see Chapter Seven). If the judge determines that there is not enough evidence to warrant the charges, the case may be dismissed and hence filtered out of the criminal justice network.

Preliminary Hearing/Grand Jury

Assuming that a case is not dismissed, the next stage in the criminal justice process is either a *preliminary hearing* or a *grand jury*, depending on the jurisdiction in which the case is being heard. Both of these mechanisms are ideally intended to ensure that innocent persons are not hastily, maliciously, or arbitrarily prosecuted. In reality, these processes are typically one-sided and almost always result in a finding that there is probable cause to warrant a person's being detained until trial (Walker 1998). This can be a major impediment to fairness in the criminal justice process, because findings of preliminary hearings and grand juries are routinely published in local media, perhaps creating assumptions among the public that named defendants are guilty of crimes, even though in fact they have not yet been convicted of anything.

In about half of the states, a preliminary hearing is held to determine if there is enough evidence to hold the case over for trial. If the judge does not find probable cause that the named person(s) committed the named offense(s), the case may be dismissed and filtered out of the criminal justice network. In cases where the judge finds probable cause, the accused is held for trial on the basis of an *information*, which is a formal charging document against the accused.

In federal cases and in other states, a grand jury is empaneled to determine if there is enough evidence to file an *indictment* charging the suspect with the named crime(s). If the *grand jury*, made up of a panel of civilians, finds that there is sufficient evidence to warrant a trial, it issues a *true bill* (which charges the defendant with a crime); if not, it issues a *no bill* (which means that the defendant is not charged with a crime) and the suspect is filtered out of the criminal justice network. Again, the vast majority of cases heard by a grand jury lead to an indictment. This has led some to call the grand jury process a "rubber stamp" for the prosecution (Walker 1998).

Arraignment

At *arraignment*, the next step in the process, the accused is read the information or indictment by the judge. The suspect then has the right to enter a plea of guilty, not guilty, or *nolo contendere* (no contest). Upon a plea of guilty or no contest, sentencing may take place immediately because a trial is not necessary to determine guilt. Pleas of guilty are not to be accepted by the judge unless several assurances from the accused are received. The reality is that *plea bargaining* occurs in more than 90% of all cases before U.S. courts, and the suspect is presumed guilty by virtually all involved, including the suspect's own attorney (see Chapter Seven).

Trial

Although the right to a *trial* is mentioned in the Declaration of Independence, three amendments to the U.S. Constitution, and numerous Supreme Court decisions, very few U.S. citizens have a reasonable expectation of a criminal trial when charged with a crime. As noted, more than 90% of defendants plead guilty to the charge(s) and thus do not need a trial. When a trial does occur, it becomes a contest between the government (prosecution) and the accused (defense) to win and secure their own interests. Ideally, our agencies of criminal justice are *adversarial* in nature, because they are supposed to feature two adversaries fighting it out for the truth. But the ideal is very different from the reality. Gaines, Kaune, and Miller (2000, p. 286) state it this way: "Television dramas often depict the courtroom as a battlefield, with prosecutors and defense attorneys spitting fire at each other over the loud and insistent protestations of a frustrated judge. Consequently, many people are somewhat disappointed when they witness a real courtroom at work." Even when trials do occur, they commonly produce cooperation rather than battle.

The typical trial process is discussed in Chapter Seven. Ideally, the truth of a suspect's guilt will emerge at trial, where guilt must be established *beyond a reasonable doubt* by the prosecution. In plea bargaining, in contrast, guilt or innocence is not determined. Instead, guilt is assumed and sentencing is the only issue to be resolved.

Trials are most likely to occur in cases where suspects are charged with serious offenses, particularly violent offenses such as murder (Cole and Smith 2000; Schmalleger 2001). Criminal trials are very expensive; for minor offenses, plea bargains are less time-consuming and therefore a much more cost-effective use of government resources to carry out justice. Criminal trials are rare precisely because, in most cases, all parties involved assume the guilt of the suspect simply because some evidence suggests that the suspect is guilty. Many ask, "If they weren't guilty, why would we be arresting them in the first place?" The answer is that the standard of evidence needed to make an arrest (probable cause) is much lower than that needed to sustain a criminal conviction (beyond a reasonable doubt). Yet even the typical defense attorney in the United States (a public defender assigned to a poor client) has little financial incentive and limited resources to determine whether due process was followed or whether his or her client is actually innocent of the charges (see Chapter Seven). So, although the ideal of American justice is the trial, in reality, trials are the exception to the rule of plea bargaining.

According to Langbein (2000, p. 25):

> We are accustomed to viewing the Bill of Rights as a success story. With it, the American constitution-makers opened a new epoch in the centuries-old struggle to place effective limits on the abuse of state power. Not all of the Bill of Rights is a success story, however . . . we would do well to take note of that chapter of the Bill of Rights that has been a spectacular failure: The Framers' effort to embed jury trial as the exclusive mode of proceeding in cases of serious crime.

Think of the Sixth Amendment to the U.S. Constitution, which states, "In all criminal prosecutions, the accused shall enjoy the right to a speedy and public trial, by an impartial jury of the State and district wherein the crime shall have been committed. . . ." Langbein (2000) writes, "'All' is not a word that constitution-makers use lightly. The drafters of the Sixth Amendment used it and meant it." Article III of the Constitution says the same thing: "The Trial of all Crimes, except in Cases of Impeachment, shall be by Jury. . . ." Today in the United States, Langbein writes, "In place of 'all,' a more accurate term to describe the use of jury trial in the discharge of our criminal caseload would be 'virtually none.'" Thus, "our guarantee of routine criminal trial is a fraud" (p. 26).

Sentencing

When defendants are found guilty by a jury of their peers or by a bench trial (where a judge determines guilt or innocence), the next step in the process is *sentencing*. When suspects are found not guilty or acquitted, they are filtered out of the criminal justice network and cannot be retried for the same offense because of the Fifth Amendment protection of freedom from double jeopardy. Sentencing addresses the questions, "What do we do with the legally guilty?" and "What punishment should be administered?" Judges typically bear the responsibility for passing sentences, which are recommended by juries. Judges have discretion within certain guidelines in *indeterminate* sentences (which specify a range of possible sanctions) but have less discretion in *determinate* sentences (which are specific to the type of crime committed) and no discretion in *mandatory* sentences (see Chapter Eight).

Appeal

Those convicted of criminal offenses, particularly serious crimes, have the right to *appeal* their convictions to appellate courts, or courts of appeals. Those convicted through plea bargains give up this right, along with many others. Convicted offenders can appeal on the basis of any matter of law—for example, that the trial court somehow failed to follow proper procedures or that Constitutional rights were violated at some point in the process. Perhaps unlawfully obtained evidence was admitted into trial, or maybe a defendant's evidence was wrongfully excluded from trial. In these cases, appeals may be allowed, yet in the vast majority of cases, appeals are denied (Meeker 1984; C. Williams 1991). Because appeals are made on matters of law rather than fact, convicted criminals cannot simply argue that they are "really innocent!" Calls to review jury decisions often fall on deaf ears.

Some claim that such appeals are based on "legal technicalities" and should be limited so criminal justice processes can operate more efficiently and effectively. Others point out that procedural errors may lead to mistakes in adjudication, meaning that innocent persons may be wrongfully convicted; therefore, Constitutional protections should not be equated with legal technicalities.

Corrections

Once a sentence is passed, correctional services such as probation, jails, prisons, and numerous other agencies administer the sanctions imposed by the court. *Probation*, a form of punishment that allows the offender to live in the community under certain rules, is the most widely used form of the criminal justice sanction in the United States (see Chapter Eight). Probation, the cheapest sanction available, is intended for less serious offenders. Jails and prisons are forms of incarceration, where offenders are deprived of their freedom and locked away from the rest of society. The destructive nature of incarceration is discussed in Chapter Nine. *Jails* are intended for persons sentenced to less than 1 year of incarceration; *prisons*, for those sentenced to more than 1 year of incarceration (Clear and Cole 1994).

Release

Once a sentence has been fully served, a person is released from the criminal justice network in what is supposed to be the final stage of the process. Offenders are also commonly released from incarceration early through the process of *parole*, which allows them to be released back into the community prior to serving their full sentence, as long as they agree to live under certain rules. In the current "get tough" environment in the United States, parole has been abolished at the federal level and in many states (see Chapter Nine).

Although release is supposed to be the final stage of the criminal justice process, the reality of release is that offenders are routinely harassed by police and/or their parole officers after being released from the criminal justice network (D. Evans 1997). When crimes are committed nearby, especially when they fit the modus operandi (M.O.) of a known offender out on parole, he or she is automatically considered a likely suspect. So much for "paying your debt to society"! Police and parole officers also may seek cooperation in developing leads for crimes committed by known associates of the offender.

From the discussion in the box, you can conclude that one thing the U.S. criminal justice network is aimed at doing is reacting to crime—catching, convicting, and punishing criminals. But is that all? Is this the only reason we have police, courts, and corrections—to deal with the nation's crime problem? Or is there something else that the criminal justice network is supposed to do?

IDEAL GOALS OF CRIMINAL JUSTICE

Believe it or not, there is no "official" source one can consult to find out what the U.S. criminal justice network is intended to do. You might find this curious: How can we possibly know how well the network is really doing if we do not know what it is intended to do? The closest we can come to a government statement of intended criminal justice outcomes is the 1967 President's Commission on Law Enforcement and Administration of Justice report, *The Challenge of Crime in a Free Society*. The authors wrote that criminal justice agencies are intended to "enforce the standards of conduct necessary to protect individuals and the community."

This seems straightforward enough, but exactly whose standards of conduct should be enforced? And what is meant by "to protect individuals and the community"? Does this mean only that the criminal justice network should protect individuals and communities from criminals? If so, how? Does it also mean that suspected criminals should be protected from the government? Does protecting the community from crime mean eroding Constitutional protections of all Americans? Answers to these questions are not clear.

This is partly due to the fact that the last national report on crime was published over 30 years ago by the Eisenhower Commission. In fact, the last time that specific recommendations for criminal justice reform were formally reported was by the 1967 President's Commission. Since that time, no president of the United States has appointed a group to analyze crime or criminal justice policy.

In the 1990s, a group called the National Criminal Justice Commission initiated an investigation of the U.S. criminal justice network (Donziger 1996). The findings of their scathing indictment, published under the title *The Real War on Crime*, are discussed at various points in this book. Their overall argument is that American criminal justice agencies mostly fail to meet their goals.

One thing we can cull from this source, and most basic introductory criminal justice texts, is that the criminal justice network has at least two goals:

- Reducing crime
- Doing justice

Reducing Crime

Police, courts, and corrections are obviously aimed at *reducing crime*, or "crime fighting," as some like to call it. This can be achieved through *reactive* means (after the crime occurs) or *proactive* means (before the crime occurs). The former type of crime fighting is generally called *crime control*, whereas the latter is often referred to as *crime prevention* (Rosenbaum, Lurigio, and Davis 1998). Amazingly, the U.S. Constitution does not list "crime control" as a responsibility of the U.S. government. Therefore, the U.S. Congress was not explicitly empowered with this authority. The Constitution does state, however, that our government must "establish Justice, [and] insure domestic tranquility," and this makes crime control an implied power of government (Marion 1995, p. 6). Because crime control activities are not specifically granted to the federal government, and because they are not specifically denied to the states, crime control has historically been the responsibility of state governments. Since the 1960s, however, crime control has become increasingly a national issue as a consequence of the politicization of crime in elections (see Chapter Two) and media coverage of crime (see Chapter Five).

In the United States, crime reduction is mostly reactive in nature. For example, American policing has historically been aimed at reacting to calls for service from crime victims (after the crimes occur). Our agencies of criminal justice try to apprehend, prosecute, convict, and punish offenders after a crime is discovered by or reported to the police. It is important to point out here that reactive criminal justice operations are not likely to reduce crime because they do not eliminate the root causes of crime. This is why the National Criminal Justice Commission claims, "We cannot expect the criminal justice system to create strong families, deliver jobs, or provide hope to young people" because it is not charged with doing so (Donziger 1996, p. 61). In fact, because the criminal justice network does little to address the major sources of criminal behavior, crime prevention through criminal justice is not likely (Sherman et al. 1997).

Crime prevention includes any means to eliminate the causes of crime so that crime does not occur and does not need to be dealt with by criminal justice agencies (Robinson 1999). Although some American criminal justice activity is aimed at crime prevention, the great bulk of it can be described as crime control. There is some evidence that crime prevention can be effective, if appropriately designed, implemented, and supported (Sherman et al. 1997).

Reducing crime is obviously a desirable goal. But the most important point to remember while reading this book is that there is another, more important goal of our criminal justice network—doing justice. Although reducing crime is an important goal, it is of secondary importance to doing justice (Cole and Smith 2000).

Doing Justice

First and foremost, the basis of the criminal justice system is *doing justice*. There are two somewhat conflicting conceptions of justice, one concerned with holding the guilty accountable for their crimes and the other with ensuring that the criminal justice process is fair and impartial. Doing justice implies both that guilty people will be punished for their wrongful acts and that innocent persons will not wrongly be subjected to the criminal justice process. Which is the most important conception of justice? If you had to emphasize one conception of justice over the other, which would you choose?

WHAT IS JUSTICE?

Arrigo (1999, p. 2) writes that the meaning of justice "is by no means easy to interpret or simple to discern." To crime victims, justice may simply mean getting even with the offenders who harmed them. For example, a rape victim may define justice for the attacker as imprisonment, or even castration or death, and might perceive anything less as unjust. When people are intentionally victimized and the guilty are not held accountable for their actions, justice clearly has not

FIGURE 1.2
The Scales of Justice

been obtained. This is because the offender has unfairly gained an advantage over the victim; the mythical scales of justice shown in Figure 1.2 have wrongfully been tilted in favor of the offender. The scales of justice depicted are in balance only when the harms inflicted on crime victims are righted by administering punishment to their offenders.

Retribution, a main reason for administering criminal sanctions to offenders (see Chapter Eight), implies that the harm inflicted by the criminal upon the victim will in some way be returned by the government to the offender. In the United States, a criminal who hurts someone is viewed as deserving of punishment: "An eye for an eye, a tooth for a tooth," so to speak. Victims now regularly view punishment of their offenders as one of their rights (Beckett and Sasson 2000). This is one conception of justice.

Justice has an alternative meaning as well. In some ways, this definition is related to the one above, for it is concerned with assuring that the scales of justice are not imbalanced. This conception of justice is based on fairness and impartiality. It assumes that all persons will be treated equally in the eyes of the law—that justice will be blind. Justice thus would not be present when any group is somehow left out or singled out for differential treatment by the law.

This conception of justice is represented by the figure of "a blindfolded woman with a scale in one hand and a sword in the other" (see the Issue in Depth at the end of this chapter for a discussion of *Lady Justitia*, whose image adorns this book). It is also what is meant by "with liberty and justice for all" in the pledge of allegiance—that the government will treat its citizens with "fairness, equity" and in a manner that is right (Kappeler, Blumberg, and Potter 2000, p. 215).

From the title of this book—*Justice Blind?*—you may guess that I am at least not sure whether our criminal justice network achieves this measure of justice. In fact, I provide evidence that our criminal justice practices are unjust in many ways. Justice must be blind or it is not just at all. I demonstrate in this book that the American criminal justice network is in some ways biased against the poor and people of color and that, to a lesser degree, it discriminates on the basis of gender (see Chapter Twelve).

The depiction of justice on the cover of this book is also reflected in the American Declaration of Independence. American settlers criticized their "British brethren" for being "deaf to the voice of justice" (Gottfredson 1999, p. 50). Ideally, this was one reason that people came to found this country in the interests of justice apart from the interests of the British monarchy. Of course, history testifies to a different reality. Early Americans wiped out numerous indigenous peoples and enslaved other groups in the name of "Manifest Destiny," a 19th-century doctrine based on the premise that the Americans had the God-given right—indeed, the duty—to expand their territory and cultural influence throughout North America (e.g., see Koning 1993). Still, early Americans envisioned a country where all "men" could live, thrive, and further their own interests without the burdens imposed by the British monarchy.

Conflicting Views of Justice

Each conception of justice is important when it comes to studying and understanding the criminal justice network. Americans will not support criminal justice practices that fail to punish those who deserve it. Ideally, they will not support them when they wrongfully convict the innocent or are biased against any group. Pound (1912) wrote long ago that justice requires that serious offenders be convicted and punished and that the innocent and unfortunate not be wrongly oppressed. Similarly, Harrigan (2000, p. 315) notes that "Justice is served neither if a guilty person is let go nor if an innocent person is punished."

These two conceptions of justice—punishing the guilty and ensuring fairness and impartiality—often conflict. The law places restrictions on the actions of criminal justice actors so that Constitutional rights of individuals are not violated. With unlimited powers, law enforcement agencies probably could do a much better job at fighting crime, but numerous liberties that we currently enjoy (such as the right to privacy) would have to be sacrificed. Imagine how much more effectively police could detect crimes if they could enter your home, peek into your windows, tap your phones, and monitor your e-mail without first having to establish probable cause!

Given the limits within which the criminal justice network must operate, it is difficult to catch, convict, and punish criminal offenders. For example, the "exclusionary rule" states that illegally seized evidence cannot be used to establish legal guilt against a defendant. The Supreme Court held, in *Mapp v. Ohio* (1961), that the rule had to be applied universally to all criminal proceedings, including those by state governments against individual citizens. This requirement may make it less likely that a factually guilty criminal will be found legally guilty in a court of law. Alternatively, our current efforts to fight crime at almost any cost have led to the establishment of measures intended to protect "victims' rights . . . [that] have lowered evidentiary requirements, eliminated the insanity defense, and weakened exclusionary rules designed to block the introduction of illegally obtained evidence" (Beckett and Sasson 2000, p. 163).

Walker (1998, p. 176) argues that many so-called victims' rights initiatives are really efforts to get "tough on crime." He writes that the President's Task Force on Victims of Crime, for example, "recommended legislation 'to abolish the exclusionary rule,' 'to abolish parole,' to permit hearsay evidence at preliminary hearings, and to authorize preventive detention." Part of the frustration that victims feel when they suffer harm at the hands of criminals stems from the fact that, technically, the only "victim" of crime is the government. This means that victims are not entitled to get justice for themselves; rather, the state is authorized to conduct crime control efforts in the interest of community safety.

Yet the U.S. justice network must strive to achieve a balance between fighting crime (to do justice for its victims) and being fair and impartial (to do justice for the accused). Justice for the community requires both. Thus, throughout our history, the priorities of American justice have shifted back and forth, much like a pendulum or a set of scales being continually rebalanced. During some periods, emphasis has been placed on apprehending and punishing criminals over ensuring fairness in the criminal justice process. At other times, crime fighting has taken a back seat to ensuring that the criminal justice network operates impartially.

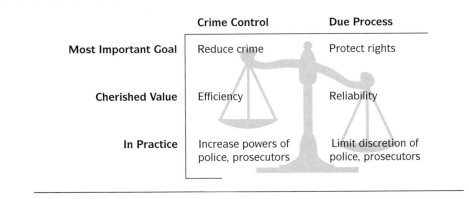

	Crime Control	**Due Process**
Most Important Goal	Reduce crime	Protect rights
Cherished Value	Efficiency	Reliability
In Practice	Increase powers of police, prosecutors	Limit discretion of police, prosecutors

FIGURE 1.3
Due Process and Crime Control Models of Justice

Due Process versus Crime Control

There has always been tension between those who believe in *due process* and those who believe in *crime control*. These terms represent two models of justice put forth by Herbert Packer (1968) in his book, *The Limits of the Criminal Sanction*. Although neither of the two models actually exists or ever can in reality, Packer attempted to describe two polar extremes—one model most concerned with preserving individual liberties and the other with maintaining order in the community and fighting crime.

Figure 1.3 depicts these models at opposite ends of a continuum. The *due process model* is aimed at ensuring that individual liberties are protected at all costs, even if guilty people sometimes go free. In other words, the due process model values individual freedom, and the way to protect individual freedom is to uphold Constitutional protections. It places a high value on the adversarial nature of justice, whereby a prosecutor and defense attorney battle it out in court to find the truth and make sure that justice is achieved. Reliability is the most important value of the due process model, for it is imperative that the right person be convicted of the crime of which he or she is accused. Packer's metaphor for this model was an "obstacle course" because, to ensure that no innocent persons were wrongfully convicted, the prosecution would have to overcome numerous obstacles in order to convict anyone.

The crime control model is aimed at protecting the community by lowering crime rates, even if, on occasion, innocent persons are mistakenly convicted. The crime control model also values individual freedom but suggests that the way to protect individual freedom is to protect people from criminals. It places a high value on informal processes such as plea bargaining (when a prosecutor and defense attorney agree out of court to an appropriate sentence for an accused criminal) to expedite criminal justice operations. In this model, very few criminal trials are held, because they are expensive and unnecessary for establishing legal guilt. Efficiency is the most important value of the crime control model, for it is imperative that the criminal justice network operate as quickly as possible to keep up with the large numbers of criminal cases that enter it each day. Packer's metaphor for this model was an "assembly line" because individual defendants would be quickly processed through the criminal justice network outside of the courtroom through plea bargaining (see Chapter Seven).

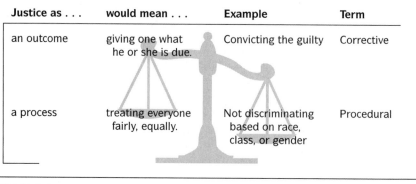

Justice as . . .	would mean . . .	Example	Term
an outcome	giving one what he or she is due.	Convicting the guilty	Corrective
a process	treating everyone fairly, equally.	Not discriminating based on race, class, or gender	Procedural

FIGURE 1.4
Justice as an Outcome and Justice as a Process

Note that justice is an important value in both models. Yet proponents of each model view justice differently. Figure 1.4 illustrates how justice can be viewed either as an outcome or as a process. People who view *justice as an outcome,* usually supporters of the crime control model, think that justice means giving people what they deserve: Guilty people deserve punishment. I call this version of justice *corrective justice.* Others, typically proponents of the due process model, see *justice as a process.* People who value what I call *procedural justice* are more concerned with ensuring that everyone is treated fairly and equally while being processed through the criminal justice network. This means not allowing discrimination on the basis of factors such as race, class, and gender.

Each of these conceptions of justice is important to many Americans, but criminal justice activity over the past few decades reflects an emphasis on corrective justice at the expense of procedural justice. In other words, U.S. policymakers are more concerned with holding the guilty accountable for their crimes than with ensuring fairness and equity in criminal justice practice, even in the face of overwhelming evidence that innocent people have been convicted of crimes they did not commit (for evidence of wrongful convictions, see the Issue in Depth at the end of Chapter Seven). This is unfortunate, because of the inherent infallibility associated with all human activity (Gaines, Kaune, and Miller 2000, p. 21).

In case you were wondering, historically Democrats have tended to support due process protections, whereas Republicans have tended to support crime control efforts. Traditionally, Democrats have been more "liberal" and have placed greater value on individual rights than on community protection, whereas Republicans have been more "conservative" and thus more supportive of government efforts to fight crime (Baker and Meyer 1980; Biskupic 1991; Van Horn, Baumer, and Gormley 1992). Because the crime control and due process models are ideals, and because of the competing values of reducing crime and doing justice, the history of criminal justice in the United States can be characterized as a pendulum swinging back and forth between the two ideals, much as the political affiliation of voters shifts over time. For example, the Warren Supreme Court (1953–1969) can be considered a "due process" court because its rulings were more consistent with upholding individual rights. The Burger Supreme Court (1969–1986) is more accurately characterized as a "crime control" court because it was less protective of individual rights and made decisions that limited *Miranda* protections (for more, see Marion 1995; O'Brien 1993; Steel and Steger 1988). Beckett and Sasson (2000, p. 59) go as far as to characterize

Burger Court activity as an "assault on defendants' rights." The Rehnquist Supreme Court (1986–present) is also generally a crime control court, as it has made it easier to convict the "factually guilty" and to avoid losing cases as a result of legal technicalities that previously made it easier for the guilty to go free. The Rehnquist Court has "given greater flexibility to the police and corrections personnel, making changes in the death penalty, unreasonable searches and seizures, and the exclusionary rule" (Marion, 1995, p. 51). Some of its rulings, however, such as *U.S. v. Dickerson* (2000), which upheld the requirement that police read suspects the *Miranda* warning prior to interrogation, have been more consistent with the due process model.

In April 2000, the U.S. Supreme Court heard arguments that reading the *Miranda* warning should no longer be required because it interferes with police officers' efforts to gain evidence necessary for criminal conviction of the guilty. The following box focuses on the Supreme Court's ruling.

The recent *Miranda* decision

In the case of *U.S. v. Dickerson* (2000), the Supreme Court upheld the *Miranda* requirements by a vote of seven to two. At issue was a 1968 federal law that allowed voluntary confessions by suspects to be admitted into court even if the defendants had not been read their rights. This law conflicted with the Supreme Court's decision in *Miranda v. Arizona* (1966).

Chief Justice William Rehnquist wrote the majority opinion of the Court, in which he stated: "We hold that *Miranda*, being a constitutional decision of this Court, may not be . . . overruled by an Act of Congress, and we decline to overrule *Miranda* ourselves. We therefore hold that *Miranda* and its progeny in this Court govern the admissibility of statements made during custodial interrogation in both state and federal courts."

Rehnquist added that because the "advent of modern custodial police interrogation brought with it an increased concern about confessions obtained by coercion," *Miranda* requirements were considered more important than ever by the Court. Rehnquist wrote, for example, that being questioned by the police places a "heavy toll on individual liberty and trades on the weakness of individuals."

Ironically, the appeal of the original 1966 *Miranda* decision did not come from a law enforcement agency. In fact, most police administrators have always believed that *Miranda* provides an important protection for all Americans. They recognize that reading *Miranda* warnings to suspects is part of their professional responsibility of upholding the Constitutional right of suspects not to incriminate themselves. Because police have always been able to use strategies to convince suspects to waive their right not to incriminate themselves (e.g., see Leo 1996), *Miranda* is not and never has been a major impediment to effective policing. Uchida and Bynum (1991) claim that very little evidence is ever excluded because of *Miranda* violations.

Edward Lazarus (2000), author of "How *Miranda* Really Works and Why It Really Matters," wrote (about 3 weeks before the decision came down):

> As matters currently stand, when police officers fail to observe *Miranda*, judges almost always limit themselves . . . to finding "technical" violations of *Miranda*, thereby allowing prosecutors to use evidence derived from challenged confessions and to keep defendants from testifying in their own defense. Judges almost never take the extra step of finding a confession to

be actually involuntary—which would deprive the prosecution of any evidence obtained as a resulted of the tainted confession.

Indeed, in practice, and wholly apart from the much-debated issue of whether *Miranda* inhibits police from obtaining confessions, the ruling has become largely symbolic. It allows judges to scold police for misbehavior and pay lip service to the right against self-incrimination, while minimizing the actual effect on police and prosecutors.

In 2000, the Court ruled that *Miranda* warnings have become intertwined with the fabric of American society. That is, *Miranda* protects a right that is crucial to being free from unwarranted government interference in our lives, a right that is so cherished by Americans that it cannot be eliminated by Court order.

Which model do you most support? Whether you would support a due process model or a crime control model may depend on which you feel is more important, protecting your individual Constitutional rights or protecting the community from crime. This may not be an easy choice, because both are worthy pursuits. Before you decide, remember that your rights as an American are the major difference between living in a democracy such as the United States and living in an authoritarian, police state such as China, Afghanistan under the rule of the Taliban, or Iraq under Saddam Hussein.

Sometimes, ensuring that all individuals' rights are protected means that guilty people will go free. Alternatively, getting all the "bad guys" means that some "good guys" may get caught up in criminal justice processes, too. Ask yourself, Which would be worse—being confronted by a criminal who was wrongly freed or being wrongfully accused of a crime by your own government? In which situation would you be more likely to win?

How you answer such questions may determine whether you are a proponent of a due process model of justice or a crime control model of justice. Whatever the case, you must remember that the U.S. criminal justice network will never be 100% representative of either the due process or the crime control model. Rather, our criminal justice network attempts to stay in balance, by upholding individual Constitutional protections while effectively fighting crime. Gottfredson (1999, p. 27) writes: "Because we value freedom, we react strongly to violations or threats of violation of our persons or property. We resist any threat to our liberty by agencies of our government. [But] [b]ecause we value safety, we expect the criminal justice system to protect us. We want both protection for ourselves and for our own liberty."

The most important lesson to be learned from Packer's (1968) discussion is that there is an inherent conflict between protecting individuals' Constitutional rights and fighting crime. It is difficult to do one well without being somewhat of a failure at the other.

Justice Today

Where are we today? And what are the implications for justice in America? The following box illustrates that most criminal justice resources go to police and corrections, with courts receiving the fewest resources. What does this suggest about whether we are following a crime control or a due process model of justice?

Resources devoted to criminal justice in the United States

A criminal justice network that places a higher value on crime fighting than on due process might allocate a larger percentage of its resources to police, because they are responsible for making arrests of suspected offenders, and/or to corrections, because its agencies have sole authority over punishing offenders. A criminal justice network that places a greater value on due process might allocate a larger share of resources to courts, because the judicial process determines the guilt or innocence of criminal justice clients. The primary protection from government overzealousness that innocent persons have is high-quality defense attorneys and neutral, objective judges. If we value due process, these actors ought to be well equipped to do their jobs.

The following discussion is organized around these issues:

- Which component of criminal justice has the most employees?
- Which component of criminal justice is allocated the most financial resources?

Employees of criminal justice

As of March 2000, the U.S. criminal justice network employed more than 2.2 million people, including over 1 million working in law enforcement, over 470,000 working in courts, and over 725,000 working in corrections. So, of the three components of justice, the fewest people work in U.S. courts (21.1% of the total employees work for courts). This is more consistent with a crime control model of criminal justice than a due process model.

There are at least 17,784 law enforcement agencies in the United States, employing a total of at least 796,518 sworn officers. There are at least 12,666 police departments, employing 440,920 sworn officers. The next largest type of agency is the county sheriff's office, with at least 3,070 departments and 164,711 sworn deputies. Special police departments totaled at least 1,376 agencies and 43,413 officers, and there are at least 623 Texas constable agencies employing 2,630 officers. Compare these numbers with the 49 primary state police agencies, which employ 56,348 officers, and the very small number of federal agencies (with more than 100 agents), which employ 88,496 officers. Clearly, law enforcement in the United States is a local phenomenon, as most police officers work for local (city and county) agencies.

Courts employ far fewer employees than police departments. Given that prosecution is a state-level phenomenon (because most crimes are acts against the state government), I limit my discussion to state courts. There are just over 2,341 state court prosecutors' offices, which employ over 79,000 attorneys, investigators, and support staff. In 2001, these employees were responsible for closing more than 2.3 million felony cases and almost 7 million misdemeanor cases. Were the millions of people in these cases convicted "beyond a reasonable doubt" by a "jury of their peers"? Given the imbalance in criminal justice employees, it would be hard to imagine having trials for all of these defendants. In fact, almost all convictions by state courts were achieved through the process of plea bargaining. Half the prosecutors' offices in the United States employed nine or fewer people and had a budget of $318,000 or less (Bureau of Justice Statistics 2003).

Given that the largest share of defendants charged with felonies in state courts is indigent clients who cannot afford their own attorneys, an examination of defense systems for these indigent clients will help us learn about the state of defense attorneys generally in the United States. In 1996, of all felony case terminations, court-appointed counsel represented 82% of state defendants in the 75 largest counties. The poor traditionally receive legal representation from assigned counsel systems and public defenders' offices (see Chapter Seven).

At the end of 2001, in the nation's 100 most populous counties, 90 had public defender programs, 89 had assigned counsel programs, and 42 had contract programs. Public defender offices in the nation's largest 100 counties employed 12,700 people in 1999. Defense attorneys for indigent clients handled 4.2 million cases in 1999, 80% of which were criminal cases. Public defenders handled 82% of these cases; appointed attorneys, 15%; and contract attorneys, 3%. Whether publicly provided counsel provide defense of a lower quality than private attorneys is a matter of interesting debate (see Chapter Seven), but the facts may speak for themselves. For example, the majority of inmates in state prisons and federal prisons were represented by publicly provided attorneys.

Private attorneys may not be any more likely than public defenders to gain acquittals for their clients or to achieve less severe sentences for them, but recall that justice is a process as much as it is an outcome. Clearly, publicly assigned defense attorneys have less financial incentive than private attorneys to assure fair and Constitutional proceedings for their clients. Given that average public defenders have more than five cases per day, 7 days per week, 52 weeks per year (assuming that they work on weekends, holidays, and vacation time), it is hard to fathom holding trials for all of these clients (Cole and Smith 2000).

It should not be hard to imagine that, with more than 2 million felony criminal convictions in any given year, correctional facilities must employ a large number of employees. In 2000, more than 725,000 people were employed in corrections. At the end of 2001, 6.6 million people were under some form of criminal justice supervision, including probation, parole, and incarceration in jail or prison. At the end of 2001, state and federal prisons housed nearly 1.3 million inmates and jails housed another 631,000. How much does all of this cost? You must be wondering, especially given that criminal justice is funded by taxpayer dollars. That's your money, after all. This is the next issue addressed.

Financial resources for criminal justice

According to the Bureau of Justice Statistics, in 1999, federal, state, and local governments spent over $146 billion for civil and criminal justice, an 8% increase over 1998. For every resident, the three levels of government together spent $521 (this means that you paid more than $500 for civil and criminal justice in 1999). State and local governments combined spent 85% of all direct justice dollars, and the federal government spent the rest. The federal government spent more than $22 billion on criminal and civil justice in 1999, compared to nearly $50 billion spent by state governments, $35 billion by counties, and $39 billion by municipalities.

This is more than twice the amount spent in 1985, when justice spending was approximately $65 billion. In Chapter Four, I review what happened to crime rates during this same time period. One might expect to have seen huge decreases in crime rates during this time period, but that is not what happened.

Most justice spending (86%) is incurred by state and local governments. The largest share of justice spending went to law enforcement ($65.4 billion, or 44.6%). Almost as much ($49 billion, or 33.4%) was spent on corrections, including jails, prisons, probation, and parole. The smallest share of resources was spent on prosecution and other legal services ($32.2 billion, or 22%). These figures are more consistent with a crime control model than a due process model of criminal justice.

In 1999, Americans in the 100 most populous counties spent only $1.2 billion to provide criminal defense to indigent clients. Let us assume that only 10% of law enforcement time and money is spent actually providing law enforcement–related activities (see Chapter Six). This would mean that 10% of the $65.4 billion (or $6.5 billion) went to fight street crime. If law enforcement activity resulted in 80% of those arrested being poor, this would mean that police spend about $5.2 billion just catching poor criminals and several billion more prosecuting them. Compare this figure with the $1.3 billion spent defending them. See where our priorities are?

In American criminal justice, government agencies allocate much more funding for police to apprehend suspected criminals and for correctional facilities to punish convicted criminals. Overburdened courts receive relatively little funding, despite the fact that it is the role of the courts to ensure that justice is served—that is, that the innocent are not wrongfully convicted and that the guilty do not go free. Implications for justice in the United States are hard to understand fully, but the bottom line appears to be that we are less concerned with spending resources to determine that we get the "right" people than we are with just getting any people and punishing them. This may be an alarming realization for Americans who believe in justice.

From the discussion in the box on resources devoted to criminal justice, it appears that we as a nation have embraced crime control values. The past several presidents of the United States have made this clear. For example, in 1994, President Bill Clinton stated:

> The American people have been very clear. . . . The most important job is to keep the streets and the neighborhoods of America safe. The first responsibility of government is law and order. Without it, people can never really pursue the American dream. And without it, we're not really free. (Quoted in Gaines, Kaune, and Miller 2000, p. 11)

Does this statement sound more in line with a crime control or a due process model? And nothing has changed under President George W. Bush (the second), who has been faced with fighting "new" forms of terrorism on our soil, as well as an explosion of corporate crimes (discussed in Chapter Four). Bush has also stepped up the nation's war on drugs (discussed in Chapter Eleven). Virtually all of the rhetoric of the Bush administration also is "tough on crime."

Other chapters in this book provide evidence that U.S. policymakers have chosen a crime control model at the expense of individual Constitutional protections. The result is that many of our civil liberties are being or have been eroded. As Beckett (1997, p. 67) writes, "Law and order politics lead to a disregard for civil rights and due process." This is particularly sad, not just because we are less free from potential government interference in our lives, but also because the criminal justice network is so ineffective at reducing crime. Perhaps if crime were eliminated, we could accept and appreciate less justice. In fact, crime rates for some types of crimes, especially homicide, in the United States are still very high. They have consistently declined since the early 1970s, but these declines are less attributable to criminal justice activity than to social and economic change (Blumstein and Wallman 2000). In essence, we have been forced to give up some of our Constitutional protections for very little in return. This is a frightening thought.

In the past three decades, the United States has witnessed a rapid expansion of American criminal justice, an expansion driven not by facts about crime or increasing crime rates but, instead, by politics, fear, and an increasingly punitive attitude toward crime and criminals (Beckett and

Sasson 2000, p. 8; Donziger 1996, p. 63). Things were probably at their worst in the 1980s—for example, state spending from 1976 to 1989 increased dramatically for correctional budgets (up 95%) but fell for non-Medicare welfare (down 41%), highways (down 23%), and higher education (down 6%) (Gold 1990, p. 16). Funding for fighting crime increased through the 1990s as well. This led Jerome Miller (1994, p. 479), affiliated with the National Center on Institutions and Alternatives, to write:

> During the 1980s and 1990s, in the midst of two decades of social neglect, America's white majority presented its inner cities with an expensive gift—a new and improved criminal justice system. This new and improved system would, the government promised, bring domestic tranquility— with particular relevance to African Americans. No expense was spared in crafting and delivering it inside city gates. It was, in fact, a Trojan Horse . . . [because} . . . [a]s governmental investment in social and employment programs in the inner city held stable or decreased, the criminal justice system was ratcheted up to fill the void. With it came a divisive philosophy, destructive strategies, and particularly vicious tactics that would exacerbate violence and social disorganization.

Miller utilized investments in criminal justice activity over the past several decades, coupled with simultaneous disinvestments in social programs, to argue that the United States has shifted its efforts to solve social problems from a "social safety net" approach to a "dragnet" approach. This means that U.S. policymakers seem more willing to spend taxpayer money catching criminals (after they commit crime) than preventing crime by helping people deal with the life-shattering effects of poverty.

In fact, corrections spending at the national level increased three times as fast as military spending in the 1980s and 1990s (Donziger 1996, p. 48). So, during this time, when you were talking about the nation's "enemy," you were much more likely to be talking about an American than at any previous time in our history. Clearly, things have changed somewhat, as we currently are fighting enemies abroad.

Was this increasingly punitive approach attributable to citizen demand? Public opinion polls show support for many current criminal justice approaches (J. Roberts and Stalans 2000), but many claim that public support for "get tough" criminal justice approaches comes from public misconceptions about who is subject to these policies. That is, when citizens answer questions about their degree of support for a particular type of punishment, they are typically thinking about violent criminals. In fact, most offenders are nonviolent and actually produce little harm to society, even those offenders in prison (see Chapter Nine). When given more information about less punitive sentencing alternatives, Americans are far less punitive than politicians seem to believe (Donziger 1996, pp. 60–61).

How has the U.S. government sold crime control to its own citizens? Goode and Ben-Yehuda (1994b, p. 31) claim that images of crime suggest that "society has become morally lax" and thus "a revival of traditional values may be necessary; if innocent people are victimized by crime, a crackdown on offenders will do the trick." This involves "more laws, longer sentences, more police, more arrests, and more prison cells." Because many of the premises on which our crime control efforts are based are false claims, some government "criminal justice–speak" amounts to propaganda: "Propaganda is a technique for influencing social action based on intentional distortions and manipulation of communications. . . . While not all media and government presentation, or even a majority of it, is a conscious attempt at propaganda, many crime myths are the product of propaganda techniques" (Kappeler, Blumberg, and Potter 2000, p. 22).

Criminal justice expansion—including placing 100,000 more police officers on the streets and constructing more than 1,000 new prisons and jails (Schlosser 1998), which are overpopulated by as much as 25%—has disproportionately affected poor people and people of color. And recently, the rate of female incarceration has increased faster than the rate of male incarceration. Not only are the poor and minorities more likely to be incarcerated and subjected to other forms of punishment, but also their families and communities are thus more likely to suffer the consequences (see Chapter Twelve). These consequences, ironically, include increased exposure to criminogenic conditions. This has led many in the criminal justice community to conclude that we now have "good reason to worry about" the implications of criminal justice expansion "for social justice and democracy" (Beckett and Sasson 2000; Currie 2000).

One threat of increased criminal justice expansion is to individual freedoms of Americans, as established in the U.S. Constitution. Remember that much of the law was set up to protect individuals from their own government. Historical accounts of the purpose of the U.S. criminal justice network suggest that it was originally created to protect innocent citizens from an arbitrary and overzealous government. The founders of the U.S. government set it up so that government practices, including criminal justice practices, would be limited by law. In Chapter Three, you will see how your Constitutional rights allow you to enjoy certain protections from unwarranted government interference in your life.

So, is the criminal justice network intended to do what criminal justice scholars claim it is intended to do? Some question these stated goals of the criminal justice network and posit that it is really intended to do something else entirely. In Chapter Two, I examine these claims and address the role of politics and ideology in criminal justice to provide a more realistic impression of what our criminal justice network achieves.

CONCLUSION

The U.S. criminal justice network is made up of police, courts, and corrections. The main responsibilities of police include investigating alleged crimes and apprehending alleged offenders, whereas the main responsibilities of courts include determining legal guilt or innocence of accused offenders and upholding the presumption of innocence supposedly enjoyed by all Americans. The main responsibility of corrections is to carry out the punishment imposed by the courts under the laws that stipulate how punishment must be imposed on convicted offenders. The U.S. criminal justice network ideally aims to do justice and reduce crime. There are at least two conflicting meanings of justice, one concerned mostly with holding the guilty accountable for their crimes and the other with ensuring fairness in the criminal justice process. American criminal justice has, over the past few decades, prioritized its crime control concerns over its due process concerns. The result has been an erosion of U.S. Constitutional protections, with little benefit in terms of crime reduction.

ISSUE IN DEPTH
Justitia—The Lady Justice

The Lady Justice who appears on the cover of this book, peeking out from beneath a blindfold, has a name. This figure, named *Justitia* after the Roman goddess of justice, may have its origins in the Greek mythological goddess

Themis, who is considered the goddess of divine justice (Hansen 1999). Justitia has also appeared in Christian imagery "as a personification of the ancient virtue" of justice (Curtis and Resnick 1987, p. 1729).

Justitia has outlasted symbols of every other virtue of humankind. As Curtis and Resnick (1987, p. 1733) write, "[S]how us a hulking woman with scales, blindfold, and sword, and the association is immediate: Justice."

What is the significance of the symbol Lady Justice? The most common understanding of this symbol today is that the figure of "a blindfolded woman with a scale in one hand and a sword in the other" demonstrates that we are dedicated to treating all Americans with "fairness, equity" and in a manner that is right (Kappeler, Blumberg, and Potter 2000, p. 215). Such a figure implies that the imposition of justice will not be affected by demographic characteristics such as race, social class, and gender.

In essence, according to the myth of Justitia, everyone deserves equal justice: "Justitia is blindfolded so that she may be impartial" (Curtis and Resnick 1987, p. 1727). Hansen (1999, p. 1) explains that she is a symbol of "the fair and equal administration of the law, without corruption, avarice, prejudice, or favor."

What follows is a summary of six main points about the Lady Justice made by Dennis Curtis and Judith Resnick (1987), published in the *Yale Law Journal.* Consider these points when deciding for yourself what "justice blind" is supposed to mean.

- Justitia is not always depicted as blind.

At many times in history, Justitia wears no blindfold but simply stares forward. In other depictions, her eyes can be seen beneath or through wide spaces in a blindfold or she is peeking out, as she does in the image on the book cover. It is claimed that the appearance of Justitia's blindfold "coincided with the establishment of professional, independent judges, who stood apart from the sovereign and were not simply acting at its behest" (1757). Thus, the blindfold signified that justice was to be carried out neither in the interests of the powerful nor in fear of the powerful. An alternative conception of the blindfold is discussed later.

- Justitia typically carries scales.

The meaning of her scales may be traced back to the Egyptian Book of the Dead (c. 1400 B.C.), the Old Testament (Job 31:6), and weighing as a symbol of judgment in the Koran. Clearly, scales imply some type of weighing, although there is disagreement about what is to be weighed. The most commonly accepted meaning of the scales is that "each man receives that which is due him, no more and no less" (1749).

- Justitia also is commonly depicted holding a sword.

The significance of the sword, like that of the blindfold, is not clear. Most agree, however, that the sword is a symbol of the power of Justitia to condemn or punish those who "fail in their public duties" (1744). It "represents the rigor of justice, which does not hesitate to punish" (1749).

- Justitia has been depicted with other ambiguous items, including a cornucopia, a fasces (bundle of rods), a scepter, books, a human skull, an ostrich or a crane, and a dog and snake.

The meaning of these symbols is not clear. Some claim that they have positive meanings, while others suggest negative meanings. For example, is the ostrich a symbol of gluttony (an ostrich will eat anything before it) or of valor and endurance (its diet might even include metal)? An ostrich puts its head in the sand. Is this an indication of forgetfulness or of stupidity? Or is the ostrich another symbol of impartiality, because its feathers are so evenly distributed across its body? (1742). Most illustrations of Justitia do not contain such items, but when they are included, no one can be certain of their significance.

- Justitia may create a false impression of what justice is.

The more negative images of Justitia have been relegated to archives, while the more common images—Justitia in white robes, with the blindfold, scales, and sword—adorn courthouses and other government buildings in the United States. Many of us have never become aware of some of the more grotesque images of Justitia, or they have disappeared from our consciousness. For example, Justitia has been depicted without hands, which may suggest that she will avoid accepting bribes or punishing the guilty too brutally (1754). Other images of Justitia surrounded by severed human heads are also generally unrecognizable. It is possible that our current conception of justice is thus sanitized so that only positive images come to mind in the presence of Justitia.

An alternative view of Justitia is possible: "Sword and scales need not only remind us that Justice can be powerful and correct; they can also be interpreted as indications of Justice as harsh, unsympathetic, and unyielding." The blindfold may be interpreted as an indication that justice is blind—to abuses that occur right under her nose. It may thus suggest "a failure to see the truth" (1756). Perhaps the blindfold symbolizes Justitia's limitations or is even a censure for past faults. Or "is she blindfolded not to see the many injuries imposed in her name?" (1757).

For these reasons, Gottfredson (1999, p. 21) argues that the blindfold should be removed from figures showing Justitia. He writes, "Much of the criticism of the criminal justice system concerns a perceived lack of fairness and evenhandedness in decisions about accused and convicted offenders. The blindfold makes a good point, but it should be removed." Gottfredson suggests that, with "eyes open," Justitia will be able to ensure that American justice will be fair, ethically sound, and more effective.

- Justitia is a symbol used by the powerful to justify their actions in the name of "justice."

For example, when a person is convicted of a crime by a jury of his or her peers, the government is granted the right to punish the person: "The imposition of judgment, with its requisite violence, is an essential, inevitable aspect of governance. How convenient, how distancing from human subjectivity and fallibility, if such decisions go forth in the name of Justice" (Curtis and Resnick 1987, 1748).

No other cardinal or theological virtue is essential to the acts of lawmakers and law enforcers in exacting justice: "All sovereigns claim (notwithstanding evidence to the contrary) that their violence goes forth in the name of Justice." Clearly, humankind is fallible—we make mistakes. In the name of justice and its implied impartiality, governments have used and will continue to use force against their citizens, to restrict their citizens' liberty, and even to execute their citizens (1734). The "conscious use of justice imagery by governments" may be an effort by them to "legitimate their exercises of power by associating themselves with the concept of justice" (1743). In some ways, Justitia is "propaganda" to reassure Americans that actions of the government are in line with a "higher right" (1746).

Images of justice may "teach, inspire, pacify, or otherwise influence viewers" (1743). In the United States, Justitia suggests to young people that this is a fair country. It inspires us as a symbol of dedication against vices and injustices. It can pacify us as well, for in the presence of Justitia, we may assume that our government is just even in the face of evidence suggesting that it is not. We may tend to ignore conspicuous injustices, perhaps because we are forced to accept the judgments of powerful people in the name of justice (1767).

Whatever Justitia is really intended to mean, I concur with Curtis and Resnick (1987, 1764) when they write, "[O]ur hopes that justice . . . simultaneously be attuned to individual nuances and be evenhanded; that objectivity and subjectivity both be present; that justice know all that is needed but not know that which might corrupt or unfairly influence; that justice be rigorous in its equality yet 'now and then' relax in compassion."

In this book, I assume that American criminal justice should be blind to factors such as race, social class, and gender; thus, the cover of the book is adorned by a blindfolded Lady Justice. She is peeking out, suggesting that perhaps American justice is not blind. Throughout the book, I examine how well the U.S. criminal justice network achieves its goals of doing justice and reducing crime. The main concern is, "How just is American criminal justice?" That is, "Is justice really blind?"

Discussion Questions

1. What is a system?
2. What is the criminal justice network?
3. List some of the reasons for the claim that *system* is not an accurate term for the operations of the criminal justice network.
4. What are the three main components or parts of the criminal justice network?
5. Outline the main stages of the criminal justice network; that is, explain how a case proceeds from commission of a crime all the way to release from corrections.
6. What are the ideal goals of the American criminal justice network?
7. What is justice?
8. Compare corrective justice (justice as an outcome) and procedural justice (justice as a process).
9. Compare the ideal models of justice described by Herbert Packer: the due process and the crime control models.
10. Which ideal model of criminal justice does American criminal justice more closely resemble? Why?
11. What are the differences between crime control and crime prevention?
12. What types of activities of police, courts, and corrections are aimed at preventing crime?
13. Which component of the criminal justice network has the most resources? Why?
14. Which component of the criminal justice network employs the most people? Why?
15. What does the symbol Lady Justitia, the Lady Justice, mean?

CHAPTER TWO

THE ROLE OF POLITICS AND IDEOLOGY IN CRIMINAL JUSTICE: REALITIES

KEY CONCEPTS

Alternative goals of criminal justice
- *Serving interests and controlling the population*
- *Box: How does population control serve interests?*

Functions versus purposes of criminal justice
What is politics?
What is ideology?
How are politics, ideology, and criminal justice related?
- *Box: Comments by politicians about crime*
- *How did criminal justice become so political and ideological?*
- *Crime, politics, and ideology today*

Conclusion
Issue in Depth: McDonaldization of America's Police, Courts, and Corrections
Discussion Questions

INTRODUCTION

Is our nation's criminal justice network really intended to reduce crime and do justice, or could there be some alternative goals? Is it a coincidence that the people who are most likely to have run-ins with police, courts, and corrections are poor and relatively powerless? This chapter introduces two alternative goals of criminal justice, serving limited interests and population control. Although I do not think that there is a criminal justice conspiracy in the United States, I do show how criminal justice activity performs functions such as serving the interests of the powerful through population control. This chapter introduces two important concepts for understanding the reality of criminal justice activity in America—power and ideology. In this chapter, I show how politics, ideology, and criminal justice are related. Finally, I examine the political nature of defining and reacting to terrorism to demonstrate its relevance for American criminal justice policy.

ALTERNATIVE GOALS OF CRIMINAL JUSTICE

As noted in Chapter One, some question the stated goals of the criminal justice network and posit that it is intended to do something else entirely besides reducing crime and doing justice. For example, Jeffrey Reiman (1998), as might be guessed from the title of his book, *The Rich Get Richer and the Poor Get Prison,* suggests that the criminal justice network is really intended to fail at reducing crime and doing justice. Although this may seem silly at first, Reiman's argument is that some failures amount to success, depending on what is really sought.

Serving Interests and Controlling the Population

Reiman (1998, p. 5) posits the *pyrrhic defeat theory,* which suggests that "the failure of the criminal justice system yields such benefits to those in positions of power that it amounts to a success." Reiman suggests that criminal justice processes are aimed at *population control* and *serving limited interests.* His main argument is that the interests of those in power are served when we focus almost exclusively on street crimes rather than other types of harmful behaviors. At the same time, those people whom we fear most (e.g., young, minority males) are routinely rounded up by the police and sent off to some form of government-controlled institution or community alternative. This amounts to a form of population control, so that the enemies in the war on crime can never win, can never achieve the types of success that are enjoyed by those with the power to achieve. The following box discusses examples of how control of criminals serves limited interests.

Among other things, Reiman (1998) argues that the label "crime" (particularly "serious crime") is not used for the most harmful and frequently occurring acts that threaten us. He claims that the criminal law distorts the image of crime so that the most dangerous threats are seen as coming

How does population control serve interests?

Think about all of the people in American prisons and jails. Currently, just over 2 million people are incarcerated in the United States. Guess what? The incarceration rate in the United States is now the highest in the world—we are number one! If there were an "Imprisonment Olympics," we would win the gold medal!

I guess this explains why some politicians celebrate our first-place standing in imprisonment as a success. For example, President Bill Clinton bragged, to a standing ovation of Congress, that the United States had imprisoned more than 1 million criminals. Why do we treat incarceration as a sign of success rather than a sign of failure? Perhaps if all Americans were safer as a result of our incarceration boom—both now and in the future—we would have reason to celebrate. Yet rates of violent crime in America, especially murders committed by handguns, are astonishingly high (see Chapter Four).

In fact, having so many people in prison is a success in many ways. For example, even though inmates are not free people working outside in the labor force, they are not counted in calculations of the unemployment rate. If we assume, as many scholars do, that a very large percentage of these inmates is not employable (because they have a low educational level, a criminal record, and many other disadvantages), what would happen to the unemployment rate if these people were free? One estimate in the mid-1990s suggested that the U.S. unemployment rate would increase by at least 1.5% if we counted all the men in our nation's prisons (Reiman 1998). Yet when politicians stand up in front of the American people and speak about unemployment, they do not have to count incarcerated people as part of the unemployment problem. This serves their own political interests, as well as those of their parties.

Additionally, some criminologists have equated crime control, especially the nation's prisons and jails, with industry. Without any doubt, crime pays tremendous dividends for business interests. Businesses now compete for contracts to provide products and services to American jails and prisons. In fact, companies such as the Corrections Corporation of America and Wackenhut run their own correctional facilities for profit. Once businesses have vested interests in making profits from crime control, it is logical that business-friendly government will do whatever it takes to ensure a steady supply of offenders, so that the criminal justice network will continue to pay off (Christie 1994). Perhaps this is why correctional officer hiring and training has become one of the "fastest-growing functions" of government (Lilly and Knepper 1993, p. 155).

It is ironic, when you stop and think about it, how many people benefit from our "wars" against crime and drugs. Kappeler, Blumberg, and Potter (2000, p. 45) write that enormous sums of money and millions of jobs are created by criminal justice, including about $65 billion spent on private security alone. Can you make a list of all the people who benefit from our crime problem? Be sure to include individuals working not only for police, courts, and corrections, but also for all the private businesses that service these agencies. Additionally, be sure to think about all the students and professors who now have something about which to study and write. If politicians in the 1970s, 1980s, and 1990s had not chosen to pursue crime with such vigor, leading to staggering increases in criminal justice spending and tremendous growth in criminal justice, what would all these people be doing right now?

from below us (i.e., from the lower class) when they really come from above us (i.e., from the upper class). In later chapters, I provide evidence that this is true by discussing how the law is biased against certain segments of the population (Chapter Three), which types of crime are actually the most dangerous (Chapter Four), and how the media portray crime (Chapter Five). Additionally, the war on crime may in effect be a war against particular segments of the U.S. population (Chapter Twelve), and our efforts to curb drug use in the United States may be aimed primarily at what are perceived to be poor people's drugs (Chapter Eleven).

The segments of the population being controlled by America's crime control efforts are poor people and minorities. Several criminologists have noted that the criminal justice network is, in effect, the primary mechanism in the United States responsible for controlling the "poor masses" (Rusche and Kirchheimer 1939), the "dangerous classes" (Shelden 2001), the "problem populations" (Spitzer 1975), and the nation's "surplus population" (Quinney 1977). Such hypotheses have been supported by evidence showing that poor, unemployed members of racial minority groups are likely to receive harsher sentences than employed minority group members and

Caucasians (e.g., see Chiricos and Bales 1991; Chiricos and Delone 1992; Nobling, Spohn, and Delone 1998).

Consistent with this evidence, Morris (1988, p. 113) writes that "the whole law and order movement that we have heard so much about is, in operation though not in intent, anti-black and anti-underclass—not in plan, not in desire, not in intent, but in operation." It is hard to imagine criminal justice processes in the United States aimed at serving limited interests and controlling certain segments of the population. Before you dismiss this possibility, however, consider that our criminal justice network may achieve certain functions without actually intending to achieve them.

FUNCTIONS VERSUS PURPOSES OF CRIMINAL JUSTICE

Criminal justice in the United States may achieve certain functions without actually intending to achieve them. This is an important distinction to understand. As Reiman (1998) points out, political processes can achieve certain outcomes without being purposeful. Reiman argues that criminal justice network failure was not set in place by some vast conspiracy of old, rich, white men who wanted to protect their limited interests. Instead, Reiman maintains, criminal justice evolved over time into processes that are unjust and that protect limited interests. Those who benefit from this obviously have no reason to change the status quo, and those harmed by the inherent biases of the criminal justice network do not have the intellectual or financial means to change it.

Herbert Gans (1995) makes a similar argument in his book *The War Against the Poor*. I return to the thrust of this argument in Chapter Twelve, but essentially Gans argues that American government has always been engaged in a war against poor people (including criminals), particularly the "undeserving underclass." Gans writes that "labeling the poor as undeserving . . . has some uses, or positive functions, or beneficial consequences, for more fortunate Americans . . . resulting in material and immaterial benefits, even though they are not immediately apparent, particularly to the people who benefit from them" (p. 91). Gans goes on to explain that functions are not the same as purposes:

> They are not what people intend to do, but are the consequences of what they actually do, whatever their initial purposes. Consequently, functions are usually neither intended nor recognized when they first emerge, and some are unintended but unavoidable because they follow from the demands of politically important groups. Whatever their origin, however, once these functions exist and produce benefits, their beneficiaries may develop an interest in them and even establish interest groups to defend them.

Figure 2.1 shows U.S. government spending on criminal justice. Notice that spending on criminal justice has increased tremendously over the years. At the same time, government funding for assisting poor people, who are disproportionately likely to be minorities (Beckett and Sasson 2000), has decreased. Welfare reform laws and welfare-to-work programs are also aimed primarily at minorities, even though most people on welfare are not minority group members (Tonry 1995). Tonry claims that such welfare reform laws are not likely to be effective in communities where African American males are absent (p. 6). And criminal justice efforts disproportionately affect minority males and their communities (see Chapter Twelve). Tonry writes, "Poor minority communities cannot prosper when so many of their young men are prevented from settling into long-term personal relationships, getting or keeping jobs, and living conventional lives" (p. vii).

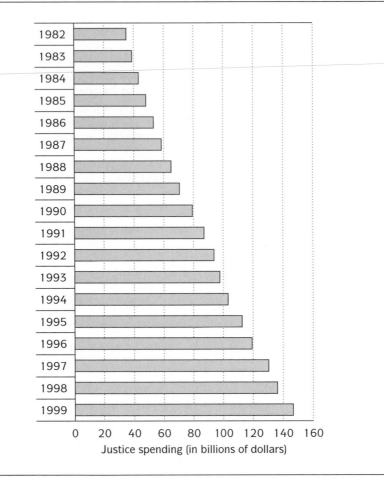

FIGURE 2.1

Spending by the U.S. Government on Criminal and Civil Justice

SOURCE: U.S. Department of Justice, *Sourcebook of Criminal Justice Statistics* (Washington, DC: U.S. Government Printing Office, 2003), p. 2.

Ironically, criminal justice policy has created these outcomes. And government policies of the 1980s "openly and successfully fought to reduce federal funding for social, educational, and housing programs and for aid to cities . . . promoted a strategy of federal disinvestment in the inner cities, which accelerated their deterioration and diminished the scope and quality of urban public services" (p. 40).

Is it possible that the criminal justice network serves functions vital to preserving the status quo in the United States, even though these functions are not intended? And if this is so, why don't those with relatively less power rise up and demand change? Reiman (1998) explains that they simply do not have the power or the will to do so. Another reason may be that the criminal justice network is highly affected by politics and ideology, two terms discussed in the following sections.

WHAT IS POLITICS?

Politics is about who gets what economic benefits in society, when they get them, and how they get them (Lasswell 1936). It is concerned with deciding who gets to keep most of the income generated in the United States and how that income will be used (Harrigan 2000). Politics is also about allocating society's values (Easton 1953), at least for those who have the ability to have their values enacted into law. Then resources are allocated for purposes of legitimating these values through government authority. One mechanism to achieve this is criminal justice. To the degree that politics is involved in criminal justice operations, an understanding of politics is necessary to understand fully the realities of criminal justice in America.

WHAT IS IDEOLOGY?

The term *ideology* was first coined by philosopher Destutt de Tracy, and referred to a "science of ideas" that he hoped would reveal people's unconscious habits of mind. Ideology today "now tends to refer to those very habits of mind—beliefs, assumptions, expectations, etc.—which are superimposed on the world in order to give it structure and meaning and which then serve to direct our political or social activities" (Cline 2002, p. 1).

There is a dominant ideology that underlies the criminal justice network in the United States. Durham (1992, p. 49) writes: "Crime and the state response to crime are highly visible processes that involve many fundamental issues regarding the application of values to law formation, the use of coercion to regulate behavior, the definition and protection of individual rights, the limits of state power, and the maintenance of social order." To the degree that this is true, an understanding of ideology is necessary to understand the realities of criminal justice in America.

HOW ARE POLITICS, IDEOLOGY, AND CRIMINAL JUSTICE RELATED?

Politics, ideology, and criminal justice are intimately linked and inseparable. Because of the close ties among them, it may be easier to understand how some interests get served while others are ignored or even harmed. For example, those with political power, or "the ability of individuals or groups to influence government as it allocates a society's resources" (Harrigan 2000, p. 25), are more likely to have their interests served at the expense of others.

Although criminal justice policy development is affected by groups other than lawmakers, including the media, voters, lobbies, and other special interest groups (see Chapter Three), politicians play the largest role in setting the crime control agenda. Politicians have the greatest ideological influence on what we do in criminal justice; this is because of their *power*. Power comes in various forms (e.g., political, economic, moral) and is "the ability to have a say, or to have influence, in what the government's policies are going to be" (Marion 1995, p. 4, citing Lowi and Ginsberg 1990). Because politicians create policies of criminal justice, they have power to determine the path of our nation's efforts to control and prevent crime. The U.S. Congress, for example, has the power to define crimes, create criminal justice agencies, provide or withhold funding for criminal justice programs (Steel and Steger 1988), and act as a public forum for public debate (Marion 1995, p. 15).

Politics and ideology are involved in criminal justice in numerous ways. The most significant is in deciding which behaviors should and should not be considered "crime." Crime is defined through a political process by a very small group of people in the United States (lawmakers or legislators) who, ideally, are representatives of the people. Richard Quinney's (1970) concept of the *social reality of crime* demonstrates that crime is imaginary rather than real; that is, it is invented by human beings with the power to do so (see Chapter Three). Therefore, all criminal justice policies that emanate from the criminal law are "merely definitions developed by people (authorities) who possess the power to shape, enforce, and administer such policies" (Arrigo 1999, p. 6). Crime and criminal justice practices are thus efforts by the powerful to control others and maintain power.

Kappeler, Blumberg, and Potter (2000), in *The Mythology of Crime and Criminal Justice*, argue that since crime is defined in a political process, crime issues and criminal justice policy decisions will be affected by the same factors that influence all political issues. These factors include partisanship (e.g., Democrats fighting Republicans) and symbolic crusading (e.g., by moral entrepreneurs, claims-makers, the media, and others with vested interests in bringing crime problems to the public's attention). What may get lost in the shuffle are key truths about crime and criminal justice.

One notable example of criminal justice policy illustrates how politics affects criminal justice processes. In September 1994, President Bill Clinton signed a $30 billion crime bill (the Violent Crime Control and Law Enforcement Act). Its stated purpose was "to prevent crime, punish criminals, and restore a sense of safety and security to the American people" (as quoted in Gaines, Kaune, and Miller 2000, p. 25). This law allowed for the hiring of 100,000 new police officers for the streets and the construction of thousands of new prison cells, changes that would supposedly make it easier to catch suspected criminals and provide living spaces for those who were ultimately convicted of criminal offenses. Also, the death penalty was expanded to cover dozens of additional murders, and some styles of assault weapons were banned. Numerous provisions were established that made it easier to convict defendants more quickly and to carry out their punishment in a less costly manner (Beckett and Sasson 2000, p. 72). Finally, limited funding was generated for crime prevention programs (Masci 1994a, 1994b), but this was ultimately cut by 1996 legislation (Beckett and Sasson 2000, p. 73).

Were any of the components of this new crime bill actually going to reduce crime rates in the United States? Reiman (1998, p. 2) writes, "No one can deny that if you lock enough people up, and allow the police greater and greater power to interfere with the liberty and privacy of citizens, you will eventually prevent some crime that might otherwise have taken place." Yet it was highly unlikely that such criminal justice policy would produce large declines in crime, given that crime rates are driven by factors beyond the control of the criminal justice network, such as employment rates, poverty rates, and the age of the population (see Chapter Four).

Here's one example of how ineffective this crime bill will likely be: Imagine the promise of 100,000 new police on the street. Assuming that we eventually achieve this goal (we have not yet), keep in mind that there will never actually be 100,000 more police on the streets at one time. It takes at least five additional officers to provide one additional officer on the street around the clock because of varied shifts, vacations, illnesses, and so forth (Bayley 1994). This means that if an additional 100,000 new police officers were hired, only 20,000 additional officers would be on the streets around the clock. If these officers were hired to police the 50 states equally, each state would gain only 400 additional officers. How many would this mean for your town or city? It is pretty clear that 20,000 additional "around-the-clock" officers will not prevent much crime.

Further, evidence suggests that much of the federal money allocated to police departments through block grants has really been used to increase technological capabilities of police departments instead of to hire new officers.

So what was this legislation really intended to do? Marion (1995, p. 1) asserts that this "legislation was merely a symbolic gesture to increase politicians' popularity in the months before the up-coming mid-term elections." Politicians did not want to be seen by the public or portrayed by their opponents as being "soft on crime." Since the 1960s, being "tough on crime" has been a necessary criterion for being a politician (Rosch 1985). Whether this approach is effective is not discussed, because in politics it is not relevant. How this approach interferes with your individual rights is virtually ignored.

The following box contains statements made by politicians of the 1990s. These comments are not casual, off-the-cuff remarks. Instead, they reflect behind-the-scenes, carefully planned strategies (especially advertisements) of some politicians to grab power and hold it, something that is not highly informed by, or beneficial to, the electorate.

Thanks to such politicians, our agencies of police, courts, and corrections now operate much like a fast food chain, aimed not only at being tough on crime but also at being as efficient as possible. In the Issue in Depth at the end of the chapter, I discuss how America's criminal justice network has become "McDonaldized."

The authors of the National Criminal Justice Commission's report, *The Real War on Crime*, describe efforts by U.S. politicians to deal with crime as a "hoax": "Politicians at every level—federal,

Comments by politicians about crime

- Texas Senator Phil Gramm said on television that he wanted a "real crime bill" that "grabs violent criminals by the throat, puts them in prison, and that stops building prisons like Holiday Inns."
- North Carolina congressional candidate Frederick Heineman proposed that the North American Free Trade Agreement (NAFTA) be used to send U.S. criminals to Mexico so that they could be "warehoused more cheaply" (in Beckett and Sasson 2000, p. 72).
- President George W. Bush (the second), in his earlier campaign to be governor of Texas, attacked the presiding Texas governor, Ann Richards, for being soft on crime, even though she supported the death penalty, increased state incarcerations, and reduced early release of violent offenders. Bush ran a political advertisement that was staged to look like footage of a real criminal attack, a man abducting a woman at gunpoint ("the people in the ad were the sound man and makeup artist of a production company") (Donziger 1996, p. 7). Then a police officer was shown covering a dead body with a blanket. The point of the ad was to criticize Richards for releasing 7,700 offenders before their scheduled release dates.
- Florida Governor Jeb Bush (brother of President George W. Bush), while campaigning for office, ran a political ad on television showing a woman who blamed his opponent, Governor Lawton Chiles, for failing to execute the killer of her daughter. The woman is shown speaking to the camera, saying, "Her killer is still on death row, and we're still waiting for justice.

> We don't get it from Lawton Chiles because he's too liberal on crime." The truth is that Chiles could not put the man to death because legal issues were still being heard in court. Chiles also had executed as many criminals as his Republican predecessor, who was supposedly tougher on crime (in Donziger 1996, pp. 80–81).
>
> - Bill McCullom, U.S. representative from Florida, talking to a radio reporter about juvenile delinquents, said, "They're not children anymore. They're the most violent criminals on the face of the earth" (in Krajicek 1998, p. 205).
> - Ernest Fletcher, candidate for a Kentucky legislative seat, ran a television ad featuring a young, blond woman named Jessica, who said:
>
> It was the worst day of my life. My attacker was convicted and got six months in jail. Ernesto Scorscone [Fletcher's political opponent] was his lawyer. He must have thought six months was too harsh, because twice Scorscone appealed just to get the case thrown out or the sentences reduced. Now Scorscone's telling us he's tough on crime. But he's not being honest with you. Everyone deserves a defense. But to me, Scorscone is more concerned with criminals' rights than victims' rights.
>
> The words "Raped," "Shot Twice," and "Left for Dead" appeared on the television screen while Jessica was speaking because Jessica had been abducted, raped, and shot by her attacker. What Fletcher did not tell viewers was that the case had happened two decades before the election, that Scorscone was a public defender who had been appointed to the case by the court, that the law at the time allowed a maximum sentence of only 4 years given that the accused was a juvenile, and that the appeals were filed because of evidence suggesting that the accused might in fact be innocent (in Kappeler, Blumberg, and Potter 2000, pp. 46–47).

state, and local—have measured our obsession, capitalized on our fears, campaigned on 'get tough' platforms, and won" (Donziger 1996, p. 2). The gist of the argument by the National Criminal Justice Commission is that the war on crime, though a victory for politicians and other limited interests, has mostly been a failure for Americans.

Since September 11, 2001, when the United States was attacked by terrorists, our focus has shifted somewhat to controlling and preventing terrorism. Thus, politics and ideology are now at work in dealing with forms of crime related to terrorism, while common crimes occupy less of our common awareness.

Whether you examine our nation's responses to street crime or terrorism, the dominant ideology underlying the policies and practices of police, courts, and corrections is conservative, characterized by unplanned policies that are tough on crime, individualistic in their focus, and nonrehabilitative (Welsh and Harris 1999). Most of our reactions to crime problems involve *unplanned change*, meaning that they are designed on a whim, without much thought or study, because they sound good or appeal to common sense. They are tough on crime in the sense that they are aimed at punishing offenders as much as possible based on the assumption that criminal behavior is freely chosen by rational people who should be held accountable for their actions regardless of the conditions that gave rise to their behaviors. And they increasingly reject any calls for treatment or a rehabilitative focus. Finally, they are explicitly nonpreventive in the sense that they are almost never aimed at ameliorating the conditions that produced the behaviors in the first place.

How Did Criminal Justice Become So Political and Ideological?

If this is true, how did we as a nation get to such a point? Numerous scholars have illustrated how crime originally became a significant political issue in the United States, used to advance a given ideological agenda (e.g., see Cronin, Cronin, and Milakovich 1981; Marion 1995; Scheingold 1984; J. Wilson 1975). Most attribute the politicization of crime at the national level to charges made by Republican senator Barry Goldwater, who ran for president in 1964 against Democratic president Lyndon Johnson. Goldwater blamed Johnson for rising crime rates and characterized the president as "soft on crime" (Rosch 1985). One statement by Goldwater illustrates his beliefs clearly:

> History shows us that nothing prepares the way for tyranny more than the failure of public offi-
> cials to keep the streets safe from bullies and marauders. We Republicans seek a government
> that attends to its fiscal climate, encourage a free and a competitive economy and enforcing law
> and order. (Quoted in Beckett 1997, p. 31)

Goldwater also attacked public assistance programs by linking them to crime:

> If it is entirely proper for the government to take away from some to give to others, then won't
> some be led to believe that they can rightfully take from anyone who has more than they? No
> wonder law and order has broken down, mob violence has engulfed great American cities, and
> our wives feel unsafe in the streets. (Quoted in Beckett 1997, p. 35)

This type of "tough" stance on crime was typical in the 1964 campaign.

Other events of the 1960s helped to make crime and criminal justice national concerns. For example, Beckett (1997, p. 28) claims that "the discourse of law and order was initially mobilized by southern officials in their effort to discredit the civil rights movement." Clearly, Southern agencies of criminal justice, in particular, law enforcement agencies, characterized and fought civil rights activities as acts of crime rather than as struggles for civil rights. Peaceful protests, sit-ins, marches, and similar methods of civil disobedience were characterized as evidence of a disrespect for law and order rather than as struggles for basic human rights. This characterization permitted and even mandated government intervention against civil rights leaders and led to the characterization of Martin Luther King, Jr., as the most dangerous man in America.

A statement from former Republican vice president Richard Nixon claimed that "the deterioration of respect for the rule of law can be traced directly to the spread of the corrosive doctrine that every citizen possesses an inherent right to decide for himself which laws to obey and when to disobey them" (in Beckett and Sasson 2000, p. 50). Some claim that, even today, crime is a code word for race, because it refers "indirectly to racial themes but do[es] not directly challenge popular democratic or egalitarian ideals" (Omi 1987, p. 120; see also Edsall and Edsall 1991).

Since the 1960s, crime has been a national issue that has been used for political gain (and loss) in each presidential election and also in hundreds of elections at other levels of government (Gest 2001; Marion 1995). The National Criminal Justice Commission claims: "Since 1968, six major anti-crime bills have passed Congress and been signed into law by presidents. In one way or another, all of these bills have been used by elected officials to convince the public that Washington was getting 'tough' on crime by increasing sentences for certain types of offenses" (Donziger 1996, p. 13). The 1994 crime bill described earlier is no exception.

The federal government seems perfectly willing to continue controlling criminal justice policy. It ensures its control over state efforts to reduce crime by promising billions of dollars to states that follow its lead—for example, by allocating prison funds to states that require offenders to serve at least 85% of their sentences and by encouraging states to try juveniles as adults (Donziger 1996). States agree to engage in such criminal justice practices so that they will not lose resources from the federal government. Hence, criminal justice policy at the state level flows less from its potential efficacy than from the states' financial concerns. The politicization of crime at the national level has created this paradox.

Crime, Politics, and Ideology Today

However crime first became such a political and ideological issue, it is clear that in today's heated political environment, even local, city-level elections sometimes deteriorate into political rhetoric about being "tough on crime." For example, in a mayoral election in Tallahassee, Florida, the incumbent charged his opponent with being soft on crime because he advocated replacing DARE (Drug Abuse Resistance Education) in schools with alternative strategies. Even though the opponent provided evidence of DARE's ineffectiveness (e.g., see Rosenbaum and Hanson 1998) and had the support of the local police chief on the issue, the incumbent was successfully reelected as a man of "good common sense."

The most notable use of a crime as a political issue was seen in the "Willie Horton" charges made against Democratic presidential hopeful Michael Dukakis by future Republican president George Bush (the first) in 1988. As governor of Massachusetts, Dukakis had supported early release programs as a means to reduce prison overcrowding and as a low-risk way to reintegrate offenders into the community through meaningful employment. An inmate from Massachusetts named Willie Horton, on his ninth furlough from prison, committed a brutal rape and assault. This incident led Bush to attack Dukakis as being "soft on crime"; Bush assured citizens that if he was elected president, he would continue to expand criminal justice powers to fight crime. Even though the "Horton case was atypical and exaggerated," it worked: Bush was successfully elected president of the United States (Merlo and Benekos 2000, p. 14).

In each election since then, it has been hard to tell Republicans from Democrats on crime control issues, because both have supported more police, more power for prosecutors, more prisons, more money for the war on drugs, more executions, limited appeals for death row inmates, and so forth.

In the 1980s, Republican presidents Ronald Reagan and George Bush (the first) wanted faster-moving, tougher criminal justice agencies and helped shift the perception of the causes of crime from society to the individual. A Reagan statement illustrates his party's stance on crime control: "Government's function is to protect society from the criminal, not the other way around" (in Beckett 1997, p. 48). Under Democratic president Bill Clinton in the 1990s, the focus was much the same, including more police on the streets and tougher sentences for convicted criminals. Clinton's 1994 crime bill, discussed earlier, allocated $8.8 billion for hiring more police and $7.9 billion for state prison grants. In the 1980s and 1990s, significant increases occurred in incarceration rates, and now both parties sell being "tough" on crime to the masses (Merlo and Benekos 2000).

Kappeler, Blumberg, and Potter (1996, p. 49) argue:

> Exaggerating and distorting the amount and shape of the crime threat is standard fare for politicians. Democrats and Republicans compete to see who can spend the most money and appear the most punitive in putting together crime control legislation. . . . It is not scientific proof which persuades, it is appeal to fear about serial killers, stalkers, drive-by-shootings, car-jackings, and violent predators. Supporting such measures will no doubt curry favor with the voting public; telling the truth could lead to premature retirement.

Currently it is appeal to fear of terrorism that convinces Americans to support American criminal justice policies, no matter how destructive they may be to the very freedoms that we are supposedly defending.

Nevertheless, proposing shortsighted and simplistic criminal justice policies not only is misleading to consumers and voters, but tends to "conceal what is really at stake" with crime-related issues (Marion 1995, p. 94, citing Scheingold 1984). The complex causes of criminal behavior are almost never discussed by politicians, at least in public. Citizens and voters allow this because they have little accurate understanding of the nature of crime and crime trends and because they place their trust in legislators to study such issues carefully. As a result, criminal justice policies that may not work and even those that have been proved ineffective are virtually never criticized from within the criminal justice network.

Merlo and Benekos (2000) claim that the Willie Horton incident taught all politicians some important lessons about winning and losing:

- Don't be portrayed as being "soft on crime";
- Portray your opponent as "soft on crime";
- Simplify the crime issue; and
- Reinforce messages with emotional context. (pp. 14–16)

These are still the dominant ideological messages driving criminal justice practice. This is why the United States leads the world in incarceration rate (the number of people locked up in prisons and jails per 100,000 citizens) (see Chapter Nine), has an ever-expanding war on drugs that is responsible for arresting, convicting, and punishing millions of people for simple possession and use of some relatively minor drugs (see Chapter Eleven), and nearly leads the world in its use of capital punishment (see Chapter Ten). Virtually no politician is willing or able to even question the logic or validity of such practices, despite their numerous flaws and lack of efficacy.

With an understanding of the role of politics and ideology in criminal justice practice, you should be able to see that: our criminal justice agencies are institutions of government social control; as institutions of government social control, our agencies of criminal justice are political enterprises; as political enterprises, the key phenomenon that drives criminal justice activity—from lawmaking through police, courts, and corrections—is ideology; the American bipartisan government structure is represented by conservative and liberal political ideologies; the conservative political ideology is currently the dominant American political ideology, ergo the behavior of our criminal justice network is presently under the dominant influence of the conservative crime control model; because the conservative crime control model is the dominant influence on our network of criminal justice, the nature and amount of our criminal justice activities will have little to do with actual crime rates and will have more to do with perceptions of crime problems generated by politicians; criminal justice processes are therefore not truly aimed at reducing crime or necessarily doing justice but, rather, at achieving certain political and ideological goals.

CONCLUSION

Instead of doing justice, the U.S. criminal justice network may serve other functions, including serving limited interests and controlling certain segments of the population. It is clear that criminal justice does not exist or occur in a vacuum. Our efforts to do justice and to reduce crime are driven by political and ideological factors even more than by actual crime rates, evidence of criminal justice failure, or concerns over eroding Constitutional protections. This in itself may be perceived as unjust by U.S. citizens and taxpayers, who should be able to expect more from their leaders than playing politics about crime and criminal justice, especially when so much is at stake.

ISSUE IN DEPTH
McDonaldization of America's Police, Courts, and Corrections

McDonaldization is a term created by sociologist George Ritzer (2000, p. 1) to describe the "the process by which the principles of the fast-food restaurant are coming to dominate more and more sectors of American society as well as the rest of the world." It is a process that represents the culmination of numerous practices of 20th-century America, including bureaucratization, scientific management, and assembly-line production.

According to Ritzer (2000), McDonaldization is made up of four elements.

1. *Efficiency* is "the optimum method for getting from one point to another" or for achieving some goal (p. 12). In the fast-food industry, efficiency is imperative, as the term *fast* implies.
2. *Calculability* is "an emphasis on the quantitative aspects of products sold . . . and services offered. . . . In McDonaldized systems, quantity has become equivalent to quality; a lot of something, or the quick delivery of it, means it must be good" (p. 12). In the fast-food industry, more for your money is better than less for your money.
3. *Predictability* refers to "the assurance that products and services will be the same over time and in all locales" (p. 13). In the fast-food industry, the goal is to make your entire dining experience completely consistent with all previous visits; no matter where you go, the product will be exactly the same.
4. *Control* means that many aspects of production and consumption are governed by strict rules and an emphasis on one way of doing things. In the fast-food industry, control is often achieved through the use of nonhuman technology (p. 236).

Any institution, system, or, in this case, network of agencies that stresses efficiency, calculability, predictability, and control can be thought of as being

McDonaldized. According to my own research, America's agencies of criminal justice (police, courts, and corrections) have been McDonaldized, which means that they tend to be aimed at efficiency, calculability, predictability, and control, perhaps even more than at justice.

Efficiency and Criminal Justice

The importance of efficiency in American criminal justice has always been stressed, perhaps never so much in our nation's history as in the past three decades. When agencies of criminal justice are more focused on controlling crime than assuring fairness and impartiality, efficiency of criminal justice becomes the most important value; informal processes such as plea bargaining are used in place of trials to expedite criminal justice operations and hold a larger proportion of criminals accountable for their criminal acts.

To the degree that cases move through the criminal justice network as on an "assembly line," criminal justice practice is much like a fast-food production line. Modern criminal justice practice aims to be efficient, even at the cost of due process rights of defendants. As you saw in Chapter One, most criminal justice resources go to police and corrections, with courts receiving the fewest resources. The result is that almost all convictions by courts are achieved through the assembly-line process of plea bargaining; less than 10% of convictions occur in criminal trials.

Allegiance to efficiency can also be seen within each of the agencies of criminal justice: police, courts, and corrections. With regard to policing, the increased use of directed and aggressive patrol techniques (including foot and bike patrol), as part of a *problem-oriented policing* strategy, provides evidence that law enforcement values efficiency. The *zero-tolerance policing* in our nation's largest cities, aimed at eliminating small problems of disorder before they grow into large crime problems, is further evidence of an allegiance to efficiency. The shift from two- to one-man police cars based on the realization that one-man cars are just as effective as those occupied by two officers provides further evidence of the importance of efficiency in policing. Finally, the growth of technology in policing, from crime analysis and crime mapping to fingerprinting and computers in squad cars, suggests that policing is much more focused on proactive strategies than it has been historically.

With regard to courts, the popularity of plea bargaining provides tremendous evidence of the significance of efficiency in American courts. The ideal of American justice is an adversarial process, whereby prosecutors and defense attorneys fight for truth and justice in a contest at trial. Yet an administrative system is in effect, as evidenced by the widespread use of plea bargaining in courts; these cases are handled informally in hallways and offices rather than in courtrooms. Instead of criminal trials, where prosecutors and defense attorneys clash in an effort to determine the truth and do justice for all concerned parties, prosecutors, defense attorneys, and sometimes judges "shop" for "supermarket" justice through plea bargaining. Criminal trials are now the exception to the rule of plea bargaining. Plea bargaining achieves only one thing—a more efficient court. Most criminologists and criminal justice scholars view plea bargaining as an unjust process driven by large caseloads, understaffed courts, and the renewed emphasis on using law enforcement to solve drug use and public order offenses (see Chapter Seven).

With regard to corrections, the renewed emphasis on efficiency is evident in the increased use of incarceration to achieve incapacitation and deterrence of large numbers of inmates. Increased use of imprisonment is discussed in the next section. Here, it should simply be noted that a greater use of imprisonment implies to consumers that the criminal justice network will be more efficient in preventing crime because it will prevent criminality by those currently locked up and instill fear in those considering committing crimes.

Other evidence of the focus on increased efficiency in corrections includes legislative efforts to expedite executions by limiting appeals and the elimination of gain time and parole by states and the federal government. The elimination of gain time and parole is a major factor contributing to prison overcrowding.

Calculability and Criminal Justice

A greater emphasis has been placed on calculability in criminal justice over the past three decades—policymakers seem much more satisfied with more criminal justice (quantity) rather than better criminal justice (quality). *Victimless crimes* have, at virtually all times in our nation's history, been criminalized and we have fought numerous wars on drugs, yet the most recent war on drugs under presidents Reagan, Bush (the first), Clinton, and Bush (the second) has stressed much more criminal justice intervention than at any other time in our nation's history. As a nation, we have spent more than $300 billion on the war on drugs since 1980; the cost of the drug war increased from just over $1 billion in federal dollars in the early 1980s to almost $20 billion in federal dollars in 2001. The largest portion of the 2001 figure (as in every previous year) was intended for domestic law enforcement, while treatment and prevention received less than this and domestic social programs have been cut dramatically to pay for the war on drugs. The largest spending increases between the end of the Clinton presidency and the beginning of the Bush presidency (1996 and 2001) were for international spending and interdiction, while prevention and treatment increased less (see Chapter Eleven).

In policing, we see calculability in the promises by politicians to place more cops on the street and to build more prisons. We also see calculability in asset forfeitures in the nation's drug war. The reward for police is being allowed to confiscate and keep some drug-related assets, including cars, houses, cash, and other property. To some degree, law enforcement officials have come to rely on drug assets to purchase equipment and conduct training so that police can exterminate drug use. The majority of law enforcement agencies in the United States have asset forfeiture programs in place (see Chapter Six).

In courts, the value of calculability is seen in the passing of longer sentences for virtually all crimes. It is also evident in laws that require offenders to serve greater portions of their sentences—the so-called "truth in sentencing" laws (see Chapter Eight).

In corrections, calculability means the construction of more prisons, more people being sent to prison, and a renewed use of capital punishment. The imprisonment rate in America has historically been relatively constant. It has fluctuated over the years, but never until the 1970s did it consistently and dramatically increase. In 1973, America began to engage in an imprisonment orgy (see Chapter Nine). Since the early 1970s there has been an approximately 6.5% increase in imprisonment each year. Most of the increase has been due to drugs; from 1980 to 1993, the percentage of prisoners serving sentences for drugs offenses more than tripled in state prisons and more than doubled in federal prisons. America now has more than twice the rate of prisoners per 100,000 citizens of any other democracy and more than five times the rate of democracies such as Canada, England, Germany, and France.

The ironic fact remains, however, that drug use trends have largely been unaffected since 1988 and drug abuse levels have always hovered at approximately the same level (see Chapter Eleven). The increased commitment to calculability—more criminal justice—has not resulted in substantial reductions in crime rates or in drug use and abuse.

Predictability and Criminal Justice

If one were to fairly assess the performance of our nation's criminal justice network in terms of crime control over the past century, one could conclude that the likelihood of being subjected to it was always very low; that is, the most predictable thing about it has been that reactive criminal justice processes fail. Even today, being apprehended, convicted, and sentenced to imprisonment is highly unlikely for all crimes other than murder.

The most important factor in the effectiveness of deterrence is the certainty of punishment, that is, the likelihood of being punished. Research on deterrence has consistently found that the severity of a sentence has less of a deterrent effect than sentence certainty (see Chapter Eight). American criminal justice performs poorly in providing certain, swift punishments that outweigh the potential benefits of committing crimes. Putting more cops on the street and increasing the use of prison sentences are efforts to make criminal justice outcomes more predictable.

In terms of policing, law enforcement officers now attempt to apprehend suspects by using offender profiling methods, which allows them to develop a picture of the offender based on elements of his or her crime. The scientific method has always been a part of policing, yet only in the past two decades has offender profiling been used by police.

Police also try to accurately predict those likely to get into trouble with the law before they commit criminal acts. They focus on particular types of people because of their own personal experience or that of their institution and profession, which suggests that certain people are more likely to violate the law. This practice, known as *police profiling*, results in startling disparities in police behavior based on class and race. Police use race, ethnicity, gender, and so forth as a proxy for risk (see Chapter Six). Using race to establish probable cause is even supported by courts as being legitimate when it is used in conjunction with other factors. Courts have stated that as long as the totality of the circumstances warrants the conclusion of the officer that the subject was acting suspiciously, race can be part of the circumstances considered by the officer. These elements of predictability in policing lead to difficulties in police–minority interactions, disproportionate use of force against people of color, and disrespect for the law generally.

American courts are also highly predictable in all they do. The main actors in this process within the criminal courts—the prosecutor, the defense attorney, and the judge—enter the courtroom each day knowing essentially what will happen before it does. Ideally, each member of the courtroom workgroup serves his or her own role and has his or her own goals; in reality, each member's main job is not to rock the boat in the daily operations of America's courts.

Because of the strong interpersonal working relationships among the courtroom crew, *going rates* are established in bail and sentencing. The process of plea bargaining, discussed earlier, serves as an excellent example. In studies of plea bargaining, cases are disposed of with great regularity and predictability, meaning that the resulting sentence is reliably predicted based on the nature of the charges and the defendant's prior record. A going rate is established for particular types of crimes committed by particular types of people, one that becomes established over time and that is learned by each member of the courtroom workgroup. Plea bargains typically closely parallel this going rate, and defendants charged with particular crimes can easily learn what sentence they likely face if they plead guilty (see Chapter Seven).

At the sentencing phase of courts, criminal penalties are highly predictable. Generally, the most important factors are the seriousness of the offense and the offender's prior record, so that the more serious the offense and the longer the prior record, the more severe the sentence will be. *Mandatory sentences* now establish a minimum sanction that must be served upon a conviction for a criminal offense. Thus, everyone who is convicted of a crime that calls for a mandatory sentence will serve that amount of time. Indeterminate sentences, which allowed parole, and determinate prison sentences, which could be reduced by good-time or earned-time credits, have been replaced by mandatory sentences across the country. Furthermore, *sentencing guidelines* have been established to make sentences more predictable and scientific based on a set of criteria including prior record, offense seriousness, and previous interactions with agencies of criminal justice. Sentencing grids reduce the discretion of judges and thus shift power to government prosecutors (see Chapter Eight).

The best example of mandatory sentences is the *"three-strikes" laws* in effect in more than half of our states. The logic of three-strikes laws is to increase penalties for second offenses and require life imprisonment without possibility of parole for third offenses (see Chapter Eight). These laws usually do not allow sentencing courts to consider particular circumstances of a crime, the duration of time that has elapsed between crimes, or mitigating factors in the background of offenders. The offender's potential for rehabilitation, ties to community, employment status, and obligations to children are also not taken into account.

Risk classification in corrections entails a great degree of prediction as well. Individuals convicted of crimes can be put on probation, incarcerated in jail or prison, or subjected to some intermediate sanction; largely their punishment is determined by offense seriousness, prior record, and behavior during previous criminal justice interventions. Yet each form of punishment entails more or less supervision, fewer or more rules to follow (e.g., probation versus intensive supervision probation), and/or greater restrictions on movement and activities (e.g., minimum versus maximum security) (see Chapter Nine). The most violent and/or unmanageable inmates are now placed in isolation or incarcerated for 23 hours of the day in supermax prisons. These issues are discussed in the following section.

Control and Criminal Justice

As you saw in Chapter One, in the past three decades, America has witnessed a rapid expansion of criminal justice. This is evidence of increased control efforts by the criminal justice network and is criticized for being a disinvestment in the nation's future.

This expansion is literally unparalleled in history, yet corresponding decreases in crime have not been achieved. Indeed, street crime decreased throughout the 1990s but only about one-fourth of this decrease is attributable to imprisonment (see Chapter Four). The clearest control issue in criminal justice revolves around corrections. Correctional facilities are now state-of-the-art in terms of their use of technology to manage inmates. Increased use of other technologies includes electronic monitoring of offenders under house arrest. *Supermaximum* prisons are the epitome of control. Offenders in *supermax* prisons have restricted contact with other inmates and with correctional personnel. Many inmates are locked in their cells for most of the day, stark cells with white walls and with bright lights on at all hours of day and night. Cells have completely closed-in front doors and no windows. In these prisons, prisoners are confined to their cells for 23 hours per day and can take showers only two or three times per week. When inmates are transferred, they are shackled in handcuffs and sometimes leg irons. Temperatures inside these facilities consistently register in the 80s and 90s.

The supermax facility gives us another interesting parallel between criminal justice and the fast-food industry. Technically, nothing can be more maximum than "maximum" custody, yet now we have supermax custody. In fast food, french fries used to come in small, medium, and large. Now they come in medium, large, and extra large; the extra large sizes are "supersized," "biggie sized," and even "super supersized" and "great biggie sized." French fries provide the fast-food industry the second-largest profit margin among its products. The McDonaldized fast-food industry tricks consumers into paying very high prices for a very small portion of one potato using deceptive terms such as super supersized and great biggie sized to convince consumers that they are getting a good deal; the McDonaldized criminal justice network creates the illusion through the term *supermax custody* that these institutions keep Americans safe. In fact, most supermax inmates will one day be released back into society, having to readjust to even living with other people. And the costs to taxpayers just to build such facilities can be more than $130,000 per inmate.

From the analysis presented, it is clear that our criminal justice agencies have fallen victim to McDonaldization. Each aims to be as efficient and predictable as possible, each uses quantity as an evaluative criterion, and each is highly controlling. Given the frequency of their exposure to the efficiency, calculability, predictability, and control of the fast food environment, people have probably come to expect these qualities from many institutions and services other than fast food restaurants. This makes it easier for politicians to tout and sell fast and easy solutions to the nation's crime problem. Unfortunately, as American police, courts, and corrections have become McDonaldized, irrational policies have resulted. Although there is more criminal justice today than 30 years ago, although much of criminal justice practice is now highly predictable, and although Americans may now believe that they are safer because the government is exerting more control over criminals, the truth is that Americans are less sure of receiving justice from their agencies of criminal justice.

Discussion Questions

1. Summarize Reiman's pyrrhic defeat theory.
2. Do you agree with Reiman? Explain.
3. What are two alternative goals of America's criminal justice network?
4. Whose interests are served by a large criminal justice network? Provide examples.
5. What is the difference between intended goals of criminal justice and functions served by criminal justice? Provide examples.
6. Compare and contrast spending on criminal justice and spending on social services over the past three decades.
7. What is *politics*?

8. What is *ideology*?
9. Identify some ways in which politics, ideology, and criminal justice are related?
10. When did American criminal justice become so political and ideological?
11. Find some examples of how recent events related to crime or criminal justice serve as evidence of their political and ideological nature.
12. What is meant by the term *McDonaldization*? In what ways has America's criminal justice network become McDonaldized?

CHAPTER THREE

THE LAW: PROVIDING EQUAL PROTECTION OR CREATING BIAS?

KEY CONCEPTS

What is the law?
- *Box: Examples of loony laws and silly statutes*

Where does the law come from?

Types of law
- *Natural law*
- *Positive law*
- *Box: The U.S. Constitution*
- *Common law*
- *Box: Some interesting North Carolina laws*
- *Criminal law and civil law*

What is the purpose of the criminal law?

Who makes the law?
- *Demographics of lawmakers*
- *Voting behavior*
- *Special interests/lobbying*

How the criminal law fails to protect Americans
- *Big Tobacco*

Conclusion

Issue in Depth: New Antiterrorism Laws

Discussion Questions

INTRODUCTION

This chapter begins with a definition of law and a discussion of where the law comes from. Distinctions are made between natural law, or law dictated by a higher source, and positive law, or law made by sovereign human beings. Different types of positive law are discussed, including

Constitutional law, statutory law, case law, and administrative law. I also demonstrate the primary differences between criminal law, which defines acts as crimes against the government, and civil law, which regulates torts or acts against individuals. This chapter also outlines the purposes of the criminal law. A vital part of this chapter is a detailed exploration of who makes the law. To illustrate that the criminal law may not represent all Americans, I examine demographic characteristics of lawmakers and voters and illustrate how rare voting is in the United States. I show how special interests shape the criminal law through lobbying and financial donations to campaigns and elections. From this investigation, it seems likely that the U.S. criminal justice network is biased in favor of the wealthy and powerful. Finally, I examine new antiterrorism laws, such as the USA PATRIOT Act, to demonstrate how the events of September 11, 2001, have affected American criminal justice operations.

WHAT IS THE LAW?

Have you ever wondered how certain acts became criminal? For example, how did killing another person become the crime of murder? Has killing always been illegal? The answer is no. Even today, there are several ways of killing someone that are still not considered crimes. These include killing someone in self-defense, killing someone in the line of duty as a police officer or military soldier, the state's executing someone through the administration of the death penalty, and killing "enemy" military personnel in times of war. Each of these means of killing is legal.

Why is it that some forms of killing are legal while other forms of killing are called "crimes"? Apparently, some forms of killing do not warrant the status of "crime." A behavior becomes a crime only when it is labeled a crime through the passage of a *law*. It is as simple as that. Rush (2000, p. 193) defines the law as "a general rule for the conduct of members of the community, either emanating from the governing authority by positive demand or approved by it, and habitually enforced by some public authority by the imposition of sanctions of penalties for its violation." Gilmer (1986, p. 194) defines the law as "a method for the resolution of disputes; a rule or action to which people obligate themselves to conform, via their elected representatives and other officials." From these two definitions, you can see that if lawmakers do not view an act as wrong, immoral, unethical, or harmful, it is not called a crime.

Thus, crimes are created when elected representatives decide to codify, or write down, behaviors as wrong, immoral, unethical, or harmful (Schmalleger 1999). As you will see in Chapter Four, a crime occurs when a person acts, fails to act, attempts to act, or agrees to act in a way that is in violation of the criminal law, without defense or justification. Because the law is what makes an act a crime, two important deductions can be made with regard to crime:

- No behavior is automatically a crime unless it is defined by the government as a crime.
- Any behavior can be made a crime.

With regard to the first point, many criminal justice scholars claim a distinction between *mala in se* crimes, acts that are inherently evil or bad, and *mala prohibita* crimes, acts that are evil or bad only because the government has labeled them criminal (Schmalleger 1999). This is really an artificial distinction, because no behavior is inherently wrong. It becomes wrong only when the government says that it is wrong. This is why there is no behavior that has been considered wrong in every society at all times in history. In numerous places, in fact, rape is still not illegal despite its atrocious nature. Some U.S. states still do not consider it rape when a man is forced into sex. Others still do not call it rape when a husband forces his wife into unwanted sexual activity.

Sheryl Lindsell-Roberts (1994) demonstrates the second point in her amusing book *Loony Laws and Silly Statutes*. In my state, North Carolina, for example, it is a crime for a man to talk to a woman who is attending an all-women's college while she is on campus. It is also a crime in North Carolina to take a deer swimming in water above its knees! In Florida, where I was born, it is against the law to take a bath with your clothes off. It is also a crime there to doze off under a hair dryer. These types of criminal laws can be found in every state.

Lindsell-Roberts's book provides examples of laws in every state that are unbelievable. The following box contains some examples from her book.

Examples of loony laws and silly statutes

- In Tennessee, it is against the law to drive while sleeping.
- In California, it is against the law for a woman to drive her car while wearing a housecoat.
- In Alabama, it is against the law to drive while barefoot or in bedroom slippers.
- In Florida, it is against the law to transport livestock aboard school buses.
- In Vermont, it is against the law to jump from a plane unless it is a true emergency.
- In Canada, it is against the law to board a plane after it has already taken off.
- In Washington, it is against the law to pretend that your parents are rich.
- In Kentucky, it is against the law to use a reptile as part of a religious service.
- In Massachusetts, it is against the law to eat peanuts while in church.
- In New Jersey, it is against the law to slurp soup.
- In Indiana, it is against the law to shoot a can of soup open.
- In Rhode Island, it is against the law to throw pickle juice on a trolley.
- In Tennessee, it is against the law to throw a banana peel on the sidewalk.
- In Wyoming, it is against the law to obstruct the view of fellow spectators by wearing a hat in a public theater.
- In Kansas, it is against the law to eat rattlesnake meat in public.
- In Minnesota, it is against the law to dance in public places.
- In Kentucky, it is against the law to remarry the same man four times.
- In Colorado, it is against the law to throw shoes at a wedding.
- In Missouri, it is against the law to carry a bear down the highway unless it is caged.
- In Washington, it is against the law to punch a bull in the nose.
- In Texas, it is against the law to milk someone else's cow.
- In Ohio, it is against the law to fish with explosives.
- In Indiana, it is against the law to take a bath during the winter.
- In Connecticut, it is against the law to chew tobacco without a doctor's permission.

- In Louisiana, it is against the law to gargle in public.
- In Oregon, it is against the law to force a dead person to serve on a jury.

SOURCE: Adapted from Sheryl Lindsell-Roberts, *Loony Laws and Silly Statutes* (New York: Sterling, 1994).

You may be wondering how such acts can be crimes. It is likely that at some time in history, these acts were considered problematic, probably because some people actually engaged in these acts and some type of harm resulted. Last year, my state of North Carolina created a new crime. It is now against the law to curse in the presence of a dead body. Apparently, a group of morticians grew tired of listening to all the foul language and thought it was disrespectful to the dead, so they lobbied to have such behavior prohibited by law. Every state has such loony laws and silly statutes on the books, even though they are not likely being enforced widely (if at all). When these laws are not enforced, do they need to be removed from the books?

WHERE DOES THE LAW COME FROM?

Acts are defined as crimes by human beings. Specifically, crimes are created by the U.S. Congress at the federal level, by legislatures at the state level, and by courts at every level of government when they interpret the law and set precedents through case law (Schmalleger 1999). Congress at the federal level and all state legislatures have the power to define behaviors as crimes. For example, at both levels of government, it is against the law to steal a car forcibly from another person; this is often called *carjacking*. Rush (2000, p. 44) defines carjacking as "the unauthorized seizure of a vehicle by the use of force, threats, or coercion." According to Rush, federal law mandates a 15-year sentence for carjacking and a life sentence if a person is killed during the offense. In Louisiana, it is currently legal for persons to use lethal force against another if they believe that they are being carjacked. This became law after a winning beauty pageant contestant made this the issue she addressed upon her victory.

Courts interpret the meaning of the written law and, in so doing, actually clarify what the written law means. For example, if a man forced a driver out of his or her car so that he could take his pregnant wife to the hospital during labor, would that be considered carjacking? A court would likely have to decide this issue and, in essence, would be making law by setting a precedent that all other courts in the same jurisdiction would be required to follow (see Chapter Seven). If a court heard a case in which a man was charged with carjacking in these circumstances and decided that such an act did not meet the definition of the crime in the statute (because the man did not intend to steal the car and thus did not intend to commit a carjacking), it would not be considered carjacking for human beings to engage in this behavior.

But where do we human beings get our law? Where did we get the notion that laws needed to be written down? The criminal law sets forth boundaries for acceptable behavior to ensure that we know what behaviors are wrong and what can happen to us if we commit wrongful acts. But where did the notions of right and wrong come from? An examination of different types of American law might answer these questions.

TYPES OF LAW

There are many types of law in the United States. Figure 3.1 depicts the main types of law and illustrates the relationships between them.

Natural Law

One type of law, known as *natural law*, is law from a higher source. If you are religious, this might be God's law—for example, the Ten Commandments delivered to Moses as explained in the Holy Bible. Natural law could also be considered "laws of the gods" (in polytheistic cultures). But natural law also exists for nonreligious people. Natural law might be the laws of "the force," for example, or laws of human nature. Natural law, whatever your beliefs about religion, is a recognition that there are wrong behaviors that are simply bad in themselves—these are the mala in se offenses. Other acts are inherently right, good, or just. Natural law in essence is greater than humankind—it was here before we got here and will be here after we depart. Schmalleger (1999, p. 16) defines natural law as those laws that "are fundamental to human nature and discoverable by human reason, intuition, or inspiration, without the need for reference to man-made laws."

The main problem with natural law is that no one can possibly know what it is. If there are universal truths, behaviors that are inherently good and bad, how can we know what they are? For example, if God has His or Her own idea about what is right and wrong, how can we know unless He or She comes down from Heaven and tells us? Since we cannot experience God directly with our empirical senses—that is, we cannot see, hear, or touch God—it is logically impossible to know God's laws.

Even if we rely on the Holy Bible to learn about natural law, which version do we use? How would we know which version is the correct one? Because religion is a matter of faith rather than evidence, you either believe it or you don't (Bohm 2001). This makes natural law useless as a

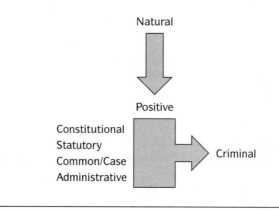

FIGURE 3.1
Types of Law

source of law for the purposes of informing us about right and wrong and of judging individuals' behaviors as right or wrong. So Americans end up disagreeing about rights and wrongs (even though we all do agree that there are rights and wrongs). Criminologists also disagree about which behaviors are wrong and thus worthy of the status of crime (see Chapter Four).

Positive Law

How do we decide whether some behavior should be considered right or wrong? How do we decide which behaviors are so wrong that they should be called crimes? We do this by electing people to make the law for us. Laws made by us—human beings—are referred to as positive law. Positive law consists of laws made by sovereign human beings. Those with the authority to make laws write them, and the rest of us have to abide by them in the face of potential sanctions for violating the law. The relationship between positive law and natural law is that natural law informs positive law. That is, positive law is based on or rooted in natural law. Legislators, on the basis of their conceptions of right and wrong and those of their constituents (natural law), define some acts as wrong by labeling them *crimes* or *torts*. A crime is an act in violation of the criminal law. A tort is an act that is harmful to an individual; it is handled in a civil court rather than a criminal court. I'll return to the differences between criminal law and civil law later in this chapter. For now, think of this example: ex–football star O. J. Simpson was accused, but found not guilty at trial, of murdering his wife and her male friend. Murder is a behavior that leads to a trial in a criminal court. Later, O. J. Simpson was tried and found liable for the wrongful deaths of Nicole Brown and Ronald Goldman. He was not convicted for the murders of two people (a crime) in criminal court, but he was found responsible or liable for their wrongful deaths (a tort) in civil court.

The advantage of positive law is that it makes the law predictable. Because the law is written down by human beings, other human beings can consult the law and know which types of behaviors are permitted and which are prohibited. This is why "ignorance of the law is no excuse" for breaking it. We also can easily find out what the possible sanctions are for violating the law. If you want to know what is illegal in your state and what can happen to you if you break a particular law, just consult the criminal statute books in any law library in your state, or simply find the laws of your state online.

Positive law comes to us from many sources. Positive law includes Constitutional law, statutory law, case law, and administrative law, all of which have been informed by common law (Cole and Smith 2000; Schmalleger 1999). *Constitutional law* comes to us from the U.S. Constitution and from the constitutions of each of the 50 states. The following box discusses the U.S. Constitution. Constitutional law establishes individual rights for people in the United States and, thus, sets forth limitations on government power. *Statutory law* comes to us from legislatures of the federal government (the U.S. Congress) and each of the 50 states. Statutory law defines crimes and sets forth potential punishments for violations of the written law. *Case law* is made by courts at the state and federal level when judges interpret statutes and make rulings on individual cases. Case law helps governments and citizens understand what statutes and constitutions mean. Rush (2000, p. 93) defines *administrative law* as "statutes, regulations, and orders that govern public agencies . . . rules governing the administrative operations of the government."

The U.S. Constitution

The Constitution of the United States grants numerous rights to individual citizens. For example, the Bill of Rights guarantees individual citizens both protection from certain acts of the federal government and, also, specific rights, including the following:

- Freedom from *unreasonable searches and seizures* (Fourth Amendment)
- Freedom from arrest or search without probable cause (Fourth Amendment)
- Freedom from *self-incrimination* (Fifth Amendment)
- Freedom from *double jeopardy* (Fifth Amendment)
- Freedom from being deprived of life, liberty, or property without due process of law (Fifth Amendment)
- Freedom from *cruel and unusual punishment* (Eighth Amendment)
- Freedom from *excessive bail or fines* (Eighth Amendment)
- Right to *speedy, public, and fair trial by jury* (Sixth Amendment)
- Right to an *impartial jury* (Sixth Amendment)
- Right to *counsel* (Sixth Amendment)

The Equal Protection Clause and the Due Process Clause of the Fourteenth Amendment extend these rights to protect citizens from acts of their state government as well. In essence, no level of American government can deprive its citizens of these rights.

These Constitutional protections demonstrate that America's founders wanted to ensure, for all time, that its citizens would enjoy certain individual rights and would be free from such forms of government oppression. Some common sayings of criminal justice reinforce this ideal. Ever hear these?

- "All suspects are innocent until proven guilty."
- "It's better to let guilty men go free than to wrongfully punish innocent ones."

These sayings reflect an inherent belief that rules of criminal procedure are important to Americans. These rules of criminal procedure are referred to as *due process*, also defined as "ensuring that laws are reasonable and that they are applied in a fair and equal manner" (Rush 2000, p. 120). No American is to be deprived of his or her life, freedom, or property without due process, because due process is required by the U.S. Constitution. Thus, when any American is subjected to some part of the criminal justice process (e.g., arrest, conviction, punishment) without due process, nothing less important than the U.S. Constitution is threatened.

The primary purpose of the U.S. Supreme Court is to interpret the meaning of individual cases for the Constitution. According to Walker, Spohn, and Delone (2000, p. 289):

> The Supreme Court consistently has affirmed the importance of protecting criminal suspects' rights. The Court has ruled, for example, that searches without warrants are generally unconstitutional, that confessions cannot be coerced, that suspects must be advised of their rights and provided with attorneys to assist them in their defense, that jurors must be chosen from a representative cross-section of the population, and that the death penalty cannot be administered in an arbitrary and capricious manner.

You might be surprised as you read this book that, despite these ideal protections, many of them are not really enjoyed by many Americans.

What was the purpose of the Constitution?

A more critical and perhaps even cynical interpretation of the Constitution suggests that the Constitution was and is biased against certain groups in society. Kappeler, Blumberg, and Potter (2000, p. 217) write, "The framers of the Constitution may have been engaged in unselfish efforts to construct an impartial rule of law, but women could not vote, and slavery was legal—constraints of the worldview at that time."

Charles Beard, in *An Economic Interpretation of the Constitution of the United States* (1913), discusses how the construction of the Constitution was a process biased against the poor. For example, of the five economic groups that existed in 1787, when the document was drafted in Philadelphia, "the four poorest groups had no representatives at the convention: women, slaves, indentured servants, and propertyless white men" (Harrigan 2000, p. 45). Every delegate involved in drafting the Constitution was a white male who owned enough property to be allowed to vote. According to Beard, of the 55 delegates, 38 owned government bonds, 24 earned their living through banking or some other financial investment, 15 owned slaves, and 14 had investments in Western lands. Feagin (2000, p. 9) suggests that of the 55 delegates, "at least 40 percent have been or are slave owners, and a significant proportion of the others profit to some degree as merchants, shippers, lawyers, and bankers from the trade in slaves, commerce in slave-produced agricultural products, or supplying provisions to slaveholders and slave-traders." Given the makeup of the delegates, was the Constitution drafted at least partly to protect their limited interests?

Harrigan (2000, p. 47) suggests that three types of provisions were written into the Constitution to protect the limited financial interests of wealthy, white male delegates.

- Those that protected their private property rights
- Those that insulated the national government from popular rule
- Those that minimized the influence of the lower-status population in the ratification process

The protections of private property rights included provisions that benefited businesses engaged in trade and economy, bankers and creditors, slave holders, and holders of securities under the Articles of Confederation.

Feagin (2000, p. 10) explains that

> at the heart of the Constitution was protection of the property and wealth of the affluent bourgeoisie in the new nation, including property of those enslaved. . . . For the founders, freedom meant the protection of unequal accumulation of property, particularly property that could produce a profit in the emerging capitalistic system. Certain political, economic, and racial interests were conjoined. This was not just a political gathering with the purpose of creating a new major bourgeois-democratic government; it was also a meeting to protect the racial and economic interests of men with substantial property and wealth in the colonies.

Popular rule was not set up in the Constitution because people did not directly vote for the president, the Court, or the Senate. Only House members were originally elected by the people, and people could vote only if their congressional districts had at least 30,000 people. This benefited the wealthy. Barriers to voting (such as property ownership requirements) were constructed to discourage a large percentage of people from voting. Because of this, Harrigan (2000) concludes:

The lower-status population did indeed have nothing to say about the drafting of the Constitution and (whether by choice or coercion) had little to say about ratifying it. Important provisions in the Constitution protected economic interests that were more valuable to the upper-status population than to the lower-status population. (p. 53)

Similarly, Joe Feagin (2000), in his book *Racist America; Roots, Current Realities and Future Reparations*, traces the roots of American racism to the U.S. Constitution and early Colonial America. He suggests that many of our country's founders, including Thomas Jefferson, Benjamin Franklin, and James Madison, were greatly influenced by assumptions in Europe about the inherent inferiority of African Americans to Caucasians. Thus, African Americans would specifically be counted as only three-fifths of a man according to Article I, Section 2, of the U.S. Constitution.

Feagin (2000, p. 14) asserts that the U.S. Constitutional Convention was something other than what we have learned about in school. He suggests the structure of the nation, as laid out in the Constitution, "was created to maintain separation and oppression at the time and for the forseeable future. The framers reinforced and legitimated a system of racist oppression that they thought would ensure that whites, especially white men of means, would rule for centuries to come."

According to Feagin (2000, p. 15), the country's founders owned slaves and benefited from the unequal treatment of African Americans and Caucasians. "Men of politics like Thomas Jefferson, George Washington, Alexander Hamilton, Patrick Henry, Benjamin Franklin, John Hancock, and Sam Houston enslaved black Americans. Ten U.S. presidents (Washington, Jefferson, James Madison, James Monroe, Andrew Jackson, John Tyler, James Polk, Zachary Taylor, and Ulysses S. Grant) at some point in their lives enslaved African Americans." Many lawmakers (members of both houses of Congress) were also slave owners, as were those who would interpret the law (members of the U.S. Supreme Court). Not surprisingly, "few major decisions made by the federal legislative and judicial branches went against the interests of the nation's slaveholding oligarchy, and foreign and domestic policies generally did not conflict with the interests of those centrally involved with the slavery system" (p. 56).

Given such an apparent built-in bias in favor of the wealthy and white, it may not have been hard to imagine that some biases would still be around today. Perhaps they would even have multiplied, expanded into areas such as tax codes and legal codes. If so, we would expect that a mechanism would need to be in place to support and maintain these biases in favor of the wealthy. Is it possible that the criminal justice network is this mechanism?

There is evidence that the American criminal justice network fails to achieve its goals of doing justice and reducing crime. In essence, it may be biased against certain groups in the United States and fail to appreciably reduce crime. The National Criminal Justice Commission concurs. They demonstrate that the criminal justice network offers little return for the massive investments we have made. For example, although from 1980 to 1993 probation increased by 154%, jail admissions increased by 177%, prison admissions increased by 188%, and the number of people on parole increased by 205%, reported Index Crimes did not decline but actually increased by 5%. The more valid National Crime Victimization Survey (NCVS) showed a reduction of only 16% for criminal victimizations during this same time period (Donziger 1996, p. 37). That hardly can be called a success. More recent data show some positive effects of criminal justice activity on crime trends, but most of the declines in crime we witnessed in the 1990s were attributable to factors outside the realm of criminal justice (see Chapter Four).

How can it be that the world's most powerful nation, capable of traveling to other worlds in space and of curing scores of illnesses, remains so blind to our criminal justice failures? One possible, though radical, rationale for our allegiance to failing methods of crime fighting is that our criminal justice network is intended to achieve goals other than doing justice and reducing crime. How likely do you think it is that the criminal justice network actually is intended to control certain segments of the population and to serve limited interests, as suggested in Chapter Two?

Common Law

Common law is a term used to describe the legal traditions of England before America was founded (Schmalleger 1999). Common law consists of the traditions and customs of British judges that were passed down from judge to judge over time. Common law was not written down as strict legal rules but, rather, included "general principles to guide judges" (Gottfredson 1999, p. 49). As noted, common law informs each of the types of positive law because American positive law grew out of the traditions and customs of England. Gottfredson explains that English common law informed American law by establishing these principles.

- The supremacy of the law
- The inviolability of person and property
- The local nature of criminal jurisdiction
- Due process of law
- The rule that no one should be compelled in any criminal prosecution to be a witness against himself or herself
- The right to a trial by jury

From these sources of positive law, we get the *criminal law*, which can be divided into two distinct types: substantive criminal law and procedural criminal law. *Substantive criminal law* is the "substance" of the law, as it defines which behaviors are illegal and what punishments can follow as a result of breaking the written law (Schmalleger 1999). The following box provides examples of substantive criminal law in my state, North Carolina.

Some interesting North Carolina laws

All of the following acts are Class 2 or 3 misdemeanors, punishable by a maximum punishment of more than 30 days' but not more than 6 months' imprisonment for Class 2 misdemeanors and a maximum punishment of 30 days' or less imprisonment (or only a fine) for Class 3 misdemeanors.

- *§ 14-72.3. Stealing a shopping cart:* It is unlawful to remove a shopping cart from the premises of a store without the consent, given at the time of the removal, of the store owner, manager, agent or employee, where "shopping cart" means the type of push cart commonly provided by grocery stores, drugstores, and other retail stores for customers to transport commodities within the store and from the store to their motor vehicles outside the store and "premises" includes the motor vehicle parking area set aside for customers of the store.

- *§ 14-400. Tattooing; body piercing:* It is unlawful to tattoo the arm, limb, or any part of the body of any other person under 18 years of age.
- *§ 14-401.17. Unlawfully removing or destroying electronic dog collars:* It is unlawful to intentionally remove or destroy an electronic collar or other electronic device placed on a dog by its owner to maintain control of the dog.
- *§ 14-113. Obtaining money by false representation of physical defect:* It is unlawful to falsely represent yourself in any manner whatsoever as blind, deaf, dumb, or crippled or otherwise physically defective for the purpose of obtaining money or other thing of value or of making sales of any character of personal property. Any person so falsely representing himself or herself as blind, deaf, dumb, crippled or otherwise physically defective, and securing aid or assistance on account of such representation, shall be deemed guilty.
- *§ 14-131. Trespassing on land under option by the federal government:* It is unlawful to, on lands under option which have formally or informally been offered to and accepted by the North Carolina Department of Environment and Natural Resources by the acquiring federal agency and tentatively accepted by said Department for administration as State forests, State parks, State game refuges or for other public purposes, cut, dig, break, injure or remove any timber, lumber, firewood, trees, shrubs or other plants; or any fence, house, barn or other structure; or to pursue, trap, hunt or kill any bird or other wild animals or take fish from streams or lakes within the boundaries of such areas without the written consent of the local official of the United States having charge of the acquisition of such lands.
- *§ 14-460. Riding on train unlawfully:* It is unlawful to, with the intention of being transported free in violation of law, ride or attempt to ride on top of any car, coach, engine, or tender, on any railroad in this State, or on the drawheads between cars, or under cars, on truss rods, or trucks, or in any freight car, or on a platform of any baggage car, express car, or mail car on any train.
- *§ 14-444. Being intoxicated and disruptive in public:* It shall be unlawful for any person in a public place to be intoxicated and disruptive in any of the following ways: Blocking or otherwise interfering with traffic on a highway or public vehicular area, or Blocking or lying across or otherwise preventing or interfering with access to or passage across a sidewalk or entrance to a building, or Grabbing, shoving, pushing or fighting others or challenging others to fight, or Cursing or shouting at or otherwise rudely insulting others, or Begging for money or other property.

These acts must have been problematic in the state of North Carolina, or they would not likely be considered crimes. Your state has similar laws based on unique problems that its citizens experience. Remember, any behavior can be made criminal at any time.

Procedural criminal law puts forth the "procedures" that governments must follow when carrying out the law (Cole and Smith 2000; Schmalleger 1999). Procedural criminal law thus establishes limits on the government's power when attempting to apprehend and prosecute suspected criminals. An example of procedural criminal law is found in the Bill of Rights of the U.S. Constitution. Recall that the Bill of Rights lays out protections that all people ideally enjoy if and when they are subjected to criminal justice processes. Ideally, if these rights are somehow violated by police, the courts, or correctional facilities, consequences can include dismissal of charges, overturning of criminal convictions, and even financial reimbursement to the victim (Peoples 2000; Stuckey, Robertson, and Wallace 2001).

Criminal Law and Civil Law

The criminal law and the *civil law* are very different. Table 3.1 illustrates these differences. For example, the criminal law is concerned with harmful acts committed against the government. All crimes are technically viewed as acts against the government rather than against individuals. Civil law, however, is concerned with harmful acts committed against individuals. The criminal law leads to trials involving the state or government against an individual—for example, the *State of California v. O. J. Simpson*. The civil law leads to trials where one individual faces another. When you think of the civil law, you may think of popular television shows like *Judge Judy*, *The People's Court*, and *Judge Joe Brown*. Criminal trials can lead to either a *criminal conviction* or an *acquittal* (a finding of not guilty). When an offender is found guilty, he or she can be punished by any of a whole range of potential sanctions (see Chapter Eight). For someone to be convicted, it must be demonstrated beyond reasonable doubt that the offender committed the named act(s) and did so intentionally (on purpose). Civil trials, however, lead to a finding of either liability or no liability. That is, the accused is either held responsible for the act or not. If found to be liable, the accused usually will be required to compensate the victim financially for the harm(s) inflicted. Intent is not required in civil court, and the standard of proof is much lower. In a civil court, the burden of proof is a *preponderance of evidence*, meaning that a simple majority of the evidence must suggest that the accused is responsible.

TABLE 3.1
Criminal Law and Civil Law

	Criminal	*Civil*
Participants	State vs. individual	Individual vs. individual
Possible outcome	Conviction	Liability
	Punishment of offender	Financially compensate victim
Intent required?	Yes	No
Standard of proof	Beyond reasonable doubt	Preponderance of evidence
Rules of evidence	Very stringent	Less stringent

One final difference between the criminal law and the civil law is that the rules of evidence are much more stringent in the criminal law, meaning that it is easier to get evidence admitted into a civil court than a criminal court. You might wonder how it is that a person can be tried twice for the same offense, given the Constitutional right to freedom from double jeopardy. Because the criminal and civil courts have different jurisdictions and are intended for different purposes, being tried in both courts does not constitute double jeopardy.

WHAT IS THE PURPOSE OF THE CRIMINAL LAW?

Early political theorists such as Hobbes, Locke, and Rousseau argued that when individuals form a society, they must enter into a *social contract* to surrender some of their individual rights in return for the protection of their personal safety and property. The social contract is codified by making law. In modern Western societies such as the United States, "crimes" are acts against the government rather than against individuals. This definition of crime gives the state the right to prosecute wrongdoers and to administer punishment in the name of the actual crime victims. At the same time, individual citizens are forbidden from engaging in vengeance or vigilantism.

For this type of system to work, the government must assure its citizens that their sacrifices are worth it. It does this primarily by providing protection, peace, and order. In other words, the government is responsible for enforcing laws, catching and punishing criminals, and protecting the community from harm (Marion 1995). These efforts are aimed at crime control, a goal of the criminal justice network discussed in Chapter One. But recall the inherent struggle between achieving our goal of crime control and achieving our goal of ensuring due process. The law must be "both an engine of government and a brake which restrains government" (Gottfredson 1999, p. 47). This means that the government can use force to make sure the criminal law is not violated, but not so much force that it interferes with the rights of individual citizens. As I discuss each of the three components of the criminal justice network later in the book, you will see how each attempts to carry out the criminal law without violating individual Constitutional protections.

For the purposes of this chapter, I focus on the function of the criminal law that is concerned with defining behaviors that are illegal. There are at least two competing interpretations of whose interests are represented when behaviors are defined as illegal. Those who believe in the *consensus view of the law* believe that the law reflects societal interests, and that "crimes" therefore are acts that a majority of the population views as immoral, wrong, and harmful. Crimes are thus deviations from the norm. This model is based on the belief that the "law reflects common consciousness and interests of society" (Marion 1995, p. 21). According to its proponents, the criminal law "serves as a banner to announce the values of society. It tells us where the boundaries of acceptable behavior lie and links those who violate the boundaries—criminals—with evil, pain, incarceration, and disgrace" (Kappeler, Blumberg, and Potter 2000, p. 216).

Several studies have shown a remarkable level of agreement among citizens about which crimes should be considered most serious. These studies typically reveal a higher level of perceived seriousness for the violent street crimes included in the Uniform Crime Reports (e.g., see Carlson and Williams 1993; Cohen 1991; Cullen, Link, and Travis 1985; Epperlein and Nienstedt 1989; Gebotys and Dasgupta 1987; Gebotys, Roberts, and Dasgupta 1988; Meier and Short 1985; Miethe 1982; O'Connell and Whelan 1996; Parton, Hansel, and Stratton 1991; Rauma 1991;

Sebba 1984; Warr 1991). Some would claim that this is evidence that the criminal law clearly serves the interests of the public. But which came first—public support for the law or the law itself? Isn't it possible that people perceive harmful acts as more or less serious based on their status in the criminal law?

I advocate a different approach to determining crime seriousness, consistent with scholars such as Friedrichs (1999). This approach would pronounce acts as more or less serious on the basis of the degree of harm that they cause. That is, more harmful acts would be considered more serious, and less harmful acts would be called less serious. The criminal law does reflect this approach in some ways—for example, murder is more serious than theft. Yet in many ways, the criminal law does not define the most harmful acts as more serious, providing evidence for proponents of the conflict model of the law.

Proponents of the *conflict view of the law* believe that the law reflects the limited interests of powerful members of society. Thus, "crimes" are not necessarily the most harmful acts; instead, they are acts committed by relatively powerless people (e.g., the poor) (Vold 1958). Those with political or economic power, and special-interest groups, are likely to have their beliefs reflected in the law, according to those who believe in the conflict model. As Goode and Ben-Yuhuda (1994b, p. 78) write, "Definitions of right and wrong do not drop from the skies, nor do they simply ineluctably percolate from society's mainstream opinion; they are the result of disagreement, negotiation, conflict, and struggle. The passage of laws raises the issue of who will criminalize whom." Similarly, Akers (1996, p. 142) writes, "The dominant groups can see to it that their particular definitions of normality or deviance will become enacted as law, ensconced in public policy, and protected by the operation of the criminal justice system."

In the United States, poor people are labeled as troublemakers more than any other group (Gans 1995, pp. 18–21). Gans writes that the process begins with the "label-makers" (in the case of crime, they are legislators). Legislators define certain acts committed by the poor as crimes and then rely on "alarmists" to spread the word about the dangers of the acts (in the case of crime, they are the media) and on "counters" to supply numbers indicating that the problem is serious or widespread (in the case of crime, they are the police and politicians). So, is the law biased against the poor? If you believe that the government should pass laws to protect us from harms, then you might feel that the law is biased if it only attempts to protect us from harms committed by poor people.

Hobbes argued that government's "sole purpose" is to give citizens the ability to "pursue their natural rights, including the rights to life, to liberty, and to enjoy personal property"—that is, to "provide safety for the citizens" (Marion 1995, pp. 4–5). To the degree that the government does not do this, the government is failing to do its job. I illustrate in Chapter Four that our government ignores many harmful acts, such as white-collar crime and corporate crime. To the degree that they ignore these harms, our government is failing to provide us with justice and to protect us from things that kill us, injure us, and take our property. A violation of the law—a crime—is clearly a potential threat to the social order. Many crimes, because of the harms they cause to society, are considered serious and thus warrant criminal justice intervention. However, other crimes are not severe enough to warrant criminal justice intervention (see Chapter Eleven for the example of drug crimes in the United States).

Failure to define intentional or other forms of culpable harms as "crimes" can also pose a threat to social order, because citizens may perceive that their government is failing to protect them. Reiman (1998, p. 59) states it this way: "The point of prohibiting an act by the criminal law is to protect society from an injurious act. . . . The label [of crime] is applied appropriately when it is used to identify all, or at least the worst of, the acts that are harmful to society. The label is applied inappropriately when it is attached to any harmless act or when it is not attached to seriously harmful acts." The label crime, especially "serious crime," is not reserved for the acts that actually threaten us the most. Instead, it is a label for harmful acts that we perceive to be crimes of the poor—that is, for street crime (see Chapter Four).

To gain a clear understanding of why this is so, it is crucial that I critically explore the legislative process in the United States, including who makes the law, who votes for the law, and how special interests shape the law.

WHO MAKES THE LAW?

The criminalization process, like all criminal justice activity, starts with the lawmaking stage. By defining crimes (substantive criminal law) and setting forth the rules that criminal justice actors must follow (procedural criminal law), the criminal law dictates what police, courts, and corrections do. That is, the criminal law sets forth what is considered a crime and what sanctions can follow from illegal behaviors. Therefore, the activities of police, courts, and corrections personnel all stem directly from the law. As introduced in Chapter One, once the law is in place, police enforce the criminal law by responding to calls for service, investigating alleged crimes, and apprehending suspects. Courts determine the guilt of suspects and impose criminal sanctions on the legally guilty. Correctional facilities and programs carry out the sanctions of the courts and administer punishment to sentenced offenders. These institutions of criminal justice thereby reinforce the validity of the law and of all stereotypes created by that law.

This section examines who makes the law by illustrating key demographics of lawmakers. I then turn to voting behavior in order to illustrate who votes for the law and who does not. Then the effects of special interests and lobbying on the law are explored. Taken together, these analyses suggest that the criminal law may be biased in favor of the wealthy and powerful.

Demographics of Lawmakers

To the degree that lawmakers are representative of all of society, it is likely that laws will represent all people in society. Table 3.2 compares demographic characteristics of state and federal legislators with those of the general U.S. population. According to the Center for Voting and

TABLE 3.2
Demographic Characteristics of Legislators

	U.S. Population	U.S. Congress	State Legislatures
Median age	35.3 years	54 years	49.4 years
Percentage women	50.9	14	22
Percentage white	75.1	86.5	89
Percentage black	12.3	8.5	8

SOURCES: U.S. Census (2003); Center for Voting and Democracy (2003); Congress Link (2003).

Democracy (2003), at the federal level, of the 435 members of the U.S. House of Representatives, 37 are African Americans (8.5%) and 19 are Hispanics (4%). The U.S. Senate includes no African Americans (0%) and no Hispanics (0%). Therefore, the majority of legislators at the federal level are Caucasians, including 86.5% of House members and 100% of senators. In terms of gender, there are 60 women in the U.S. House (14%) and 13 women in the U.S. Senate (13%). Therefore, the majority of federal legislators are men, including 86% of House members and 87% of senators. In fact, there are 426 white men in Congress (79%), including 339 members of the U.S. House (77%) and 87 members of the U.S. Senate (87%). In terms of age, there are only 43 members of the U.S. Congress under the age of 40 years (8%), including 42 members of the U.S. House (9%) and 1 senator (1%). The average age of federal legislators is approximately 53 years in the U.S. House, 58 years in the Senate, and 54 years old overall (Congressional Quarterly 1999). Thus, we can confidently say that the typical federal legislator is an older, white male.

At the state level, according to the Center for Voting and Democracy (2003), 605 of the 7,380 state lawmakers are African Americans (8%) and 206 are Hispanics (2.8%). Therefore, the majority of legislators at the state level are Caucasian (89%). In terms of gender, 401 of 1,961 (20%) state senators are women, and 1,244 of 5,421 (23%) representatives are women. Therefore, 1,645 of 7,382 (22%) lawmakers at the state level are women; 78% are men. The average age of state legislators is approximately 49.4 years. Thus, we can confidently say that the typical state legislator is an older, white male.

When we compare these numbers with the U.S. general population, we see that demographically, lawmakers look very different from the average American. In 2000, according to the U.S. Census, the average age of the population was 35.3 years. Legislators at both federal and state levels are older on average than the general population. Women make up 50.9% of the U.S. population. Women are thus underrepresented as federal and state lawmakers. Caucasians now make up 75.1% of U.S. citizens, whereas African Americans make up 12.3% of the population and Hispanics make up 12.5% of the population. Caucasians are thus overrepresented as lawmakers at the federal and state level, while African Americans and Hispanics are underrepresented. It can be concluded that lawmakers are not representative of the general population in terms of demographic characteristics such as race, ethnicity, gender, and age.

Lawmakers are also much wealthier than the average person. For example, according to Congress Link (2003), members of Congress received $154,700 in base salary in 2003. Congressional leaders received $166,700 per year, whereas speakers received $192,600. This is nearly four times the average pay of Congress' constituents. According to the U.S. Census, the average income of all households in 2001 was $42,228, including $44,517 for Caucasian households, $33,565 for Hispanic households, and $29,470 for African American households.

Base salary is only what legislators get paid; it does not include their net worth or the numerous benefits and perks they receive. According to Common Dreams (2003), 27 of the 63 incoming freshman lawmakers (43%) are millionaires, compared with only 1% of the American population. And based on recent financial disclosures of U.S. Senators, at least 40 of the 100 are millionaires. Additionally, many claim that these millionaire lawmakers have potential conflicts of interest given their financial interests in various corporations. This issue is discussed later in the chapter.

At the state level, legislator pay varied widely across the country. In my state of North Carolina, pay varies based on the office held. According to the North Carolina General Assembly, pay of lawmakers in the state's House and Senate ranges from $17,048 to $38,151, with an expense allowance of $666 per month. Keep in mind, however, that this is pay for a part-time job!

Voting Behavior

These elected "representatives" may still represent the voter, but most people do not vote regularly. For example, according to the U.S. Census, only 63.9% of people eligible to vote (18 years or older) are registered to vote, and only 54.7% reported voting in the 2000 elections. This is significant because the 2000 elections were predicted to be among the closest ever in our history, yet only half of registered voters even turned out to vote. Harrigan (2000, pp. 178–79) explains that in an indirect, representative democracy such as the United States, "without meaningful elections, there is no meaningful democracy."

Before I move on to whether voters are representative of the population generally, think about this: If people do not vote, how do representatives know what normal citizens think? The law cannot represent the masses, and the *collective conscience* of society cannot be incorporated into the criminal law, if people do not vote. Figure 3.2 shows what I call Extrasensory Political Participation (ESP), which is the only way that representatives can represent the people if the people do not speak for themselves.

FIGURE 3.2

Extrasensory Political Participation (ESP): How Politicians Know What We Want When We Don't Vote

TABLE 3.3
Voting Behavior, by Age (2003)

	Registered to Vote	Voted in 2002 Elections
Ages 65 and older	76.2%	69.9%
Ages 18–24	45.4%	32.3%
Whites	70%	60.4%
Blacks	64.3%	51.1%
Hispanics	34.9%	27.5%
Earning $75,000 per year or more	78.4%	71.5%
Earning less than $5,000 per year	44%	28.2%

SOURCE: U.S. Census (2003; www. census.gov/).

Voters are not representative of the general population demographically either. As Table 3.3 shows, voting behaviors are positively related to age. This means that as one's age increases, the likelihood that one will be registered to vote and will bother to vote increases. The age group most likely to be registered to vote and to actually vote is people over 65 years of age (76.2% and 69.9%), whereas the group least likely to be registered to vote and to actually vote is people 18 to 24 years old (45.4% and 32.3%).

As for race and ethnicity, 70% of Caucasians are registered to vote, and 60.4% reported voting, versus only 64.3% and 54.1% of African Americans and only 34.9% and 27.5% of Hispanics, respectively. Voter registration and voting rates are slightly higher for females than males (65.6% and 56.2% versus 62.2% and 53.1%, respectively).

Voting is highest among the most educated as well, as 79.4% of people with an advanced college degree are registered to vote and 75.5% reported voting, versus 36.1% and 26.8% of people with less than a ninth-grade education and 60.1% and 49.4% of people with high school diplomas, respectively. Voter participation is highest for government employees, as 79.2% of them are registered to vote and 72.4% reported voting.

Finally, in terms of income, there is a positive relationship between income and voting behaviors. For example, the highest level of voter registration and reported voting is for people who earn more than $75,000 per year (78.4% and 71.5%), versus only 44% and 28.2% of people who earn less than $5,000 per year.

Voting is generally lowest in the South, where poverty and minority residence are very high. According to Harrigan (2000), lower rates of voting by the poor should be attributed to the fact that poor people have been systematically shut out of the electoral process, not that they are bad citizens. In essence, economic stress threatens good citizenship.

From these data, we see that voters are not demographically representative of the population either. Voters tend to be older, disproportionately Caucasian, and wealthier (just like the lawmakers).

Voters can have tremendous power to the degree that politicians fear that voters will be antagonized. Yet Harrigan shows how very powerful interest groups have their will enacted into law, even when the interests of the voting public are not served.

Special Interests/Lobbying

Let there be no doubt about two key facts when it comes to American politics:

- There is a lot of money involved in the political system.
- Money determines the outcomes.

Table 3.4 illustrates just how money is involved in the federal system. During the 2001–2002 election cycle, Republicans raised $652.1 million, 62% in hard money and 38% in hard money. Democrats raised $466.1 million, 53% in soft money and 47% in hard money.

According to the Center for Responsive Politics (2003), in 2002, 1,296 House candidates raised a total of $637.9 million to run for office, and 146 Senate candidates raised a total of $325.9 million to run for office. This translates into an average of $492,235 for House candidates and $2.2 million for Senate candidates. The 435 winning House candidates raised a total of $420.3 million, and the winning 34 Senate candidates raised $170.5 million. This translates into an average of $966,343 for winning House candidates and $5 million for winning Senate candidates.

Where does this money come from? Well, it does not come from average Americans. According to the Center for Responsive Politics (2003), in 2002, far less than 1% of the U.S. adult population (0.31%) gave more than $200 to a political candidate, party, or lobbying group, and only 0.12% gave more than $1,000.

Instead, the money comes from *political action committees* (PACs) and wealthy individuals in the form of *hard money* and *soft money*. Hard money is money given by individuals and groups to individual candidates and is limited by law. Soft money is money given by individuals and groups to political parties, which until 2002 was not prohibited by law. As explained by Common Cause (2003):

> Simply put, soft money is money, which, by definition and law, is not supposed to be part of our federal campaign finance system. It is precisely the kind of money which federal law and policy have sought to exclude from national campaigns. . . . Since 1907, it has been illegal for corporations to spend money in connection with federal elections. . . . Since 1947, it has been illegal for labor unions to spend money in connection with federal elections. And since 1974, it has been illegal for an individual to contribute more than $1,000 to a federal candidate, or more than $20,000 per year to a political party, for the purpose of influencing a federal election. Soft money is money which violates these rules. It is the corporate donations, the union tributions and the large—$100,000, $250,000 or even $1 million—contributions given by wealthy individuals to the political parties.

As explained by Harrigan (2000, p. 194), "Soft money is a rich person's game, and soft money contributions and issue ad expenditures by interest groups also reflect a bias" against the poor. Donation of goods and services also is unlimited. Many corporations give more than $100,000 each to the major political parties because Federal Election Commission rules allow unlimited donations by corporations of goods and services, which are not counted as money.

TABLE 3.4

Money in Federal Politics (2001–2002)

	Republicans	Democrats
Total raised	$652.1 million	$466.1 million
Hard money	62%	47%
Soft money	38%	53%

SOURCES: Center for Responsive Politics (2003); Common Cause (2003).

According to Common Cause (2003), the problem of soft money was not exploited until 1988. Then in 1992, political parties raised $86 million in soft money for the presidential campaign. This grew to $260 million for the 1996 election and $440 million during 2001–2002. Several notable corporations are among those in the top 50 contributors of soft money to political parties. For example, between 1995 and 2001, the tobacco company Philip Morris (which has been successfully sued numerous times for fraud, negligence, and recklessness) ranked 2nd, at $9.2 million ($7.8 million to Republicans), the now-defunct energy giant Enron (which is implicated in unbelievable fraud) ranked 15th, at $4 million ($3 million to Republicans), corporate criminal WorldCom (also implicated in widespread fraud) ranked 25th, at $3.3 million ($1.9 million to Republicans), and RJ Reynolds (RJR) Tobacco (also sued for fraud, negligence, and recklessness) ranked 28th, at $3.1 million ($2.7 million to Republicans).

PACs are another source of money. PACs are groups organized to raise and spend money on political campaigns. According to the Center for Responsive Politics, PACs typically represent corporate, labor, and ideological interests and are allowed to give $5,000 to any candidate per election, $5,000 to any other PAC, and $15,000 to any national party annually. Individuals can also donate up to $5,000 to any PAC. Table 3.5 illustrates the top PACs for the 2001–2002 election cycle for federal elections. The data show that both major parties are well funded by PACs

TABLE 3.5

Top Political Action Committees (PACs) in Federal Politics (2001–2002)

Republicans	Democrats
National Assoc. of Realtors	Assoc. of Trial Lawyers of America
National Auto Dealers Assoc.	Laborers Union
National Beer Wholesalers Assoc.	American Federation of State/ County/Municipal Employees
American Medical Assoc.	United Auto Workers
National Assoc. of Home Builders	Machinists/Aerospace Workers Union
United Parcel Service	International Brotherhood of Electrical Workers
Associated Builders & Contractors	Teamsters Union
Credit Union National Assoc.	Carpenters & Joiners Union
National Rifle Assoc.	Communications Workers of America
American Bankers Assoc.	National Assoc. of Realtors
Americans for a Republican Majority	United Food & Commercial Workers Union
FedEx Corporation	Service Employees International Union
SBC Communications	National Educational Association
KPMG LLG	American Federation of Teachers
Verizon Communications	AFL-CIO
WalMart Stores	Ironworkers Union

SOURCES: Center for Responsive Politics (2003); National Institute on Money in State Politics (www. followthemoney.org/).

and that Democrats are most represented by groups of workers and teachers, whereas Republicans are most represented by corporations. According to the Center for Responsive Politics, strongly Democratic industries include unions, lawyers, and entertainment (TV, movies, music), whereas strongly Republican industries include insurance, pharmaceuticals, and oil and gas.

To even run for office takes a tremendous amount of money. Of the $637.9 million raised by House candidates, $325.6 million came from individuals (51%) and $216.9 million came from PACs (34%). As for the $325.9 million raised by Senate candidates, $218.1 million came from individuals (67%) and $61.9 million came from PACs (19%). As it turns out, to win office costs even more. It is fair to say that American politics is essentially a fund-raising contest: Whomever raises the most money (and spends it) is almost guaranteed to win. For example, the average winner of a House seat outraised his or her opponent by $898,221 to $198,888 and the average Senate winner outraised his or her opponent $5.7 million to $985,112! According to the Center for Responsive Politics, in 2002, the ratio of winners to losers is as high as 10 to 1 for amount spent on campaigns.

The picture is the same at the state level. The Center for Public Integrity (2003) claims that private interests basically govern our states. According to the National Institute on Money in State Politics (online), candidates for legislative and statewide offices raised more than $1.4 billion during the 1998 election cycle. Given that only about one-third of voters turned out for these elections across the country (36.3% in 45 states studied), the "average contribution-dollar-per-voter figure" was $20.44. This means that each vote costs candidates approximately $20! In the 2002 election cycle, state party committees raised $570 million, 46% of which came from soft money transferred from national party organizations aimed at swing states (such as Florida) needed to determine the election.

In the 1998 elections in North Carolina, candidates for 120 House seats and 50 Senate seats raised a total of $17.1 million, according to the National Institute on Money in State Politics. The average candidate for seat in the state House of Representatives raised $37,419 (Democrats) and $49,677 (Republicans), whereas candidates for the state Senate raised $35,349 (Republicans) and $152,463 (Democrats). Again, winners outraised losers: In the House, winners outraised losers $58,192 to $31,840, and in the Senate, winners outraised losers $128,804 to $34,570. Only five members of the House won without the advantage of being an incumbent or raising the most money in their race, 92% of the winners raised the most money, and 88% were incumbents. The largest percentage of this money came from industries such as finance, insurance, health, general business, construction, lawyers, energy, agriculture, communications, transportation, and labor (together totaling 65.6%), followed by political party contributions (22.6%), small contributors like me (15.3%), and candidate contributions (10.6%).

A study by Democracy North Carolina (2003) found that in 2002, candidates for the state legislature spent $22.4 million on their campaigns. The average spent by winning candidates was $101,384, including $61,060 for a House seat and $198,150 for a Senate seat. The candidate who spent the most money won 82% of the legislative races.

Even though PACs and wealthy individuals seem to have a stranglehold on lawmakers, groups other than powerful elites are involved in the codification of criminal law. For example, the general public makes demands, and events such as media reporting and some 40,000 lobbying actions among more than a dozen interest groups affect legislation (Brunk and Wilson 1991; also see Hagan 1989; McGarrell 1993; Walker, Spohn, and Delone 1996; Wright 1993). *Interest groups* are collectives of individuals with a common interest or goal who seek to influence public policy (Berry 1984). Most of the 40,000 lobbying groups in the United States represent U.S. and foreign corporations (Simon and Hagan 1999, p. 47), but some represent average Americans. Common Cause, noted above, introduced the bill that became the law banning soft money contributions to federal candidates. This law is being challenged and its constitutionality was recently upheld five to four by the U.S. Supreme Court.

Interest groups are the "core of democracy, because they represent channels through which people can band together to counteract the advantages that the economic elite have in a political system" (Harrigan 2000, p. 165). But given that the poor are the least likely to belong to interest groups (J. Davis and Smith 1996), and that the richest one-third of U.S. citizens are nearly twice as likely as the poorest one-third to belong to such a group, interest group activity is biased in favor of the wealthy. D. Simon and F. Hagan (1999, p. 13) thus claim that "the richest 1 to 5 percent of the population pays for political campaigns. The resultant system is something of a corrupt gravy train that only the rich and powerful may board." The voter is left with the realization that his or her vote, letter, phone call, fax, e-mail, or personal visit carries relatively little weight in a political process driven by money.

HOW THE CRIMINAL LAW FAILS TO PROTECT AMERICANS

Given that the law is made by people who are very different from the typical U.S. citizen, that most people do not inform the law through voting, and that lobbying and special interests influence the law so greatly, is it possible that the law does not really provide protection from the harms that most threaten us? Morgan-Sharp (1999, p. 383) explains that because the law is made "mainly by rich white men and persons who share their interests" but is sold as defining behaviors that are unacceptable to the majority of Americans, we may mistakenly believe that the law protects us. One example proves the point.

Big Tobacco

According to Common Cause (1999), tobacco companies gave nearly $30 million in political contributions to national parties between 1987 and 1998, including $11.9 million in PAC money and $16.7 million in soft money. Between 1987 and 1997, three of four members of Congress (319 representatives and 76 senators) accepted money from Big Tobacco.

Between 1987 and 1998, $13.6 million of the tobacco soft money contributions to national parties (81%) and $6.9 million of the PAC money (58%) went to Republicans. Not surprisingly, in June 1998, Senate Republicans defeated legislation that would have raised more than $500 billion over 25 years through a $1.10 tax increase on a pack of cigarettes (Common Cause 1999; Salant 1999). The bill was aimed at reducing smoking among children, which has been shown to save lives. According to Common Cause, on June 17, 1998, senators who voted against the bill "received on average more than four times the tobacco industry. . . . PAC contributions during the three most recent election cycles as those voting to move the bill forward."

Common Cause (1999) reports that, between January 1993 and March 1998, the 43 senators who voted against the bill received an average of $20,761 from tobacco PACs, versus $4,970 received on average by the 57 senators voting for the bill. Given that more than 80% of tobacco money goes to Republicans, it is not surprising that 40 of the 42 senators voting against the bill were Republicans.

But most significant is that both sides of the aisle regularly accept money from the same lobbying groups. For example, in 1997–1998 alone, 20 tobacco donors gave nearly $1.9 million to Democrats ($900,000 from Philip Morris) and 29 donors gave almost $9.7 million to Republicans ($4.3 million from Philip Morris) (Common Cause 1999; Salant 1999). Between 1987 and 1997, Philip Morris gave $6.1 million in soft money contributions and $4.3 million in PAC money to national parties, while RJR Tobacco gave $3.8 million in soft money contributions and $3.9 million in PAC money. These are the two leading donors to political parties.

Meanwhile, the public (75% of whom are not smokers) suffers tremendous harm as a result of tobacco use. Given the harmfulness of this drug, its legal status does not make sense considering that some far less deadly drugs are illegal. Politicians routinely justify the illicit nature of many drugs on the grounds that they are dangerous or deadly. Yet according to the federal government, the number of deaths caused by all illicit drugs combined is approximately 19,000 each year, versus 440,000 for tobacco (see Chapter Eleven). That's right, according to our own government, tobacco kills more than 22 times more people than all illegal drugs combined. It is the leading cause of preventable death and illness in the United States every year.

Tobacco executives have avoided criminal convictions for their negligent and reckless behaviors in part because of the tobacco lobby's historical stranglehold on Congress (which has recently tightened even in the wake of increased realization of industry deception). At the same time, people continue to smoke and die because of Big Tobacco's seemingly bottomless advertising budget and willingness to target even children to ensure the sale of its products. In the 2001–2002 election cycle, tobacco PACs donated a total of $2.4 million to federal candidates (77% to Republicans), including $896,500 from Philip Morris and $624,750 from RJR Tobacco.

In Chapter Four, you will see how other corporations also commit harmful acts, many of them explicitly illegal. And you will learn how their acts cause far more damage than all street crimes combined, including more deaths than murder and more property loss than theft and bank robbery.

CONCLUSION

The law, which defines the behaviors that will be pursued by agencies of criminal justice and those that will be broadcast by the media, is created by human beings through a legislative process that is heavily skewed in favor of the wealthy and powerful. (Perhaps this is why some have said that there are two things you just do not want to see being made: sausage and the law.) Because legislators are predominantly Caucasian, male, and wealthy, because voters are also predominantly Caucasian, financially better off, and well educated, and because monied interests have greater access to legislators than other citizens do, the law is heavily biased against powerless groups in society. The first result of this is that the label "crime" may not be used to identify those acts that are really the most dangerous to society.

ISSUE IN DEPTH
New Antiterrorism Laws

Although the September 11, 2001, terrorist attacks against the World Trade Center in New York City and the Pentagon in Washington, DC, may seem like the first time that America was attacked by terrorists, this is not the case. There have been several notable attacks, even in recent history.

For example, on February 26, 1993, a rented van packed with explosives blew up in a basement parking garage in the World Trade Center, killing 6 people and injuring more than 1,000. The convicted bombers received life sentences for the crime, whose aim was to kill many more people using cyanide canisters that did not explode as planned. On April 19, 1995, a rented van packed with explosives blew up in front of the Murrah Federal Building in Oklahoma City, killing 168 people and injuring more than 400. The convicted murderer was executed by lethal injection in Terre Haute, Indiana.

As a result of such events, our federal government has passed various laws that are of great importance for the activities of police, courts, and corrections at all levels of government. They also have great import for the main issues of this book, especially the balance between proponents of the crime control and those of the due process model of criminal justice.

What follows is a brief summary of some of the most important antiterrorism laws and some commentary on their meaning for justice in the United States. First, *The Antiterrorism and Effective Death Penalty Act of 1996* was signed into law on April 24, 1996. According to the U.S. State Department, this law:

- prohibits U.S. foreign assistance to governments that provide assistance or lethal military equipment to terrorist-list governments;
- prohibits sales or licenses for export of defense articles or defense services to countries that the president determines are not fully cooperating with U.S. antiterrorism efforts;
- authorizes exclusion of aliens who are members or representatives of foreign terrorist groups designated as such by the secretary of state;
- directs the Federal Aviation Administration to require foreign air carriers serving the United States to use the identical security measures utilized by U.S. carriers;
- criminalizes numerous forms of terrorism, such as possessing certain chemical and biological materials and conspiring to commit acts of terrorism; and
- makes dozens of types of killings involving terrorism grounds for the death penalty.

The aspects of the law that are most controversial deal with limiting *habeas corpus petitions*, which are judicial mandates to prison officials requiring that inmates be brought to the court to determine whether or not they are lawfully imprisoned based on the facts of their cases and the law. According to The

Federal Judiciary, the law "creates one-year deadlines for filing habeas petitions, limits successive petitions, and generally restricts the review of state prisoner petitions if the claim was adjudicated on the merits in the state courts." The law also "establishes special habeas corpus procedures for capital cases in states with mechanisms for the appointment, compensation, and payment of reasonable litigation expenses of counsel in state post-conviction proceedings brought by indigent prisoners" and "establishes a 180-day time frame in which a petitioner must file a habeas petition, restricts the scope of federal review." When it comes to the death penalty, we know that expediting the process by limiting appeals increases the likelihood that errors (in this case, fatal errors) will be made (see Chapter Ten). Any time an innocent person is punished for a crime, justice is not achieved. Finally, the law makes it easier to deport aliens by streamlining the deportation process after they serve their sentences.

The Aviation and Transportation Security Act was signed into law on November 19, 2001. According to the GOP (Grand Old [Republican] Party), this law:

- establishes a new Transportation Security Administration (TSA) within the Department of Transportation (DOT) responsible for security for all modes of transportation and headed by a new Under Secretary;
- requires that the federal government assume responsibility for all passenger and baggage screening at commercial airports in the United States;
- requires that the TSA hire, train, and deploy federal screeners, federal security managers, federal security personnel, and federal law enforcement officers;
- requires the TSA to adopt new, stricter standards for airport baggage screeners;
- requires that 100% of checked baggage be screened;
- requires the deployment of Federal Air Marshals for certain flights; and
- directs the new Under Secretary, in consultation with the Federal Aviation Administration (FAA), to take action to strengthen cockpit doors and provides for pilots to carry firearms to defend their aircraft.

The aspects of the law that are most controversial deal with directing pilots to be armed. Many Americans feel uncomfortable with pilots being armed and/or pilots firing weapons while flying airplanes. Even pilots spoke out against being responsible for defending their planes, suggesting that the government and the airlines ought to take responsibility for preventing acts of violence in the air.

The most controversial law to be passed in the wake of the attacks of September 11, 2001, is the *USA PATRIOT Act* (Uniting and Strengthening America by Providing Appropriate Tools Required to Intercept and Obstruct Terrorism), which was signed into law with almost no debate on October 24, 2001 (only 45 days after the attacks). The bill was 342 pages long, yet many members of Congress say that they did not even read it before voting in favor of it.

The stated purpose of the law was "to deter and punish terrorist acts in the United States and around the world, to enhance law enforcement investigatory tools, and for other purposes." It is these "other purposes" that have legal experts and normal citizens very worried. This law is very complicated and modifies several existing laws, but essentially it allows the Federal Bureau of Investigation (FBI), Central Intelligence Agency (CIA), and other agencies of the Office of Homeland Security to:

- access medical, financial, library, educational, and other personal records of any people as long as a "significant purpose" is for "the gathering of foreign intelligence";
- tap any and all phones of such people and monitor their Internet use, tracking every phone call made and received, and every Web site visited;
- detain such people against their will and refuse them access to a lawyer, based on secret evidence; and
- label people "domestic terrorists" if they violate the criminal law and "influence the policy of a government by intimidation or coercion" or "intimidate or coerce a civilian population."

Legal experts have suggested that the law erodes elements of the First, Fourth, Fifth, Sixth, and Eighth Amendments to the U.S. Constitution, because it is possible that the U.S. government will use its unlimited authority to spy on American citizens without any evidence of criminal activity and to do so in secret, without judicial oversight, and without any accountability to the American people.

Perhaps this is why, at the time of this writing, more than 200 towns and counties have already passed resolutions against this law. Three states have also done so, and more than 100 other towns and counties are working to do the same. Furthermore, numerous bills proposed in Congress would substantially weaken the USA PATRIOT Act.

Still, according to The Center for Public Integrity, the U.S. Department of Justice apparently wants to expand the USA PATRIOT Act. The Center for Public Integrity obtained a draft of *The Domestic Security Enhancement Act of 2003*, dated January 9, 2003, and written by the staff of Attorney General John Ashcroft, which has not been officially released or proposed to Congress. The draft of the bill, which is being referred to as *PATRIOT Act II*, would:

- limit the type of information released through Freedom of Information requests;
- create a DNA database of suspected terrorists;
- lessen restrictions on local police departments seeking to gather information on individuals;
- encourage (or mandate) detention of people charged with any offenses connected to terrorism; and
- expatriate American citizens who give financial or material support to a group considered a "terrorist organization" by the federal government.

Parts of PATRIOT II were passed by the U.S. Congress and signed into law by President Bush, as part of an intelligence appropriations bill. Thus, it received little media attention and generated little public concern. These laws, and Americans' reactions to them, serve as a good example of the struggle to maintain a balance between security (crime control or crime prevention) and individual liberty (due process). At the current time, it is safe to conclude that efforts are being made by the U.S. government to restrict the liberties of all Americans in order to prevent or reduce the threat of terrorism on our soil. The Bill of Rights Defense Committee tracks developments in these laws. For the latest, see www.bordc.org.

Discussion Questions

1. Define the law.
2. Explain the difference between so-called mala in se and mala prohibita crimes. Provide examples of each. Do you think this distinction is an important one? Why or why not?
3. Make a list of different types of law, and define each.
4. What is the difference between natural law and positive law?
5. Try to think of some behaviors that you think violate natural law but not positive law. Also, are there behaviors that violate positive law but not natural law? Examples?
6. Where do the following types of law come from: Constitutional law? statutory law? case law? and administrative law?
7. How did common law shape American criminal law?
8. Contrast substantive and procedural criminal law.
9. What are the main purposes of the law?
10. What do you think is the most important purpose of the criminal law?
11. Describe the typical lawmaker in the United States. How does he or she differ from the average American?
12. Describe the typical voter in the United States. How does he or she differ from the average American?
13. What is a PAC?
14. What is soft money? How is it different from hard money?
15. Provide an example of how money shapes the law.
16. Do you think the law represents the interests of Americans? Why or why not?
17. Which is more accurate in explaining the interests served by the law—the consensus model of lawmaking or the conflict model of lawmaking? Why?
18. What is the USA PATRIOT Act? In your opinion, is this law necessary to protect America from terrorism?

PART II

CRIME: IMAGES AND REALITIES

CHAPTER FOUR

CRIME: WHICH IS WORSE, CRIME ON THE STREETS OR CRIME IN THE SUITES?

INTRODUCTION

Close your eyes and picture a crime. What do you see? What does the offender look like? What about the victim? The image that you probably see is likely consistent with those vigorously pursued by American criminal justice agencies and portrayed in the American mass media. But what is a crime? Why are some crimes considered more serious than others? How do we know how much crime there is in the United States? Is the crime problem getting worse or is it getting better? This chapter answers these questions. I argue that crime in the United States is probably not as bad as you think it is, unless you are thinking of some violent crimes and corporate crime. I also show that our criminal justice network is focused almost exclusively on street crimes committed by a small segment of our population. Implications for justice are discussed.

WHAT IS A CRIME?

When you think of the word *crime,* you probably have a good idea of what it means. Although there is a straightforward legal definition of crime, most of us think of crimes as any behaviors that are done intentionally and cause physical or financial harm to another person. For example, if you were standing on a street corner minding your own business, and someone came up and poked a pencil into your eye, causing a loss of vision, you would probably feel that you had been victimized by crime. Even if it was not against the law, you would probably think it should be. If a corporation manufactured a toaster that shot sparks into your eyes, you might also feel like a victim of crime, even if it was not specifically a violation of the criminal law to manufacture such a toaster. Whether or not any act violates the law, you may feel like a crime victim when you are harmed by another. The *natural definition of crime* is any act that is seen as "fundamentally wrong, strongly disapproved, and deserving of punishment," regardless of whether it is legal (Gottfredson 1999, p. 47). Recall the discussion of natural law in Chapter Three. Some argue that behaviors that violate natural law should be considered crimes.

This natural view of crime, which appeals to our common sense, is very similar to the *legal definition of crime,* with one significant exception. Legally, a crime occurs only when an act violates the criminal law. As you saw in Chapter Three, there is no crime without law. Clearly, there are scores of behaviors that kill and injure us and take our property; many of them are committed intentionally but are not against the criminal law. Such acts are not legally considered crimes, even if we all think the act is wrong, immoral, deviant, or bad. What makes the act a crime is that it is written down as a crime by the government.

This means that crime is made up—invented—by people. Quinney (1970, p. 15) makes this point clear in his book *The Social Reality of Crime* when he writes:

> Crime is a definition of behavior that is conferred on some persons by others. Agents of the law, representing segments of a politically organized society, are responsible for formulating and administering criminal laws. Persons and behaviors, therefore, become criminal because of the formulation and application of criminal definitions. Thus, crime is created.

Crime does not exist in nature. It is something that human beings have invented and continue to invent every day.

This is not to say that there is no harmful behavior in nature. Many behaviors in nature kill and produce harms. For example, on the plains of Africa, lions and hyenas fight for the right to kill zebras and other animals. This is part of Darwin's concept of "survival of the fittest." When lions and hyenas kill zebras or even one another in order to eat, defend their territory, or gain mating advantages, the zebra police are not called out to round up the killers in the interests of justice. Why not? I hope the answer is obvious—because zebras do not call such killings crimes. It is not illegal for lions or hyenas to kill zebras. Human beings are the only species to legislate killing as a crime (and only in certain circumstances, because there are plenty of ways to kill people, even intentionally, without committing a crime).

Since crime is invented, no behavior is inherently criminal, and any behavior can be defined as a crime. These commonsense points are important to remember when thinking about crime. If you can remember these points, it will be much easier for you to understand this book. For example, in Chapter Eleven, I explore drug legalization as an alternative to the war on drugs. In that chapter, you will see that many "drug crimes" are not really all that harmful. They are illegal only because human beings have made them illegal. Drugs that are illegal can also be made legal (whether they should be is discussed in Chapter Eleven).

Because crime is a human invention, there is some disagreement among those who study crime for a living about what behaviors should constitute crime. Most criminologists and criminal justice scholars tend to limit their studies to behaviors that violate the criminal law, and a very large share of them study only *street crimes* or crimes committed on the streets of America.

Legal Definition of Crime

Legally, a crime occurs when a person acts, fails to act, attempts to act, or agrees to act in a way that is in violation of the criminal law and without defense or justification. This legal definition of crime is made up of several elements. The first element, *acts,* includes any behaviors that are actually carried out, such as intentionally taking the life of another (murder) or taking someone's wallet from his or her back pocket (theft). *Attempts* are acts that are not successfully carried out, such as unsuccessfully trying to break into someone's home through a locked front door (attempted burglary). Agreeing to act is called a *conspiracy*. An example is verbally agreeing with a friend to kill the president of the United States even if you do not ever attempt to do so. Examples of *failures to act* include not paying your taxes and not paying child support. The most important element of the definition of crime is the criminal law, which is made up of federal or state statutes that specify what behaviors are in violation of the criminal law. As noted, without the law, there is no crime.

The final element of this definition is *without defense or justification*. This is an important element, for a person may commit an act *(actus reus)* that is against the law, and even may do so with intent *(mens rea),* yet may not be a criminal if he or she has a valid reason for committing the act (Schmalleger 1999). Examples of valid defenses include an alibi, a justification, an excuse, or a procedural defense (Schmalleger 2001, p. 143). In addition to an *alibi,* which is a statement that suggests that the defendant was somewhere else at the time of the crime and thus truly innocent, there are defenses that can be used that acknowledge that the defendant did in fact commit the act. They are based on the premise that even though the defendant committed the act, he or she is still not responsible for the crime and thus not legally guilty.

Justifications assert that the crime was necessary in order to avoid some greater evil. *Excuses* assert that the crime can be accepted based on some special condition or emergency. *Procedural defenses* suggest either some form of discrimination by criminal justice officials or some form of misconduct, either intended or not. Examples of each are provided in the following box.

Valid defenses to criminal charges

Justifications

- *Self-defense:* If you are afraid for your life and act to protect it (and sometimes to protect your property)—for example, if you attack someone who breaks into your house—you may plead not guilty because of self-defense.
- *Necessity:* If you are personally at risk of dying or becoming ill unless you commit a crime—for example, if you find yourself in danger of freezing to death unless you break into someone's cabin in the middle of the woods—you may plead not guilty because of necessity.

Excuses

- *Duress:* If you are coerced or forced to commit a crime by another—for example, if someone shoves a gun in your face and demands that you help rob a bank—you may plead not guilty because of duress.
- *Immaturity:* If you are too young to understand right from wrong—for example, if you are 5 years old and you playfully aim a gun at a playmate and pull the trigger—you may plead not guilty because of immaturity.
- *Insanity:* If you are unable to understand the difference between right and wrong or are unable to adjust your behavior accordingly—for example, if you have been diagnosed with a severe mental illness that impairs your thought processes—you may plead not guilty because of insanity.
- *Involuntary intoxication:* If you become impaired by the action of another—for example, if someone slips a drug into your drink and you violently attack another person—you may plead not guilty because of involuntary intoxication.

Procedural defenses

- *Entrapment:* If a government agent such as a police officer approaches you and offers you the opportunity to commit a crime, and the offense did not originate in your own mind—for example, if you buy drugs from an undercover officer who has come to your door while you are at home enjoying dinner with your family—you may plead not guilty because of entrapment.
- *Selective prosecution:* If some people are singled out for a particular punishment based on extralegal factors such as race—for example, if you are pulled over for speeding and learn that blacks are more likely to be pulled over and ticketed, as well as prosecuted because of "police profiling"—you may plead not guilty because of selective prosecution.

Additionally, for an act to be legally considered a crime, it must be committed with *culpability* (or responsibility). This includes acts that are committed in any of the following circumstances.

- *Intentionally:* Committed with a guilty mind, on purpose
- *Negligently:* Committed as a result of a failure to meet normal or recognized expectations

- *Recklessly:* Committed without due caution for human life or property
- *Knowingly:* Committed with knowledge that an outcome is likely

Generally, acts committed with intent are considered more serious than those committed negligently, recklessly, or knowingly. Considering that a person who is killed negligently, recklessly, or knowingly is just as dead as one killed intentionally, you may question the logic of such distinctions.

TYPES OF CRIME IN THE UNITED STATES

Serious/Street Crime

Remember what I asked you to do at the beginning of this chapter? Close your eyes and picture a crime. What do you see? What does the offender look like? What is he or she doing? What about the victim?

Chances are, if you do this, you will see a particular type of crime committed by a particular type of person against another particular type of person. To avoid biasing your images, I will not tell you what you probably saw when you closed your eyes and pictured a crime, a criminal, and a victim—not yet, anyway.

In all likelihood, you saw a crime that is consistent with what our government perceives as *serious crime,* that which is visible to us as ordinary U.S. citizens. What does "serious" mean?

You may consider something serious that is important to you, perhaps something you fear or are worried about. You might consider crimes serious if they cause or threaten great danger and harm (either physical or financial).

The term *serious* also might be related to the frequency of a behavior. For example, a behavior may be very harmful but may occur so rarely that it does not create fear or worry in citizens. Would this type of act be considered serious?

The U.S. government has an answer to this question. The Uniform Crime Reporting Program, discussed later in this chapter, is a source of crime information compiled by the Federal Bureau of Investigation (FBI) each year. This source of data was created because of a need to gather and disseminate national crime statistics. In the 1920s, the International Association of Chiefs of Police (IACP) formed a committee to create a uniform system for recording police statistics. Crimes were originally evaluated on the basis of the following criteria:

- Harmfulness
- Frequency of occurrence
- Pervasiveness in all geographic areas of the country
- Likelihood of being reported to the police

After a preliminary compilation in 1929 of a list of crimes that met these criteria, the committee completed their plan for developing the Uniform Crime Reports (UCR). Statistics on these crimes were collected beginning in the 1930s.

As noted in each year's UCR publication, "Seven offenses were chosen to serve as an index for gauging the overall volume and rate of crime." These offenses, known as *Part I index offenses*, include the violent crimes of murder and nonnegligent manslaughter, forcible rape, robbery, and aggravated assault and the property crimes of burglary, theft, and motor vehicle theft. In 1979, arson was added to the UCR list, for a total of eight "serious" crimes. These terms are defined in the following box.

Serious crimes: Part I offenses of the UCR

- *Criminal homicide:* Includes murder and nonnegligent manslaughter: the willful (nonnegligent) killing of one human being by another. Deaths caused by negligence, attempts to kill, suicides, and accidental deaths are excluded. Justifiable homicides are classified separately, and traffic fatalities are excluded.
- *Forcible rape:* The carnal knowledge of a female forcibly and against her will. Rapes by force and attempts or assaults with the intent to rape, regardless of the age of the victim, are included. Statutory offenses (where no force is used but the victim is under the legal age of consent) are excluded.
- *Robbery:* Taking or attempting to take anything of value from the care, custody, or control of a person or persons by force or threat of force or violence and/or by putting the victim in fear.
- *Aggravated assault:* An unlawful attack by one person on another for the purpose of inflicting severe or aggravated bodily injury, which usually is accompanied by the use of a weapon or by means likely to produce death or great bodily harm. Simple assaults are excluded.
- *Burglary:* The unlawful entering of a structure to commit a felony or a theft. Attempted forcible entry is included.
- *Larceny–theft:* The unlawful taking, carrying, leading, or riding away of property from the possession or constructive possession of another. Examples are thefts of bicycles or automobile accessories, shoplifting, pocket-picking, or the stealing of any property or article that is not taken by force and violence or by fraud. Attempted thefts are included. Embezzlement, confidence games, forgery, worthless checks, and so on are excluded.
- *Motor vehicle theft:* The theft or attempted theft of a motor vehicle, defined as a vehicle that is self-propelled and runs on the surface and not on rails. Motorboats, construction equipment, airplanes, and farming equipment are specifically excluded from this category.
- *Arson:* Any willful or malicious burning or attempt to burn, with or without intent to defraud, a dwelling house, public building, motor vehicle or aircraft, or personal property of another.

Given their own discussion of what constitutes a serious offense, you might expect that the street crimes listed in the box would be the ones that cause the greatest harm (either physical or financial), occur with great frequency, are pervasive throughout the country, and are likely to be reported to the police. Since the majority of crimes overall are not reported to the police, you may wonder why some crimes (e.g., theft) that are highly unlikely to be reported to the police are included.

In the discussion of the eight types of serious crime in each annual UCR report, it is claimed that "these are serious crimes by nature and/or volume." That is, these crimes supposedly cause the most harm, occur with the greatest frequency, and are the most widespread.

Other types of crimes, known as *Part II offenses* of the UCR, are literally considered "less serious." Presumably, it is because they either cause less harm, occur with less frequency, or are not as pervasive throughout the country. This list of Part II offenses is provided in the following box. As a justification for their inclusion in this list, the FBI explains:

> Not all crimes, such as Embezzlement, are readily brought to the attention of the police. Also, some serious crimes, such as Kidnapping, occur infrequently. Therefore, for practical purposes, the reporting of offenses known is limited to the selected crime classifications because they are the crimes most likely to be reported and most likely to occur with sufficient frequency to provide an adequate basis for comparison.

No explanation is offered for their exclusion from the list of Part I or "serious" offenses based on the degree of relative harm they cause, how frequently they occur, and/or how pervasive they are throughout the country.

Less serious crimes: Part II offenses of the UCR

- *Simple assaults:* Assaults and attempted assaults in which no weapon is used and which do not result in serious or aggravated injury to the victim.
- *Forgery and counterfeiting:* Making, altering, uttering, or possessing, with intent to defraud, anything false in the semblance of that which is true. Attempts are included.
- *Fraud:* Fraudulent conversion and obtaining money or property by false pretenses. Confidence games and bad checks, except forgeries and counterfeiting, are included.
- *Embezzlement:* Misappropriation or misapplication of money or property entrusted to one's care, custody, or control.
- *Buying, receiving, or possessing stolen property:* Buying, receiving, and possessing stolen property, including attempts.
- *Vandalism:* Willful or malicious destruction, injury, disfigurement, or defacement of any public or private property, real or personal, without consent of the owner or persons having custody or control. Attempts are included.
- *Prostitution and commercialized vice:* Sex offenses of a commercialized nature, such as prostitution, keeping a bawdy house, procuring, or transporting women for immoral purposes. Attempts are included.
- *Sex offenses:* Statutory rape and offenses against chastity, common decency, morals, and the like. Attempts are included.
- *Drug abuse violations:* State and/or local offenses relating to the unlawful possession, sale, use, growing, and manufacturing of narcotic drugs.
- *Gambling:* Promoting, permitting, or engaging in illegal gambling.
- *Offenses against the family and children:* Nonsupport, neglect, desertion, or abuse of family and children. Attempts are included.
- *Driving under the influence:* Driving or operating any vehicle or common carrier while drunk or under the influence of liquor or narcotics.
- *Liquor law violations:* State and/or local liquor law violations except drunkenness and driving under the influence. Federal violations are excluded.

- *Drunkenness:* Offenses relating to drunkenness or intoxication. Driving under the influence is excluded.
- *Disorderly conduct:* Breach of the peace.
- *Vagrancy:* Begging, loitering, and the like. Includes prosecutions under the charge of suspicious person.
- *Curfew violations and loitering:* Offenses relating to violations of local curfew or loitering ordinances where such laws exist.
- *Running away:* Limited to juveniles taken into protective custody under provisions of local statutes.

Why are such acts considered less serious? We return to that issue later in this chapter, when we compare harms caused by serious crimes with harms caused by other types of behaviors. I illustrate that the acts we focus on least actually cause more harm, both physically and financially, and occur with greater frequency than the crimes we consider the most serious. You might correctly wonder, then, whether legal definitions of crime are appropriately limited. If not, why not? Recall the examination of who makes the law in Chapter Three. Why would legislators, who are predominantly older, wealthy Caucasian males, define acts committed by people like themselves and their financial backers as crimes?

Apparently, even the federal government is aware of the contradiction in what they claim to be the most serious crimes and those that actually cause the most damage. The result is the creation of the *National Incident Based Reporting System* (NIBRS). This is a data set that includes information on individual criminal incidents, including arrests. The NIBRS includes 22 categories of offenses and 46 specific crimes (called *Group A offenses*), as well as 11 categories of offenses for which only arrest data are collected (called *Group B offenses*). In the NIBRS data set, typical street crimes such as theft have been combined with white-collar crimes such as embezzlement and fraud, which makes sense, as each is a form of stealing someone else's property. However, the NIBRS was not created to finally recognize the seriousness of white-collar crimes by treating them as "serious crimes." Instead, the NIBRS is aimed at gathering more specific information about individual criminal incidents (such as time and place of occurrence and characteristics of victims and offenders) to provide law enforcement with better information in their fight against crime. The following box lists the NIBRS offenses. (Note: The offenses are not defined by the FBI except when listing specific types of offenses that fall into each category.)

NIBRS Offenses

Group A offenses

- *Arson*
- *Assault offenses*—aggravated assault, simple assault, intimidation
- *Bribery*
- *Burglary/breaking and entering*
- *Counterfeiting/forgery*
- *Destruction/damage/vandalism of property*
- *Drug/narcotic offenses*—drug/narcotic violations, drug equipment violations

- *Embezzlement*
- *Extortion/blackmail*
- *Fraud offenses*—false pretenses, swindle, confidence game, credit card/automatic teller machine fraud, impersonation, welfare fraud, wire fraud
- *Gambling offenses*—betting/wagering, operating/promoting/assisting gambling, gambling equipment violations, sports tampering
- *Homicide offenses*—murder and nonnegligent manslaughter, negligent manslaughter, justifiable homicide
- *Kidnapping/abduction*
- *Larceny/theft offenses*—pocket-picking, purse-snatching, shoplifting, theft from building, theft from coin-operated machine or device, theft from motor vehicle, theft of motor vehicle parts or accessories, all other larceny
- *Motor vehicle theft*
- *Pornography/obscene material*
- *Prostitution offenses*—prostitution, assisting or promoting prostitution
- *Robbery*
- *Sex offenses, forcible*—forcible rape, forcible sodomy, sexual assault with an object, forcible fondling
- *Sex offenses, nonforcible*—incest, statutory rape
- *Stolen property offenses (receiving, etc.)*
- *Weapon law violations*

Group B offenses

- *Bad checks*
- *Curfew/loitering/vagrancy violations*
- *Disorderly conduct*
- *Driving under the influence*
- *Drunkenness*
- *Family offenses, nonviolent*
- *Liquor law violations*
- *Peeping Tom*
- *Runaway*
- *Trespass of real property*
- *All other offenses*

According to the FBI:

> NIBRS has the capability of furnishing information on nearly every major criminal justice issue facing law enforcement today, including terrorism, white collar crime, weapons offenses, missing children where criminality is involved, drug/narcotics offenses, drug involvement in all offenses, hate crimes, spouse abuse, abuse of the elderly, child abuse, domestic violence, juvenile crime/gangs, parental kidnapping, organized crime, pornography/child pornography, driving under the influence, and alcohol-related offenses.

In fact, the NIBRS still does not go far enough because it does not collect data on the behaviors that pose the greatest threats to Americans.

Other Conceptions of Crime: White-Collar Deviance

As noted at the onset of this chapter, you may feel like a crime victim when you are victimized by an act that is committed against you on purpose. But if this act was not legally defined as a crime at the time it was committed against you, then legally, you were not a crime victim.

Does this mean that you were not victimized? Of course not. You may be victimized by acts outside the scope of the criminal justice system. For example, *white-collar deviance* is a term put forth by D. Simon and Hagan (1999, pp. 3–4) in their book of the same name. It includes not only criminal acts but also unethical acts, civil and regulatory violations, and other harmful acts committed intentionally, recklessly, negligently, or knowingly. *White-collar deviance* is a term that encompasses *white-collar crime* (Sutherland 1977a, 1977b), *elite deviance* (D. Simon and Eitzen 1993), *corporate violence* (N. Frank and Lynch 1992), and those *crimes by any other name* (Reiman 1998) committed by our *trusted criminals* (Friedrichs 1999). These are acts that cause tremendous physical, financial, and moral harms to Americans.

Here's one example of white-collar deviance: Many Americans criticize "big government" for wasting tax money on social programs. Yet when money is wasted on national defense, Americans seem less concerned (this is not to say that national defense spending itself is a waste of money). Sherrill (1997) describes many defense-spending scandals. According to Sherrill, $13 billion paid to weapons contractors between 1985 and 1995 was simply "lost," and another $15 billion remains unaccounted for. D. Simon and Hagan (1999, p. 33) claim that military waste and fraud cost taxpayers $172 billion per year. President Bush's (the second) defense budget for 2003 was $399 billion (not including the costs of the war in Iraq and rebuilding costs). Bush requested more than $70 billion for the war and we spent nearly $4 billion per month in 2003 in Iraq. Is losing money intended for national defense a crime? No. Is anyone held criminally accountable for such losses? No.

Another example of white-collar deviance is what Sennott (2000) calls "corporate welfare," which he claims costs Americans at least $150 billion per year. Essentially, businesses are subsidized by taxpayers in the form of trade missions, funding for support services, tax breaks, and state offices that guide corporations in their business affairs. Frivolous spending by the government also might be considered white-collar deviance. For example, members of Congress enjoy $78 million in free mailing privileges each year (about $120,000 each). They also pay no sales tax on items bought in Washington, DC, and pay no income taxes there. On top of that, all members of Congress are allowed an extra $3,000 income tax deduction and can have their tax returns prepared free of charge by professionals. They are also accorded free transportation in chauffeured limousines. Most shocking, given that more than 40 million Americans do not have any medical insurance, is that members of Congress receive free medical and life insurance as well as very generous retirement plans (D. Simon and Hagan 1999, pp. 43–44). None of this is criminal, even though many acts of white-collar deviance produce victims.

What Is Victimization?

Currently, the criminal justice network seldom views a person as a victim unless that individual person becomes a victim (suffers financial or physical harm) specifically as a result of a criminal act. Rush (2000, p. 353) defines *victimization* as "the harming of any single victim in a criminal incident." Champion (1997, p. 128) defines *victimization* as a "specific criminal act affecting a specific victim." The UCR definition of *homicide* also illustrates how crimes are typically perceived as being committed against one person by another. Murder is the "willful . . . killing of one human being by another."

Notice the common elements in these definitions:

- A single victim
- Suffering harm
- From a criminal act

According to these definitions, victimization occurs when one person suffers some harm from a behavior that violates the criminal law. Yet people obviously are victimized by behaviors that do not meet these conditions. Table 4.1 sets forth a typology of victimization that illustrates four basic types:

- Harmful acts committed by an individual person against another individual person (Cell 1)
- Harmful acts committed by an individual person against an entity (e.g., a group of people or a corporation) (Cell 2)
- Harmful acts committed by an entity (e.g., a group of people or a corporation) against an individual person (Cell 3)
- Harmful acts committed by an entity (e.g., a group of people or a corporation) against another entity (e.g., a group of people or a corporation) (Cell 4)

Table 4.1 also provides examples of specific behaviors that would fall into each cell: one example of an act that causes financial harm to victims and one of an act that causes physical harm. Examples in Table 4.1 of harmful acts committed by an individual against another individual include theft (e.g., taking property from another without consent and without the use of force or the threat of force) and battery (e.g., physically striking or beating another person with force). Examples of harmful acts committed by an individual against a group of people or a corporation include forgery (e.g., signing another person's name to a check that is not yours in order to cash it) and terrorist acts (e.g., planting and detonating explosives at a building occupied by other people). Examples of harmful acts committed by a group of people or a corporation against an individual person include fraud (e.g., making false or deceptive claims about a product to trick the buyer into purchasing it) and manufacturing and selling defective products (e.g., making a car that explodes in a low-impact

TABLE 4.1
A Typology of Victimization

| | Offender | |
Victim	Individual	Group/Corporation
Individual	Cell 1 Theft Battery	Cell 3 Fraud Defective products
Group/Corporation	Cell 2 Forgery Terrorist acts	Cell 4 Price fixing Hazardous conditions

crash because of a faulty part). Finally, examples of harmful acts committed by a group of people or a corporation against another group of people or corporation include price fixing (e.g., when two large corporations keep prices artificially high by agreeing to set a specific price on their products and simultaneously exclude smaller competitors that cannot lower prices to compete for buyers' business) and forcing or allowing employees to work under hazardous conditions (e.g., not complying with federally required safety regulations or ignoring warnings of potential problems).

Although these four types of victimization are mutually exclusive, the examples provided in Table 4.1 are not. That is, some of the examples provided could also fit well into another category of victimization. For example, acts of fraud can also be committed by an individual against another individual (as when a person sells a fake fur coat to someone after claiming that it is "a genuine mink coat") or by a group of people or a corporation against an individual (as when a corporation sells a product guaranteed to "make you younger!"). Likewise, theft can be committed by individuals against other individuals or against groups and corporations. The examples simply serve to help illustrate the four types of victimization defined.

The significant point is that victimization encompasses many more types of behaviors than can be adequately understood according to its most common definition in criminology. As noted by Karmen (1996, p. 2), the term *victim* most accurately "refers to all those people who experience injury, loss, or hardship due to any cause." In other words, a broader definition is:

> people who experience any harmful behavior, such as "accident victims, cancer victims, flood victims, and victims of discrimination and similar injustices" and people who have been "physically injured, economically hurt, robbed of self-respect, emotionally traumatized, socially stigmatized, politically oppressed, collectively exploited, personally alienated, manipulated, co-opted, neglected, ignored, blamed, defamed, demeaned, or vilified." (Karmen 1996, p. 2)

Although this definition is too broad, legal conceptions of crime and victimization are too restrictive to encompass the wide range of purposive behaviors that create victims, particularly given the fact that "crime" is a label applied by persons with power to have their will enacted into law while simultaneously creating a criminal law not focused on their own harmful and deviant acts (see Chapter Three). A compromise between the traditional definition of victim and the broader one proposed here would be a recognition of a specific set of harmful behaviors that more accurately captures the range of culpable behaviors that cause harm to their victims. As has been discussed, the key word pertaining to criminal justice is *culpability,* which indicates some degree of blameworthiness or responsibility for a resulting action. Because culpability encompasses more than intentionality, acts causing harm can lead to findings of responsibility even when they were not committed intentionally.

I have suggested that the concept of victimization be broadened to include any act that produces financial or physical harm and is committed intentionally, negligently, recklessly, or knowingly (Robinson 2002). Following this logic, a new understanding of the term *victim* is in order, one that consists of individual persons, groups of people, or corporations that are victimized by acts committed intentionally, negligently, recklessly, or knowingly. Scholars such as Friedrichs (1983), McShane and Williams (1992), and Phipps (1986) have also been critical of the traditional conception of victims, for at least the following reasons.

- Current images of victims reinforce a focus on the state rather than the actual person(s) who suffered physical or financial harm. This "is a logical extension of a legal system which defines crimes as offenses against the state" (Zehr and Umbreit 1982, p. 64).

- Current images of the state as victim reinforce a "conservative crime control agenda" or ideology "and have increased the power of the state in criminal proceedings" (McShane and Williams 1992, p. 258).
- Criminal justice is focused on street crimes by the poor rather than on white-collar crimes and deviance, which allows white-collar offenders to escape relatively unscathed and unpunished despite their culpability (e.g., see D. Simon and Hagan 1999).

Such criticisms have led scholars to call for a widening of the scope of criminal justice beyond street crimes committed by individuals against other individuals.

This is not to say that street crime is not tremendously harmful; it is just not as harmful as other acts that are either not against the law or not vigorously pursued by agencies of social control. Even violent crime, which Americans fear the most, is unlikely to result in actual harm to its victims. For example, fewer than 1 in 10 victims of violent crime will seek treatment for injuries at an emergency room (Donziger 1996). In fact, the most common violent street crimes, simple assault and aggravated assault, do not even require any injury to be counted in the UCR. An attempt to injure is all that is required. As Kappeler, Blumberg, and Potter (2000, p. 122) explain, "All the violent crime, all the property crime, all the crime that we concentrate our energy and resources on combating is less of a threat to society than the crime committed by corporations."

A Comparison of Harms Associated with Crimes and "Noncrimes"

The label "crime" is not a function of what is most harmful to society. If you believe that you are more likely to be victimized by street crime than by acts of white-collar deviance committed by wealthy individuals or corporations, you are wrong. The belief that white-collar deviance is less harmful than street crime is a myth (Kappeler, Blumberg, and Potter 2000).

There is considerable evidence that white-collar deviance causes more physical and property damage than all eight serious crimes combined. Kappeler and coworkers (2000) estimate that just the economic losses due to corporate crime cost somewhere between 17 and 31 times as much as those due to street crime, although the total losses caused by corporate crime cost much more than this (see the Issue in Depth at the end of this chapter for some stunning examples). And this says nothing about lives lost due to corporate crime. One example proves this point: Tobacco use kills more people annually (approximately 440,000) than murder (approximately 16,000) and causes more financial loss ($100 billion in direct health care costs) than all street crime combined (less than $20 billion). Whereas murder by definition is intentional, manufacturing and promoting the use of tobacco for the specific purpose of killing people are not intentional. Yet lawsuits against the tobacco industry have shown that the tobacco industry's recklessness and negligence have produced hundreds of thousands of deaths in the United States each year. Thus, some scholars claim that the law should criminalize any act that causes harm to others, as long as the act is done intentionally, negligently, recklessly, or knowingly, as discussed earlier.

Can a corporation be held responsible for a crime? According to Podgor and Israel (1997, p. 16):

> The initial common law view was that a corporation could not be held criminally liable, although the individual members of the corporation could. Lacking a mind, the corporation could not form the *mens rea* necessary for criminality. Not having physical attributes, there was no *actus reus*. Additionally, even if convicted of an offense, the corporation could not be imprisoned for the crime.

Currently, however, corporations can be held liable for their harmful acts. For example, Section 2.07 of the Model Penal Code suggests that corporate agents can be held responsible for harms inflicted in the course of their work, including harms resulting from a failure to act, and for actions authorized, performed, or recklessly tolerated by the board of directors. The problem is that corporations are rarely held criminally responsible for the harms they inflict on Americans. Why not? Because the "most powerful organization in our society is the corporation. Corporations have become more powerful than governments, or religious institutions, or labor unions" (Mokhiber and Weissman 1999, p. 96).

Other harms associated with legal acts and/or "crimes" that are not considered serious or worthy of criminal justice and media attention demonstrate that the label "crime" is not reserved for the most harmful acts in society. For example, Frank and Lynch (1992, pp. 1–11) document the costs of physical damage to individuals and society by means of deadly pollutants, preventable work-related "accidents" (as they are called), occupational diseases and deaths, and faulty consumer products. D. Simon and Eitzen (1993, pp. 49–73, 113–14, 121–56) discuss individual cases of fraud by companies in the United States and trace harms to the savings and loan (S&L) scandals and tax breaks given exclusively to the rich. They also document the dangers associated with unsafe working conditions and unsafe products, including food products. Friedrichs (1995, pp. 70–88) shows the harms associated with corporate violence against the public, consumers, and workers, and illustrates harms resulting from fraud, tax evasion, price fixing, price gouging, false advertising, and so forth. Weisburd and Schlegel (1992, pp. 22–38) document the nature and extent of antitrust violations, multiple types of fraud, bribery, tax violations, and embezzlement. Rosoff, Pontell, and Tillman (1998) discuss numerous examples of white-collar crimes, including medical crime and computer crime, which demonstrate cold, calculated acts of individuals and corporations that result in mind-boggling financial and physical harms.

Reiman (1998, p. 113) estimates the costs of white-collar crimes to be at least $208 billion annually, far more than that of all street crimes combined, but even this number is an underestimate. Only one estimate of street crime costs has exceeded this estimate: A 1996 Justice Department report estimated that street crimes led to $450 billion per year in losses, but most of this was due to "quality of life costs" (T. Miller, Cohen, and Wiersma 1997). The S&L scandals of the 1980s alone will cost Americans $500 billion over the next 40 years. Yet the "average prison term for savings and loan offenders sentenced between 1988 and 1992 was 36 months, compared to 56 months for burglars and 38 months for those convicted of motor vehicle theft," even though the average loss in an S&L case was $500,000 (*Criminal Justice Newsletter*, December 5, 1994, p. 5, reported in Reiman 1998) while the loss in an average property crime is $1,251 (Reiman 1998, p. 128). In 2003 evidence came to light that Enron, WorldCom, and other large corporations, with assistance from the accounting firm Arthur Andersen and numerous banks, engaged in numerous forms of white-collar deviance that caused thousands of Americans to lose their life savings and retirement resources. Their misdeeds are discussed in the Issue in Depth at the end of the chapter.

Reiman (1998), using both official and unofficial sources of data, shows that every year far more people are killed and injured by preventable occupational diseases and hazards than by crime. He convincingly argues that the majority of these—totaling nearly 35,000 deaths and 3.5 million injuries—are as much beyond the control of the workers as being murdered is beyond the control of the murder victim (pp. 74–75). The fact that many of these deaths and injuries result from the negligence or recklessness of people who work for corporations demands our attention. McCaghy, Capron, and Jamieson (2000) suggest that as many as 100,000 workers each year die because of hazardous working conditions. Another 30,000 people die from unsafe and defective merchandise (Coleman 1998). Additionally, studies show that nearly 100,000 die from hospital errors (negligence and recklessness) every year, and another 90,000 die each year because of poor diets, in part due to high levels of large portions of high-fat foods.

The negligent and reckless acts that produce such harms are undeniably disproportionately committed by wealthier Caucasians. I illustrate this in Figure 4.1, which compares the typical offenders and victims of street crime and white-collar deviance.

Whereas African Americans are rounded up for street crimes, particularly drug crimes (see Chapter Eleven), white-collar and corporate criminals typically walk away unscathed or with a slap on the wrist. Studies show that prosecution of white-collar criminals represents the "road not taken" (S. Shapiro 1995) and that most white-collar criminals are repeat offenders but are nonetheless punished only with administrative sanctions or simple warnings (Weisburd, Chayet, and Waring 1990). Reiman (1998, p. 110) writes that when we are talking about

> the kinds of crimes poor people almost never have the opportunity to commit, such as antitrust violations, industrial safety violations, embezzlement, and serious tax evasion, the criminal justice system shows an increasingly benign and merciful face. The more likely that a crime is the type committed by middle- and upper-class people, the less likely it will be treated as a criminal offense. When it comes to crime in the streets, where the perpetrator is apt to be poor, he or she is even more likely to be arrested and formally charged. When it comes to crime in the suites, where the offender is apt to be affluent, the system is most likely to deal with the crime noncriminally, that is, by civil litigation or informal settlement.

Reiman (1998) even compares arrest data for street crimes that result in the loss of property with the crime of embezzlement (a property crime whereby property is misappropriated—that is, stolen from its rightful owner after being left in the care or trust of another). He finds that the number of arrests for property crimes is 140 times greater than that for embezzlement and that there is "one arrest for every $7,000 stolen [versus] one arrest for every $742,000 'misappropriated'" (p. 115). Arrests of white-collar offenders are made unlikely by deregulation efforts of politicians. *Deregulation* occurs when a government passes laws to limit its own control over an industry. In the 1980s, budgets of the Consumer Product Safety Commission, Occupational

	Street		White-Collar	
	Offender	Victim	Offender	Victim
Gender	Male	Male	Male	All
Age Group	Young	Young	Older	All
Race/Ethnicity	Minority*	Minority*	Caucasian	All
Income Level	Low	Low	High	All

FIGURE 4.1

The Typical Offender and Victim of Street Crime and White-Collar Deviance

* Self-report studies and victimization surveys generally do not find the pronounced differences in offending by race and ethnicity that are evident in arrest and conviction statistics.

Safety and Health Administration, and Federal Trade Commission were slashed, and requirements relating to pharmaceutical and automotive safety were lifted or softened (Kappeler, Blumberg, and Potter 2000, p. 135). Most of these changes in policy were attached as "riders" to large bills in Congress.

In fact, the history of government regulation has been one of businesses regulating themselves for their own benefit and gain. Many regulators are former corporate executives or go to work for corporations after their regulating days are over (Hagan 1998). Thus, there is a double standard of justice in the United States. While we spend billions each year fighting street crimes that produce relatively minor harms, we allow businesses to police themselves, and we give "little effort to enforce the law against [white-collar] criminals. When we do catch them at their nefarious deeds, we tap them on the wrist, make them say they are sorry, and send them about their criminal business" (Kappeler, Blumberg, and Potter 2000, p. 134). Some just change their names—e.g., Philip Morris Tobacco has become Altria and WorldCom is now MCI.

Why do white-collar and corporate offenders rarely receive "justice"? In their book *Corporate Predators,* Mokhiber and Weissman (1999, p. 9) claim that it is because of their power to shape the definition of the law and to influence prosecutors not to bring criminal charges. To this I would also add that they can afford the best defense that money can buy.

In Chapter Three, I showed how this owes itself to the criminal law, which does not usually label such acts "crimes"; when it does, they are not considered "serious." In defining what is bad, evil, wrong, harmful, and criminal, the criminal law thus creates myths about crime that cause people to view certain acts as the most serious and harmful, even though they are not, and produces fear of certain actions and people instead of others that pose even greater threats.

The government basically views victims of white-collar deviance as deserving their own victimization. The phrase "Let the buyer beware" is a prime example: "American business has followed 'caveat emptor' (let the buyer beware) and 'laissez faire' economics (the doctrine of government noninterference in business)" (D. Simon and Hagan 1999, p. 158). The former doctrine suggests that if you get ripped off by fraudulent salespeople, it is your own fault; you should have known better. The latter doctrine suggests that the government has no legitimate role in regulating business. Of course, if your house is burglarized because you left the windows unlocked, it is not your fault; you are seen as a victim of a "serious" crime, and the government has a legitimate role intervening in this type of activity.

Why does our own government fail to define the acts that are most dangerous to us as the most serious crimes? Kappeler and coworkers (2000) state:

> The government has a vested interest in maintaining the existing social definition of crime and extending this definition to groups and behaviors that are perceived to be a threat to the existing social order. . . . Similarly, the government has an interest in seeing that the existing criminal justice system's response to crime is not significantly altered in purpose or function.

According to these authors, the government's interests are served by promoting myths about crime and criminal justice. These myths are not only false but dangerous—dangerous because they allow harmful acts to be committed against innocent people by others with virtual impunity, even when done intentionally. And they are promoted by the mass media, which are owned by powerful U.S. corporations (see Chapter Five). In essence, the definition of crime is a threat to justice in the United States, because people who intentionally, recklessly, negligently, and knowingly kill and injure Americans do so with virtual impunity.

SOURCES OF CRIME INFORMATION: DO WE REALLY KNOW HOW MUCH CRIME IS OUT THERE?

Now that you have a better understanding of what crime is (and perhaps what it should be), how much of it is out there? To answer this question, you first need to understand where we get our information about crime. Most people get their crime information from media outlets such as television and newspapers, as well as from popular forms of entertainment such as movies, books, and the Internet (see Chapter Five).

The government also collects information about crime. Government sources tend to be more representative of what street crime really is than media sources of crime information. I use these government sources to illustrate the nature of crime in the United States.

We get our information about street crime from two main sources produced by the U.S. government. One may be better than the other, depending on what you want to learn. Major sources of crime data in the United States include the Uniform Crime Reports, the National Crime Victimization Survey, and self-report studies. Each of these, as well as sources of data on other forms of harmful behaviors, are discussed next.

Uniform Crime Reports

The *Uniform Crime Reports* (UCR) is perhaps the most commonly cited source of crime data in the United States. The UCR is a city, county, and state law enforcement program that provides a national source of crime data based on the submission of crime statistics by law enforcement agencies across the country (UCR Handbook 1999). More than 17,000 city, county, and state law enforcement agencies, employing more than 700,000 officers and representing roughly 260 million inhabitants of the United States (96% of the U.S. population), voluntarily send their crime statistics either directly to the FBI or to their own state's bureau of investigation or department of law enforcement for inclusion in the UCR.

The UCR collects data primarily on a group of index offenses (serious crimes), including both *violent crimes* and *property crimes*. These crimes are listed as Part I and Part II offenses in boxes earlier in this chapter. The UCR has essentially been expanded to include the Group A and Group B offenses of the National Incidence Based Reporting System (NIBRS), also discussed earlier. Of the many limitations of the UCR (see Gove, Hughes, and Geerken 1985), the most troubling in terms of both crime frequencies and crime trends is that it measures only *crimes known to the police*. Most crimes are not known to the police, so the measure does not reflect actual crime frequencies accurately. Crimes not known to the police, commonly referred to as the *dark figure of crime,* are not addressed by the UCR. Statistics from the Bureau of Justice Statistics (BJS; 1997) suggest that victims report only about one of every three property crimes and that victims are most likely to report their victimizations to the police when they are violent in nature, when an injury results, when lost items are valued at $250 or more, or when forcible entry has occurred.

Additionally, because factors that affect the UCR figures fluctuate from one year to the next, it is not clear how valid the measure is of crime rates over time, known as *crime trends*. For example, rates of forcible rape may appear to be increasing according to the UCR when in fact they may be decreasing or remaining steady over time. For example, if police across the United States get better at detecting rape or if citizens report more rapes to the police, the UCR will show an increase in rape rates even though the actual rate may not have changed at all. One of the most striking limitations of the UCR as a source of valid crime data is that evidence is now available suggesting that police downgrade or upgrade serious crimes to less serious or more serious ones for political purposes (McCleary, Nienstedt, and Erven 1982; Seidman and Couzens 1974). Gaines, Kaune, and Miller (2000, p. 43) discuss evidence showing that police departments in Atlanta, New York, and Philadelphia seriously manipulated their crime data.

Despite these weaknesses, and keeping in mind that these figures represent only crimes known to the police, the UCR does teach some interesting facts about crime. The most common crime according to the UCR is theft, making up nearly 60% of all crimes known to the police. The least common type of crime in the United States is murder, which makes up only 0.1% of all crimes known to the police. Most crimes known to the police, including theft, burglary, and motor vehicle theft, are committed against property. If you include robbery, which is committed against individuals but is done for property gain, then property crimes make up more than 90% of all crimes known to the police. Given that property crimes are less likely to be reported than violent crimes, it is safe to assume that the true distribution of street crime in the United States would be more like 99% property crimes and 1% violent crimes. Figure 4.2 illustrates the percentage of each type of crime known to the police.

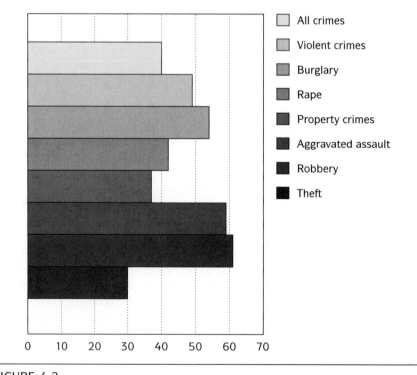

FIGURE 4.2
Percentage of Crimes Known to the Police (2001)
SOURCE: Sourcebook of Criminal Justice Statistics (2003).

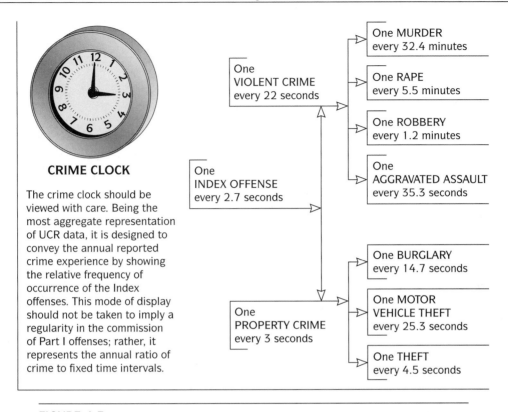

CRIME CLOCK

The crime clock should be viewed with care. Being the most aggregate representation of UCR data, it is designed to convey the annual reported crime experience by showing the relative frequency of occurrence of the Index offenses. This mode of display should not be taken to imply a regularity in the commission of Part I offenses; rather, it represents the annual ratio of crime to fixed time intervals.

FIGURE 4.3
The Crime Clock (2002)

SOURCE: Federal Bureau of Investigation (2003).

Figure 4.3 depicts some alarming statistics from the UCR. This "crime clock" suggests that an Index offense occurs in the United States on average every 2.7 seconds, including a violent crime every 22 seconds and a property crime every 3 seconds. There is on average one murder every 32.4 minutes and a theft every 4.5 seconds! These time estimates are based on the total number of crimes known to the police per year. They do not imply regularity of crime occurrences. Table 4.2 shows how many actual offenses of each type were known to the police in 2002, the latest year for which full data were available at the time of this writing.

Of the 11,877,218 crimes known to the police in 2002, 10,450,893 were property crimes (88%) and 1,426,325 were violent crimes (12%). Thefts comprised the majority (59%) of all crimes known to the police in 2002, followed by burglary (18%), motor vehicle theft (10.5%), aggravated assault (7.5%), robbery (3.5%), rape (0.8%), and murder (0.1%).

From these numbers, you might conclude that the United States is plagued by unusually high crime rates. In fact, this is not the case, with the exception of murder, which many attribute to the violent culture, economic and racial inequality, and availability of guns in the United States (Beckett and Sasson 2000, p. 8). This has led some to claim that "crime is not the problem"— instead, the problem is lethal violence (Zimring and Hawkins 1997).

TABLE 4.2

Number of Crimes Known to the Police (2002)

Murder	16,204 (0.1%)
Rape	95,136 (0.8%)
Robbery	420,637 (3.5%)
Aggravated assault	894,348 (7.5%)
Motor vehicle theft	1,246,096 (10.5%)
Burglary	2,151,875 (18.1%)
Theft	7,052,922 (59.4%)
Total	**11,877,218 (100%)**

SOURCE: Federal Bureau of Investigation (2002).

National Crime Victimization Survey

In part to uncover some of the dark figure of crime—to assess some of the crimes not being reported to the police—the U.S. Department of Justice, BJS, designed the *National Crime Victimization Survey* (NCVS), originally known as the National Crime Survey (NCS). The survey was redesigned in the late 1980s, in part to improve survey techniques to increase people's ability to recall events, including previously undetected victimizations, and the first annual results for the redesigned survey were published for the year 1993.

The NCVS is a survey of roughly 100,000 people age 12 years and older in approximately 50,000 households. The survey explores the experiences with criminal victimizations of a sample of respondents made up of a nationally representative group of individuals living in U.S. households. Demographic variables such as age, sex, race, and income are used to compare rates of victimization for different subgroups within the population. The NCVS collects crime data on both personal crimes and household crimes, as noted in Table 4.3.

These crimes are very similar to those contained in the UCR, with the notable exception of homicide; the NCVS does not include statistics on homicide simply because it is impossible to ask a homicide victim how many times he or she has been murdered in the past 12 months. Neither the UCR nor the NCVS measures victimizations resulting from white-collar deviance.

TABLE 4.3

Crimes Documented in the Uniform Crime Reports (UCR) and National Crime Victimization Survey (NCVS)

UCR	NCVS
Murder	—
Forcible rape	Rape
Robbery	Robbery
Aggravated assault	Aggravated assault
Motor vehicle theft	Motor vehicle theft
Burglary	Burglary
Theft	Theft
Arson	—

TABLE 4.4

Criminal Victimization in the United States (2002)

Rape	247,730 (1%)
Robbery	512,490 (2.2%)
Aggravated assault	990,110 (4.3%)
Motor vehicle theft	988,760 (4.3%)
Burglary	3,055,720 (13.4%)
Theft	13,494,750 (59%)
Total (includes other offenses)	**22,880,630**

SOURCE: Sourcebook of Criminal Justice Statistics (2003).

Twice each year, citizens are asked about their experiences of victimization by various street crimes. Because the NCVS includes both crimes that citizens report to the police and those that they do not report, it is a more valid measure of actual street crime rates than the UCR. This is why the NCVS always indicates higher rates of crime than the UCR. Table 4.4 shows how many offenses of each type were actually reported to NCVS researchers in 2002.

As you can see, in 2002, U.S. residents 12 years or older suffered 22.9 million criminal victimizations, including 17.5 million property crimes (77%) and 5.3 million violent crimes (23%). Property crimes included approximately 13.4 million thefts, 4.3 million household burglaries, and 1 million motor vehicle thefts. Violent crimes included 4.6 million assaults (3.6 million of these were simple rather than aggravated), 512,490 robberies, and 247,730 rapes and sexual assaults. In 2002, for every 1,000 people age 12 years old or older, there were 1 rape or sexual assault, 1 assault with injury, and 2 robberies.

From these data, we can conclude that the vast majority of street crime is property crime, and the most common crime is theft. The most common violent crime is aggravated assault, but relatively little crime in the United States is violent (although, as noted, the United States is plagued by an alarmingly high murder rate).

Other than this, the U.S. crime rate is comparable to those of other industrialized countries. Findings from the *International Crime Victim Survey* (ICVS), first administered by the Dutch Ministry of Justice in 1988, suggested that crime rates are high in the United States but not much higher than in many other countries (Beckett and Sasson 2000). More recent data from the ICS suggest that other countries have overtaken the United States as leaders in homicide rates. According to Barclay and Tavares (2002), the average rate of homicides in European Union countries from 1998 to 2000 was 1.7 homicides per 100,000 citizens, with the highest rates in Northern Ireland (3.1), Spain (2.8), Finland (2.6), Scotland (2.2), and Sweden (2.1). Non-European nations with the highest rates include South Africa (54.3), Russia (20.5), Estonia (11.4), Lithuania (8.9), Latvia (6.5), and the United States (5.9).

Barclay and Tavares (2002) report that although official crime rates fell by 14% in the United States from 1996 to 2000 and by 11% in Canada, they rose in many European countries. Crime rates did fall in other European nations, however. Some European nations saw large increases in violent crime during this time period, including Spain (38% increase), France (36% increase), the Netherlands (35% increase), Portugal (28% increase), Italy (20% increase), Denmark (17% increase), and England and Wales (15% increase). The only decreased rate was for Ireland (49% decrease). Other countries that saw large increases in violent crime from 1996 to 2000 include Japan (72% increase), Poland (49%), Slovenia (26%), Lithuania (23%), and Slovakia (19%).

Key findings of the 2000 ICVS, conducted in 17 industrialized countries (van Kesteren, Mayhew, and Nieuwbeerta 2001), are as follows.

- Countries where more than 24% of citizens were victims of any crime included Australia, England and Wales, the Netherlands, and Sweden.
- Countries where between 20% and 24% of citizens were victims of any crime included Canada, Scotland, Denmark, Poland, Belgium, France, and the United States.
- Countries where less than 20% of citizens were victims of any crime included Finland, Spain, Switzerland, Portugal, Japan, and Northern Ireland.

The most common crime in any country is a crime against property, typically theft of one person's property by another.

In terms of an individual's risk for criminal victimization from specific crimes, the 2000 ICVS finds the following:

- The highest risks for contact crime (robbery, assaults with force, and sexual assaults) were in Australia, England and Wales, Canada, Scotland, and Finland (all more than 3%).
- The highest risks for theft were in Australia, Sweden, and Poland (between 5% and 6%).
- The highest risks for burglary were in Australia (7%), England and Wales (5%), and Canada, Denmark, and Belgium (all at 4%).
- The highest risks for car theft were in England and Wales (2.6%), Australia (2.1%), and France (1.9%).

Why, then, does the United States incarcerate more people than any other country? The answer—that we are tougher on crime than any other country—probably goes against all you have heard from "get tough" politicians attacking their "soft on crime" opponents. In fact, the notion that the U.S. criminal justice network is lenient is a myth, say Kappeler and coworkers (2000, p. 257), who write, "We lock up more people, for longer sentences, for more offenses than any nation on the face of the earth." Walker (1998, p. 146) writes that "the alleged 'loophole' of being soft on dangerous offenders does not exist." In fact, the opposite is true with regard to street crime. The United States is highly punitive against violent street criminals. It is only our response to white-collar and corporate crime that is "soft."

The NCVS is also considered a better measure of crime trends than the UCR because the factors that affect victim recall and reporting to researchers are more constant than the factors affecting UCR crime trends. "The victimization surveys are clearly superior to UCR data in that they measure both reported and unreported crime, and they are unaffected by technological changes in police record keeping, levels of reporting by victims and the police, and other factors which call into question the validity of UCR data" (Kappeler, Blumberg, and Potter 2000, p. 35). According to the NCVS, street crime rates are at their lowest since the inception of the survey and have almost consistently declined since 1973. The next section examines these street crime trends.

American Crime Trends, According to the UCR and NCVS

In the 1990s, the bottom fell out of crime, meaning that street crime rates fell consistently during that decade. Figure 4.4 illustrates *crime trends* according to the NCVS. Several books have examined the causes of these declines. For example, *The Crime Drop in America* (Blumstein and Wallman 2000) and *Why Crime Rates Fell* (Conklin 2002) examine the effects of criminal justice (police, corrections) and non–criminal justice (economic, social) factors on crime.

Approximately 25% of the decline in crime in the 1990s can be attributed to higher rates of imprisonment. More significant are factors such as the ebbing of the crack cocaine epidemic (see Chapter Eleven) and improvements in the U.S. economy since the 1980s. Blumstein and Wallman (2000) summarize what likely led to declines in street crime: "The number of very tenable explanations for the crime drop, none of which inherently excludes any of the others, leads to the conclusion that there is no single explanation but that a variety of factors, some independent and some interacting in a mutually supportive way, have been important" (p. 2). The factors analyzed in the book include economic improvement, an aging population, the stabilization of the illicit drug trade, reductions in gun crimes, and prison. The authors conclude that "no single factor can be invoked as *the* cause of the crime decline of the 1990s. Rather, the explanation appears to lie with a number of factors, perhaps none of which alone would have been sufficient and some of which might not have been of noticeable efficacy without reinforcement from

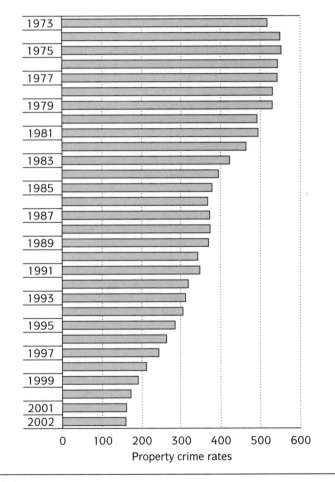

FIGURE 4.4
Trends in American Crime (NCVS)
SOURCE: Bureau of Justice Statistics (2003).

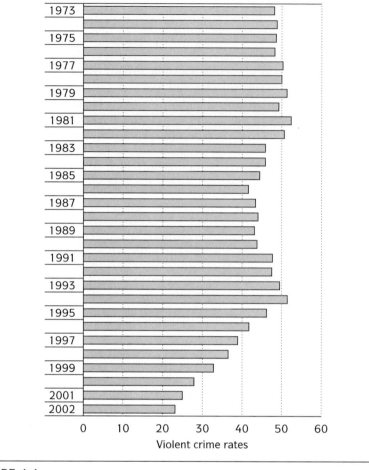

FIGURE 4.4
(continued)

others" (p. 11). It should be pointed out that the author who wrote the chapter on prisons (Spelman 2000) concludes that "the prison buildup was responsible for about one-fourth of the crime drop. Other factors are responsible for the vast majority of the drop" (p. 123). He adds, " . . . Most of responsibility for the crime drop rests with improvements in the economy, changes in the age structure, or other social factors" (p. 125).

Kappeler and coworkers (2000, p. 36) write, "Let us be very clear about this. The only reliable, scientific data we have on crime in the United States tells us that crime is decreasing." These authors are referring to the NCVS, which indicates that street crime has decreased consistently since the 1970s. So, believe it or not, you are safer from street crime today than at any time in recent U.S. history. Although fear of crime remains high, the belief that crime is increasing is nothing more than a myth (Kappeler, Blumberg, and Potter 2000; Walker 1998).

Gallup polls taken every year show that public concern about crime is not a function of fluctuations in actual crime rates. Figure 4.5, for example, compares trends in violent crime rates as measured in the NCVS (top) with Gallup polls (bottom) in the 1990s. Note how the percentage of people who ranked crime as the nation's number one problem increased dramatically in the early 1990s even though crime rates were actually going down. In Chapter Five, I attribute these increases to the politicization of crime and resulting media coverage.

Walker (1998, p. 14) writes:

> Crime plagues our daily lives like a plague, affecting the way we think, the way we act, the way we respond to one another. Fear of crime has a corrosive effect on interpersonal relations, making us wary of small acts of friendliness toward strangers. It distorts the political process, with politicians offering quick-fix solutions that offer no realistic hope of reducing crime. Fear and frustration about crime produce irrational thinking.

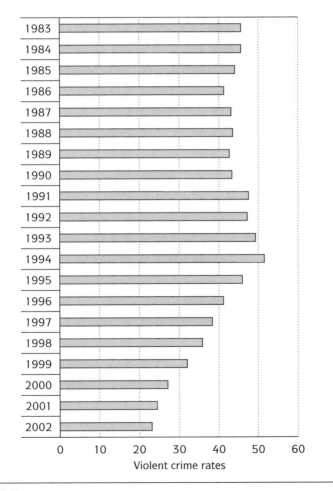

FIGURE 4.5

Public Opinion of Crime

SOURCES: Bureau of Justice Statistics (2003); Sourcebook of Criminal Justice Statistics (2003).

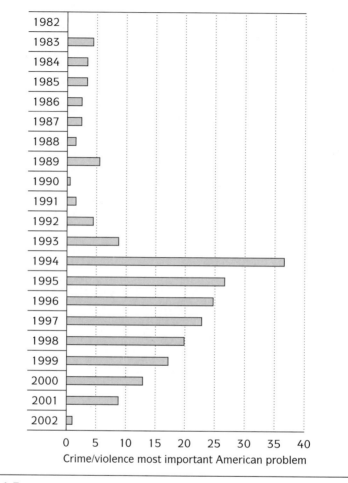

FIGURE 4.5
(continued)

Even though street crime rates are very low compared with other times in U.S. history, Americans are afraid. Although crime rates in the United States are no higher for most categories than in other industrialized countries, Americans report feeling less safe walking in their own neighborhoods after dark than citizens of other countries with higher crime rates (e.g., see Mayhew and Van Dijk 1997).

Why are Americans so concerned about street crime even though it has decreased consistently since the 1970s? Is it that we see so much of it in the news and in television shows and movies? Kappeler and coworkers (2000, pp. 14–15) suggest that our own government must exaggerate the harms associated with street crime in order to justify intervening in it. Think about the massive criminal justice expansion detailed in Chapters One and Two. Does it make sense that we are spending more now than at any other time in U.S. history to fight crime even though street crime rates are at their lowest rates in many years?

Kappeler, Blumberg, and Potter (2000) argue that myths about crime and criminal justice are portrayed in ways that ensure that Americans will spend their tax dollars to expand the criminal justice network. They claim that this portrayal involves several steps.

- A distinct population is identified as "deviant" or "different" and then targeted.
- The harms associated with this population pose a threat to American norms, lifestyles, and traditions.
- Victims are portrayed as "innocent" or "helpless."
- Those who take on the dangerous class of offenders are portrayed as "virtuous" and "brave."

Is this how you see crime and criminal justice? While politicians and the media overemphasize street crime, more harmful acts of white-collar deviance are ignored. This is not consistent with either of the criminal justice network's goals, reducing crime and doing justice.

Self-Report Studies

Another way that criminologists have learned about crime is by studying actual offenders through *self-report studies,* including discussions with both incarcerated offenders and active offenders.

In general, these studies suggest that virtually all people have committed crimes during the course of their lives, including crimes for which they could have been incarcerated for at least 1 year. Even recent self-report studies measuring serious criminality and delinquency show that most people admit to committing harmful acts that are prohibited by law. M. Robinson and Zaitzow (1999a) even found that the nation's crime experts—members of the American Society of Criminology—admit to illegal, deviant, and unethical behaviors.

The main problems associated with self-report studies revolve around reliability and validity issues. In self-report research, *reliability* refers to the likelihood that an offender will give the same answer to a question if the researcher asks it more than once over time. *Validity* means the likelihood that the offender is giving an honest, accurate answer. One thing we have learned about human behavior is that people misrepresent, exaggerate, and sometimes forget the truth. This makes self-report studies somewhat questionable. As stated by Nettler (1984), "Never bet on an animal that talks" (quoted in Jeffery, 1990).

What we have learned about offenders from self-report studies is still considered valuable by most criminologists. For example, we know that almost all offenders admit to having committed a crime for which they could have been incarcerated for at least 1 year. Self-report studies also indicate that much of what we do to fight crime in the United States does not work. Offenders tell us that they are not highly concerned about getting caught or punished for their criminal acts. Instead, they are motivated by potential gains from their crimes, and they know from experience that the criminal justice network is highly ineffective at even detecting crimes (e.g., see Cromwell 1995).

The following box contains some key truths about crime in the United States, taken from NCVS data. How do these trends compare to what you have been led to believe about street crime in your life?

Key truths about crime

- There is no crime wave in the United States. Victimizations from street crime have been steadily declining since the 1970s.
- The overwhelming majority of street crimes are minor, causing neither serious bodily damage nor major economic losses.
- Most acts of violence on the streets are committed by people whom the victim knows.
- In most street crimes, especially acts of violence, the victim and the perpetrator are of the same race.

SOURCE: Adapted from V. Kappeler, M. Blumberg, and G. Potter, *The Mythology of Crime and Criminal Justice*, 3rd ed. (Prospect Heights, IL: Waveland Press, 2000).

Sources of Data on White-Collar Deviance

According to leading consumer advocate Ralph Nader, also the Green Party presidential candidate in 2000:

> Our country does not collect statistics on corporate crime the way that it does on street crime. For to do so would begin to highlight a little-attended agenda for law enforcement and other corporate reforms. Neither the Congress nor the White House and its Justice Department have made any moves over the years to assemble from around the country the abuses of corporations in quantifiable format so as to drive policy. (Mokhiber and Weissman 1999, Introduction)

In fact, there are no national sources of data on white-collar deviance as there are on street crime: "No private or public institution—not the FBI, not the U.S. Department of Commerce—keeps up-to-date statistics on the cost of white collar crime. . . . The last public record was issued by the Department of Commerce in its 1974 *Handbook on White-Collar Crime*" (Kappeler, Blumberg, and Potter 2000, p. 123). This fact alone is proof that the U.S. government is less concerned with white-collar deviance than with street crime:

> Every year, the Federal Bureau of Investigation (FBI) issues its Crime in the United States report which documents murder, assault, burglary, and other street crimes. . . . The FBI does not issue a yearly Corporate Crime in the United States report, despite strong evidence indicating that corporate crime and violence inflicts far more damage on society than all street crime combined. (Mokhiber and Weissman 1999, pp. 8–9)

With the invention of the NIBRS program, discussed earlier, at least there is a source of national white-collar crime data available that tells us something. Unfortunately, what we can learn from the NIBRS data is very limited because (1) the FBI's definition of white-collar crime is very limited, (2) the NIBRS only measures a handful of white-collar offenses, and (3) UCR data on white-collar offenses are limited to arrests. The FBI defines white-collar crime as "those illegal acts which are characterized by deceit, concealment, or violation of trust and which are not dependent upon the application or threat of physical force or violence . . . [committed] . . . to obtain money, property, or services, to avoid the payment or loss of money or services, or to secure personal or business advantage" (Barnett 2003, p. 1). This definition ignores most acts committed by corporations, as well as all acts of violence committed by corporations and wealthy individuals through their work, referred to earlier as white-collar deviance.

So, how do we learn about harms associated with acts of white-collar deviance? Most of the evidence comes from studies of wealthy people, governments, corporations, and institutions, conducted by a handful of social scientists. These studies clearly demonstrate that the U.S. criminal justice network is failing to pursue the acts that most threaten us.

CONCLUSION

Clearly, the label "crime" is applied to only a small portion of acts that are harmful to Americans. The label "serious crime" is reserved for those acts that the government perceives to be committed primarily by the poor. This explains the focus in the United States on street crime rather than on white-collar deviance, even though the latter is far more dangerous. The sources we rely on for understanding how much crime there is in the United States reflect this bias—we rely on the error-prone Uniform Crime Reports more than we do on more valid measures such as the National Crime Victimization Survey. Yet both sources show that street crime has declined significantly in the 1990s, mostly in spite of criminal justice policy. Meanwhile, sources of data on white-collar deviance in the government are almost nonexistent, forcing us to rely on individual studies of corporations and wealthy citizens to learn about the harms caused by white-collar deviance. If we know that white-collar deviance is far more dangerous and costly than street crime, why do we, as a nation, fear street crime more? This issue is addressed in Chapter Five.

ISSUE IN DEPTH
Enron, WorldCom, Tyco, and the Other Corporate Bandits

Next to the terrorist attacks that shook our country on September 11, 2001, the largest crime story since 2001 has been the massive frauds committed by dozens of major corporations—which I refer to here as the "corporate bandits."

According to Cable News Network (CNN), the accused corporations include Arthur Andersen, Enron, WorldCom, Qwest, Tyco, ImClone, Global Crossing, Dynergy, CMS Energy, El Paso Corp., Halliburton, Williams Cos., AOL Time Warner, Goldman Sachs, Salomon Smith Barney, Citigroup, J.P. Morgan Chase, Schering Plough, Bristol–Myers Squibb, Kmart, Johnson & Johnson, Adelphia, Merrill Lynch, Rite Aid, and Coca-Cola.

Many of these corporations are accused of the same basic fraudulent activities—essentially "cooking the books" to inflate profits by hiding debts so that investors will be more likely to invest money in the corporations. Many of the corporations allegedly treated debts as revenue in order to look more profitable. Think of it this way—imagine that you wanted to get a loan from your local bank and you treated every check that you wrote in the past month not as a debt against your account but as a payment made to you by the company to which you sent the check: This is what many companies in the United States allegedly did.

Several of the corporations have been accused of more, including Coca-Cola. Coca Cola has been accused of knowingly allowing malfunctioning machines to leave metal residue in their products, rigging marketing tests to win business with Burger King, racial discrimination, antitrust violations, and accounting irregularities that boosted its net worth.

According to CNN/*Money's* "Fraud Inc.," this is what the following companies are accused or convicted of:

- *Adelphia Communications*—This major cable company filed for bankruptcy protection after it was discovered that the Rigas family used billions of dollars in loans to cover investment losses. Adelphia filed its own racketeering lawsuit against Rigas and other members of his family. The company faces civil charges by the Securities and Exchange Commission (SEC) and an ongoing Justice Department investigation.
- *AOL Time Warner*—This major corporation is under investigation by the SEC and the Justice Department for questionable accounting practices at the company's America Online unit in 2000 and 2001.
- *Arthur Andersen*—This major accounting firm was found guilty by a jury of obstructing justice for shredding Enron documents and received the maximum sentence of a $500,000 fine and 5 years' probation. This firm also served as the accounting agency for numerous other companies accused of crimes.
- *Bristol–Myers Squibb*—This drug-maker has restated sales by $2 billion, and federal regulators are investigating whether it purposely inflated sales by offering incentives to wholesalers.
- *Citigroup*—This financial services company agreed to pay $240 million to settle "predatory lending" charges in the largest consumer protection settlement in the history of the Federal Trade Commission (FTC). It has also been charged with helping Enron manipulate its finances to deceive investors.
- *Credit Suisse First Boston Corporation*—This company agreed to pay $100 million for taking millions of dollars from customers through inflated commissions in exchange for allocations of "hot" initial public offerings.
- *Enron*—This large energy company is accused of obscuring its finances with business partnerships (invented companies to hide debts) and questionable accounting practices that fooled debt-rating agencies, Wall Street analysts, and investors. Enron was forced to file for bankruptcy, causing billions of dollars of losses for investors and Enron employees, many of whose company retirement accounts became worthless. Many Enron rivals (including Dynergy, El Paso Corp., CMS Energy, and Halliburton and Williams Cos.) are also under investigation because of questionable accounting and trading activities. The Halliburton case concerns an accounting practice introduced at the company when it was headed by now Vice President Dick Cheney.
- *Global Crossing*—This telecommunications company is being investigated for using "swap deals" with other telecom carriers to inflate sales. The company is

suspected of selling capacity on its fiber-optic network to other carriers and then buying back a like amount, which is improper. Global Crossing filed for Chapter 11 bankruptcy protection and agreed to sell a majority stake in its fiber-optic network to two Asian investors for about $250 million in cash.

- *Goldman Sachs*—This investment bank has been asked to turn documents over to the House of Representatives, which is investigating potential conflicts of interest and the distribution of stock as companies went public.
- *ImClone*—This company's former Chief Executive Officer (CEO) was convicted on charges of insider trading for allegedly trying to sell his stock and tipping off family members after learning that the federal Food and Drug Administration (FDA) would refuse to review the company's application for the promising cancer drug Erbitux.
- *Johnson & Johnson*—This company is under investigation by the FDA for false record-keeping at a plant that makes an anemia drug linked to serious side effects.
- *J. P. Morgan Chase*—This company is charged with helping Enron with $8 billion in financial dealings that made Enron look rich in cash rather than heavily indebted.
- *Kmart*—This major retailer filed for Chapter 11 bankruptcy protection. It is under investigation by the FBI and the SEC and has closed hundreds of stores and cut 22,000 jobs.
- *Merrill Lynch*—This Wall Street brokerage firm agreed to pay $100 million to settle charges from New York that its research analysts knowingly promoted stocks that they privately ridiculed in order to win business for Merrill's investment banking unit.
- *Qwest*—This telecommunications company is being investigated by the SEC after admitting that it improperly accounted for about $1.2 billion in revenue for part of 2000 and all of 2001, most of it from swap deals it made with other companies. It restated $950 million in revenue derived from making sales to other carriers and then buying back a similar amount.
- *Rite Aid*—Three former executives and one suspended executive of this drugstore company were indicted on charges that they cooked the books to make it appear more profitable. It restated results going back 3 years.
- *Tyco*—The former CEO and former Chief Financial Officer (CFO) have been charged with looting $600 million from Tyco, but both men have pleaded not guilty. Tyco has sued its former CEO for at least $730 million.
- *WorldCom*—This company, now known as MCI, filed the largest bankruptcy in U.S. history. It has admitted that it overstated profits by hiding more than $7 billion in expenses over five quarters. Several former WorldCom executives have been charged and others have pleaded guilty.
- *Xerox*—This major company was forced to restate earnings to reflect $1.4 billion less in pretax profits over the past 5 years as part of a settlement with the SEC. It was forced to pay a $10 million penalty.

The total combined harms of the above corporate crimes are unknown, but estimates are in the hundreds of billions of dollars. Additionally, tens of thousands of people have lost their jobs, hundreds of thousands have lost money from their retirement accounts, and millions have lost money from the resulting stock market crash.

Ariana Huffington (2003), in her book *Pigs at the Trough*, reports the following statistics related to the above scandals.

- Kmart CEO Charles Conaway received about $23 million compensation over 2 years, after which Kmart filed for bankruptcy, 283 stores closed, and 22,000 people lost their jobs.
- Tyco CEO Dennis Kozlowski received nearly $467 million in compensation over 4 years, after which Tyco's stockholders lost $92 billion.
- Enron CEO Kenneth Lay earned more than $100 million in cash the year before Enron's collapse, after which Enron lost $68 billion in market value, 5,000 people lost their jobs, and workers lost $800 million.

Additionally, Huffington reports that American corporate executives earned $66 billion by selling company stock "even while their companies crashed and burned" (some even forbade their employees from selling their stock). This amount could buy 66,000 homeless people houses, each worth $100,000. She also claims that the total loss in market value caused by Enron, Global Crossing, Tyco, Qwest, and WorldCom alone was $427 billion. With this money, we could get every state in the country out of debt several times over, or we could give $356 to every man, woman, and child living in poverty on the Earth.

Whatever the actual harms, there is no doubt that the financial harms exceed those caused by street crime in any year by dozens of times (and numerous people have committed suicide as a result of losing all their money and/or killed their spouses and family members as a result of the stress of losing their jobs).

Keep in mind that these corporations are not nameless, faceless entities. Each is run by a CEO, a CFO, and a Board of Directors—in other words, real people who made real decisions and who can be held accountable for their actions. At the time of this writing, the toughest sanction handed down was for ImClone's CEO, Sam Waksal, who was sentenced to 87 months in prison for his role in an insider trading scandal that has shed negative light on Martha Stewart. Waksal pleaded guilty to obstruction of justice, perjury, bank fraud, and sales tax evasion. He also was sentenced to pay a fine of $3 million and more than $1.2 million in restitution. The most serious alleged offenders have not even gone to trial yet.

In response to these crimes, Congress passed the Sarbanes–Oxley Act, which doubled the potential sentences that such corporate criminals can face. President George W. Bush (the second) signed the bill into law, appointed a corporate fraud task force (to be headed by the director of a credit card company that paid more than $400 million to settle fraud lawsuits), and allocated millions to the SEC to conduct investigations. Yet Jeffrey Reiman and Paul Leighton (2003) claim that mostly the response has been "huff and puff and . . . do little" in responding to these actions. According to their analysis of the law, it will now be more difficult to prosecute alleged offenders in similar cases because the law raised the standard of proof from "recklessly" to "knowingly."

In fact, most of the companies have, as of this writing, paid fines to get out of trouble. For example, WorldCom is now to pay $750 million to settle the case against it, an alarmingly high figure. Yet considering that investors lost $175 billion because of WorldCom, the company is being charged about 0.4% of the amount of financial harm they caused. Imagine going to a bank and robbing it of $100,000, then being forced to pay back only 0.4% of it (which is $400)!

The banks that were involved with illegal loans to help these corporations hide their losses and the accounting firms that oversaw them and turned a blind eye are each facing their own investigations. One notable example is that federal and state regulators settled with 10 Wall Street investment firms (including Citigroup, Merrill Lynch, J. P. Morgan Chase, and Credit Suisse First Boston) for knowingly pushing bad stocks and conducting and publishing flawed research and for conflicts of interest. They have agreed to pay $1.4 billion in fines and to separate their investment banking activities and research activities. Most of these firms have not admitted guilt, and some have changed their names to distance themselves from these scandals.

Although these scandals have left the front pages of the paper, Caffrey (2003) reports that the FBI has launched about four new investigations of fraud per month, each of which has surpassed $100 million in damages. The FBI is, at the time of this writing, investigating about 100 new cases, and the Corporate Fraud Task Force is investigating another 100 cases.

Discussion Questions

1. Compare and contrast the terms *natural crime* and *legal crime.*
2. List and define the eight "serious" crimes of the Uniform Crime Reports (UCR).
3. What does the term *serious* mean?
4. List and define the main elements of a crime.
5. Is it possible to show that a person committed an act with intent? Why or why not?
6. Outline some defenses that can be used when charged with a crime.
7. List and define the main types of culpability, including *intentionality, recklessness, negligence,* and *knowingly.*
8. In your opinion, are there any less serious crimes (Part II offenses of the UCR) that should be considered serious crimes (Part I offenses of the UCR)? Why or why not?
9. What is victimization?
10. Discuss how the definition of criminal victimization is too limited.
11. Define white-collar deviance and provide a few examples.
12. Which is more harmful to Americans, street crime or white-collar deviance?
13. What interest does the U.S. government have in maintaining the current image of crime and criminals?
14. Identify and discuss the main sources of crime data in the United States, including the UCR, the NCVS, and self-report studies.

15. What is meant by the "dark figure of crime"?
16. What does the crime clock show us about crime in the United States?
17. Does the United States have more crime than other countries? Why or why not?
18. Why do you think that the American criminal justice system does not collect national statistics on white-collar deviance?
19. How do the harms caused by the corporations reviewed in the preceding Issue in Depth compare to street crimes? Were the harms caused by these corporations committed intentionally or with some other form of culpability? Explain.

CHAPTER FIVE

"THE SKY IS FALLING! THE SKY IS FALLING!"—MEDIA PORTRAYALS OF CRIME AND CRIMINAL JUSTICE

INTRODUCTION

This chapter introduces you to the *media*, a term that includes a wide range of sources of news-related information. I examine what the media do and do not do, and then turn to how much people are exposed to the media in the United States. In discussing how the U.S. media cover crime and criminal justice, I show what the media cover, what they ignore, and why the media are so inaccurate when portraying crime and criminal justice. I also examine media coverage of terrorism and the war on terror. Implications of media inaccuracy for justice are discussed.

AN INTRODUCTION TO THE MEDIA

Many of society's problems are blamed on the *media*. We hear, for example, that the prevalence of violence in the United States is "because of the media." When school shootings rocked communities across the country in the late 1990s, parents and community leaders called for tougher standards for showing violent content in "the media" because of their suspicion that the media are responsible for copycat crimes.

But what are the media? Surette (1992, p. 10) defines the mass media as "media that are easily, inexpensively, and simultaneously accessible to large segments of a population." These sources include newspapers, magazines, books, television, radio, film, and recordings.

Media sources are organized within a hierarchy of controlling institutions. Hess (1981) describes the media as having an inner ring, a middle ring, and an outer ring. These sources of media information are depicted in Figure 5.1

The *inner ring of the media* includes the major television networks such as ABC, NBC, CBS, and CNN; major news magazines such as *Time, Newsweek,* and *U.S. News & World Report;* national newspapers such as *The New York Times,* the *Washington Post, USA Today,* and *The Wall Street Journal;* and the Associated Press (AP) wire service. The *middle ring of the media* and the *outer ring of the media* are more prevalent but have far less influence on the news than the institutions in the inner ring.

These inner-ring sources are Americans' main sources of information about many issues (Lewis 1981; Marion 1995). Crime, as a major issue for society, is usually news (Merlo and Benekos 2000). The Center for Media and Public Affairs, for example, found that almost 30% of local news is devoted to crime and criminal justice (Center for Media and Public Affairs 2000).

The media are our main source for news about crime and criminal justice policy. As noted by Krajicek (1998, p. 139), "The press provides our window on public problems, on the government's strategies to solve them, and on how well those strategies succeed (or fail)." The media sources in the inner ring have greater influence than other sources. According to Harrigan (2000, p. 120), "The organization at the top of the media hierarchy decides what counts as news." This is true because most journalists consult these sources for their own news (Weaver and Wilhoit 1986). Reporters of crime news commonly "copy" what other media reporters are doing. When reputable sources cover crime problems in the media, other reporters take their lead and follow with very similar stories.

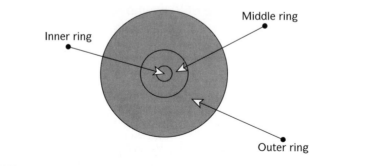

FIGURE 5.1
Organization of the Media

As one example, virtually all of the 1,700 newspapers in the United States subscribe to the AP, the largest news organization in the world. The AP is a nonprofit cooperative that serves more than 6,000 television and U.S. radio stations and more than 8,500 media outlets throughout the world through AP online. The AP compiles thousands of stories each day, of which only a couple of dozen are sent to the local, regional, national, and international wires for inclusion in various media outlets (Krajicek 1998). Historically, crime has been considered newsworthy by the media. Because newsworthy events are determined by media outlets that are owned by large corporations, the public's image of crime is at least partially defined by the wealthy and powerful. The issue of corporate ownership of the media is discussed in the following box.

The media and business

The major news media are owned and thus controlled by major corporations: "By the late 1980s, eight corporations controlled eight of the inner-ring media and a host of middle- and outer-ring media, including 40 television stations, over 200 cable television systems, more than 60 radio stations, 59 magazines, and 41 book publishers" (Parenti 1993, p. 26). Half of the nation's newspapers are controlled by just 10 large chains, and only about 2% of cities have competing newspapers (Graber 1996). About 24 corporations control most of the U.S. culture industry (Herman and Chomsky 1988).

Ben Bagdikian's book *The Media Monopoly* (2000) chronicles the ever-growing stranglehold that major corporations have on news in the United States. Since the 1980s, ownership of the media has narrowed. In 1983, 50 corporations owned the media. As of 2002, according to *The Nation,* just 10 corporations control all the mainstream news and entertainment media. Amazingly, only five corporations now own most of the mainstream news. For example:

- General Electric (GE), with revenues of $129.9 billion, owns NBC, CNBC, and part of MSNBC, at least 13 television stations and numerous other channels, Internet companies, sports teams, and various other business such as aircraft engines and medical equipment.
- AOL/Time Warner, with revenues of $36.2 billion, owns CNN, Headline News, CNNfn, CNN/SI, at least 64 magazines, more than 40 music labels, several book companies, Internet companies, and sports teams and is the second largest provider of cable television.
- Walt Disney, with revenues of $25.4 billion, owns ABC, ESPN, ESPN2, at least 10 television stations, and several magazines and book companies, as well as sports teams, movie companies, radio stations, and theme parks.
- Viacom, with revenues of $20 billion, owns CBS, MTV, MTV2, at least 39 television stations, major movie companies, several book companies, magazines, more than 100 radio stations, and Internet companies.
- News Corporation, with revenues of $11.6 billion, owns Fox, Fox News Channel, at least 26 television stations, major satellite and cable companies, books, newspapers, movies, and magazines, as well as sports teams.

Although the Federal Communications Commission (FCC) has historically prohibited a corporation or individual from owning both a local television station and a newspaper in the same area to prevent a monopoly on news, this rule was recently challenged and the FCC voted 3–2 to relax it (despite overwhelming public sentiment by liberals and conservatives). Additionally, the FCC allowed large media corporations to grow larger and broadcast to larger segments of the U.S. population.

Many viewers are unaware that the crime news they see on TV and in the newspapers is the version that large corporations choose to air. Would it be logical to expect these corporations to focus on their own acts of deviance and harmful behaviors? As discussed later in this chapter, there is substantial evidence that the media tend to ignore corporate crimes.

Perhaps this is why street crime is more likely to be the focus of news than the more harmful behaviors of white-collar deviance discussed in Chapter Four. The disproportionate focus on street crime is a form of labeling whereby certain segments of the society are identified as bad, deviant, or immoral (Gans 1995). In this process, evil is dramatized and the notion of "us" versus "them" is reinforced, because we tend to think of criminals as being different from us. This "dualistic fallacy" is troubling because media coverage of crime is more reflective of crime myths than of realities (Kappeler, Blumberg, and Potter 2000). As images of crime tend to depict certain groups of society as bad, deviant, and immoral, they reinforce stereotypes created by U.S. criminal law.

At the same time, the media do not enlighten the public about other occurrences, such as "a $40 million misleading advertising campaign by the tobacco industry in its successful bid to defeat a 1998 tobacco bill that would have forced tobacco companies to absorb some of the public health costs of dealing with tobacco addiction" (Harrigan 2000, p. 122). The tobacco industry characterized the tobacco bill as an $800 billion tax increase that would be passed on to U.S. citizens. Why didn't the media discuss the harms of tobacco and depict the negligence and recklessness of tobacco companies that perpetuate these harms?

This example demonstrates that U.S. corporations, through the inner ring of media outlets they own and control, define problems, identify crises, and thereby determine "what issues will be brought to the attention of political leaders" and U.S. citizens (Harrigan 2000, p. 124), while other issues and problems are ignored.

D. Simon and Hagan (1999, p. 12) place the media among the nation's group of elite individuals, corporations, and institutions. They suggest that the media have a direct impact on policies, including criminal justice activity, "because they set limits on the breadth of ideological views that enter the policy-making debate in the United States. The media also choose which stories to emphasize and which to ignore. . . . Finally, the media are merely a group of corporations that are owned by other corporations and financial institutions."

A political action committee (PAC) called *Move On* has worked to educate Congress about the potential negative effects of corporate control of the media. *Move On* joined with dozens of other groups from all political affiliations (including the National Rifle Association) to fight the recent FCC ruling, but lost. *Move On* (2002) writes, "At networks owned by multibillion-dollar conglomerates like General Electric, Viacom and Disney, the news divisions solemnly report every uptick or downturn of the markets. In contrast, when was the last time you heard Tom Brokaw [NBC], Dan Rather [CBS], or Peter Jennings [ABC] report the latest rates of on-the-job injuries or the average wait times at hospital emergency rooms?" I would add to this, When was the last time you heard any news about hospital error, which, according to the Institute of Medicine's *To Err Is Human* (Kohn et al. 2000), kills nearly 100,000 people every year!

If one of the fundamental purposes of government is to protect innocent human life, and if one of the fundamental duties of the media is to report truths (e.g., hospital errors kill more than six times as many people as murder), where is the coverage? Why is there so much media focus on murder? It is because corporations benefit from media ignorance that this occurs.

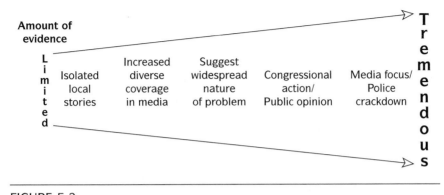

FIGURE 5.2

The Growth of a Crime Problem

Figure 5.2 illustrates how the media can transform a minor problem into a major one. Try to imagine a recent crime story, for example, one related to a threat of terrorism against some place in your community. How does this threat become newsworthy in your community and, ultimately, to the whole nation? I suggest in Figure 5.2 that crime problems (such as terror threats) are actually created and spread because of media coverage. For example, when a terror threat is received, local radio and television stations and newspapers will cover the story, leading to isolated local stories. As other, unrelated terror threats are received in other locations, the problem of terror threats becomes more newsworthy and leads to increased, diverse coverage in the media. To the consumer of news, with the increased coverage of terror threats, it appears that the problem is widespread or even happening everywhere. With each new threat, all previous threats are rehashed, leading the viewer with the perception that these threats are more common than they truly are and even that they are connected. Now the public becomes concerned and legislative bodies begin to discuss what can be done about the problem, ultimately leading to some tough talk by politicians in the media and even some new laws. Any time politicians talk tough or pass new laws, there is more coverage of the problem, some analysis, and justifications for the changes in law. To the news consumer, even though the problem may not be much of a problem in reality, it appears that it has grown immensely, because there is much more evidence of the problem in all forms of media. So, in essence, the media are involved in constructing or creating crime problems.

What the Media Do and Do Not Do

Because people do not simply absorb ideological propaganda (Potter and Kappeler 1998, p. 19), the media do not tell the public what to think, but they may tell the public what to think about (Bennett 1980; Iyengar and Kinder 1987; McCombs and Shaw 1972). Whatever is covered in the media is perceived to be important and worthy of viewer attention. Whether the attention is actually warranted on the basis of the nature and severity of the issue being covered is debatable.

Without question, the news media, in their broadcasts and editorials, alert and even alarm the public and lawmakers about important events and issues (Hollinger and Lanza-Kaduce 1988).

Given that people are "passive consumers" of most forms of the media (such as television), it is not surprising that media coverage shapes their conception of reality: "People use knowledge they obtain from the media to construct a picture of the world, an image of reality on which they base their actions" (Surette 1992, p. 2).

As explained by Potter and Kappeler (1998, p. 7), "Media coverage directs people's attention to specific crimes and helps to shape those crimes as social problems." The main problem with media coverage of crime, as you will see, is that it is dangerously inaccurate. Marion (1995) argues that the media alter the perceptions people have of criminal justice activity (Van Horn, Baumer, and Gormley 1992) and distort the facts about crime.

Marion explains that the "early steps in the [criminal justice] process (law enforcement, investigation and arrest) are emphasized, and the other steps are almost invisible, especially informal procedures such as plea bargaining. Lawyers are often shown as actively investigating crimes, which rarely occurs" (Potter and Kappeler 1998, p. 108). This is especially true in the everyday cases of poor people represented by publicly assigned counsel (see Chapter Seven).

In fact, most criminal justice cases receive no coverage by the media (Haltom 1998, p. 157). Those rare cases that are covered tend to be atypical. As a result, false conceptions of what is "ordinary" are generated by these extraordinary cases. The O. J. Simpson trial wrongly showed Americans that the criminal justice network works too slowly and is more focused on defendants' rights than on victims' rights. For wealthy clients in highly publicized cases, the process of justice will be slow and deliberate. Yet most court clients are poor and do not receive a trial; instead, they are convicted through the informal process of plea bargaining (see Chapter Seven).

According to Haltom (1998, p. 157), media coverage of crimes in U.S. courts "tends to emphasize 'Crime Control' values" such as assuring "security from wrongdoers, just deserts, and punishment" while simultaneously devaluing due process concerns such as Constitutional protections of the accused. Haltom maintains that only in celebrated cases do the media highlight due process values. From his analysis, it is clear that media coverage of criminal justice in the courts is partly responsible for the United States' shift to a crime control model of criminal justice.

Given that reporters rely on insiders for information, it is logical that media coverage of courts will support crime control values. The result is that reporters will be encouraged to "cover some aspects of the news more than others" (Haltom 1998, p. 158). It is a symbiotic relationship in which the reporters get information and court personnel ensure the type of coverage that is favorable to their daily activities (Schlesinger and Tumber 1994). Haltom suggests that "court sources 'feed' court reporters, and thus the news is largely what the reporters have 'eaten.'"

There are several reasons that crime control values are emphasized over due process values. As noted earlier, the main reason is that members of the U.S. crime control bureaucracy are more likely to interact with the media than advocates of due process. Another reason that media slant their coverage of criminal justice in a manner more consistent with a crime control model is that it is simply

> easier to understand for reporters, their editors, and their audiences. Struggles between cops and robbers, good guys and bad guys, protectors and perpetrators are easy to write, to source, and to read or to view. Arcane rules and technicalities elude readers and viewers, many of whom have no idea what the rules are or what they mean. (Haltom 1998, p. 165)

One reason that it is easier is that reporters often rely on prosecutors' offices for their stories. Dreschel (1983) suggests that prosecutors are more helpful to reporters than defense attorneys in terms of clarifying facts and offering tips about stories. Because prosecutors are more concerned with crime control than with due process, logically their biases are reflected in any subsequent media coverage.

Of course, the media are not the only source of information from which a person constructs his or her own reality. According to Surette (1992, p. 4), four primary sources are used—personal experiences, significant others (peers, family, friends), other social groups and institutions (schools, churches, government agencies), and the mass media (Altheide 1984; Quinney 1970; Tuchman 1978): "knowledge from all of these sources is mixed together, and from this mix, each individual constructs the 'world.'" Logically, the influence of the mass media likely increases as the influence of the other sources declines (Cohen and Young 1981; Lichter 1988).

Given that 90% of Americans will not be victimized by serious street crime (Barkan 1997; Kappeler, Blumberg, and Potter 2000) and that most people do not know anyone who chooses to talk about a personal experience of criminal victimization, the media are a prime source of information about crime (Potter and Kappeler 1998). Other scholars make the same claim, that the U.S. media are basic sources about crime and criminal justice (Barak 1994; Ericson, Baranek, and Chan 1989; Graber 1980).

An alarming realization is that the media tend to cover the same crime repeatedly as it processes through the criminal justice network. With any recent development in a case, the details of the original crime are rehashed, fostering an impression that the crime occurred more than once. When the case goes to trial or is plea bargained, when a sentence is passed down, and so on, the news consumer learns these details from the media once more. The effect is a general feeling that there is much more crime out there than there really is.

To the extent that media coverage of crime is repetitive and pervasive, it is more likely that it will affect people's attitudes about crime (Surette 1992, pp. 86–87). This is true in terms of not only what the media cover, but also what they fail to cover: "by emphasizing or ignoring topics, [the media] may influence the list of issues that are important to the public" (p. 87). Corporate crimes are virtually ignored by the media; thus most people, even criminology and criminal justice students, do not perceive such acts as threatening to their own personal safety (M. Robinson 1999).

In this chapter, I examine how and why media coverage of crime is inaccurate and dangerous. The chapter compares the realities of crime examined in the previous chapter with the way crime is portrayed on television, in the newspapers, and in popular entertainment. First, I examine the degree to which people actually are exposed to media sources.

DOES IT MATTER? ARE PEOPLE EXPOSED TO THE MEDIA?

Selective media coverage might be less problematic if viewers did not expose themselves to it. A study by the Pew Research Center for the People and the Press (1998) shows that only one in four Americans follows national news closely. Yet the nature of crime news is that it does not have to be followed closely, particularly at the national level. As illustrated later, crime news is prevalent at all levels of news coverage, even the local level. It should not be surprising, then, that the media are the people's main source of information about crime (Beckett and Sasson 2000). Tunnell (1992, p. 295) cites a National Crime Survey that found that 96% of Americans reported they relied on the media for information about crime. Fields and Jerin (1999, p. 94) cite research showing that most Gallup poll respondents report believing that the media are accurate in their depictions of crime.

Televison is a more significant source of news than newspapers: 60% of Americans rely on TV for news information (Angolabahere, Behr, and Iyengar 1993). According to Klain (1989), the average American spends more than 4 hours per day—roughly one-third of his or her recreational time—watching TV (Stossel 1997). The average American child watches television for between 3 and 4 hours per day (American Academy of Pediatrics 2000; Center for Media Education 2000). People are less exposed to other sources of news information, such as newspapers, because television is more easily consumed; it can be taken in passively and does not require the ability to read in order to watch (Surette 1992).

According to the Gallup Organization (2003), which polls Americans on a variety of topics, "Americans are more likely now than at any point in the previous 15 years to say that news organizations' stories and reports are inaccurate. Additionally, about half of Americans perceive that there is a bias towards one political party or the other in the way news organizations report the news, and by a two-to-one margin, those who feel there is a bias say it favors the Democrats." Given that the mainstream media are owned by large corporations, as discussed earlier, this is an interesting finding!

A recent Gallup poll (2003) showed that a majority of Americans believe that crime increased on a national scale over the previous year. According to the Gallup Organization (2003), "The poll was conducted as the news media were covering a series of sniper shootings in the Washington, D.C. area, which could affect the public's perceptions about the crime rate." Even though respondents were no more likely to report being worried about being crime victims and were no more likely to report taking precautions to prevent their own victimization, this poll shows the power of the media when it comes to informing public opinion. As noted earlier, when the media cover crime more, it leads to the perception that crime is increasing, even when it is not.

MEDIA COVERAGE OF CRIME AND CRIMINAL JUSTICE

Perhaps the most fascinating research on the media and crime is found in *Scooped!*, written by a former crime reporter, David Krajicek (1998). The subtitle of this inside look at media coverage of crime reflects its author's informed opinion: *Media Miss Real Story on Crime While Chasing Sex, Sleaze, and Celebrities*. Krajicek's main claim about the media is this: "Take a predisposition toward simplicity and anecdote, add unsophisticated reporting, a degenerating peer culture, an overworked news staff, the rapture of sex and celebrities, and—poof!—you've got today's crime journalism" (p. 180).

Disgusted with this type of crime reporting, Krajicek quit his job as a reporter. Why? In his words, he explains:

> While we [reporters] were sitting in vans counting arrests, we missed the most important story on the crime beat: the collapse of the U.S. criminal justice system as an effective means of fighting crime, maintaining order, ensuring public safety, and meting out equitable justice. . . . I came to conclude that the media had been scooped by myopia, sleazy story distractions, and an unhealthy devotion to the official police agenda. (p. 111)

Krajicek argues that the media misrepresent reality, much like what Reiman (1998) points out about the image of crime in U.S. society. As you may recall from Chapter Two, Reiman describes the American conception that crime is a problem of the poor as distorted, much like a reflection in a carnival mirror. In Krajicek's (1998) words, "Today, reading a newspaper or watching a news telecast can be like looking at the country's reflection in a fun-house mirror. The society we see presented in the news is a warped place, often morbid and alarming" (p. 4). It should be no surprise to you that for a lot of people, "the term crime evokes an image of a young African American male who is armed with a handgun and commits a robbery, rape, or murder. In the minds of many Americans, crime is synonymous with black crime." Why? Because those "crimes that receive the most attention—from the media, from politicians, and from criminal justice policy makers—are 'street crimes' such as murder, robbery, and rape" (Walker, Spohn, and Delone 2000).

As explained by Krajicek (1998, pp. 5–6), the media provide crime-anxious Americans with excited accounts of horrible crimes; present tenuous evidence that the crimes, however anomalous, could happen to each of us; seek out the accountable individuals (judges and probation officers); devise snappy slogans to package the problem neatly; and serve up images of scowling politicians thumping their lecterns about the latest legislation that surely would stop such atrocities: "We're finally getting tough on crime. We're no longer coddling criminals. We're making America's streets safe again."

Whether crime news is based on fact and is representative of the truth is irrelevant—"the politicians wanted expedient answers, not information"—"efficacy means nothing; image is everything" (Krajicek 1998, pp. 5, 17). I return to the issue of how politics is involved in the "framing" of crime and criminal justice later in this chapter.

In terms of criminal justice, TV coverage inaccurately portrays the U.S. criminal justice network. For example, despite all the controversial issues regarding TV in the courts (e.g., see Surette 1992), the most troubling aspect of the TV camera in the courtroom is the fact that what people see is not representative of the typical court case. While people see trials in their entirety on *Court TV* and in part on shows such as *Dateline NBC*, the reality is that more than 90% of cases do not lead to trial but are handled informally through plea bargaining (see Chapter Seven). People think that trials are the rule when, in fact, they are the "exceptional case" (Cole and Smith 2000). The media thus "emphasize the rare-in-reality adversarial criminal trial," which leads the viewer to believe that the typical court case in the United States is "a high-stakes, complicated, arcane contest practiced by expert professionals and beyond the understanding of everyday citizens" (Surette 1992, p. 40), even though the reality is the assembly-line justice of plea bargaining. In other words, people think we are following a due process model of criminal justice when in fact we are using a crime control model. At the same time, corrections is the least-shown aspect of criminal justice, so that the farther one moves into the system, the worse the image of American criminal justice becomes (p. 41).

Media coverage of policing is plagued by numerous problems as well. Typically, police television shows such as *COPS* and *World's Wildest Police Videos* misrepresent crime, criminals, and typical police work. They tend to focus on the most violent, random, and bizarre stories while ignoring more routine calls for service. They also tend to characterize criminals as minorities, who are typified as being very threatening or suffering from some form of insanity (Chiricos and Eschholtz 2002; Perlmutter 2001).

The Focus of Media Reporting on Crime: What the Media Cover and Ignore

As explained before, media portrayals of crime are "selectively determine[d]" by media outlets (Merlo and Benekos 2000, p. 5). Generally, decisions are made to feature "the most sensational, emotional, significant, and universally appealing aspects" of crime for public viewing (Sacco 1995). As Krajicek (1998, p. 95) said about his own work, crime reports focus on the miserable, the deviant, the strange, and the "particularly cruel." The common saying, "If it bleeds, it leads," accurately characterizes the philosophy of the media in the United States. Platt (1999) calls nightly news "Armageddon—Live at 6 (PM)!" Sabato (1993), in his book *Feeding Frenzy,* claims that American media coverage of politics is comparable to an attack of sharks on a helpless victim. Although his research focuses on politics generally, his arguments apply to media coverage of crime and criminal justice as well. Metaphorically speaking, if there is blood in the water, the media will likely cover a story about crime.

Research clearly demonstrates that crime news is focused on the most violent types of crime (Potter and Kappeler 1998), at least those that occur at the street level (e.g., see Chiricos 1995; Kooistra, Mahoney, and Westervelt 1999). Of particular interest to the media are the rarest and "most egregious examples" of crime.

Television news generally shows violence at a rate much higher than its incidence in society would seem to justify (Newman 1990). As noted by Krajicek (1998, p. 4), "Murder and sexual offenses are the marquee offenses . . . and certain cases, generally based upon nubility or celebrity, are anointed for extravagant coverage." A study cited by Surette (1992, p. 68) showed that 26% of news stories were focused on murder, even though murder regularly accounts for only 0.1% of all crimes known to the police. Although murder may be the most heinous of all crimes, this disproportionate focus does not seem justified by its prevalence in the United States. At the same time, even though about half of the crimes that are reported to the police are nonviolent, they made up only 4% of the stories in the same study. Additionally, it is the most heinous and bizarre of all murders that tend to be discussed most widely in the media (e.g., see Paulsen 2000).

Terrorism is no different. As horrible as the events of September 11, 2001, were, the fact is that four planes were crashed that day by terrorists, of approximately 40,000 that were in the air that day. Consider this: If roughly 40,000 flights per day landed successfully before the terrorist attacks and roughly the same number per day since then (but less given our increased fear of flying), how was the intense media coverage of those flights justified? The rare nature of the event and the horrifying result are what is used to justify the coverage. The problem, however, is that such coverage may lead viewers to conclude wrongly that flying is unsafe and/or that such terrorism is likely to happen to them when they fly.

Marsh (1991) conducted a review of studies of media coverage and crime and found that for every two stories of property crimes, there were eight stories of violent crimes. Newspapers in the mid-1980s covered the violent crimes of murder, rape, robbery, and assault four times more than they did the property crimes of theft, burglary, and motor vehicle theft, even though property crimes make up at least 90% of street crimes in any given year (see Chapter Four).

By focusing on certain types of crimes over others, the media are thus involved in "constructing" the typical view of crime, even when they are only reporting "extreme, dramatic cases: the public is more likely to think they are representative because of the emphasis by the media" (Chermak 1994, p. 580). Potter and Kappeler (1998, p. 7) explain, "Media coverage directs people's attention to specific crimes and helps to shape those crimes as social problems." This means that Americans are much more concerned with violent crimes such as murder, even though they are much more likely to be victimized by property crimes such as theft and burglary and acts of white-collar deviance that receive virtually no coverage.

The media are also preoccupied with random crime (Merlo and Benekos 2000), which partly explains the focus on terrorism, which is very rare in the United States. Not surprisingly, one type of crime that has received a tremendous amount of coverage in recent years is school violence. After the tragic mass murder of a dozen students and a teacher at Columbine High School in Littleton, Colorado, in 1998, the national news on each of the three major networks (ABC, NBC, CBS) devoted no less than half of each night's newscasts to this subject for approximately a month after the murders. But despite a commonsense impression to the contrary, in fact, school violence was not increasing during this time period, but rather, was decreasing!

Even though the media give much attention to crime, they typically ignore harmful acts committed by the wealthy, such as white-collar crime (Potter and Kappeler 1998; Surette 1992) and corporate crime (Evans and Lundman 1987; Randell 1995). This is troubling precisely because, in any given year, the harms associated with such acts clearly dwarf those resulting from all street crimes combined (see Chapter Four). Neglect of this topic stems from the risk of libel suits, interrelationships between the media and business, the probusiness orientation of the media, and difficulties associated with investigating white-collar crime (Potter and Kappeler 1998, p. 15; citing Mintz 1992). The media focus almost exclusively on street crimes, so that three classes of people are depicted—the upper class, the middle class, and the "criminal class" (Barak 1994).

When ABC's *Prime Time Live* investigated allegations and uncovered actual examples of food contamination at a Food Lion grocery store in 1996, for example, ABC was successfully sued by Food Lion for using deceptive media techniques to investigate claims of contaminated food products. The fact that Food Lion had intentionally sold unsafe food products to consumers was lost in the resulting coverage. This type of coverage is rare, however, and is limited to news magazine shows such as *Prime Time Live*. This is one result of the intimate relationship between the media and corporate America.

Recently, in the wake of the corporate scandals that sent our stock market crashing, led to hundreds of billions of dollars in losses to investors, and resulted in tens of thousands of Americans losing their jobs and retirement savings, the media finally began to tell the story of corporate crime in America. We learned of the fraud and embezzlement of Enron, Andersen, WorldCom, Tyco, and dozens of other corporations (recall the Issue in Depth at the end of Chapter Four). Unfortunately, once new laws were passed that supposedly "cracked down" on "bad apples," our attention was diverted away from such crimes toward a coming war with Iraq. And now, as if corporate crime is a thing of the past, the media rarely even mention it.

All of this is problematic precisely because the media serve as the major source of information about crime for most people (Beckett and Sasson 2000). As I show in Figure 5.3, crime stories funnel out to media viewers, but they are in no way accurate about what most crime really is; nor is public perception of crime.

Historically the media also have not paid much attention to costly and misguided criminal justice policies. Krajicek (1998) writes, "Collectively, journalists were scooped on the biggest crime story of the last quarter of this century by neglecting to adequately inform a puzzled public that

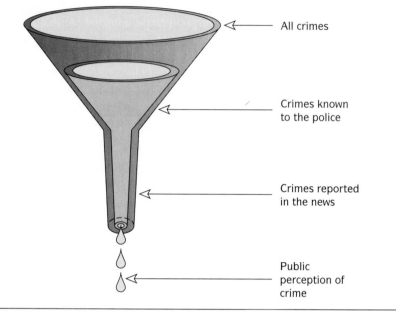

All crimes

Crimes known
to the police

Crimes reported
in the news

Public
perception of
crime

FIGURE 5.3
How the Media Shapes Public Opinion of Crime

our system of law enforcement and punishment, cobbled together with razor wire and prison bars, has been an expensive folly" (p. 5).

The media typically do not challenge the legal institution when it needs to be challenged. Although the media may question a particular enforcement (e.g., the vicious beating of Rodney King by Los Angeles police officers, captured on videotape), they rarely challenge the legal institution as a whole (Reiman 1998). What about police corruption and police brutality as a regular, everyday occurrence for some Americans? What about the way police discretion in the United States permits and perhaps even encourages such actions? The media rarely discuss such issues. As a result, media reporting reinforces the validity of law and the myths inherent in the law: "Crime news . . . tends to be ideological insofar as it represents a worldview of state managers" (Welch, Fenwick, and Roberts 1998, p. 220).

Some specific events (e.g., Willie Horton's crimes, committed after he was released early on a prison furlough) have been used by politicians, through the media, to reinforce a need for new laws that crack down even harder on street crimes and poor minorities. In these cases, the media act as mouthpieces for sound-bite politicians.

Crime Trends

Even when crime is going down, stories about declines in crime are like "a dinghy bobbing in a rolling sea" of stories about individual, thoughtless, and salacious crime reports (Krajicek 1998, p. 12). Individual stories erroneously suggest that crime is increasing (Beckett and Sasson 2000).

This is one example of how media activity reinforces myths about crime: People believe that crime is increasing even when it is not (Kappeler, Blumberg, and Potter 2000). The media achieve this by providing "a steady diet of the growing and omnipotent danger of interpersonal crime" (Barak 1995, p. 133).

For example, in the mid-1990s, when violent crime was decreasing to its lowest levels in 20 years, crime coverage on television and in the newspapers increased in one city by more than 400% (Chiricos, Eschholtz, and Gertz 1997). In 1993, the three major news networks ran 1,632 crime stories on their evening newscasts, up from 785 in 1992 and 571 in 1991. This occurred even though victimization rates of the National Crime Victimization Survey (NCVS) and crime rates of the Uniform Crime Reports (UCR) were down during this time (Potter and Kappeler 1998, p. 3). Not surprisingly, in 1994, 88% of Americans thought that crime was at an all-time high (Barkan 1997; D. Jackson 1994). Additionally, between 1992 and 1993, major network evening news coverage of homicide tripled even as homicide rates remained unchanged, and from 1993 to 1996, major network news increased coverage of homicide by 721% (National Center on Institutions and Alternatives 1999).

Studies of violent crime rates and drug use rates versus media coverage of violent crime and drug crimes on television and in the newspapers show clearly that amount of coverage is not directly related to actual trends of violence or drug use. Instead, coverage tends to increase for reasons unrelated to actual crime trends. And public concern about crime peaks along with media coverage, rather than actual crime trends (MacCoun and Reuter 2000).

Approximately one-fifth of local television news relates to crime, as does more than one-tenth of national news and about one-quarter of newspaper space (Ericson, Baranek, and Chan 1989; Surette 1998). The main problem with this overreporting is that news stories about crime are not rational and tempered. They are not in-depth, critical, informative accounts. Instead, they amount to numerous "raw dispatches about the crime of the moment, the frightening—and often false—trend of the week, the prurient murder of the month, the sensational trial of the year" (Krajicek 1998, p. 4).

Lack of Critical Coverage: Where's the Context?

Critical coverage about crime and criminal justice is typically lacking in American news. In terms of criminal justice policy, the media simply "cover" what politicians pledge and promise about getting tough on crime because the media are caught up in the same moral panic about crime, because they have become so caught up in the chase that they have forgotten to expose the public to intelligent crime reporting, and because crime news is inexpensive and attracts viewers (Krajicek 1998, pp. 6–7).

A *moral panic* occurs when

> a condition, episode, person or group of persons emerges to become defined as a threat to societal values and interests; its nature is presented in a stylized and stereotypical fashion by the mass media; the moral barricades are manned by editors, bishops, politicians, and other right-thinking people; socially accredited experts pronounce their diagnoses and solutions. (S. Cohen 1972, p. 9)

Escholtz (1997, p. 48) adds that because moral panics "typically involve an exaggeration of a social phenomenon, the public response also is often exaggerated and can create its own long lasting repercussions for society in terms of drastic changes in laws and social policy."

One example of a recent moral panic is the threat of terrorism faced by the United States since September 11, 2001. The federal government developed an alert system wherein a color indicates the relative degree of risk faced by our country. The color has been changed numerous times since the system was developed, generally based on anonymous and usually false information about alleged terrorist plots. When pressed to explain what normal Americans should do when the threat is increased, we citizens are told not to actually change our daily activities but rather to be "more vigilant" and "watchful for anything out of the ordinary." We are not told specifically to look for anything or anyone or to avoid any given place at any given time, so many now question why the government should tell us anything unless it is very specific information that may help us avoid becoming victims of terrorist crimes.

So, why do the media create moral panics about real problems such as terrorism and crime by blowing them out of proportion? Harrigan (2000, p. 130) claims that the media are biased in favor of "visually dramatic or sensational events that will attract a wide viewing audience."

Such media depictions of crime problems are inherently inaccurate—they have to be. The alternative is to tell the truth, which is virtually guaranteed to be more mundane and therefore will not attract as many TV viewers. Imagine how many Americans have experienced sleepless nights and great worry over anonymous and very vague terrorist threats when the government has claimed that it does not know how, where, when, or if America might be attacked but that "intelligence" indicates that "recent chatter" among terrorist suspects "has increased."

Stories about crime and terrorism do not provide much real information about problems of crime and terrorism. Krajicek (1998) claims that media coverage of crime almost never attempts to answer the most important question of all: "So what?" Instead, the majority of crime coverage can be depicted as "drive-by journalism—a ton of anecdote and graphic detail about individual cases . . . but not an ounce of leavening context to help frame and explain crime" (p. 7). Zuckerman (1994, p. 64) writes, "Television, in particular, is so focused on pictures and so limited by time that in the normal run of reporting it cannot begin to provide the context that gives meaning and perspective." Think of news reporters you have seen on the news, standing live at the scene of a crime that happened hours ago. The fact that there is nothing going on there now is apparently irrelevant. Because the reporter is there live, the illusion of importance is maintained.

How many times have you seen reporters broadcast from the scene of "ground zero" since September 11, 2001? What is added when news people report from the scene of an empty space? Preliminary studies on reporting since the terrorist attacks against the United States suggest that the coverage has been mostly superficial and fails to provide any context for the attacks (see the Issue in Depth at the end of this chapter). Why do some people hate us so much that they would sacrifice their own lives to spill blood on American soil? What are their goals? Where do they come from? Why didn't we see this coming? Why didn't we take action, given the clear warnings we had? What would be the best way to prevent such attacks in the future? Questions such as these have not been answered; in fact, they rarely even been asked by members of the mainstream media.

Lack of context in the news does not serve Americans well because it misinforms them. It is beneficial for politicians who want to put forth brief and simplistic stances on crime and terrorism, most commonly depicted as the 10- or 15-second "sound bites" heard in any election year (Harrigan 2000). The president's claim that terrorists are "evil" and we are "good" is one example of simplifying the problem of terrorism.

One night on my local news, a reporter discussed a series of crime-related stories. The news began with the alarmed-looking news reporter, who came on with a "video box" above his left shoulder announcing a "CRIME EXPLOSION!" This video image stayed above his left shoulder as he reported on a local rape, another crime that had occurred elsewhere in the state, and still another heinous act that had been committed somewhere else in the United States. After he finished reporting on these stories, the reporter said, in a hushed voice, "Actually, crime statewide is down according to official statistics." The reporter did not elaborate on this statement, did not explain what he meant by "official statistics," and did not provide any insight into how there could be a crime explosion in the midst of declining crime rates. In other words, he failed to place the individual crime stories in the overall context of declining crime rates.

Is this atypical? Is it unique to the recent past? McGucken (1987) suggests that the media may have always been focused disproportionately on crime, at least during the 20th century. Her analysis of stories featured in the *New York Times* during the first half of the 20th century showed that crime was covered by anecdote and that little attention was given to contextual criminal justice policy discussions. As noted by McGucken, the *New York Times* coverage was consistently brief, superficial, and purely descriptive.

This is troubling not just because readers of the *New York Times* are exposed to simplistic crime discussions, but also because, as an inner-ring source, the *New York Times* is a primary source of information for other media outlets. Another study (Lichter, Lichter, and Rothman 1994) compared violent crimes on television with real-world violent crime rates from the mid-1950s through the mid-1980s. The authors found that homicide was represented on prime-time television shows at 1,000 times its actual rate over this time period.

One of the most popular types of television programs since the 1950s has been the police drama: 20% to 40% of prime-time television programs are police-related (Surette 1992). Because the most effective law enforcers in the media are those who do whatever it takes to beat crime, including using excessive force, engaging in vigilantism, and ignoring due process procedures (Culver and Knight 1979; Dominick 1978), viewers may view the courts as "handcuffing the police" and as favoring the "rights of criminals" (Beckett and Sasson 2000; Merlo and Benekos 2000). This type of biased coverage would logically promote crime control values over due process values, perhaps explaining in part why American criminal justice has moved in this direction, as discussed in Chapter One.

Media and Fear of Crime: The Chicken Little Phenomenon

One claim about media coverage of crime that has recently been confirmed is that it is related to the level of fear of crime (Livingston 1996). In particular, so-called crime-time news leads to increased fear among its viewers (S. Cohen and Solomon 1994).

Consider the prevalence of violence depicted on the nightly news. Kappeler, Blumberg, and Potter (2000, p. 42) provide an example of a study that illustrates the amount of violence in the television news: "The Center for Media and Public Affairs found that crime has been the most prominently featured topic on the evening news since 1993, with 7,448 stories, or about 1 in 7 evening news stories." And 1 in 20 stories since 1993 has been about murder (Center for Media and Public Affairs 1997). A study of single crime stories featured on *ABC World News Tonight,*

CBS Evening News, and *NBC Nightly News* by the Center for Media and Public Affairs (CMPA, 2000) found that murder led all stories by far, followed by gun control, the death penalty, and terrorism. Other studies by the CMPA show clearly that the coverage of crime in the news is not related to crime trends—as crime rates go down, coverage does not typically decrease but fluctuates in ways unrelated to crime rate changes.

Why do people who are exposed to media become afraid of crime? I suggest that it is because of what I call the *Chicken Little phenomenon.* News broadcasts merely cover violence without providing any context, leaving viewers with no real sense of their relative risks of violent crime victimization. All viewers, regardless of where they live or who they are, come to believe that their risk of victimization is significant and, therefore, become afraid. Media coverage of crime stories creates the sense that the sky is falling!

According to the CMPA (1999), "The American Psychological Association [APA] estimates that the average twelve-year-old has seen 8,000 murders and 100,000 acts of violence on network television." Also, the National Institutes of Mental Health (NIMH) illustrate the harmful effects of violent entertainment, including increased aggression among young viewers and "a callousness toward violence directed at others." The American Medical Association (AMA) thus passed a resolution declaring that TV violence "threatens the health and welfare of young Americans."

Krajicek (1998, p. 7) calls the result a "tattooing of the national psyche." The National Criminal Justice Commission demonstrates how the media have created the illusion that all Americans have a realistic chance of being murdered by strangers, even though murder is the rarest of all crimes and is most likely committed by people known to the victims (Donziger 1996, p. 9). In the mid-1990s, *USA Today* published a headline that claimed, "Random Killings Hit a High." The subtitle claimed "All have 'realistic chance' of being victim, says FBI" (R. Davis and Meddis 1994). This was absolutely false. According to Kappeler, Blumberg, and Potter (2000, p. 39), the chance of any U.S. resident over the age of 11 years being murdered was was only 1 in 14,286 in 1996.

Generally, the more viewers are exposed to television, the more likely they are to see the world as a "mean and scary place" and to distrust others, feel insecure and vulnerable, and view crime as a serious problem (Gerbner et al. 1980; Morgan and Signorielli 1990; Signorielli 1990). Heavy TV exposure also leads to an increased fear of crime, an overestimation of the likelihood of becoming a victim of violence, beliefs that one's neighborhood is unsafe, assumptions that crime rates are increasing, and increased support for punitive anticrime measures (Gerbner 1994). Another result of TV viewing is that it can "dull the critical-thinking ability" of Americans and lead to apathy (Harrigan 2000, p. 131), thereby making simplistic solutions to complex problems more appealing and making Americans less interested in important issues.

An analysis of crime news and fear of crime by Chiricos, Eschholtz, and Gertz (1997) found that frequency of exposure to television news and radio news was related to fear of crime. Yet reading newspapers was not found to be related to fear of crime, even though most newspaper crime coverage is violent or sensational in nature (Marsh 1991). According to their analysis, the effects of television viewing depend on who is doing the viewing (also see Heath and Gilbert 1996). In their research, television viewing and fear of crime were related only in Caucasian females between 30 and 54 years of age. Chiricos and his colleagues suggest that this finding can be attributed to the fact that the most likely depicted crime victims on television are middle-age or older Caucasian women.

Thus, for "the media have the ability, indirectly at least, to manipulate the fear of crime" (Tunnell 1992, p. 300). Eschholtz (1997, p. 50) summarizes the research by claiming that

for newspaper consumption the character of the message is important: local, random, and sensational stories evoke the most fear, whereas, distant, specific, and less sensational stories may have a calming effect on individuals. For television, the quantity of television viewed in general, violent programming in particular, and certain audience characteristics are generally associated with higher levels of fear.

Few go as far as to suggest that the media intentionally create fear in viewers. But the fear that is created reinforces mythology about crime and criminal justice (Kappeler, Blumberg, and Potter 2000), causing citizens to avoid, and police to apprehend, people who are perceived as posing the greatest threats to our well-being (e.g., see Culverson 1998; Rome 1998). As argued in Chapter Four, these people tend to be darker in skin color and lacking in wealth compared to the average American. Michael Moore, in his Oscar-winning documentary film *Bowling for Columbine,* implies that media coverage of crime leads Americans to become afraid and spend more time at home, watching television, where they are thus exposed to more commercial messages from the corporations that own the media and pay to advertise their products.

Given all this coverage of crime in the United States, for many citizens "the United States must seem to be a hopelessly savage place that stands teetering on the lip of the Apocalypse" (Krajicek 1998, p. 4). Gallup polls conducted throughout the 1980s and 1990s show that even as crime declined, people were more likely to call it the number one problem facing the nation. Additionally, the percentage of people who fear walking alone at night has been highly variable over the years despite relatively consistent declines in crime since the early 1970s. In March 1994, the Times Mirror Center for the People and the Press reported a poll showing that 50% of the respondents feared that they would be victims of crime. Another 30% said that crime was the nation's number one problem. Compare this with the Gallup polls discussed in Chapter Four, which showed that in 1994 a large number of citizens thought that crime was the most important problem facing the country. Perhaps it is not surprising to learn that coverage of crime on the three major networks peaked a year earlier, in 1993.

Some research links fear not only to media coverage but also to the extent to which politicians highlight crime as a major concern (Lichter, Lichter, and Rothman 1994). Perhaps this is why public concern about crime peaked, at 52%, in the same month in which President Clinton signed the 1994 federal crime bill into law.

EXPLANATIONS OF MEDIA INACCURACY

According to S. Cohen and Young (1981), there are two competing explanations for the news media's inaccuracy in covering crime. According to one explanation—the *market model*—crime is considered newsworthy because of the public interest in it, and thus it is covered. According to the other explanation—the *manipulative model*—crime is of interest to the owners of the media and is purposefully distorted to shape public interests in line with those of the owners of the media. Surette (1992, p. 57) describes both models as simplistic and inadequate, and puts forth an alternative explanation—the *organizational model*—which posits that crime is inherently subjective and thus distorted, but also allows owners to generate profit from using crime.

Move On (2002) asserts that

> the main problems with media are profoundly structural. The airwaves are supposed to belong
> to the public, but they've been hijacked by huge companies. With the government assisting the
> monopolization process, all the major forms of media—such as broadcasting, cable, newspa-
> pers, magazines, books, movies, the music industry, and, increasingly, the Web—are now dom-
> inated by the interests of capital, devoted to maximizing private profit. Some investors benefit;
> the public gets shafted.

This is a good starting point. In examining the literature in this area, however, there are other reasons that the media focus on crime and tend to be inaccurate in their coverage of it. Each of these
reasons is discussed next. I begin with a discussion of organizational factors.

Organizational Factors: Entertainment for Profit

Reporters do not deserve all or even most of the blame for providing inaccurate coverage of
crime and criminal justice. Most are simply following orders from their superiors. Instead, blame
resides in "the moguls, stockholders, owners, and publishers" as well as the "editors, reporters,
and photographers" (Krajicek 1998, p. 5). Those who set the agenda for the media are the most to
blame for inaccuracies about crime and criminal justice in the media.

Let's face it: Crime is almost always the top story. Studies of news by the CMPA show that
crime is usually the top story in any given year, and at no time in the 1990s did it drop below the
top five stories. Part of the reason that crime is so newsworthy is that violence is so prevalent in
entertainment media, apparently because Americans like to watch it. Studies of American television shows, movies, and music illustrate that violence is a main theme. The good news is that a
recent study by the CMPA (1999–2001) found that the "amount of sexual material in television
entertainment fell by 29 percent and the amount of serious violence decreased by 17 percent."
Yet violence remains high in our entertainment media, particularly after the terrorist attacks on
our country and the U.S. "wars" in Afghanistan and Iraq.

Given the finite resources of reporters and news space, the fact that crime is so prominent in
the news means that other issues, such as international affairs, are not adequately addressed. Is
this intentional? According to Krajicek (1998, p. 13), "The process of journalism—collecting,
organizing, and disseminating information—happens in a series of priority-setting decisions
about how to use . . . resources." Those that prioritize crime over other vexing social problems are
the most accountable.

Who decides, then, what will be newsworthy? Beckett and Sasson (2000, p. 81) claim that news
is simply defined as what is out of the ordinary (Ericson, Baranek, and Chan 1989). Thus, television news comes to be seen as a form of entertainment, whereby the media are highly selective in
what they broadcast. Violence is more "sellable" than the mundane aspects of theft and other
forms of property crime. This explains what Surette (1992, p. 14) calls the recent blurring of news
and entertainment in media outlets.

However, according to Surette (1992, pp. 22, 32), crime has been the "single most popular
story element in the forty year history of U.S. commercial television, with crime-related shows
regularly accounting for one-fourth to one-third of all the three major networks' prime time
shows" from the 1960s to the 1990s. Why is this so? Since the media are businesses, economic
factors are inherently involved in selecting content. The content of the media is shaped in line

with the economic interests of the organization that owns the media outlet (Potter and Kappeler 1998, p. 19).

According to Stevens and Garcia (1980), TV programming is aimed at attracting and keeping large audiences because the "larger the audience, the more that sponsors are willing to spend for advertising and the greater the profits" (Surette 1992, p. 31). Given the organizational needs of the media, including profit-generating news (Beckett and Sasson 2000; Marion 1995), crime is valuable because it attracts viewers and because it is relatively easy to write about given the abundance of official sources of information in law enforcement personnel and politicians (Fishman 1978; Sherizen 1978). These officials are considered legitimate, authoritative, reliable, and consistently available (Beckett 1997; Gans 1979; Schlesinger and Tumber 1994; Sigal 1973).

Beckett and Sasson (2000, p. 118) conclude that crime entertainment narratives promote three related messages:

- Most offenders are professional criminals.
- Community safety is threatened by judges and defense attorneys who are too much concerned with offenders' rights.
- Criminal justice personnel are out there every day, fighting the war on crime.

These messages have the potential to be highly misleading to the general public. Therein lies the danger to doing justice, as well as to more honest crime control efforts. They also shift support toward a crime control model of criminal justice.

Peer Culture

Additionally, the "peer culture among journalists is as intense as that at any junior high school. Reporters and editors look to one another—both colleagues and competitors—to determine what is appropriate. If everyone else is doing it, that deserves an affirmation" (Krajicek 1998, p. 35). Consistent with *social learning theories* of crime, the media imitate what others in the business are doing and are likely to continue to cover stories when the coverage is positively reinforced (Akers 1996).

As noted by Fishman (1978), simple *imitation* also plays a role. Once a news agency picks up on a crime story or theme, other news organizations are likely to pick it up as well. When the theme runs throughout the media industry as a whole or through the mainstream media discussed earlier, it can lead to a "media crime wave" or moral panic. As noted earlier, the inner-circle media—who are owned by large corporations—are the ones that determine what is newsworthy.

Lack of Criminal Justice Education

The problem with the peer culture of the media is that few reporters have expertise on crime and criminal justice. As Krajicek (1998) puts it, they do not know the difference between a VCR and the UCR. If media owners, reporters, and editors do not understand basic facts of crime and criminal justice, they will merely report what they are told by official sources. For example, you have likely seen headlines and stories about rising and falling crime rates that base their arguments on rising or falling arrest rates. Arrest rates are not valid measures of crime rates but, instead, are a function of what police are doing. It is doubtful that many in the media understand the difference.

The journalist writes crime stories to get on the front page, much as the academic criminologist or criminal justice professor writes articles to get published in the best journals. The goal of each is not necessarily to make an actual difference in criminal justice policy but, rather, to play the game successfully within the rules laid out by the discipline. Ultimately, personal and even financial reward may be gained by each, as well as by their respective employers.

While academics practice "real criminology" and have been highly critical of recent criminal justice policy, their findings do not seem to inform criminal justice policy. Politicians practice "kindergarten criminology" (Krajicek 1998, p. 5), and reporters have not held politicians or criminal justice policymakers accountable for it.

The Role of Politics in the "Framing" of Crime

Ironically, the media, by reporting what such official sources report, create perceptions of the crime problem in viewers, thereby also creating support for particular crime control policies (J. Roberts and Doob 1990; J. Roberts and Edwards 1992). Because government sources are typically cited in crime reports, it is not surprising that Americans support "more police, more arrests, longer sentences, more prisons, and more executions" (Potter and Kappeler 1998, p. 3). State managers cited in media reports about crime also tend to emphasize a crime control perspective over a due process model of criminal justice (Welch, Fenwick, and Roberts 1998).

Logically, as news becomes routinized—as it follows similar formats to what has proved acceptable to owners of the media and news consumers and to what has evolved in line with needs of advertisers (Potter and Kappeler 1998, p. 19)—sources that have been relied on in the past are relied on regularly. This makes getting the news relatively easy. Government sources can be also be cited as "official" and thus reliable (Surette 1992).

Given that the media are dominant institutions in society, they share similar characteristics with other dominant institutions, such as the state and corporations (Potter and Kappeler 1998, p. 17). They reproduce the status quo, which is beneficial to them (Alvarado and Boyd-Barrett 1992; Gurevitch et al. 1982; Lapley and Westlake 1988; McQuail 1994; Stevenson 1995; Strinati 1995). An example can be characterized as a form of media inbreeding. Given that "media professionals are trained, educated, and socialized in a way as to internalize the values and norms of the dominant, mainstream culture . . . [they will] interpret or mediate news, information, and complex issues in a way that is usually consistent with the dominant culture and with the interests of powerful groups" (Potter and Kappeler 1998, p. 18).

The media will also amplify viewpoints of the powerful, especially when these views are already shared by members of society because they appeal to our "common sense." Anything offensive to consumers, advertisers, or owners will be discouraged (Potter and Kappeler 1998, p. 18). News stories about crime also often include "commentary from public officials" (Merlo and Benekos 2000, p. 2) or "state managers" (Welch, Fenwick, and Roberts 1998), which supposedly provide expert opinion about crime-related problems. Thus, politicians attempt to "capitalize on the news to further support their political agendas and to gain support of voters" (Merlo and Benekos 2000, p. 2).

The best of these politicians—the most effective claims-makers about crime—have their views of crime turned into media coverage; thus, they determine the focus of crime coverage by the media (Edelman 1988; Gusfield 1967; Hilgartner and Bosk 1988; Kitsuse and Spector 1973). Strangely enough, politicians then see media coverage of crime problems as heightened public concern over crime (Beckett and Sasson 2000). Yet most scholars posit that political action occurs before public concern and that public concern stems from actions of politicians, rather than the other way around.

For example, Gans (1995) outlines the labeling process of the "underclass" in the United States. The process he discusses is similar to the process whereby politicians create images of crime that are then picked up by media outlets. As discussed in Chapter Three, legislators apply labels to people by defining their acts as criminal. Then media outlets serve to alarm others about who should be feared. Finally, the media rely on official sources of information about crime (called "counters" by Gans) to prove that their claims-making activities are valid.

In the media, the most common way in which crime is framed is as a failure of criminal justice agencies (Beckett and Sasson 2000). For example, misleading and misinforming media coverage of crime highlights the failures of criminal justice agencies and characterizes the justice network as being inefficient and soft on crime (J. Roberts 1992; J. Roberts and Doob 1990). This is one of the paradoxes of news coverage of criminal justice. Although the media depict the criminal justice network as ineffective, "the cumulative effect of these portraits appears to be increased support for more police, more prisons, and more money for the criminal justice system" (Surette 1992, p. 14).

In other words, media coverage of criminal justice advances the status quo of big government when it comes to fighting crime by reinforcing the dominant ideology in American criminal justice (Fishman 1978; Graber 1980). That is, discourse on crime control is limited to present, get-tough policies (Potter and Kappeler 1998, p. 7). Given that the media focus disproportionately on law enforcement crime-fighting activities, the result is increased support for a crime control model rather than a due process model (Surette 1992).

As if due process rights were the cause of crime in the United States, politicians have made us all less free in an effort to fight a crime problem that is actually less problematic today than it has been in a long, long time. This attack on due process is consistent with *social control theories* of crime, which hold that criminality is normal and should be expected in the absence of meaningful societal controls on individual behavior (Hirschi 1969).

Even as the United States has been cast by "get tough" politicians as "a victim of its own liberty"—"U.S. society is too free for its own good and insufficiently fearful of authority" (Krajicek 1998, p. 16)—the media have not alerted citizens to how their Constitutional protections have been eroded in the move toward a crime control model of criminal justice. As explained by Krajicek (1998, p. 139), "The media have uncritically reproduced official, conservative, 'law-and-order' perspectives with little fundamental analysis of their success or failure."

The media tend to amplify politicians' claims about crime (Beckett and Sasson 2000). Sasson (1995, p. 13) states it this way: "People do crimes because they know they can get away with them. The police are handcuffed by liberal judges. The prisons, bursting at their seams, have revolving doors for serious offenders." Thus, the way to reduce crime is to reduce "loopholes and technicalities that impede the apprehension and imprisonment of offenders" and increase the "swiftness, certainty and severity of punishment"—in other words, to erode due process protections that interfere with the crime-fighting capacity of our criminal justice network (Surette 1992, p. 14).

CONCLUSION

Clearly, the media shape our worldview about crime and criminal justice. Once the law has defined certain acts as crimes, the media tend to cover those acts that are the most unusual, bizarre, and violent. Coverage of criminal justice is front-loaded, focused on police but rarely on corrections or the reality of plea bargaining in courts. Because the inner ring of the American media is controlled by large corporations, which are concerned first and foremost with ensuring profits, the media sell crime to Americans—"if it bleeds, it leads." The media's coverage of criminal justice is biased in favor of "get tough" approaches to reducing crime. All of this threatens justice and due process in the United States. Using the media as their mouthpieces, politicians have become like Chicken Little, trying to incite the public about impending doom in the form of crime in this country. They claim that we need a "war" to stop crime. When politicians and the media use terms like *war*, it suggests to the public that crime must be "fought" rather than "prevented." The costs to Americans include the failure to either do justice or reduce crime.

ISSUE IN DEPTH
Media Coverage of September 11th and the War on Terror

On September 11, 2001, the United States was attacked by terrorists as it had never been attacked before. Even the December 7, 1941, attacks on Pearl Harbor by the Japanese were not as deadly.

And of course, clearly there were differences. Pearl Harbor was a military base, and civilians were not the intended targets. Additionally, military planes and weapons were used in the attacks on Pearl Harbor. The attacks in New York City were intended to kill and injure civilians, and our own civilian airliners were used as weapons. Only the Pentagon was a targeted military facility, and one of the four doomed planes crashed into it. People have speculated that the fourth plane was intended for a government target in Washington, DC, such as the White House or the U.S. Capitol building; that plane crashed into a field in rural Pennsylvania. But of course, you know all this.

What I have done in briefly describing the September 11, 2001, attacks, to set the stage for this discussion of media coverage of them and America's subsequent "war on terror," is what mainstream media outlets did for months every time these issues were discussed. Think about it: How many times did you see the planes fly into the World Trade Center buildings? How many horrific images from that day—people running for cover, dead bodies and injured people, crushed police cars and fire engines, photos of missing persons posted on walls and fences—have you seen?

The media coverage of these attacks has been very similar to their typical coverage of crime and criminal justice discussed in Chapter Five: disproportionately focused on violence, creative of misperceptions of one's true risk of becoming a victim of such terrorism, ignorant of some key facts and issues about the causes and effects of terrorism, neglectful in failing to provide a context for the attacks, and creative of much fear and anxiety.

Coverage of the war on terror has been plagued by similar problems and distortions of its own. As you must know, the United States has responded to these attacks by launching two separate "wars"—one on the Taliban government in Afghanistan and one on the Saddam Hussein government in Iraq.

According to polls, most Americans cannot even identify these countries on a map, much less discuss the relationships that our government has had with these countries. Perhaps this is why some claim that the problem with the media coverage of the terrorist attacks began before the attacks even came. For example, Nisbet (2001) points out how American media essentially ignore world affairs, especially those that are complex and cannot be summarized in sound bites and short stories.

Many have characterized media coverage of the terrorist attacks and the looming wars as prophetic (Schecter 2003). In essence, the media beat the drums of war with unique prowar headlines and theme songs, making war seem inevitable, even before the United States launched any attacks. Americans just had to prepare for what was coming.

Early reports, beginning immediately after the attacks and continuing for months, focused almost exclusively on the human elements of the attacks. What was left out was any type of context for how rare these attacks were, where they came from, why they were initiated, the role the United States itself played in the motivations, international reactions, appropriate or inappropriate responses from Congress and the president of the United States, or any information on what normal, everyday Americans should do in the wake of such events.

Lule (2002) focused on editorials in the *New York Times,* a member of the inner ring of the media, and found that their writers focused on four myths to portray the events of September 11, 2001: the end of innocence, the victims, the heroes, and the foreboding future. In essence, even editorials in top newspapers were simplifying the attacks and not providing any critical coverage of where the attacks emerged or why. Why did the attackers choose us? Why did they hate us so much that they were willing to give their own lives to kill innocent civilians? Since the *New York Times* is a member of the inner ring of the media, its coverage affects most other media outlets in America.

Questions like those above were not answered because they were not asked by inner ring media. The reporters and commentators who asked such questions received predictable answers given whom was being asked—disproportionately those appearing on news broadcasts and talk shows were government and military spokespersons who simplified the motives for the attacks as jealousy of the United States and pure evil.

Not surprisingly, one study found that prowar voices in America dominated news coverage, outnumbering antiwar voices by a margin of about 25 to 1

(Rendell and Broughel 2003). Zerbisias (2003) summarizes this study, conducted by Fairness and Accuracy in Reporting (FAIR):

> FAIR found a mere 3 per cent of U.S. sources represented or expressed opposition to the war, and that includes senators and members of Congress. With more than 1 in 4 U.S. citizens opposing the war and much higher rates of opposition in most countries where opinion was polled, none of the networks offered anything resembling proportionate coverage of anti-war voices. . . . The anti-war percentages ranged from 4 per cent at NBC, 3 per cent at CNN, ABC, PBS and FOX, and less than 1 per cent—1 out of 205 U.S. sources—at CBS. . . . Anti-war voices were almost universally blown off in one-sentence sound bites while 42 per cent of them were never identified by name, labeled instead as "protester" or "antiwar activist."

Some outer ring and middle ring media agencies investigated the motivations for the war on Iraq and reported it for about a year before the war started, yet it was not until after the war began that any inner ring media outlets even mentioned the *Project for a New American Century* (PNAC) or the *American Enterprise Institute* (AEI), two neoconservative think tanks that had called for an invasion of Iraq. Shockingly, the founders and other key members of the PNAC are now in the White House, and at least one key writer for the AEI has unfettered access to President Bush on foreign policy matters. These groups have planned the Iraqi war for more than 10 years!

As the nation prepared for military action against Afghanistan and ultimately Iraq, mainstream media outlets provided little in the way of information about these countries, their cultures, and previous interactions between these countries and the United States. For example, the U.S. government recently viewed the Taliban government as an ally in the war on drugs for destroying massive amounts of opium poppies. Since the Taliban government in Afghanistan had no air force and virtually no defenses, the U.S. military could easily move into and around Afghanistan, running nearly flawless air strikes against whatever military targets they located.

The Afghanistan "war" quickly was replaced by much bigger news, especially the large corporate crime stories of Enron, World Com, and so forth (see Chapter Four). This was the focus of the news for an unprecedented few weeks, until President Bush signed a new law toughening sanctions for corporate crime and began openly discussing the possible invasion of Iraq, which then became the lead story. Coverage of the continuing "war" on Afghanistan—including the facts that Americans are still dying in Afghanistan and Iraq and that the Taliban are regrouping—is not widespread.

Almost nightly, the television news reported that the United States was already striking targets in Iraq, as they had been doing since the end of the first Gulf War with Iraq (for about 12 years). Yet rarely did we hear more than one sentence about the attacks, what their intended targets were, or how many civilians were killed in these bombings (Schechter 2003). As military actions against Iraq seemed imminent, despite overwhelming worldwide opinion against it, the media again began preparing the American people for the inevitable. Broadcasters on each of the major networks and writers for each of the major newspapers began predicting when the war would start and asked top officials in the U.S. government when they would launch the "war." Absent were questions pertaining to the just or unjust nature of the war (Cohen 2003).

Once it finally began, television news stations provided around-the-clock coverage initially, and major newspapers carried in-depth coverage and analysis of the war, including targets, weaponry, military personnel on both sides, and similar issues. Mainstream media developed special graphics with American flags, to be continuously broadcast on their television screens, which waved in the background or foreground as people were interviewed about the war. Some claim that the media thus were involved in selling the war rather than reporting it (Schecter 2003). When President Bush declared an end to major combat operations only a few weeks into the military actions, the media began returning to normal, everyday stories, such as coverage of celebrity and random, violent crimes.

Prior to the war, the leading story was the disappearance of a young woman who had some kind of relationship with a congressman from California. Although no evidence ever surfaced to suggest that the congressman was involved in her disappearance or death (she was found dead in a public park long after she disappeared), intense media coverage followed the every move of the congressman. The attacks of September 11, 2001, were supposedly a wake-up call to mainstream media: Many reporters even said this directly on the air, how they felt so bad for wasting so much time discussing the disappearance of one young woman and missed other, far more important stories. September 11th was going to teach us what was really important. Yet 2 years later the lead stories in the news dealt with the disappearance of a collegiate basketball player and the alleged sexual assault committed by a professional basketball player.

There has been almost no discussion of civilian deaths in Iraq despite clear evidence that deaths are in the thousands (like in Afghanistan)(Schechter 2003). Only occasionally do the media mention the continuing deaths and injuries of U.S. soldiers in Iraq and even Afghanistan. There has been very little in-depth analysis or investigative reporting about the conditions in Iraq, except by international news institutions such as the British Broadcasting Corporation (BBC) and a few public media institutions such as the Public Broadcasting System (PBS). The media have completely ignored the deterioration of Afghanistan and the efforts to return to power by the Taliban government.

Even before the highest-ranking officials of the Taliban government and the Hussein regime were captured or killed, mainstream media began asking who the United States will attack next in the war on terror. Top military officials have appeared on television making their own predictions about countries like Iran, Syria, Lybia, and North Korea.

Before the "war" on Iraq, mainstream media institutions failed to provide coverage of the initial antiwar rallies in the United States, even though they were the largest-ever rallies against a war that were launched before the war started (Schechter 2003). When the media began covering these events as they grew still larger (the largest since the 1970s), in an effort to be fair, they gave equal time to the counter-protesters even though the counter-protesters were vastly outnumbered. Most media outlets did not investigate the claims of those against the war, such as that the evidence against Iraq had been manipulated, misrepresented, exaggerated, and even fabricated and that the war was actually against the law (Schechter 2003).

At the time of this writing, these claims are finally being investigated. Stories of this nature are becoming more routine, questioning the intelligence that implicated the Hussein regime in attempting to obtain weapons of mass destruction. What is still not being asked, however, is whether it matters that Hussein possessed or was attempting to possess these weapons. Could he reach us with them? Did he have any reason to? Would we be able to stop him without initiating a war? What would be the implications for the law, which explicitly forbids launching preemptive wars, and for our allies, who uniformly stood against the invasion? Such questions need answers.

As you saw in this chapter, media inaccuracies such as these stem, first and foremost, from the organizational nature of the media. Mainstream media are owned by corporations and will inevitably cover stories in a way that serves their own interests (including ignoring stories that call their interests into question). The media also attempt to give us what they think will help us sell the products that they advertise on their stations and in their newspapers. Since violence is so important and even celebrated in America, wars fit our preoccupation with violence nicely. Additionally, the effects of the peer culture help explain the immense focus on the terrorist attacks and the war on terror. Once inner-ring media begin reporting on such stories, other media agencies follow so as not be left out. Furthermore, as the lack of criminal justice education partly explains the inaccurate media coverage of crime and criminal justice, so too does the lack of political science education partly explain the incomplete media coverage of the terrorist attacks on this country and the war on terror. Finally, as politics plays a role in "framing" crime, the war on terror has also been framed for a significant political reason—it reinforces patriotism and an unquestioning allegiance to government leaders who promote war rather than peace—even when the facts do not justify war (Nacos 2002; Norris, Korn, and Just 2003).

According to Jeff Cohen, founder of FAIR, the news media promote ignorance about important issues such as the war on Iraq. He writes:

> That half or more Americans think Iraq was involved in the 9/11 attack—perhaps the most media-covered event in our history—stands as a horrific indictment of U.S. media today. Such levels of ignorance can't be found in other countries. . . . The run-up to the Iraq war offers a case study in news bias: how mainstream media, especially television, were incapable of getting the truth out in the face of administration lies and innuendo about Iraq's 9/11 role and weapons of mass destruction.

The "truth" includes the following facts: Iraq did not attack the United States on September 11, 2001; Iraq was not linked meaningfully with al-Qaeda; and the majority of people in the world opposed the war (even among the countries that participated in it, aside from in the United States).

So perhaps it is not surprising that a study by the Program on International Policy at the University of Maryland reports that a majority of Americans have significant misperceptions and these are highly related to support for the war with Iraq (Kull et al. 2003). The study found that 48% incorrectly believed that evidence of links between Iraq and al-Qaeda has been found, 22% believed that weapons of mass destruction have been found in Iraq, and 25% believed that world public opinion favored the United States going to war with Iraq. More than half (60%) had at least one of these three misperceptions.

The misperceptions were also found to be related to support for the war on Iraq. For example:

- Among those with none of the misperceptions, only 23% reported supporting the war.
- Among those with one of the misperceptions, 53% reported supporting the war.
- Among those with two of the misperceptions, 78% reported supporting the war.
- Among those with all three misperceptions, 86% reported supporting the war.

The frequency of Americans' misperceptions varied depending on their primary source of news. Viewers of Fox were most likely to have at least one misperception (80%), followed by CBS (71%), ABC (61%), and NBC and CNN (55%). Only about half (47%) of people who reported relying on print sources had at least one misperception, followed by only 23% of listeners of National Public Radio (NPR) and viewers of the Public Broadcasting System (PBS).

When Americans misperceive the facts after watching news coverage, it is clear that the media are failing to do their job. Because the free flow of information is at the heart of democracy, there is no greater threat to democracy than media that fail to do their job.

Discussion Questions

1. What is meant by the term *media?*
2. Discuss how the "inner ring" of the media has more control over the stream of information than less well-known media outlets.
3. What are the main types of media that cover crime and criminal justice stories?
4. Explain how the media help shape our worldview.
5. Why do you think the media are so heavily relied on for information about crime and criminal justice?
6. Why do the media tend to ignore white-collar deviance even though it causes so much harm?

7. What components of the criminal justice system do the media focus on most? Why?
8. Why do you think the media focus so much more on violent crimes than on property crimes?
9. Provide a few examples of how the media fail to provide the proper context when reporting about crime and criminal justice.
10. Do the media promote fear of crime? Why or why not?
11. Which reasons discussed in the chapter do you think best explain why the media are so inaccurate when reporting about crime and criminal justice?
12. On the basis of the research discussed in the chapter, do you the think the media are biased against any particular group in society? Why or why not?
13. What are some likely effects of media coverage of terrorism and American wars on our approach to criminal justice?

PART III

COMPONENTS OF CRIMINAL JUSTICE: POLICE, COURTS, AND CORRECTIONS

CHAPTER SIX

LAW ENFORCEMENT:

TO SERVE AND PROTECT?

INTRODUCTION

What do images of police from television and movies suggest to you about American policing? What lessons does Hollywood teach you about what police do? This chapter shows how police are mischaracterized in the United States. While police perform valuable functions for the

American people, including crime victims, police spend very little time fighting crime. This is one significant reason that the criminal justice network is very ineffective at reducing crime. In this chapter, I discuss the basics of law enforcement in the United States, including how policing is organized and the basic roles and responsibilities of American police. I also show that, because police are responsible for enforcing the criminal law, any biases in the criminal law will also be found in the activities of law enforcement. The term for unintended biases in law enforcement is *innocent bias*. In this chapter, I explain from where innocent bias against the poor and people of color arises.

THE ORGANIZATION OF POLICING IN THE UNITED STATES

The allocation of police officers to various government levels (i.e., city, county, state, and federal governments) in the United States will have major effects on what police do. Policing at different levels of government is focused on different forms of behaviors. An examination of the levels of government at which the police work in the United States provides a good picture of the types of harmful behaviors to which U.S. police generally dedicate their efforts.

As of 2000, there were 17,784 police agencies in the United States and 796,518 full-time sworn police officers. As shown in Table 6.1, a total of 12,666 (71%) of the police agencies were local police departments, and another 3,070 (17%) were county sheriff departments. Local police agencies have *jurisdiction* over cities and sheriff departments have *jurisdiction* over counties. Thus, 87% of police agencies are responsible for policing what can be thought of as local governments, or cities and counties.

As shown in Table 6.2, in 2000, city police departments employed 440,920 full-time officers (55% of the total), whereas sheriff departments employed 164,711 deputies (21% of the total). This means that 76% of police officers in the United States work for local cities and counties. Thus the typical police agency and the typical officer in the United States are at the local level of government. Meanwhile, only 56,348 officers work for state agencies (7% of the total), and 88,496 officers work for the federal government (11% of the total).

Most police departments are relatively small, as 5,894 departments (47%) employ fewer than 10 sworn officers. Almost 75% of local police departments serve communities with fewer than 10,000 people. Many sheriff's offices are also small, as 844 offices (27.5%) employed fewer than 10 personnel. Yet almost two-thirds of offices employed more than 100 officers.

TABLE 6.1

American Police Agencies (2000)

Total agencies	17,784 (100%)
City police	12,666 (71%)
County police (sheriff)	3,070 (17%)
State	49 (<1%)
Special jurisdiction	1,376 (8%)
Texas constable	623 (3.5%)

SOURCE: Bureau of Justice Statistics (2002).

TABLE 6.2
American Police Employees (2000)

Total officers	796,518 (100%)
City police	440,920 (55%)
County police (sheriff)	164,711 (21%)
State	56,348 (7%)
Special jurisdiction	43,413 (5%)
Texas constable	2,630 (<1%)
Federal	88,496 (11%)

SOURCE: Bureau of Justice Statistics (2002).

From these data, we can conclude that police activities are very much a local phenomenon and that most law enforcement officers work for small departments that serve small geographic areas. What types of harmful behaviors do local police agencies focus on? The answer is street crimes, such as the "serious" crimes listed in Chapter Four, as well as drug offenses and public order offenses. Later in this chapter, I show which of these types of offenses produce the most arrests (you may be surprised!). For now, keep in mind that most police agencies and officers are not focused on acts of white-collar deviance, the acts shown in Chapter Four to cause the most harm to Americans.

The following box lists some of the main policing agencies at the federal level in the United States. The responsibilities of each are also discussed.

American federal law enforcement agencies

U.S. Department of Justice

- *Immigration and Naturalization Services (now Bureau of Citizenship and Immigration Services)*—Enforces U.S. immigration and naturalization laws and attempts to prevent illegal entries into the United States
- *Federal Bureau of Prisons*—Responsible for providing safe and secure living environments for federal inmates
- *Federal Bureau of Investigation*—Investigates violations of all federal laws that are not covered in the jurisdiction of other federal agencies, including bank robberies, kidnapping, treason, civil rights violations, extortions, and attacks against federal government employees
- *Drug Enforcement Administration*—Enforces laws relating to the unlawful distribution and use of illicit drugs
- *U.S. Marshals Service*—Provides security for federal court proceedings by maintaining order, guarding prisoners, and serving orders of the courts and provides transport to court proceedings and to and from federal correctional centers for all federal prisoners

U.S. Department of the Treasury

- *U.S. Customs Service (now U.S. Customs and Border Protection)*—Collects duties and taxes on goods and services exported from or imported into the United States and investigates some forms of thefts and the smuggling of illegal narcotics

- *U.S. Secret Service*—Protects the president of the United States, the vice president, former presidents, and heads of foreign states while in the United States, provides security for federal buildings, and investigates many crimes relating to counterfeiting
- *Internal Revenue Service*—Investigates alleged tax fraud and enforces tax codes
- *U.S. Bureau of Alcohol, Tobacco, and Firearms (now U.S. Bureau of Alcohol, Tobacco, Firearms, and Explosives)*—Enforces laws relating to alcohol, tobacco, firearms, and explosives

According to the Bureau of Justice Statistics, the majority of federal officers (17,654, or 20%) work for the Immigration and Naturalization Service (INS), Bureau of Prisons (13,557, or 15%), Federal Bureau of Investigation (FBI; 11,523, or 13%), and U.S. Customs Service (10,522, or 12%). Whereas most INS workers are border patrol agents, FBI officers have broad investigative responsibilities for more than 250 federal crimes, including bank fraud, embezzlement, and kidnapping.

In 2000, the main functions of federal law enforcement officers included criminal investigation (41%), police response and patrol (19%), corrections (18%), noncriminal investigation and inspection (13%), court operations (4%), and security and inspection (3%). The numbers of agents assigned to each federal police agency has definitely changed since the terrorist attacks against the United States and the creation of the new *Department of Homeland Security,* as have some of their basic responsibilities. The data are not yet available, but it is clear that the attention of the FBI, for example, has shifted from white-collar crime to terrorism, thus meaning that there is even less of a focus on criminal acts of the powerful than probably at any time in our nation's history.

Of all federal officers in 2000, women accounted for only 14.4% and minorities made up just 30.5%, including 15.2% Hispanics and 11.7% African Americans. In 2000, less than 11% of local officers were women and less than 23% were minorities, including less than 12% African Americans and just over 8% Hispanics. Less than 13% of sheriff deputies were women and only about 17% were minorities, including less than 10% African Americans and just over 6% Hispanics. So, at all levels of government, women and minorities are underrepresented among police officers.

BASIC ROLES AND RESPONSIBILITIES OF POLICE OFFICERS: WHAT POLICE DO AND HOW THEY DO IT

Americans are exposed to a stereotypical view of policing from television entertainment shows and daily crime news. The typical view of police shows them encountering hardened criminals on a daily basis and fighting for their very survival each day (see Chapter Five). One surprising reality of policing in the United States is that police actually spend most of their time not dealing with crime. This fact runs counter to the image of high-speed car chases and "good guys versus bad guys" depicted in the media. In fact, most of what American police do on a daily basis is mundane and routine. According to Wrobleski and Hess (2000), police officers in the United States serve five basic roles.

- *Enforcing laws:* This includes investigating reported crimes, collecting and protecting evidence from crime scenes, apprehending suspects, and assisting the prosecution in obtaining convictions.
- *Preserving the peace:* This includes intervening in noncriminal conduct in public places that could escalate into criminal activity if left unchecked.
- *Preventing crime:* This includes activities designed to stop crime before it occurs, such as education campaigns, preventive patrols, and community policing.
- *Providing services:* This includes performing functions normally served by other social service agencies, such as counseling, referring citizens for social services, assisting people with various needs, and keeping traffic moving.
- *Upholding rights:* This includes respecting all persons' rights regardless of race, ethnicity, class, gender, and other factors and respecting individual Constitutional protections.

Of these five roles, the *typical police officer* spends most of his or her time each day not fighting crime (Fyfe et al. 1997). So how do police spend their time? According to Wrobleski and Hess (2000, p. 128), "Approximately 90% of a police officer's time is spent in the social service function." Services provided by police include checking buildings for security violations, regulating traffic, investigating accidents, providing information to citizens, finding lost children, providing first aid, handling animal calls, mediating disputes, and negotiating settlements between citizens (Cox and Wade 1998, pp. 99, 103). As noted by Manning (1997, p. 93), "Of the police functions or activities most central to accumulated police obligations, none is more salient than supplying the range of public services required in complex, pluralistic, urban societies." So, although "law enforcer" or "crime fighter" is the stereotypical image of the police officer, the typical city patrol officer or county sheriff in the United States spends the smallest amount of his or her day dealing with crime.

Others, such as Bayley (1994), claim that police spend about 75% of their time on routine patrol or administrative tasks. In fact, according to the Bureau of Justice Statistics, almost 70% of full-time local police officers were regularly assigned to responding to calls for service in 2000. Whatever the case, police spend only about 5% to 10% of their total time handling criminal matters (Cox and Wade 1998, p. 99). An examination of activities of police officers at various levels of government illustrates this point equally well. According to the Bureau of Justice Statistics, approximately two-thirds of officers have primary responsibility for answering calls for service. Fewer than 1 in 5 have primary responsibility for investigative duties (15%), and fewer than 1 in 10 have primary responsibility for duties that are administrative or technical, or that involve training, jail-related duties, and court-related duties. When comparing city and county officers, the main difference is that city officers are more often on patrol, whereas county officers are more likely to have jail duties given that county sheriff departments often operate jails.

At the state and federal levels, the picture is very similar. State officers are most frequently assigned to responding to calls for service, followed by investigative duties; administrative, technical, and training duties, and court-related duties. At the federal level, most officers have primary responsibility for investigations and enforcement, followed by corrections-related duties, police services, court operations, and security and protection.

When Bill Clinton, as president of the United States, promised to put 100,000 more police on the streets in the 1990s, he did not bother to tell us that it would probably make little difference in the fight against crime. Do you find it ironic that politicians have emphasized how important it is to put more police on the streets, even though they spend so little time actually fighting crime? Given that fewer than one in two crimes is even known to the police (and this counts only street crimes), and only one in five of these leads to an arrest, it is not surprising that police have some free time on their hands (see Chapter One). How could this time be better spent? I discuss this issue in Chapter Thirteen. Politicians offer more of the same—more police—even though the evidence suggests that what we need is not more but better policing (Sherman et al. 1997).

These moves—to hire more police, arm police better, and allow increasingly tough and intrusive policing to crack down on relatively minor offenders—all interfere with one responsibility of police: to safeguard citizens' Constitutional protections. A significant problem with "get tough," "law and order" approaches to reducing crime is that they interfere with citizens' Constitutional rights. One example is the *exclusionary rule*, discussed in the following box.

The exclusionary rule

The *exclusionary rule* was applied to the states by the Supreme Court case, *Mapp v. Ohio* (1961). It states that if evidence is obtained illegally, it cannot be used against the accused in court. This rule grew out of the Fourth Amendment, which reads, "The right of the people to be secure in their persons, houses, papers, and effects, against unreasonable searches and seizures shall not be violated, and no Warrants shall issue, but upon probable cause, supported by Oath or Affirmation, and particularly describing the place to be searched, and the persons to be seized." Any evidence obtained without a valid warrant thus would not be admissible in court.

Yet, as we have become more and more entrenched in a crime control model of criminal justice, numerous exceptions have been created that allow police to get around the exclusionary rule, including the following.

- *Searches incident to lawful arrests:* Police may search the area within the immediate control of suspects upon arresting them.
- *Searches with consent:* Police may search any area if citizens voluntarily consent.
- *The plain view doctrine:* Evidence in plain view of the police may be seized without a warrant.
- *The plain touch doctrine:* Evidence that is felt by the police while they are legally searching a person or place may be seized without a warrant.
- *The good faith exception:* If it can be determined that a police officer was acting in good faith that a warrant was valid even though it was not, seized evidence can still be used against the accused.
- *Inevitable discovery:* Police can use illegally seized evidence against a suspect if they can demonstrate that the evidence would have ultimately been discovered by lawful means.
- *Exigent circumstances:* During emergencies, police may find evidence that can ultimately be used against a citizen.

These exceptions seem logical enough, but are they necessary? Fyfe (1983) has demonstrated that the exclusionary rule really does not make it harder for the police to gather and use meaningful evidence against guilty criminals. As explained by Walker (1998, p. 87), "[T]he police solve crimes when they immediately obtain a good lead about a suspect, from either the victim or a witness. Physical evidence, independent of some other kind of identification of the suspect, is rarely the primary factor in making an arrest and convicting the offender." This means that even fewer cases will be dismissed because of evidence that is thrown out as a result of the exclusionary rule. Fyfe described such a likelihood as "minuscule" and "infinitesimal." Does such a small likelihood that a guilty person will go free justify allowing courts to use illegally seized evidence against accused criminals?

Walker concludes that the exclusionary rule is valuable and in fact is supported by most police administrators. For example, former FBI Director William Sessions stated that "protections that are afforded by the exclusionary rule are extremely important to fair play and the proper carrying out of the law enforcement responsibility" (cited by Walker 1998, p. 89). In essence, the exclusionary rule results in better police work and lowers the possibility that citizens will be wrongfully convicted by overzealous agents of government.

How Police Serve Crime Victims

Although police officers spend most of their time not dealing with crime, they do provide valuable services to victims of crime. Generally, as police "are the first representatives of the criminal justice network that victims encounter after being victimized," they serve victims in the following ways.

- Responding quickly to calls for help
- Launching thorough investigations into alleged crimes
- Preserving and collecting evidence
- Solving crimes by capturing suspected offenders
- Assisting with criminal prosecutions of criminal suspects. (Karmen 1996, p. 166)

Technically, all crime-related police work is in service to victims—recording crimes, investigating crimes, collecting and preserving evidence, apprehending and arresting suspects, interviewing witnesses and victims, interrogating and booking suspects, testifying in court, and so forth (Cox and Wade 1998, p. 99). Such services are crucial to achieving justice as an outcome for victims of crime. The main problem with American policing is that it is structured to be reactive to crime, or *incident-driven*, rather than proactive, or *problem-oriented*.

Because street crime is "the product of social and economic disadvantage, much of it traceable to racial bias and discrimination" (Tonry 1995, p. 3), police have little effect on crime rates. Such factors are beyond the reach of criminal justice agencies. Police themselves know this. For example, Klockars (1991, p. 250) writes:

> All of the major factors influencing how much crime there is or is not are factors over which police have no control whatsoever. Police can do nothing about the age, sex, racial, or ethnic distribution of the population. They cannot control economic conditions; poverty; inequality; occupational opportunity; moral, religious, family, or secular education; or dramatic social, cultural, or political change. These are the "big ticket" items in determining the amount and distribution of crime. Compared to them what police do or do not do matters very little.

This, in part, explains why American policing has shifted toward the community policing ideal. Wrobleski and Hess (2000, p. 161) explain that community policing is more proactive and problem-oriented—a "customer service" approach to law enforcement.

THE MOVE TO COMMUNITY POLICING

The main buzz word in policing today is *community policing*, which refers to a crime prevention partnership between the police and the community (Wrobleski and Hess 2000). Although the term has no clearly defined set of characteristics in practice, in philosophy it is aimed at solving problems before they become crimes rather than merely reacting to crimes after they occur. That is, it is an approach aimed at identifying problems with the community before they lead to crime (Goldstein 1990).

Community policing is rooted in a problem-solving approach and is sometimes referred to as problem-oriented policing. Problem-oriented policing is based on the following principles, as described by the Bureau of Justice Assistance (1993, p. 5).

- A problem is something that concerns the community.
- A problem will likely indicate a pattern of related incidents that will require unique police interventions.
- Problem solving is a long-term strategy requiring increased police creativity and initiative.

Community policing in its current forms began to take hold in the United States during the 1970s. It grew out of the recognition that professional policing was unsuccessful at reducing crime, as well as unpopular with certain segments of the public. From roughly 1920 to 1970, American policing was more professional in nature; that is, it placed a high value on efficiency and crime fighting while being separate and distinct from public influence. In the *professional policing model*, police intentionally keep themselves separate from the public in order to reduce corruption and special favors. Unfortunately, this leads to isolation from the community and hinders the ability of police to achieve cooperation from citizens. It also fosters hostilities in some neighborhoods where the police become seen as occupiers rather than service providers. Community policing places more emphasis on providing services to the community and developing police–community relations (Gaines, Kaune, and Miller 2000, p. 178).

Research demonstrates that the success of formal social control depends, at least in part, on informal social controls in a community (M. Robinson 2004). Police know that they need the help of communities to fight crime. Social control can be understood as "attempting to persuade persons or groups to conform to group expectations" (Cox and Wade 1998, p. 94). *Formal social control* achieves that conformity through the use of official or governmental means, such as law enforcement, whereas *informal social control* is achieved through families, peers, teachers, and others. Coercing people to abide by the law (formal social control) depends to a great degree on a criminal justice network that can efficiently detect crime and apprehend criminals. Clearly, American criminal justice is highly inefficient. In part, this is because many Americans avoid getting involved in the process—for example, by not calling the police when they witness crimes. Given that there are only 2.86 police officers per 1,000 citizens in the United States, it is highly unlikely that formal social control mechanisms will effectively deter would-be lawbreakers. This "should be enough to convince us that the likelihood of detection and apprehension for those who violate laws is quite low if we rely totally on the police for such detection and apprehension" (Cox and Wade 1998, p. 94).

Community policing is also theoretically based on sound *crime analysis*, so that police resources and personnel are assigned to geographic areas where and when they are most needed. This goes back to a notion of Sir Robert Peel, who in 1829 founded the London Metropolitan Police Department in England. The following box illustrates the core ideas of Sir Robert Peel and discusses how and why they are still important for American policing. Compare this with the realities of policing discussed in this chapter.

Key ideas of Sir Robert Peel

American policing evolved from English policing traditions. As the early colonists brought over their customs and traditions to this new country, they also brought over their law enforcement customs and traditions. In 1829, Home Secretary Sir Robert Peel established the London Metropolitan Police Department (LMPD) in England. The officers became known as "bobbies," after their founder. Peel put forth certain principles that he believed police should follow for law enforcement to be successful. As consistent as they are with today's version of community policing in the United States, keep in mind that he actually posited these ideas more than 175 years ago!

Peel insisted that the police be chosen from the people so that they would be familiar with and essentially the same as the people whom they policed. He insisted that police be uniformed and be unarmed except for a small truncheon beneath their coats. Peel clearly laid out his vision of the personality of the ideal police officer. Police, he said, should be highly trained, stable, quiet yet determined, and in control of their tempers. Peel also thought that officers should keep up a good appearance in order to gain respect.

Peel insisted that the police force be under government control and organized in military fashion to maximize accountability and ensure cohesiveness. He also held that officers should be required to keep records of all of their interactions with citizens, also for accountability purposes. Keeping records of all interactions would also allow the police to track incidents by time and place. Thus, Peel believed in what we now call *crime analysis*, which would allow police to deployed to those areas and at those times when they were needed most. This would also permit the police department to distribute crime news for the benefit of the public (as is done in today's police newsletters).

Peel envisioned a police force whose officers would be hired on a probationary basis (much like today's probationary patrol officer, fresh out of the police academy). This would permit police officers to be adequately trained while on the street and would reduce the possibility of hiring negligent personnel. Unlike the current situation, in which law enforcement success has been measured in terms of more and more arrests, Peel believed that police efficiency could be demonstrated by the absence of crime—that is, by crime prevention.

In the 1850s, Peel's law enforcement ideas spread across England, and England's police force became the largest and most organized in the world. Eventually, legislators from New York actually visited the LMPD to copy their ideas and to build a similar foundation for American police forces.

Has American policing become detached from its roots? Have we lost our way? Or is community policing a means to return to Robert Peel's core ideals?

According to the National Criminal Justice Commission, community policing is based on the notion that police "should serve residents in a neighborhood rather than simply police them" (Donziger 1996). Yet one significant problem with community policing is that many minority communities "feel both *overpoliced and underprotected*—overpoliced because the drug trade flourishes with the same vitality as before, and because police are often slow to respond to 911 calls from minority neighborhoods" (p. 160; emphasis in original).

Legislators have voted to place more police in these neighborhoods on the basis of the belief that there is more crime there and that the presence of more police will reduce crime. The evidence from studies such as the now famous Kansas City Patrol Study (Kelling et al. 1974) and its replications (Police Foundation 1981) suggests that more police will not reduce crime. These studies found no evidence that patrol activities of police, whether proactive, reactive, or even absent, had any effects on crime rates. This is why the National Criminal Justice Commission concludes that "we need to learn how to police *better* before we add new police" (Donziger 1996, p. 160).

Walker (1998, p. 79) explains why adding more police will have no effect on crime rates. He argues that patrol will always be spread thin in a geographic area, so that its crime-preventive benefits will be minimal. He also suggests that many crimes are not suppressible by patrol because they happen in private areas between people who know one another.

There is some research suggesting that adding more police to large cities will reduce street crime there, especially when patrols are directed at *hot spots of crime* (Sherman et al. 1997). The number of violent street crimes, as measured in the Uniform Crime Reports (UCR), declined 34% between 1990 and 2000, and the number of UCR property crimes fell by 31%. During this time, the number of full-time officers increased 17% (Bureau of Justice Statistics 2003). Policing likely had something to do with these declines but was not responsible for most of them (see Chapter Four).

President Clinton boasted that crime rates fell in the nation's cities because he had put 100,000 new "community police officers" on the street. In fact, we still have not hired those additional 100,000 officers, and most of those that we did hire are not engaged in community policing. The good news is that in 2000, of all city police departments, 66% had full-time sworn officers engaged in community policing activities, as did 62% of sheriff's departments. Almost 70% of local police departments had a community policing plan of some type. The bad news is that only 18% of local police departments (who employed 52% of all officers) had a formally written community policing plan, and only 17% of departments offered training to citizens on community policing issues. As for sheriff's offices, 55% had some community policing plan, and 62% used full-time community policing officers. Yet less than one-third (31%) of departments, employing 51% of deputies, trained all new recruits in community policing, and only 13% had formal policies on community policing. Only 9% of sheriff's offices included problem-oriented projects in performance evaluations for officers and only 8% surveyed citizens regarding perceptions of crime problems in the community. Thus, it is safe to say that community policing is more of a buzzword than a widely used approach to crime prevention.

I suggest that even if we add more police, policing will probably be ineffective in reducing crime because police still will not spend a substantial amount of time fighting crime. Of crime calls, which make up only a small minority of calls for service, "almost all calls come when it is too late to catch the perpetrator" (Donziger 1996, p. 162). These are known as *cold crimes*. The fact that about 75% of offenders are not caught at the scene of the offense is what makes arrest the weakest stage of the criminal justice process. Such facts have led even police chiefs to make statements such as, "Adding more police may be good politics, but it will do little to reduce crime and violence in America" (Moran 1994; quoted by Krajicek 1998).

Alternatively, better policing may reduce crime. A small portion of officers nationwide is assigned to crime prevention efforts. If we want to prioritize community policing, we must invest more resources in problem-solving approaches that are proactive rather than reactive.

HOW POLICE ARE SUPPOSED TO BEHAVE

Now that you have a better understanding of how policing is organized in the United States, what police do in a typical day, and what is happening with policing in the United States, you may be wondering how police actually behave. In fact, police are expected to behave in a very specific manner at all times. The following box contains *The Law Enforcement Code of Conduct* passed by the International Association of Chiefs of Police (IACP). Consider this the ideal of American policing.

The law enforcement code of conduct

All law enforcement officers must be fully aware of the ethical responsibilities of their position and must strive constantly to live up to the highest possible standards of professional policing.

The International Association of Chiefs of Police believes it important that police officers have clear advice and counsel available to assist them in performing their duties consistent with these standards, and has adopted the following ethical mandates as guidelines to meet these ends.

Primary responsibilities of a police officer

A police officer acts as an official representative of government who is required and trusted to work within the law. The officer's powers and duties are conferred by statute. The fundamental duties of a police officer include serving the community, safeguarding lives and property, protecting the innocent, keeping the peace and ensuring the rights of all to liberty, equality and justice.

Performance of the duties of a police officer

A police officer shall perform all duties impartially, without favor or affection or ill will and without regard to status, sex, race, religion, political belief or aspiration. All citizens will be treated equally with courtesy, consideration and dignity.

Officers will never allow personal feelings, animosities or friendships to influence official conduct. Laws will be enforced appropriately and courteously and, in carrying out their responsibilities, officers will strive to obtain maximum cooperation from the public. They will conduct themselves in appearance and deportment in such a manner as to inspire confidence and respect for the position of public trust they hold.

Discretion

A police officer will use responsibly the discretion vested in his position and exercise it within the law. The principle of reasonableness will guide the officer's determinations, and the officer will consider all surrounding circumstances in determining whether any legal action shall be taken.

Consistent and wise use of discretion, based on professional policing competence, will do much to preserve good relationships and retain the confidence of the public. There can be difficulty in choosing between conflicting courses of action. It is important to remember that a timely word of advice rather than arrest—which may be correct in appropriate circumstances—can be a more effective means of achieving a desired end.

Use of force

A police officer will never employ unnecessary force or violence and will use only such force in the discharge of duty as is reasonable in all circumstances.

The use of force should be used only with the greatest restraint and only after discussion, negotiation and persuasion have been found to be inappropriate or ineffective. While the use of force is occasionally unavoidable, every police officer will refrain from unnecessary infliction of pain or suffering and will never engage in cruel, degrading or inhuman treatment of any person.

Confidentiality

Whatever a police officer sees, hears or learns of that is of a confidential nature will be kept secret unless the performance of duty or legal provision requires otherwise.

Members of the public have a right to security and privacy, and information obtained about them must not be improperly divulged.

Integrity

A police officer will not engage in acts of corruption or bribery, nor will an officer condone such acts by other police officers. The public demands that the integrity of police officers be above reproach. Police officers must, therefore, avoid any conduct that might compromise integrity and thus undercut the public confidence in a law enforcement agency. Officers will refuse to accept any gifts, presents, subscriptions, favors, gratuities or promises that could be interpreted as seeking to cause the officer to refrain from performing official responsibilities honestly and within the law. Police officers must not receive private or special advantage from their official status. Respect from the public cannot be bought; it can only be earned and cultivated.

Cooperation with other police officers and agencies

Police officers will cooperate with all legally authorized agencies and their representatives in the pursuit of justice.

An officer or agency may be one among many organizations that may provide law enforcement services to a jurisdiction. It is imperative that a police officer assist colleagues fully and completely with respect and consideration at all times.

Personal–professional capabilities

Police officers will be responsible for their own standard of professional performance and will take every reasonable opportunity to enhance and improve their level of knowledge and competence.

Through study and experience, a police officer can acquire the high level of knowledge and competence that is essential for the efficient and effective performance of duty. The acquisition of knowledge is a never-ending process of personal and professional development that should be pursued constantly.

Private life

Police officers will behave in a manner that does not bring discredit to their agencies or themselves.

A police officer's character and conduct while off duty must always be exemplary, thus maintaining a position of respect in the community in which he or she lives and serves. The officer's personal behavior must be beyond reproach.

Compare the above ideal of police behavior with your own experiences with police. Are they generally consistent? I have personally had both good and bad experiences with police—sometimes I dealt with officers who behaved precisely the way the IACP expects they will, and sometimes I dealt with officers who took job-related events personally and let it affect their behavior.

The vast majority of police likely follow the IACP mandate. Yet, because of structural impediments, the reality of policing in the United States clearly runs counter to the ideals we expect. I would argue that for police to carry out the above mandate successfully, they would have to be highly educated. In 2000, almost all (98%) local police departments had some type of educational requirements for new officer recruits, but most (83%) required only a high school diploma. Only 15% of city police departments and 11% of sheriff's officers had college education requirements for new officers, including only 1% of local departments that required a 4-year degree. New police recruits were required to complete between 800 and 1,600 hours of academy and field training, depending on the city size. It is estimated that less than one-third of new officers work for departments that require college education (Law Enforcement Management and Administrative Statistics 2003). The bottom line with police education requirements is that they are simply too low. Perhaps this is why the average starting salary of new officers in local police departments in 2000 was $25,500, whereas for sheriff deputies it was only $23,700.

What can we realistically expect from our police officers who are held to such high standards when they are not required to have a college education and when they are paid so poorly? I argue that we should not expect the reality of policing to match the ideal. And you should be concerned about this. In 2000, local police departments spent nearly $37 billion, for an overall cost per resident of $179, whereas sheriff's departments spent almost $18 billion for $65 per resident (Bureau of Justice Statistics 2003). This is your money.

INNOCENT BIAS: HOW POLICING IS ORGANIZED IN THE UNITED STATES

If individual police officers are biased against certain groups of people, we may conclude that they are involved in unjust activity. Yet bias in policing does not require "bad cops." Biased law enforcement only requires bad law. In Chapter Three, it was shown that the criminal law is biased against poor people and people of color. Given this fact, enforcement of this law (through policing) will logically reinforce the bias within the law.

This means that even if each individual police officer was not biased, prejudiced, or bigoted, American law enforcement would still be biased because it simply reflects the biases of the law. This is what I call *innocent bias.*

Innocent bias can arise from the following factors.

- The use of police discretion
- The use of "police profiling"
- The location of police on the streets of the United States
- The particular focus of police on certain types of crimes
- Policing of the "war on drugs"

The Use of Police Discretion

Discretion is the ability of an agent to act according to his or her own professional judgment rather than some preset rules or procedures. Even though all criminal justice decision making must occur within limits imposed by the U.S. Constitution, state constitutions, state laws, and precedents set forth by previous courts, many actors within the criminal justice network have wide discretion. The very nature of policing, whereby officers are entitled to use their own unchecked discretion to make decisions (e.g., see National Association of Criminal Defense Lawyers 1996), allows racial stereotypes and myths of crime to infiltrate police work, resulting in racial disparities in stops, arrests, and police use of force (Cole 1999).

Pratt (1992, pp. 99–100) argues that police officers are given discretion to act or not act on the basis of their own judgment because we assume that they are honest and trustworthy. In addition, extensive in-service training leaves police officers uniquely qualified to judge which behaviors pose significant threats to society. Finally, police must be allowed to use discretion for their own protection.

According to Bittner (1970, p. 107), police officers have "a greater degree of discretionary freedom in proceedings against offenders than any other public official." After all, if the police do not take people into custody, make arrests, and issue citations, the criminal justice network has no clients and thus cannot operate. This is why D. Gottfredson (1999, p. 30) writes about police, "To a great extent, they exercise discretion in deciding whether to invoke the criminal justice system."

When police are given discretion over criminal matters, the potential for abuse is clearly there. The National Criminal Justice Commission writes that American police have the power to decide how to apply the law and determine the crime-fighting agenda of a community:

> They have wide discretion to decide who will be stopped and searched, which homes will be entered into, and which businesses will be inspected. If misused, that power can cause every-thing from a minor inconvenience to the destruction of life and property. If used properly, it can save lives and help make neighborhoods safer. (Donziger 1996, p. 161)

Corruption in police departments and discrimination by the police were factors that led to the move by police away from the community and toward neutral, professional models of policing in the early 20th century (Fyfe et al. 1997).

Discretion seems vital to the success of American policing; the problem is determining how to ensure that it will not be misused. It seems more likely that police will misuse their discretion when the political climate of their communities, states, and country is so focused on fighting street criminals that they lose sight of what should be the real goals of law enforcement: to serve citizens and reduce harmful behaviors while simultaneously upholding Constitutional protections.

A prime example of misused discretion is seen in the enforcement of speeding laws. The police cannot possibly enforce laws regulating speeding on all roads at all times, so they selectively choose roads and times to patrol for speeding and even target individual cars. Cox and Wade (1998, p. 98) write, "While an officer is writing a citation to one speeder, several other speeders may escape his or her attention." The threat of a speeding ticket may deter some drivers from intentionally speeding at some times, but it is evident that most drivers exceed the speed limit at times, sometimes even intentionally. M. Robinson and Zaitzow (1999b) found that more than 90% of American criminologists admitted to speeding intentionally. There are times when one must speed to stay out of the way of other drivers or to keep up with the flow of traffic. This may explain why many speeders get upset with police officers for selecting them out of the dozens of surrounding vehicles on the roads.

The point is not that speeding should be allowed, speed limits should be lifted, or people should be free to drive as fast as they want. Rather, I want to demonstrate what can happen if police are looking for particular types of cars, or even types of people, to pull over for speeding. Because police have a wide range of discretion in deciding who to pull over, very little can stop them from abusing this discretion and applying the law differentially to different types of people.

Racial, cultural, or gender differences may lead officers to stop and arrest individuals from some groups of people more than others. African Americans may be more fearful and thus may run from or refuse to cooperate with the police. Hispanics may not make direct eye contact with officers, and this may be misinterpreted as a lack of respect. If police are not trained to recognize such group differences, their discretion may be biased against groups who are unlike the officers.

At the arrest stage, the police officer "possesses considerably discretionary power . . . [where] there is no one physically present to supervise the officer's actions, and he or she may respond to a variety of cues . . . [such as] the age, gender, race, dress, prior history, or location of a suspect" in deciding to arrest or not (Cox and Wade 1998, p. 101). Granting police this awesome power is asking for trouble if police are dishonest, partial, bigoted, or unethical.

Cox and Wade (1998, p. 101) claim:

> It is the existence of discretion by individual police officers in thousands of police–citizen encounters everyday that helps shape public attitudes toward the police. . . . If an officer arrests one person for a particular offense but allows another who has committed the same offense to go free, the arrested party . . . can hardly be expected to feel that the criminal justice network is just.

Nor are everyday citizens who become aware of such discrepancies likely to think that the criminal justice network is just. Decisions about who to stop, pull over, and suspect of criminal activity are informed by images of crime created by the criminal law and broadcast in the news media. Therefore, what is known as police profiling begins with the biases built into the law and the news media.

The Use of Police Profiling

American police focus on particular types of people because of their own personal experience or that of their institution and profession, which suggests that certain people are more likely than others to violate the law. For example, during police academy training, officer candidates may learn about crime rate differentials among different groups in society, using official rates of street crime from the UCR. Also, during the time probationary officers spend with a *Field Training Officer* (FTO), new police officers may pick up subtle hints of whom to be on the look out for, whom to stop and question, and so forth, from their senior officers. These experiences allow race and other extralegal factors to affect police decision making. This practice, known as *police profiling*, results in startling disparities in police behavior (D. Harris, 1999; D. Roberts, 1993; Son, Davis, and Rome, 1998).

One study found that although African Americans made up about 17% of drivers and only 17.5% of traffic violators, they made up nearly 73% of those pulled over and searched by the police (Gaines, Kaune, and Miller 2000, pp. 645–46). The Bureau of Justice Statistics reports that about one in five (or 20%) of Americans had face-to-face contact with the police in 1999. The most frequent cause of these interactions was traffic stops, making up 52% of all interactions. In 1999, the latest year for which data were available, 19.3 million drivers were stopped by the police. Only 10.3% of all drivers were stopped by the police.

Among young males, ages 16–24 years, neither African Americans nor Hispanics were more likely than Caucasians to be stopped by police. Yet African Americans (75.7%) and Hispanics (79.4%) were more likely than Caucasians (66.6%) to be ticketed for speeding. In this age group, African Americans (15.9%) and Hispanics (14.2%) were more likely than Caucasians (7.9%) to have their cars or persons searched.

Among males over the age of 24 years, African Americans (13.8%) were more likely than Caucasians (10.7%) to be stopped by police, and African Americans (3.2%) were more likely than Caucasians (2%) to be stopped by police more than one time. In this age group, African Americans (15.5%) and Hispanics (11.1%) were more likely than Caucasians (5.8%) to have their cars or persons searched. African American males over the age of 24 years faced searches of their persons during 11.4% of stops, versus only 5.8% of Hispanics and 4% of Caucasians.

Interestingly, African Americans (74%) and Hispanics (81.6%) were less likely than Caucasians (86%) to report that they felt the stop was legitimate. African American (32%) and Hispanic (34.7%) males over age 24 years who were stopped more than once by police were far less likely than Caucasian (16.5%) males over 24 years to say that the stop was illegitimate.

Given that the chance of arrest was not much greater for African Americans searched by police than for Caucasians (41.5% versus 37.3%), do these statistics suggest anything in particular? The Bureau of Justice Statistics suggests that, among nonarrested motorists (those for whom there was either no evidence or not enough evidence to warrant an arrest), African American males were more likely than Caucasian males to be searched (9.9% versus 5.1%). This seems like clear evidence of profiling, based on the assumption that people of color need to be searched more than Caucasians.

When police use race as a proxy for risk, being young, African American, and male equals probable cause (Gaynes 1993), a phenomenon that is even supported by courts as legitimate when race is used in conjunction with other factors. Police profiling may explain why police target minority communities—"where drug dealing is more visible and where it is thus easier to make arrests"—more than other areas (Walker, Spohn, and Delone 2000, p. 265).

Most of this perceived "social threat" to communities (Jackson 1997) results from an honest, unintentional exaggeration of risk on the part of police, but it creates significant disparities nevertheless. "Race dependent policing erodes the difficult-to-maintain habit of individualizing persons and strengthens the reflex of lumping people together according to gross racial categories" (D. Kennedy 1997, p. 157).

Other outcomes of police profiling of particular offenders include "a climate of alienation, hostility, social unrest, and violence in the nation's inner cities" and a basic distrust and resentment of the police. Not surprisingly, several studies reflect a lower view or approval of law enforcement and government among African Americans than among whites (e.g., see Donziger 1996). In areas where it is the worst, such as Washington, DC, courses are available to teach citizens how to handle themselves if stopped by the police (R. Miller 1997, p. 26). Some studies show that police may overcharge arrestees with crimes they did not commit in order to make some charges stick (e.g., see P. Smith 1990). Some of these arrests and overcharging practices have been found to be racially motivated (e.g., see Nazario 1993). Therefore, jury nullification on the part of African Americans who refuse to convict other African Americans charged even with violent crimes may suggest that, for this targeted group, outrage against violent criminals may be dwarfed by apathy or hostility toward the justice network (J. Miller 1997).

Profiling may be part of what Eddings (2000, p. 197) calls *stealth racism* in the United States. The term *stealth racism* suggests that racism is not gone but, rather, has become harder to see. It is more subtle because it is less likely to be admitted or is passed off as part of a legitimate function, such as maintaining order. Eddings suggests several examples of stealth racism—taxis that do not stop for minorities, shoppers who are identified as suspicious on the basis of their race, and customers who receive unequal service because of race. In Chapter Twelve, I explain how discrimination based on race persists in the United States even today.

The Location of Police on the Streets of the United States

Police are disproportionately located in some areas of our country while being nearly absent from others. Specifically, more police are allocated to the nation's inner cities. Why? First, there is more demand for police services in these areas. Second, the nation's inner cities are characterized by very high poverty rates. According to the U.S. Census (2001), the average poverty rate in central cities in 2001 was 16.5% (26.1% for African Americans, 13.4% for Caucasians), versus 11.1% in metropolitan areas (21.4% for African Americans, 9.3% for Caucasians) and only 8.2% in metropolitan areas not in central cities (14.7% for African Americans, 7.5% for Caucasians). This may explain why there are more police patrols directed at these areas. Residents in these areas have less power and are less able to resist police presence. Benjamin and Miller (1991, p. 21) provide an example with drug crimes. They claim that "the inner city is an expedient locale for police to rack up impressive arrest numbers, with little fear for consequences if mistakes are made."

The result of a differential location of police by city size and type is that police will make more arrests of the people who live in the areas where they patrol. Since poverty is higher in the nation's central cities, and since the poverty rate is highest among African Americans in these areas, we would expect police to disproportionately arrest poor people and African Americans.

The Particular Focus of Police on Certain Types of Crimes

Local policing in the United States focuses on street crime, the eight "most serious" Part I index offenses of the UCR: theft, burglary, motor vehicle theft, arson, homicide, aggravated assault, forcible rape, and robbery (see Chapter Four). These acts are generally perceived by society and government agencies alike to be the behaviors that cause the most physical and financial harm and occur with the greatest frequency. As pointed out by Wrobleski and Hess (2000, p. 132),

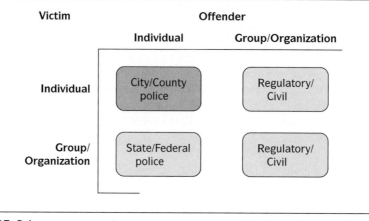

FIGURE 6.1

Focus of Law Enforcement on Victimization

"Usually [police] departments concentrate law enforcement activities on serious crimes—those that pose the greatest threat to public safety and/or cause the greatest economic losses." The main conclusion is that the general focus of law enforcement in the United States is on a very small number of criminal acts and an even smaller number of culpable harmful acts. The majority of types of victimizations, even those that stem from harmful, culpable behaviors, are virtually ignored by law enforcement in the United States.

Figure 6.1 illustrates the way in which law enforcement in the United States is most focused on criminal victimizations of individuals caused by acts of individual persons. The shaded region in Figure 6.1 indicates the main focus of police when it comes to victimizations. Law enforcement is much less concerned with victimizations against individuals that are committed by entities such as groups or corporations (these are usually under the jurisdiction of state or federal law enforcement). Victimizations against individuals or entities such as groups and corporations committed by other entities are generally not handled by the criminal justice network and hence do not fall within the primary domain of law enforcement. Instead, harms and victimizations resulting from such acts are handled through civil law (as in the case of major lawsuits against large tobacco corporations) or regulatory agencies (as in the case of outbreaks of bacterial contamination in food products). Other harmful culpable behaviors, especially those that do not violate any law, are completely ignored.

These facts indicate that people can be victimized by acts that result in death, physical injury, and/or loss of property, with virtual impunity from the U.S. criminal justice network. Given that doing justice implies that the guilty will be punished for their actions, the fact that our justice network ignores harmful acts committed with culpability means that the criminal justice network does not achieve justice as an outcome. It also means that our network of justice is ineffective at reducing these types of crimes.

Policing the War on Drugs

One main focus of policing in the contemporary United States seems to be on drug offenses. Our nation's police spend a significant amount of time and resources fighting the war on drugs (see Chapter Eleven). In 2000, almost 90% of local police departments regularly engaged in drug enforcement activities, and 95% of sheriff's offices engaged in drug operations. More than 20% of local police departments participated in a multidrug task force, and another 15% assigned officers full-time to a special drug unit. Nearly 30% of sheriff's offices had special units for drug enforcement and 40% had deputies assigned full-time to drug task forces. Not surprisingly, then, of the nearly 13.7 million total arrests in 2001, 1.6 million (11.4%) were for drug offenses. Our courts are now backlogged with too many cases (see Chapter Seven), and our prisons and jails are filling up with drug offenders at unprecedented rates (see Chapter Nine).

One outcome of the police focus on drug offenses is that police forces have become increasingly militarized, with more paramilitary units and better technology and weaponry (Kraska and Kappeler 1997). In spite of this, the war on drugs is generally focused on low-level offenders engaged in illegal activity related to certain types of drugs. For example, 81% of all drug arrests in 2001 were for possession, 46% were for marijuana-related offenses, and 41% of the total were for marijuana possession. This means that the largest share of drug arrests in any given year in the United States is for simple possession of marijuana. In Chapter Eleven, I show that marijuana is much less harmful than legal substances such as alcohol and tobacco. Is this a wise use of police resources?

One indicator of innocent bias in the war on drugs is racial disparities in arrests, convictions, and sentences to prison for drug offenses. In 2000, African Americans made up just under 13% of the U.S. population but 34.5% of the arrests for drug abuse violations. Given that most drug arrests are for simple possession, are African Americans that much more likely to possess drugs? According to the Substance Abuse and Mental Health Services Administration's (SAMHSA) National Survey on Drug Use and Health (NSDUH), only 9.7% of African Americans and 8.5% of whites report using some illegal drug in the previous month (current users). In other words, African Americans are no more likely than Caucasians generally to use an illegal drug. So how can we explain the differential for race in drug arrests? One possible answer is that police are disproportionately located in the neighborhoods where poor African Americans live, thus making it more likely that they will be arrested.

The U.S. government has chosen to take a reactive approach to drug use rather than a proactive approach. This means that American law enforcement spends more money attempting to reduce the supply of drugs coming into the United States than it spends on efforts to reduce the demand for drugs (see Chapter Eleven). According to a 1998 investigation into police corruption related to the war on drugs by the General Accounting Office (GAO), police officers have become frustrated with their inability to stop drug use in their communities, despite their best efforts. This, along with general cynicism and dissatisfaction, leads to *police corruption*. Add to this the tremendous potential for profits to be made from stealing money and drugs from dealers, selling drugs, and so on, and it is easy to understand how some good cops turn bad (Gray 2001; Merlo and Benekos 2000). The Issue in Depth at the end of this chapter discusses corruption in the criminal justice network.

Additionally, in 1999, almost 40% of local police departments reported drug asset forfeiture receipts, and they seized $320 million in cash, goods, and property. The average seizure was $5,000. More than half (53%) of sheriff's offices had receipts for asset forfeitures as a result of drug crimes. Sheriff's departments seized $137 million. The average seizure was $14,700. Guess what this money is used for? That's right, fighting the war on drugs!

With the U.S. war on drugs, police officers on our streets have been using more and more aggressive techniques. I believe that our nation's law enforcement leaders are ignoring lessons from the past. In 1968, the National Advisory Commission on Civil Disorders, commonly referred to as the Kerner Commission, published a report that found a direct relationship between aggressive police patrols and tensions between police and minority communities. The type of intrusive law enforcement that is occurring in the United States' inner cities is aggravating racial tensions between citizens and the police in particular and worsening racial relations in the United States generally. Ironically, some claim that law enforcement techniques used in the war on drugs run counter to the Law Enforcement Code of Conduct, discussed earlier. Police end up abusing their discretion, using excessive force, and occasionally even sullying their private lives.

AMERICAN STOP RATES AND ARREST RATES

Technically, anyone suspected of committing a criminal act can be arrested. An arrest occurs when a person is legally detained to answer to criminal charges (Rush 2000, p. 20). *Black's Law Dictionary* (1991, p. 72) defines *arrest* as follows: "To deprive a person of his liberty by legal authority. Taking, under real or assumed authority, custody of another for the purpose of holding or detaining him to answer a criminal charge. . . ." Wrobleski and Hess (2000, p. 344) elaborate on this definition by demonstrating that arrest includes four main elements: (1) the officer must have intent to make an arrest, (2) the officer must have authority to make an arrest, (3) the person must be seized or restrained, and (4) the person must understand that he or she is being arrested. Typically, a *warrant* is required to make an arrest, but officers do not need warrants when crimes are committed in their presence or when they are responding to the scene of a crime and an offender is at the scene (Wrobleski and Hess 2000).

The Supreme Court has explained that an arrest is not the same thing as a *stop*. A stop must only be justified by reasonable suspicion that some wrongdoing has occurred or is likely to occur (*Terry v. Ohio*, 1968). An arrest requires *probable cause*, meaning that all the facts and circumstances known to the officer would suggest to a person of reasonable caution that a crime has been committed or is likely to be committed (*Draper v. United States*, 1959).

Essentially, a stop will occur if police officers come upon a person they reasonably feel looks suspicious or is acting suspiciously. For their own protection, police officers are justified in conducting a frisk or pat-down search of the suspect if they feel the suspect is armed (Hess and Wrobleski 1997, p. 122), called a *Terry stop* after the Supreme Court case, *Terry v. Ohio* (1968). The Supreme Court ruled in *United States v. Cortez* (1981) that reasonable suspicion should be based on the *totality of circumstances*, including the officer's inferences and deductions. A police officer who is carrying around a mental stereotype of the *typical criminal* may be more likely to stop some types of people than others.

If you can imagine that police might stop some people more than others, then consider the following scenario: A police officer sees a dark-skinned man (race unclear to the officer) lurking outside a store late at night and feels that the man looks suspicious. The man looks suspicious in part because the store is getting ready to close and because the neighborhood is mostly inhabited by Caucasians. The police officer approaches the man, stops him, and conducts a pat-down search of the man's outer clothing. In doing so, the officer feels something hard in the man's jacket pocket and then reaches inside to find a knife. If, by being in possession of the knife, the man has violated state law, the police officer would be justified in making an arrest of the man. This type of stop would likely be considered legal given that the officer is allowed to use his or her discretion to justify the stop and frisk, regardless of the man's intent. This man would likely have committed a crime against his state law. But what if the man was simply waiting for his girl-friend to get off of work and was carrying the knife for his own protection? This probably would not matter to the police officer or to the court.

Now, what if the man outside the store was a Caucasian? Would the officer think that a Cau-casian man hanging around a store at closing time in a Caucasian neighborhood was suspicious? Justifying a stop on the basis of the totality of circumstances allows officers to use their own dis-cretion to determine who looks dangerous and who does not. This may allow police profiles of the typical criminal, created by the criminal law and reinforced by media coverage of crime and crim-inal justice, to come into play.

If every group in the United States committed equal amounts of crime and if police did not discriminate against any group, we would expect to see relatively equal stop rates and arrest rates for all groups. Any diversion from this expectation would suggest either that some groups commit more crime, that the police discriminate against some groups, or both.

Evidence suggests that Hispanics, African Americans, and other people of color are more likely to have run-ins with police (Bureau of Justice Statistics 2003). Friedman and Hott (1995) found in a survey of high school students that people of color were more likely to report that they had been stopped by the police and treated in a disrespectful manner. Chicago police were found to be using an unconstitutionally vague loitering statute to stop and question people of color (D. Roberts 1993). This pattern has also been found in other big cities, such as Los Angeles and New York. Clearly, race is used as a cue for potential trouble-making activity on the part of citizens. In essence, police allow their personally held stereotypes to invade their professional work (J. Skolnick 1994).

The significance of being stopped by the police cannot be understated. Logically, being stopped would increase a person's risk of being arrested or of having force used against him or her, especially to the degree that the person does not cooperate with the police. Beyond this, being stopped can be bothersome and even intimidating if the police have bad attitudes or if a person is constantly harassed for no valid reason. Disproportionate arrest rates are accompanied by disproportionate harassment by the police (Chambliss 2000).

The typical arrestee in the United States is a young, urban, poor, African American male: "This is the Typical Criminal feared by most law-abiding Americans. Poor, young, urban, [dispropor-tionately] African American males make up the core of the enemy forces in the war against crime" (Reiman 1998, p. 55). Kappeler, Blumberg, and Potter (2000, p. 221) concur, "The vast majority of people arrested and processed through the criminal justice system are poor, unem-ployed, and undereducated."

Given that police focus on crimes of the poor, because the law defines their acts as criminal more often than those acts of the wealthy, the police target particular populations they perceive to be threatening, especially within inner cities. This calls into serious question official statistics suggesting that African Americans commit more than their "fair share" of criminal behavior. As noted by Kappeler, Blumberg, and Potter (2000, p. 222), "Research on the police clearly shows that suspects from lower socioeconomic groups and suspects who are members of minority groups are arrested more frequently, on weaker evidence, and for more crime than their white, affluent counterpoints."

The fact that police typically arrest urban street criminals should not be surprising. Arrest rates from the UCR consistently are four to five times higher for African Americans over age 18 than for Caucasians over 18 and two to three times higher for African Americans under age 18 than for Caucasians under 18. It is alarming that African Americans make up roughly one-third of arrests in any given year even though they account for only 12% to 13% of the U.S. population. The percentage of African American arrests is also higher in cities (30.8% African American in 2001) than in suburban communities (21.3% African American) and rural areas (15% African American), as expected given their relative residential concentration in inner cities (Sourcebook of Criminal Justice Statistics 2003). Walker, Spohn, and Delone (2000) claim that the arrest rate for African Americans is two and one-half times higher than it would be if simply predicted by their proportion of the population.

American police officers in 2001 made an astounding 13.7 million arrests, the majority of which were not for "serious" street crimes. R. Miller (1997, p. 484) is thus correct when he asserts, "Most of the frenetic law enforcement in the black community has nothing to do with violent or serious crime." In fact, less than 2.3 million arrests were for index offenses of the UCR (16.4%), including 1.6 million arrests for property crimes and just over 625,000 arrests for violent crimes. Of arrests in 2001, 28.1% were of African Americans, who, as noted, account for less than 13% of the U.S. population. As shown in Table 6.3, African Americans are overrepresented in every category of arrests, with the exceptions of arson, vandalism, sex offenses, driving under the influence (DUI), liquor law violations, suspicion, curfew and loitering, and runaways. They made up (37.6%) of arrests for serious violent crimes and 31.4% of arrests for serious property crimes.

African Americans are generally no more "criminal" than other groups of people (see Chapter Twelve). Even when evidence does show that African Americans account for a disproportionate amount of some "serious" crimes (such as murder and robbery), *serious* is a term defined by lawmakers. As you learned in Chapter Three, legislators are less likely to be African American and not at all likely to be poor. Thus, if you learn that African Americans made up (53.8%) of all arrests for robbery and 48.7% of all arrests for murder in 2001, perhaps you should ask yourself, What is "robbery" and what is "murder"? No one would argue that these crimes are not serious or not harmful. But there are many ways to take someone's money by force or to kill a person that are not currently considered robbery or murder, respectively. The fact that these acts are not legislated as criminal or treated as serious is a function of who makes the law (see Chapter Three). The disproportionate

TABLE 6.3
Arrests in the United States, by Race (2001)

	White	Black
Murder & manslaughter	48.4%	48.7%
Forcible rape	62.7%	34.8%
Robbery	44.5%	53.8%
Aggravated assault	64%	33.7%
Burglary	69.4%	28.5%
Theft	66.1%	31.2%
Motor vehicle theft	57.5%	39.8%
Drug abuse violations	64.2%	34.5%

SOURCE: Sourcebook of Criminal Justice Statistics (2003).

focus of law enforcement on poor, minority communities, though rooted to a degree in the criminal law, is nevertheless extremely detrimental to minority communities. As R. Miller (1997) writes, "[A] major contributor to breakdown in the inner cities is the criminal justice system itself."

According to Walker, Spohn, and Delone (2000, p. 99), officers are more likely to arrest a suspect when there is strong evidence that he or she is guilty, when the crime is of a serious nature, when a victim requests that an arrest be made, when the alleged offender is a stranger rather than a person known to the victim, and when the suspect is disrespectful to the officer. The bulk of the evidence also suggests that race does matter when it comes to arrest because police are more likely to arrest alleged offenders when the victim is a Caucasian and the suspect is a member of a minority group.

USE OF FORCE

Limits have been placed on police use of force to protect citizens and police officers alike. Ideally, use of force by the police is determined by the behaviors of citizens with whom police come into contact. Police use of force can range from verbal commands to deadly force, whereby a citizen is actually killed. Figure 6.2 shows a continuum of options for the use of force available to police based on the behavior of citizens. As the figure illustrates, the more resistant a citizen is to the police, the more force can be legally used against him or her.

A report by the U.S. Department of Justice entitled "National Data Collection on Police Use of Force" (1996) summarizes this issue very well:

> The feature distinguishing police from all other groups in society is their authority to apply coercive force when circumstances call for it. Police may be called on to use force when making an arrest, breaking up an altercation, dispersing an unruly crowd, or performing a myriad of other official activities during their daily routines. The force may range from pushing a person to get his attention to using a firearm. Between those extremes are several other types of force, including firm grips on an arm, use of debilitating chemical agents, and blows with a baton. Whatever method is used, police are expected to apply only the force necessary to resolve a given situation.

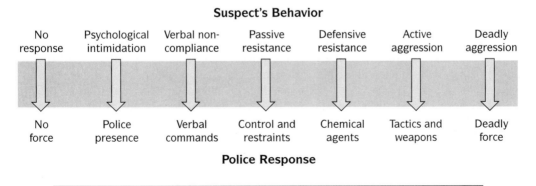

FIGURE 6.2
Law Enforcement Use of Force Continuum

The necessary degree of force to be used against a citizen is determined in the officer's own judgment (i.e., his or her discretion), based on the behaviors of the citizen. It is also constrained by the U.S. Constitution (Hall 1992). McEwen and Leahy (1994) place force techniques along a continuum from no force to verbalization techniques to deadly force, with several nonlethal mechanisms somewhere in the middle, including the following.

- Impact weapons (e.g., batons and flashlights)
- Chemical weapons (e.g., pepper spray)
- Electrical weapons (e.g., electronic stun guns)
- Other less-than-lethal weapons (e.g., projectile launchers)

In 1999, the year when the latest data were available, nearly all (93%) local police departments had a formal policy pertaining to the use of deadly force and 87% of local police departments had a formal policy pertaining to the use of non-deadly force. As for sheriff's offices, nearly all (92%) had a formal policy pertaining to the use of deadly force and 85% had a formal policy pertaining to the use of non-deadly force.

Luckily for both citizens and the police, use of police force is relatively rare. Force is used in only about 1% of all citizen encounters (Bureau of Justice Statistics 1996). In 1996, for example, American police officers questioned almost 4.5 million people as suspects in crimes, and in less than 2% of cases was force used or threatened (Bureau of Justice Statistics 1997). Of all people stopped in cars by the police in 1999, only 3% were arrested. Of all drivers, more than 420,000 people age 16 years and older (roughly 2%) report that the police used or threatened to use force against them. Yet less than 1% of drivers (0.7%) actually had force used against them or had excessive force used against them (0.5%) (Bureau of Justice Statistics 2003).

A large majority of instances of the uses of force are deemed justified. A national study of police use of force by Pate and Fridell (1994) found what one might expect about police use of force: Less serious types of force are used more frequently than more serious types. Their study also found that citizen complaints for excessive force were rarely filed. Nationally, the rate for city police departments was 11.3 complaints per 100,000 people.

We cannot know for certain the prevalence of excessive use of force by police. We do know, however, that it is minority men who are most likely to be subjected to it (Ross 1999). In a 1991 Gallup poll, respondents were asked, "Have you ever been physically mistreated or abused by the police?" Five percent of all respondents said that they had been physically mistreated or abused by the police. Nine percent of non-Caucasians answered in the affirmative to the question of physical mistreatment or abuse by the police, and 20% of respondents said that they knew someone who had been physically mistreated or abused by the police (U.S. Department of Justice 1996). A study in Cincinnati, Ohio, found that African Americans were more than four times as likely as Caucasians to indicate that they had been hassled by the police (Browning et al. 1994). According to the American Civil Liberties Union (ACLU), polls conducted in the 1960s showed similar results:

- A 1965 Gallup poll showed that 35% of African American men believed that there was police brutality in their areas, compared with only 7% of Caucasian men.
- A 1966 survey conducted for a U.S. Senate subcommittee found that 60% of African American residents of the Watts neighborhood in Los Angeles who were between 15 and

19 years of age believed that there was some police brutality; 50% said that they had witnessed such conduct.
- A 1967 Urban League study of the Detroit riot area found that 82% believed that there was some form of police brutality.

Apparently, fear of police hostility persists among people of color. Things have improved much since the 1960s. We can also tell that minorities suffer from higher levels of police use of force and harassment because they file a disproportionate number of citizen complaints against the police.

Walker, Spohn, and Delone (2000, p. 289) claim:

> Pervasive evidence indicates that racial minorities suffer discrimination at the hands of the police. They are more likely than whites to be shot and killed, arrested, and victimized by excessive physical force. In addition, there is evidence of police misconduct directed at racial minorities, as well as evidence that police departments fail to discipline officers found guilty of misconduct.

Studies show that minorities in the United States are more likely to have force used against them by the police (Geller and Toch 1995). In 1999, Caucasians comprised 78% of all people who had face-to-face contacts with the police but only 58.9% of all people who experienced force; African Americans were 10.6% of all people who had face-to-face contacts with the police but 22.5% of all people who experienced force; and Hispanics accounted for 8% of all people who had face-to-face contacts with the police in but 15.5% of all people who experienced force. Thus, African Americans and Hispanics are overrepresented among people who experience force.

African Americans are also most likely to be shot and killed by the police, followed by Hispanics and then Caucasians (Geller and Scott 1992). Disparities in police involvement in shootings have lessened since the Supreme Court abolished the fleeing felon rule in the 1985 case *Tennessee v. Garner*. Walker, Spohn, and Delone (2000) suggest that since this case, police officers are less able to justify shooting a fleeing felon on the basis of his or her race alone as a sign of dangerousness. Thus, the law has made it more difficult for police to use their own stereotypes to inform split-second decisions about whether or not to kill a suspect.

The 1999 and 2000 shootings of Amadou Diallo and Malcolm Ferguson, two unarmed African American men, by New York City police show that questionable police shootings still persist. These two men were shot only two blocks away from each other by the New York City Police Department's Street Narcotics Enforcement Unit. Given that both men were unarmed, the police have been accused of using excessive force. Although the four officers in the first case, who shot a combined 41 rounds at the fleeing Diallo, were acquitted of criminal charges because they shot Diallo as he reached for his wallet (which the officers thought was a gun), many Americans are not satisfied with the verdicts, and marches on New York City and Washington, DC, were organized in protest of these shootings.

I do not bring these cases up to question whether they were justified shootings. Technically, the officers followed their training and acted in an appropriate manner given their beliefs that the men were armed and their fear for their own personal safety. Yet I find the shootings unjustifiable, not because they did not follow proper procedure but, instead, because the situation that precipitated the shooting should never have happened. It is never appropriate for police to approach a suspect (who is presumed innocent) in a militaristic manner, wearing all black and with weapons drawn. The *war on crime* cannot actually be fought like a war, because the United States is not a war zone and its citizens will not tolerate this on their own soil.

The report by the U.S. Department of Justice (1996) states, "When police go beyond reasonable force to use excessive force during an arrest or in precipitous response, as during the decades of protest demonstrations involving labor, civil rights, or other controversial issues, citizens become victims of police, and the public's confidence in a police force can plummet." I now turn to the issue of how citizens view the police.

DIFFERENTIAL VIEWS OF THE POLICE

An outcome of even innocent bias in policing is that those who are most subjected to police activity will likely view the police differently than those who are not generally targeted by the police (Weitzer and Tuch 1999). Even in the wake of all of the recent stories about police corruption and excessive use of force by the police, you may be surprised to learn that most Americans generally have a positive view of the police.

Data published in the *Sourcebook of Criminal Justice Statistics* (2003) show that when asked how they would rate the honesty and ethical standards of people in various professions, Americans rank police near the top. Table 6.4 shows that 59% of Americans rank police as very high or high, 33% rank them as average, and only 8% rank them as low or very low. This puts police behind only firefighters, members of the U.S. military, nurses, and clergy, and ahead of more than a dozen other professions. Additionally, Table 6.4 illustrates that 58% of Americans have a great deal or quite a lot of confidence in police to protect them from violent crime, versus only 31% who have not very much confidence and 9% who have none at all. Additionally, Americans seem satisfied with police performance in their own communities. In response to the question, "How much respect do you have for the police in your area?" 60% said a great deal, 30% said some, and only 9% indicated hardly any respect. To the question, "How would you rate the police in your community?" 68% reported either excellent or good for police responding to calls, 67% for police not using excessive force, and 73% for police being helpful/friendly. Sixty-six percent reported either

TABLE 6.4

Americans' Views of the Police (2002)

Honesty and ethical standards	
Very high or high	59%
Average	33%
Low or very low	8%
Rating of the police in community	
Being helpful/friendly	73% excellent/good
Responding to calls	68% excellent/good
Not using excessive force	67% excellent/good
Treating people fairly	66% excellent/good
Solving crime	61% excellent/good
Confidence in police to protect from violent crime	
A great deal/a lot	58%
Not very much	31%
None	9%

SOURCE: Sourcebook of Criminal Justice Statistics (2003).

excellent or good to police treating people fairly and 6% to police preventing crime. Finally, 61% reported either excellent or good to police solving crime.

Despite this good news for police, there seems to be variation in views of police by race and other demographic characteristics. For example, whereas 63% of Caucasians report having a great deal or quite a lot of confidence in the police, only 31% of African Americans report that they do. At the same time, only 6% of Caucasians have very little confidence in the police, versus 28% of African Americans. Additionally, whereas 62% of Caucasians would rate the honesty and ethical standards of police as very high or high, only 41% of African Americans would. To the question, "Do you think the police in your community treat all races fairly?" 57% of Americans answer yes, but the difference between the races is apparent: 61% of Caucasians report that they think the police treat all races fairly, versus 41% of Hispanics and only 43% of African Americans.

To the question, "Are there any situations you can imagine in which you would approve of a policeman striking an adult male citizen?" 66% of Americans answer yes. The percentage of Caucasians who answer yes (71%) is higher than that of African Americans (44%). It is also higher for those who earn more money each year than for those who make less. For example, 77% of those who make $50,000 or more per year say that they can imagine approving of a policeman striking an adult male citizen, versus 56% of those who make less than $20,000 per year.

What accounts for these different views of police in the United States? Could they reflect differential treatment at the hands of police? As I have shown, there is evidence that people of color are disproportionately likely to suffer at the hands of the police. Extensive human rights abuses by police against poor minorities (such as immigrants) have been documented and reported by various agencies such as Amnesty International (e.g., see *The Economist* 1998b; Federal Bureau of Investigation 1994). Although Constitutional constraints are placed on the use of force by law enforcement officers (e.g., see Hall 1992), the abuse of police discretion and the existence of racial bias in policing may subvert such restraints.

According to Ross (1999), Caucasian officers are most likely to be resisted, and the average person who resists police authority is a 22-year-old male. African Americans are disproportionately likely to resist the police, as they make up less than 13% of the population but 43% of suspects who resist. It is unclear why African Americans are more likely to resist than Caucasians, but it is not inconceivable that African Americans may fear police more than Caucasians do. This may stem both from deep-seated historical roots of police oppression and brutality against minorities and from the recent stories of widespread police corruption in major American cities.

African Americans and poorer Americans do report being more afraid that they will be stopped and arrested by the police in circumstances in which they are completely innocent. Whereas 21% of all Americans are afraid of this, 42% of African Americans are afraid, versus only 16% of Caucasians. More than one-third (36%) of Americans who earn annual salaries of $15,000 or less report that they are afraid that they will be stopped and arrested by the police even when they are completely innocent, versus only 16% of those who earn over $75,000 per year.

Finally, in response to the question, "Do you think there is any police brutality in your area?" 30% of Americans say yes. This includes 53% of African Americans who answer yes, versus only 28% of Caucasians. The percentage of people who say yes is also higher for urban dwellers (46%) than for those who live in the suburbs (30%) and in rural areas (15%). This means that there is a greater perception among minorities and people who live in cities that police brutality is a problem.

CORRUPTION IN AMERICAN POLICING

Corruption, a perversion of policing stemming from a lack of integrity or honesty, is widespread and highly likely to affect poor people and people of color. Goldstein (1975, p. 3) defines *corruption* as a misuse of police authority "in a manner designed to produce personal gain." That is, corruption results in some benefit to the officer, even if the benefit is only emotional.

One recent example shocked even those who had a negative view of police to begin with. In the summer of 1997, a Haitian immigrant, Abner Louima, was attacked by four police officers. Two officers used the baton of one of the officers to sodomize Louima and then shoved the baton into his mouth, knocking out several of his teeth, as if they hated him personally. These officers were fired and convicted on criminal charges. Is this type of police attack common?

In fact, we do not know how extensive and prevalent police corruption is in the United States because problems such as citizen mistreatment and falsification of records and evidence have never been subjected to a national study (Donziger 1996, p. 163). However, there are numerous well-known examples, particularly within larger American cities, of alarming corruption in American police departments (see the Issue in Depth at the end of this chapter). For example, the Mollen Commission (1994) in New York found evidence of police involvement in theft, drug trafficking, drug use, falsification of police reports, lying in court, and police brutality. Shockingly, the most common form of corruption in New York was not police brutality (although the city has lost over $100 million in lawsuits recently for brutality); rather, it was falsifying police records and testimony at criminal trials, a practice known as *testilying,* whereby officers often made up testimony to ensure criminal convictions. They would invent stories to justify their illegal and unethical police techniques, which violated suspects' Constitutional rights.

There can be no greater threat to justice—including the presumption of innocence and equality before the law—than such police misconduct. Imagine yourself, an innocent citizen, facing arrest, charges, and the threat of criminal prosecution for crimes you did not commit. Because you happened to be in the wrong place at the wrong time (e.g., in an inner-city neighborhood where police were patrolling), and because a police officer lied in his reports and is willing to lie at trial, you know you are likely to be convicted. What would you do? Would you consider accepting a lesser sentence through a plea bargain? I return to the issue of how plea bargaining interferes with justice in Chapter Seven.

Other large police departments have witnessed major corruption scandals, as well. In Washington, DC, partly as a result of a massive hiring of unqualified officers, some of whom even had criminal records, since 1989 more than 200 police officers have been arrested and charged with crimes, including 79 officers in 1993 (Harriston and Flaherty 1994). Departments that were faced with losing millions of dollars in federal funding if they did not hire more officers are the same ones that ended up hiring some very bad people.

In Philadelphia in 1995, officers confessed to planting evidence, personally profiting from the illegal drug trade, and making false arrests. This led to the reexamination of 2,000 criminal cases that may have led to wrongful convictions because of bad policing. Additionally, nearly 200 police officers in New Orleans were disciplined for their questionable activities, and 4 were charged with murder related to their involvement in drug offenses (Cromwell 1995). The Christopher Commission in Los Angeles found "a significant number of LAPD officers who repeatedly misuse[d] force and persistently ignore[d] the written policies and guidelines of the Department regarding force" (Christopher 1991).

More recently, Bernard Parks, chief of police for Los Angeles, issued the report of the Rampart Area Corruption Incident. This involved police officers being involved in a bank robbery, false imprisonment and beating of a handcuffed arrestee at a police substation, and the theft of 3 kilograms of cocaine from a police evidence room (see the Issue in Depth at the end of this chapter).

The most recent allegations of corruption revolve around the planting of cocaine in the automobiles of unsuspecting Mexican immigrant laborers in Dallas, Texas, and the framing of dozens of African Americans in Tulia, Texas, for drug crimes they did not commit. In Dallas, Police Chief Terrell Bolton admitted that "bricks of cocaine" seized as evidence actually turned out to be ground sheetrock. Two undercover police officers and a paid informant who received $200,000 for his tips reported that drugs had been sold or shown to them, which led to dozens of arrests. Prosecutors dismissed 86 drug cases and released dozens of defendants (all of them Mexican immigrants or legal Hispanic residents). In Tulia, 43 residents of the small town were arrested for alleged drug offenses (40 of them were African Americans, accounting for 10% of the entire town's African American population). The only evidence against them was the testimony of one undercover officer, Tom Coleman, who worked alone and had no audio tapes, video surveillance, or eyewitnesses. Essentially, these people were framed and have all subsequently been released.

Amazingly, the National Criminal Justice Commission reports that in several of the cases in Los Angeles, superiors were to some degree aware of the police corruption, yet decided not to intervene because of their fear of bad press (Donziger 1996). Meanwhile, citizens were learning about corruption firsthand from the actions of the officers on the streets. Daily activities are far more important to the way police are perceived by citizens than public relations campaigns or bumper stickers aimed at promoting partnerships between citizens and the police (Wrobleski and Hess 2000).

Unfortunately, several aspects of police corruption differentially affect the poor and citizens of color, which may explain the differential view of police by people of color and the poor. Police use of force is a significant problem in our inner cities, where the poor and African Americans are more likely to reside. Not surprisingly, then, in the 1990s, a majority of adults believed that the police were more likely to beat minorities than Caucasians (National Association for the Advancement of Colored People [NAACP] 1993). This is why the authors of the NAACP report claimed that African Americans were more likely to be shot by police and bitten by police dogs and, thus, concluded that the "risk of abuse, mistreatment or even death" accompanied any minority interaction with the police (p. vi).

Current law enforcement strategies revolving around zero-tolerance approaches exacerbate such problems. For example, the National Criminal Justice Commission discusses an antigang sweep of streets called Operation Sunrise, which led to 63 arrests in Los Angeles. Of those arrested, only 1% were charged with a violent felony. Such efforts were characterized as part of the "squeegee strategy," named after the street dwellers who, uninvited, wash the windows of cars that stop at red lights on city streets (Donziger 1996, p. 169).

Zero-tolerance policing runs counter to community policing and logical crime prevention efforts. To whatever degree street sweeps are viewed by citizens as brutal, suspect, militaristic, or the biased efforts of "outsiders," citizens will be discouraged from taking active roles in community-building activities and crime prevention initiatives in conjunction with the police. Perhaps this is why the communities that most need neighborhood watch programs are least likely to be populated by residents who take active roles in them (Sherman et al. 1997). Zero-tolerance policing will fail because its practice destroys several important requisites for successful community policing, namely, police accountability, openness to the public, and community cooperation (Cox and Wade 1998, p. 106).

Some link these types of police corruption to the unique nature of policing, particularly the *police subculture* that "exalts loyalty over integrity" and "a hostility and alienation between the police and the community in certain precincts which breeds an 'Us versus Them' mentality" (Mollen Commission 1994). Walker (1998, p. 15) argues that this allows police officers to treat suspects as if they did not have the same Constitutional rights as the rest of us. This police subculture results in part from the nature of police work, but also from how citizens interact with police.

A subculture is a group of people in a larger society with its own way of life, norms, beliefs, attitudes, and values. The existence of a police subculture suggests that in some very real way, police are different from "civilians." These differences are attributable in part to the work environment of policing. According to Cole and Smith (2000), the main elements of the police subculture include the following.

- *Working personality of the officer:* The personality of the officer changes over time as he or she is exposed to the threat of danger and is forced to exert his or her authority over citizens who do not automatically defer to the officer's authority.
- *Social isolation:* Police officers separate themselves from civilians professionally and personally because of the nature of their jobs. In part, this is because they are expected to live exemplary lives and are always on duty. Police officers use technical jargon to discuss their work and often literally speak in codes.
- *Stress:* Police officers face numerous sources of stress and thus suffer high rates of suicide, divorce, heart disease, alcohol and other drug abuse.

Other research suggests that the police officer personality can be described as being authoritarian and cynical in nature (Skolnick 1966). Officers can also become suspicious, insecure, hostile, and prejudiced, in addition to several other characteristics (Schmalleger 2001).

Cox and Wade (1998, p. 98) claim, "Many segments of the public are uncooperative with the police and some openly hostile a good deal of the time. Other segments criticize the police for being unable to do anything about the crime problem or appear largely apathetic regardless of police action or inaction." Thus, the police become "equally critical of and hostile toward some segments of the population." Others link police corruption to a lack of understanding on the part of the police of the people they are policing. Consistent with this are the findings that the largest police departments show more indications of police corruption and also tend to be the least diverse in terms of race and ethnicity (Donziger 1996).

CONCLUSION

Police, the first component of the criminal justice network, are responsible for enforcing the criminal law. Despite the presence of the Law Enforcement Code of Conduct, which stipulates how police must behave, the practice of law enforcement in the United States results in innocent biases against the poor and people of color. This innocent bias owes itself to the use of police discretion, the particular focus of police on certain types of crimes, the location of police on the streets of the United States, the use of police profiling, and policing of the war on drugs. Not only does policing create innocent bias, which in turn results in injustice, but also it is highly ineffective at reducing crime. Some police behavior, as well intentioned as it certainly is, is inconsistent with the goals of the U.S. criminal justice network.

ISSUE IN DEPTH
Corruption in the Criminal Justice Network

Recall the discussion in Chapter Two about the role of politics in criminal justice. The American criminal justice network was created by and is currently maintained by people with tremendous power. For example, legislators are the only people in the country who can define your behavior as a crime, even if it is relatively harmless or harms only you. Police officers are the only people in the country who can legally use force against you—in some cases, lethal force—if you violate the law. Criminal justice processes in the United States can thus be viewed as a system of oppressive power: "Criminal justice is, literally, state power. It is police, guns, prisons, the electric chair" (L. Friedman 1993, p. 462). The problem with power is that it "corrupts; and power also has an itch to suppress."

With corruption comes wrongdoing and, potentially, criminal acts on the part of criminal justice officials. These crimes of the criminal justice network itself are virtually ignored, but according to Henderson and Simon (1994, p. xi), "[T]here is clearly evidence that deviance, corruption, and immorality exist in the system." Crimes within the criminal justice network are "remarkably frequent" and "constant throughout the system" (p. iii). They include corruption, abuse of authority, jury tampering, bribe taking and payoffs, brutality, sexual exploitation of prisoners, and formal approval of such acts by administrators. Such acts cause physical, financial, and moral harm.

Because power corrupts, "politicians probably represent the single most corrupt group involved with the criminal justice system" (Henderson and Simon 1994, p. 61). Yet because of the long history of corruption in American policing, it is the component of the criminal justice network most often identified with corruption (e.g., see Fyfe and Skolnick 1993).

Research into police corruption has "consistently unearthed substantial and wide-ranging forms of police bribery" (e.g., see Coleman 1990), including about a hundred drug-related cases that are heard by courts each year (Henderson and Simon 1994). Drug law enforcement may present the most significant opportunity for police bribery (Gray 2001; Kellner 1988). Police corruption also includes violation of search-and-seizure laws, evidence tampering (J. Douglas and Johnson 1977), and perjured testimony (Kittel 1986). Abuse of authority in corrections also has been described as a "nationwide problem" (Henderson and Simon 1994, p. 47).

A recent example of a highly publicized corruption case in criminal justice is the Rampart Scandal in Los Angeles. According to the "Board of Inquiry into the Rampart Corruption Incident, Executive Summary":

a. In late 1997 and early 1998, three incidents occurred in which Los Angeles Police Officers were identified as suspects in serious criminal activity. The incidents began on November 6, 1997, when three suspects robbed a Los Angeles Bank of America. The investigation into that robbery led to the arrest of Officer

David Mack, who was assigned to West Los Angeles Area at the time, and his girlfriend, an employee of the bank. The second incident occurred on February 26, 1998, and involved the false imprisonment and beating of a handcuffed arrestee at the Rampart Substation. The officer who beat the suspect was Rampart CRASH Officer Brian Hewitt. Two other CRASH officers, one of whom was Ethan Cohan, were present and acquiesced to the beating. The third incident involved the March 2, 1998, theft of three kilograms of cocaine from the Department's Property Division. The investigation into that theft led to the arrest of Officer Rafael Perez, who was assigned to Rampart CRASH.

b. The investigations into these incidents disclosed that the suspect officers were closely associated, either as working partners or close friends, and all but one of them were assigned to Rampart Area. The only exception, David Mack, had previously been assigned to Rampart and was a close friend of Rafael Perez. Due to the seriousness of the criminal activity, commonality among the officers and potential for involvement of more Department employees, Chief of Police Bernard C. Parks formed a special criminal Task Force in May 1998 to investigate these incidents.

c. Hewitt and Cohan were terminated following their Board of Rights hearings, but the third officer was found not guilty by his board. (In Los Angeles, a three-member Board of Rights, composed of two staff or command officers and one community member, hears allegations of major misconduct. Each accused officer may select a separate Board and the Chief of Police can impose no greater penalty than the Board recommends.) The case against Hewitt has been presented to the District Attorney on two occasions, but was rejected both times for a lack of sufficient evidence. The District Attorney's Office is now reconsidering the case. The case has also been presented to the State Attorney General's Office, which declined to take further action on the matter. David Mack was convicted in federal court of bank robbery and resigned from the Department in lieu of termination. He has been sentenced to 14 years and 3 months in prison. The $722,000 stolen in the robbery has not been recovered, and his two accomplices have not been identified.

d. Rafael Perez's first trial resulted in a jury deadlock, eight to four in favor of a guilty verdict. The Department's investigative efforts during and after the first trial produced additional evidence that Perez was responsible for three additional cocaine thefts. He was also identified as being closely associated with known narcotics dealers, one of whom accompanied Perez, Mack, and a third officer on a trip to Las Vegas immediately after Mack committed the bank robbery.

e. As the evidence against Perez mounted, Perez offered to plead guilty to the charges and cooperate with the LAPD Task Force detectives in exchange for a reduced prison sentence. Perez indicated that he could provide information on other Rampart officers who were involved in serious criminal activity and misconduct. Just prior to the second trial in September 1999, an agreement was reached for a reduced prison sentence in return for Perez' guilty plea and cooperation in providing information on corruption activities within the Department. Subsequent interviews of Perez have indicated that much deeper corruption was occurring at Rampart than was originally suspected. The Task Force, in conjunction with the Los Angeles District Attorney's Office and Office of the United States Attorney General, is pursuing that investigation. On September 21, 1999, Chief Parks convened a Board of Inquiry (BOI) to assess the totality of the Rampart corruption incident without infringing on the work of the Task Force.

The final report was organized around more than 100 recommendations for positive change within the LAPD, in the following areas.

- Testing and screening of police officer candidates
- Personnel practices
- Personnel investigations and management of risk
- Corruption investigations
- Operational controls
- Anticorruption inspections and audits
- Ethics and integrity training
- Job-specific training

Despite the scores of breakdowns within the LAPD that led to this corruption scandal, the final report recommended that no outside investigation by the FBI take place.

According to news reports, LAPD Rampart officers routinely and unnecessarily punched, kicked, and choked suspects in an effort to intimidate them. The officers then fabricated stories in police reports to account for their victims' injuries. The corruption probe uncovered information about unjustified shootings, evidence planting, and even false arrests of innocent people. More than 50 convictions have been overturned, and more than 20 officers have been relieved of duty, have been fired, or have quit because of the scandal.

At a 1999 press conference, District Attorney Gil Garcetti expressed his concern about one very troubling aspect of the Rampart scandal—the fact that innocent people were coerced into confessing for crimes that they did not commit. Garcetti said, "It raises the specter, obviously, that they pleaded guilty to something [even though] they were telling their lawyer, 'I'm not guilty, I'm innocent.' That raises a question for everyone in the criminal justice system."

Because crimes of the criminal justice network are not widely studied, we do not know precisely why they occur, but here are some likely reasons: There is only a small chance of such acts leading to punishment, criminal justice personnel become jaded over time in their fight against crime, and these crimes are supported to some degree by institutional factors (Henderson and Simon 1994).

This book does not directly address the issue of criminality within the criminal justice network. Instead, I argue that even with completely "noncriminal" criminal justice personnel—that is, even in the absence of corruption—the criminal justice network fails to do justice or reduce crime effectively. At the same time, the criminal justice network tends to focus its attention on acts that, though harmful, are not the most harmful behaviors in the United States. All of this amounts to what I consider a "crime"—not in the legal sense, of course, but in the sense that it is not right or just.

Discussion Questions

1. Identify the main roles of police officers in the United States, and provide a few examples of behaviors that fit into each role.
2. To which role do police officers devote most of their time? Why?
3. Compare the main functions of local police versus state and federal police.
4. Do you think that more police on the streets will reduce crime in the United States? Why or why not?
5. What is the exclusionary rule? How does it protect you?
6. List some exceptions to the exclusionary rule. Do you think that these exceptions are reasonable? Why or why not?
7. In what ways do police serve crime victims?
8. What is community policing?
9. Contrast the community police officer with the stereotypical view of the police officer.
10. Discuss the main tenets of Sir Robert Peel.
11. What does the term *innocent bias* mean?
12. What factors produce innocent bias in policing?
13. What do you think are the most important elements of the Law Enforcement Code of Conduct? Explain.
14. Why is it so important that police have discretion in deciding who to stop, detain, arrest, and so on?
15. On which types of crimes are American police most focused? Why?
16. Do you think there is a valid rationale for police profiling? Explain.
17. Why do more police officers work for local governments (e.g., cities, counties) than for states or the federal government?
18. Explain the difference between a *stop* and an *arrest*.
19. Explain why people of color are disproportionately more likely to be stopped by and arrested by the police.
20. In your opinion, when has excessive force been used by police against a citizen?
21. Why do you think that Americans rate the police so highly in public opinion polls?
22. How does zero-tolerance policing run counter to the notion of community policing?
23. Identify and discuss the main elements of the police subculture.
24. What produces corruption in the criminal justice network?

CHAPTER SEVEN

RIGHT TO TRIAL?
INJUSTICE IN PRETRIAL
AND TRIAL PROCEDURES

INTRODUCTION

This chapter continues the assessment of the criminal justice process by examining the operation of American courts. I begin with a brief examination of the U.S. court structure and then go on to discuss what courts actually do. Because of an imbalance in the courts in favor of the government, criminal proceedings are inherently biased against individual defendants. Additionally, because most defendants are indigent and therefore are appointed defense attorneys, biases against the poor and people of color continue in the courts. The institutions of bail, plea bargaining, and trials often do not promote the ideal goals of the criminal justice network. Trial processes also are fundamentally tilted in the favor of the state and the wealthy. Finally, I examine the issue of wrongful conviction to identify why it occurs.

WHAT ARE THE COURTS?

The Organization of Courts in the United States

Because of the separation of powers clause of the U.S. Constitution, the United States has a *dual court system*; that is, federal and state governments each have their own distinct court systems, and the two systems operate independently of each other (Marion 1995). As of 1998, there were 208 court systems in the states; Washington, DC; and Puerto Rico, including 71 statewide trial courts systems with general jurisdiction. There were also 132 courts of appeal.

State and federal courts can be differentiated by their *jurisdiction*—that is, where they have "the authority or power to hear a case" (Cox and Wade 1998, p. 130). Where a case is heard depends on what type of law is violated. Crimes against states are typically handled in state courts, whereas crimes against the federal government are held in federal courts. And yes, cases can be heard in both courts without violating suspects' Fifth Amendment rights to freedom from double jeopardy. If both federal and state laws are violated, both courts can and often do hold trials.

Courts with *general jurisdiction* can hear most types of cases, whether they be criminal or civil matters, whereas courts of *specific* or *limited jurisdiction* can only hear cases within their specific expertise (e.g., juvenile courts hear only juvenile cases). Courts with original jurisdiction are typically trial courts, because their jurisdiction grants them the power to hear facts of cases initially. *Appellate courts*, or courts of appeals, do not decide matters of fact but, rather, matters of law. They hear cases that were first heard by courts with original jurisdiction and then appealed. The power of appeals courts lies in their ability to set precedents. Once a decision is made, a *precedent* is created that, under the principle of *stare decisis* (let the decision stand), must be followed by all other courts within the same jurisdiction.

There is no stereotypical court in the United States because the system is decentralized. Instead, there is a variety of types of courts, each with their own distinct names, purposes, and functions served (Cole and Smith 2000; Schmalleger 2001). Federal courts in the United States include 94 trial courts (called *district courts*) and 12 appeals courts (called *circuit courts*). Of course, the United States also has an appeals "court of last resort," the U.S. Supreme Court, made up of 9 justices. State courts include trial courts of original jurisdiction, intermediate courts of appeals in about half of the states, and appellate courts of last resort (state supreme courts). As indicated earlier, not all states have intermediate courts of appeals, but states with larger populations tend to have them to relieve the burden on the state supreme courts (Chapper and Hanson 1990). State courts are very diverse; Cox and Wade (1998, p. 132) write that the term that best describes state courts is *variation* because "there is no one state that adequately depicts the other fifty systems."

Most criminal justice scholars also differentiate between lower courts (e.g., courts that hear traffic cases or misdemeanors) and higher-level courts (e.g., courts that hear felony cases). They are differentiated on the basis of how they ideally process defendants. Lower courts tend to emphasize speed and routinization of cases, so that large numbers of cases are disposed of

quickly through fines, community service, and other such sanctions. Higher-level courts are ideally less characterized by "assembly-line justice" and more accurately described as adversarial. The reality of even higher-level trial courts for most defendants, as you will see later in this chapter, is that trials are the rare exception to the assembly-line nature of plea bargaining.

Types of crimes handled by federal and state courts are often very different. In 2001, state prosecutor offices closed more than 2.3 million felony cases and 7 million misdemeanor cases (Bureau of Justice Statistics 2003). Of all felony defendants in the nation's largest 75 counties in 1998, the largest percentage were charged with drug offenses (37%), followed by property offenses (29%), violent offenses (24%), and public order offenses (10%) (Sourcebook of Criminal Justice Statistics 2003). In federal district courts, prosecutors investigated cases against 121,818 suspects in 2001. Of these, 40% were for public order offenses, 31% were for drug offenses, 24% were for property offenses, and only 5% were for violent offenses. Accused drug offenders (78%) were more likely than accused violent offenders (60%), accused public order offenders (56%), and accused property offenders (53%) to be prosecuted of all offenders in federal courts in 2000.

State and federal courts convict most defendants who come before them. In the nation's largest 75 counties, state courts convicted 68% of all defendants. Conviction rates tend to be highest in state courts for drug offenses (72%). Almost all convictions come through plea bargains rather than jury trials (less than 6% of all convictions with the exception of murder came by way of guilty pleas). Defendants charged with murder are most likely to go to trial. More than three-fourths (77%) of trials end in convictions.

State and federal courts convicted nearly 1 million adults of felonies in 2000. Table 7.1 shows the types of felonies leading to convictions in each court in 2000. In the nation's 75 largest counties, most defendants (87%) were not convicted of violent crimes. Drug trafficking (15%) and other drug offenses (17%) made up the largest portion of felony convictions in state courts, whereas crimes such as rape and murder made up 1% or less of felony convictions (Bureau of Justice Statistics 2003).

TABLE 7.1
Convictions in American Courts (2000)

	State Courts	Federal Courts
All offenses	924,700 (100%)	68,156 (100%)
Vilolent offenses	173,200 (18.7%)	2,676 (3.9%)
Murder/manslaughter	8,600 (0.9%)	345 (0.5%)
Sexual assault/rape	31,500 (3.4%)	347 (0.5%)
Robbery	36,800 (4%)	1,514 (2.2%)
Aggravated assault	79,400 (8.6%)	286 (0.4%)
Property offenses	262,000 (28.3%)	12,814 (18.8%)
Burglary	79,300 (8.6%)	58 (0.0009%)
Theft	100,000 (10.8%)	1,470 (2.2%)
Motor vehicle theft	11,900 (1.3%)	150 (0.2%)
Fraud/forgery/embezzlement	82,700 (8.9%)	9,085 (13.3%)
Drug offenses	319,700 (34.6%)	24,886 (36.5%)
Public order offenses	n/a	19,683 (28.8%)
Other offenses	141,600 (15.3%)	18,689 (27.4%)

SOURCE: Sourcebook of Criminal Justice Statistics (2003).

At the federal level, only 66,452 cases were actually filed in 2002 (Sourcebook of Criminal Justice Statistics 2003). The largest percentage was for drug crimes (28.9%), whereas only 16% were for some form of white-collar crime (12% for fraud, 2% for forgery and counterfeiting, 2% for embezzlement). Of all felony charges, 43% were for drug offenses.

Thus, the majority of people convicted of felonies in each court were not convicted for violent crimes. Compare this with media coverage of crime in Chapter Five. Perhaps you are surprised that at this stage of the criminal justice process, most cases are not violent in nature.

Not surprisingly, in light of our examination of American police, court defendants are disproportionately poor; *indigents* make up more than 80% of people charged with felonies in the United States (Gaines, Kaune, and Miller 2000). According to the Bureau of Justice Statistics, in 1996 and 1998, 82% of felony defendants in state courts within the nation's largest 75 counties and 66% of federal defendants were given publicly financed defense attorneys.

Characteristics of both federal and state court defendants demonstrate who our criminal justice network pursues. In federal courts, most felony defendants were men (86%), African American (57%), and younger than 35 years of age (66%). African Americans made up 60% of defendants charged with violent crimes, 53% of defendants charged with property crimes, 59% of defendants charged with drug crimes, and 52% of defendants charged with public order crimes. Also, Hispanics (41%) and African Americans (25%) were disproportionately likely to be sentenced under federal sentencing guidelines in 2000 (Sourcebook of Criminal Justice Statistics 2003). In state courts, 83% of convicted felons were men in 2000, and 44% were African American. This includes 44% of violent felony convictions, 39% of property felony convictions, and 46% of drug felony convictions.

What Courts Do

When citizens are arrested by police, they become clients for the courts. What do courts do?

> Simply stated, a court is a place where arguments are settled. The argument may be between the federal government and a corporation accused of violating environmental regulations, between business partners, between a criminal and the state, or any other number of parties. The court provides an environment in which the basis of the argument can be settled through the application of the law. (Gaines, Kaune, and Miller 2000, p. 270)

In deciding arguments, the primary function of American criminal courts is to determine the legal guilt of the accused—that is, to determine if a person is guilty of committing a crime beyond a reasonable doubt (Peoples 2000; Stuckey, Robertson, and Wallace 2001). The National Criminal Justice Commission writes of the courts: "Their responsibility is to be fair to all citizens charged with a crime and to impose a just punishment on those found guilty" (Donziger 1996, p. 181). These are the key functions served by American courts.

But courts do much more than determine guilt or innocence. They also are "responsible for determining bail, conducting preliminary hearings (or grand juries), ruling on the admissibility of evidence, and determining the appropriate sentence when a finding of guilty has been reached" (Cox and Wade 1998, p. 130).

Essentially, courts take over where the police leave off. As I show later in this chapter, the U.S. courts are demonstrably biased against poor people and people of color. Pretrial procedures such as bail and plea bargaining, as well as trial procedures, are biased against relatively powerless groups. This bias begins with an imbalance in the power of the courtroom workgroup and occasionally results in wrongful convictions (see the Issue in Depth at the end of this chapter).

The Courtroom Workgroup

To ensure justice, the court is supposed to be impartial. Ideally, this means that neutral actors are involved in objectively determining the relevant facts of each case in order to ensure that the guilty are convicted and the innocent are not. The importance of this is explained by Gaines, Kaune, and Miller (2000, p. 271): "In theory, each party in a courtroom dispute must have an equal chance to present its case and must be secure in the belief that no outside factors are going to influence the decision rendered by the court."

Keep in mind as you read this chapter that the people who work in the courts are very different from the people who are typically processed through the courts. Minorities and women are underrepresented in American courtroom workgroups (Bonsignore et al. 1998; Spire 1990). Graham (2000) demonstrates how African Americans are underrepresented as attorneys and judges. Thus, much as legislators are not representative of Americans (see Chapter Three), those who work to convict or acquit suspected criminals also are not representative of Americans. Whether this is sufficient to explain injustice in the courts is unclear, but an unrepresentative courtroom workgroup is probably less likely to produce an outcome of justice than a representative workgroup.

Formal rules of procedure also are supposed to assist with objectivity. For example, "there are limitations as to how evidence may be introduced, what types of evidence may be admitted, and what types of questions may be asked" (Cox and Wade 1998, p. 130). Later in this chapter I return to whether the American criminal courts really act in an objective manner. First, I examine who works in the courts.

The *courtroom workgroup* is a term used to describe the main actors in this process within the criminal courts—the prosecutor, the defense attorney, and the judge (Cole and Smith 2000; Cox and Wade 1998; Schmalleger 2001; Walker 1998). A workgroup can be understood as a collective of individuals who interact, share goals, follow court norms, and develop interpersonal relationships (Fleming, Nardulli, and Eisenstein, 1992). This concept is important because it helps us understand why the workgroup's overriding concern is speeding up the process and getting rid of cases as efficiently as possible rather than "doing justice."

Ideally, each member of the courtroom workgroup plays its own roles and has its own goals. In reality, each member's main job is not to rock the boat in the daily operations of American courts, which are described as follows:

> Every day, the same group of courthouse regulars assembles in the same courtroom, sits or stands in the same places, and performs the same tasks as the day before. The types of defendants and the nature of the crimes they are accused of committing also remain constant. Only the names of the victim, witnesses, and defendants are different. (Neubauer 1998, p. 41)

The prosecutor

The *prosecutor*, as a representative of the court, fights for the "people" in an effort to "get justice" (as an outcome) for the crime victim and the community. His or her main job is to decide whether to press charges on the basis of the amount of quality evidence available to obtain a conviction. If the prosecution decides to press criminal charges, the next decision is which charges to press. This decision will ultimately have a great effect on the resulting criminal sentence, as you will see in Chapter Eight.

Criminal charges come in the form of an *indictment* (if the state uses a grand jury system) or an *information* (in cases of a preliminary hearing). The primary difference between grand juries and preliminary hearings is that grand juries are one-sided presentations by the prosecution, whereas preliminary hearings are adversarial in nature. Some have called the grand jury a "rubber stamp" for the prosecutor because grand juries almost never fail to return an indictment. Both grand juries and preliminary hearings result in a determination of whether there is enough evidence to pursue the case further (e.g., to a criminal trial).

A prosecutor must consider numerous factors when deciding either to accept a case for prosecution or to reject the case. Most cases that come before prosecutors' offices do not lead to a prosecution. In fact, just under half of arrests lead to prosecution. Despite what you may have heard about "legal technicalities," most cases are in fact dropped because of a lack of high-quality evidence. Of course, decisions to prosecute do not emanate from formal rules but from informal relationships with people such as the police, victims, and other community members. This is another reason that it is imperative that positive relationships be established and maintained among citizens, police, and other criminal justice officials.

Walker (1998, p. 46) reviews the evidence of factors that influence prosecutors' decisions to accept cases for prosecution and concludes that the largest share of cases that are not prosecuted are dropped because of evidence problems—not enough high-quality evidence to obtain a conviction at trial. He claims that "due process problems—illegal searches or confessions—are not a major cause of rejections or dismissals." Thus, those who argue that legal technicalities should be disallowed may be off the mark. Pizzi (1999), in his book *Trials Without Truth*, claims that trials are too focused on winning and losing rather than on truth. One reform he advocates is eliminating the exclusionary rule as a means of convicting more guilty criminals. His reforms are aimed at achieving justice as an outcome rather than ensuring justice as a process. On the basis of the review of evidence in Chapter Six, I disagree that the exclusionary rule should be abolished.

The prosecutor also serves as *trial counsel for police* (fighting crime) and *house counsel for police* (giving legal advice) (Cole and Smith 2000). Examples of the role of trial counsel for the police include zealously prosecuting suspected criminals and pursuing community crime control interests to achieve justice as an outcome. Examples of the role of house counsel for the police include "providing legal advice to [the police], providing training for police on criminal law and legal processes, preparing drafts of search warrants and wiretapping applications, participating in decisions regarding court administration, and engaging in a wide variety of public information and community relations programs" (Holten and Jones 1982, p. 185). In both cases, the prosecutor can be accurately understood as a partner with the police in the fight against crime.

As a *representative of the court*, the prosecutor also must be concerned with justice as a process. A prosecutor is "obliged to protect the rights of the defendant" (Cox and Wade 1998, p. 148), just as a police officer is obligated to uphold the Constitutional rights of a suspect (Wrobleski and Hess 2000). There is evidence, however, that many prosecutors ignore possible indications of innocence of defendants simply to gain convictions and clear cases.

Prosecutors have tremendous power in the criminal justice process. This power imbalances the court in favor of the state rather than the defendant. "Ideally, this power is balanced by a duty of fairness and a recognition that the prosecutor's ultimate goal is not to win cases, but to see that justice is done" (Gaines, Kaune, and Miller 2000, p. 302). The American Bar Association (1993, 1997), for example, expects that prosecutors will "seek justice, not merely convict" criminals because they have the "responsibility of a minister of justice." Justice Sutherland wrote in *Berger v. United States* (1935) that the prosecutor "may prosecute with earnestness and vigor—indeed he should do so. But, while he may strike hard blows, he is not at liberty to strike foul ones."

Yet most prosecutors are also elected officials, meaning that at times they will be concerned with what they perceive their community wants, as well as with the underlying philosophy of the voters (DeFrances and Steadman 1998; Merlo and Benekos 2000). Gershman (2000, p. 286) demonstrates that the typical jury is biased toward the prosecution, meaning that jurors will be more tolerant of misconduct by prosecutors than by defense attorneys, including promises made about evidence in opening statements of a trial but not delivered during the trial and purposeful mention of inadmissable evidence. Ensuring high conviction rates sends a signal to the community that the prosecutor is tough on crime. The desire to be tough on crime while simultaneously being fair and making sure that innocent people are not convicted seem to conflict.

Are prosecutors biased against any particular group of people? That is, is there any evidence that they are more likely to press charges against some groups of people? The *Harvard Law Review* (1988) suggested that prosecutors sometimes abuse their discretion by upgrading charges against minorities and downgrading them against Caucasians. In Chapter Ten, you will see clear evidence of bias toward minorities in death penalty cases. The main source of this bias is prosecutor discretion.

The defense attorney

The *defense attorney* represents the "defendant" and has the main duty of being an advocate for the defendant. This is the main actor in the criminal justice process who is responsible for ensuring that Constitutional protections of the accused are upheld and protected. Defense attorneys are the actors in the court process responsible for upholding the due process function of the court, protecting "individuals from the unfair advantages that the government—with its immense resources—automatically enjoys in legal battles" (Gaines, Kaune, and Miller 2000, p. 271). Standard 4–1.2(b) of the American Bar Association's Standards for Criminal Justice (1991) states that the basic duty of the defense attorney is "to serve as the accused's counselor and advocate with courage and devotion, and render effective, quality representation." The ideal functions of defense attorneys include the following (Siegel 1998, pp. 487–88).

- Investigating the facts of the case against his or her client
- Preparing his or her client's case for trial
- Submitting motions in favor of his or her client's case
- Representing the defendant at trial
- Negotiating the sentence with the prosecutor if the client is convicted
- Appealing convictions

The reality is that these functions may be carried out by some defense attorneys but not by others. It all depends on what type of defense attorney a person can afford. At the state level, defense attorneys include *nationally known attorneys*, other *private attorneys*, and *courthouse regulars* (e.g., public defenders) (Cole and Smith 2000). There are generally three types of systems available to defend those who cannot hire their own attorneys:

- *public defender systems*—a salaried staff of government attorneys paid for by taxpayers
- *assigned counsel programs*—private attorneys assigned to particular cases by courts
- *contracting attorney programs*—private attorneys hired to defend a group of defendants for a specified period of time (Bureau of Justice Statistics 2003).

In the nation's 100 most populous counties, 90 had public defender programs, 89 had assigned counsel programs, and 42 had contract programs (Bureau of Justice Statistics 2003). Public defender offices in the nation's largest 100 counties employed 12,700 people in 1999. Defense attorneys for indigent clients handled 4.2 million cases in 1999, 80% of which were criminal cases. Public defenders handled 82% of these cases, followed by 15% by appointed attorneys and 3% contract attorneys.

At the federal level, the following types of defense are available for the indigent.

- *Panel attorneys*—appointed by the court from a list of attorneys on a case-by-case basis
- *Community defender organization*—incorporated service lawyers under grant by the Administrative Office of the U.S. Courts

Panel attorneys were available in all 94 districts, whereas community defender organizations were available in 74 districts. Of federal defendants, 36% used panel attorneys and 30% used attorneys from the Federal Defender Organization.

These systems are necessary primarily because the majority of defendants in criminal cases are indigents, or people who cannot afford their own attorneys. The Supreme Court, in *Gideon v. Wainwright* (1963), held that the right to fair trial was jeopardized if state court defendants were not granted assistance by defense. In *Mempa v. Rhay* (1967), the Supreme Court extended the right of indigents beyond trial to other critical stages of the criminal justice process, including arraignment, preliminary hearing, entering of the plea, sentencing, and first appeal.

The typical defendant is not a wealthy person out to beat the system: "The average defendant in a criminal proceeding is indigent and not capable of hiring the 'best attorney money can buy.'" Instead, he or she is assigned a courthouse regular, who is usually paid a very low salary, works in a depressing environment, and has very few support services available (Merlo and Benekos 2000, p. 57). Harrigan (2000, p. 319) writes that "the quality of state-provided representation seldom equals the representation you would obtain if you could afford to hire your own criminal lawyer." This is in part because they are "often so overloaded with cases they find it impossible to devote much of their time or effort to any specific case." Also, "because assigned lawyers get paid on a per-case basis rather than on an hourly basis, they have a great incentive to speed up the cases as much as possible." This led Blumberg (1967) to call many defense attorneys "double agents" and "cons" often working against the interests of their clients (Uphoff 2000). Others assert that public defenders do as well at defending their clients as private attorneys do (Hansom and Ostrom, 1993). In Chapter Ten, you will learn about how incompetent defense attorneys are one of the most significant problems in death penalty cases.

The judge

The *judge*, as leader of the courtroom workgroup, has the goal of ensuring that proper legal procedures are followed as a case is processed through the courts. The roles of judges include *adjudicator* (passes sentence), *negotiator* (referee between parties), and *administrator* (keeps up the docket). Judges decide if arrests are based on probable cause, inform charged suspects of their rights, determine if bail will be granted to defendants, rule on motions filed by the prosecution and the defense, officiate trials to make sure they are fair, and impose sentences on the legally guilty.

Ideally, judges embody justice and ensure due process, but in reality, judges spend most of their time in the administrative role, which includes such activities as preparing budgets, scheduling cases, supervising employees, and maintaining court records (Cole and Smith 2000; Cox and Wade 1998). Because of the number of cases they must handle, and because of the amount of time courthouse employees spend together, the group may generally share the overriding goal of disposing of cases as quickly as possible more often than they may fight for justice. As more and more citizens have "run-ins with the law"—that is, as more police are put on the street and as American police make more arrests—the courts suffer the consequences. Today, the courts are forced to handle too many cases. As a result, many cases are simply dismissed before they are even considered (Donziger 1996). Walker (1998, p. 13) writes, "The justice system can only handle so much business. It does not 'collapse' like a building. It keeps on going, but only through adjustments that are often undesirable."

AN IMBALANCE OF POWER IN THE COURT: FROM JUDGE TO PROSECUTION

The intimate nature of the daily operations of American courts makes the courtroom workgroup a "community" (Nardulli, Eisenstein, and Flemming 1988) because the members develop shared understandings of what cases should be worth and "reach a general consensus about how different kinds of cases should be handled" (Walker 1998, p. 51). This means that even though prosecutors and defense attorneys are supposed to be adversaries, they rarely act this way.

By examining the reality of courtroom interactions today, you can learn a great deal about American priorities. For example, it is clear that prosecutors have much more power in the criminal justice process than judges or defense attorneys. Power is the ability to influence actions of others (see Chapter Two). The judge is ideally the most powerful member of the court, in that he or she can decide matters of law that affect courtroom operations and in that he or she presides over trials: "Since they are deciding benefits, judges are political actors with power" (Marion 1995). Yet since the "final decision about whether an alleged offender will be brought to court rests with the prosecutor" exclusively, the prosecutor has an enormous amount of discretion and is clearly the most powerful member of the court. Cox and Wade (1998, p. 147) state, "The decision not to prosecute (*nollee prosequi*), in addition to the discretion in determining the number and severity of charges, renders the prosecutor a very powerful figure in the court process." Stated plainly, if the prosecutor decides not to prosecute a case, the defense attorney and judge will in essence have no say in the outcome of that case. It is the discretion of the prosecutor to act or not to act that gives him or her so much power (Albonetti 1987).

A former U.S. attorney general once claimed, "The prosecutor has more control over life, liberty, and reputation than any other person in America" (in Cox and Wade 1998, p. 147). This is especially true when large numbers of cases are sent from the police to courts. As American courts have become bogged down with more cases, judges have lost significant power, because they are even more reliant on prosecutors to determine which cases merit charges, trials, and justice (Marion 1995). The power of judges also has been significantly reduced by new sentencing rules (see Chapter Eight). Milovanovich (2000, p. 516) claims that the power of the prosecutor in the United States is essentially unchallenged.

Because of this imbalance of power in the court, justice is severely threatened. Ideally, if Americans value justice, due process, "innocent until proven guilty," Constitutional protections, and equality before the law, it seems that defense attorneys would have more power and a greater share of resources to ensure that their clients are processed fairly through the criminal justice network. Because most criminal defense attorneys work for the government (e.g., as public defenders), they have heavy caseloads, limited resources to investigate the facts of a case, and little or no financial incentive to take a case to trial (Casper 1972; Cole and Smith 2000). This may result in unequal justice for the rich and the poor: "The general suspicion is that equal justice is not available to rich and poor alike . . . indigents receive a lower quality of legal service, which results in their being more likely to suffer harsher penal sanctions than similarly situated defendants who can afford to buy good legal talent" (Sterling 1983, p. 166). Despite this suspicion, others assert that because public defenders are members of the courtroom workgroup, they have the advantage of assuring a reasonable sentence from prosecutors with whom they interact on a daily basis (Skolnick 1967; Wice 1985).

PRETRIAL PROCEDURES AND JUSTICE

Everything that goes on in the criminal justice process between arrest, booking, and the criminal trial is called the *pretrial phase* (Peoples 2000; Stuckey, Robertson, and Wallace 2001). The term can be misleading in that it is called *pretrial* whether or not a trial actually results. The pretrial phase contains two major decisions that must be made before a case can proceed to trial (or be disposed of through some other means). These two decisions concern the issuing of bail and whether a case gets plea bargained. Next, I examine each of these processes and demonstrate how each severely threatens justice.

Bail as an Injustice

First, there is the decision about bail. After suspects are arrested and brought to court to make an *initial appearance* (where they are notified of the charges against them and advised of their rights), they may be released from the supervision of the court through the process of bail. *Bail* is a specified sum of money paid to the court for suspects' release, to be paid back to the suspects if they return for their court date. That is, bail is not the same thing as a fine, because it is not meant to be a form of punishment. It is important to point out that people are not supposed to be punished unless they commit a crime (under the policy of *nulla poena sine crimine*). Instead, bail is meant to ensure the presence of the defendant at trial. The logic is that if suspects pay a sum of money to the court, they will come back to have the money returned.

Types of bail are described in the following box.

Types of bail

- *Percentage bail:* The defendant must pay only a percentage of the bail amount set by the judge up front, with the rest due if the defendant does not show up for the next trial date.
- *Fully secured bail:* The defendant must pay the entire bail amount set by the judge up front.
- *Unsecured bail:* The defendant must not pay any of the bail amount set by the judge up front but must pay the full amount if he or she does not show up for the next trial date.

Bail is based on the premise that no one—since everyone is supposedly innocent in the eyes of the law at this point—should be unduly burdened by being held against his or her will until the trial date. Because many crimes are relatively minor, holding many offenders would be a waste of taxpayer money. It would not be fair to interrupt suspects' lives—to separate them from their families and force them to stop working and lose important wages—just to ensure that the state has the right to prosecute someone accused of a criminal offense.

There are, however, cases in which bail is not granted to suspected offenders. In some cases, people are detained in jail until their trial dates. For example, ex–football star O. J. Simpson spent two of his birthdays in jail while awaiting trial and during his trial. He was detained because it was feared that if he was let out, he would *abscond* or *jump bail* and not return for his court date. It was also feared that he might be dangerous to the community, given that he was accused of two heinous murders. The fact that Simpson was later *acquitted* (found not guilty) led some to question whether he was entitled to any compensation for his time served.

The answer is no. According to the Bail Reform Act of 1984, accused criminals can be held in jail in *preventive detention* for two primary purposes: to prevent them from fleeing the state's jurisdiction and to protect the community. Thus, judges may deny bail when there is either a flight risk or some potential danger to the community. The constitutionality of this practice was upheld by the Supreme Court in *U.S. v. Salerno* (1987).

Bail, however, cannot be "excessive," according to the Eighth Amendment to the U.S. Constitution, although there is no clear understanding of what excessive really means. Instead, prosecutors may ask for a certain amount of bail, defense attorneys may ask for a reduction, and judges ultimately decide what the acceptable bail amount will be. Ideally, defense attorneys ensure that bail is not excessive for their clients; in reality, however, they rarely challenge the amount (Gaines, Kaune, and Miller 2000, p. 312). A *going rate* for particular crimes seems to develop over time so that persons charged with a particular crime may have a rough idea of what they will have to come up with to be granted bail. The nature of the charges; the defendant's prior record (if any); and extralegal factors such as employment status, ties to the community, and status in the community are also considered when bail is being determined (Nardulli, Eisenstein, and Flemming 1988).

The application of bail has several major problems. First, it is biased against certain groups in the United States. Erving and Houston (1991) found evidence of judges using excessive bonds against minorities. Spohn and Delone (2000) found that pretrial detention was disproportionately used against African Americans and Hispanics in two cities and against African Americans in another. Other studies show biases against the poor and minorities (Ayers and Waldfogel 1994; Harmsworth 1996). Such findings suggest that the bail decision can be biased against certain Americans. Kappeler, Blumberg, and Potter 2000, p. 226) claim that "[b]ail itself is inherently discriminatory." Logically, people who cannot afford bail are less likely to come up with the money or property to make bail and thus are forced to sit in jail awaiting trial. This may explain why jails are considered the poorhouses of the 20th and 21st centuries (Cole and Smith 2000): They are filled with poor criminals and accused criminals who could not afford bail.

Second, bail flies in the face of "innocent until proven guilty"—How can persons be detained if they have not been found guilty by a jury of their peers for any criminal act? In reality, approximately half of the people in jail in any given year are awaiting trial and thus have not been convicted of any criminal offense, yet they are living away from their families, in the company of convicted criminals, mentally ill citizens, and homeless people detained for minor crimes.

Third, courtroom workgroups inflate bail amounts for those they want to detain, meaning that two people charged with the same crime or same type of crime may see drastically different bail amounts. This practice is contradictory to equal justice under the law.

Fourth, bail may encourage guilty pleas. After all, if accused of relatively minor crimes, many would likely take a guilty plea and receive probation or a fine rather than being forced to sit in jail awaiting trial.

Fifth, preventive detention may increase the likelihood that a defendant will be convicted and sentenced to prison. Walker (1998, p. 118) reports findings from the National Pretrial Reporting Program illustrating that defendants held in preventive detention were more likely to be convicted of both felonies and misdemeanors. Whether this is because detained citizens appear in court wearing "jail garb" and thus "look guilty," while freed clients appear wearing normal clothes, is unknown. Logically, it would seem that seeing a person wearing jail clothing and perhaps in handcuffs or shackles would suggest to the normal citizen that "this person must be guilty if he or she is in jail." Another possible explanation of why detained suspects are more likely to be convicted is that when suspects are in jail, they are far less able to gather evidence in their defense. If the defense attorney is a public defender, the defendant will not receive quality efforts from the attorney, as is illustrated later in this chapter. In their study, Spohn and Delone (2001) found that those offenders held in pretrial detention were somewhat more likely to be sentenced to incarceration. Of course, it is possible that pretrial detainees are more often convicted and sentenced to prison because they are actually guilty and perhaps committed more serious crimes.

Finally, preventive detention may not generally be necessary, because most people who are let out on bail do not commit another crime while awaiting trial (Walker 1998, pp. 121–22). The bottom line is that it is impossible to predict who might be dangerous if let out: "[T]here are no reliable methods for either measuring or predicting future offense rates" (Greenwood and Turner 1987, in Walker 1998, p. 126). As stated by Fagan and Guggenheim (1996, p. 445), "The accuracy of prediction of dangerousness during the pretrial period remains questionable." Some crime control model advocates might conclude that we should therefore keep all people in jail until trial to protect our communities from those few who might become dangerous. The other extreme is advocated by Fagan and Guggenheim, who conclude that "preventive detention appears to be unjustified" (p. 448).

Given these limitations, there are also alternatives available to judges, as outlined in the following box.

Bail alternatives

- *Release on own recognizance:* The defendant is released on the basis of his or her promise to appear.
- *Release into third-party custody:* The defendant is released into the custody of another person (e.g., a parent), who agrees to ensure that the defendant will show up for his or her next court date.
- *Conditional release:* The defendant is released on the basis of his or her promise to follow certain rules while free.

In 2000 nearly two-thirds (64%) of defendants charged with felonies in the 75 most populated counties were released from jail at some point in the court process prior to the disposition of their case. Of these, 34% were released on bond and 18% were released on their own recognizance

(ROR) (Sourcebook of Criminal Justice Statistics 2003). More than one-third (36%) of defendants charged with felonies in the 75 most populated counties were detained until the final disposition of their cases, including 7% who were denied bail.

Of all those released by state courts, 31% failed by either violating a condition of their release or getting arrested for committing a new crime. Most were not arrested for committing a new crime (84%), but charged drug offenders were most likely to be rearrested for a new crime (20%), versus 14% of property offenders and 13% of violent offenders (Sourcebook of Criminal Justice Statistics 2003). In federal courts, fewer than one in five (18%) defendants failed by either violating a condition of their release or getting arrested for committing a new crime. Only about 2% were arrested for committing a new felony.

Defendants charged with murder by states (13%) were least likely to be released, followed by robbery (38%), rape (47%), burglary (50%), and motor vehicle theft (50%). Defendants charged with fraud (84%) were most likely to be released. Defendants charged with murder (47%) were also the most likely to be denied bail. This same pattern is found in federal courts. Since most cases in federal courts deal with drugs, it is interesting to note that 84% of drug offense defendants in 2000 were detained until the final disposition of their cases (Sourcebook of Criminal Justice Statistics 2003). Nearly the same percentage of murder defendants (83%) in 2000 were detained until the final disposition of their cases, versus only 36% of property offenders (including 15% of those charged with embezzlement and 38% of those charged with fraud). Thus, at both the state and the federal levels, accused white-collar offenders are most likely to be released.

According to the Sourcebook of Criminal Justice Statistics (2003), in federal courts, Caucasians (74%) and African Americans (68%) were detained at about the same rates, yet Hispanics (92%) were more likely to be detained than non-Hispanics (58%). Less educated and unemployed were also less likely to be released than higher educated and employed.

With America's "war on terror," the U.S. military and various investigative and intelligence agencies, such as the FBI and CIA, have rounded up hundreds of suspects (more than 600) and detained them in Guantanamo Bay, Cuba, at Camp X-Ray, which the British Broadcasting Corporation calls "an island, on an island, on an island. It is a sealed off zone within the US naval base at Guantanamo Bay, which is itself sealed." The BBC describes the camp this way: "It is a maze of chain-link fences, razor wire and guard towers. There are dog patrols and snipers. You can see into the prisoners' cell block quite clearly, as its walls are also made from chain-link. The cells are protected from the elements only by a metal roof . . . the prisoners in their bright orange jumpsuits spend most of their time in their cells, sitting on the floor or lying on foam sleeping mats, trying to keep cool in the incredible heat."

Plea Bargaining as an Injustice

The ideal of American justice is an "adversarial" process whereby prosecutors and defense attorneys fight for the truth and justice in a contest at trial. Yet "the reality is that an administrative system is in effect, with a high degree of consensus and cooperation" (Walker 1998, pp. 51–52). Most cases are handled informally in hallways and offices rather than in courtrooms, as in a crime control model rather than a due process model. Instead of criminal trials in which prosecutors and defense attorneys clash in an effort to determine the truth and do justice for all concerned parties, prosecutors, defense attorneys, and sometimes judges "shop" for "supermarket" justice through plea bargaining (Feeley 1979).

Shockingly, more than 90% of felony cases in the United States in any given year are disposed of via plea bargaining. This led Cole and Smith (2000) to call trials the "exceptional case" and Cox and Wade (1998) to call trials a "great American myth." Criminal trials are a formalized means of determining the legal guilt of your fellow citizens. Meanwhile, plea bargaining is an informal process whereby defendants plead guilty to lesser charges in exchange for not taking up the court's valuable time or spending the state's money on trials. Clients give up their Constitutional rights to cross-examine witnesses, to present a defense, not to incriminate themselves, to testify on their own behalf, and to appeal their convictions, all in exchange for a dismissal or reduction in charges, and/or a lesser sentence (Blumberg 1967; Casper 1972). Gaines, Kaune, and Miller (2000, p. 294) write that this type of assembly-line justice, consistent with a crime control model, "implies injustice. The term suggests that defendants are being hurried through the process, losing the safeguards built into our criminal justice system in the blur."

There are three basic types of plea bargaining: horizontal, vertical, and charge bargaining. In *horizontal bargaining*, additional charges or counts are not filed against the accused in exchange for a guilty plea. *Vertical bargaining* involves reducing the severity of charges—for example, being charged with manslaughter instead of murder. Finally, charge bargaining suggests that some provable charges simply will not be pressed against the defendant on the basis of his or her guilty plea (Milovanovich 2000).

Walker (1998, p. 157) claims that "[v]irtually all of the studies of plea bargaining have found a high degree of regularity and predictability in the disposition of cases," meaning that the resulting sentence can be reliably predicted on the basis of the nature of the charges and the defendant's prior record (e.g., see Nardulli, Eisenstein, and Flemming 1988). Thus, another type of *going rate* is established for particular types of crimes committed by particular types of people, one that becomes established over time and is learned by each member of the courtroom workgroup. Plea bargains typically closely parallel this going rate, and defendants charged with particular crimes can easily learn what sentence they likely face if they plead guilty.

Plea bargaining is a process driven by large numbers of caseloads, understaffed courts, an imbalance between the prosecution and the defense, and the renewed emphasis on using law enforcement to solve drug use and public order offenses. Of the 2.3 million felony cases in 2001, prosecutors participated in 67,000 jury trials that ended in verdicts (Bureau of Justice Statistics 2003). Thus, only about 3% of felony cases disposed of were handled by jury trials. There are so few trials in part because large prosecutor offices closed an average of 12,079 felony cases, medium officers closed an average of 3,162 felony cases, and small offices closed an average of 288 felony cases. There are simply too many cases to have trials and not enough personnel or money to handle them all, and most of criminal spending and employees are devoted to police and corrections (see Chapter One).

According to the Bureau of Justice Statistics, the average court budget in 1998 accounted for only about 1.5% of all state budget appropriations. In 1996, there were 2,341 state court prosecutor offices, with 79,000 staff. Total budgets for state prosecutor offices totaled more than $4.6 billion in 2001. Recall from Chapter Six that local police departments spent $37 billion in 2000. Thus, we spend at least $40 billion catching and prosecuting mostly street criminals, the vast majority of which are poor. In 1999, Americans in the 100 most populous counties spent only $1.2 billion to provide criminal defense to indigent clients. Nearly three-fourths (73%) was spent on public defenders, and 21% was spent on assigned counsel programs, plus another 6% on contract defense. This figure of $1.2 billion makes up only 3% of all local criminal justice expenditures used for police, courts, and corrections in these counties. In other words, we spend far more money catching and prosecuting indigent defendants than defending them. Since 1994, the amount of money Americans have spent prosecuting street criminals at the state level has increased 61%. During this time, the amount spent defending the indigent has not changed—just more evidence of our crime control values.

Not surprisingly, plea bargaining results in a bias against poor clients, who are typically minorities, as well as the uneducated, who may not even know what is being done to them in the criminal justice process (Gorr 2000; Kaminer 1999; Palermo, White, and Wasserman 1998). Stephen Bright, director of Atlanta's Southern Center for Human Rights, says it this way: "If you're the average poor person, you are going to be herded through the criminal justice system about like an animal is herded through the stockyards" (in Herbert 1998, p. 15).

Some may argue that no one would enter a guilty plea for a crime he or she did not commit, but a person living in conditions of poverty who is charged with a minor crime and refuses to plead guilty will only guarantee himself or herself a longer stay in jail awaiting a hearing—often longer than the likely sentence to be imposed upon conviction through a guilty plea (R. Miller 1997). If a public defender is representing the case, chances are the defendant will not have much of a chance to win at trial even if he or she is actually innocent, because "in many jurisdictions, public defenders and state appointed attorneys are grossly underpaid, poorly trained, or simply lack the resources and time to prepare for a case—a pattern documented in cases ranging from the most minor to the most consequential, capital crimes" (Weitzer 1996, p. 113).

The U.S. Supreme Court has granted the defendant the right to a defense attorney during the plea bargaining process (*Brady v. United States*, 1969). It is also required that the defendant voluntarily give his or her guilty plea (*Boykin v. Alabama*, 1969). When prosecutors offer a particular sentence in exchange for a guilty plea, they must keep their promise related to the sentence (*Santabella v. New York*, 1971). Finally, when defendants enter a guilty plea, they are asked numerous questions by the judge to ensure that they understand that they are giving up many Constitutional rights and that the guilty plea was not coerced.

Coercion is not clearly defined for the defendant in this process. Pleas might be understood as coerced if one considers the quality of defense provided by public defenders. Oftentimes, defendants plead guilty because of the threat of losing at trial and receiving a much more severe sentence. Langbein (2000, p. 27) claims that "the plea bargaining system operates by threat." In the face of threats by the prosecution, defense attorneys essentially may tell their clients, "So you want your Constitutional right to jury trial? By all means, be our guest. But beware. If you claim this right and are convicted, we will punish you twice, once for the offense and once again for having displayed the temerity to exercise your Constitutional right to jury trial." In other words, the goal of the public defender is to coerce his or her clients into surrendering their rights by threatening them with the possibility of greater sanctions.

The work environment of public defenders, who are responsible for defending the indigent (those who cannot afford their own attorneys), is typically depressing. Public defenders have large caseloads and limited resources relative to the prosecution, they work long hours, and they receive low pay (Cole and Smith 2000). The indigent defendant must know that the likelihood of winning is remote. The result should not be surprising: "Some public defenders seem to have little interest in using every possible strategy to defend their clients. On numerous occasions, legal errors are made by prosecutors and judges to which the public defender raises no objection. In addition, appeals are sometimes not initiated by public defenders even when chances of successful appeal seem to be good" (Cox and Wade 1998, p. 149).

Note that the U.S. Constitution does not guarantee a competent attorney. In *Strickland v. Washington* (1984), the Supreme Court set forth the standard for competence. In essence, a defendant must be able to prove that his or her sentence was directly affected by the conduct of the defense attorney—an impossible standard to prove.

Factual guilt is not determined in plea bargaining as it would be at a criminal trial. Guilt is assumed rather than established. Langbein (2000, p. 31) calls plea bargaining "condemnation without adjudication"—that is, sentencing without an establishment of guilt. Little investigation of the case against the defendant is conducted. Witnesses and victims are not present to see or approve of justice being meted out to the guilty. The question addressed by plea bargaining is not whether the defendant is actually guilty of the charges but, rather, what to do with the defendant. And one more thing—when guilty people plea bargain, they receive relatively lighter sentences than those convicted at trial for all crimes (D. Smith 1986). This means that people convicted at trial for murder, rape, robbery, aggravated assault, burglary, drug possession, and drug trafficking get longer sentences than people convicted through plea bargains (Bureau of Justice Statistics 1998). And victims of crime have no say in the matter.

For all of these reasons, everyone seems to be against plea bargaining. It is surprising, then, that it happens so often:

> Conservatives believe it is a major loophole through which criminals beat the system and avoid punishment. Liberals, meanwhile, believe that it is a source of grave injustices: prosecutors deliberately "overcharge"; defense attorneys make deals rather than fight for their clients; defendants are coerced into waiving their right to a trial; some defendants get much better deals than others. (Walker 1998, p. 153)

Cox and Wade (1998, p. 139) write, "Victims, the public, and the police are frequently unhappy about this practice, but if it were to be discontinued, the delays would be unconscionable." Thus, the large number of cases before today's courts seem to be driving the American plea-bargaining binge. Bradley (2000, p. 507) writes that the original approval of plea bargaining by the Supreme Court in *Santobello v. New York* (1971) "was based largely on the pragmatic concern that the criminal justice system could not afford to accord every defendant his constitutional rights, rather than on a claim that such a practice was inherently desirable."

When we shine a light on the outcome of justice in the United States, we see that the reality of plea bargaining is not consistent with the American ideal of the criminal trial, which is mentioned in the Declaration of Independence, three amendments to the U.S. Constitution, and scores of Supreme Court cases. Remember the two conceptions of justice discussed in Chapter One— justice as an outcome and justice as a process. Then ask yourself, Does plea bargaining achieve either of these forms of justice? Donziger (1996, p. 182) answers that plea bargaining bestows "lenient treatment on the guilty" and "coercive treatment on the innocent." Either way, it is unjust. Plea bargaining achieves neither justice as a process nor justice as an outcome.

THE UNEQUAL RIGHT TO A DEFENSE IN THE UNITED STATES: PUBLIC VERSUS PRIVATE ATTORNEYS

Think about the so-called Dream Team that O. J. Simpson employed during his double murder trial in 1995. Not only did Simpson enjoy the talents of one of the best attorneys in the world, but also he enjoyed the talents of many of the best attorneys in the world, as well as some of the top expert witnesses. Yet the "overwhelming majority of people accused of crimes" cannot afford even one attorney, and certainly not even one expert witness. In such cases, a defendant is granted one attorney, who will have few resources and thus little ability to subject the evidence against his or her client to any scrutiny. This explains how, in the face of evidence against their clients, public defenders see their clients as guilty anyway and thus not worthy of a trial (Cole and Smith 2000), especially since they carry 350 cases or more at a time and they receive so little of the criminal justice resources in any given year (Donziger 1996).

The American Bar Association calls the underfunding of defense attorneys for the indigent a "crisis of extraordinary proportions" (Tuohy 1995). As explained by the National Criminal Justice Commission, "The constitutional right to an attorney is meaningful only to the extent that resources are available to adequately prepare a defense," which "includes access to investigators, expert witnesses, paralegals, and support staff, as well as time to research the law and prepare the legal motions" (Donziger 1996, p. 189).

Everyone in the United States does have the right to counsel, as granted by the Sixth Amendment to the U.S. Constitution. And the U.S. Supreme Court granted indigents the right to a defense in felony cases in the case of *Gideon v. Wainwright* (1962). But although the poor thus have an equal right to counsel, they clearly do not have the right to equal counsel (Cole 1999; Reiman 1998). The average courthouse regular who is assigned by the court to indigent defendants has more than 1,000 cases a year to handle (Cole and Smith 2000); he or she has no time to investigate the facts of a case and put on an appropriate and thorough defense. Compare this with prosecutors, "who can draw on big police departments, teams of investigators and lawyers to prepare their cases." It's no wonder many prosecutors enjoy conviction rates of more than 90%. Even the "typical murder defendant has little money and is represented by an underpaid, overworked public defender" (Streisand 1994, p. 63). Adding to the built-in bias against the typical criminal defendant in the United States is the fact that criminal defense attorneys are usually from "less prestigious law schools, have less training, and come from lower socioeconomic backgrounds" (Kappeler, Blumberg and Potter 2000, citing Ladinsky 1984).

Why would a public defender, who is ideally responsible for upholding the Constitutional right to due process of law for the most vulnerable of all citizens—poor defendants faced with the incredible power of the government—take part in plea bargaining? Reiman (1998, p. 118) answers, "Because the public defender works in day-to-day contact with the prosecutor and the judge, the pressures on him or her to negotiate a plea as quickly as possible, instead of rocking the boat by threatening to go to trial, are even greater than those that work on court-assigned counsel."

Various court rulings also permit and even encourage judges to treat inadequate defense attorneys as effective even when they fail to investigate the facts of the case or to cross-examine crucial witnesses, fall asleep during testimony, or even come to court drunk (Cole 1999). Perhaps it is easy to understand the claim of Kappeler and coworkers (2000, p. 225) that public defenders are generally less likely than private attorneys to get cases against their clients dropped or to achieve an acquittal: "In essence, justice is correlated with the ability to pay by the hour."

According to surveys of state and federal inmates, African Americans (77%) and Hispanics (73%) were more likely than Caucasians (69%) to use public defense attorneys. Among federal prison inmates, African Americans (65%) were more likely than Hispanics (57%) and Caucasians (56%) to use public defense attorneys. Those represented by public attorneys met with their attorneys later in the criminal justice process and less frequently than those represented by private attorneys (Bureau of Justice Statistics 2003). This may lead you to believe that private attorneys must do a better job than public attorneys.

Yet when one compares the various outcomes of court processes when clients have publicly provided defense attorneys (such as public defenders) and private attorneys (at both the state and the federal level), the following facts emerge.

- Defendants with private attorneys are more likely than defendants with public attorneys to be released prior to the disposition of their cases.
- Conviction rates of defendants with public and private attorneys are nearly identical.
- Defendants with private attorneys are less likely than defendants with public attorneys to be sentenced to prison for their crimes and more likely to be sentenced to probation.
- Of those defendants sentenced to prison, those with public attorneys are sentenced to shorter sentences than defendants with private attorneys (Bureau of Justice Statistics 2003).

The Bureau of Justice Statistics asserts that the type of crime is most likely what determines the type of attorney one has and the likely outcome of the case (this means that the relationship between attorney type and outcome is spurious or dependent on other factors). This does not deny a bias in the criminal justice process, it just means the bias is in the criminal law, which defines some harmful acts as more harmful and more serious than others. As you learned in Chapter Four, the acts of the poor are more likely to be defined as serious crimes. Since the poor are, by definition, indigent, they will be more likely to be served by public attorneys. This means that they will be less likely to be released until their cases are disposed of, more likely to sit in jail while their cases are processed, and more likely to be sentenced to prison for their crimes. The fact that they spend less time than those with private attorneys when sentenced to prison serves as evidence of the effects of the courtroom workgroups on American justice: public counsel are part of the courtroom workgroup and can gain lower sentences for their clients through bargaining.

In federal courts, defendants charged with white-collar crimes are most likely to use private attorneys, including 63% of those charged with regulatory offenses and 43% charged with fraud. This means that they will be more likely to be released until their cases are disposed of, less likely to sit in jail while their cases are processed, and less likely to be sentenced to prison for their crimes. So, even though public defenders are "experts" in criminal practice, whereas private attorneys may not be, public attorneys are often "among the most inexperienced" lawyers, often recent law school graduates in "positions . . . typically characterized by low salaries and limited support services" (Merlo and Benekos 2000, p. 57).

THE "EXCEPTIONAL CASE" OF TRIAL

Cases that are not dismissed by the prosecutor and are not plea bargained end up going to trial. That is, a trial results only when other forms of case disposition are either not sought or not obtained (Schmalleger 2001). As noted earlier, trials are the exception to the rule of plea bargaining. They are very rare.

There are significant problems with the American trial process, most notably how rarely trials occur. Aside from that, several stages of the criminal trial process seem to result in biases against the poor and people of color. Before I move on to those stages and outline the main problems associated with bias, I want to point out that Americans charged with crimes are "innocent until proven guilty" of their crimes at trials. Americans ideally enjoy this *presumption of innocence* before and during trials. Former U.S. Supreme Court Justice Thurgood Marshall once said that American "principles of justice declare that the defendant is as innocent on the day before his trial as he is on the morning after his acquittal" (in Gaines, Kaune, and Miller 2000, p. 338). This is the ideal, but do all Americans equally enjoy this presumption?

Stages of the Criminal Trial

Stages of the typical American trial include voir dire, opening statements, the presentation of the prosecution's case, the presentation of the defense's case, the calling of rebuttal witnesses, closing arguments by the prosecution, closing arguments by the defense, and jury instructions by the judge. After these stages, the jury is given the case by the judge and the deliberations begin. Finally, the jury issues its verdict, and if the defendant is found guilty, the sentence is subsequently handed down by the judge (Peoples 2000; Stuckey, Robertson, and Wallace 2001).

Voir dire

Voir dire, meaning "to speak the truth" (Gaines, Kaune, and Miller 2000, p. 343), is an examination of potential jurors to ensure a fair trial for the defendant. Its ideal purpose is to gain a cross section of the community so that the defendant can have a jury of his or her "peers." Potential jurors must answer questions about their potential biases verbally and/or in writing. Ideally, voir dire will result in an impartial jury for the trial of the accused. We want juries "to have no axes to grind, no prejudgments about the people or issues they confront. We also want them to have the ability to empathize with others, to evaluate credibility, to know what is fair" (Minow 2000, p. 365). Thus, an unlimited number of jurors can be eliminated through *challenges for cause*, if a potential bias is identified. A limited number also may be eliminated through *peremptory challenges*, where no cause needs to be identified. A person may be excused from the jury in a death penalty case for cause if he or she absolutely refuses to impose the death penalty on a convicted murderer in any circumstances (see Chapter Ten). A person may be excused from a jury for cause if he or she has racist feelings and the case deals with an interracial crime.

There are at least three significant problems with the first stage of the criminal trial. First, some groups are underrepresented in jury pools. Second, peremptory challenges can be used against certain groups without explanation. Third, jury consultants can be used to help select sympathetic juries. Each of these problems results in a bias in favor of people with greater resources. I discuss these problems next.

Jury pools for state trials come mostly from voter registration, though some states select juries from other sources, such as motor vehicle registration, telephone directories, and tax rolls. Since voting lists are the primary source of jury pools, juries tend to be less representative of poor people, people of color, the young, and the uneducated, because these members of society are less likely to vote. As a result, poor people, people of color, and young people are less likely to be represented by juries who are like them. If this affects the outcomes of cases, it would likely do so in a manner biased against these groups. The *Capital Jury Project*, discussed more in Chapter Ten, shows that Caucasian males are more likely to vote for a death sentence for a convicted murderer, in part because they are more likely to see future dangerousness in the convicted offenders. African American males are less prone to vote for a death sentence for a convicted murderer, in part because they are more likely to see remorse in the convicted offenders.

Prosecutors and defense attorneys can use peremptory challenges to eliminate potential jurors without any explanation. Thus, lawyers can reject people for jury service on the basis of their style of dress or their demeanor without giving any valid reason. Bradley (2000, p. 508) claims that "peremptory challenges are largely a matter of wild guesses about how jurors will decide the case based upon their answers to one or two questions in the voir dire." Even if this is true, peremptory challenges allow a very troublesome practice. As in the use of drug courier profiles by police, these challenges allow attorneys to eliminate people they feel "look wrong" (*The Economist* 1998a; Kadish 1997). Additionally, racial minorities can be, and often are, denied the opportunity to serve on juries, even though rejecting potential jurors on the basis of race is specifically illegal based on the Supreme Court case, *Batson v. Kentucky* (1986) (Bohm 1999). Lawyers use race as a proxy to develop peremptory challenges, in part because of racial myths and stereotypes, in part because courts allow subjective qualifications for jury service, and in part because it simply benefits their cases (R. Kennedy 1997). Minorities are simultaneously inhibited from jury service for a variety of other reasons, many intimately related to their social class, social status, and past runins with the law.

The reality of jury selection, very different from the ideal, is that neither the defense nor the prosecution actually seeks an impartial jury. Barber (1994) explains that each side seeks out a jury that is likely to be partial to their side of the story. The problem with this for justice is that poor people and people of color are less able to hire professional jury consultants to analyze potential jurors so that they can select a jury more likely to sympathize with the defendant (P. Smith 1993; Varinsky 1993). Wealthy individuals, such as O. J. Simpson, can afford to hire the best jury consultants that money can buy and, in essence, have a much greater chance that a jury sympathetic with the defendant will find reasonable doubt and thus vote to acquit (McElhaney 1998; P. Smith 1993; Varinsky 1993). The jury in the O. J. Simpson case was handpicked with the help of a millionaire jury consultant who surveyed thousands of people prior to voir dire to identify the type of person who would make a sympathetic juror. The defense was able to isolate eight questions from an 85-page questionnaire that would identify jurors sympathetic to the defense's argument (M. Miller 1995). The final O. J. Simpson jury was made up entirely of people who did not regularly read the newspaper, 75% of whom thought that Simpson was not likely to have committed the murders because he excelled at football, and 42% of whom thought that it was acceptable to use force on a family member (M. Davis and Davis 1995). Clearly, everything about the O. J. Simpson case was unusual. Yet it serves as an excellent example of how jury consultants can be used to create a jury that will find reasonable doubt.

The National Criminal Justice Commission outlines many other problems with the American jury system. Jurors are exposed to endless waiting, must put up with insensitive questioning, are sometimes sequestered from their families, may lose substantial income, and can be eliminated without just cause through peremptory challenge (Donziger 1996, p. 184).

Opening statements

After a jury is empaneled, both sides of the case (the prosecution and the defense) make *opening statements* to lay the foundation of their cases. Opening statements are not allowed to be argumentative and cannot be considered as evidence by the jury. Opening statements are road maps laying out where each side intends to take its case.

The prosecution presents its case

Because the prosecution has the burden of proving its case beyond a reasonable doubt, it presents its case first. Its goal is to present relevant facts to the jury that prove that the named defendant(s) committed the named crime(s). Ingraham (1994) explains that because defendants are innocent in the eyes of the law, they do not have to present a case unless they feel that the prosecution can prove its case that they are guilty of crimes beyond a reasonable doubt. Rush (2000, p. 113) defines *reasonable doubt* as "[t]he state of mind of jurors in which, after the comparison and consideration of all the evidence, they cannot say that they feel an abiding conviction, a moral certainty, of the truth of a criminal charge against a defendant." Essentially, if another theory of the crime for which the defendant is accused is reasonably likely to be true, jurors are required by law to find the defendant not guilty of the crime, even if they think the person is actually guilty of the act(s). Why do we have such a high standard of proof to establish legal guilt at criminal trials? "This high standard of proof in criminal cases reflects a fundamental social value—the belief that it is worse to convict an innocent individual than to let a guilty one go free." At least, that is the ideal (p. 113).

The reality of the prosecution is that it is generally much more powerful and better equipped to present its case than the defense. Most accused criminals, who are indigent and thus cannot hire private attorneys, do not have the resources to subject the state's evidence to meaningful scrutiny. This means little or no investigation of the charges against the defendant, no expert witnesses to rebut or refute the prosecution's case, and very short trials. The presumption of innocence may be a myth for most criminal defendants in the United States.

The defense presents its case

If the defense attorney feels that the defense must answer the charges of the prosecution, the defense will present its own case. It is not required that the defense present a case. If the defense feels that the prosecution's case is weak, it can ask that the charges be dropped against the defendant through a *directed verdict*. If the defense puts on its case, it will either provide contrary evidence to the prosecution, offer an *alibi* (e.g., that the accused was somewhere else at the time of the crime), or present an *affirmative defense* (which admits that the defendant committed the act or acts of which he or she is charged but that the defendant is nevertheless not guilty of a "crime"). The purpose of the defense presentation is to raise reasonable doubt so that the defendant will not be convicted. Once again, wealthier clients who can afford better attorneys are more likely to ensure that reasonable doubt will be found because they are more likely to subject the evidence to independent examinations, to construct alternative theories of the crime, and to hire expert witnesses in their defense.

Rebuttal witnesses

After each side has presented its primary case, both sides have the option of calling *rebuttal witnesses* to discredit the testimony of previous witnesses for the other side. Clearly, poor clients and people of color are generally at a disadvantage here because of their lack of resources and the quality of their attorneys.

Closing arguments

At the end of each side's case, prosecutors and defense attorneys are permitted to make *closing arguments* to the jury that present the facts in a manner that is most favorable to their side. Prosecutors might choose to ignore evidence pointing to the innocence of the defendant, and defense attorneys might choose to point out alternative theories of who committed the crime(s). Truth is irrelevant here; what counts are the strong points of each side's case. Obviously, attorneys with some incentive to argue vehemently for the benefit of their clients will make better closing arguments on their clients' behalf.

Jury instructions

After closing arguments, the judge instructs the jury as to how the law bears on their decisions. At a minimum, the *jury instructions* will include a definition of "reasonable doubt" and will explain what elements of the crime or crimes must be established to show guilt of the defendant. Both sides will meet with the judge and hammer out the specific content and wording of the instructions. Because of the importance of jury instructions, "one would expect jury instructions to be carefully drafted to maximize juror comprehension, but they are not" (Steele and Thornburg 2000, p. 118). Some research shows that jurors may not even understand jury instructions given to them, a frightening thought given that the jurors are expected to follow these instructions carefully when deliberating about the guilt or innocence of the accused (Dattu 1998; Steele and Thornburg 1991). Once again, private attorneys of powerful and wealthy citizens have a significant advantage here, as they can assure that the instructions are most favorable for their clients. In death penalty cases, there is disturbing evidence that juries often do not understand much of the jury instructions (see Chapter Ten).

Jury deliberations

Once juries are given the case by the judge, they may consider only the evidence entered into the trial to determine whether the person(s) charged with the crime(s) is/are legally guilty beyond a reasonable doubt. In almost every state, the verdict must be unanimous, or the result is a *hung jury* or a *mistrial*. It is hard to know whether juries follow the law in making decisions because of the secrecy afforded to jury deliberations. Much research into jury deliberations (mainly from mock trials) shows that jurors consider a lot of what they are not supposed to consider, including the defendant's appearance, his or her past record, and other facts not admitted to trial but learned about from other sources (Devine 1988). Postinterview verdicts with jury members, mock juries, a few televised jury deliberations, and even transcripts of jury deliberations on the Internet show that juries frequently consider evidence that they should not consider (Kassin 2000; MacCoun 1990). This is why some argue that jury deliberations should be open to judicial review, to make sure that justice is being done according to the law (e.g., see Ruprecht 1997). Gershman (2000) maintains that jurors consider strong opening statements (which may include promises of evidence to be presented even when such evidence is not delivered during trial) and purposefully mentioned inadmissible evidence, which is not supposed to be considered by the jury.

CONCLUSION

Scholars have argued that no trial system is deserving of public respect if it cannot be trusted to acquit the innocent and convict the guilty, if it fails to treat those who come into contact with the system with respect, and if does not appropriate judicial resources wisely. The American court system, highly consistent with a crime control model of criminal justice, handles cases in an administrative manner rather than an adversarial manner. More resources are given to prosecutors than to defense attorneys, adding to the immense power of American prosecutors. The clear evidence of bias in plea bargaining and the use of bail and preventive detention, as well as the low quality of defense afforded to those most in need, provides further evidence that the criminal justice network fails to do justice as expected. In essence, the courts have been left to do the best they can with increasing numbers of cases and relatively less resources than police and corrections.

ISSUE IN DEPTH
Wrongful Convictions

It is impossible to know how many innocent people each year are convicted of crimes that they did not commit. Huff, Rattner, and Sagarin (1996, p. 53), in their book *Convicted but Innocent: Wrongful Conviction and Public Policy*, write, "Quite clearly, there is no accurate, scientific way to determine how many innocent people are convicted, or put another way, how many of those convicted of crimes are innocent." Unfortunately, we also do not know how many innocent people are executed for crimes they did not commit. One study, published as the book *In Spite of Innocence* (Radelet, Bedau, and Putnam 1992), found that 400 persons were wrongfully convicted of capital crimes, including 23 who were actually executed and 22 others who came within 72 hours of being executed. I revisit the issue of wrongful convictions in capital cases in Chapter Ten. What follows here is a brief discussion of some actual cases in which people have been wrongfully convicted of crimes, as well as the factors that produce wrongful convictions in the United States.

Of most importance for the main argument of this book is that wrongful convictions are obviously a direct threat to justice—to justice as an outcome (because the factually guilty are not punished for their wrongdoings and because innocent people do not deserve to be punished) and to justice as a process (because wrongful convictions suggest that the criminal justice network is not fair and unbiased). In the Foreword to Huff, Rattner, and Sagarin's book, Dinitz (1996, pp. xii–xiii) states it this way:

> Wrongful convictions, however infrequent, are anathema to the American due process system and to all who believe in the fairness of our law enforcement and judicial systems and the constitutional protections guaranteed individual citizens. Not only do such wrongful convictions violate trust in our system, but . . . such convictions undermine public safety by leaving the "true" positives—the guilty—in the community to commit future grave offenses.

So, a lot is at stake when wrongful convictions occur. First, the "conviction of the innocent leaves the guilty free to commit more crimes, thus threatening public safety" and "each instance of the conviction of an innocent enhances the possibility that there will be more not-guilty verdicts against the truly guilty" (Huff, Rattner, and Sagarin 1996, p. 12) because of a distrust in the government resulting from wrongful convictions.

As I have stated, no one can know for sure how often errors are made, but a statement by Huff and coworkers (1996, p. xxii) suggests the significance of the problem. They write, "The American criminal justice system is so large and has so many arrests each year that even if the system were 99.5% accurate, it would still generate more than 10,000 wrongful convictions a year for the eight serious index crimes alone" and even more for relatively less serious crimes. Huff et al. mailed a survey to various actors in the Ohio criminal justice network to estimate how frequently wrongful convictions occur; they make what they call "a conservative prevalence estimation made by a largely conservative sample," mostly because the people they surveyed would have reasons to deny the wrongful conviction of the innocent (p. 55). After throwing out cases where there were serious and reasonable doubts about the innocence of the convicted parties, along with cases in which people were punished and subsequently released but their innocence was not clearly established, they were left with individual cases where actual innocence is known. Some of these cases are discussed below. The first of these would not be included by Huff and coworkers, for there is still some doubt about the convicted man's guilt, yet I include it because it points out the absurdity of how our criminal justice network sometimes operates.

- James Hicks was a 31-year-old man who had served 7 years of a 10-year sentence for the murder of his wife after she disappeared in Maine. On the stand he denied that he had killed his wife and also admitted to having been living for about 5 years with another woman, with whom he had fathered two children. After being sentenced to prison, he attempted to marry his girlfriend but was denied a marriage license because there was no death certificate for his presumed dead wife. Huff, Rattner, and Sagarin (1996, p. 7) write, "So, although he was convicted of murdering his wife on the basis of evidence that convinced 12 men and women beyond a reasonable doubt, the authorities entertained some doubt that his wife was dead."

In the remaining cases, we know that the wrong people were actually convicted and/or punished for crimes they did not commit:

- David Fedderson is a Caucasian man convicted of raping a woman he did not know in Dubuque, Iowa. The victim identified Fedderson as her attacker as he walked in a crowd of people after her attack. Fedderson was walking along a street he normally walked along, and he had no history of violent behavior, but he also had no alibi for his whereabouts at the time of the crime. Only one person, the victim, saw the attacker, so her eyewitness testimony alone led to his conviction for rape. When Fedderson rose to speak on his behalf after his conviction, he did not express remorse for his actions or sympathy for the victim, for he knew he was actually innocent of the crime. Fedderson spent 2 years in prison before he was finally able to convince all parties that he was in fact innocent. The same judge who had convicted him then set him free and stated that the fact that an innocent man could be convicted "is scary."
- Nathaniel Carter was sentenced to life imprisonment after being convicted of the stabbing death of Clarice Herndon. His conviction was based almost solely

on the testimony of the actual killer, his ex-wife, who was found by police at the scene with blood on her hands (they assumed that she, too, had been attacked). Carter had spent 2 years in prison when his ex-wife came forward, after being promised immunity from being prosecuted, and testified that she had committed the murder.

- Johnny Binder is an African American man convicted in Houston, Texas, for a robbery committed by a group of African Americans driving a yellow Cadillac similar to Binder's car. Binder lived in Houston but was in Dallas at the time of the crime. Binder had no criminal record and knew he was innocent of the crime, but after hearing about the make and color of the car involved in the crime, he voluntarily went to the police to tell them that he was not involved. Binder was arrested and then convicted by an all-white jury, despite the fact that several eyewitnesses claimed that he was not involved. After Binder had spent 4 years in prison, the real criminals were discovered, and Binder was taken back to court, where, however, he could not be set free or given a new trial by the judge. Binder was returned to his cell. An appeal for a writ of habeas corpus was denied because "it was not the appropriate route to be taken when there is a claim for a new trial based on newly discovered evidence" (Huff, Rattner, and Sagarin 1996, p. 18). Binder was eventually set free by the judge, even though she did not have the authority to do so, and the state granted him a special pardon, which did not say anything about Binder's actual innocence.

- Todd Neely was a young man in Florida convicted of raping one of his neighbors. A woman in Neely's apartment complex had been raped by a boy she described as no older than 16 who wore braces on his teeth. Neely was 18 years old, did not have braces, and was 11 miles away having dinner with his parents at the time of the rape. The victim picked out a photograph of Neely from a photo line-up, but the photograph was several years old and showed Neely at an age more similar to that of the attacker. It turned out that the real rapist was a 14-year-old boy who also lived in the complex and who had a history of exhibitionism and voyeurism in the neighborhood (he also had told friends that he was the one who committed the rape). Neely was eventually freed, after spending 92 days in jail, mostly because his family spent $300,000 of their own money investigating the case. This case shows what can happen when the police and prosecution zero in on a suspect and ignore obvious evidence of his or her innocence.

Given all of these shocking cases, you may wonder why such wrongful convictions occur. According to Huff, Rattner, and Sagarin (1996), the most common cause, responsible for more than half of wrongful convictions, is eyewitness identification—that is, victims and witnesses who pick out the wrong person even though they may truly believe that the people they have identified are the real criminals. Also of significance is

police and prosecutorial overzealousness: the anxiety to solve a case; the ease with which one having such anxiety is willing to believe, on the slightest evidence of the most negligible nature, that the culprit is in hand; the willingness to use improper, unethical, and illegal means to obtain a conviction when one believes that the person at the bar is guilty. (p. 64, emphasis in original)

Eyewitness Testimony

Consider the case of Jeffrey Streeter, convicted and sentenced to a year in jail for the assault of an elderly man. Streeter, who was uninvolved in the case, had been sitting outside the courtroom when the defense attorney asked him to come in and sit in the defendant's usual place. Although the defendant was also in the courtroom, three eyewitnesses to the assault picked Streeter as the man who had committed the crime, as if, because Streeter was sitting where the defendant normally sits, he must be guilty. Streeter spent one night in jail before the error was realized. As this defense atorney had set out to demonstrate, eyewitness testimony is patently unreliable. Yet many consider it to be undeniable proof of guilt, and cases lacking eyewitness identification are often dismissed as "purely circumstantial" and thus inherently weaker.

Research demonstrates that human brains (of witnesses and victims of crimes, for example) store information from environmental experiences in chemical bits and pieces. When attempting to recall events, our brains actually reconstruct these events from the fragments stored in our brains. During the stages of acquisition, retention, and retrieval, falsehoods are pulled into our memories so that we "remember" things that really did not happen (Loftus 1979). As one example, a victim of crime may retrieve pieces of information gleaned from discussions with friends and families, news clippings, and other sources, and may wrongly attribute these recollections to the criminal event. Buckhout (1974, p. 23) explains why eyewitness identification is inherently unreliable:

> Research and courtroom experience provide ample evidence that an eyewitness to a crime is being asked to be something and do something that a normal human being was not created to be or do. Human perception is sloppy and uneven, albeit remarkably effective in serving our need to create structure out of experience. In an investigation or in court, however, a witness is often asked to play the role of a kind of tape recorder on whose tape the events of the crime have left an impression. . . . Both sides, and usually the witness, too, succumb to the fallacy that everything was recorded and can be played back through questioning.

The criminal justice process serves to reinforce the likelihood that innocent people will be wrongly convicted. For example, witnesses and victims may see a photo lineup or actual physical lineup of real people and then choose one as the offender. From that point on, the face of the person picked will be the offender, even if it is not the actual offender. When asked to pick out the offender in court, witnesses and victims will point to that person as the offender because his or her identity matches that of the person picked out from the lineup. The memory of the face from the crime may be replaced with the memory of the face from the lineup. That this may be the wrong face is not considered by the person, who is convinced that he or she has chosen the right person (e.g., see Brown, Defenbacher, and Sturgill 1977).

As a college student, I was one of two witnesses to a failed burglary attempt. Ironically, I had just watched a video in one of my criminology classes about the unreliability of eyewitness identification. In the video, a college professor set up an experiment whereby a stranger walked into the classroom, took the professor's bag from the desk, and then ran away. After the offender had left, the professor said, "All I recall is that the man had a large nose." Many of the subjects noted to the police that they recalled the man having a distinctive nose (even though he did not). One witness (who was wearing a hat) said he remembered the man wearing a hat (even though he did not). Most of the students could not pick out the actual offender from a photo lineup when the offender's photo was included. When the actual offender's photo was not included, many of the student witnesses picked out an innocent person.

So, when I witnessed the burglary attempt, I made sure I was prepared to provide a perfect description to the police. Here's what happened: Late one night I was up sick, unable to sleep. I heard someone hanging around outside, checking the doors and window screens. After listening for a while, I heard someone trying to force his way into my next door neighbor's bedroom window. I went outside to see what was going on, as did another neighbor, and we scared the offender away. He ran right by me, so I got a great look at him. I followed him down the stairs and proceeded to watch him climb a fence to get away. As I watched him run away, I took mental notes about the offender's appearance.

When the police arrived, they asked me what he looked like. My description was very precise and included details about the offender's height, weight, hair color and style, approximate age, clothing, shoes—even shoelaces! About 2 hours later (around 4:00 A.M.), the police came back to my apartment and asked me to accompany them to the rear of an abandoned house, where they had apprehended someone who resembled the offender. Upon arriving, the police shone a bright spotlight on the man and asked me if this was the offender. This man had been tracked by police dogs from the scene of the attempted burglary (when he climbed the fence to get away, his watch, along with his scent, got stuck at the top of the fence). The apprehended man was exactly like the man I described, with one significant exception—he was slightly shorter and heavier than I remembered. The police asked me if I could be sure that this was the man (I could not ethically say that I was 100% sure it was he, even though it had to be, based on the dogs tracking his scent). He was too stocky to be the offender I saw.

As we waited in a police squad car, I asked the other witness what he had told the police, and he said that he thought the offender was taller and thinner than the man they had apprehended. This made me very uncomfortable—How could it be that we both had been so wrong about what we thought the offender looked like, given that the man the police apprehended was wearing the same outfit, including the same shoes and even shoelaces, had the same hair color and braids as I had described, and was also a Hispanic male? As I have thought about that experience over the years, I realized that my run-in with the burglar was not unlike the experiences of most crime victims and witnesses: I saw the man very briefly, it was late at night, I was tired when I witnessed the crime; and so on. Why shouldn't I expect to be wrong about some details? More importantly, how can the criminal justice network be so dependent on eyewitness identifications such as this one when they are so unreliable? Yet prosecutors are more willing to press charges and pursue convictions in court when eyewitnesses are part of the case, and jurors are more likely to convict given eyewitness testimony, even given results like those in the cases described here. Cases lacking an eyewitnesses are often described as merely circumstantial in nature and therefore are seen as less reliable.

Overzealousness

As for overzealousness by police and prosecutors, I restrict my comments to the following main point: We must expect our police and prosecutors to pursue arrests and convictions zealously (in the pursuit of justice as an outcome); it is the current "tough on crime" environment that makes overzealousness more likely. Huff, Rattner, and Sagarin (1996, p. 71) write that such overzealousness

> might come from a desire to add points to a scorecard, to enhance a reputation as a tough and successful prosecutor because of an impending election, or to receive commendation and promotion in the police department for having nabbed a vicious criminal and solved a difficult case . . . may sometimes derive from the inability, unwillingness, or lack of funds and personnel available to police to make true and proper investigations . . . [and] might also conceal bigotry and racism, or sometimes greed.

Other sources of overzealousness may be "the inability, unwillingness, or lack of funds and personnel available to police to make true and proper investigations."

Partly because of the overzealousness of the police and prosecution, as well as because of the presumption of guilt that accompanies an arrest and the immense power of the prosecution relative to the typical defense attorney, many innocent people will plead guilty (and some even confess to the police) to crimes they did not commit. Many of these plea bargains result in immediate freedom for the accused, through either release for time served or a probation sentence. Remember—a plea of guilty is not necessarily an admission of guilt. It can be as much a strategy for avoiding punishment as a not guilty plea is by a factually guilty suspect.

Consider this case involving presumption of guilt: Willie Jones, a 33-year-old African American man with a criminal record involving many minor criminal acts, was arrested for using Connecticut subway tokens in the New York City subway system. Jones was remanded to jail to await his arraignment, referred to a public defender, and thereafter confronted with a long rap sheet of serious crimes and an outstanding warrant for jumping bail on another charge. Jones correctly pointed out that the rap sheet was not his, that it must belong to another Willie Jones. The other Jones had a file with no photo and no fingerprints, so the police and his own attorney did not believe that he was really "innocent." He spent 3 months in jail awaiting trial because he refused to plead guilty to the serious charge for which the other Jones was accused. On his trial date the mistake was realized, and Jones was released. So much for "innocent until proven guilty."

I will concede that many of those wrongfully convicted, like Willie Jones, do in fact have criminal records. Some may assert that this gives the police reason to suspect them of future criminal activity. I want to point out the irony of this expectation: Society gets upset when criminals continue to offend after their punishment, even though we simultaneously seem to expect them to commit more crimes.

At the extreme end of overzealousness are false confessions. Police may occasionally resort to any and all tactics necessary to gain convictions of people they truly believe to be guilty so that the end—a conviction or justice as an outcome—justifies the means in their minds, violating justice as a process. In fact, some early texts on criminal interrogations and confessions encourage trickery by police to encourage confessions, which is actually allowed by courts (e.g., see Inbau and Reid 1967). Cases of false confessions abound in the United States.

The case of James Richardson, a poor African American farm worker with an IQ of only 77, stands out. Richardson confessed to poisoning seven of his own children and stepchildren and was imprisoned and sentenced to death in 1968. Richardson served 22 years before being freed for these crimes, which he did not commit. The prosecution, suggesting that Richardson laced his children's lunches with poison and planned their deaths in advance, showed evidence that Richardson had sought life insurance policies for his children right before their deaths (in fact, a door-to-door insurance salesman had visited the day before and simply left his card). The children's babysitter, who was ultimately admitted to medical care for Alzheimer's disease, admitted more than 100 times that she had killed the children. Richardson said that he had been beaten into confessing his crime. The sheriff's deputy who allegedly coerced the confession out of Richardson probably believed that Richardson was guilty, but his unjust means resulted in an unjust outcome.

Such cases serve as the ugliest incidents uncovered by the research of Huff, Rattner, and Sagarin (1996), cases that "involved outright lying, the fabrication and alteration of evidence, the intimidation and coaching of witnesses, and perjury and the suborning of perjury" (p. 143). As I stated earlier, my assertion is that these tactics, and thus wrongful convictions, are more likely in the current get tough attitude promoted by politicians and emphasized in media coverage of crime and criminal justice. The research shows that wrongful convictions often start with a presumption of guilt on the part of criminal justice actors (characteristic of a crime control model of justice) and are made more likely because of numerous system breakdowns (which occur more often in the assembly-line process of American criminal justice).

Discussion Questions

1. Why is the U.S. court system called a dual court system?
2. Define the term jurisdiction.
3. Contrast trial courts with appellate courts.
4. List and discuss the key functions of U.S. courts.
5. Identify the main actors in the courtroom workgroup and discuss the main roles of each member.
6. What factors affect whether prosecutors decide to press charges against accused criminals?
7. What important decisions are made during the pretrial phase of courts?
8. What is bail?
9. What is meant by saying that "Bail is not intended to be punishment"?
10. Identify the main types of bail and discuss alternatives to bail.
11. How is preventive detention justified?
12. What are some of the main problems associated with the administration of bail?
13. What is plea bargaining?
14. Explain how plea bargaining is inconsistent with the ideal of justice as a process.
15. Do you think that guilty pleas are ever coerced? Why or why not?
16. Is there a difference in the quality of the defense offered by private versus public defense attorneys? Why or why not?
17. Given how rare trials are in the United States, does the typical defendant have a reasonable expectation of trial?
18. Identify and discuss the main stages of the criminal trial.
19. What are some problems with the voir dire process?
20. What factors produce wrongful convictions?

CHAPTER EIGHT

PUNISHMENT: DOES IT WORK AND IS IT FAIR?

INTRODUCTION

This chapter examines the posttrial phase of the criminal courts—sentencing of the guilty by the courts to some form of punishment. I illustrate types of sentences available to sentencing judges and methods of punishment in the United States, including probation, imprisonment, and intermediate sanctions. A detailed discussion of why we punish provides insight into what's wrong with the American approach to punishment. I also show what we have learned about the effectiveness of various types of punishment. The chapter concludes with an examination of bias in the sentencing process. Again, clear evidence of some forms of sentencing bias is illustrated, lending support to the notion that the criminal justice network fails to do justice.

AN INTRODUCTION TO SENTENCING

A *sentence* is a penalty or sanction imposed on a person by a court upon conviction for a criminal offense (Rush 2000, p. 295). For example, when persons are convicted of murder, they may be sentenced to the death penalty, life in prison, some other term of imprisonment, or, in rare cases, a long term of probation and/or house arrest.

A sentence, then, is any criminal sanction or punishment. Herbert Packer, in his book *The Limits of the Criminal Sanction* (1968), defines *punishment* as inflicting pain or unpleasant circumstances for an offense against legal rules on an offender or alleged offender for his or her offense, intentionally administered by human beings within a legal system that grants authority to do so. He argued that the only valid justifications for punishment are deterrence and retribution for an offender whose moral responsibility has been established beyond a reasonable doubt. Deterrence refers to creating fear through punishment to make would-be offenders not commit crime. Retribution is punishment of offenders to give them what they deserve based on the wrongs they inflicted on society. Each term is discussed more later in the chapter. Similarly, Hart (1968, p. 4) defined punishment as the infliction of pain for offenses against legal rules, applied to the actual offender, that is intentionally administered by a legal authority (cited by Jeffery 1990).

Types of Sentences

The three primary forms of sentences are determinate sentences, indeterminate sentences, and mandatory sentences. *Determinate sentences* set forth a specified criminal sanction for a particular type of crime. Based on the severity of the offense, determinate sentences are generally the same for each person convicted of a particular type of crime. Although determinate or *fixed sentences* are generally set by law, judges have limited discretion when it comes to passing each sentence, based on certain aggravating and mitigating factors. As defined by Rush (2000, p. 8), *aggravating factors* are "circumstances relating to the commission of a crime which cause its gravity to be greater than that of the average instance of the given type of offense." For example, any crime committed with a weapon is considered more serious than one without a weapon, so the presence of a weapon would be an aggravating factor at sentencing. Thus, a rape committed at gunpoint may lead to a greater sentence than a rape without a weapon. *Mitigating factors* reduce the perceived seriousness of crimes (Rush 2000, p. 216). Any motives of the offender that may make crimes more understandable to the court may be considered mitigating factors. For example, a bank robber who is unarmed, does not pretend to have a weapon, and is truly motivated by the hunger of his children may receive a less severe sentence than a ruthless, armed bank robber motivated only by monetary gain.

Indeterminate sentences are not fixed on the basis of the crime but are a function of characteristics unique to each offender. Thus, indeterminate sentences, or *minimum–maximum sentences*, establish a range within which each individual offender may be sanctioned, somewhere between the minimum and the maximum sentences allowed in the law. Indeterminate sentences give judges more discretion in establishing what any given offender may receive for his or her crimes. The advantage of indeterminate sentences is that they allow judges to take into account both aggravating and mitigating factors. One murder may be either more or less serious than other murders; indeterminate sentences allow judges to reflect this in the sentences they hand down. The main drawback of indeterminate sentences is that they allow judges to abuse their discretion. That is, there is at least the potential that longer sentences will be passed down against particular groups of people who are convicted of the same offenses as other groups. For example, judges may consciously or subconsciously treat African Americans more harshly than Caucasians for identical offenses, especially given that African Americans are not well represented in courtroom workgroups (see Chapter Seven).

To address such concerns, many states and the federal government have passed *sentencing guidelines* that minimize the amount of discretion to which judges are entitled when considering sentences for convicted offenders. Judges weigh various factors in determining the most appropriate sentence. Generally, the most important factors include the seriousness of the offense and the offender's prior record; the more serious the offense and the longer the prior record, the more severe the sentence will be. Relying on offense seriousness and previous record allows for biases in the criminal law and policing to affect sentences.

Federal sentencing guidelines were put into effect in 1987. The range of possible sentences was reduced, meaning that judge discretion was minimized, and discretionary early release from prison was abolished. Generally speaking, prison terms increased as a result of such revisions. A fundamental problem with these federal sentencing guidelines is that those criminal offenders who have information on other crimes may get lesser sentences than those without. This is because of Section 5K1.1 of the guidelines, which in essence allows prosecutors to use their discretion in charging to give breaks to cooperative defendants (Walker 1998, p. 136). Given the definitions of justice in Chapter One, such practices can be considered unjust, as small-time offenders who have no information to give to prosecutors may get more severe sentences than big-time offenders who simply know more.

Mandatory sentences simply establish a minimum sanction that must be served upon conviction for a criminal offense. Thus, everyone who is convicted of a crime that calls for a mandatory sentence will serve that amount of time. As explained by Walker (1998, p. 130), "Mandatory sentencing usually means two things: mandatory imprisonment for a certain crime and/or a mandatory minimum prison term." Judges have no discretion in mandatory sentencing because, by definition, the sentence is mandatory. A specified imprisonment term must be given to the convicted offender by law. The war on drugs is responsible for a large share of mandatory sentences. Consider, for example, 20-year-old Nicole Richardson of Mobile, Alabama, who was dating a drug dealer. When approached by an undercover officer about where to buy some drugs, Nicole said to talk to her boyfriend. Her sentence was 10 years in prison with no possibility of parole; her boyfriend, who cooperated with authorities, received a 5-year imprisonment sentence (Donziger 1996, p. 25). Sentencing judges, with no discretion in mandatory sentencing, are generally opposed to it: Sileo (1993) reports that 90% of federal judges and 75% of state judges do not support mandatory sentences. Gray (2001), a judge himself, also reports that most judges are against mandatory sentences.

Good examples of mandatory sentences are the so-called *three-strikes laws* that have been passed by more than half the U.S. states. These laws usually require that upon conviction for a third felony, offenders will be sentenced to a period of imprisonment for the remainder of their natural lives: "Neither the particular circumstances, nor the seriousness of the crimes charged, nor the duration of time that has elapsed between crimes is given consideration" in three-strikes laws (Beckett and Sasson 2000, p. 180). These laws also mandate that judges must "ignore mitigating factors in the background of offenders, as well as their ties to community, employment status, potential for rehabilitation, and obligations to children." Tonry (1995) argues that mandatory sentences are unwise because they do not allow judges to consider mitigating factors such as economic deprivation.

I discuss whether three-strikes laws make any sense at all later in this chapter. The following box highlights some important facts about these laws.

Facts about three-strikes laws

- According to a 1997 National Institute of Justice (NIJ) report, between 1993 and 1995 alone, 24 states and the federal government passed three-strikes laws. In 20 of these states, the law requires three strikes for a mandatory sentence. In many of these states, at least one strike must be a violent felony. And in 12 of these states, the mandatory term of punishment is life without the possibility of parole.
- Now more than half the states have three-strikes laws, as does the federal government, although only a handful of states have used these laws to any real degree (led by California).
- California's law, which has been the most scrutinized, only requires that two of the offenses be serious felonies, whereas the last strike can be for any crime. This explains why one person was sentenced as a three-strikes offender for stealing four chocolate chip cookies from a restaurant (Elikann 1996).
- The logic of three-strikes laws is to increase penalties for second offenses and to require life imprisonment without possibility of parole for third offenses.
- Many states, such as California, passed laws that were intended primarily for violent offenders but that failed to specify this intent. Many nonviolent offenders are being incarcerated under this law. Perhaps this is why California's law was estimated to cost about $5 billion or more each year—five times more than originally expected (Greenwood et al. 1994). The NIJ (1997, p. 1) report states, "The vast majority of California 'strike' inmates have been sentenced under the two-strikes provision and for nonviolent crimes."
- Three-strikes laws are based on a false premise that "an increasingly larger portion of serious crimes are committed by recidivating felons" (W. Walsh and Harris 1999, p. xii).
- Three-strikes laws grew out of a crime hysteria or moral panic caused by a publicized violent crime in California, and the idea was promoted by the National Rifle Association.
- Experts estimated that every single dollar of new money in the state would have to be used to pay for this effort.
- In California, 42,000 inmates have been sentenced under either a second- or a third-strike offense, including 7,000 third-strikers.

- The average cost of a third-strike incarceration is $26,500 per inmate per year.
- Approximately 52% of third-strikers in California were sentenced for nonviolent or nonserious crimes, including 344 for petty theft and 647 for drug offenses.
- Three-strikes inmates in California are far more likely to be African Americans than Caucasians—approximately 45% of all third-strikers are African American.
- One "three-striker" is Michael Garcia, who stole a $5.62 package of chuck steak from a grocery store after his mother's Social Security check failed to arrive on time (Schiraldi, Sussman, and Hyland 1994). His previous strikes also were nonviolent offenses.
- Early in the implementation of the law, the California three-strikes law was about four times as likely to be used against a person for marijuana possession than for murder, rape, and kidnapping combined. Specifically, 85% of California's sentenced inmates were for nonviolent offenses, including 192 for marijuana possession (versus 40 murderers, 25 rapists, and 24 kidnappers).
- In California, almost three of four (74%) second-strikers and third-strikers are minorities.
- In California, African Americans make up 8% of the general population and 21% of arrests but 37% of second-strikers and 44% of third-strikers.
- Most Americans support three-strikes laws. According to Lacayo (1994), 81% of Americans support life imprisonment for persons convicted of three serious crimes. One Gallup poll found that 78% of respondents believed that their local courts did not deal harshly enough with criminals (Maguire and Flanagan 1997).

Truth-in-sentencing laws are also examples of mandatory sentences. At least 29 states now have these laws on the books, and the first was imposed in 1984. Most of these states require inmates to serve at least 85% of their sentences. By the end of 2000, at least 16 states have also abolished *parole* to reduce early release from prison. At least five other states have also abolished parole board release for some offenders, such as violent or felony offenders. Although truth-in-sentencing laws may sound logical, what they do is eliminate reductions in sentencing for good behavior and mandate that correctional facilities keep inmates in prison for longer periods of time than they would normally serve. In some states, these longer sentences have created an extraordinary burden because of the added expense to correctional budgets and the growth of overcrowding problems.

Walker (1998, p. 136) concludes that mandatory sentences are responsible in part for the shift of power in the courts to prosecutors, as well as for "unduly harsh" punishments for some crimes. Tonry (1992, p. 243) states it very clearly: "Mandatory penalties do not work." The American Bar Association has concluded that no mandatory sentencing should be in effect for any category of offenses.

In 2003, the Supreme Court upheld California's three-strikes sentencing law in the cases of *Ewing v. California* (01-6978) and *Lockyer v. Andrade* (01-1127), ruling five to four that long prison terms are constitutionally permissible even for minor offenders. The court upheld sentences of

25 years to life and 50 years to life for a thief who shoplifted clubs from a golf course pro shop and for a man who stole a handful of videotapes from Kmart, respectively. In the former case, Sandra Day O'Connor wrote, "We do not sit as a super-legislature to second-guess [the legislature's] policy choices. It is enough that the state of California has a reasonable basis for believing that dramatically enhanced sentences for habitual felons advances the goals of its criminal justice system in any substantial way." Only time will tell whether she was right or wrong. It should be noted that many eminent criminologists believe that California's law is a major mistake and a burden on California rather than a blessing.

Although the longest time a person can actually serve is the term of his or her natural life, as in the case of mandatory life sentences, the longest sentence actually imposed by a court is 10,000 years! The sentence was imposed in Tuscaloosa, Alabama, on Dudley Wayne Kyzer, age 40, for a triple murder in 1981. Obviously, no one can ever serve such a sentence—they are handed down by judges who want to make political or moral statements. In fact, the longest sentence ever served for a crime was by Paul Geidel, convicted of second-degree murder in 1911, as a 17-year-old in New York City; he served 68 years, 8 months, and 2 days (Rush 2000, p. 295).

METHODS OF PUNISHMENT

When you think of punishment, what do you see? Prisons? The death penalty? These are currently considered valid sentencing options for judges who are responsible for meting out punishments in the United States (death is available in 38 states). However, prison and death are two punishments that are relatively infrequently administered. I say "relatively infrequently" not to suggest that their administration is not plagued with problems, but to make the point that, relative to probation, imprisonment and death are rare. In Chapters Nine and Ten, I take a close look at incarceration and the death penalty, respectively.

Generally speaking, four main categories of punishment are used in the United States—including probation, incarceration, intermediate sanctions, and death. These are depicted along a continuum in Figure 8.1. Punishments (also known as *criminal sanctions*) on the left in this figure are generally less restrictive and less expensive than those to the right of the continuum.

Probation, the least restrictive of punishments depicted in Figure 8.1, is also the most commonly used criminal sanction in the United States. According to the U.S. Department of Justice,

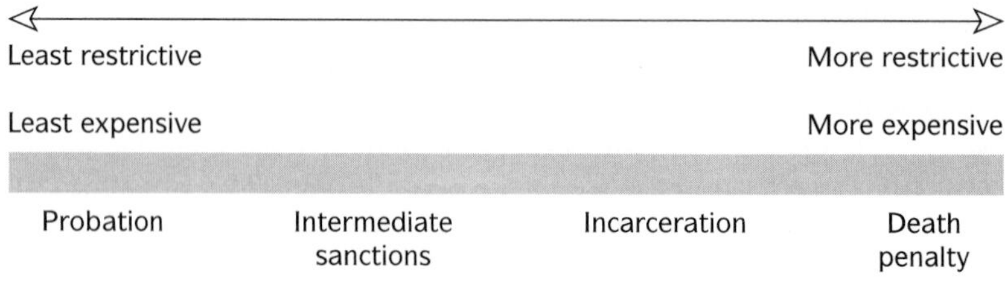

FIGURE 8.1
Continuum of American Punishments

probation is the court-ordered community supervision of convicted offenders by a probation agency, requiring the adherence to specific rules of conduct while living in the community. The following box lists some of these requirements. If they are violated, probation can be revoked and the offender sent to prison or jail, whatever was stated in the original sentence by the judge.

Typical rules of probation

- Pay supervision fees.
- Pay fines.
- Pay court costs.
- Attend substance abuse treatment.
- Gain and maintain employment.
- Participate in drug testing.
- Pay victim restitution.
- Perform community service.
- Gain education and/or training.
- Have no contact with the victim.
- Remain drug-free.
- Attend counseling.
- Abide by driving restrictions.
- Abide by movement restrictions.

Probation is not intended for serious, repetitive, violent criminals. Generally, it is not intended for people convicted of multiple charges, for people who were arrested while on probation or parole, for repeat offenders, for drug addicts, or for violent offenders (Petersilia and Turner 1986). In fact, in recent history the offense most likely to lead to a sentence of straight probation or a split sentence between incarceration and probation has been simple drug possession, while the least likely has been murder, followed by rape. For every type of crime, people sentenced to probation generally receive shorter sentences than those sentenced to prison.

Walker (1998) claims that we use probation for various reasons. First, as noted, many crimes are relatively minor and thus do not warrant a term of incarceration. Second, there are not enough prison and jail cells for those we have already sentenced to incarceration, which is why U.S. prisons are operating above maximum capacity. Third, probation is much cheaper than prison. Walker estimates that it costs about $600 per year per offender for probation. He maintains that it costs about 37 times as much to incarcerate an offender for a year in prison (plus the fact that you don't have to build a facility to house people on probation). Fourth, probation is no less effective than prison. In fact, probation is actually more successful at reducing recidivism than more severe sanctions.

Incarceration takes many forms, notably being sent to prison or jail. It involves having one's freedoms taken away while one is locked away from society. A *prison* is a state or federal correctional facility used to house those sentenced to more than 1 year of incarceration. A *jail* is a local correctional facility used to hold persons awaiting trial, awaiting sentencing, serving a sentence of less than 1 year, or awaiting transfer to another facility. Incarceration is used more for violent criminals than for property criminals and is a sanction supposedly intended for more severe offenders.

Unlike those on probation, people who are incarcerated are not allowed to live in the community. They are taken away from their families and loved ones and are subjected to numerous discomforts (see Chapter Nine). Think of being locked away from free society, not being able to come and go as you please, being told what to do, when to do it, and how to do it. Does this sound like soft punishment?

Imprisonment costs approximately $24,000 per year per inmate. Since most offenders do not warrant incarceration, and because probation may not be tough enough for some offenders, a wide array of *intermediate sanctions* has become available to sentencing judges. The following box lists several of these.

Some types of intermediate sanctions

- *Boot camps:* Usually intended for juveniles, these facilities are run as paramilitary organizations, attempting to instill discipline in wayward youth through hard work and exercise and to increase educational and vocational skills.
- *House arrest:* This is intended for less severe offenders, who are required to stay within a certain distance of their actual residence.
- *Electronic monitoring:* This is usually used in conjunction with house arrest. Offenders are monitored via an electronic device attached to their leg, which assures that they do not violate the terms of their house arrest.
- *Community service:* This is typically used for the least severe offenders, who are required to spend a specified number of hours serving their community by picking up garbage or performing other necessary tasks.
- *Day reporting center:* This is a facility where probationers are sent to attend treatment and counseling sessions each day.

Punishment Facts

In 2000, state and federal courts convicted just over 1 million adults of felonies, the vast majority of which were handled by state courts. As shown in Table 8.1, of all felons convicted by state courts in 2000, 68% were sentenced to incarceration (40% to prison and 28% to jail), and 32% were sentenced to probation. Incarceration was more likely for violent offenses (78%) than drug offenses (67%) and property offenses (64%). The felony offense most likely to lead to incarceration was murder (95%) while the least likely were fraud, forgery, and embezzlement (54%).

At the federal level, 74% of convicted defendants were sentenced to prison in 2001, up from 65% in 1994. Almost all (92%) convicted federal drug offenders were sentenced to prison in 2001. Of those sentenced to prison, the average sentence was 57 months, down from 63 months in 1994. Those convicted of violent felonies were sentenced on average to 91 months, versus 87 months for weapons felonies and 74 months for drug felonies. Even though average sentences fell from 1994 to 2001, average time served increased from 27 months to nearly 44 months. In 2000, violent offenders served an average sentence of nearly 54 months, drug offenders served just over 41 months, public order offenders served nearly 20 months, and property offenders served just over 16 months.

TABLE 8.1

Types of Sentences Imposed on Convicted Felons (2000)

	Prison	Jail	Probation
All offenses	40%	28%	32%
Violent offenses	54%	24%	22%
Murder/manslaughter	93%	2%	5%
Sexual assault/rape	64%	20%	16%
Robbery	74%	15%	11%
Aggravated assault	40%	31%	29%
Property offenses	37%	27%	36%
Burglary	52%	24%	24%
Theft/motor vehicle theft	33%	30%	37%
Fraud/forgery/embezzlement	29%	25%	46%
Drug offenses	38%	29%	33%

SOURCE: Sourcebook of Criminal Justice Statistics (2003).

As shown in Table 8.2, the average sentence of these convicted felons in state courts was 36 months, including 55 months for those sentenced to prison, 38 months for those sentenced to probation, and 6 months for those sentenced to jail. Sentences for convicted violent felons were longer (66 months overall) than for property offenses and drug offenses (27 and 30 months, respectively). Murderers were sentenced to the longest average sentences (242 months), whereas motor vehicle thieves were given the shortest average sentences (18 months), followed by those convicted of drug possession (20 months).

As for intermediate sanctions, additional sentences imposed by state courts on convicted felons included fines to courts (25%), restitution to victims (14%), community service (5%), treatment (7%), and other sentences (7%). These additional sentences were generally more likely to be handed down to property and drug offenders than violent offenders.

TABLE 8.2

Average Sentences Imposed on Convicted Felons (2000)

	Number of Months		
	Prison	Jail	Probation
All offenses	55	6	38
Violent offenses	91	7	44
Murder/manslaughter	248	18	64
Sexual assault/rape	108	8	64
Robbery	94	11	52
Aggravated assault	59	6	40
Property offenses	42	6	38
Burglary	52	7	41
Theft/motor vehicle theft	34	6	37
Fraud/forgery/embezzlement	34	6	37
Drug offenses	47	6	36

SOURCE: Sourcebook of Criminal Justice Statistics (2003).

At the end of 2001, of all people under jail supervision, 2.5% were sentenced to community service, 2% were in weekender programs, 1.4% were supervised with electronic monitoring, 0.7% were in treatment programs, 0.7% were involved with work programs, 0.5% reported to day reporting centers, and 2% were involved in some other program or type of supervision.

Although the average sentence imposed by state courts for convicted felons was nearly 5 years in 2000, the average time served was about 47% of the sentences imposed. According to the Bureau of Justice Statistics, in 1996 violent offenders served only 45 months of their sentences of 85 months in prison. Drug offenders and property offenders also serve just under half of their sentences.

Average sentences actually served increased from 1990 to 1996 for every crime except robbery (Bureau of Justice Statistics 2003). Yet even though time served has increased, the average criminal sentences imposed by courts have declined. For example, between 1990 and 1996, the average sentence for all offenses declined or remained the same except for murder and nonnegligent manslaughter and some forms of sexual assault (Bureau of Justice Statistics 2003). Interestingly, as of 1999, states without truth-in-sentencing laws sentenced violent inmates to longer average sentences (104 months) than truth-in-sentencing states (93 months) and offenders served more time (55 months versus 50 months) (Sourcebook of Criminal Justice Statistics 2003).

At the federal level, sentences increased significantly between 1986 and 1997. Average prison sentences increased from 39 months to 54 months, and average time served increased from 21 months to 47 months. Sentences for weapons and drug offenders more than doubled during this time period. Offenders entering federal prison in 2001 could expect to serve 87% of their sentences, up from 65% for those who entered in 1990.

At the end of 2002, more than 6.7 million people were under some form of correctional supervision in the United States (including probation, prison, jail, and other forms of criminal sanctions). This includes 4 million people on probation, 1.4 million people in prison, 753,141 on parole, and 665,475 in jail. Thus, 4.7 million were under community supervision (probation and parole) and 2.1 million people were incarcerated in 2002 (prisons and jail). Figure 8.2 shows the number of people under each of these forms of correctional supervision. About 3.1% of the U.S. adult population, or 1 in every 32 adults, is under some form of correctional supervision.

The rate of incarceration (prisons and jails) in 2002 was 701 per 100,000 residents, number one in the world. The rate of imprisonment (prisons only) was 476 per 100,000 people and the rate of jail incarceration was 257 per 100,000 people. One in every 142 residents was in prison or jail in 2002. The rate of imprisonment growth is alarming and unprecedented in our nation's history. The use of probation tripled from 1980 to 1997, a rate equal to the increase in the use of incarceration (Gaines, Kaune, and Miller 2000, p. 420). You might think that because most convicted criminals do not go to prison, this is proof that the United States is "soft on crime," but in fact the U.S. leads the world in incarceration rates.

The rate of growth of the nation's prison population has gradually slowed over the past 5 to 7 years, especially the past 2 years. During 2002, the overall rate of growth was 2.8%, compared with an average annual growth of 3.8% since 1995. According to the Bureau of Justice Statistics, the smallest growth in prison populations since 1972 was in 2001 at 1.1%. In the last 6 months of 2001, the number of state inmates actually declined, but less than 1% (0.3%). Yet in the first half of 2002, the nation's incarceration population grew again, by 2.8%, with the largest increase in federal prisoners.

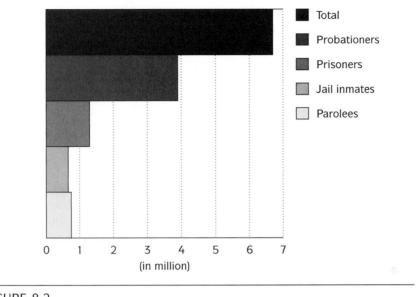

Total
Probationers
Prisoners
Jail inmates
Parolees

0   1   2   3   4   5   6   7
(in million)

FIGURE 8.2
Correctional Population in the United States (2002)

Between 1995 and 2001, jail populations grew 3.7% per year, prison populations increased by 3.6% per year, probation populations grew 3.4%, and parole populations increased by 1.2%. In 2001, state prison populations grew only 0.4%, while jail populations grew 1.6%. Yet federal prison populations grew 7%. This is evidence of a *federalization of incarceration* in recent years. In the first 6 months of 2002, federal prison populations grew the fastest, accounting for more than 40% of the growth during this time. As of 2001, the federal prison system was the third largest system in the United States, following only Texas and California.

In 2001, state prisons were operating at between 1% and 16% over capacity, and federal prisons were operating at 31% over capacity. According to the Bureau of Justice Statistics, 22 states and the federal government were at or above capacity and 26 states were below capacity. Private prisons housed 5.8% of state inmates in 2001, as well as 12.3% of federal inmates.

The adult probation population in 2002 grew 1.6%, less than the average 3.4% growth per year since 1995. The adult parole population grew 2.8%, and mandatory release made up 55% of those released. Only 36% of all offenders released from prison to parole were released through discretionary parole, down from 59% in 1990.

WHY DO WE PUNISH?

Punishment is natural: "Parents punish children by taking away privileges. The punishment is often characterized as 'teaching a lesson.' Teachers discipline students who don't follow the rule; managers penalize unproductive employees" (Kappeler, Blumberg, and Potter 2000, p. 234). Given that punishment is natural, it is unlikely that we can ever put a complete end to the use of punishment as a means to control crime. Yet many criminal justice scholars do believe that the United States is overrelying on punishment in general and on certain forms of punishment in particular.

Here I assess why American criminal justice administers punishment to offenders. John Stuart Mill (1859) argued that we should punish people only to prevent harms to others. Sir James Stephen (1883) disagreed with this position and stated that the purpose of punishment is to enforce the morality of the community—to allow the community to hate criminals and to get revenge against them. Similarly, Immanuel Kant saw punishment as virtuous because the guilty deserve to suffer. However, Kant did not believe that punishment should be used to deter others who had not yet done anything wrong, nor did he believe in rehabilitation (cited by Jeffery 1990, p. 63). The great legal scholar Oliver Wendell Holmes did not support vengeance; he believed that the only justifications for punishment were deterrence and reform.

Lord Patrick Devlin (1959) attacked Mill's position and supported Stephen's view that punishment should be used to enforce morality. H. L. A. Hart (1968, p. 231) defended Mill and argued that the law could not successfully be used to enforce morality. Hart thought that the only justification for punishment was the prevention of harm. Hart did support retribution as well and claimed that "the justification for punishing men (who have committed wickedness) is that the return of suffering for moral evil voluntarily done, is itself just or morally good."

Whatever your own personal beliefs, most criminal justice scholars agree that there are four primary justifications for criminal punishment.

- Retribution
- Incapacitation
- Deterrence
- Rehabilitation

Each of these justifications for punishment is discussed next.

Retribution

Retribution implies "an eye for an eye, a tooth for a tooth." That is, when a criminal harms a victim, he or she deserves to suffer a similar if not identical harm. In Western societies, the notion of retribution has evolved out of religious convictions found in the Old Testament.

Retribution has two related meanings. The first deals with the natural human emotion of *vengeance*—the desire to give the offender his or her "just deserts." At various times in U.S. history, notable people have attempted to achieve such literal retribution. For example, Thomas Jefferson proposed to the legislature that for the crime of murder by poisoning, poisoning be the just penalty. For the crime of rape, he proposed castration of the rapist as retributive justice. For treason, he suggested that the offender be buried alive (Gottfredson 1999, p. 3).

The second meaning of retribution deals with a more rational approach to justice. It assumes that when an offender commits a harm against a victim, the offender gains an unfair advantage to which he or she is not entitled under the law. To balance the scales of justice, punishment must be administered to counteract the advantage gained through crime. In essence, when rules are broken, rule breakers must be punished. The basic differences between vengeance and retribution are as follows.

- Retribution is rooted in the law (and thus is legal) and vengeance is not.
- Retribution is public (i.e., decided by legislators and judges) and vengeance is private (i.e., carried out by family members of victims).

- Retribution is something offenders pay back to society for their crimes (e.g., years of their lives, restitution to victims), whereas vengeance is something society pays back to offenders (e.g., punishment, pain).

With regard to the first meaning of retribution, Beckett and Sasson (2000, p. 164) claim that "those [victims of crime] who believe that revenge will bring them relief often discover that it does not" (e.g., see Prejean 1993; Shapiro 1997). When you or a loved one becomes a crime victim, the desire to get even with the offender is natural and easy to understand. Yet this does not mean that getting even will give you a sense of justice or relief. Given the long delays in the administration of justice, the fact that victims are not highly involved in this process, and the fact that punishment is so detached from the victim, it is just as logical to assert that the criminal justice network cannot effectively make victims feel better.

It is tough to argue against the logic of the second meaning of retribution. If people freely choose to commit crime, they deserve some form of punishment for the harms they have inflicted on society. After all, one conception of justice, discussed in Chapter One, requires that the guilty be held accountable for their crimes in order for justice to be achieved as an outcome. Yet as I have attempted to demonstrate throughout this book, we should not let our goal of punishing the guilty so interfere with our goal of being fair and impartial in the criminal justice process that humans become generally less free, especially when this burden is imposed on some groups in society more than on others.

One clear benefit of retribution administered by the criminal justice network is that it limits the likelihood that *escalation* will occur (Glaser 1997). That is, if victims were allowed to get "justice" for themselves, without the assistance of their government, the desire for vengeance would not be limited by the law. Thus, a single murder might lead to two more deaths—the death of the guilty offender and perhaps also the death of someone standing next to the offender when the victim's family opens fire. This in turn could lead to a desire for vengeance on the part of the offender's family and the family of the innocent bystander. Without state-controlled retribution, where would the cycle of vengeance and escalation end?

Incapacitation

Incapacitation involves restricting the freedom of offenders so that they cannot offend again. The logic of incapacitation is summed up by L. Friedman (1993, p. 237) as follows: "[A] burglar in jail can hardly break into your house. This effect is called 'incapacitation. . . .' If all the crooks are behind bars, they cannot rape and loot and pillage." Most people think of prisons and jails when they think of incapacitation, because they envision the offender being removed from society, but in fact, the most typical form of incapacitation is not incarceration; probation is more commonly used to restrict the freedom of offenders, as you read earlier.

Unless you believe in reincarnation, the ultimate form of incapacitation is death. When an offender is killed, he or she can no longer offend against society. Thus, incapacitation becomes a justification for the death penalty (see Chapter Ten). Aside from death, however, we cannot be assured that offenders who are locked up behind bars will not continue to offend against society, and there is overwhelming evidence of crimes committed within prisons and jails against other inmates and correctional personnel. Because such crimes are not widely discussed or broadcast in the news, society can easily ignore them, but this does not make them any less real or harmful.

It also does not deny that offenders who are locked away with other criminals will ultimately learn to be better offenders (see Chapter Nine).

One thing we can conclude is that the United States is currently on an incarceration binge that is unprecedented in the history of the world. Yet Americans seem to be generally unconcerned with the long-term social and economic implications of this trend for the United States. Incapacitation, whether it be achieved through incarceration or through the death penalty, suggests an "I give up" attitude toward crime and criminals. If we are unwilling to treat those who are sick, unwilling to change those environments that are conducive to street crime, and unwilling to invest in long-term approaches to crime prevention, then the easiest alternative is simply to lock people away from society (or kill them) so that we do not have to think about them.

Incapacitation takes two main forms—general and selective (Walker 1998). *General* or *collective incapacitation* occurs when society uses incarceration and other forms of incapacitation as a general punitive strategy for many forms of criminality. This type of incapacitation is aimed at all forms of criminality, regardless of the likelihood of *recidivism*, or repeat offending. It is based on the belief that incarceration and other forms of incapacitation are effective means of controlling crimes. *Selective incapacitation* occurs when these punishment mechanisms are reserved for the most dangerous offenders, those in most need of incapacitation because of their likelihood of repeating their criminality. Selective incapacitation is based on scientific research demonstrating that a small percentage of offenders commits a very large portion of all crimes (e.g., see Wolfgang, Figlio, and Sellin 1972).

The main problem with general or collective incapacitation is that not every offender deserves or warrants it, especially given the enormous costs associated with incarcerating and executing offenders. Collective incarceration may make us feel safer, but incarcerating more people has a "limited capacity to actually make us safer" (D. Gottfredson 1999, p. 431). As for selective incapacitation, the main problem is known as the "prediction problem" (S. Gottfredson and Gottfredson 1994). Because we simply are unable to predict accurately which offenders pose the greatest risk of repeating their crimes, it is difficult to use selective incapacitation accurately (Walker 1998). We do know that the most minor offenders are the ones who are most likely to reoffend. For example, thieves are more likely to commit more thefts after release than murderers are to commit more murders. Yet the costs of incarceration do not seem to be warranted for these minor offenders on the basis of the minor harms they are likely to inflict on society. Keeping thieves in jail or prison because of the likelihood that they will reoffend is not good criminal justice policy.

Deterrence

Deterrence is based on the logical notion that being punished for criminal activity will create fear in people so that they will not want to commit crime. There are two types of deterrence, special or specific deterrence and general deterrence. *Special* or *specific deterrence* means punishing offenders with the specific intent of instilling fear in them so that they will not commit crimes in the future. *General deterrence* involves punishing offenders to instill fear in society generally so that the rest of us will not want to commit crimes. Special or specific deterrence is aimed at stopping a known criminal offender from committing future crimes, whereas general deterrence is aimed at teaching the rest of us a lesson about what might happen to us if we were to commit crimes. Deterrence is evident in all that we do in the United States to fight crime, as discussed in the following box.

Deterrence in American punishment

- *Probation:* Offenders on probation are "hassled" by their probation officer and must follow many rules that they would not have to follow even in prison. Thus, they should be deterred from committing future crimes for fear that they might be put on probation again.
- *Incarceration:* Prisons and jails are horribly violent and repressive places. Any criminal who goes to prison ought to be afraid to go back. Additionally, all of society should fear suffering the pains of imprisonment. Thus, crime will be specially and generally deterred.
- *Boot camps:* Juvenile offenders sentenced to boot camps are forced to go to classes, work, and train through various physical fitness activities. It is hoped that these juveniles will fear being forced to experience such conditions again in the future, so that boot camps will deter juvenile delinquency.
- *Chain gangs:* Forcing inmates to work on the side of the road doing hard labor will not only instill fear in them, but also show others what can happen if they commit crimes. Thus, crime is both specially and generally deterred.
- *Death penalty:* Not only does the death penalty incapacitate the offender, it sends a message to all of society that anyone who commits murder can be executed for his or her offense.

Deterrence as a justification for punishment is based on several assumptions:

- Offenders are hedonistic or pleasure-seeking (e.g., crime provides various pleasures).
- Offenders seek to minimize costs or pains associated with crimes (i.e., they do not want to get caught and be punished).
- Offenders are rational (i.e., they choose to commit crime after weighing the potential costs or punishments and benefits or rewards).

Many criminologists believe that human beings are rational, are motivated by desire for personal pleasure, and want to avoid pain (Bohm 2001). Yet numerous human behaviors seem quite irrational. Most forms of criminality, it has been argued, are impulsive, short-sighted, stupid, and risky behaviors (see M. Robinson 2004). Many types of crimes are committed with only short-term gain in mind and with little or no thought of likely outcomes. This is not consistent with the view of the rational criminal.

To deter would-be offenders effectively, punishment must be certain (or at least likely), swift (or at least not delayed by months or years), and severe enough to outweigh the pleasures associated with crimes. Of these requirements, the most important is the *certainty of punishment*. The more likely that punishment is to follow a criminal act, the less likely that the criminal act will occur. Think of this example: If a lightning bolt was guaranteed to strike an offender who stole property, how many thefts do you think we would have each year? Probably not many. If it was absolutely certain that some higher being would strike you dead upon stealing someone else's property, everyone would know this and would refrain from committing theft in order to remain alive.

Such punishment would be certain, swift, and severe. But this example is misleading. For deterrence to be effective, it must be certain and somewhat swift, but it has to be only severe enough to outweigh the pleasure gained by committing the offense. For most crimes, certain death by lightning strike is not required! The noted Italian criminologist Cesare Beccaria wrote, in *An Essay on Crime and Punishments* (1776):

> The certainty of punishment, even though it be moderate, will always make a stronger impression than the fear of one more severe if it is accompanied by the hope that one may escape that punishment, because men are more frightened by an evil which is inevitable even though minor in nature. Further, if the punishment be too severe for a crime, men will be led to commit further crimes in order to escape punishment for the crime. . . . It is essential that it be public, prompt, necessary, minimal in severity as possible under given circumstances, proportional to the crime, and prescribed by the laws.

Contemporary research supports Beccaria's original statement. For example, Blumstein (1995, pp. 408–9) writes: "Research on deterrence has consistently supported the position that sentence 'severity' (that is, the time served) has less of a deterrent effect than sentence 'certainty' (the probability of going to prison). Thus, from the deterrence consideration, there is clear preference for increasing certainty, even if it becomes necessary to do so at the expense of severity."

What do you think? Is American criminal justice doing a good job of providing certain, swift punishments that outweigh the potential benefits of committing crimes? The evidence says no.

For every 100 serious street crimes (as measured in the National Crime Victimization Survey [NCVS]), only about 40 are known to the police (as measured in the Uniform Crime Reports [UCR]). Of these 40, only about 10 will lead to an arrest. Of those arrested, some will not be prosecuted, and some will be prosecuted but not convicted. Only about 3 of the original 100 crimes will lead to an incarceration. Punishment is anything but certain in the United States. Offenders know this. They tell criminologists that they know from personal experiences and from the experiences of fellow criminals that their risks of being apprehended by the police and convicted in court are very low (Cromwell, 1995). Because there are only 2.86 police officers in the United States for every 1,000 citizens (see Chapter Six), is this surprising?

What many offenders do tell us, and what is evident from their offending patterns, is that the great bulk of criminal behavior seems to be motivated by the desire to obtain short-term, immediate pleasures and gains. Long-term concern about potential punishment seems not to enter the minds of most offenders. If they thought that there was a good chance of getting caught, after all, offenders would not likely engage in their criminal behaviors, especially if they are as rational as criminologists tell us.

The main problem with deterrence as a justification for punishment is that it is impossible to demonstrate empirically that deterrence works. How can one prove the absence of criminal activity as a result of some criminal justice policy or program? This is why many criminal justice scholars argue that there is no empirical evidence supporting deterrence (Bohm 2001).

Even if the threat of punishment does deter some would-be offenders from committing crimes, our common experiences also suggest that deterrence is a myth.

Rehabilitation

Rehabilitation, probably the least popular of all justifications for punishing people today, is justified to the degree that something within offenders or their environments causes them to commit crime. Rehabilitation is aimed at eliminating the causes of crime by making offenders "better"— restoring them to a healthy condition—or altering conditions in their "sick" environments.

Rehabilitation would also include what Glaser (1997, p. 36) calls "anticriminal enculturation" ("[c]lassifying and separating inmates, promoting good staff–inmate relations, encouraging non-criminal visitors, providing law-abiding role models"), "retraining" ("[p]roviding academic and vocational instruction and employment during confinement, providing postrelease aid and personal counseling"), and "reintegrative shaming" ("[c]ondemning the offense but accepting the offender's apology, and granting public respect").

There is very little rehabilitation in American punishment today, mostly because of the widespread but false belief that we do not know what works or how best to use it. A major report by Martinson (reprinted in 2000, p. 23), a criminologist, stated that "with few and isolated exceptions, the rehabilitative efforts that have been reported so far have had not appreciable effect on rehabilitation." Such reports led to the decline of the rehabilitative ideal in the 1970s. In fact, some forms of *nurturant strategies* are likely to be highly effective at eliminating crime before it even happens (see M. Robinson 2004).

There is very little going on in the world of corrections today that we can call rehabilitation (D. Gottfredson 1999, p. 420). This can be attributed, in part, to the use of crime as an election issue by politicians seeking to get elected and maintain power through law-and-order, get-tough-on-crime rhetoric. The shift from rehabilitative to law-and-order approaches coincided with the use of crime for national political gain, as discussed in Chapter Two. Beckett and Sasson (2000, p. 55) explain how the rehabilitative ideal collapsed in the United States

> in the context of a growing chorus of criticism, from scholars and activists across the political spectrum, of "rehabilitation" as a primary justification for punishment. Conservatives opposed rehabilitation on the grounds that punishment must be harsh and painful if it is to deter crime. Liberals also criticized policies associated with rehabilitation, arguing that the open-ended ("indeterminate") sentences designed to facilitate "correction" created the potential for the intrusive, discriminatory, and arbitrary exercise of power.

Dozens of reviews of the ineffectiveness of rehabilitation were published in the 1960s and 1970s (see D. Gottfredson 1999, p. 423).

Walker (1998, p. 203) explains that we must, at least to some degree, still be committed to rehabilitation, because we still call the facilities that punish offenders "corrections" (which suggests that we hope to correct their behavior). Public opinion polls of Americans show that there is widespread support for rehabilitation, treatment, and crime prevention as alternatives to punitiveness (Roberts and Stalans 2000). In fact, some treatment does work for some people (see D. Gottfredson 1999, p. 434). In Chapter Thirteen, I argue that the future of criminal justice policy must be directed toward programs that are less punitive and more treatment-based.

Punishment: A Summary

The most severe sanctions are generally handed down for violent offenders and repeat offenders. Although judges ultimately hand down sentences to convicted offenders, the law is the instrument that sets forth minimum and maximum sentences. This gives legislators tremendous power in determining the direction of U.S. sentencing practices: "If lawmakers feel that the other two bodies—judges and officials of the executive branch—are being too lenient in their sentencing decisions, they can pass truth-in-sentencing laws that require convicts to serve the amount of time indicated in criminal codes" (Gaines, Kaune, and Miller 2000, p. 382).

We can also conclude, by comparing punishment in the United States with that in other countries, that the U.S. is very "tough" on crime. In fact, the United States sentences convicted murderers and robbers to roughly the same length of incarceration as Canada and England do (and we have the death penalty!). For relatively petty offenses, we sentence offenders to much longer terms of incarceration than these countries do (Beckett and Sasson 2000, p. 29). Thus, the notion that the U.S. criminal justice network is lenient on criminals is simply a myth (Kappeler, Blumberg, and Potter 2000).

The bottom line is that punishment should be aimed toward the future, not the past. When we say, "Don't cry over spilled milk," we mean that it does very little good after the milk is spilled to cry about it. The milk should be cleaned up, and precautions should be taken so that no more milk will be spilled in the future. If this requires punishing the offender for being careless, being reckless, or even intentionally spilling the milk, so be it. But it would not make much sense to punish the milk-spiller simply to get even with him or her. It would not get the floor clean (unless the punishment included cleaning the floor), it would not increase the likelihood that more milk would not be wasted in the future, and it might even be detrimental or destructive to the future of the milk-spiller, particularly if the punishment far exceeded the act. We wouldn't want to do anything that would make it more likely that the milk-spiller would spill more milk in the future, would we?

I argue that our system of punishment should be future-based, aimed at crime prevention, and rooted in utilitarianism. *Utilitarianism* (based on the writings of John Stuart Mill, for example) holds that actions should be aimed at doing the greatest good for the greatest number of people. Some of what we do may ideally be based on utilitarian goals of crime prevention through deterrence, but most of what we do in the United States to punish criminals is based on retribution, which is backward looking: It aims to get even with the offender for past wrongs. The methods of punishment available to the U.S. network of criminal justice are not being best utilized to achieve the goals set forth in Chapter One.

IS PUNISHMENT EFFECTIVE?

There are several sources of information to consider when attempting to determine which types of punishment are effective. One valuable source is offenders themselves. Another is criminal justice research, which sheds some light on the effectiveness of various kinds of punishment. Next, I summarize what these sources suggest about the effectiveness of punishment in the United States.

What We've Learned from Offenders

Many scholars have spent time with known offenders, both incarcerated and free, to discover their motivations and mechanisms for committing crimes. Offenders report that they have learned from personal experience that their likelihood of getting punished is extremely low in the United States. Figure 8.3 illustrates the likelihood of being caught by the police, convicted by the courts, and sentenced to some form of incarceration (prison or jail) for various crimes. The numbers in the first column represent the percentage of criminal victimizations (NCVS) in 1998 that led to an incarceration in either prison or jail. The numbers in the second column represent the percentage of crimes known to the police (UCR) in 1998 that led to an incarceration in either prison or jail. As you can see, the only crime for which there exists a substantial risk of

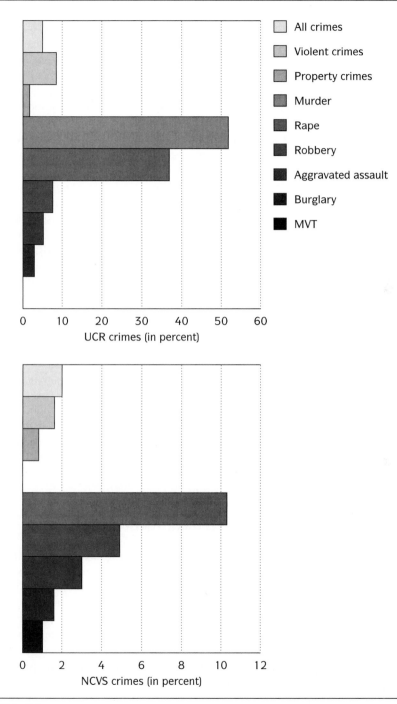

FIGURE 8.3
Likelihood of Incarceration, by Crime Type (1998)

arrest, conviction, and imprisonment is murder. The risk of incarceration for murder in 1998 was 52%, and the next highest risk was for rape (10%). No other crime ever neared a 10% risk for incarceration, including all violent crimes at 1.6% and all property crimes at 0.8%. Even using crimes known to the police as a measure of crime in the United States, other than murder, only rapists face some significant threat of incarceration (37%).

The crime of burglary, committed by rational offenders who carefully choose their targets on the basis of certain environmental characteristics, provides an excellent example of how the threat of punishment can never deter would-be offenders (Wright and Decker 1994). First, consider when burglars choose to commit their offenses. Many burglary studies show that residences are at highest risk for burglary when they are left unoccupied—that is, when no one is home. Burglar interview studies (Cromwell, Olson, and Avary 1991; M. Maguire and Bennett 1982; D. Walsh 1980; Wright and Decker 1994) and analyses of times of burglary (Reppetto 1974; Waller and Okihiro 1978; Winchester and Jackson 1982) have both demonstrated the importance of nonoccupancy in the occurrence of burglary. Scarr (1973) found, in a study in Washington, DC, that residential burglary occurred during the daytime and on weekends, following relatively regular patterns of nonoccupancy. Approximately half of all residential burglaries in Scarr's study occurred during the 6-hour period between 10:00 AM and 4:00 PM. Rengert and Wasilchick (1985) also found that the occurrence of burglary corresponded with occupants' schedules, because burglaries occurred during times when dwellings were left unoccupied.

Offenders tell researchers that they prefer not to enter residences that are occupied (Cromwell 1995). According to Cromwell, Olson, and Avary (1991, p. 37), 28 of the 30 burglars in their ethnographic study of breaking and entering indicated that they would never intentionally enter an occupied residence. In Wright and Decker's (1994) study of residential burglary, occupancy served as the major risk factor associated with the decision not to enter a potential target residence. Thus, the major risk to burglars is not law enforcement, courts, and corrections, but instead, the threat of run-ins with residential occupants. Consider also what these offenders tell researchers about their likelihood of being punished by criminal justice agencies. They know from experience that this likelihood is very low. As many offenders have stated, "If I thought I was going to get caught, I wouldn't be doing it, now would I?" Criminal justice data confirm that the risk of getting caught and incarcerated is slim.

What We've Learned from Other Criminal Justice Research

Research shows that, overall, American punishment is highly ineffective at reducing crime. Regardless of the type of punishment, virtually every type of criminal sanction fails to reduce recidivism. In the Issue in Depth at the end of this chapter, Professor C. Ray Jeffery of Florida State University provides some reasons why American punishment does not reduce crime.

According to the Bureau of Justice Statistics, "At least 95% of all state prisoners will be released from prison at some point; nearly 80% will be released to parole supervision." For example, in 2000, more than 570,000 inmates were released to community supervision after imprisonment. According to the data, most of these inmates will one day be back in trouble with the law. For example, a study of recidivism of prisoners released in 1994 from 15 states found that more than two-thirds (67.5%) were rearrested after 3 years and more than half (51.8%) returned to prison. Almost half (46.9%) were reconvicted of new crimes, and one-quarter (25.4%) were returned to prison with a new sentence (Sourcebook of Criminal Justice Statistics 2003). Failure rates were highest for property and drug offenders, as well as for males and African Americans. According to The Sentencing Project (2003), about one-third of inmates were rearrested within 6 months, 44% were rearrested within the first year, 59% were rearrested by the second year, and 67.5% were rearrested by the third year.

As for inmates released from federal prisons in 1994, almost one-fifth (18.6%) were returned to prison within 3 years of their release. The highest rates of failure were for violent offenders at the federal level.

Most data on recidivism concern only the percentage of offenders who successfully complete the conditions of their release within the time period during which they are being supervised. These data are more suggestive of success, but they are not as accurate in terms of characterizing the widespread failure of probation and parole because they do not measure long-term change in offenders.

At the end of 2002, more than 650,000 adults were under state parole supervision. Among those discharged in 1999, only 42% successfully completed their supervision term. As for probation, more than three in five state parolees successfully met the conditions of their probation in 2001, whereas 13% were incarcerated because of a rule violation or new offense, 11% also failed to meet their conditions but were not incarcerated, and 3% had absconded.

Of all federal offenders on probation in 2000, 80% successfully completed their conditions of probation, whereas 18% violated the conditions of their probation. Only 6% were arrested for committing new crimes. Violent offenders (36%) were most likely to violate the conditions of probation, followed by drug offenders (18%), property offenders (15%), and public order offenders (10%). Violent offenders (14%) were also most likely to commit new crimes, followed by drug offenders (7%), property offenders (5%), and public order offenders (4%).

As for parole, only 46% of those released on parole in 2001 successfully met the conditions of their release, while 40% were returned to incarceration for a rule violation or a new offense. Another 2% failed but were not reincarcerated and 9% absconded.

Success for those on parole was lower still, at only 55%, whereas 26% committed technical violations and 14% were arrested for committing new crimes. Once again, violent offenders (60%) were most likely to violate the conditions of their release, followed by public order offenders (36%), drug offenders (30%), and property offenders (28%). Violent offenders (21%) were also most likely to commit new crimes, followed by drug offenders (12%), property offenders (11%), and public order offenders (10%).

Success for those federal prisoners released on *supervised release* was lower, at 64%, whereas 21% committed technical violations and 13% were arrested for committing new crimes. Again, violent offenders (56%) were most likely to violate the conditions of their release, followed by public order offenders (36%), drug offenders (32%), and property offenders (29%). Violent offenders (20%) were also most likely to commit new crimes, followed by public order offenders (16%), drug offenders (12%), and property offenders (10%).

Those most likely to violate probation, supervised release, and parole were those with a history of drug abuse, those with lower education backgrounds, and younger males. Thus, our most disadvantaged criminals are most likely to continue offending. Our approach to crime control does not address the root problems, so why should we expect success?

Given the horrors of prison life (see Chapter Nine), it does not surprise many that prison fails so badly to stop repeat offenders. What is amazing to many is that even our most used criminal sanction—probation—appears to be largely a failure. Probation fails to stop recidivism about half the time (Walker 1998).

A couple of important factors explain the failure of probation. First, only about one-tenth of the corrections budget in any given year is allocated to probation, even though two-thirds of people under the supervision of corrections are on probation (Petersilia 1998). Also, even though probation populations have grown since 1980, funding for probation has remained virtually unchanged (Langan 1994). Further, individual probation officers have large caseloads, making their jobs difficult if not impossible. Given that offenders spend very little or no time being supervised by probation officers, and that this form of punishment does nothing to change the social conditions that produce criminality, maybe we should not expect probation to be effective.

In terms of other punishment strategies, many have been reviewed for their effectiveness of preventing crime. For example, Sherman et al. (1997) published a congressionally mandated evaluation of state and local crime prevention programs funded by the U.S. Department of Justice. The study, titled *Preventing Crime: What Works, What Doesn't, What's Promising*, clearly lays out the few programs that we know work to reduce crime, the many more that we know don't work, and the largest share that appear to be promising.

The authors proceeded from the assumption that crime prevention means "any practice shown to result in less crime than would normally occur without the practice." Programs aimed at crime prevention, including reducing drug abuse and youth violence, were assessed and placed in the "seven local institutional settings in which these practices operated": in communities, in families, in schools, in labor markets, in places, by police, and by courts and corrections (Sherman et al. 1997, p. 2).

The authors identified the hundreds of programs operated under U.S. Department of Justice funding and then developed the Maryland Scale of Scientific Methods so that the effectiveness of each study could be determined. As mentioned before, each individual type of crime prevention program was categorized as either something that works, something that does not work, something that is promising, or something that is unknown. These terms are defined as follows.

- *What works:* Programs that the authors believe are "reasonably certain" to prevent crime or reduce risk factors for crime.
- *What doesn't work:* Programs that the authors believe are "reasonably certain" to fail to prevent crime or reduce risk factors for crime.
- *What's promising:* Programs for which the level of certainty is too low to make firm conclusions but for which, on the basis of the limited evidence, there is some reason to expect some successful reduction in crime.
- *What's unknown:* Programs that the authors could not classify into one of these categories because of a lack of studies testing the programs' effectiveness

The following box presents the main findings of the study.

What works, what doesn't, what's promising

According to the authors, the following worked.

- *For older male ex-offenders:* Vocational training reduces repeat offending.
- *For high-risk repeat offenders:* Monitoring by specialized police units reduces the crimes committed by repeat offenders on the streets. Incarceration of high-risk offenders keeps them from committing crime on the streets.

- *For drug-using offenders in prison:* Therapeutic community resident programs reduce repeat offending after release.

According to the authors, the following did not work.

- *Correctional boot camps* using traditional military basic training
- *"Scared Straight" programs* wherein minor juvenile offenders visit adult prisons
- *Shock probation, shock parole, and split sentences* adding jail time to probation or parole
- *Home detention with electronic monitoring*
- *Intensive supervision on parole or probation*
- *Rehabilitation programs using vague, unstructured counseling*
- *Residential programs for juvenile offenders using challenging experiences in rural settings*

According to the authors, the following can be considered promising.

- *Prison-based vocational education programs* may be beneficial for adult inmates in federal prisons.
- *Drug courts* may reduce repeat offending.
- *Drug treatment in jails followed by urine testing in the community* may reduce subsequent drug use.
- *Intensive supervision and aftercare of juvenile offenders* may reduce repeat offending.
- *Fines* may reduce repeat crimes.

SOURCE: Sherman et al. (1997).

BIAS IN THE SENTENCING PROCESS

Recall from Chapter One that for a criminal justice process such as sentencing to be just, it must be fair and "not be affected by extraneous factors, such as race, gender, or socioeconomic status" (Kappeler, Blumberg, and Potter 2000, p. 228). Instead, sentences should be based on legal factors such as seriousness of offense and prior criminal record. The use of legal factors to determine appropriate sentence, though obviously less troublesome than sentencing based on extralegal factors, is still problematic. Using prior record and seriousness of offense to determine sentence allows biases of the criminal law and police behavior to come into play.

According to Kappeler and coworkers (2000, p. 28), "The empirical research done by criminal justice scholars has demonstrated with remarkable regularity that minority group members (particularly African Americans) and the poor get longer sentences and have less chance of gaining parole or probation, even when the seriousness of the crime and the criminal record of the defendants are held constant." T. Pratt (1998) illustrates how race will continue to play a role in sentencing into the 21st century. Such conclusions would lead you to believe that power has a direct influence on justice because relatively fewer powerful groups in the United States don't receive equal justice. For example, a study of incarceration in Florida found that the people most likely to be imprisoned were unemployed African American males, even when the seriousness of the offense and the prior record of the defendant were held constant (Chiricos and Bales 1991).

Walker, Spohn, and Delone (2000, p. 218) conclude that sentencing in the 1990s was characterized by discrimination because they found evidence of bias in many court jurisdictions in various areas related to sentencing. They write:

> Judges in some jurisdictions continue to impose harsher sentences on racial minorities who murder or rape whites, and more lenient sentences on racial minorities whose victims are of their own racial or ethnic group. Judges in some jurisdictions continue to impose racially biased sentences in less serious cases; in these "borderline cases" racial minorities get prison, whereas whites get probation. In jurisdictions with sentencing guidelines, judges depart from the presumptive sentence less often when the offender is African American or Hispanic than when the offender is white. Judges, in other words, continue to take race into account, either explicitly or implicitly, when determining the appropriate sentence.

It is in borderline cases, then, the only cases in which discretion can come into play, where discretion does come into play. In other words, race and class biases affect sentencing when it is possible for them to do so. Luckily, what mandatory sentencing has done for us, through sentencing guidelines and truth-in-sentencing laws, is make it harder for prosecutors, judges, and juries to be discriminatory in sentencing matters.

If one were to look at sentencing nationally without distinguishing between types of offenses, sentencing generally does not appear to be biased against any race of people; that is, African Americans and Caucasians appear to receive the same sentences within the same categories of offenses. An earlier review of sentencing and race by the National Academy of Sciences claimed that factors other than racial discrimination in sentencing account for most of the disproportionate representation of blacks in U.S. prisons, although "racial discrimination in sentencing may play a more important role in some regions or jurisdictions, for some crime types, or in the decisions of individual participants" (Blumstein et al. 1983, p. 13).

The average prison sentences imposed on convicted felons by state courts are virtually identical for African Americans and Caucasians for violent, property, drug, weapons, and other felonies. Yet there is evidence of clear sentencing bias against African Americans and Hispanics at the federal level, particularly with regard to drug offenses (Albonetti 1997).

African Americans also are no more likely than Caucasians nationally to be sentenced to a term of imprisonment by state courts for violent crimes and are even less likely to be sentenced to imprisonment for property offenses. African Americans are, however, more likely than Caucasians to be sentenced by state courts to incarceration in prison for drug offenses. Finally, there is evidence of discrimination against people of color, because there are patterns of discrimination in some cities (Walker, Spohn, and Delone 2000, p. 183).

It is unclear why African Americans appear to be discriminated against when sentenced to imprisonment for drug felonies but not for violent and property felonies. It is also not clear why African Americans are sentenced to longer jail terms than Caucasians but not prison terms generally. With regard to drugs, African Americans probably receive longer average sentences than Caucasians because of prior record, which thus reflects a bias—not a court bias, but a policing bias—as African Americans are more likely to be arrested for drug offenses (see Chapter Eleven). The use of discretion by prosecutors in the charging phase of the criminal justice process probably explains the apparent biases against African Americans in jail terms. In serious felonies that will likely result in substantial prison terms, it would be very difficult for prosecutors to use their discretion in a biased manner. It would, however, be substantially easier for them to be biased in relatively minor felonies, where they have substantially more discretion to charge defendants with more or less severe offenses. The same would be true for judges, whose discretion is limited when sentencing for major felonies but substantially wider in less serious felonies that may lead to jail time rather than imprisonment.

This may be why some studies have found sentencing bias against minorities for crimes where the nature of the crime and the offender's prior record do not point clearly to the appropriate sentence (e.g., see Unnever and Hembroff 1988). Such findings suggest that in at least some jurisdictions, when prosecutors and judges have discretion, they may be more likely to be biased against minorities than Caucasians. Other studies, in larger states and in areas where income inequality is higher, have found sentencing disparities based on race, even after controlling for legal factors (e.g., see Bridges and Crutchfield 1988; Myers 1987; Petersilia 1995).

There is also evidence of discrimination in sentences to probation. Caucasians are overrepresented among probationers, leading Walker, Spohn, and Delone (2000, p. 270) to suggest that the less severe sentence of probation is more likely to be reserved for Caucasians, especially in borderline cases where probation and a short sentence of incarceration are both options.

Some court clients are subjected to sentencing laws that are clearly biased. For example, the three-strikes laws introduced earlier in this chapter are disproportionately aimed at relatively non-serious minority offenders. Harvard Medical School researcher William Brownsberger claims that they are "wasting prison resources on non-violent, low-level offenders and reducing resources available to lock up violent offenders" (quoted in National Center on Institutions and Alternatives 1999). Walker (1998, p. 137) writes that three-strikes laws "have been almost universally condemned by criminologists and other experts on sentencing."

Researchers confidently conclude that the laws cost billions of dollars, cause lengthy delays in the criminal justice process, and are biased against members of the poor and racial minorities. A Rand Corporation study estimates that if California fully carried out its version of the three-strikes law, it would cost more than $5 billion per year (Greenwood et al., 1994). The likely result: a drastic drop in street crime (about 28%, they estimate, mostly in assaults and burglaries), but also a simultaneous pillaging of the state's higher education and social welfare budgets. Three-strikes laws are disinvestments in America's future.

And who is getting caught? The shocking fact is that most offenders sentenced are not repeat violent murderers, rapists, and robbers. After the first 5 years in California, only 25% of third-strikers were convicted of violent offenses, including 294 murderers, 241 child molesters, and 136 rapists. The largest category of "violent" third-strikers was robbers, and most of these committed their crimes to get drugs and/or did not actually hurt anyone. The following box lists some people sentenced under three-strikes laws.

Victims of three-strikes laws

- Jerry Williams, who stole a piece of pizza
- A woman who bought $20 worth of cocaine, 14 years after her second conviction
- A robber of a sandwich shop in Washington who stole $151 (his two previous robberies netted $460) (Walker 1998, p. 139)
- A teenager sentenced to life for stealing a cellular phone (Dominick 1997)
- A man sentenced to 25 years to life for stealing a bottle of vitamins from a grocery store (Gaines, Kaune, and Miller 2000, p. 394)

- A man convicted of stealing a carton of cigarettes from Target, with prior offenses 15 years earlier of burglary and assault
- A woman who gained $5 in a cocaine sale, whose prior offenses included robbery, burglary, and prostitution
- A man convicted of receiving stolen property (a 1985 car), whose prior offenses included burglary, drug possession, and a robbery that involved the theft of a pack of cigarettes from another inmate
- A homeless man, whose only possession was a bicycle, charged with stealing a $2 bicycle lock
- A severely retarded 34-year-old woman, who was homeless and living in a park, charged with possession of a $5 rock of cocaine
- A man who allegedly bought a crushed macadamia nut from the police, charged with attempting to possess drugs (Dodge and Harris 2000, pp. 355–56)

SOURCES: (1) Families to Amend California's Three-Strikes. 2001. Facts about California's 3-strikes law. http://www.facts1.com/general/facts1.htm. (2) Hughes, W. 2002. Three strikes laws: Only the poor need apply. http://www.counterpunch.org/hughes1112.html. (3) The Sentencing Project. 1999. "Three strikes" five years later. http://www.sentencingproject.org/pubs/3strikes.pdf. (4) The Sentencing Project. 2001. Aging behind bars: "Three strikes" seven years later. http://www.sentencingproject.org/pdfs/9087.pdf. (5) Sunde S. 2001. Blacks bear brunt of '3 strikes' laws. http://seattlepi.nwsource.com/local/strk20.shtml. (6) Wood, D. 1999. The impact of 'Three strikes' laws. http://csmweb2.emcweb.com/durable/1999/03/08/fp1s1-csm.shtml.

Many three-strikers are drug offenders, including those who were convicted and sentenced simply for possessing drugs. Meanwhile, the Rand Corporation claims that mechanisms such as drug treatment, parent training, delinquent supervision, and graduation incentives are up to seven times more effective at reducing recidivism than mandatory prison terms and are more cost-effective as well (Robinson 2000). Three-strikes laws have shifted the power in courts from judges to prosecutors, have led to backlogs in court dockets, and have led to more pretrial detention for inmates charged with third-strike offense (because they are considered a high flight risk), sentence length has increased (but only for minor crimes), prisons are overcrowded, funding for social services has been cut, and racial and class-based disparities have worsened.

Although street crime is down in California in the first 5 years since the laws were implemented, criminologists have attributed such declines to factors beyond the scope of criminal justice (see Chapter Four), crime was already declining prior to the passage of the laws, crime declined in other states without the laws, and crime declined more in the counties that used the laws less than in those that used it more.

When drug offenses are included in mandatory sentencing, such sentencing laws become a major source of criminal justice bias. For example, in 2000–2001, African Americans accounted for only 6.8% of monthly drug users (versus 6.9% for Caucasians), and they accounted for 34.5% of arrests for drug abuse violations (versus 64.2% for Caucasians). Earlier data showed that African Americans made up more than half (55%) of convictions for drug offenses and almost three of four (74%) prison sentences for drug offenses (Mauer and Huling 1995a). Additionally, whereas 39% of crack users were African American, 89% of people sentenced for federal crack crimes were African American. Throughout the United States, convicted drug offenders are disproportionately low-income minorities. And according to the Bureau of Justice Statistics (2003), African Americans are sentenced to prison more than half the time for drug offenses, whereas Caucasians are sentenced to incarceration only about one-third of the time for the same offenses. From 1990 to 1996, the number of African Americans in federal prisons for violent and property crimes decreased by 726 persons, but for drug offenses the number increased by 12,852!

The impact of sentencing laws on minorities (especially African Americans) is greatest at the federal level. Thus, the number of federal inmates in 1980 who were minorities was 8,085 (33%), but this increased to 65,000 (64%) by 1995 (Coalition for Federal Sentencing Reform 1999). Such bias counters the myth that the criminal justice network is fair. Some even suggest that the war on drugs amounts to genocide "because African Americans constitute a disproportionate number of those subjected to arrest, prosecution, and incarceration for illicit drug trafficking" (e.g., see Meddis 1993).

Federal sentencing against drug dealers demonstrates clear evidence of bias against people of color. One study, for example, found that African American and Hispanic drug offenders received longer sentences than Caucasian drug offenders, even after controlling for relevant legal factors (Albonetti 1997), and that Caucasian defendants received more benefit from departures from federal sentencing guidelines. Albonetti concludes that her findings "strongly suggest that the mechanism by which the federal guidelines permit the exercise of discretion operates to the disadvantage of minority defendants" (p. 818).

In the wars against drugs and violence, federal sentencing has become much more complex. And the prosecutor, who decides what to charge and how many counts to charge (among the thousands of offenses in the federal criminal code), thereby effectively determines the likely sentence. Such concentration of power creates bias in favor of the government and against the client, who is supposedly innocent until proved guilty. Also, judges have little oversight in the process, and only prosecutors can reward suspects for turning state's evidence against other suspects.

Federal sentencing is also viewed as unfair. For example, Judge Gray (2001) reports that most judges want to modify guidelines to increase their sentencing discretion. A 1992 survey of judges found that they believed that only one in four sentences imposed under guidelines is appropriate (Coalition for Federal Sentencing Reform 1997). A particularly striking unfair pattern is the 100:1 ratio for sentences for crack cocaine and powder cocaine, meaning that to receive a mandatory sentence of 5 years' imprisonment, a person would need 100 times as much powder cocaine as crack (500 grams of powder versus 5 grams of crack). No one can say for sure if this discrepancy is racially motivated, but in the late 1990s, African Americans accounted for 39% of crack cocaine users (and for only 13% of the general population) but 89% of those sentenced for federal crack crimes (Coalition for Federal Sentencing Reform 1999). Media portrayal of crack use reinforces the stereotype or myth that it is an "African American drug" (e.g., see Reeves and Campbell 1994). Because harms associated with crack cocaine (e.g., "crack babies") were so broadly portrayed and discussed, not even a single African American member of Congress spoke out against the sentencing disparities between crack and powder cocaine at the time that the law was originally proposed and debated (D. Kennedy 1997).

Of course, bias in sentencing can be found when we look at crimes committed by the wealthy. As noted by Kappeler, Blumberg, and Potter (2000, p. 230), this is where the courts tend to be "kinder and gentler." One study compared people who were convicted of grand theft versus those convicted of fraud in the health care industry. The study (Tillman and Pontell 1992) showed that those who were convicted of fraud were only half as likely as those convicted of grand theft to be sentenced to prison, even though the damages they caused were 10 times greater. The average sentence given to offenders in the savings and loan crisis in the 1980s was 36 months, versus 38 months for people who committed auto theft and 56 months for burglars (Pontell, Calavita, and Tillman 1994). The average sentences for white-collar offenders in the most recent cases have been modest as well. Failing to sentence the guilty simply because of their social class and skin color is as unjust as sentencing a small group of the guilty more harshly because of their social class or skin color. White-collar deviance (see Chapter Four) is one place where Justitia, the Lady Justice, truly is not blind. Instead, she knowingly shrugs off the harms caused by wealthy Caucasian criminals.

CONCLUSION

Sentencing is the process whereby persons who have been convicted of a crime or crimes are sanctioned for their wrongdoings by a court. In the United States, we punish offenders because we want them to suffer (vengeance), we want them to pay us back for the harms they inflicted on us (retribution), and we want to scare them so that they will not commit crimes in the future (deterrence). Yet most of what we do to fight crime does not get even with offenders and does not prevent future criminality. American criminal justice is dedicated to sentencing criminals to punishments that have clearly been proven ineffective, particularly imprisonment. Meanwhile, punishment in the United States is also biased in some ways against poor people, people of color, and women. Although biases in sentencing are not institutional, there is clear evidence of sentencing disparities based on class, race, and gender. These biases serve as further evidence of unjust practices of the U.S. criminal justice network.

ISSUE IN DEPTH
Professor C. Ray Jeffery on Why Punishment Does Not Work

Professor C. Ray Jeffery (1990), on the basis of psychological theories of behavior, outlined significant reasons that American punishment does not work to reduce crime and may, in certain circumstances, actually increase crime. His main points include the following.

- To be successful, the time lag between the behavior and the punishment must be short . . . punishment must be swift. . . . Punishment is anything but swift, with long delays between the crime, arrest, conviction, sentencing, and imprisonment. Today it may take years before a criminal is punished.
- To be successful, punishment must be certain. In our system of criminal justice we have many unknown and unreported crimes, which can run as high as five unreported crimes for one reported crime. Of those crimes reported, few arrests are made, few convictions are made, and few criminals are sentenced to prison. . . . For the same crime the sentence can vary in many ways. . . . To be effective, punishment must overcome positive reinforcement. . . . When a reinforcer such as money can be gotten by an illegal response, persons can weigh the risk of punishment versus the monetary gain. Since the risk of punishment is low, criminals have

the odds in their favor as they commit crimes. The prospect of gaining money immediately outweighs the threat of punishment in the distant future.

- To make punishment effective, we must provide the person with alternative means for reinforcement. If a person is offered an alternative to the punished response, the punished response will be diminished or eliminated. This implies the establishment of crime prevention programs that block the illegal opportunities structure, as well as behavioral programs that create legitimate opportunities.

- Punishment can become a conditioned stimulus for positive reinforcement. If a child is spanked and then given candy, the child will misbehave to get candy. If the only time a child is noticed by the parent is when the parent is punishing the child, the child will act in an antisocial manner to get attention.

- Punishment creates escape and avoidance behaviors. . . . A person does not learn through punishment to obey the law; rather, he or she learns how to commit crimes and to escape punishment. Criminals can avoid punishment by avoiding detection and arrest; if arrested, they can give an alibi or hire lawyers; if charged, they can falsify statements and attempt to win an acquittal; if found guilty, they can tell the social worker a story that may result in probation; if sentenced, they can try to manipulate the prison community to gain privileges and an early release. The criminal justice system is one huge escape and avoidance conditioning system. Rather than conditioning people to legal behavior, it conditions them to escape and avoid the law.

- Punishment creates aggression in those who are punished. This aggression can be operant—that is, against the aggressor, to remove the aggression—or reflexive. Reflexive aggression occurs when pain is administered to a person and the person strikes out against any object or person in the environment. When we put people in prison, we make them more vicious and hateful than before. This is a major failure of our prison system to rehabilitate.

- Any stimulus associated with punishment can become a conditioned stimulus for punishment. A child who avoids or hates a parent or teacher may run away from home or become a truant from school. Many delinquent careers start with such behavioral problems at home or in school. The use of punishment to control behavior creates major behavioral problems of its own.

- If an animal is conditioned to receive unavoidable shocks, with no possibility of escape or avoidance, the animal will not learn to avoid shock even later, when the shock is avoidable. This is called learned helplessness, and it is also an important aspect of psychological depression. Punishment of prisoners can create learned helplessness. The ability to control one's environment is an important aspect of healthy adaptive behavior; criminal behavior, in contrast, can reflect learned helplessness, a trust in fate, and a loss of control over the environment.

- The punisher (lawyer, parent, teacher, police officer) may be angry or hostile toward the person punished. Aggression rewards those doing the punishing. It allows for a feeling of power over others, it releases feelings of revenge and hatred, and it allows one to be aggressive in a legitimate manner. Aggression can be either lawful or unlawful. The criminal justice system continues to punish and execute criminals not because of the impact of punishment on the criminal but because of the impact of punishment on those doing the punishing, including you and me.

- Punishment, then, is not a successful way to control criminal behavior, because it is so disruptive to other, lawful behaviors.

C. Ray Jeffery's main point is that we ought not to expect American punishment to reduce crime given the many ways in which it may actually encourage people to initiate and maintain criminal careers. Jeffery has always advocated a more rational and preventive approach to crime reduction, one that identifies the risk factors that increase the likelihood of antisocial behavior in children. Ultimately, if we can reduce one's exposure to these risk factors, we should see less juvenile delinquency and ultimately less adult criminality.

Professor Jeffery was President of the American Society of Criminology, the world's largest and most prestigious criminological organization and is the author of several books, including *Crime Prevention through Environmental Design* (1971, 1977) and *Criminology: An Interdisciplinary Approach*. In these books, Jeffery advocates shutting down the entire criminal justice apparatus and using the money instead to research the causes of criminal and antisocial behavior so that it can more effectively be prevented. While this is certainly radical and idealistic, Jeffery's ideas rest on proven practices of crime prevention rather than reactive measures of crime control that have been called into question by much research.

Discussion Questions

1. What is sentencing?
2. Identify and discuss different types of sentences.
3. Identify some of the drawbacks to determinate and indeterminate sentences.
4. Why do you think judges are generally opposed to mandatory sentences?
5. What types of crimes generally receive the longest sentences? Why?
6. Identify and discuss the main justifications for punishment.
7. Why has the U.S. criminal justice network largely given up on rehabilitation?
8. Identify and discuss the main methods of punishment in the United States.
9. Which type of punishment is the most used? Which is the least used? Why?
10. Why are some people sentenced to probation and others sentenced to terms of incarceration, even though they are convicted for the same crimes?
11. Why is the administration of punishment in the United States so ineffective at reducing crime?
12. Identify the main sources of bias during the sentencing process.
13. How does criminal sentencing reflect biases of the criminal law and policing?
14. Identify and discuss the main problems with the so-called three-strikes laws.
15. Why do you think the criminal justice network pursues crime prevention strategies that have been proved ineffective?
16. Why is American punishment a failure according to C. Ray Jeffery?

CHAPTER NINE

INCARCERATION: LOCK 'EM UP
AND THROW AWAY YOUR MONEY

INTRODUCTION

The result of the criminal justice process is our corrections system. The corrections system in the United States is made up of a group of agencies and programs that are responsible for administering punishment to people accused and convicted of criminal offenses. As discussed in

Chapter Eight, forms of punishment include incarceration in prisons and jails, probation in the community, and a wide array of intermediate sanctions. This chapter gives separate attention to incarceration, mostly to imprisonment, because it is one of the most destructive and expensive forms of punishment in the United States. It is also a method that clearly does not achieve the ideal goals of the criminal justice network.

THE ORGANIZATION OF CORRECTIONS IN THE UNITED STATES

Currently in the United States there are thousands of agencies of *institutional corrections*, including more than 1,000 state prisons, 80 federal prisons, and countless jails operated by local governments. Additionally, there are thousands of agencies of *community corrections*, typically governed by counties, which run probation and parole services and some forms of intermediate sanctions. Together, these correctional agencies supervise more than 6.7 million Americans who were convicted of criminal offenses. As you saw in previous chapters, *prisons* are run by states and the federal government and are intended for people convicted of "serious" crimes and sentenced to more than 1 year of incarceration. *Jails* are typically run by cities and are intended for people convicted of less serious crimes and sentenced to 1 year or less of incarceration. Jails also hold some people waiting to have their cases heard in court, as well as people picked up by the police for disturbing the peace or awaiting transfer to other institutions. *Probation* is a sentence imposed by the court for relatively minor offenders that requires inmates to complete a term of supervision in the community under certain rules; *parole* is similar to probation, but it is not a sentence imposed by the court; it is instead a term of supervision to be served after release from incarceration. Finally, *intermediate sanctions,* which are not widely used in the United States, are more restrictive than probation but less restrictive than incarceration.

AMERICA'S INCARCERATION RATE

As you saw in the last chapter, the United States has the highest rate of incarceration in the world, just ahead of Russia's and more than five times higher than that of most industrialized nations (Beckett and Sasson 2000; Irwin and Austin 1997). This is due to massive increases in incarceration in the last 30 years (e.g., see Beck 1998). Just how many people are incarcerated in the United States? If we took all the people who are incarcerated and put them in one place, it would be the sixth largest city in the country. As you saw in the last chapter, the rate of incarceration (prisons and jails) at mid-year 2002 was 701 per 100,000 residents, number one in the world. Considering only prisons, the rate of imprisonment was 476 per 100,000 people.

The National Criminal Justice Commission writes, "Since 1980, the United States has engaged in the largest and most frenetic correctional buildup of any country in the history of the world" (Donziger 1996, p. 31). This is true for incarceration in prisons and jails and also for probation and parole populations. Collectively, these correctional populations have swelled to 6.7 million people, including more than 2 million people incarcerated.

Think about the irony of this. Professor Todd Clear, an expert on corrections, writes in the foreword to Irwin and Austin's (1997) book, *It's About Time: America's Imprisonment Binge:*

> As Americans, we think of ourselves as a free people. And we think that our freedoms are central to what sets us apart from the rest of the world. . . . It is ironic, then, that in America more people are denied these freedoms by law than in any other Western nation: we lock up more citizens per capita than any other nation that has bothered to count its prisoners. (p. xiii)

Without much doubt, the U.S. imprisonment rate alone (which does not include jail populations) stands as a testament to how far our nation's leaders are willing to go to fight crime—or, more accurately, to fight some types of crime committed by some types of people.

Walker (1998) describes recent crime control efforts in the United States as "an imprisonment orgy." Figure 9.1 documents the unprecedented explosion of *imprisonment* in the United States from the early 20th century through the 1990s. First, note how the U.S. imprisonment rate has

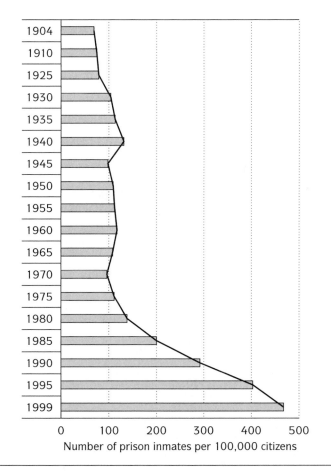

FIGURE 9.1
Trends in America's Imprisonment Rate

historically been relatively constant. It has fluctuated over the years, but never until the 1970s did it consistently and dramatically increase. In fact, scholars had written about the *stability of punishment* because there was so little fluctuation in the nation's incarceration rate for so long (Blumstein and Cohen 1973). Second, note how the imprisonment explosion began in the early 1970s. Between the early 1970s and the mid-1990s, there was an approximately 6.5% increase each year (Blumstein 2000, p. 6). As you learned in the Chapter Eight, the rate of growth has slowed to between 3% and 4% per year from 1995 to 2001.

According to Kappeler, Blumberg, and Potter (2000, p. 161), the number of sentenced prisoners in both state and federal prisons increased almost seven times from 1972 to 1998 alone. The United States now has more than twice the number of prisoners per 100,000 citizens as any other democracy, and more than five times the rate of democracies such as Canada, England, Germany, and France (The Sentencing Project 1997). Also, jail, probation, and parole populations in the United States have tripled since 1980.

Figure 9.2 shows the key years during the imprisonment explosion and identifies some key events. You see in the figure the years in which public concern about violent crime and drugs peaked. Keeping in mind what you learned about the media in Chapter Five, you should remember that the public did not become concerned about these crimes and demand more imprisonment. In part, it is logical to expect that increased media coverage of crime and of mass imprisonment actually made people more afraid, which then led to an even greater criminal justice response.

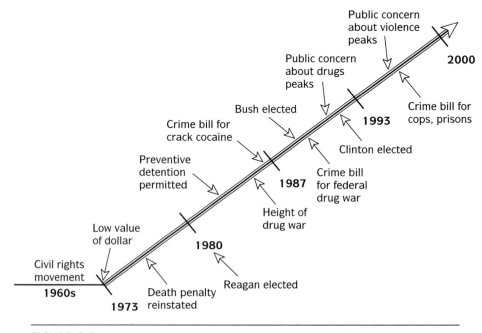

FIGURE 9.2

Key Events in America's Imprisonment Boom

Much of the increase in prisons has been due to drug convictions (including a 478% increase in drug offenders sentenced to state prisons and a 545% increase in drug offenders sentenced to federal prisons from 1985 to 1996). From 1980 to 1993, the percentage of prisoners in state prisons serving sentences for drug offenses more than tripled; in federal prisons, it more than doubled (Welch 1999, p. 52). Meanwhile, drug treatment in prison is insufficiently funded, although it is supported by most Americans (p. 62). According to the Bureau of Justice Statistics, between 1990 and 2000, violent offenders comprised 53% of the growth in prison populations, whereas drug offenders made up 20%, public-order offenders made up 15%, and property offenders made up 12%. Given that when Americans think about crime, they think about violent crime, most would probably be surprised to learn that only about half of the increase in the prison population is because of violent offenders.

Does sound, scientific evidence suggest that mass imprisonment will work to make us safer? My answer would be, "To a small degree, temporarily." In the book, *The Crime Drop in America,* Blumstein and Wallman (2000) identify the factors that account for reductions in street crime over the past decade and conclude that there is no single explanation. The factors analyzed in the book include economic improvement, an aging population, the stabilization of the illicit drug trade, reductions in gun crimes, and prison. The authors conclude that "no single factor can be invoked as *the* cause of the crime decline of the 1990s. Rather, the explanation appears to lie with a number of factors, perhaps none of which alone would have been sufficient and some of which might not have been of noticeable efficacy without reinforcement from others" (p. 11). The author who wrote the chapter on prisons (Spelman 2000) concludes that prisons were responsible for only about one-fourth of the crime drop. He adds, "Most of responsibility for the crime drop rests with improvements in the economy, changes in the age structure, or other social factors" (p. 125).

J. May (2000, p. xvi), editor of a series of essays on prison titled *Building Violence,* suggests that "[t]he United States is conducting a social experiment unparalleled in its size and implications" and that "[c]riminological research has not been able to demonstrate convincingly that the incarceration of more people, and longer sentences, ultimately provide more security." Given the conclusion by Sherman et al. (1997) that incarceration of repeat offenders "works" to reduce crime, it seems honest to conclude that some of the decline in street crime in the 1990s was attributable to locking up some of the "right offenders." The problem is that a lot of offenders we have locked up are probably not the right offenders. Additionally, any gains in crime reduction must be understood as temporary, given that about 95% of prisoners will one day be released (Bureau of Justice Statistics 2003). If these offenders are angry and want revenge, we should expect them to commit more crime later.

Let me state unequivocally that the dramatic upward shift in the U.S. imprisonment rate is not attributable to increases in street crime. In Chapter Four, you saw that most forms of street crime have decreased since 1973. The murder rate has held relatively constant prior to and after the boom in incarceration. One trend that corresponds with the increased use of imprisonment as a criminal sanction is an upward shift in income, documented nicely by Phillips (1991) in *The Politics of Rich and Poor* and by Barlett and Steele (1992) in *America: What Went Wrong?* These authors demonstrate how, during the 1980s, the wealthiest Americans got richer while most Americans actually lost ground. In an environment of corporate-friendly legislation, including the deregulation efforts and tax breaks of Presidents Reagan and Bush (the first), many more Americans found themselves living in conditions conducive to criminality. For example, from 1977 to

1988, the average after-tax family income for Americans in the bottom 10% declined nearly 11%, while for the upper 10% it increased almost 25%, and for the top 1% it increased almost 75%. Also, compensation for CEOs of corporations increased more than 100%, and the number of millionaires and billionaires increased by 250%. Do you think that any of these figures are relevant for understanding why the United States is incarcerating so many people?

If you compare these rising imprisonment rates to crime rate declines since the early 1970s, you might conclude that incarceration is an effective means of reducing crime. But this conclusion would be, at best, incomplete and, at worst, wrong. First, there has not been a dramatic drop in crime during this same time period, as you would expect given that incarceration rates are nearly four times what they were 20 years ago (Blumstein 2000). Second, according to the experts, the modest declines in crime rates are more likely due to non–criminal justice interventions. One major reason that street crime rates have declined in the United States is that Americans have gotten older. Street crime is generally a young male phenomenon, so an older population means less crime. Irwin and Austin (1997, p. 144) attribute 60% of the decline in U.S. crime rates between 1980 and 1988 to reductions in the size of the population aged 15 to 24 years old.

Todd Clear, in the foreword to Welch's (1999, p. ix) *Punishment in America: Social Control and the Ironies of Imprisonment,* claims that the U.S. incarceration rate has little to do with crime rates in the United States: "Prison populations continue to grow, despite five consecutive years of falling crime; indeed, since 1975, we have had 10 years of declining crime rates and then 13 years of increasing crime rates—but prison populations have gone up every year regardless." Welch claims that prison populations are being driven more by economic and market forces than by crime. He claims that

> political leaders, rather than simply treating lawbreakers firmly but fairly, are becoming increasingly intolerant and vindictive. In a sense, the state appears to have crossed the line from "getting tough" to "getting rough" by encouraging institutions and authorities to bully individuals lacking the power to defend themselves adequately against an ambitious and overzealous criminal justice system. (p. xix)

Statistics from The Sentencing Project (2003) are particularly revealing. Between 1984 and 1991, states that increased their incarceration rates at above-average levels (by 89%) experienced 15% increases in street crime, versus 17% increases in crime for states that increased their incarceration rates at average levels (by 37%). Between 1991 and 1998, states that increased incarceration at above-average levels (by 72%) experienced 13% reductions in street crime, versus 17% decreases in crime for states that increased incarceration at average levels (by 30%).

The U.S. imprisonment binge is ironic given that numerous scholars and organizations have demonstrated that incarceration is destructive to the United States and that our war on crime "has made things worse: that it has not deterred crime, that it is racially biased, and that it has contributed to the destruction of inner-city communities" (Walker 1998, pp. 10–11). Currie (1998, pp. 56–57) demonstrates that there is not clear evidence showing that states and countries that incarcerate more people have lower crime rates. Irwin and Austin (1997, p. 146) show that states that incarcerate more people do not necessarily have lower crime rates; in fact, the opposite is true overall, although the differences between states are inconsequential. Within the academic disciplines of criminology and criminal justice, a consensus has emerged against over-relying on incarceration, yet we continue to lock up more and more people. You will recall from earlier chapters that crime is a political issue that can be "sold" to voters and viewers of the mass media, and that politicians must appear "tough on crime" to get elected and stay in office (see Chapter Five). Nevertheless, criminal justice policies motivated by politics are not in line with the scientific knowledge generated within the academic disciplines of criminology and criminal justice.

Irwin and Austin (1997, pp. xvii–xviii) discuss the main tenets of the political agenda that justifies more and more prisons, which include the following.

- The War on Poverty, which sought to fight crime through education, job training, and rehabilitation in the 1960s and 1970s, was a total failure.
- Dangerous criminals repeatedly go free because of liberal judges or decisions made by the liberal Supreme Court that help the criminal but not the victim.
- Swift and certain punishment in the form of more and longer prison terms will reduce crime by incapacitating the hardened criminals and making potential lawbreakers think twice before they commit crimes.
- Most inmates are dangerous and cannot be safely placed in the community.
- In the long run, it will be far cheaper for society to increase the use of imprisonment.
- Greater use of imprisonment since the 1980s has in fact reduced crime.

Does any of this sound familiar to you? It is likely that these are the kinds of statements you have heard from politicians of both major political parties in the last several election cycles. For example, on C-SPAN, I recently saw a congressional representative from my home state of Florida who made a simplistic association between falling crime rates in New York and tougher, zero-tolerance law enforcement. His argument was that if we engaged in tougher law enforcement across the nation, crime rates would fall everywhere. In fact, crime rates are already falling everywhere and they have fallen in major cities that have not pursued zero-tolerance policing as much as, if not more than, in New York. Furthermore, crime rates began declining in New York before the implementation of the zero-tolerance law enforcement policies. The member of Congress was either misinformed or dishonest about the issue.

What It Costs

It is difficult to put a price tag on the U.S. corrections system, because the cost of building and maintaining prison cells varies from state to state. Additionally, true costs of building prisons cannot be known unless one considers the added costs of interest over time on loans to build prisons. Irwin and Austin (1997, p. 139) write that

> when a state builds and finances a typical medium-security prison, it will spend approximately $268,000 per bed for construction alone. . . . [I]n the states that have expanded their prison populations, the cost per additional prisoner will be about $39,000 per year [which] includes the cost of building the new cell amortized 30 years. In other words, the 30-year cost of adding space for one prisoner is more than $1 million.

For every $100 million spent on prison construction, the government will ultimately have to pay $1.6 billion over the next 30 years (Ambrosio and Schiraldi 1997, p. 5).

Incarceration in the United States costs nearly $50 billion annually, with over 11 million new admissions each year (National Center on Institutions and Alternatives 1999). As you saw in

Chapter One, operating criminal justice agencies costs over $100 billion annually, due in part to the $100,000 it takes to build a new cell, $200,000 over 25 years to pay off debt for construction, and an average of $24,000 per year per cell (National Center on Institutions and Alternatives 1999). To accommodate new correctional clients, 38 federal prisons were built between 1980 and 1995, compared with only 41 built between 1900 and 1980. More federal prisons are currently under construction. With correctional populations exploding from 24,000 in 1980 to 143,337 in 2001, federal prisons are operating at 131% of capacity (Bureau of Justice Statistics 2003). States are also embarking on "record-level prison construction programs. Between 1990 and 1994, the bed capacity of the country's prison system increased by nearly 200,000 prison beds" (Irwin and Austin 1997, p. 65).

For every inmate that is incarcerated, the cost, at least $24,000 per year, is equivalent to the tax burden of at least four American families (Coalition for Federal Sentencing Reform 1997). Additional costs come in the form of cuts in educational funding, student loans, libraries, work incentives, opportunity-creating programs, employment programs, and highway repair and construction (J. Miller 1997). As such programs were being cut, in the 1980s alone, federal, state, and local expenditures increased 416% for police, 585% for courts, 1,019% for prosecution and legal services, 1,255% for public defenders, and 986% for corrections. Federal justice spending overall increased 668%, county justice spending increased 711%, and state spending increased 848% (J. Miller 1998).

The evidence suggests that the U.S. war on crime not only is costing us dearly now but will continue to do so in the future. Every dollar we spend on fighting crime, for example, we take away from other social services, including education, public health, and the infrastructure of roads and bridges. Ironically, crime funding may actually exacerbate criminogenic factors. For example, the three-strikes laws in California will produce shortfalls in education funding for at least an entire decade (see Chapter Eight). Less money for education means less access to education. Less education can lead to less opportunity for legitimate success, leading in turn to conditions of strain, which historically have been linked to increased risk for criminality (Agnew 1993; Merton 1938a). "If education has historically been an investment in the future of society, then the cuts in education to finance prison represent a *dis*investment in the future" (Walker 1998, p. 13; emphasis in original). According to the National Association of State Budget Officers (1996, pp. 77, 98), the total cost of state-issued bonds to build prisons surpasses the total issued to build colleges. Also, as the burdens of imprisonment fall disproportionately on some communities, incarceration creates a condition known as *social disorganization*, which has been associated with higher rates of street crime (M. Robinson 2004).

WHO'S IN PRISON AND JAIL?

Why do we lock up so many more of our citizens than other countries do, even though we have no more crime overall? One primary reason is that criminal justice in the United States is much harsher toward relatively minor criminals than in other countries (Donziger 1996, p. 10). In fact, for a large part of our history, the majority of people in our nation's jails and prisons were convicted of nonviolent offenses. For example, 84% of prison admissions between 1980 and 1993 were for nonviolent offenses (Bureau of Justice Statistics 1994). These statistics may explain why many prison wardens feel that up to half of the offenders under their supervision could be released without making the country any less safe (J. Simon 1994). Ingley (2000, p. 21) summarizes who's in prison:

> Today's corrections reality is such: the fastest growing [prison] populations are those captured from our "war on drugs," the deinstitutionalization of our mental health system, and mandatory minimum sentencing policies. . . . [T]he majority of our prisoners are chronic substance abusers, functionally illiterate, indigent, or possess few, if any, job skills.

In fact, according to the Bureau of Justice Statistics, at the end of 2001, nearly half (49%) of state inmates were serving time for violent offenses, followed by 20% for drug offenses, 19% for property offenses, and 11% for public-order offenses. As shown in Figure 9.3, the number of drug offenders surpassed that of property offenders in 1999.

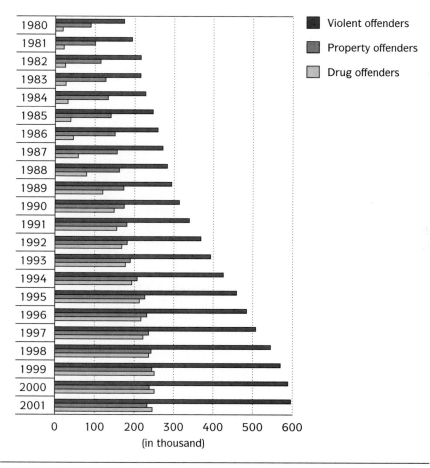

FIGURE 9.3
Trends in Incarceration, by Crime Type
SOURCE: Bureau of Justice Statistics (2003).

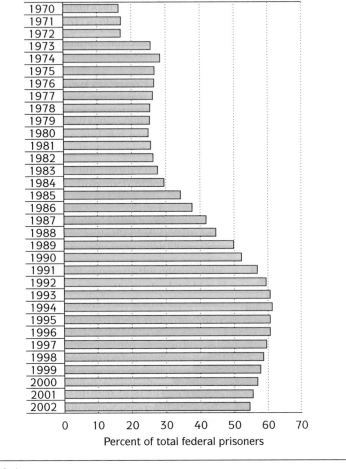

FIGURE 9.4
Trends in Federal Drug Imprisonment
SOURCE: Sourcebook of Criminal Justice Statistics (2003).

As you can see in Figure 9.4, 55% of all federal prison inmates were incarcerated for drug crimes at the end of 2002, versus only 10% for immigration offenses, 10% for violent offenses, 9% for weapons offenses, 7% for property offenses, and 6% for other offenses. White-collar offenders made up 0.7% of all federal inmates in 2002. The number of drug offenders in federal prisons rose 41% between 1990 and 2000, but the fastest growth was for immigration offenses (691% increase) and weapons offenses (247% increase).

So, a significant portion of state and federal prisoners has been incarcerated for nonviolent crime. What has happened in the United States has been likened to a bait-and-switch scam, because politicians have talked tough about violent criminals and promised tougher punishment for them, yet many of the people being sent to prison are not violent offenders (Donziger 1996, p. 18). This works because Americans see "crime" and "violence" as essentially the same thing

(Zimring and Hawkins 1997). Most incarcerated criminals are not violent criminals, nor are most incarcerated criminals "career criminals" (Irwin and Austin 1997). Americans may support imprisonment as punishment for repeat, violent criminals. It is doubtful that they would support it for relatively minor offenders. It is, after all, their money that pays for prisons. Yet mass releases of prisoners will certainly not occur, even with the realization that it may be cost effective and relatively safe to release nonviolent and drug offenders from prison to serve probationary parole sentences (Bureau of Justice Statistics 1995).

A possible danger of incarcerating relatively minor offenders is that as Americans become aware of this, some may begin to disrespect law generally. Rold (2000, p. 45) claims, "People are more likely to follow laws when they agree with them and respect the legitimacy of the community and agency administering the laws." Because prisons are used against many relatively harmless offenders, what is threatened is "the fabric of our social order and our view of ourselves as a compassionate nation." This is also the argument of Packer, whose crime control and due process models of criminal justice are discussed in Chapter One. Packer suggests that victimless crimes (such as drug use and prostitution) should be decriminalized because their illegal status leads to disrespect for the law generally.

Recall from Chapter Two the discussion of alternative goals of the criminal justice network. I suggested that the criminal justice network may be serving limited interests by controlling certain segments of the population. According to Alexander (2000, p. 52), the only Fortune 500 company to employ more people than corrections is General Motors. Companies lobby and make hundreds of thousands of dollars in political contributions to maintain a stranglehold on criminal justice. Additionally, politicians benefit from the incarceration boom by getting elected to office. An irony is that as the nation's economy provides substantially more wealth to the richest of Americans, more of the rest of us support more prisons simply because they provide us with jobs that allow us to enjoy some of the benefits of the good economy.

American prisons and jails are used disproportionately against the nation's "riffraff." J. Williams (2000, p. 72) writes that the nation's "lost souls find their only productive social role is as fodder for the ever-growing number" of prisons and jails. Irwin and Austin (1997, p. 8) write that what explains the U.S. reliance on incarceration as a means to control serious crime is "the American people's strong desire to banish from their midst any population of people who are threatening." Rothman (1971) makes a similar point in his book, *The Discovery of the Asylum*, by analyzing the history of American corrections. Rothman shows that the United States has always set aside the poor, mentally retarded, and mentally ill under the guise of corrections. A study by del Carmen and Robinson (2000) shows how both tuberculosis and crime prevention efforts used at the turn of the century in the nation's big cities were aimed primarily at poor immigrants.

It is estimated that roughly 1 in 10 of the nation's prisoners is mentally ill (Weisman 2000, p. 105), although some suggest that the figure may be more like 40% (Torrey et al. 1992). The Sentencing Project (2003) reports that as of 1998, American jails and prison housed at least 238,800 people with mental illnesses (versus only 70,000 people with mental illnesses housed in public psychiatric hospitals). The mentally ill are in jail largely because the nation's mentally ill populations were released from state hospitals with the expectation that they would be able to get treatment in their communities. But community treatment programs are not available in many communities, and in places where such programs are available, systems are not in place to ensure that people who need them will obtain treatment. Over the past decade, 400 new prisons have opened and 40 state mental hospitals have closed. Thus, "jails and prisons have become the de facto providers of mental health services in this country" (Weisman 2000, p. 106). In most states, the largest provider is the prison system; the nation's largest provider is the Los Angeles County Jail.

Jail may represent the largest waste of resources on offenders: Most people in county jails who were convicted of crimes committed very minor crimes, and the average sentence they will serve is a few days. Prisoners, in contrast, will serve longer sentences because of the perceived severity of their offenses. I focus on prisons in this chapter because of the prolonged stay of their inmates. Yet jail populations serve as further evidence of whom we pursue through our agencies of criminal justice, so I briefly mention them here. Welch (1999, p. 89) calls the jailing of offensive but nondangerous populations a form of "social sanitation" reserved mostly for the urban underclass or our nation's "rabble" (Irwin 1985). People in jail are generally "either members of the working poor or permanent members of the underclass," with low educational attainment and "limited means to survive economically" (Welch 1999, p. 94).

Do Americans really support these policies? Public opinion research has consistently shown that Americans prefer that inmates in the nation's prisons be granted access to rehabilitation (Roberts and Stalans 2000). It is doubtful, too, that many Americans truly understand who is in prison. The typical prisoner, as you have seen, is not a repetitive, violent criminal. Rather, he or she (most likely "he") is typically a property or drug offender. Slightly less than half of Irwin and Austin's (1997, p. 40) sample of incarcerated prisoners were characterized as "career criminals." Of those who were, about 60% were imprisoned for what Americans view as "petty crimes." Of the 25% of their sample who were serving lengthy sentences, many did not warrant these sentences on the basis of the relative nonseriousness of their offenses.

Thus, Irwin and Austin (1997, p. 57) write: "Most crimes are much pettier than the popular images promoted by those who sensationalize the crime issue (such as politicians and the media). More than half of the persons sent to prison committed crimes that lacked any of the features the public believes compose a serious crime." Even the high-risk inmates, the career criminals, are typically uneducated, unskilled, and underemployed. From public poll results, Irwin and Austin claim that if Americans knew this, they would not likely support the massive use of incarceration as a means to reduce crime.

Consider an alarming possibility about U.S. prisons, then: One of their functions may be to warehouse a significant portion of the population that is not employable. Consider that most convicted offenders sentenced to a term of imprisonment are poor, uneducated, and underemployed. To the degree that people are targeted, then, one function served by incarceration is a reduced need to provide social services to those people. In fact, virtually everyone in prison is poor. According to the 1996 *Survey of Inmates in Local Jails* (U.S. Department of Justice 2003), only 20% had a private attorney.

Table 9.1 illustrates that many people in prison were underemployed (i.e., not employed full-time) in the year prior to their incarceration, that most offenders in prison earned less than $10,000 per year, and that the vast majority of offenders in prison did not go to college. These statistics prove that the war on crime disproportionately affects poor people. Americans view street crimes (committed by the poor) as "our problem," when in reality it is mostly "their problem" (because criminal victimization is disproportionately directed at the poor). Our criminal justice reactions, particularly imprisonment, aimed at making it better for "us," actually make it

TABLE 9.1

Characteristics of American Inmates

Male	93%[1]
Black	46%[1]
Hispanic	16%[1]
Sentenced for nonviolent crimes	70%[2]
Did not complete high school	68%[3]
Earning less than $1,000 per month	64%[4]
Under influence of drugs at time of crime	60%[4]
Unemployed	36%[4]

[1]All prison inmates, 2001.
[2]Sentenced state prison inmates, 1998.
[3]State prison inmates, 1997.
[4]Jail inmates, 1996.
SOURCE: The Sentencing Project (2003).

worse for "them." This is another ironic, unintended consequence of U.S. criminal justice practices (Walker 1998).

As noted throughout this book, incarceration also disproportionately affects people of color. Is this a recent phenomenon? According to Cahalan (1986), we can confidently say that prison populations have been disproportionately made up of African Americans since 1926, the first year that national prison statistics were collected. In that year, African Americans made up 9% of the population but 21% of the prison population. At the end of 2001, African Americans made up less than 13% of the U.S. population but 46% of all inmates in state and federal prisons, versus 36% Caucasians. The first time that more African Americans than non-African Americans were admitted to U.S. prisons was in the late 1980s, during the height of the war on drugs. Even worse, only about 10% of those seeking college degrees are African American (Walker, Spohn, and Delone 2000, p. 260). Hispanics now make up 15% of the nation's prison inmates, and their incarceration rate since the mid-1980s has increased twice as much as those of African Americans and Caucasians (Walker, Spohn, and Delone 2000, p. 261). The picture in American jails is very similar, as Caucasians made up 43% of inmates at the end of 2001, African Americans made up 42%, and Hispanics made up 15%. This means that the majority of jail inmates were people of color (Gilliard 1999). I return to the issue of bias at the end of this chapter, but first I dispel some myths about what it is like to be in prison.

WHAT HAPPENS IN PRISON? PAINS OF IMPRISONMENT

Most people who are in prison will one day get out (see the section on parole later in the chapter). It may be easy to lock up criminals and believe that we are somehow safer for it. But 9 of 10 inmates will one day be released. Thus, Americans must realize that their own safety depends on what happens to prisoners while they are incarcerated. And prison, contrary to popular belief, is a horrendous place.

Contrary to the mythical view of the comfortable prison, American prisons are terribly hot, loud, and violent places to live (and work—keep in mind that many people in prison simply work there). The myth of "country club" prisons has led state lawmakers to pass some laughable legislation and make startling threats. The National Criminal Justice Commission reports the following examples:

- a Mississippi law forbidding individual air conditioners, even though no inmate actually had an individual air conditioner;
- a Louisiana law forbidding inmates from taking martial arts classes, even though such classes were not currently available; and
- a complaint by the governor of Connecticut about the landscaping outside a prison, even though the plantings were made at the request of residential neighbors (Donziger 1996, p. 45).

Add to these examples efforts by state lawmakers to take away inmates' cigarettes (which contain the addictive drug nicotine and are used as a form of currency within prisons), other efforts to prevent inmates from lifting weights or watching television, the resurgence of chain gangs in many Southern states, and other efforts to humiliate inmates by making them wear orange, pink, or striped jumpsuits. From all these efforts to make prison less pleasant, you might imagine that prison is a pretty nice place to be. In fact, because of the numerous *pains of imprisonment* (Sykes 1958), the typical prison is not anything like a country club.

Gresham Sykes (1958), in his groundbreaking work *The Society of Captives*, outlined the major pains of imprisonment:

- Loss of liberty
- Loss of autonomy
- Loss of security
- Deprivation of heterosexual relationships
- Deprivation of goods and services

To these, I add three more:

- Loss of voting rights
- Loss of dignity
- Stigmatization

I discuss each of these in turn.

Loss of Liberty

First and foremost, prisoners suffer from a *loss of liberty*. Many Americans seem to conceive of prisons as comfortable places where offenders watch televison free of charge, eat three square meals per day at no cost, enjoy various extracurricular activities such as weight lifting and basketball, and get a free education. Most of these conceptions are false. The Florida Department of Corrections maintains a Web page where myths about its prisons are disputed, as shown in the following box.

Myths about Florida prisons

1. *Inmates don't work.* On June 30, 2002, there were 73,553 inmates in the Florida prison system. Private prisons housed 3,998 inmates and the remaining 69,555 were in Department of Corrections (DC) facilities. On June 30, 2002, 83% of the inmates in DC institutions and facilities were assigned to work, assigned to participate in a substance abuse program or vocational education or adult education program, or assigned to some other program activity. The remaining 17% were medically unable to work or were participating in the reception and orientation process, assigned to a disciplinary work squad as a result of rule infractions, assigned to a restricted labor squad, or in some type of confinement for management purposes, including death row.

   Inmate labor is used to perform work on farms and gardens managed by the department, construct new correctional facilities, perform repairs and renovations to facilities, and otherwise support and maintain the ongoing operation of correctional institutions. Inmates also prepare and serve all meals, maintain prison grounds, participate in sanitation and recycling processes, and work in Prison Rehabilitative Industries and Diversified Enterprises or Prison Industry Enhancement work programs. Additionally, inmates are assigned to Community Work Squads provided by the department. These inmates perform services under agreements with the Department of Transportation, other state agencies such as the Division of Forestry, counties, cities, municipalities, and nonprofit organizations. In fiscal year (FY) 2001–2, the DC's Community Work Squad Program saved Florida taxpayers more than $33 million through inmate labor.

2. *Inmates have cable television and satellite dishes.* There are no correctional facilities with cable television. The few prisons that have satellite dishes use them for staff training and academic classes for inmates as part of the Corrections Distance Learning Network (CDLN). The CDLN saves money by training staff throughout the state simultaneously and teaching inmates via satellite. Most prisons have televisions available to inmates for use when inmates are not working or attending educational programs. The televisions are located in dormitory dayrooms for group viewing. Most of the department's televisions were paid for by proceeds from sales to inmates from the inmate canteens. However, state law now prohibits the purchase of televisions for recreational purposes.

3. *Inmates should grow their own food and save taxpayers some money.* Inmates do grow some of their own food and expansion of the Bureau of Field Support Service's edible crops program continues. In FY 2001–02, the Bureau cultivated approximately 1,200 acres and harvested 5.5 million pounds of produce. In 2002–3, approximately 1,500 acres were cultivated and it was expected that 7.5 million pounds of produce would be harvested. The number of inmates assigned to the edible crops program continues to increase, due largely to the expanded use of close-custody inmates supervised by Field Force Officers. Field Force Officers, mounted on horseback, supervise

close-custody inmates who are assigned to work in the fields cultivating the edible crops. Usually the squad is made up of four mounted, armed officers and one unarmed (on the ground) supervisor who control up to 75 close-custody inmates. These squads currently exist at Applachee Correctional Institution (CI), Florida State Prison, and De-Sort Annex. With the privatization of food service delivery in our department, the edible crops program is moving toward more centralized operations on our large-scale farms, thus allowing greater efficiency in processing and distributing harvested products.

4. *The Department of Corrections determines how long inmates serve in prison.* The DC does not determine the length of prison sentences or the length of time inmates serve in prison. Judges and juries, in accordance with state laws and sentencing guidelines, make these decisions. The department is solely responsible for the care and custody of offenders under its jurisdiction. In FY 2001–2, the average sentence length was 5.0 years for whites, 5.2 years for blacks, and 5.6 years for all others.

5. *Inmates still aren't serving most of their sentences.* Offenders who committed their offenses on or after October 1, 1995, are required to serve a minimum of 85% of their court-imposed sentences prior to their release. More than 8 of every 10 inmates released in March 2003 (83.3%) had one or more sentences that fell under the minimum 85% of sentence served law and they served an average of 82.5% of their sentences. That number has been climbing steadily. For example, all inmates released in FY 1997–98 served an average of 74.0% of their sentences, compared to 82.7% for all inmates released in FY 2001–2.

6. *Prisons are air-conditioned.* Only 10 of the 51 major state-managed prisons in Florida have air-conditioning in some portion of the facility housing inmates, and many of these are located in South Florida. The five Florida prison facilities built under the privatization contract are also air-conditioned.

7. *Inmates who get life sentences don't really stay in prison for life.* Since 1995, anyone sentenced to life in prison is serving a life term with no possibility of parole. Offenders sentenced to life for noncapital crimes committed between 1983 and 1993 are serving life sentences without any chance for release. Ironically, offenders sentenced to life for capital crimes committed between 1983 and 1993 are parole eligible after serving 25-year mandatory sentences. These sentencing provisions appear to be reversed, but they are correct. This anomaly in the law lasted from 1983 to 1994. Since 1995, anyone sentenced to life in prison is serving a life term with no possibility of parole. On June 30, 2002, there were 8,473 inmates in prison serving life sentences. A total of 4,069 were serving life with the possibility of parole and 4,404 were serving life sentences without the possibility of parole.

SOURCE: Florida Department of Corrections, www.dc.state.fl.us/oth/myths.html.

Prisons in most states are similar in their conditions. For example, the following box describes a day in the North Carolina Department of Correction Division of Prisons.

Twenty-four hours in the North Carolina Department of Correction Division of Prisons

Hour	Type of Facility		
	Minimum	Medium	Close
Morning			
5:00	Sleep	Wake up	Sleep
6:00	Wake up	Breakfast	Wake up
7:00	Breakfast	Travel to work site	Breakfast
	Travel to work site	Work	Go to work in prison
8:00–10:00	Work		
11:00	30 minutes for lunch	30 minutes for lunch	Work
Afternoon			
12:00	Work	Work	30 minutes for lunch
1:00–2:00	Work	Work	Work
3:00	Work	Work	Work day ends
	Travel to prison	Travel to prison	Time on prison yard
		Off duty	
4:00	Off duty	Time on prison yard	Return to cell
	Time on prison yard		
5:00	30 minutes for supper	30 minutes for supper	30 minutes for supper
Evening			
6:00–7:00	Time for religious and specialized programming such as religious services, Narcotics Anonymous, anger management		
8:00	Return to dorm	Return to dorm	Return to cell block
9:00–10:00	Remain in housing area	Remain in housing area	Remain in housing area
11:00	Lights out; go to sleep	Lights out; go to sleep	Lights out; go to sleep
12:00–4:00	Lights out; sleep	Lights out; sleep	Lights out; sleep

Close-Custody Inmates at Central Prison

In close-security prisons, inmates remain in the prison 24 hours a day and have no assignments outside of the prison. Movement from one area of the prison to another is restricted. Armed correctional officers man security towers to stop escape attempts.

At 3:30 A.M., the first inmates are awakened. They are the kitchen workers, who get up to prepare the morning meal. These inmates live and work together. Correctional officers escort them to the kitchen as a group. Each worker is thoroughly frisk-searched before entering the kitchen. The first-shift kitchen workers arrive at the kitchen for duty at 4 A.M. to begin preparing for breakfast and the day's other meals.

All inmates are awakened at 6 A.M. for the formal inmate count. Correctional staff count and recount inmates over and over throughout the day. At about 7 A.M., the feeding of breakfast begins. All inmate workers report to their jobs at 7:30 A.M. Second-shift inmate workers may use the gyms, recreation yard, and canteens.

Inmates work in the kitchen, license tag plant, or laundry or perform maintenance or janitorial tasks during the day.

At about 3 P.M., inmates usually check their mail and spend some time on the recreation yard prior to returning to the dining hall for the evening meal at 4 P.M. After the evening meal, inmates will have access to the gym, auditorium, or recreation yard. Depending on the day of the week, they may be involved in some organized recreational activities. On Wednesdays, Fridays, Saturdays, and Sundays, there is noncontact visitation with individuals who are on the inmates' approved visitors list. The visits are usually from 1 hour to 1.5 hours in duration.

At approximately 6:30 P.M., inmates may attend classes in the school or take part in other activities such as Alcoholics Anonymous, Narcotics Anonymous, Freedoms Journey Classes, and Jaycees. At 8:30 P.M., another formal count is conducted. At 9 P.M., inmates return to their housing area and are allowed to watch television, play checkers, chess, or cards, or write letters.

At 11 P.M., the inmate is locked into his cell and the lights are dimmed for the night.

Medium-Custody Inmates Working on a Road Squad at Pender Correctional Institution

In medium-security prisons, most inmates remain in the prison 24 hours a day. Armed correctional officers supervise squads of inmates who leave the prison to work on road squads cutting brush or work the fields at the state prison farm. Armed correctional officers man security towers to stop escape attempts.

Inmates wake up at 5:30 A.M. and have 45 minutes to shower, clean up, and make their beds. They go to the dining hall and eat breakfast in shifts beginning at 6:15. The inmates assemble for the count, search, and assignment to the road squads at 8 A.M. and, over the next 30 minutes, travel to their work site. The squads work in Pender and three surrounding counties. Travel time may vary, but all squads are busy at work by 9 A.M.

Squads work until noon, when they get a 30-minute break for lunch. They continue the work until about 3 P.M. As they arrive at the prison at 3:30, all inmates must be searched.

Inmates get cleaned up and prepare for dinner, which begins at 4:30 P.M. Afterward, they may exchange clothing at the prison clothes house, report to staff for counseling or medical appointments, or go to the prison yard.

Inmates are locked into the dormitory at 7 P.M. They may leave only to take part in religious, educational, or other programs in the prison's chapel, education center, or programs building.

All programs end at 9:30 P.M. and inmates return to their dorms to be counted. At 10 P.M., lights are dimmed in the sleeping area and inmates may remain in adjacent dayroom space. The inmates may watch television or play cards or table games. The 32 inmates on each dorm wing share a television and watch programming selected by inmates and preapproved by staff.

At 11:30 P.M., inmates are required to go to their dormitory beds and lights are dimmed.

Minimum-Custody Inmates Working on a Community Work Squad at Umstead Correctional Center

Inmates must be within 5 years of release to enter minimum custody. Minimum-security prisons prepare inmates for return to the community. While those entering minimum custody are assigned to jobs and remain at the prison, inmates in later phases leave the prison for work assignments. In the final stage of minimum custody, inmates may take part in work release jobs, family visits, and community volunteer visits, where they leave the prison in the custody of an employer, family member, or volunteer.

One of the many work assignments for minimum-custody inmates is the community work squad, where inmates are supervised by correctional officers in short-term, manual-labor jobs for local governments or public agencies.

At 6 P.M., inmates are awakened and have time to shower, dress, make up their beds, and prepare for breakfast. They eat in the dining hall at 6:45 and then prepare for the day's work.

A correctional officer assembles the community work squad inmates, who prepare their equipment and travel by prison van to their work site. By 8 A.M., the inmates are hard at work. They work on short-term manual-labor jobs like clearing brush from ditches, painting public buildings, and improving community parks. The work crews get 30 min to eat a bag lunch prepared by inmate kitchen workers.

The squads may work up to 5 P.M. if the job requires it. Normally, they wrap up work and return to the prison at about 3–4 P.M. They get cleaned up and attend to any unit duties they may have. At 5 P.M., they go to the dining hall for dinner. After dinner, they may have some time on the prison yard. Between 7 and 9 P.M., they may participate in specialized or religious programming such as Bible studies or Narcotics Anonymous.

By 9, inmates return to the dormitory they share with up to 150 other inmates. They may talk, play cards, or watch the dorm's one television. At 12 A.M., dorm lights go out and inmates are required to stay in their bunks.

Correction officers, constantly watching, patrol the dorms.

Inmates repeat this routine day after day after day.

SOURCE: North Carolina Department of Correction, www.doc.state.nc.us/dop/HOURS24.htm.

Although recreation is permitted and even encouraged within most U.S. prisons, it is allowed for the safety of correctional personnel. And funding for educational, vocational training, and treatment programs within prisons has been slashed dramatically. In part, treatment is lacking because of prisoners' protections from government intervention. McLaughlin (2000, p. 24) states, for example, "Federal regulations for the Protection of Human Subjects . . . are extended to prisoners due to past abuses and the concern that prisoners may be limited in their ability to give truly informed consent." Many, if not all, medical treatments are discouraged because of these strict requirements. In essence, the criminal justice network can stick a needle in a person's arm for punishment, but not for treatment. At the same time, "behavioral interventions . . . are developed and conducted frequently by people with little or no training in the area, no monitoring or thought as to the potential damage that an intervention may cause, and no informed consent" (pp. 24–25). Although somewhere between 70% and 85% of inmates need substance abuse treatment, only about one-tenth actually receive it (National Center on Addiction and Substance Abuse 1998; Simpson, Knight, and Pevoto 1996). This is true even though studies have proved how much more effective drug treatment is than expanding the use of prisons in reducing recidivism (Caulkins et al. 1997; MacCoun and Reuter 2000).

Some Americans might prefer to throw inmates into freshly dug holes in the ground and provide them with nothing but the bare minimum to survive. Others would like to "make 'em break rocks" (McGinnis 2000, p. 35). Former Massachusetts governor William Weld publicly stated that life in prison should be "akin to walking through the fires of hell" (p. 35). But these people misconceive the purpose of imprisonment. We send people to prison as punishment, not for punishment. As explained by Ingley (2000, p. 20), "The incarceration itself [is] supposed to be the punishment, not an occasion for the state to arbitrarily inflict additional punishment." In other words, the main part of the punishment is losing one's freedom. Individual freedom may be the most cherished part of being American. Prisoners, because they are locked up, away from friends and family, have lost their liberty. This means that they are not free to do all the things you and I can do as they see fit. Their activities are decided by others.

Loss of Autonomy

Related to loss of freedom is the *loss of autonomy* that accompanies being incarcerated. Inmates do not decide for themselves when or where to sleep, wake up, shower, eat, engage in recreation, or live. They are told when and how to do virtually everything they do. Thus, prisoners lose the capacity and, some argue, the ability to govern their own lives and behaviors. What are the implications of this for society? If we want people to be responsible for themselves, their lives, their families, their children, wouldn't it make sense to equip them with the ability to live in the free world? Is our desire to make prisoners suffer more important than protecting us from their future acts of crime and violence?

May (2000, p. xvii) claims that incarceration can "foster dependency" and, for some, actually "becomes a way of life—even a generational phenomenon." For them, the criminal justice network "becomes their only source of social support, structure, discipline, validation, and even power and respect." These people typically have family and friends who have been processed through the criminal justice agencies and live in communities where incarceration is simply an expected part of life.

Loss of Security

Prisoners are subjected to numerous forms of victimization that are much more prevalent in correctional facilities than outside in the free world, and thus suffer from a *loss of security*. Prisoners are subjected to psychological victimization, economic victimization, social victimization, physical victimization, and sexual victimization. May (2000, p. 134) describes prisons this way:

> Prisons are violent places, and prisons teach violence. Anyone walking into a prison for the first time can feel the tension. The concrete and steel walls and floors serve to echo and intensify the noises of chains, steel doors slamming, yelling, cursing, and beatings. For an inmate who

must make the prison his or her home, whether for months, years, or even a lifetime, avoiding a violent attack becomes a daily concern. The need to maintain constant vigilance creates stress, tension, and chronic anxiety. Even in their sleep, they do not feel safe. They almost instinctively react to provocation with violence, as adjustments to this sense of vulnerability.

J. Page (2000, pp. 138, 141) claims that "[v]iolence is a dominant and defining thread running through the fabric of jail and prison life" and describes facilities of incarceration as "factories of rage and pain."

As explained by the National Criminal Justice Commission, "Inmates learn to strike first and seek strength in gangs often comprised of dangerous offenders. Sexual assaults are frequent and usually go unpunished" (Donziger 1996, p. 43). Rather than being a deterrent to future criminality, the commission concludes that "the violent subculture of the correctional facility increasingly acts as a vector for spreading crime in our communities" (p. 44). Ironically, then, imprisonment escalates the very behavior it is intended to deter (Marx 1981) because it increases violence instead of decreasing it (Poporino 1986; Welch 1999).

American criminals who are imprisoned are locked away in overcrowded warehouses and forced to live in closet-sized rooms (C. Clark, 1994). Most are subjected to some type of physical abuse and many to sexual abuse (Donaldson 1995). Violence inflicted for the purpose of causing pain or as punishment is illegal and prohibited by the American Correctional Association (Martin 2000, p. 114). Additionally, many of the inmates who become victims in prison were convicted of relatively minor acts—acts that many of us may have committed at one time in our lives. And remember, most of these inmates will one day get out of prison. Some of these include inmates who have gone on to earn their doctoral degrees and now teach in criminology and criminal justice. They are now known as the *Convict School of Criminology* and are examined in the Issue in Depth at the end of this chapter.

Human rights violations are commonplace in prison. As examples, Welch (1999) discusses chain gangs, inhumane prison conditions, and the use of political imprisonment in the United States. He writes, "American prisons are neither *civilized* nor *civilizing*. Simply put, inmates are subjected to a degrading prison environment, then returned to the community" (p. 199; emphasis in original).

Deprivation of Heterosexual Relationships

Although not everyone is heterosexual, most Americans are. Incarceration means being forced to suffer from a *deprivation of heterosexual relationships*. This is likely worst for married couples who are separated by imprisonment. But for any heterosexual person, being imprisoned generally means living without sexual contact with a member of the opposite sex. Consequently, heterosexuals may have to abstain completely from sexual encounters, turn to self-gratification, or engage in homosexual encounters. Even if a prisoner chooses to abstain, there is, of course, the risk of being forced to engage in homosexual relations because of the threat of rape in prison. And even though prison administrators know that rapes occur within the walls of American prisons, these attacks generally are not investigated or prevented (Mariner 2000, p. 129).

A growing number of American prisoners are being deprived of virtually all relationships, including contact with other people. One reason is that more and more prisons are being built in rural areas, far from the offenders' family members and significant others. In rural communities prisons are promoted as a blessing—a source of jobs to boost the local economy. Another reason is that the United States has begun incarcerating some of its most dangerous offenders in *supermaximum* or *supermax* prisons. These facilities restrict inmate contact with other inmates and with correctional personnel. Many inmates are locked in their cells for most of the day, stark cells with white walls. Cells have completely solid front doors, no windows, and bright lights that stay on at all hours of day and night.

Examples of supermax facilities include Marion (Illinois) and Pelican Bay (California). Welch (1999, p. 200) describes the conditions in these prisons:

> [In Marion] all prisoners are confined to their cells for 23 hours per day, granted 1 hour of exercise outside of their cell, and allowed to shower 2 or 3 days a week. Handcuffs are fastened to inmates while they are transported within the facility . . . [and they are chained] "long-term . . . to their beds."

> [In Pelican Bay] [i]nmates are confined to their 8- by 10-foot cells, where the temperature registers a constant 85 to 90 degrees, for twenty-two and a half hours per day. The unrelenting heat produces headaches, nausea, and dehydration and drains the inmates of their mental and bodily energy.

Human rights violations in supermax facilities, of course, are hidden from the public. When abuses of prisoners in other types of prisons become known, Americans do not become concerned because state-controlled media outlets do not construct these harms as social problems (Welch 1999, p. 208). The Pelican Bay facility in California was built at a cost of $278 million for 2,080 maximum-security inmates. That's $134,000 per inmate! The organization Human Rights Watch calls these expensive facilities "a clear violation of human rights" and a breach of an international treaty implemented by the United States in 1992 (Weinstein 2000, p. 120). Yet Americans are generally unaware of or unconcerned about human rights violations against convicted criminals.

Deprivation of Goods and Services

Another significant loss associated with imprisonment is the *deprivation of goods and services*. Imagine all of your worldly possessions being inaccessible to you, along with virtually every service and product that a free person can enjoy. This would be a major loss associated with having your freedom taken away. More and more, prison life is becoming a boring, uniform routine with what inmates consider to be "chickenshit rules" (Irwin and Austin 1997, p. 75). Some prisoners may become *prisonized* and unable to make it in the real world (Clemmer 1940).

Loss of Voting Rights

According to The Sentencing Project (2003), 48 states and the District of Columbia prohibit inmates incarcerated for felonies from voting, 33 states prohibit people from voting while they are on parole, and 29 states prohibit people from voting while on probation. The Bureau of Justice Statistics maintains that all states impose some form of *collateral damage* on inmates. Although you may not consider the *loss of voting rights* an important loss, especially if you do not currently vote, it is inconsistent with the goal of integrating ex-convicts into free society. Members of free society have the right to vote and thus to help shape the direction of their lives, as well as those of their families and communities. In a representative democracy, when a person cannot vote, by definition, that person's voice cannot be heard and he or she is not represented.

According to The Sentencing Project (2003), about 4 million Americans (1 in 50 adults) have lost their rights to vote because of felony convictions. In the United States, the loss of the right to vote is a burden disproportionately imposed on poor people and people of color. The rate of *felony disenfranchisement* is seven times higher than the national average for African American males; now about 13% of African American males cannot vote. In the state of Florida, 600,000 people could not vote in the 2000 presidential elections.

Loss of Dignity

Associated with each of the losses described here is a *loss of dignity*. Prisoners are treated not as individual human beings, but as numbers. At worst, they lose respect for themselves because of this treatment. They come to be dependent on the government to live their lives. They are also subjected to various labels, such as "convict," "ex-convict," "criminal," "dangerous," and "antisocial." According to M. Robinson (2004), when such labels are applied to offenders and would-be offenders in a destructive, mean-spirited manner, their risk of offending actually increases rather than decreases. This is predicted by the theory of *reintegrative shaming*.

Stigmatization

As I showed earlier in this chapter, most people in U.S. prisons are truly disadvantaged: poor, uneducated, underemployed. Irwin and Austin (1997) illustrate that the typical offender enters prison with a 10th-grade education and leaves with a 10th-grade education plus the stigma of being an "ex-con." Most inmates "leave prison with all their previous disadvantages plus the additional stigma of a felony conviction" (Kappeler, Blumberg, and Potter 2000, p. 251). Perhaps this is why estimates suggest that inmates will lose about 70% of the income level they were accustomed to prior to entering prison (The Sentencing Project 1998), a level that was already low relative to the national average. Not surprisingly, then, when prisoners are released, the pain of *stigmatization* (e.g., the ex-con label) makes it difficult for them to find places to live and work.

Labeling theory asserts that when people are labeled by the criminal justice network as "criminals," "convicts," or "offenders," the label can affect how these offenders view themselves, thus potentially changing their self-concepts. Once they begin to see themselves as "deviant" or "different," they will continue committing crime to live up to the expectations that society has set forth for them (Bohm 2001). Sampson and Laub (1997) suggest that employers use the ex-con label as a warning against hiring former offenders. According to Bushway (2000, p. 144), "Federal legislation explicitly denies ex-felons employment in *any* job in the financial sector, as well as in other areas such as child care and private investigations. Most states also have legislation mandating screening on the basis of criminal history records for literally hundreds of jobs" (emphasis in original).

Irwin and Austin (1997, p. 82) summarize the issue this way:

> The disturbing truth is that growing numbers of prisoners are leaving our prisons socially crippled and profoundly alienated. Moreover, they understand that they will be returning to a society that views them as despicable pariahs. They are also aware that they will have major difficulty finding employment than formerly, and consequently their expectations are low.

Shouldn't we be able to expect more out of a system of "corrections"? As May (2000, p. xvii) correctly points out, the term *corrections* is really a misnomer.

Summary: Pains of Imprisonment

Given these pains of imprisonment, it's no wonder that most released prisoners will end up back in prison. As Irwin and Austin (1997, p. 62) explain, "Because most will be released within two years, we should be deeply concerned about what happens to them during their incarceration." We have to decide, as states and as a nation, what we think is most important—punishing offenders to get retribution or preventing their future crimes. If we want to make inmates mad at society and want to create a sense of vengeance in them, we should continue doing what we are doing. If we want them to become part of legitimate U.S. society, we must witness a change of direction in punishment.

For the past several decades, U.S. prisons have done little more than warehouse inmates. Irwin and Austin (1997, p. 62) describe it this way:

> Convicted primarily of property and drug crimes, hundreds of thousands of prisoners are being crowded into human (or inhuman) warehouses where they are increasingly deprived, restricted, isolated, and consequently embittered and alienated from conventional worlds and where less and less is being done to prepare them for their eventual release. As a result, most of them are rendered incapable of returning to even a meager conventional life after prison.

Simultaneously, as indicated earlier, opportunities for education, vocational training, and recreation have substantially decreased in the prevailing punitive environment of American punishment. Irwin and Austin (1997, p. 80) suggest that fewer than 20% of all prisoners are enrolled in any type of educational program.

Incarceration also hurts more than the criminal. Effects of imprisonment on families can be tremendous. Obviously, imprisonment runs counter to the goal of maintaining a two-parent family. The National Criminal Justice Commission writes:

> For many young women in the inner city, there is a scarcity of available men of marriage age because so many are going in and out of jails and prisons. . . . In some inner-city areas, virtually every resident has a close relative and over 50 percent have a parent who is in prison, on probation, on parole, in jail, or hidden because there is a warrant out for their arrest. (Donziger 1996, p. 47)

Whitehead (2000, p. 87) reports that in a study of inner-city women, some African American females (15 to 19 years old) reflected on this situation in their comments on dating. They were asked, "What recommendations would you have for other young women your age who have met a new boy with whom they are thinking of entering into a relationship?" Some of their answers were "Make sure the police isn't looking for him" and "Make sure he didn't recently get out of jail" (Whitehead 1997). Think of the irony of politicians speaking of the value of two-parent families while simultaneously promoting policies that split them up. Is it any wonder that about 60% of prisoners have been there before and will end up there again?

Given that prison is such an awful place, does imprisonment reduce crime? That is, is it a deterrent to future criminal activity? I explained earlier that most of the recent declines in crime are not attributable to massive increases in imprisonment. Research findings do not support politicians' claims that imprisonment is an effective method of reducing crime rates and making people safer. Politicians, in essence, promote a failing means of crime reduction to Americans who have sworn an allegiance to it, even though it does not work. Even if you believe that imprisonment is a special deterrent (a punishment that instills fear in offenders, making it less likely that they will commit crimes in the future), consider this possibility: For individuals who see no promising options in the legitimate economy, for whom life on the street is very risky anyway, and who have not been effectively socialized against committing crimes, the prospect of spending time in prison, perhaps with others they know, of being assured meals and a bed (even if far from luxurious), may not deter them from criminal activity. Prison may not be a very attractive option, but its increment of pain is likely to be far less than it is to middle-class populations (Blumstein 2000, p. 10).

There is also substantial evidence that prisons serve as *colleges of crime.* Think about it: A logical outcome of placing large numbers of convicted criminals together is that they will teach one another new tricks of the trade. Amazingly, although we know that having criminals live in close proximity to one another will ultimately produce more crime, for this reason and others, we still continue to build more and more facilities to house more and more inmates. Politicians who claim that crime is down because of increased use of imprisonment are, at best, misinformed and shortsighted. The long-term effects of mass imprisonment will be disastrous and costly.

Walker (1998, p. 14) shows how the United States' fight to reduce crime by means such as imprisonment parallels efforts of some overweight people to lose weight: "Just as people go on crash diets, lose weight, put it all back on, and then take up another diet fad a year later, so we tend to 'binge' on crime control fads." Many people fail to recognize that fighting fat through fad diets will never work, and that weight-loss fads result in billions of dollars of profit each year for those who misrepresent even the most bizarre programs and products. It is ironic that people who want to lose weight are most likely to try approaches that actually increase their weight. Similarly, reducing crime cannot be achieved through fad crime control policies that are proposed for purely symbolic reasons by politicians and inadequately designed by criminal justice policymakers. Even though they are enormously profitable for some, prisons do not reduce crime. There is no "miracle cure" for crime. Reducing crime, like losing weight, requires dedication and time. In Chapter Thirteen, I explore some criminal justice options that might work to reduce crime in the United States.

Yet we continue with our "crime control theology," rooted not in empirical evidence and sound scientific argument, but rather in belief and common sense. As discussed in Chapter Two, politicians have pledged to put more police on the streets and put more people in prison. Even though these measures are only a temporary fix, they are widely supported by the public (Walker 1998, p. 75). Irwin and Austin (1997) suggest that imprisonment is rooted in a false image of the typical offender, created by politicians and by media attention to violent crimes and rooted in what they call "voodoo criminology." They write that

> the idea that increased penalties will reduce crime is based on a simplistic and fallacious theory of criminal behavior [that] starts with the idea that every person is an isolated, willful actor who makes completely rational decisions to maximize his or her pleasure and to minimize his or her pain. . . . If penalties for being caught are small or nonexistent, then many persons who are not restrained by other factors . . . will commit crimes . . . a lot of crimes. Only by increasing the certainty and severity of punishment, this thinking goes, will people "think twice" and be deterred. (p. 156)

These are fallacious assumptions about the motivations for criminal behavior. It's no wonder that prison fails so consistently.

After some period of confinement in a prison, offenders typically are not yet off the hook. Even after their term of imprisonment is reduced (or when they are released early), they typically will still be under some form of criminal justice supervision. In the next section, I address how one such mechanism—parole—can increase the risk of repeat offending.

FORGIVING THE OFFENDER: WHY HARASS PAROLEES?

Parole means conditional release to community supervision, whether by parole board decision or by mandatory conditional release after serving a prison term. On December 31, 2002, 753,141 individuals were on parole. More than 650,000 adults, or more than 1 in every 320 adults, were under parole supervision by states. The rest were supervised by the federal government. According to the Bureau of Justice Statistics, 55% of those entering parole in 2001 were *mandatory releases* from prison rather than *discretionary releases*. Mandatory releases occur because of a sentencing statute or good-time provision in the law. Discretionary releases are granted by parole boards. In 1995, mandatory releases made up 45% of all parole releases. Parolees are subject to being returned to jail or prison for rule violations or other offenses. This is because parole can be revoked when a person either commits another criminal act or violates one of the rules of release.

If rearrest is a sign of parole failure, then parole is a failure. Irwin and Austin (1997, p. 113) write, "In general, most inmates are rearrested at least once after being released from prison." This does not mean that they committed new crimes, only that they either were suspected of having committed a new crime or violated some rule of their parole. In some ways, police harassment of parolees makes sense.

When a crime is committed in the vicinity of a known offender, especially one that fits his or her modus operandi (M.O.), the ex-con becomes a logical suspect. Yet some feel that once an offender has paid his or her debt to society, police should not automatically assume that an "innocent" person is guilty of a crime.

In fact, most people who fail parole fail not because they committed new crimes but because of *technical violations*. As you saw in Chapter Eight, of all state parolees discharged in 1999, only 42% successfully completed their supervision term. Success for federal parolees in 2001 was only 55%. At both levels of government, failures were attributable more to technical violations than to new crimes. Irwin and Austin (1997, pp. 116, 123) attribute parole failures to increased supervision capacities of parole officers and to an increased focus on the law enforcement function of parole as opposed to its social service function. Parolees are typically required to follow the same general rules of those on probation, including obeying all laws, reporting to their parole officers, permitting their parole officers to visit them, remaining in the jurisdiction, maintaining employment, abstaining from associating with known felons, paying fines and court costs, engaging in community service, and participating in treatment and/or training.

Irwin and Austin (1997) lay out the main reason that people who go to prison will likely end up back there eventually after their release. They suggest that, in addition to the pains of imprisonment discussed earlier and the harassment of parolees by the police, the following reasons make it easy to understand why the prison experience followed by parole fails to reform prisoners.

- Reentering society is literally a shock to offenders, who are used to the routine of prison life, lived under government-controlled rules and orders.
- Finding a job is next to impossible, given ex-prisoners' lack of employment skills, educational deficits, and criminal record.

In essence, prisons are not really supposed to make people better; they are just supposed to warehouse criminals for only short-term benefit to society.

HOW AND WHY CORRECTIONS REFLECTS CRIMINAL JUSTICE BIAS

Because corrections represents the end of the criminal justice process, it is the ideal place to look for *disparities* that suggest injustices in the law, media coverage of crime, police activity, and court processes. Imagine that small biases exist within each of these institutions. The outcome would probably be large disparities in correctional populations.

Clearly, U.S. prisons reflect a significant disparity in punishment in the United States. This led Irwin and Austin (1997, p. 164) to write, "In effect, we are gradually putting our own apartheid into place." According to The Sentencing Project, the characteristics of those who regularly end up in state prisons and jails include the following: 93% of state prisoners are male, 68% of state prisoners did not complete high school, 64% of jail inmates earned less than $1,000 per month at the time of their arrest, 60% of jail inmates self-report being under the influence of drugs when committing their offenses, 46% of prison inmates are African American, and 36% of jail inmates were unemployed prior to their incarceration.

As shown in Table 9.2, African American males are disproportionately likely to be under all forms of correctional supervision. According to The Sentencing Project (2003), African American males have a 29% chance of serving time in prison at some point in their lives, versus 16% of Hispanic males and 4% of Caucasian males.

At the end of 2001, black males between 20 and 39 years of age made up 34% of all state and federal prison inmates. The war on crime is clearly having its greatest effects on young African American males. For example, the Bureau of Justice Statistics reports that at mid-year 2002, 12.9% of all African American males between 25 and 29 years of age were in prison, versus only 4.3% of young Hispanic males and 1.6% of young Caucasian males. Thus, young African American males are seven times more likely than young Caucasian males and two times more likely than young Hispanic males to be in prison. At mid-year 2002, 12% of African American males in their 20s and 30s were in prison or jail, compared with 4% of Hispanic males in this age group and only 1.3% of Caucasian males. In fact, at mid-year 2002, African American males in their 20s and 30s made up an astounding 596,400 of all 2,021,223 inmates in the United States, or nearly 30% of all people locked up in America.

Figure 9.5 shows the rates of sentenced prisoners for various groups in the United States. The larger the number, the more people per 100,000 in that group in society are incarcerated. The focus of imprisonment in America is on men of color. African Americans made up 46% of all inmates in state and federal prisons at the end of 2001, versus 36% Caucasians and 15% Hispanics. African American females were also 2.3 times more likely than Hispanic females and 4.5 times

TABLE 9.2

African Americans in Correctional Populations

	Percentage Black
Prisoners	46 (2001)
Jail inmates	40 (2002)
Probationers	31 (2000)
Death row inmates	43 (January 2003)

SOURCE: Sourcebook of Criminal Justice Statistics (2003).

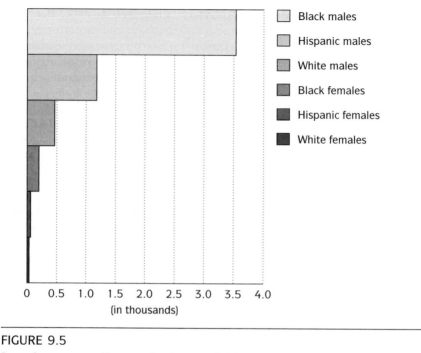

FIGURE 9.5

Imprisonment Rates, by Race (2001)

more likely than Caucasian females to be imprisoned in 2001. In 1950, African Americans made up about 35% of state and federal prisoners, but in 2010 it is expected that they will account for about 68% (National Center on Institutions and Alternatives 1999).

Blakemore (1998, p. 4) asserts that the prison industry is being built "on the backs of blacks." In fact, there are more African American males incarcerated than enrolled in higher education. While we build and build and build new prisons, 38 states and the District of Columbia witnessed an increase in racial disparity in their rates of incarceration from 1988 to 1994.

Of the nation's jail populations at the end of 2002, Caucasians made up 44% of inmates, African Americans made up 40%, and Hispanics made up 15%. The rate of jail incarceration for African Americans was 4.6 times higher than for Caucasians and 1.6 times higher than for Hispanics.

As for probation, at the end of 2002, men made up 78% of probationers and women made up 22%. Caucasians made up 55% of probationers, African Americans made up 31%, and 12% were Hispanics. As for parolees, at the end of 2002, 88% were men and 12% were women. African Americans made up 41% of parolees, 39% were Caucasians, and Hispanics made up 19%. From these statistics, it is clear who is suffering most from our current criminal justice policies. Young, poor, minority men (and, increasingly, women) are most affected by mass imprisonment and other forms of punishment.

The result of such disparities is devastating. For example, one in seven African Americans cannot vote because of felony convictions (Mauer 1997). Almost 80% of African American males can expect to have been arrested by age 35 (National Center on Institutions and Alternatives 1999;

also see Tillman 1987). Whereas approximately 1 in 3 African American males is somehow involved in the criminal justice network, only about 1 in 15 young Caucasian males and 1 in 8 Hispanic males are (The Sentencing Project 1997). In the late 1990s, African Americans made up 3% of California's population but 40% of its inmates (J. Miller 1997, p. 28).

J. Miller (1997) claims that contact with the criminal justice network is now a "rite of passage" for young African American men. As a result,

> it is now a sad reality that most of the young African American men can anticipate being at least briefly ushered through a series of hothouses for sociopathy: prisons, jails, detention centers, and reform schools—all of which nurture those very characteristics that can subsequently be labeled as pathological.

Blakemore (1998, p. 5) calls contact with the criminal justice network a "badge of honor" for some African American males and claims that punishment thus loses its deterrent effect for them. Also, criminal justice network targeting of minorities exacerbates problems such as single parenthood and unemployment (Blakemore 1998), which undoubtedly increases the likelihood of criminality. For example, in 1999, more than 1.5 million minor children had parents in prison. More than 640,000 state inmates and nearly 80,000 federal inmates were parents to children under the age of 18 years. In 1997, 55% of inmates said that they had minor children and 45% reported living with their children at the time of their admissions.

Other minorities and disenfranchised groups suffer as well. For example, the percentage of Hispanics in state and federal prisons doubled between 1980 and 1993, to over 14% (Mauer and Huling 1995b). The greatest increase in incarceration between 1989 and 1994 was 78% for African American women (Mauer and Huling 1995b). From 1986 to 1991, the number of African American women incarcerated for drug offenses in state prisons increased 828% (Mauer and Huling 1995b). More and more African American women are being incarcerated, partly because they do not have anything to offer the prosecutors who are looking for "bigger fish," so the "small fish" in the drug markets go to prison (J. Miller 1997).

Only 7% of state and federal prison inmates were women at the end of 2002. Yet since 1995, the number of female inmates had grown faster (36% increase) than the number of male inmates (24% increase). This accelerated growth has disproportionately affected minority women, and a significant portion is attributable to the war on drugs. Thus, since 1990, 33% of the total increase in female inmates is for drug offenses, versus only 19% for male inmates. Similarly, more of the growth among African American inmates is attributable to drug offenses (27%) than for Caucasian inmates (15%) or Hispanic inmates (7%).

There has been a dramatic increase in drug offender imprisonment, as drug offenders now make up 55% of all federal inmates (Bureau of Justice Statistics 2003). As explained earlier, at least half of state prison inmates were convicted of crimes that are considered petty by the American public. Drug offenders made up 1 in 11 offenders in 1983 but now make up about 1 in 4 inmates nationally, costing billions of dollars per year, in part because the probability of imprisonment for drug offenses has increased 500% since 1980 (Beck 1998).

So there is clearly a correlation among punitiveness in the United States generally, the U.S. wars on crime, and on drugs in particular, and racial disparities in the criminal justice network. Whether intended or not, our nation's crime control efforts disproportionately affect poor people and people of color. Perhaps part of these disparities can be explained by differences in offending patterns (see Chapter Twelve). But most of them cannot. Thus, the most valid explanation of these disparities is discrimination in the criminal justice network, beginning with bias in the criminal law, reinforced by the media, and continuing with the police and courts. Discrimination in the criminal justice network makes criminal justice operations incompatible with its ideal goal of being fair, neutral, unbiased, and nondiscriminatory. In other words, correctional populations serve as evidence of an unjust U.S. criminal justice network.

CONCLUSION

This chapter illustrates how the use of imprisonment will ultimately add to the crime problem in the United States, even if it temporarily locks some criminals away from society. Imprisonment, a main component of the unprecedented U.S. incarceration rate, has increased dramatically since the early 1970s. This chapter demonstrates that this increase had little or nothing to do with crime, is incredibly expensive, and is very unlikely to make Americans safer. In fact, given that most people in prisons are not repeat, violent offenders, many have claimed that we are wasting too much money on relatively harmless offenders such as drug criminals. This chapter also demonstrates that, contrary to the myth of the comfortable prison, prisons in the United States are rough places in which to stay and serve as more than sufficient punishment for most crimes. Because of these pains of imprisonment and because we harass parolees after they complete their sentences, it is very difficult for street criminals to "go straight" upon their release. Thus, we are guaranteeing our failure by choosing to imprison so many of our citizens. Most important for the theme of this book, imprisonment serves as a clear example of how the U.S. criminal justice network fails to meet its ideal goal of doing justice. Plainly stated, the use of imprisonment in the United States is biased against the poor and people of color.

ISSUE IN DEPTH
The Convict School of Criminology

The *Convict School of Criminology* was formalized in 2001 with the appearance of a journal article and in 2003 with the publication of the book *Convict Criminology* (Ross and Richards 2003). This new "school of thought" within the discipline of criminology came about when a handful of criminologists with criminal records met over time in their graduate school programs, at academic conferences, and through correspondence via e-mail and telephone.

As criminologist John Irwin (2003, p. xvii) notes: "It seemed to me that convicts were springing up like toadstools in the clear and pure fields of academe; one of the unintended consequences of laws recently casting a larger and larger net and catching, in addition to the usual suspects, a whole bunch of more educated and educable felons." As explained by Ross and Richards (2003), convict criminology

consists primarily of essays and empirical research conducted and written by convicts or exconvicts, on their way to completing or already in possession of a Ph.D., or by enlightened academics who critique existing literature, policies, and practices, thus contributing to a new perspective on criminology, criminal justice, corrections, and community corrections. This is a "new criminology" . . . led by exconvicts who are now academic faculty. These men and women, who have worn both prison uniforms and academic regalia, served years behind prison walls, and now, as academics, are the primary architects of the movement.

John Irwin's (2003) case is particularly interesting, one that he describes quite well:

> I served five years for armed robbery in the mid-1950s at Soledad Prison in California. Soledad was planned to be the model rehabilitative prison in the California system. We prisoners were forced to participate in educational and vocational training programs. I repeated many high school courses . . . and earned 24 college units from the University of California Extension Division. Though after release I was discouraged by parole authorities, I immediately entered San Francisco State College, then transferred to UCLA and earned a B.A. in sociology. (p. xx)

Upon graduating with his bachelor's degree, Irwin was encouraged to go to graduate school by another notable criminologist, with whom Irwin would ultimately go on to publish. He then received financial assistance and a position with the help of yet another notable criminologist and, ultimately, earned his Ph.D. at the University of California, Berkeley, and was hired to be a sociologist who would study crime by yet another criminologist at San Francisco State University.

Irwin (2003) explains the significance of all this: "The point is, I made my transition from the life of a thief, drug addict, and convict to one of a 'respectable' professional during a period when there was growing tolerance toward us condemned wrongdoers. The doors were opening. Then, in the mid-1970s, they slammed shut again" (p. xx). Yes, as I claim in Chapter Nine of this book, prisons are horrible places with few opportunities for rehabilitation.

Among the explicit claims of convict criminologists are the following.

- Prisons are being used as a solution to a social problem that does not respond to prison.
- America's prisons and correctional agencies are clearly flawed.
- Efforts to reform America's prisons have failed.
- The level of incarceration in the United States is at its highest ever.
- The major justifications for America's unprecedented prison expansion are unwarranted.
- Every cell built in a new prison costs approximately $100,000 and is money that is not spent on other vital social services such as education.
- Prisons do not reduce crime.
- Prison expansion has disproportionately affected people of color.
- One dramatic result of mass imprisonment is that as many as 2 million people of color currently are denied the right to vote.
- Prison expansion has disproportionately affected the nation's poor, especially poor men of color, who are seen as being marginal to America's political economy.

- Most people have not noticed how rapidly the prison population has grown, in part because the people who have the greatest voice in today's culture are not largely affected by the expansion of prisons.
- Prisoners are extremely demonized and marginalized despite being human beings.
- Vocational programs have been reduced in prisons as privileges were reduced simultaneously, so that there is virtually no rehabilitation in American prisons.
- The treatment of prisoners inside is permitted mostly because people (including the academic criminologists who study crime for a living) do not understand what it is like to be inside and the culture that is unique to prisoners.
- Most inmates are normal, relatively harmless people who made bad decisions and committed relatively harmless but bothersome crimes.
- Not only are too many people incarcerated, but also they are generally held for too long.
- Even the motivations of serious offenders in prison can typically be understood without invoking negative personality traits or character flaws (this is not to justify their behavior, but rather to explain it).
- When released, prisoners reenter a society that fears and loathes them, and do so with meager resources and virtually no preparation.

In essence, most of the claims of convict criminologists match what I have written in this chapter about America's prisons and its imprisonment boom. What is unique about convict criminologists is their insight into prison life and their way of telling their stories to so clearly cast grave doubts on our entire method of punishment in the United States.

Although convict criminologists appear to be taken seriously within the academic discipline of criminology, it is hard to say how a group of current and former prison inmates (even with doctoral degrees) would be viewed by legislators and general members of society. Given the politicization and intense media coverage of crime, and America's overall fear of both criminals and the unknown, it is unlikely that any reforms suggested by convicts and ex-convicts would be taken seriously. Thus, other conditions in society must be changed before the reforms suggested by convict criminologists can be implemented. For more on such recommendations, see Chapter Thirteen.

Convict criminologists advocate at least the following reforms.

- Reduce the number of people in prison through diversion to probation and other community sanctions.
- Close large prisons where thousands of inmates are warehoused and forced to live in conditions like animals at the slaughterhouse, and replace them with smaller and safer prisons with individual cells.
- Increase the quality of prisoners' food and clothing to reduce resentment and violence within prisons.
- Better fund prison programs, including employment programs, vocational training, higher education, and family skills training.
- Restore voting rights for all ex-convicts.
- Provide voluntary drug education therapy.

- Provide inmates with 3 months' pay for food and rent upon their release, to give them a fair chance at reform.
- Use victim–offender reconciliation programs and other forms of restorative justice to relieve some of the burden on criminal justice.
- End the drug war.

I advocate many of these same reforms given the research presented in this chapter. The drug war is discussed in Chapter Eleven.

Discussion Questions

1. Why is the United States' incarceration rate so high compared with rates of other countries?
2. Differentiate prisons and jails.
3. Do you think there is a link between crime rates and incarceration rates? Why or why not?
4. Identify the claims of politicians that would justify building more prisons.
5. What are some of the costs associated with imprisonment?
6. In what ways might imprisonment increase crime?
7. Describe the typical prisoner.
8. Why do you think politicians have passed laws that have led to the removal of educational, vocational, and drug treatment opportunities within prisons?
9. Think back over the course of your life and try to recall any crimes you may have committed that could have led to your own imprisonment. What made you commit those crimes?
10. What is parole?
11. What are the typical conditions required of parolees?
12. Outline the ways in which the use of imprisonment can be considered a failure.
13. What is the Convict School of Criminology?

PART IV

BAD CRIMINAL JUSTICE POLICY
AND HOW TO FIX THIS MESS

CHAPTER TEN

THE ULTIMATE SANCTION:

DEATH AS JUSTICE?

KEY CONCEPTS

A brief history of capital punishment
Death penalty facts
- *Box: Death penalty offenses at the state level*
- *Box: Death penalty offenses at the federal level*

Public support for capital punishment
Justifications for capital punishment: Logical or not?
- *Vengeance*
- *Retribution*
- *Box: Capital punishment in the Bible*
- *Incapacitation*
- *Deterrence*

What's wrong with the death penalty? Alleged problems with the administration of death
- *Box: Inmates executed despite doubts about their guilt*

Conclusion
Issue in Depth: A Broken System, Parts I and II
Discussion Questions

INTRODUCTION

The death penalty, also known as *capital punishment,* is the ultimate punishment imposed by any society. America has had a long and sordid history with this criminal sanction, including both state-sanctioned killings and the murders of African American men through lynchings carried out in the name of "punishment" for alleged wrongdoings. This chapter briefly examines this history and then turns to the issue of whether the death penalty makes any sense. The questions of whether capital punishment is moral or immoral, right or wrong, good or bad, necessary or unnecessary, just or unjust, and so forth, have been asked and answered numerous times throughout history. There is no one answer on which all people agree, but most of us have made up our own minds as to what side of the debate we are on. However you feel about the death penalty personally, capital punishment is a highly emotional issue. As you read this chapter, you should attempt to put your personal opinions aside and understand that your personal opinion may not be supported by empirical evidence. In this chapter, I critically analyze the justifications for the death penalty and conclude with a discussion of what's wrong with the application of capital punishment in the United States.

A BRIEF HISTORY OF CAPITAL PUNISHMENT

The earliest recorded execution in America was in 1608, of Captain George Kendall, a member of the Virginia colony. His punishment was for the crime of spying for Spain (Espy and Smykla 1987). Since that time, about 22,500 people have been executed in America (Espy, personal correspondence, cited by Bohm 1999, p. 2). Another 10,000 or so were lynched in the 19th century (Bedau 1982). Most of those executed have been men—only 2% were women—and the largest share of those executed were put to death prior to 1866 (Schneider and Smykla 1991). Originally, death sentences were mandatory for certain crimes, such as murder, but this began to change in 1838 when Tennessee enacted a discretionary death sentence (Acker and Lanier 1998). Today mandatory death sentences are considered unconstitutional. In the case of *Woodson v. North Carolina* (1976), the Supreme Court ruled five to four that the death penalty statutes in question were "cruel and unusual" because they violated the Eighth and Fourteenth Amendments to the U.S. Constitution. In essence, the Supreme Court found that mandatory death sentences violated the evolving standards of respect for human life implicit in the Eighth Amendment to the Constitution.

The decade that saw the largest number of executions was the 1930s, when the average number of executions per year was 167 (Schneider and Smykla 1991). Between 1977 and 2003, there were only 885 people executed in the United States, or about 33 per year (see Figure 10.1).

According to Costanzo (1997, pp. 13–15), there have been four consistent trends in the application of the death penalty over the past two centuries:

• A dramatic shrinking in the number and types of crimes punishable by death
• Attempts to lessen the cruelty of executions
• Attempts to ensure that death sentences are imposed fairly and rationally
• Efforts to sanitize executions by making them private

As you will see in this chapter, the combined effect of these death penalty trends is a freakish experience with executions in America.

Throughout U.S. history, many states have temporarily abolished the death penalty, and the United States as a whole briefly witnessed a *moratorium* on the death penalty from 1967 to 1977. Other states, including Illinois since 2002, have also instituted temporary halts to capital punishment. Cases heard by the U.S. Supreme Court about racial discrimination in the administration of capital punishment, particularly cases of alleged rapes of Caucasian women by African American men, led to an "unofficial suspension" of the death penalty after June 1967

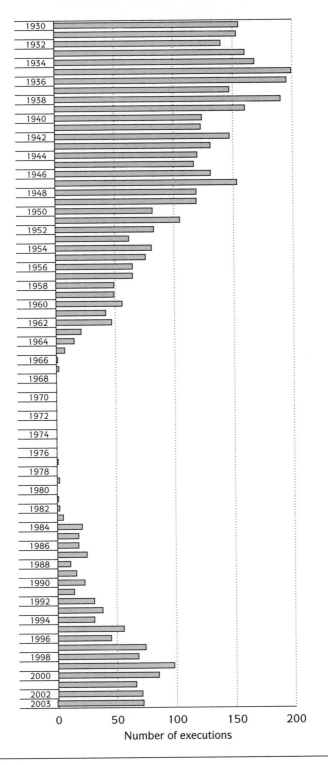

FIGURE 10.1

Trends in American Executions

SOURCE: Bureau of Justice Statistics (2003).

(Bohm 1999, p. 13). The Supreme Court formally prohibited capital punishment in *Furman v. Georgia* (1972) but later ruled it Constitutional in *Gregg v. Georgia* (1976). I discuss each of these cases later in the chapter.

The first person executed after the death penalty was reinstated in 1976 was Gary Gilmore, who requested to be killed by the state of Utah (Bohm 1999, p. 13). Gilmore insisted that he be put to death by the state, and he was, in 1977 by shooting squad. Gilmore's brother now discusses how ironic it is that his brother's last gift to mankind, created by his own push to be executed as rapidly as possible, was a return to capital punishment in the United States.

The U.S. is the only Western, industrialized country still practicing the death penalty. Most of our European allies abolished capital punishment after the horrors of World War II (Zimring and Hawkins 1986). This may suggest that American respect for life is less than in other countries. In 1961, the law professor Gerald Gottlieb wrote that "the death penalty was unconstitutional under the Eighth Amendment because it violated contemporary moral standards, what the U.S. Supreme Court in *Trop v. Dulles* . . . referred to as 'the evolving standards of decency that mark the progress of a maturing society'" (Bohm 1999, p. 11). In the case of *Weems v. United States* (1910), the Supreme Court held that punishments are excessive only if they violate "evolving social conditions." The fact that we administer the death penalty in the United States must mean that the courts do not believe that our country has evolved enough socially to warrant a cessation of capital punishment. Public opinion shows widespread support for capital punishment generally.

Although we continue to use the death penalty, its use began to decline after World War II as our allies moved to abolish it. For example, 1,289 people were executed in the 1940s, but only 715 were executed in the 1950s. From 1960 through 1976, only 191 were executed (Bedau 1982). Recently, the United States has witnessed a rebirth of capital punishment, despite evidence that the death penalty is highly discriminatory and erroneously applied. Here is some evidence of the resurgence of capital punishment in the United States during the 1990s.

- In 1992, Robert Alton Harris was the first person executed in California in a quarter-century.
- Presidential candidate Bill Clinton interrupted his 1992 campaigning to fly back to Arkansas to preside over two executions.
- In 1993, Wesley Allan Dodd became the first person executed in Washington in almost 30 years.
- In 1994, Maryland carried out its first execution in more than 30 years, Nebraska killed its first citizen in 35 years, and Idaho began executing citizens again after 36 years.
- In 1995, New York reinstated the death penalty.
- In 1996, Congress passed a law allowing death row inmates only one federal appeal unless new evidence proves clearly and convincingly that the person is innocent. In that same year, Oregon carried out its first execution in 34 years.
- In 1997, Arkansas executed three prisoners in one night (Costanzo 1997, p. 1).

Figure 10.2 shows that the number of people on death row began to increase in the 1970s as our nation moved more toward a crime control model of criminal justice.

As I mentioned above, the case of *Furman v. Georgia* (1972) led to a temporary abolition of capital punishment in the United States. William Henry Furman, a 25-year-old African American with an IQ of only 65, was convicted of the murder of Wiliam Micke, Jr., a Coast Guard petty officer in Georgia who was also the father of four children and the stepfather of six others. This case,

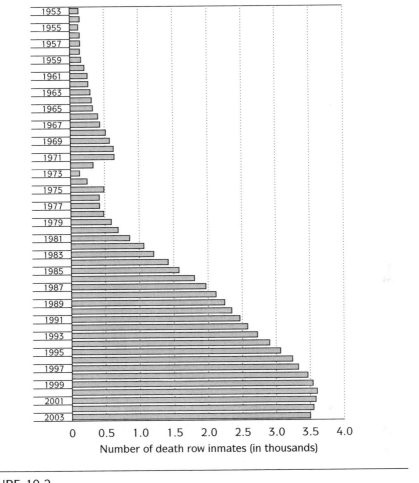

FIGURE 10.2

Trends in America's Death Row Population

SOURCE: Bureau of Justice Statistics (2003).

in which Furman was convicted of killing his victim in a failed burglary attempt, was not the stereotypical killing in the United States. Most murders are intraracial—that is, committed against a person of the same race as the murderer—and historically, most have been committed by persons known to the victims rather than by strangers. Because Furman was an African American and a stranger, and his victim was a Caucasian as well as a family man who served in the military, Furman's chance of not receiving the death penalty was slim, especially in a Southern state with a history of racial unrest.

Furman's attorneys argued to the Supreme Court that capital punishment in Georgia was unfair because capital trials essentially gave the jury unbridled discretion about whether to impose a death sentence on convicted defendants. The Furman case was only one of three heard by the Supreme Court at the same time, all dealing with death sentences imposed against African

American men. The other two cases specifically involved rapes of Caucasian women by African American males (Coyne and Entzeroth 1994), a crime that has been a primary source of discriminatory punishment in American history.

The *Furman* case led to nine separate opinions by each of the justices of the Supreme Court, and the ruling was five to four that the death penalty statutes in question were "cruel and unusual" because they violated the Eighth and Fourteenth Amendments of the U.S. Constitution. In essence, the Supreme Court found that capital punishment was being imposed "arbitrarily, infrequently, and often selectively against minorities" (Bohm 1999, p. 23). So it was not the death penalty itself that was at issue; it was how this penalty was being applied arbitrarily and disproportionately to certain groups of people.

Bohm (1999, citing K. Anderson 1983) writes, "A practical effect of *Furman* was the Supreme Court's voiding of 40 death penalty statutes and the sentences of 629 death row inmates." The Supreme Court, however, did not conclude that the death penalty per se was unconstitutional. It was unconstitutional only to the degree that it was imposed arbitrarily and unfairly. Thus, "36 states proceeded to adopt new death penalty statutes designed to meet the Court's objections" (p. 24). States, concerned with their image as much as with the public safety of their citizens, quickly passed death penalty laws that would be considered Constitutional by the Supreme Court.

Nearly one-third of states enacted mandatory death sentences for some crimes (Acker and Lanier 1998), taking the issue of discretion of judges and juries out of the picture. Most states passed "guided discretion" statutes that would give juries and sentencing judges some guidelines to follow when considering death sentences (Bohm 1999, p. 25). The mandatory death sentence statutes were rejected five to four as unconstitutional by the Supreme Court in *Woodson v. North Carolina* (1976), but in the case of *Gregg v. Georgia* (1976), the Court ruled by a vote of seven to two that guided discretion statutes were acceptable in death penalty cases. The Court also upheld the use of bifurcated trials, where guilt or innocence would be decided in the first phase and sentencing decided in the second, as well as automatic appellate review of convictions and sentences and, finally, proportionality reviews to compare sentences of particular cases against similar cases to ensure just sentencing practices. Thus, suggestions made in 1959 by the American Law Institute's Model Penal Code and aimed at making the death penalty fairer were finally put into place.

Almost all of the 38 states that still practice the death penalty provide an automatic appeal of all death sentences, whether the defendant wants it or not (Snell 1997). The use of appeals supposedly makes it less likely that a death sentence will be inappropriately handed down. Automatic appeals do not, however, lessen the likelihood that an innocent person will be wrongfully executed, for evidence pointing to the defendant's innocence may arise or be discovered only years later. Contrary to popular belief, many discretionary appeals initiated by defendants are not frivolous. In fact, since 1976, there have been nearly 2,000 cases in which defendants have either had their convictions overturned or had their sentences reduced by appeals courts (Death Row, U.S.A. 2003). Using such statistics, Bohm (1999, p. 45) estimates that approximately 21% to 32% of imposed death sentences "have been found faulty" by appeals courts, for reasons such as ineffective counsel, prosecutors referring to defendants' refusal to testify (as if this is a sign of guilt rather than a Constitutional right), denial of an impartial jury, and use of bad evidence such as coerced confessions of guilt (Freedman 1998). A more recent report shows an even higher incidence of serious reversible error (see the Issue in Depth at the end of this chapter).

Despite the implementation of these reforms, little has changed in the outcome of death penalty cases. Steiker and Steiker (1998, p. 70) claim:

> The Supreme Court's death penalty law, by creating an impression of enormous regulatory effort, while achieving negligible effects, effectively obscures the true nature of our capital sentencing system. The pre-Furman world of unreviewable sentencer discretion lives on, with much the same consequences in terms of arbitrary and discriminatory sentencing patterns.

In other words, the death penalty still does not pass Constitutional muster in practice.

Yet the last time the death penalty was seriously challenged, the Court failed to abolish capital punishment once and for all. In *McCleskey v. Kemp* (1987), the Supreme Court heard testimony from a sociologist (Dr. Baldus) who showed that the death penalty was applied disproportionately to African Americans in Georgia. The study utilized a multiple regression analysis including 230 variables likely to affect the outcome of death penalty cases to test the hypothesis that race of defendant and race of victim played a role in death penalty sentences. This study found that only 1% of Caucasians received the death penalty in homicide cases between 1973 and 1979, whereas 11% of African Americans did. Additionally, the study found that 22% of African Americans who killed Caucasians received death sentences, versus only 3% of Caucasians who killed African Americans. The Court recognized the validity of these findings and even acknowledged a general pattern of discrimination in the application of death sentences in Georgia. Yet the Court held that an individual defendant must demonstrate discrimination in his or her specific case for the case to be considered unconstitutional. That is, he or she must be able to demonstrate that the prosecutor acted in a discriminatory fashion in the individual case or that the legislature intended to make discriminatory law. Can this standard ever be met by an individual person?

Bohm (2002) reviews executions in Georgia since the *McKleskey* decision and finds that racial disparities still exist. Specifically, killers of Caucasians are far more likely than killers of African Americans to be sentenced to the death penalty, especially when African Americans are convicted of killing Caucasians.

The point is this: We know, and the Supreme Court even acknowledged in this case, that the death penalty is disproportionately applied to African Americans who harm Caucasians, yet the Court failed to use this evidence to overturn the death penalty. A majority of Americans still say that they support the use of capital punishment.

DEATH PENALTY FACTS

At year end 2003, the 38 states with the death penalty and the federal government held 3,504 prisoners who had been sentenced to death. Of the men and women (mostly men) who sit on the nation's death rows, some have been there only months while others have been there for more than 20 years. Although I discuss the issue of deterrence and the death penalty later in this chapter, it is impossible not to point this out at the outset: The death penalty is rarely administered in the United States. Consider, for example, the following statistics pertaining to the infrequent use of capital punishment in America.

- According to the Death Penalty Information Center, between 1976 (when the death penalty was reinstated after a brief moratorium) and 2001, only 749 people were executed.
- According to the NAACP Legal Defense Fund's *Death Row, U.S.A.*, as of January 1, 2002, there were 3,711 people on death row in the United States.

Combining the two numbers means that 4,460 people either were executed since 1976 or were on death row at the end of 2001. Another 93 people were released from death row between 1976 and 2001 (Death Penalty Information Center 2003). Therefore, a total of 4,553 people have been executed, are on death row, or were sentenced to death but subsequently released between 1976 and 2001.

During the same time period, between 1976 and 2001, there were 482,116 murders and incidents of nonnegligent manslaughter in the United States (Federal Bureau of Investigation 2003; Sourcebook of Criminal Justice Statistics 2000). Thus, less than 1% (0.9%) of people who committed a murder or nonnegligent manslaughter were either executed or sentenced to death between 1976 and 2001. This number is low for many reasons, most importantly the fact that only aggravated murderers are eligible for the death penalty.

Why do we kill so few of our nation's killers? As you will see later, only some types of killings are eligible for the death penalty—most notably, *aggravated murder*. Yet, even of aggravated murderers, we sentence only about 1% to 2% to the death penalty (Bohm 1999, p. 144). Bohm claims that "not only are the vast majority of capital offenders able to escape execution, but there is no meaningful way to distinguish between the eligible offenders who were executed and those who were not." This is one reason that death penalty opponents argue that capital punishment is applied so arbitrarily that it is not fair.

Since 1990, the United States has executed an average of 61 persons per year, and since 1977, only 31 per year. "Even during the peak of executions in the United States in the 1930s, only 20 percent of all death-eligible offenders were executed." How can it be that our nation, supposedly devoted to justice, tolerates a punishment that is, and always has been, so arbitrarily applied? Bowers, Pierce, and McDevitt (1984, p. 188) call the application of the death penalty "an occasional product of chance—an unpredictable occurrence." Even with the modifications to the death penalty after the *Furman* ruling, its application is still "rare," "uncommon," and "freakish" (Bohm 1999, p. 146).

Of the 1,367,856 inmates in the nation's prisons and the 665,475 inmates in local jails at the end of 2002, only 3,692 were on death row. This means that of the 2,021,223 people in our nation's correctional facilities, the 3,557 death row inmates account for only 0.17% of the nation's inmates. Of death row inmates, most are Caucasians, but minorities are overrepresented. As shown in Figure 10.3, in early 2003, there were 1,610 Caucasians (46%), 1,490 African Americans (42%), 344 Hispanics (10%), and 81 people of some "other" race (2%) on death row. The increase in Americans on death row since 1990 has been higher for African Americans than for Caucasians and other ethnic groups. Almost all (99%) death row inmates are males. The average age of death row inmates is less than 30 years. I visit the issue of bias in the application of the death penalty in the United States later in this chapter.

In 2003, 65 people in 11 states were executed. The average time on death row for those executed was nearly 11 years—hardly proof of a swift system. Table 10.1 illustrates which states executed people in 2003. As you can see, Texas leads the nation in executing its killers, proving once again, "Don't Mess with Texas!" Between 1993 and 2003, Texas executed 38% of all people put to death by capital punishment in the United States! Executions are so infrequent in most states (even in Texas) that it is almost laughable to assert that the death penalty deters would-be murders. But if there were a deterrent effect anywhere, it should be in Texas. Yet the murder rate in Texas in 1999 was 6.1 per 100,000 people, higher than the national average of 5.7 per 100,000 and number 19 in the country. Its overall violent crime rate is 15th.

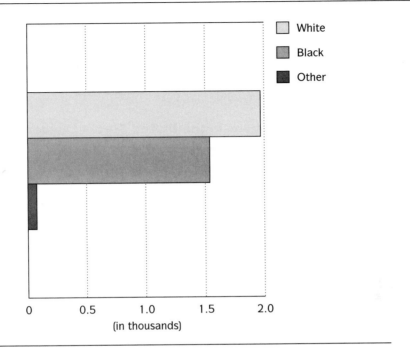

FIGURE 10.3
America's Death Row Population, by Race (January 2003)

TABLE 10.1
Executions in the United States (2003)

Texas	24
Oklahoma	14
North Carolina	7
Alabama	3
Florida	3
Georgia	3
Ohio	3
Indiana	2
Missouri	2
Virginia	2
Arkansas	1
Federal	1
Total	65

SOURCE: Death Penalty Information Center (2003).

You might expect that California would have a low murder rate as well, given that it has more death row inmates than any other state. Yet the murder rate in California in 1999 was 6.0 per 100,000 people, also higher than the national average and number 20 in the country. Its overall violent crime rate is 11th. Table 10.2 shows the states with the most death row inmates in 2002.

TABLE 10.2
Death Row Populations in the United States (January 2003)

California	624
Texas	454
Florida	381
Pennsylvania	244
North Carolina	217
Ohio	208
Alabama	193
Arizona	124
Georgia	117
Oklahoma	114
Tennessee	105
Louisiana	96
Nevada	86
South Carolina	77
Missouri	70
Mississippi	67
Arkansas	42
Indiana	41
Kentucky	38
Oregon	29
Virginia	26
U.S. government	25
Idaho	21
Delaware	19
Maryland	15
New Jersey	15
Washington	12
Utah	11
Connecticut	7
Illinois	7
Kansas	7
Nebraska	7
U.S. military	7
Colorado	6
Montana	6
New York	6
South Dakota	4
New Mexico	3
Wyoming	2

SOURCE: Death Penalty Information Center (2003).

TABLE 10.3
Method of Executions (2003)

	Number
Lethal injection	64
Electrocution	1

SOURCE: Death Penalty Information Center (2003).

Again, there is Texas, trying to displace California as the nation's leader. Jurisdictions without the death penalty include the District of Columbia, Alaska, Hawaii, Iowa, Maine, Massachusetts, Michigan, Minnesota, North Dakota, Rhode Island, Vermont, West Virginia, and Wisconsin.

Most people executed today are killed by lethal injection. Table 10.3 documents the method of execution of the 65 people executed in 2003. As you can see, all but one were killed using lethal injection. There has been a move to make execution as sanitary and "clean" as possible, so that allegations of cruel and unusual punishment against states that use capital punishment will be harder to prove.

Methods of capital punishment have evolved with evolving standards of decency; that is, as beliefs about what is acceptable punishment have changed, so too have methods of capital punishment. Bohm (1999) notes that hanging has been the most common form of capital punishment in American history, although electrocution was the most commonly used form of the death penalty in the 20th century. It is likely that the future will see new forms of capital punishment developed; until then, lethal injection is likely to be the most popular from of capital punishment in the United States in the 21st century. Currently authorized options for methods of executions include lethal injection (36 states), electrocution (10 states), lethal gas (5 states), hanging (3 states), and firing squad (3 states). The U.S. government and the U.S. military utilize lethal injections as well. Most of these states actually use only lethal injection because the other methods are typically authorized only for people convicted of capital crimes under previous statutes; in some cases, inmates have the choice among available methods.

America has made great strides to make its executions more humane, so that they will not be considered cruel and unusual. Prior to the *Furman* decision, individual methods of punishment were considered cruel and unusual only if they involved torture, unnecessary cruelty, or lingering death due to inhuman and barbarous punishments (Bohm 1999, p. 20). Of course, human beings have historically been subjected to executions that today would be considered cruel and unusual. Bedeau (1982, p. 14) writes about some historical examples of methods of execution, including "flaying and impaling, boiling in oil, crucifixion, pulling asunder . . . burying alive, and sawing in half."

One highly recognized example of a brutal execution is that of Robert-François Damiens, who in 1757 attempted to assassinate King Louis XV of France. His execution is described by D. Jones (1987, p. 26):

> At seven o'clock in the morning of his execution day, Damiens was led to the torture chamber, where his legs were placed in "boots" that were squeezed gradually as wedges were inserted. A total of eight wedges were inserted, each at fifteen-minute intervals, until the attending physicians warned that an additional wedge could (prematurely) provoke [Damien's death]. Thereupon, Damiens was removed to the place where he would be executed. . . . The condemned man was placed on a scaffold, where a rope was tied to each arm and leg. Then,

Damiens' hand was burned with a brazier containing burning sulphur, after which red-hot tongs were used to pinch his arms, thighs, and chest. Molten lead and boiling oil were poured onto his open wounds several times, and after each time the prisoner screamed in agony. Next, four huge horses were whipped by attendants as they pulled the ropes around Damiens' bleeding wounds for an hour. Only after some of the tendons were cut did two legs and one arm separate from Damiens' torso. He remained alive and breathing until the second arm was cut from his body. All parts of Damiens' body were hurled into a nearby fire for burning.

Executions often were public spectacles of excess. Adler, Mueller, and Laufer (1995, p. 56) write that, at the execution of Damiens, so many people wanted to watch the hour-long killing that window seats overlooking the site were sold at high prices. Criminal defendants in Europe were stretched on their backs, in public, and had large rocks or iron weights placed on their chests until they confessed or died.

Early methods of execution included stoning, "death by a thousand cuts," hanging, drawing and quartering, "parboiling" (cooking in salt and cumin seed), drawing, beating, beheading, "breaking on the wheel," pressing to death, and burning at the stake (Costanzo 1997).

Even in the United States, executions have been carried out in public. Costanzo (1997, p. 7) describes how public executions in America were similar to those in Europe: "The condemned was forced to take a slow wagon ride to the gallows, often sitting atop the very coffin he or she would soon occupy. The rowdy crowds who witnessed the hangings often numbered in the thousands." Bohm (1999, p. 4) notes that the first state to "hide executions from the public" was Pennsylvania, in 1834. The last public execution in the United States was in Galena, Missouri, in 1937, before a crowd of nearly 20,000 (Costanzo 1997, p. 9). Since this time, executions have occurred in the nation's prisons, in isolated rooms, inaccessible to the general public, late at night, without much attention by the media. This is to prevent or reduce the "public disorder, rioting, and even murder," as well as public knowledge of botched executions and disappointment associated with last-minute reprieves, that accompanied public executions (Bowers, Pierce, and McDevitt 1984, p. 8; Denno 1994, p. 564).

You may imagine that executions should be public as a deterrent to would-be criminals, but there is no evidence to support this assertion. In fact, when executions were public in Europe just prior to the French Revolution, large crowds of witnesses would attract pickpockets, who would steal from witnesses watching the public spectacle. Yet theft was a crime punishable by death (Adler, Mueller, and Laufer 1995)! I return to the issue of deterrence later in this chapter.

As I have mentioned, most people are executed today after being convicted of aggravated murders. The following box lists specific death penalty offenses at the state level.

Death penalty offenses at the state level

- Alabama: Capital murder with a finding of at least one of nine aggravating circumstances (Ala. Code Sec. 13A-5-40 and Sec. 13A-5-49)
- Arizona: First-degree murder accompanied by at least 1 of 10 aggravating factors
- Arkansas: Capital murder (Ark. Code Ann. 5-10-101) with a finding of at least 1 of 10 aggravating circumstances; treason

- California: First-degree murder with special circumstances; train wrecking; treason; perjury causing execution
- Colorado: First-degree murder with at least 1 of 13 aggravating factors; treason. Capital sentencing excludes persons determined to be mentally retarded.
- Connecticut: Capital felony with nine categories of aggravated homicide (C.G.S. 53a–54b)
- Delaware: First-degree murder with aggravating circumstances
- Florida: First-degree murder; felony murder; capital drug trafficking
- Georgia: Murder; kidnapping with bodily injury or ransom where the victim dies; aircraft hijacking; treason
- Idaho: First-degree murder; aggravated kidnapping
- Illinois: First-degree murder with 1 of 15 aggravating circumstances
- Indiana: Murder with 16 aggravating circumstances (IC 35-50-2-9). Capital sentencing excludes persons determined to be mentally retarded.
- Kansas: Capital murder with seven aggravating circumstances (KSA 21-3439). Capital sentencing excludes persons determined to be mentally retarded.
- Kentucky: Murder with aggravating factors; kidnapping with aggravating factors
- Louisiana: First-degree murder; aggravated rape of a victim under age 12; treason (La. R.S. 14:30, 14:42, and 14:113)
- Maryland: First-degree murder, either premeditated or during the commission of a felony, provided that certain death eligibility requirements are satisfied
- Mississippi: Capital murder (97-3-19[2] MCA); aircraft piracy (97-25-55[1] MCA)
- Missouri: First-degree murder (565.020 RSMO)
- Montana: Capital murder with one of nine aggravating circumstances (46-18-303 MCA); capital sexual assault (45-5-503 MCA)
- Nebraska: First-degree murder with a finding of at least one statutorily defined aggravating circumstance
- Nevada: First-degree murder with 13 aggravating circumstances
- New Hampshire: Six categories of capital murder (RSA 630:1 and RSA 630:5)
- New Jersey: Purposeful or knowing murder by one's own conduct; contract murder; solicitation by command or threat in furtherance of a narcotics conspiracy (NJSA 2C:11-3C)
- New Mexico: First-degree murder in conjunction with a finding of at least one of seven aggravating circumstances (Sec. 30-2-1 A, NMSA)
- New York: First-degree murder with 1 of 12 aggravating factors. Capital sentencing excludes persons determined to be mentally retarded.
- North Carolina: First-degree murder (N.C.G.S. 14–17)
- Ohio: Aggravated murder with at least one of eight aggravating circumstances (O.R.C. Secs. 2903.01, 2929.01, and 2929.04)
- Oklahoma: First-degree murder in conjunction with a finding of at least one of eight statutorily defined aggravating circumstances
- Oregon: Aggravated murder (ORS 163.095)

- Pennsylvania: First-degree murder with 18 aggravating circumstances
- South Carolina: Murder with 1 of 10 aggravating circumstances (Sec. 16-3-20[C][a]). Mental retardation is a mitigating factor.
- South Dakota: First-degree murder with 1 of 10 aggravating circumstances; aggravated kidnapping
- Tennessee: First-degree murder
- Texas: Criminal homicide with one of eight aggravating circumstances (TX Penal Code 19.03)
- Utah: Aggravated murder (76-5-202, Utah Code annotated)
- Virginia: First-degree murder with 1 of 12 aggravating circumstances (VA Code Sec. 18.2-31)
- Washington: Aggravated first-degree murder
- Wyoming. First-degree murder

At the federal level, the situation is much the same. Most crimes punishable by death involve murder. Laws such as the 1994 crime bill discussed throughout this book and the 1996 *Anti-Terrorism and Effective Death Penalty Act* specifically increased the number of crimes punishable by death to more than 50, but only 4 of them do not involve the crime of murder. The following box lists specific death penalty offenses at the federal level.

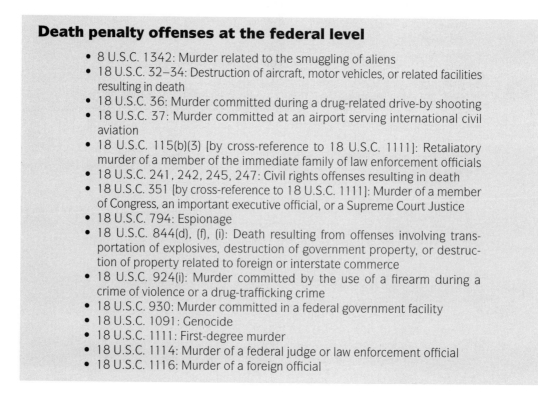

Death penalty offenses at the federal level

- 8 U.S.C. 1342: Murder related to the smuggling of aliens
- 18 U.S.C. 32–34: Destruction of aircraft, motor vehicles, or related facilities resulting in death
- 18 U.S.C. 36: Murder committed during a drug-related drive-by shooting
- 18 U.S.C. 37: Murder committed at an airport serving international civil aviation
- 18 U.S.C. 115(b)(3) [by cross-reference to 18 U.S.C. 1111]: Retaliatory murder of a member of the immediate family of law enforcement officials
- 18 U.S.C. 241, 242, 245, 247: Civil rights offenses resulting in death
- 18 U.S.C. 351 [by cross-reference to 18 U.S.C. 1111]: Murder of a member of Congress, an important executive official, or a Supreme Court Justice
- 18 U.S.C. 794: Espionage
- 18 U.S.C. 844(d), (f), (i): Death resulting from offenses involving transportation of explosives, destruction of government property, or destruction of property related to foreign or interstate commerce
- 18 U.S.C. 924(i): Murder committed by the use of a firearm during a crime of violence or a drug-trafficking crime
- 18 U.S.C. 930: Murder committed in a federal government facility
- 18 U.S.C. 1091: Genocide
- 18 U.S.C. 1111: First-degree murder
- 18 U.S.C. 1114: Murder of a federal judge or law enforcement official
- 18 U.S.C. 1116: Murder of a foreign official

- 18 U.S.C. 1118: Murder by a federal prisoner
- 18 U.S.C. 1119: Murder of a U.S. national in a foreign country
- 18 U.S.C. 1120: Murder by an escaped federal prisoner already sentenced to life imprisonment
- 18 U.S.C. 1121: Murder of a state or local law enforcement official or other person aiding in a federal investigation; murder of a state correctional officer
- 18 U.S.C. 1201: Murder during a kidnapping.
- 18 U.S.C. 1203: Murder during a hostage taking
- 18 U.S.C. 1503: Murder of a court officer or juror
- 18 U.S.C. 1512: Murder with the intent of preventing testimony by a witness, victim, or informant
- 18 U.S.C. 1513: Retaliatory murder of a witness, victim, or informant
- 18 U.S.C. 1716: Mailing of injurious articles with intent to kill or resulting in death
- 18 U.S.C. 1751 [by cross-reference to 18 U.S.C. 1111]: Assassination or kidnapping resulting in the death of the president or vice president
- 18 U.S.C. 1958: Murder for hire
- 18 U.S.C. 1959: Murder involved in a racketeering offense
- 18 U.S.C. 1992: Willful wrecking of a train resulting in death
- 18 U.S.C. 2113: Bank robbery–related murder or kidnapping
- 18 U.S.C. 2119: Murder related to a carjacking
- 18 U.S.C. 2245: Murder related to rape or child molestation
- 18 U.S.C. 2251: Murder related to sexual exploitation of children
- 18 U.S.C. 2280: Murder committed during an offense against maritime navigation
- 18 U.S.C. 2281: Murder committed during an offense against a maritime fixed platform
- 18 U.S.C. 2332: Terrorist murder of a U.S. national in another country
- 18 U.S.C. 2332a: Murder by the use of a weapon of mass destruction
- 18 U.S.C. 2340: Murder involving torture
- 18 U.S.C. 2381: Treason
- 21 U.S.C. 848(e): Murder related to a continuing criminal enterprise or related murder of a federal, state, or local law enforcement officer
- 49 U.S.C. 1472–1473: Death resulting from aircraft hijacking

PUBLIC SUPPORT FOR CAPITAL PUNISHMENT

According to public opinion polls, most people in the United States support the death penalty. In fact, the percentage of Americans who report that they support capital punishment increased consistently from the 1960s but leveled off in the 1990s. According to Bohm and Vogel (1994) most people who support the death penalty are Caucasian and believe that the death penalty achieves revenge against offenders and deters would-be murderers. Other research shows that support for the death penalty is associated with stereotyping of people of color and antipathy toward African Americans (Barkan and Cohn 1994).

TABLE 10.4
Public Support for Capital Punishment (Harris Polls)

	Believe in It	Opposed to It	Not Sure/Refused to Answer
1965	38%	47%	15%
1969	48%	38%	14%
1970	47%	42%	11%
1973	59%	31%	10%
1976	67%	25%	8%
1983	68%	27%	5%
1997	75%	22%	3%
1999	71%	21%	8%
2000	64%	25%	11%
2001	67%	26%	7%

SOURCE: Sourcebook of Criminal Justice Statistics (2003).

This apparently clear-cut support for the use of the death penalty becomes more ambiguous when citizens are provided with alternatives; the percentage of Americans who say that they support the death penalty for convicted murderers declines when the option of life imprisonment without the possibility of parole is given as a sentencing option. Perhaps if people were better informed about capital punishment facts, they would change their opinions to an anti–capital punishment stance. Haas and Alpert (1999, p. 167) predict that increased use of capital punishment will reveal its flaws to more people and ultimately lead to its abolition. They write that they will "become convinced by the weight of the evidence that the death penalty is useless, dangerous, and self-defeating" (p. 186).

Results from the Harris poll question, "Do you believe in capital punishment, that is, the death penalty, or are you opposed to it?" are listed in Table 10.4. These figures show that although a majority of Americans still say that they support the death penalty, the percentage who say that they do declined somewhat in the late 1990s. Polls generally show that support is higher among males than females and higher among Caucasians than Hispanics or African Americans. It is also higher for older people than for younger people and higher for people with less than a college education than for people with some graduate school. Generally, people with higher incomes are more apt to support the death penalty. Finally, support is higher among Republicans than Independents or Democrats.

Gallup polls show that when asked, "What do you think should be the penalty for murder—the death penalty, or life imprisonment with absolutely no possibility of parole?" most Americans favor the death penalty. As shown in Table 10.5, support for capital punishment is far from universal. A study by Sandys and McGarrell (1995) found that only about 9% of respondents in their survey of Indiana residents could be categorized as universally supportive of the death penalty. Their findings suggest that many Americans may simply accept capital punishment without actually supporting it.

A Gallup poll conducted in 2002 found that, for persons convicted of murder, 70% favor the death penalty while 25% do not. As in the Harris poll, support is higher among males (76%) than females (64%) and among Caucasians (72%) than nonwhites (63%) and African Americans (53%). It is also higher among people with less than a college education (71%) than among people with graduate school education (59%). Support is higher among people living in rural areas

TABLE 10.5
Public Support for Capital Punishment (Gallup Polls)

	Yes, in Favor	No, Not in Favor	No Opinion
1965	45%	43%	12%
1969	51%	40%	9%
1971	49%	40%	11%
1972	57%	32%	11%
1976	66%	26%	8%
1981	66%	25%	9%
1985	75%	17%	8%
1995	77%	13%	10%
1999	71%	21%	11%
2000	66%	28%	6%
2001	68%	26%	6%
2002	70%	25%	5%

SOURCE: Sourcebook of Criminal Justice Statistics (2003).

(72%) than those living in urban areas (63%). Finally, support is higher among Republicans (80%) than Independents (65%) or Democrats (64%).

Table 10.6 shows reasons that Americans gave in 2001 for favoring the death penalty. More than half (59%) said that they support the death penalty because of retribution (an eye for an eye, they took a life, punishment fits the crime, fair punishment, biblical reasons, to serve justice). Another 10% supported it for its deterrent value, and 10% supported it for incapacitation (they will repeat their crime, keeps them from repeating it, don't believe they can be rehabilitated, life sentences don't always mean life sentences). Another Harris poll, from 2001, asked, "Do you feel that executing people who commit murder deters others from committing murder, or do you think such executions don't have much effect?" Less than half (42%) reported that they felt it deterred others, while more than half (52%) said that it did not have much effect.

Let me now turn to the issue of whether these beliefs of Americans are justified on the basis of either logic or empirical evidence. If you support the death penalty, I think you will be surprised by much of what you will read.

TABLE 10.6
Reasons for Supporting Capital Punishment (2001)

Retribution	59%
(an eye for an eye, they took a life, punishment fits the crime, fair punishment, biblical reasons, to serve justice)	
Deterrence	10%
Incapacitation	10%
(they will repeat their crime, keeps them from repeating it, don't believe they can be rehabilitated, life sentences don't always mean life sentences)	

SOURCE: Sourcebook of Criminal Justice Statistics (2003).

JUSTIFICATIONS FOR CAPITAL PUNISHMENT: LOGICAL OR NOT?

Why do we have a death penalty? There seem to be only four possible justifications: vengeance, retribution, incapacitation, and deterrence. Vengeance and retribution are the most commonly cited reasons that people support the death penalty; incapacitation is the second most often stated justification for supporting the death penalty. Americans today rarely mention deterrence as a reason for supporting capital punishment, and most criminologists and criminal justice scholars no longer think that capital punishment is a deterrent to murder.

Vengeance

Costanzo (1997), in his book by the same name, suggests that the death penalty is *Just Revenge*. *Vengeance* is a "vengeful, aggressive act . . . performed in cold blood, after the damage has been done, and . . . is not a defense against immediate danger . . . which is of great intensity, often crude, vicious, and insatiable" (Marongiu and Newman 1987, p. 2, citing Erich Fromm). You can see how the death penalty fits this definition of vengeance in that the penalty is administered years after the criminal offense after the damage has been done. The death penalty also is not administered in the face of any immediate danger: Once an offender is properly confined in custody, he or she no longer poses a threat to society.

This may be one limitation to vengeance as a justification for punishment. As stated by the criminologist Frederic Faust (1995), "No other species will expend the energy to kill the enemy after it is clear that it has already won." Yet once a person has been arrested and convicted for murder and is thus no longer capable of killing another free member of society, we may still kill the person.

What needs to be understood about vengeance is that it is a human emotion. Nothing is wrong with feeling the desire to get even with someone who hurts you; indeed, this is probably natural. The problem arises when we try to justify a state response to crime based only on a human emotion. Since crimes are acts against the state, including murder, the emotional state of victims and their families is not relevant for deciding the proper punishment. The punishment in a rational system of punishment must be based on reason rather than emotion.

Retribution

One major reason we administer capital punishment in the United States is to do to offenders what they have done to someone else, to get even with offenders, or, stated differently, to give offenders their *just deserts*. This is related to vengeance, except that *retribution* is a rational desire to have the offender pay something back to society to rebalance the scales of justice.

A benefit of state-sanctioned *retribution* is that it limits the emotional aspects of vengeance, which often prompt retaliation on the part of victims and ultimately lead to escalation rather than resolution of the situation. For example, when a murder has been committed, only the state has the legal authority to seek justice for the harm inflicted. In the absence of this formal system of justice, victims would be left to seek out revenge for their loved ones and would likely end up killing not only the offender, in the name of justice, but whoever happened to be with the offender when the vengeance was carried out. This would ultimately lead to the killing of even more people in the name of justice for the new victims, with little hope of a successful ending to the killing. Mahatma Gandhi said that the problem with "an eye for an eye" is that it leaves the whole world blind.

State-sanctioned retribution, ideally, does provide the advantage of preventing retaliation and escalation that is produced by vengeance. Without punishment of the guilty, "there [would] exist the typical progression or spiraling process by which each offense [would be] countered by another offense more severe until the complete destruction of one of the parties [would be] achieved. It is the establishment of a social order that attempts to break this cycle of destruction" (Marongiu and Newman 1987, p. 4). There is certainly evidence of such escalation in history, which may justify state-sanctioned and state-administered vengeance. In ancient tribes, before the establishment of the Magna Carta in A.D. 1215 and the philosophy on which it was based (*lex talionis*, or "an eye for an eye"), retaliation threatened the social order as a result of "blood feuds." As stated by Jeffery (1990, p. 61), "Tribal law was based on revenge and the blood feud. The offended group carried out revenge against the offending group until some form of restitution was made by the offending group." If one individual offended against another, retaliation ensued, which led to escalation, clearly a destructive force. The only solution to this problem, according to Marongiu and Newman (1987, p. 5), is the development of an acceptable formal means of social control, such as a criminal justice network.

By limiting retaliation to "an eye for an eye," no more than one "eye" could be paid to right a wrong. The process of escalation should effectively be wiped out by punishing a guilty party for his or her acts. As explained by Jeffery (1990, p. 62):

> Legal systems emerged . . . to control the blood feud and private vengeance. The law said, "You cannot kill another person in retaliation for an injury to you or your tribe." However, the political state proceeded to establish criminal law based on the basis of public vengeance; that is, the state arrested, convicted, and killed the offender through legal procedures. Although the victim or his family is not allowed to kill the offender, the state is. Public vengeance replaced private vengeance.

This is an important point to remember when considering the validity of any punishment. But why do we have to kill people rather than subject them to some other form of punishment? "An eye for an eye" does not mandate plucking an eye from one who plucks an eye from you; it means that this is the most you can possibly do to the offender (S. Johnson 2000). Similarly, when one person kills another, we do not have to kill the offender; we just cannot do more to the offender (e.g., torture and kill the offender).

That is, retribution does not mandate an eye for an eye (Erez 1981). The state could easily administer some other punishment to achieve retribution. After all, the state does not rape rapists, burn the property of arsonists, or assault people who assault others (Amsterdam 1982).

One reason people support the death penalty as a form of retribution is the perception that it is supported by the Bible. In fact, among the earliest justifications for the death penalty in Colonial America were religious passages, quoted in early criminal statutes (Bohm 1999, p. 1). Costanzo (1997, p. 11) writes:

> Early justifications for killing wrongdoers rested on religious authority. Religious leaders insisted that executions were means of carrying out the will of God. According to the laws of Moses, the death penalty was a way to appease God and avert famines, plagues, and other misfortunes that might result from "God's fierce anger" against any community that failed to punish sinners.

The following box provides a summary of the death penalty and the Bible by a criminal justice scholar. His analysis shows less support for capital punishment than one might think.

Capital punishment in the Bible

S. Johnson (2000) focuses on instances where the Bible either mandates, explicitly acknowledges, or implicitly implies a state-sponsored execution. He writes: "People often cite specific verses of the Bible to justify a particular position on capital punishment, but these passages are frequently acontextual, failing to consider the significance of the passages containing these verses or the Bible as an entire document" (p. 15). Because the Bible is more ambiguous on the death penalty than one might believe, both supporters and opponents can find evidence supporting their arguments in the Bible.

Consider that "[t]he majority of biblical statements that support capital punishment are found in the Old Testament, more specifically the first five books of the Old Testament ... the Pentateuch ... the books of Genesis, Exodus, Leviticus, Numbers, and Deuteronomy." These are the oldest books of the Bible and they "clearly mandate the use of the death penalty for premeditated homicide" (p. 17). They also allow for capital punishment for the crimes of blasphemy and sacrifice to false gods, dishonoring parents, disrespecting priests or elders, adultery, incest, and homosexuality.

The New Testament, a more recent testimony to God, "provides no overt statement in which Jesus or New Testament authors endorse the use of death as a punishment for crimes" and "also fails to reveal any overt rejection of capital punishment," although death was clearly used as a state-sanctioned punishment during this time (p. 23). Yet the New Testament "also contains many passages that seem to refute the death penalty" (p. 26). For example, the Bible at times argues against taking revenge and seems to advocate forgiveness. Jesus even says:

> You may have heard that it was said, "An eye for an eye and a tooth for a tooth." But I tell you to resist an evil person . . . whoever slaps you on your right cheek, turn the other also. . . . You have heard that it was said, "You shall love your neighbor and hate your enemy." But I say to you, love your enemies, bless those who curse you, do good to those who hate you, and pray for those who spitefully use you or persecute you . . . . (Matthew 5:38–45)

Perhaps the clearest example of ambiguity about the death penalty in the Bible comes in the form of the outcomes of people in the Bible who committed murder. S. Johnson (2000, p. 29) identifies 22 murderers in the Bible, only 4 of whom (18%) are executed by the state. As explained by Johnson, "It seems difficult to suggest that the Bible sincerely endorses state sponsored capital punishment, when so few murderers in the Scriptures receive the death penalty" (p. 31).

Considering the lack of a clear mandate for executions in the Bible, Bohm (1999, p. 182) poses an interesting question: How can people, "particularly people whose lives are governed by the Bible . . . endorse revenge, support or oppose capital punishment, and use the Bible as a basis of their support or opposition, when they know the Bible is ambiguous on the subject"?

Even though the Bible may not provide the answer, consider that the "leaders of most organized religions in the United States no longer support the death penalty and actually openly favor its abolition" (Bohm 1999, p. 177). This includes Pope John Paul II and the National Conference of Catholic Bishops, who suggested that death by execution is "uncivilized," "inhumane," "barbaric," and assaultive of human life (Gow 1986, p. 80).

Since human life is precious, shouldn't we mourn the loss of any human life, including that of the offender? Keep in mind that when a person is executed, his or her family is victimized by the loss of their own loved one. In many ways, the loss of the convicted killer is just as bad as the loss of the innocent victim. Consider these points by Vandiver (1998, p. 486):

- The families of condemned prisoners know for years that the state intends to kill their relatives and the method that will be used. They experience a prolonged period of anticipatory grieving, complicated by the hope that some court or governor will grant relief.
- Their relatives' deaths will come about as the result of actions of dozens of respected and powerful persons. Their deaths are caused not by a breakdown in social order, but by a highly orchestrated and cooperative effort of authority.
- Their relatives are publicly disgraced and shamed; they have been formally cast out by society and judged to be unworthy to live.
- The deaths of their relatives are not mourned and regretted as other violent deaths are; rather, the death is condoned, supported, and desired by many people and actively celebrated by some.

Whatever the case, all acts of retribution and vengeance are motivated by concerns for equality, justice, and reciprocity, as well as the safety of society (Marongiu and Newman 1987). This means that people who support capital punishment seek to achieve legitimate and positive goals for society. Even the U.S. Supreme Court, in the case of *Gregg v. Georgia* (1976), recognized that retribution is a legitimate purpose of administering capital punishment; the Court even suggested that executing the guilty serves the purpose of satisfying the feelings and needs of the public for revenge (Bedau 1987). A significant drawback to their reasoning is that family members who survive murder victims are not well served by the execution of their loved ones' killers. Vandiver (1998) shows that there are many reasons that family members of murder victims do not want the killers executed, including the following.

- They do not support capital punishment.
- An execution would diminish the memory of their relative.
- They do not want to be forced to have prolonged contact with criminal justice agencies.
- They do not want the condemned killer to have any added public attention for his or her wrongdoing.
- They prefer the finality of a sentence of life imprisonment without the possibility of parole and the obscurity of prisoners over the continued uncertainty and publicity of the death penalty.
- They want the offender to reflect on his or her wrongdoing for life and to feel remorse.
- They may hope to develop, from the offender, a sense of understanding of why he or she committed the act.

There are many limits to retribution as a justification for punishment. For example, Jeffery (1990, p. 64) writes, "Retribution perpetuates the human urge for revenge, and it brutalizes societies and individuals by its use. . . . Although retribution is justified as a moral position, it is an immoral, vulgar, and self-defeating response to human behavior." Such statements are representative of those who feel that getting even to make us feel better is, simply stated, evil.

Others point to the hypocritical assertion that we can teach people that killing people is wrong by killing people who kill people: "[Some may] reap revenge in order to cancel out an offense, yet those same persons are perpetrating the very same behavior that they wish to avenge" (Marongiu and Newman 1987, p. 3). As asked on the bumper stickers you may have seen on cars, "Why do we kill people who kill people to show them that killing people is wrong?" The idea that the death penalty is hypocritical was also put forward by the British criminologist Jeremy Bentham, who claimed that the state could no more justly take the life of a person than could an individual person. In essence, the crime and the punishment become indistinguishable.

Obviously, not everyone feels that the death penalty is evil or hypocritical, given Americans' support of capital punishment. Virtually every politician claims to support the death penalty, at least publicly. To be against the death penalty today is virtually to ensure that you will not get elected. Many philosophers have claimed that retribution is a valid justification for punishment by positing that offenders who harm others are deserving of punishment. By killing, killers give up their right to life.

Many politicians echo these statements to justify their own support of capital punishment. A prosecutor in Florida said publicly in 1995 that the state should speed up the process of administering the death penalty by using "electric bleachers." Even though he was probably joking, his point was not only that he supported capital punishment, but also that he was fed up with how long it takes to carry out an execution.

Other supporters of the death penalty claim that it is the only form of justice to which individual victims are entitled. For example, Ernest Van den Haag states that punishment is a "collective reaction aimed at the satisfaction of the desire for retaliation by the injured party" (cited in Marongiu and Newman 1987, p. 3). Perhaps this is so, but the question remains: Could we more effectively and humanely achieve retribution through some alternative method of punishment?

Incapacitation

Without question, the death penalty achieves the goal of *incapacitation* of the offender. Once an offender has been executed, there is no chance that he or she will commit another crime, unless you believe that people get another go-round on the planet through reincarnation. Yet, because the death penalty is so rare, we incapacitate only about 1% of killers.

The question is, Can we achieve incapacitation with a form of punishment other than the death penalty? The answer is Yes: Incapacitation can be achieved with life imprisonment without the possibility of parole.

Luckily for taxpayers, the costs associated with life imprisonment without the possibility of parole for one offender are actually less than the costs associated with the execution of the same offender. Administering this alternative punishment also eliminates the possibility of killing innocent people, as we now know has been done.

The alternative I would likely advocate is life imprisonment without the possibility of parole, plus restitution (LWOP+R)—that is, where people convicted of aggravated murders would spend the rest of their lives behind bars and be required to work to pay for part of their incarceration costs and repay the families of victims of their crimes. Costanzo (1997, p. 163) claims that "detailed surveys of attitudes toward the death penalty show that Americans favor LWOP+R because it reduces the cost of incarceration, provides some form of restitution to victims, and is more likely to teach murderers to accept responsibility for their crimes." Since most jurors are reluctant to impose death sentences (regardless of their general support of capital punishment), because errors are inevitable, and because appeals in death penalty cases are numerous, LWOP+R sentences are swifter, surer, and more final, and we would never again have to worry about killing an innocent person.

Deterrence

Another supposed reason for administering capital punishment is to achieve *deterrence*—to stop other would-be murderers from committing murder. I should point out from the outset that most people probably no longer really believe that the death penalty is a deterrent to murder. It is currently the least mentioned reason for supporting the death penalty.

Recall from Chapter Eight that there are two types of deterrence—*special or specific deterrence*, aimed at preventing one offender from committing future crimes; and *general deterrence*, aimed at preventing members of society from engaging in criminality by making examples of criminals who already have. Some assert that the death penalty is at the very least a special deterrent, but this is an incorrect statement based on a misunderstanding of the meaning of special deterrence. Special deterrence implies that a convicted offender will fear punishment for future offenses and will thus refrain from committing crimes in the future. Since an execution results in the death of an offender, it is not a special deterrent because it does not create fear in the offender. Instead, it kills the offender, meaning that he or she is incapacitated.

So, is the death penalty a general deterrent? That is, when a person is executed, does it create a sense of fear in other Americans so that they will refrain from committing murder? If so, the death penalty would save lives (Costanzo 1997, p. 12). Logically, when Americans learn of executions, they should get the clear message: "SEE WHAT CAN HAPPEN TO YOU IF YOU GET CAUGHT COMMITTING SUCH AN OFFENSE!" Recall that much of what we do to punish criminals is based on logic. It appeals to our common sense that the death penalty should deter would-be murders. The problem with common sense is that it is often more "common" than "sense." Common sense would suggest, for example, that the sun revolves around the Earth, but we know that the opposite is true (Costanzo 1997, p. 95).

A significant problem comes from the assumption about murderers on which the death penalty is based. As explained by Costanzo (1997, p. 104), when we elect to impose a death sentence on murderers, we assume "that potential killers engage in a dispassionate weighing of the costs and benefits of killing." In other words, we assume that offenders choose to commit murder because the pleasure outweighs the potential pains associated with committing murder; thus, if we can somehow make the potential pains outweigh any benefits gained from committing murder, would-be murderers would not choose to commit murder. Costanzo claims, "This assumption is simply wrong." Most people who kill do not carefully weigh the pleasures and pains associated with committing a murder; most, instead, act in the heat of the moment, without much thought about getting caught, convicted, and punished for their acts. In 2001, 63% of murders were firearm related, and 49% were committed with handguns. How long does it take to grab a gun and pull the trigger? Is it likely that these murderers even thought of the death penalty in the short time it took to pull the trigger?

Van den Haag (1982, p. 326) sums up the logic of deterrence by suggesting that since "our penal system rests on the proposition that more severe penalties are more deterrent than less severe penalties," logic would dictate that "the most severe penalty—the death penalty—would have the greatest deterrent effect." Bohm (1999, p. 84) responds by saying that this assertion "is based on a debatable assumption and a testable proposition with no scientific evidence to support it." Van den Haag's assumption that the death penalty is more severe than life imprisonment is debatable and has been contested for hundreds of years. Perhaps it is far worse to have to live in prison for the rest of your life than to be executed after spending only 10 years on death row. However you feel about this issue personally, the fact remains that "[t]here is no evidence that capital punishment deters more than an alternative noncapital punishment, such as life imprisonment without opportunity for parole. Instead, statistics indicate that capital punishment makes no discernible difference on homicide or murder rates" (Bohm 1999, p. 85).

It does not matter if one compares states with and without the death penalty, nations with and without the death penalty, or jurisdictions before and after executions—all methods show no valid empirical evidence that the death penalty deters murders. In fact, more studies show a *brutalization effect* of the death penalty—that is, that capital punishment increases the rate of murder rather than decreasing it (Bailey 1998; Cochran, Chamlin, and Seth 1994; Death Penalty Information Center 2003).

The brutalization hypothesis suggests that the death penalty shows people that killing is an acceptable means for settling disputes; thus, when an execution occurs, murders actually increase for a short period of time. Although effects on homicide tend to be relatively small, the point is that homicides seem to increase in the short term after an execution, rather than decreasing. Even if these findings turn out to be false, there still is absolutely no valid scientific evidence showing a deterrent effect on homicides. It may be that the death penalty has no effect, overall, on murders in the United States (Bohm 1999).

Bowers, Pierce, and McDevitt (1984, p. 90) write:

> The evidence that capital punishment has no deterrent advantage over imprisonment is now stronger and more consistent than when the Court last considered this issue. . . . Indeed, a comprehensive review of previous studies and recent analyses of refined statistical data both support the contention that the death penalty has a "brutalizing" rather than a deterrent effect—that executions can be expected to stimulate rather than to inhibit homicides.

Supporters of capital punishment typically draw cautious conclusions about the evidence. For example, Pojman (1998, p. 38) says, "We must conclude that we lack strong statistical evidence that capital punishment deters. . . . There is no such evidence for nondeterrence either. The statistics available are simply inconclusive." And Van den Haag (1997, p. 449) says, "Statistics have not proved conclusively that the death penalty does or does not deter murderers more than other penalties." After an exhaustive review of the deterrence literature, Bailey and Peterson (1997, p. 155) make a more assertive claim. They write, "We feel quite confident in concluding that in the United States a significant general deterrent effect for capital punishment has not been observed, and in a probability, does not exist."

Why might we expect the death penalty to increase rather than decrease murders? In effect, would-be murderers see that killing is an acceptable means of righting a wrong against a person who has offended them, so that the lesson of capital punishment may be that lethal vengeance is acceptable.

Perhaps this is one reason that the American Society of Criminologists—the largest association of crime experts in the United States—passed a resolution calling for the abolition of the death penalty in 1989. As pointed out by Bohm (1999, pp. 90–91), "A recent survey of 67 current and past presidents of the top three criminology professional organizations—the American Society of

Criminology, the Academy of Criminal Justice Sciences, and the Law and Society Association—found that about 90 percent of them believe that the death penalty 'never has been, is not and never could be a deterrent to homicide over and above life imprisonment.'" The American Society of Criminology's National Policy Committee concludes that there is "little evidence that the death penalty has a deterrent effect on violent crimes. A comparison of homicide rates both pre- and post–death penalty eras have not shown a deterrent effect, either within a single state or between states." Also opposed to the death penalty are medical organizations, the American Bar Association, and the widow of Martin Luther King, Jr. (Costanzo 1997).

The rarity of the application of the death penalty alone, as I have mentioned, suggests that it can never deter offenders. Recent legislative initiatives have increased the number of offenses punishable by death in an effort to increase its application, presumably to send a message to criminals that "Crime does not pay." Yet the reality is, and always will be, that most murderers are not even charged with capital offenses and therefore do not receive the death penalty.

Despite all this, supporters of capital punishment rely on what they call the best-bet hypothesis and rely on anecdotal evidence of deterrence. The *best-bet hypothesis* suggests that if we do not know that the death penalty is a deterrent, we should bet that it is. They say that it would be better to assume that there is a deterrent (when there is not) and use the death penalty than to assume that there is not a deterrent (when there is) and not use the death penalty. In the former case, we would only be unnecessarily killing guilty murderers, whereas in the latter case, we would be allowing innocent victims to die. *Anecdotal evidence* of deterrence comes from offenders who claim that they did not commit murder (when they could have) because of their fear of the death penalty. If these stories are true, no one can deny that the death penalty may deter some people, perhaps even more than life in prison. But given the weight of the evidence, it is safe to conclude that there is virtually no deterrent value to capital punishment. And it is no wonder, given that we rarely execute anyone.

WHAT'S WRONG WITH THE DEATH PENALTY? ALLEGED PROBLEMS WITH THE ADMINISTRATION OF DEATH

There are many reasons that the application of capital punishment is unjust (Nelson and Foster 2001). Streib, in the Foreword to *Death Watch* (2001), suggests: "We have given capital punishment ample opportunity to prove whether or not it can reduce violent crime. It has made us only more violent and less sensitive to human suffering. We now must put this barbaric practice behind us and confess our shame at having used it for so many centuries before seeing the light."

Some view the death penalty as being wrong. For example, the National Coalition to Abolish the Death Penalty (NCADP) asserts that the death penalty is wrong because it is plagued by racial disparities, costs more than life in prison, and is used against innocent people, the mentally retarded and, potentially, people who committed their crimes as juveniles. Bedau (1997, p. 101) agrees, saying, "I think it is unnecessary for deterrence or incapacitation . . . [is] arbitrary and discriminatory in the retribution it inflicts . . . and therefore [is] an affront to our civilized sensibilities."

Others view capital punishment as cruel and unusual punishment. For example, Bedau (1997, p. 103) suggests that the application of capital punishment violates due process and equal protection of the law, rights he claims are "not forfeitable and cannot be waived. . . . Individuals cannot do anything that . . . nullifies his or her 'moral worth' or standing as a person."

Regardless of how you feel about capital punishment in theory, it exists only in practice. Therefore, we should assess its practice—the reality of capital punishment in America. When we do this, we see the following problems.

- ### *The death penalty is a political process more than a criminal justice process.*

Capital punishment is an issue that serves one significant purpose in America's political system: It gives politicians something to talk tough about. Seriously, when was the last time you heard a politician speak out against the death penalty? Taking a tough stand on crime by supporting capital punishment is easy and has no risks.

The last time I recall a serious presidential candidate speaking out against the death penalty was Governor Michael Dukakis of Massachusetts in the 1988 presidential debates. When asked the question, "Governor, if [your wife] Kitty Dukakis were raped and murdered, would you favor an irrevocable death penalty for the killer?" he answered, "No, I don't. . . . And I think you know that I've opposed the death penalty all of my life. I don't see any evidence that it's a deterrent, and I think there are better and more effective ways to deal with violent crime. We've done so in my own state." Dukakis lost the election to George Bush (the first).

More recently, in the 2000 presidential debates, both George W. Bush (the second) and Al Gore were asked about their support for capital punishment. Bush answered, "I believe it saves lives. . . . I'm proud that violent crime is down in the state of Texas." Gore said, "I think it is a deterrence [*sic*]. . . . I know that's a controversial view but I do think it's a deterrence [*sic*]." To a follow-up question about whether they thought that the death penalty deters murderers, Bush answered, "I do. It's the only reason to be for it. . . . I don't think you should support the death penalty to seek revenge. I don't think that's right." Gore also said, "Yes. If it was not, there would be no reason to support it."

Given that there was virtually no difference between Bush and Gore on any issue, it is not surprising that the election was so close. What is sad is that neither Bush nor Gore seemed to know that virtually every expert on capital punishment does not think that the death penalty is a deterrent to crime. That is, the views of Bush and Gore are not consistent with the scientific evidence. Since this is a political issue, it does not seem to matter.

We have to be concerned about the political nature of capital punishment because politics is not supposed to decide issues such as who lives and who dies. Ideally, murders that receive the death penalty, and those that do not, should be decided based on legal factors such as the presence of *aggravating factors* and *mitigating factors* (state laws require that aggravating factors outweigh mitigating factors for a death penalty sentence to be imposed). Unfortunately, research suggests that death penalty murders and non–death penalty murders are typically not distinguishable based on legal factors, but rather can be distinguished based only on extralegal factors, or factors outside the law.

For example, whether one heinous murder receives death is often determined by factors such as the county where the crime occurred, the state where the crime occurred, the region of the country where the crime occurred, the racial makeup of the jury, and the race of the defendant and his or her victim (Bedau 1997). In an ideal system of punishment, such factors would be irrelevant for justice.

Because of the way our courts operate, it is entirely up to the discretion of the prosecution whether a murder case leads to a capital trial or a noncapital trial. Research shows that prosecutors in the southern United States, particularly in Texas, are tougher on crime. For example, the Death Penalty Information Center (DPIC) reports that between 1976 and early 2004, 82% of all executions occurred in the South, 67% occurred in five states (Texas, Virginia, Oklahoma, Missouri, and

Florida), 46% occurred in just two states (Texas and Virginia), and 36% occurred in Texas alone. In 2002, the state of Texas carried out 46% of all executions.

Should the location where a crime occurs determine whether murderers live or die? When it plays a role, ultimately we see a *geographic disparity* in the administration of capital punishment. The best justification for this problem is that state laws vary and murderers ought to be smarter than to commit their crimes in states that are tougher on crime.

• *The death penalty is arbitrarily applied and is discriminatory in nature.*

Because the death penalty is not mandatory, is so rare, and is decided by discretion, and because of the problem of inadequate representation for the indigent (see Chapter Seven), its application is necessarily *arbitrary*. This means that it is not decided by legal factors but is more a matter of random chance. We see the arbitrary nature of capital punishment in the numerous forms of *disparity* based on factors such as gender, class, and race.

Recall from Chapter One that for something to be just, it must be fair. Justice requires that all persons will be treated equally in the eyes of the law. Injustice is present when any group is singled out for differential treatment by the law. Using this definition, the application of the death penalty in the United States is clearly unjust (McAdams 1998).

According to Nakell and Hardy (1987, p. 16), *discrimination* is deliberate, whereas disparities may not be (see Chapter Twelve for more discussion). There is no doubt that capital punishment in the United States is applied in a disparate fashion. The question is, Is this disparity intentional? I say that when it comes to deaths intentionally caused by the government, it does not really matter. Injustice does not require intentional discrimination by police, courts, and correctional personnel. As I have argued throughout this book, it can also arise out of innocent biases created in the criminal law and reinforced by media coverage of crime.

Beginning with gender, women make up more than 10% of all murder arrests in any given year but only about 2% of all death sentences imposed, less than 2% of the people on death row, and only about 1% of all executions (Bohm 2002). The death penalty is highly unlikely to be used against women for no other reason than that they are not men.

As for social class, it may be true that we have never executed a wealthy killer, in part because their forms of killing typically either are not illegal or are not viewed as serious crime (see Chapter Four), but also because prosecutors are less likely to seek and achieve death sentences when clients have private attorneys and numerous resources at their disposal to win lesser sentences from juries. In fact, approximately 95% of death row inmates were represented by public defenders (Bedau 1997). While every American ideally has the right to a competent defense attorney, in fact not every American can afford a high-quality defense. Recall from Chapter Seven the distinctions between private and publicly appointed attorneys. Costanzo (1997, p. 75) claims, "The sad, shameful fact is that money makes the difference between life and death for many defendants." This is true because publicly appointed attorneys are often inexperienced at capital cases and have limits on how much they can spend to prepare their defense.

As for race, we see clear disparities in both the federal and the state capital punishment systems. Of the 18 inmates awaiting executions in the federal system at the end of 2002, 69% were African Americans and 77% were minorities. According to the study "The Federal Death Penalty System: A Statistical Survey, 1988–2000," 50% of all defendants approved for death penalty prosecution were African Americans and 75% were minorities (U.S. Department of Justice 2001). According to the study "Racial Disparities in Federal Death Penalty Prosecutions, 1988–1994," "racial minorities are being prosecuted under federal death penalty law far beyond their proportion in the general population or the population of criminal offenders" (Committee on the Judiciary 1994).

The picture is somewhat different at the state level. As you saw earlier, African Americans make up 42% of death row inmates and have accounted for only 35% of all people executed since 1976, even though they account for about 50% of murderers. Scholars have determined that the race of the victim explains this discrepancy. For example, between 1976 and early June 2003, 81% of completed capital cases involved Caucasian victims, even though nationally Caucasians made up only 50% of murder victims. Prosecutors are more likely to seek death when the victim is Caucasian and juries are more likely to impose it when the victim is Caucasian, especially when the offender is not. Thus, between 1976 and early June 2003, 178 African Americans were executed for killing Caucasians, but only 12 Caucasians were executed for killing African Americas, even though interracial killings are extremely rare (Death Penalty Information Center 2003).

In the state of Georgia since 1976, 56% of the people executed have been Caucasian, whereas 35% have been African American. African Americans who killed Caucasians make up 22.5% of all executions, whereas Caucasians who killed African Americans make up only 1.4% of all executions (Bohm 2003). Perhaps the most comprehensive study of race and capital punishment at the state level is "Race and the Death Penalty in North Carolina," which assessed how race affected all capital sentences between 1993 and 1997. It found that the odds of receiving a death sentence were 3.5 times greater for killers of Caucasians (Unah and Boger 2001).

A review of 28 similar studies conducted by 21 sets of researchers with 23 data sets by the U.S. General Accounting Office found "a pattern of evidence indiciating racial disparities in the charging, sentencing, and imposition of the death penalty" (Bedau 1997, p. 271). The study found that "in 82 percent of the studies, race of victim was found to influence likelihood of being charged with capital murder or receiving the death penalty. . . race of victim influence was found at all stages of the criminal justice system process" even after controlling for legally relevant variables.

Such disparities are not proof of discrimination. In fact, there are various forms of discrimination (discussed in Chapter Twelve). Yet we know that the application of the death penalty is plagued by significant disparities, some of which are based on the race of the defendant and race of the victim.

Rather than stemming from overt racism, the problem today lies in abuse of discretion. The entire network of criminal justice agencies is "saturated with discretion" that works to the disadvantage of people of color and the poor (C. Black 1974, pp. 90–91). In deciding whether to arrest, police discretion is at issue; in deciding whether to charge, whether to plea bargain or go to trial, or whether to seek the death penalty, prosecutor discretion is at issue; when conviction or acquittal and sentencing are at hand, the discretion of the jury and/or judge is at issue; and so on. The accumulated effects of these discretionary decisions result in the discriminatory application of the death penalty in the United States.

The death penalty, because it is applied in a discriminatory fashion, threatens justice. If you look up the word *discrimination* in any dictionary, you will find definitions suggesting that it means "distinguishing" or "differentiating." Human beings, who assign blame and punishment, distinguish and differentiate on the basis of their own perceptions and preferences. This means that all punishments, including the death penalty, will inevitably be applied in a discriminatory fashion. The significant problem with the death penalty is that it is final: Once it is administered, it cannot be "taken back" or undone.

In studies, most racial bias is found to come from prosecutorial discretion, meaning that it is up to the whim of the prosecutor which heinous murderers deserve to die and which deserve to live. Apparently, in our nation's courts, killers of Caucasians are more deserving of death than killers of minorities. According to the research, part of this problem also stems from problems with capital juries.

- ### *Death penalty juries are often confused and incompetent and are not representative of the population.*

As you've seen in this chapter, most Americans say that they are in favor of capital punishment, generally, and for aggravated murderers specifically. The juries that are faced with making decisions about whether convicted murderers ought to live the remainder of their natural lives in prison or be executed by the government are not representative of the general population. First, the groups least likely to be represented on juries are the ones most likely to be processed through the criminal justice network. This is also true for capital juries.

Equally important, jurors who refuse to consider death as a valid option at sentencing are routinely denied service on capital juries. Bohm (2003) cites research indicating that *death-qualified juries*, as they are called, are more conviction prone and more likely to recommend a sentence of death (Dillehay and Sandys 1996; Ellsworth 1991; Luginbuhl and Burkhead 1994; R. Robinson 1993). Defendants accused of capital crimes are at a significant disadvantage when the jurors who will determine their fate are more likely to hold crime control values consistent with the goals of the prosecution rather than due process values more in line with the defense. Stated differently, capital juries are more likely to be concerned with justice as an outcome (i.e., giving the alleged offender what he or she deserves) rather than justice as a process (i.e., making sure that the trial is fair).

A continuing study sponsored by the National Science Foundation, known as the *Capital Jury Project*, has shown us a great deal about how capital juries function. Researchers have conducted interviews with 1,115 jurors from 340 capital cases in 14 states. This study shows that juries are a significant cause of arbitrary sentencing. Capital juries often do not understand fundamental legal issues such as the meaning of aggravating and mitigating factors and how to weigh them to decide if a convicted defendant lives or dies (see Bedau 1997). The study shows that capital juries often engage in premature decision making (e.g., they may determine that a defendant should be executed during the guilt phase of a trial) and they often do not understand jury instructions and misperceive their sentencing responsibility (e.g., they may mistakenly believe that upon agreement of the presence of an aggravating factor, they are required to vote for death and/or that a judge will overrule their sentence if he or she feels that the jury has made a mistake). Although jury instructions do explain to capital jurors the meaning of aggravating and mitigating factors, juries are typically instructed to "weigh" these factors. Many scholars conclude that this type of setup is confusing to juries, given that judges are "loath to offer any clarification beyond the vague charge of the jury instructions." Therefore, it is likely that jurors will have tremendous difficulty assessing which convicted people deserve death and which do not (Costanzo 1997, p. 36).

Race of the capital juries matters greatly to trial outcomes. Research shows that African American males are more sympathetic toward defendants and are more likely to sense remorse that justifies lesser sentences, whereas Caucasian males are less sympathetic toward defendants and are more likely to see signs of future dangerousness that warrant death sentences. As noted earlier, race of the victim also matters. When the victim is Caucasian, capital juries are more likely to return death sentences. Finally, we also know that juries make critical mistakes. This leads us to the issue of innocence.

• *The death penalty is sometimes used against the innocent.*

Recall the logic of the due process model of criminal justice, discussed in Chapter One. The most important values in this model are liberty, individual freedom, and the protection of Constitutional rights from unnecessary government intervention. Proponents of the due process model would argue that it is far better to let guilty people go free than to punish even one innocent person. The killing of even one innocent individual, especially when it is state-sanctioned and carried out by state officials, is the ultimate evil. It might also be considered unacceptable to kill people who acted because of biological brain disorders (the mentally ill) or who cannot develop the full mental capacity or intent to be held accountable for their actions (the mentally incompetent).

The U.S. Supreme Court ruled in *Herrera v. Collins* (1993) that a claim of actual innocence is not relevant for decisions about whether new hearings should be granted in federal courts (Bohm 1999, p. 37). Because only issues of law are decided by appeals courts, issues pertaining to factual guilt or innocence are not relevant for these courts. Only when state courts violate Constitutional procedures are federal appeals courts really able to correct wrongful convictions. This leaves the wrongfully convicted with little hope of being set free other than executive clemency, which, for political reasons, is rarely granted.

How often are the innocent actually executed? With the recent renewal of debate about the death penalty in the United States, many politicians have claimed that there is absolutely no evidence that a single innocent person has been executed in the United States. Yet, Espy (reported by Bohm 1999, p. 125) estimates that of the 19,000 executions since 1608, 5% have been of innocent persons: About 950 wrongful executions have been carried out.

Between 1976 and early 2004, 108 people have been released from death row, while only 885 have been executed. This means that for every 8 people we execute, we release 1 from death row. We do not know for sure whether all of these people are truly innocent, but the answer is a function of how innocence is defined. The largest study ever on wrongful convictions, *In Spite of Innocence* (Radelet, Bedau, and Putnam 1994), found that at least 400 people have been wrongly convicted. Of these, 23 were executed and 22 were freed within 72 hours of execution. Since this study, approximately 5 wrongful convictions have been discovered each year! Given that most mistakes are discovered by luck or chance, based on the work of student groups and people in the media, it is unlikely that we catch them all.

There is no question that our country has wrongly convicted and executed innocent people. In my state of North Carolina, for example, between 1910 and 1961, the state executed 71 rapists (87% African American) and 11 burglars (100% African American). These are crimes for which eyewitness identification is inherently unreliable (see Chapter Eight), and no DNA tests were available during this time. Thus, it is certain that some of these executions were of innocent people, especially in the cases where African Americans were alleged to have raped Caucasian women.

It is, of course, hard to say how likely it is today that we will execute an innocent person. But executions of the innocent are less likely under *super due process*. Bohm (1999, p. 131) claims, "As many as a dozen people (and likely more) may have been executed in error in the United States since 1976 and the implementation of super due process. That represents nearly three percent of all executions through April 1, 1998." A study conducted by the Columbia Law School found that at least 7% of all death penalty cases appealed between 1973 and 1995 were found to be innocent (see the Issue in Depth at the end of this chapter).

There is no way to know for sure how many innocent people we have executed. This is partly because politicians do not seem to want to know. For example, consider the cases in the following box, as described by the Death Penalty Information Center.

Inmates executed despite doubts about their guilt

- **Roger Keith Coleman** (executed in Virginia, 1992)—Coleman was convicted of raping and murdering his sister-in-law in 1981, but both his trial and his appeal were plagued by errors made by his attorneys. The U.S. Supreme Court refused to consider the merits of his petition because his state appeal had been filed 1 day late. Considerable evidence was developed after the trial to refute the state's evidence, and that evidence might well have produced a different result at a retrial. Governor Wilder considered a commutation for Coleman but allowed him to be executed when Coleman failed a lie detector test on the day of his execution.
- **Joseph O'Dell** (executed in Virginia, 1997)—New DNA blood evidence has thrown considerable doubt on the murder and rape conviction of O'Dell. In reviewing his case in 1991, three Supreme Court justices said that they had doubts about O'Dell's guilt and whether he should have been allowed to represent himself. Without the blood evidence, there is little linking O'Dell to the crime. In September 1996, the Fourth Circuit of the U.S. Court of Appeals reinstated his death sentence and upheld his conviction. The U.S. Supreme Court refused to review O'Dell's claims of innocence and held that its decision regarding juries being told about the alternative sentence of life without parole was not retroactive to his case. O'Dell asked the state to conduct DNA tests on other pieces of evidence to demonstrate his innocence but was refused. He was executed on July 23rd.
- **David Spence** (executed in Texas, 1997)—Spence was charged with murdering three teenagers in 1982. He was allegedly hired by a convenience store owner to kill a girl but killed the three victims by mistake. The convenience store owner, Muneer Deeb, was originally convicted and sentenced to death but then was acquitted at a retrial. The police lieutenant who supervised the investigation of Spence, Marvin Horton, later concluded, "I do not think David Spence committed this crime." Ramon Salinas, the homicide detective who actually conducted the investigation, said, "My opinion is that David Spence was innocent. Nothing from the investigation ever led us to any evidence that he was involved." No physical evidence connected Spence to the crime. The case against Spence was pursued by a zealous narcotics cop who relied on the testimony of prison inmates who were granted favors in return for their testimony.
- **Leo Jones** (executed in Florida, 1998)—Jones was convicted of murdering a police officer in Jacksonville, Florida. He signed a confession after several hours of police interrogation but later claimed that the confession was coerced. In the mid-1980s, the policeman who arrested Jones and the detective who took his confession were forced out of uniform for ethical violations. The policeman was later identified by a fellow officer as an "enforcer" who had used torture. Many witnesses came forward pointing to another suspect in the case.
- **Gary Graham** (executed in Texas, 2000)—On June 23, 2000, Gary Graham was executed in Texas, despite claims that he was innocent. Graham was 17 when he was charged with the 1981 robbery and shooting of Bobby Lambert outside a Houston supermarket. He was convicted

primarily on the testimony of one witness, Bernadine Skillern, who said she saw the killer's face for a few seconds through her car windshield, from a distance of 30–40 feet. Two other witnesses, both of whom worked at the grocery store and said that they got a good look at the assailant, said that Graham was not the killer but were never interviewed by Graham's court-appointed attorney, Ronald Mock, and were not called to testify at trial. Three of the jurors who voted to convict Graham signed affidavits saying that they would have voted differently had all of the evidence been available.

SOURCE: Death Penalty Information Center (2003), http://www.deathpenaltyinfo.org/article.php?scid=6&did=111#Released.

Even if you still doubt that innocent people have been executed, remember that we also know that more than 100 wrongfully convicted Americans have been set free from death row since 1976. Consider these two cases:

- In 1996, Rolando Cruz was freed after 11 years on death row. He had been convicted of the rape and murder of a 10-year-old Chicago girl on the basis of phony evidence invented by the police. The real murderer confessed to the crime 8 years prior to Cruz's release, but Cruz was not released until a DNA test proved that he had not committed the crime.
- In 1993, Walter McMillan was released from death row in Alabama after the state admitted that it had withheld evidence that an eyewitness had lied. Kirk Bloodworth was also released that year in Alabama after a DNA test proved him to be innocent.

Wrongly convicted Americans typically spend about 10 years in prison for crimes that they did not actually commit, in isolation from their families and even from other inmates. More than 100 such cases can be read about online at the Death Penalty Information Center Web site. Bohm (1999, p. 126) writes that these inmates would have been executed if "not for sheer luck." Politicians who use these cases as evidence that the system works to (eventually) set the innocent free, while simultaneously promoting policies to speed up the system and limit appeals of death row inmates, are hypocritical and a threat to justice in the United States.

Why are innocent people wrongfully convicted of capital crimes, even with all the protections put into place by states to ensure that this does not occur? The answers are straightforward and not surprising. The bottom line is that errors are inevitable. Not to make mistakes is beyond the capabilities of human beings. Many wrongful convictions stem from errors made by eyewitnesses to crimes (Huff, Rattner, and Sagarin 1986). Think of the recent execution of Gary Graham in Texas. Graham was convicted on the basis of the eyewitness identification of one person. Another five people claimed that Graham was not the actual offender but did not testify to the court.

Another major reason that people are wrongfully convicted of capital crimes is the incompetence of their defense attorneys. In the Graham case, two of his attorneys reportedly never made an effort to interview or call to the stand the witnesses who claimed that Graham was not the offender. A 1990 study found that many capital defense attorneys "had never handled a capital trial before, lacked training in life-or-death cases, made little effort to present evidence in support of a life sentence, or had been reprimanded, disciplined, or subsequently disbarred" (Bohm 1999, p. 134). The standard for a competent attorney in capital cases is very low and is inconsistent with justice as a process. According to the standard set forth in *Strickland v. Washington* (1984), an individual defendant must show that his or her attorney was deficient in performance and that this deficiency contributed to the outcome of the case. Given that virtually every capital defendant lacks the resources necessary to prove such deficiencies, this is an impossible standard to meet.

Apparently, the thought of executing the innocent does not bother Americans enough to diminish their overwhelming support of capital punishment. A recent Gallup poll found that, if they knew for a fact that the death penalty resulted in the wrongful execution of 1% of people subjected to it, three-fourths of those polled would still support the death penalty for people convicted of murder. This serves as evidence that Americans value justice as an outcome rather than justice as a process, and prefer crime control values over due process ones.

Research suggests that mistakes are more likely the more we carry out capital punishment, when cases are politicized, when police and prosecutors zealously pursue executions, and when we limit appeals. In the Issue in Depth at the end of this chapter, you'll see that, unfortunately, these factors continue to produce wrongful convictions.

• *The death penalty costs more than life imprisonment.*

Administering the death penalty to a convicted murderer costs 2.5 to 5 times as many taxpayer dollars as locking up an offender for life without the possibility of parole. When you add the costs of posttrial reviews, executions become about 24 times as expensive as life imprisonment without parole. The death penalty is so much more expensive than life imprisonment because of the high rates of error that occur at each stage and the persistence of high error rates over time and across the nation, which mandate multiple, expensive judicial inspections (Liebman, Fagan, and West 2000).

Consider these statistics:

- Taxpayers in California could save about $90 million each year if the state abolished the death penalty (Magagnini 1988).
- California spent more than $1 billion on its death penalty system between 1977 and 1996 but executed only five people, one of whom asked to be killed (Costanzo 1997, p. 61).
- In Florida, the average cost of an execution is $3.2 million (Von Drehle 1988).
- Texas capital cases cost about $2.3 million (Hoppe 1992).
- In North Carolina, capital cases cost taxpayers an additional $2.16 million, added onto the costs of the typical murder case (Cook, Slawson, and Gries 1993).

The added costs mount simply by maintaining an elaborate system of capital punishment. When they do occur, capital trials are more complex and time-consuming, and appeals are costly. Costanzo (1997, p. 66) reviews these statistics and concludes, "Massive resources are squandered, courts and prisons are strained, just so that, eventually, a few condemned prisoners can be killed." Thus, he concludes that the death penalty is an elaborate, costly charade.

The social costs are harder to identify, but the bottom line is this: The death penalty does not teach Americans that killing is wrong; it teaches them that killing is acceptable in certain circumstances. Humankind says, through its criminal law, that killing is sometimes acceptable; only murder is wrong. Killing, to humans, is not always wrong, but "no matter if done by a legitimate authority such as the state under the term of 'retribution' or if done by a private citizen in the name of 'vengeance,' the act of killing becomes no more moral, only more legitimate" (Marongiu and Newman 1987, p. 6).

The United States stands out as a shining example of injustice, ironic given that this country is supposed to be a beacon of justice and freedom for the rest of the world. In fact, by continuing to administer capital punishment, we place ourselves in the company of other countries such as China, Iraq, Afghanistan, Iran, Libya, Nigeria, and Uganda, countries whose civil rights violations we deplore.

CONCLUSION

America's long and sordid history with capital punishment has provided plenty of rationale for abolishing the death penalty, something that many states have in fact done. The United States briefly witnessed a moratorium on the death penalty in the face of overwhelming evidence that it was being applied in an arbitrary and discriminatory fashion, but capital punishment has since been reinstated and is now being increasingly used despite the evident bias and inequity in its application. One exception is the state of Illinois, which recently had a moratorium on executions after realizing that 13 innocent people had been freed from death row since 1977, while only 12 persons had been executed. Public support for capital punishment, though apparently widespread, is not as clear-cut as it may seem from opinion polls, and without doubt is lessening. With knowledge that the death penalty does not achieve its goals of retribution and deterrence, and that incapacitation can be achieved more fairly, humanely, and cheaply through life imprisonment without the possibility of parole, public support for capital punishment will likely dwindle in the years to come.

ISSUE IN DEPTH
A Broken System, Parts I and II

An alarming study was recently published by James S. Liebman, Jeffrey Fagan, and Valerie West (2000). Part I of the study is titled *A Broken System: Error Rates in Capital Cases, 1973–1995*. These authors undertook "the first statistical study ever undertaken of modern American capital appeals (4,578 of them in state capital cases between 1973 and 1995)" and found that capital trials end up placing people on death row who do not belong there (either because serious errors were made during their cases or because they were innocent of the crimes of which they were charged) and that it takes a long time to carry out death sentences in the United States because of the numerous errors in the process. According to the findings of this report, "American capital sentences are so persistently and systematically fraught with error" that their reliability is seriously undermined. The authors claim that capital punishment in the United States is "collapsing under its own mistakes . . . a system that is wasteful and broken and needs to be addressed."

Here are some of the key findings of the report.

- Nationally, the overall rate of prejudicial error was 68%—that is, "Courts found serious, reversible error in nearly 7 of every 10 of the thousands of capital sentences that were fully reviewed during the period."
- Serious error was "error substantially undermining the reliability of capital verdicts."
- "Capital trials produce so many mistakes that it takes three judicial inspections to catch them—leaving grave doubt whether we *do* catch them all" (emphasis in original). State courts dismissed 47% of death sentences because of errors, and a later federal review dismissed 40% of the remaining cases.
- The most common errors found in the cases were (1) egregiously incompetent defense attorneys who missed evidence of the defendant's innocence or evidence that he or she did not deserve a death sentence, and (2) suppression of evidence by police and prosecutors.
- Eighty-two percent of those whose death sentences were overturned by state courts were found to be deserving of less than a death sentence, and 7% were found to be innocent of the crimes for which they were convicted.
- Serious errors have been made every year since the death penalty was reinstated, and more than half of all cases were found to be seriously flawed in 20 of the 23 study years.
- Serious errors are made in virtually every state that still executes people, and over 90% of these states make errors more than half of the time.
- "In *most* cases, death row inmates wait for years for the lengthy review procedures needed to uncover all this error. Then, their death sentences are *reversed*" (emphasis in original).
- "This much error, and the time needed to cure it, imposes terrible costs on taxpayers, victims' families, the judicial system, and the wrongly condemned. And it renders unattainable the finality, retribution and deterrence that are the reasons usually given for having a death penalty."
- The death penalty costs from 2.5 to 5 times more than life imprisonment without parole. When you add the costs of posttrial reviews, executions become about 24 times more expensive than life imprisonment without parole. The death penalty is so much more expensive than life imprisonment because of the high rates of error that occur at each stage and the persistence of high error rates over time and across the nation, which mandate multiple expensive judicial inspections.
- The death penalty is rarely applied—of the 5,760 state death sentences handed down between 1973 and 1995, only 313 (5.4%) led to an execution during this time. Additionally, since 1984, when post-*Furman* executions began in earnest, we have executed only about 1.3% of our nation's death row inmates each year. This makes "the retributive and deterrent credibility of the death penalty" very low.
- Homicide rates were slightly higher in death-sentencing states than in non–death-sentencing states during the study years.

From their findings, Leibman, Fagan, and West (2000) conclude that the administration of capital punishment in America is nothing less than irrational. On the basis of their research, capital punishment is also a farce. They note: "Death penalty states sentenced 22 times more defendants per 1,000 homicides than they executed. And they sentenced 26 times more defendants per 100,000 population than they executed" (p. 45). I would characterize these types of findings as bizarre. Consider this: "There is no relationship between death-sentencing and execution rates" (p. 92). It is as if death sentences really have nothing to do with justice, but more to do with politics.

In fact, the study found a not-so-surprising relationship between politics and the death penalty—that political pressure plays a role in capital punishment. The authors explain:

> In general, the more electoral pressure a state's judges are under, the higher the state's death-sentencing rate, but the lower the rate at which it carries out its death sentences. [This] suggests that political pressure tends to impel judges—or to create an environment in which prosecutors and jurors are impelled—to impose death sentences, but then tends to interfere with the state's capacity to carry out the death sentences that are imposed . . . a desire to curry favor with voters may lead elected prosecutors and judges to cut corners in an effort to secure that premium—simultaneously causing death-sentencing rates, and error rates, to increase. (p. 103)

In Part II of the study; *A Broken System, Part II: Why There Is So Much Error in Capital Cases*, Liebman et al. (2002) assessed the causes of the errors in America's capital punishment processes. According to the authors:

> This study uncovered a number of conditions related to error in capital cases, including politics, race, crime control and the courts. But running through all the data was a simple finding—the more a state or county sentences people to death, the more often they make mistakes. . . . Everything else being equal, when death sentencing increases from the lowest to the highest rate in the study, the reversal rate increases six-fold, to about 80%. The more often states and counties use the death penalty for every, say 10 or 100 homicides, the more likely it is that any death verdict they impose will later be found to be seriously flawed, and the more likely it is that the defendant who was found guilty and sentenced to die will turn out to be not guilty. (Death Penalty Information Center 2003)

Additionally, the authors found that there are four key factors which lead to errors:

> homicide risk to whites and blacks; the size of the black population; the rate at which police catch and punish criminals; and politically motivated judges. . . . Everything else being equal, when the risk of a white person getting murdered is high relative to the risk of an African-American getting murdered, twice as many appeals are reversed than where that risk is low . . . when whites and other influential citizens feel threatened by homicide, they put pressure on officials to punish as many criminals as severely as possible—with the result that mistakes are made, and a lot of people are initially sentenced to death who are later found to have committed a lesser crime, or no crime at all.

> The more African-Americans there are in a state, the more likely it is that serious mistakes will be made in death penalty trials. This could be because of fears of

> crime driven by racial stereotypes and economic factors. . . . It is disturbing that
> race plays a role in the outcome of death penalty cases, whatever the reasons.
> (Death Penalty Information Center (2003)

On the basis of this research, as well as that reported throughout this chapter, I agree. I will conclude by saying that the continued administration of the death penalty in the United States is proof that our criminal justice network fails to achieve justice. In fact, the death penalty is one practice that is a clear failure.

Discussion Questions

1. What are the main means of execution in the United States?
2. Why do you think more men are executed than women?
3. Why do you think so many of our allies have abolished the death penalty?
4. Why do you think that executions declined in the United States between the 1930s and the 1970s?
5. What are the main factors that lead to legal errors in death penalty cases?
6. Why didn't the Supreme Court abolish the death penalty with the case of *McClesky v. Kemp*?
7. Why do so few murders lead to executions in the United States?
8. Why do the vast majority of executions take place in the southern states?
9. Is there any evidence that suggests that public executions would deter murderers?
10. Discuss why most Americans say they support the death penalty.
11. Identify and discuss the main justifications for capital punishment.
12. Is there support for the death penalty in the Bible? Why or why not?
13. Does the death penalty deter murders? Why or why not?
14. In your opinion, do the errors in American capital punishment warrant a halt to executions? Explain.

CHAPTER ELEVEN

THE "WAR ON DRUGS":
FOCUSING ON THE WRONG DRUGS?

INTRODUCTION

This chapter introduces you to the U.S. war on drugs. The drug war is a prime example of a war on crime that serves limited interests and is used to control certain segments of the U.S. population, notably the poor and people of color. The chapter shows who is most affected by the nation's drug war and how ineffective the war is for reducing illicit drug use. You will learn what a drug is, how prevalent drug use is in the United States, and harms associated with various drugs. An interesting issue arises: Why are the most harmful drugs legal, while some relatively less harmful drugs are criminalized? I conclude the chapter with an assessment of legalization and decriminalization as strategies for American criminal justice.

THE WAR ON DRUGS

The *war on drugs* is the phrase used to describe the American approach to reducing drug use and abuse in the United States. Unless you've been asleep for the last 20 years, you must have heard something about it. President George Bush (the first) declared in a nationally televised message that drug abuse was "our nation's most serious domestic problem" (Beckett 1997, p. 6). Earlier, President Reagan had diverted more than $700 million from education, treatment, and research to law enforcement programs to fight the war on drugs. Reagan also gave more money to prisons and to the Drug Enforcement Administration, the federal agency responsible for preventing illicit drug use (Kraska 1990, p. 117). Now our federal government spends almost $12 billion annually fighting the drug war (this figure does not include state and local government costs). Figure 11.1 depicts federal dollars spent on the war on drugs over the years.

What are we spending this money for? The Office of National Drug Control Policy (ONDCP) stated the goals of the war in 2000:

- To educate and enable America's youth to reject illegal drugs as well as alcohol and tobacco (reduce drug use)

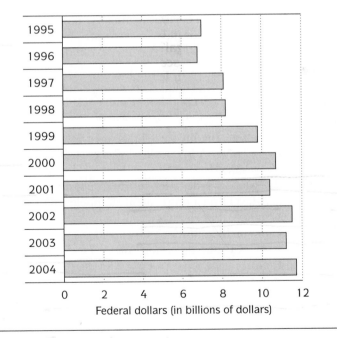

FIGURE 11.1
Trends in Federal Spending on the Drug War
SOURCE: Sourcebook of Criminal Justice Statistics (2003).

- To increase the safety of America's citizens by substantially reducing drug-related crime and violence (reduce crime)
- To reduce health and social costs of illegal drug use to the public (reduce harm)
- To shield America's air, land, and sea frontiers from the drug threat (control border)
- To break foreign and domestic drug sources of supply (eradicate and interdict)

In 2002, the ONDCP put forward some revised goals, including the following.

- Stopping drug use before it starts; education and community action (reduce drug use)
- Healing America's drug users; getting treatment resources where they are needed most (reduce harm)
- Disrupting the market; attacking the economic basis of the drug trade (eradicate and interdict)

Given these goals, the key questions to assess America's war on drugs are:

- Is drug use down?
- Is crime down?
- Are health and social costs down?
- Are drug users more healthy?
- Are drugs less available?
- Is treatment more available?
- Are our borders secure?

If the answer to these questions is Yes, then America's drug war has succeeded.

Unfortunately, most scholars suggest that the answer to the above questions is No. Take, for example, this statement by Glaser (1997, p. 116):

> Narcotics are the bane of our criminal justice system, and control efforts have been much more extensive than for any vice except possibly alcohol use during Prohibition. Attempts to diminish the use of drugs by punishment have been tremendously costly, but usually seem to have no effect on the prevalence of drug abusers and their predations.

In this chapter, I assess our nation's performance in its war on drugs and show that the answer to most of the questions above is No. Additionally, I demonstrate that the war has probably caused more harm than it has prevented.

The main elements of the war on drugs include three policies: crop eradication efforts, interdiction efforts, and street-level drug enforcement (Kappeler, Blumberg, and Potter 2000, p. 159). *Crop eradication* is aimed at destroying crops before they are cultivated and sold as illicit drugs. *Interdiction* efforts include border control and strategies aimed at intervening in countries where drugs are grown and harvested. *Street-level drug enforcement* includes undercover drug busts and seizures of drugs. Treatment of drug abusers and drug prevention education are also involved in the drug war, but these efforts have received far less funding over the years. Finally, *asset forfeiture* involves the seizure by police of cash profits and property generated by drugs.

The majority of American drug war spending is reactive rather than proactive or preventive, as shown in Figure 11.2. Table 11.1 shows what the war on drugs looks like, using data from various government sources. It illustrates how many people are arrested, charged, and sent to some form of correctional supervision for drug offenses.

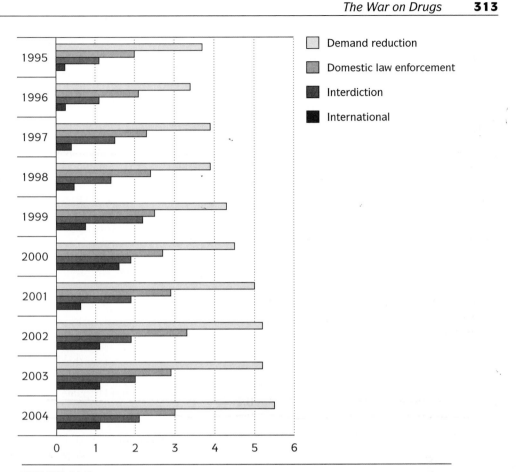

FIGURE 11.2

**Trends in Federal Spending on the Drug War, by Area
of Spending**

SOURCE: Sourcebook of Criminal Justice Statistics (2003).

The Sentencing Project (2003) summarizes what the drug war has looked like:

> Arrests for drug offenses nearly tripled from 580,900 in 1980 to 1,579,566 by 2000. Nearly
> 315,000 persons were sentenced in state courts for a drug offense in 1998. Of these, 43% were
> sentenced to prison, 26% to jail, and 32% to probation and/or treatment. The number of
> inmates incarcerated for drug offenses at all levels—state and federal prisons and local jails—
> has skyrocketed by more than 1,000% from 40,000 in 1980 to 453,000 by 1999. At that point,
> there were 251,200 drug offenders in state prisons incarcerated at a [conservative] cost of
> about $5 billion annually.

According to a study by the U.S. Sentencing Commission, most people sentenced to time in federal prisons for drug offenses are low-level (55%) or midlevel dealers (34%). Further, according to
The Sentencing Project, three-quarters of state prison inmates were convicted of drug and/or nonviolent crimes, and most sentenced drug offenders in state and federal prisons (58%) have no

TABLE 11.1

Key Facts of the War on Drugs

Drug arrests, 2000	1.6 million (11% of all arrests)
Most common arrest, 2000	Possession of drugs (81% of all drug arrests)
Marijuana arrests, 2000	73,600 (46% of all drug arrests, mostly possession)
State court drug convictions, 2000	319,700 (35% of all felony convictions)
Federal court drug convictions, 1998	27,274 (35% of all felony convictions)
Drug offenders in corrections, 2001	55% of federal prisoners 25% of state and federal prisoners 22% of jail inmates 24% of probationers

SOURCE: Bureau of Justice Statistics (2003).

history of violence or high-level drug activity. Additionally, more than one-third (35%) of drug inmates have criminal histories that are limited to drug offenses and 21% are first-time offenders. Finally, four of every five drug offenders are African American (56%) and Hispanic (23%).

Virtually every law enforcement agency has a drug budget, including virtually every federal agency, 3 of 4 state-level agencies, and more than 9 of 10 local agencies. In 2000, police officers made 1.6 million arrests, 11.4% of all arrests that year. Most (81%) were for simple possession of drugs, and 46% were for marijuana crimes (41% of the drug arrests were for marijuana possession) (see Chapter Six). In state courts, 35% of all convictions were for drug offenses. In federal courts, 35% of all people convicted were drug offenders. Now drug offenders make up 55% of all federal prisoners and 25% of all inmates in state and federal prisons. They also make up 22% of all people in jail and 24% of all people on probation (see Chapter Nine).

Each year our nation spends tens of billions of dollars on drug law enforcement and incarceration. As a nation, we have spent hundreds of billions of dollars on the war on drugs since 1980 (Merlo and Benekos 2000, p. 19). The cost of the drug war increased sixfold between 1986 and 1996, and most of this money went to domestic law enforcement at the local and state levels of government (Gaines, Kaune, and Miller 2000, p. 610). Meanwhile, domestic social programs have been cut dramatically to pay for the war on drugs (Goetz 1996).

Consider this irony: Police departments in the United States have begun to profit from drug seizures and asset forfeitures of drug dealers. American police can seize assets accumulated as a result of illicit drug trafficking and keep a share of the proceeds to fund training and equipment (Gaines, Kaune, and Miller 2000). If the police have come to need these funds for their own operating budgets, what would happen if they completely eliminated illicit drugs from our society?

The drug war is aimed at stopping *drug-related crimes* (e.g., acts of violence caused either by the pharmacological effects of drugs on people or by the need to obtain money to buy drugs), *crimes associated with a drug-using lifestyle,* and *drug-defined crimes* (crimes committed because of coming into contact with drug dealers and other users) (Walker 1998). In similar terms, Beckett and Sasson (2000, p. 40), discuss types of drug-related homicides, including *psychophar-macological homicides,* caused directly by effects of drugs on the brain. Ironically, the war on drugs also creates drug-defined crimes, such as possession and sale of drugs, which obviously would not be "crimes" if drugs were not illegal (ONDCP 2002).

Despite the common image of a drug-crazed criminal, most crimes committed by people involved with drugs are not caused by the pharmacological effects of the drugs on behavior. Some criminal justice statistics promote this myth about the overall harmfulness of drugs. For example, research by the National Center on Addiction and Substance Abuse (1998) at Columbia University found that 80% "of prisoners in the United States were involved with alcohol or other drugs at the time of their crimes." This sounds like clear proof of the link between drug use and crime. But consider what this research actually means: "That is to say, 80 percent were either under the direct influence of alcohol or other drugs while committing the crime, had a history of drug abuse, committed the crime to support a drug habit, or were arrested for violating drug or alcohol laws" (Gaines, Kaune, and Miller 2000, p. 51). Considering all that being "involved with drugs" includes, it is hard to imagine any prisoner who is not "involved with" alcohol or other drugs at the time of his or her crimes.

Drug-related crimes include what Beckett and Sasson (2000) call *economic compulsive homicides*—murders motivated by the need to obtain money to buy high-priced drugs. Others are *systemic homicides,* such as turf war killings aimed at protecting illicit drug markets. In essence, the illegal status of drugs creates *criminal subcultures,* such as gangs, that develop their own norms: being tough, getting respect, and making money through illicit activity. Reiman (1998) calls such crimes *secondary crimes,* which could be virtually eliminated if drugs were not illegal. Inciardi (2002, p. 193) lists several types of systemic violence, including "territorial disputes between rival drug dealers; assaults and homicides committed within dealing and trafficking hierarchies as means of enforcing normative codes; robberies of drug dealers, often followed by usually violent retaliations; elimination of informers; punishment for selling, phony, adulterated, or otherwise bad drugs; retribution for failing to pay one's debts; and general disputes over drugs and drug paraphernalia."

Although the United States has always engaged in wars against drugs, the current drug war really started in the 1970s under President Richard Nixon. In 1973, Nixon created the *Drug Enforcement Agency (DEA)* within the Department of Justice as the federal government's lead agency for suppressing drugs in the United States (Lyman and Potter 1998). Since that time, drug use has been blamed for "the dramatic rise in the murder rate in the 1980s [and] gang violence." The resulting focus on drugs by U.S. criminal justice agencies, however, has produced something perhaps more disastrous—"the soaring prison population, the worsening crisis in race relations, and the steady erosion of individual rights in the Supreme Court" (Walker 1998, p. 243).

Walker links these outcomes directly to U.S. drug policy, which he calls "nonsensical." Sensible discussion about drugs, Walker claims, does not occur because of the public hysteria accompanying our war against drugs. The national outcries over "reefer madness" in the 1930s and "crack babies" in the 1980s, discussed later in this chapter, are prime examples of hysterias that led politicians to promote myths about drug use and crime and to talk tough about how to reduce Americans' use of drugs. The result has been our war on drugs.

Judge James Gray, who served a career as a judge fighting the war on drugs, wrote a book that condemns the war as a failure. In his book, *Why Our Drugs Laws Have Failed and What We Can*

Do About It, Gray (2001) argues that there are actually two sets of Bills of Rights now in place, one for the war on drugs and one for everything else. Gray provides numerous examples of how the Constitution has been eroded to allow the nation's police to fight the drug war, despite its continued failures.

Why, then, have Americans supported the addition of police and prisons in efforts to stop drug use, which is mostly "casual and recreational and does not lead to either addiction of criminal activity" (Walker 1998, p. 247)? Why has the war on drugs become such a powerful force in the United States? Gaines and Kraska (1997, p. 4) claim:

> Most people do not question the political/media cries to do something about our "drug problem"; to wage wars on "drugs"; or that "drug use" destroys a person's, or even an entire community's well-being. Drug war ideology lulls us into assuming a number of properties about drugs. We refer to certain drugs . . . as if they were little demons committing crimes. Waging war on drugs—as if the drugs themselves constitute our "drug problem"—allows us to overlook the underlying reasons why people abuse these substances. . . . The language of ideology fools us into thinking that we're waging war against drugs themselves, not real people. . . .

These authors describe our war on drugs as "hypocritical, exploitative, and dangerously misleading" (p. 5).

Best (1999, p. 144) explains the value of the war metaphor:

> Declaration of war on social problems are dramatic events; they call for society to rally behind a single policy, against a common foe. Typically, the initial pronouncements receive favorable attention in the mass media; the press details the nature of the problem and outlines the efforts designed to wage war against it. Usually, the enemy . . . has no one speaking on its behalf. There is the sense that society is united behind the war effort. Declaring war seizes the moral high ground.

According to Jensen and Gerber (1998, p. ix), misguided drug policies result from at least three factors: political opportunism, media profit maximization, and desire among criminal justice professionals to increase their spheres of influence. Politicians create concern about drug use to gain personally from such claims; they achieve this largely by using the media as their own mouthpiece.

Jensen and Gerber (1998) suggest that concern over drugs typically occurs in a cycle whereby some government entity claims the "existence of an undesirable condition" and then legitimizes the concern, garnering public support through the media by using "constructors" (similar to what Gans has called "counters") who provide evidence of the problem. Claims-makers "typify" the drug problem by characterizing its nature (Best 1989). For example, drugs are typified as "harmful" even if they are being used recreationally. They are characterized as bad regardless of the context in which they are being used. Any drug use is wrong even if it is not abuse (Jensen and Gerber 1998, p. 5). Most troubling, drugs are connected to other social problems to make them seem even worse. Recently, illicit drugs were tied to acts of terrorism in television commercials and print ads, paid for by taxpayers. I return to the specific role that the media have played in creating public concern about drugs later in this chapter.

Several myths about drugs exemplify this typification. For example, the "dope fiend mythology" promulgated by the U.S. government in the early 1900s contained these elements: "The drug addict is a violent criminal, the addict is a moral degenerate (e.g., a liar, thief, etc.), drug peddlers and addicts want to convert others into addicts, and the addict takes drugs because of an abnormal personality (Lindesmith, 1940)" (p. 8). Another example typified the use of marijuana, as indicated in a pamphlet circulated by the Bureau of Narcotics in the 1930s:

> Prolonged use of Marihuana frequently develops a delirious rage which sometimes leads to high crimes, such as assault and murder. Hence Marihuana has been called the "killer drug." The habitual use of this narcotic poison always causes a marked deterioration and sometimes produces insanity . . . .

> While the Marihuana habit leads to physical wreckage and mental decay, its effects upon character and morality are even more devastating. The victim frequently undergoes such moral degeneracy that he will lie and steal without scruple. (Quoted by Bonnie and Whitebread, 1974, p. 109)

The propaganda circulated by the Bureau of Narcotics included the story of a "murder of Florida family and their pet dog by a wayward son who had taken one toke of marijuana" (Kappeler, Blumberg, and Potter 2000, p. 9). Evidence about the relative harmlessness of marijuana was ignored.

Amazingly, the federal government recently called marijuana more dangerous than all other illegal drugs combined! The ONDCP now claims that aggressive antisocial behavior among youths is linked to frequency of marijuana use and that marijuana use is linked to cutting class, stealing, and property crime.

The main effects of the war on drugs have included pressure on police to arrest drug violators, the use of drug assets for police benefits (what Jensen and Gerber [1998] call "policing for profit"), and increased militarization of police departments (Kraska and Kappeler 1997). As the soldiers in the war on drugs, police departments have been encouraged by policies first instituted by President Reagan in the 1980s to pursue drug offenders; as a reward, they are allowed to confiscate and keep some drug-related assets (M. Gray 1998). Again, think of the irony of law enforcement officials coming to rely on drug assets to purchase equipment and conduct training so that police can exterminate drug use (Rasmussen and Benson 1994). It may be startling to realize that the majority of law enforcement agencies in the United States have such asset forfeiture programs in place (Jensen and Gerber 1998; McAnamy 1992).

According to Webb and Brown (1998), such "wars" on drugs as inanimate objects "tend to be concerned less with the drugs they purportedly target than with those who are perceived to be the primary users of the drugs (Morgan and Signorielli, 1990)" (p. 45). For example, the war on opium in the late 1800s and early 1900s was focused on Chinese laborers who represented unwanted labor competition. Thus, the Harrison Act of 1914, which forbade importation and manufacture of opium by the Chinese, excluded the "Chinese living in the United States from fully participating in the labor market" (p. 46). The war on marijuana in the 1930s was grounded in racism against Mexican immigrants, who were characterized as "drug-crazed criminals" taking jobs away from Americans during the Great Depression (Sandor 1995, p. 48). Finally, "the use of crack by the urban poor provided political leaders (in the 1980s) with a convenient scapegoat for both diverting attention from pressing social and economic problems and blaming a specific powerless group for social disaster" (Belenko 1993, p. 9).

Other effects of wars on drugs include overloaded court systems, increased punitiveness in the form of stiff mandatory sentences for drug offenses, exploding prison populations, and, ultimately, a worsening of racial disparities in criminal justice (Jensen and Gerber 1998, pp. 1–2). This chapter examines the American war on drugs in an effort to determine if such effects are justified.

In the next section, I examine what a drug is and then discuss types of drugs. Then, I explore the extent of drug use in the United States and document harms associated with each type of drug.

WHAT IS A DRUG?

What do you think of when you hear the word *drug*? The meaning of the word really depends on who is asked. To a doctor or pharmacist, for example, a drug is something very different than it is to a homeless person living on the street (Liska 2000).

The term *drug* does have a clear definition. Lyman and Potter (1998, pp. 59–60) begin their examination of drugs in American society with a discussion of the dictionary definition of the term. Liska (2000, pp. 3–4) writes that drugs are used to fight infection, reverse a disease process, relieve symptoms of illness, restore normal functioning of human organs, aid in diagnosing sickness, inhibit normal body processes, and maintain health. This is a relatively positive view of drugs.

Have we as a nation declared a war on substances that help fight disease and maintain health? Clearly not. Obviously, there must be another meaning of drugs. Lyman and Potter (1998, p. 60) define a drug as "any substance that causes or creates significant psychological and/or physiological changes in the body." Liska (2000, p. 4) defines a drug as "any absorbed substance that changes or enhances any physical or psychological function in the body." But these definitions of a drug would include coffee, tea, and cigarettes—in fact, virtually any substance. Have we declared war on these substances? Obviously not.

Merriam-Webster's Collegiate Dictionary (2003) includes as its last acceptable definition of the word *drug*, "something and often an illegal substance that causes addiction, habituation, or a marked change in consciousness." Is this the focus of our war on drugs? Clearly, it is. Our American "war on drugs" is being waged against illegal forms of drug use and the activities that permit it (manufacturing, distribution, sales, possession, etc.).

All drugs, whether legal or illegal, affect the brain by interacting with naturally occurring brain chemicals known as *neurotransmitters* (such as dopamine): "The major drugs of abuse—e.g., narcotics like heroin or stimulants like cocaine—mimic the structure of neurotransmitters, the most powerful mind-altering drugs the human body creates" (Lyman and Potter 1998, pp. 60–61). By altering the brain's chemistry, drugs alter people's behavior. When their effects are dangerous or simply unintended, such as interfering with a person's family, work, or social relations, drugs can be harmful to the user (Lyman and Potter 1998, p. 60). In fact, every drug—from legal drugs such as aspirin to illegal drugs such as cocaine—is potentially harmful.

The effects of any drug depend on numerous factors, including the type of drug, its potency and quantity, the method in which it is ingested, the setting in which it is ingested, the frequency of use, the mood of the user, and the user's biological and psychological makeup (Gaines and Kraska 1997; Lyman and Potter 1998). Effects of particular types of drugs are discussed later.

Keep in mind the clear distinction between *drug use* and *drug abuse*. Drug use is generally understood as any consumption of a drug, including recreational or occasional use. Remember President Bill Clinton explaining, as a candidate in 1992, that he had tried marijuana in college, didn't inhale it, and didn't like it? That's drug use, as is the alleged cocaine use of President George W. Bush (the second).

Drug abuse implies a problematic level of use, or overuse, of drugs. Lyman and Potter (1998, p. 60) define drug abuse as "illicit drug use that results in social, economic, psychological or legal problems for the drug user." They also note that the Bureau of Justice Statistics defines drug abuse as "the use of prescription-type psychotherapeutic drugs for nonmedical purposes or the use of illegal drugs."

Drug use, even of illegal substances, is not the same as drug abuse. It is possible to use illegal drugs without abusing them, although this is a lesson that seems to be lost on U.S. criminal justice agencies. We treat drug use as a crime rather than a recreational habit and do not recognize that most people who use drugs do not abuse them. In fact, most drug-related arrests are for simple possession, not for manufacturing, distributing, or selling drugs (Beckett and Sasson 2000, p. 172).

Drug abuse varies by individual: "Abuse occurs when the use of the drug—whether aspirin, beer, caffeine, cigarettes, marijuana, diet pills, or heroin—becomes a psychological, social, or physical problem for the user" (Gaines and Kraska 1997, p. 6). Only a small portion of drug users, somewhere between 7% and 20%, depending on the type of drug in question, actually become drug abusers (Kraska 1990). In fact, depending on one's definition of a drug, we all use drugs as part of our everyday lives: "Some form of drug use is an everyday part of living for most Americans" (Lyman and Potter 1998, p. 11).

Drugs are useful because they can alter our moods, create feelings of pleasure, stimulate brain activity, or aid in sedation or enhanced physical and psychological performance (Lyman and Potter 1998). Some suggest that drug use is innate or natural, as much as the need for food or sex. Weil (1998, p. 4) writes, "The use of drugs to alter consciousness is nothing new. It has been a feature of human life in all places on the earth and in all ages of history." Hamid (1998, p. vii) suggests that "the human use of psychoactive drugs is both primordial and nearly universal. In almost every human culture in every age of history, the use of one or more psychoactive drugs was featured prominently in the contexts of religion, ritual, health care, divination, celebration (including the arts, music, and theater), recreation, and cuisine." People use drugs in certain rituals in groups, such as during "Happy Hour" or at parties with friends. People may use drugs to relieve boredom (Glassner and Loughlin 1987), to alter their moods, to inspire creativity, and sometimes for medicinal and religious purposes.

For numerous reasons, then, people use drugs without experiencing significant problems associated with drug abuse. This does not mean that drug use should be promoted or supported by government, but it does raise the question of why we spend so many physical and financial resources fighting something that is considered normal by most people at some point in their lives, is relatively harmless, and is not likely to be stopped through criminal justice mechanisms. I would argue that drug abuse (which is only a small portion of all drug use) should be of concern to our government because of its possible outcomes, regardless of whether the drug being abused is legal.

Lyman and Potter (1998, p. 62) list several outcomes of drug abuse:

- *Physical dependence:* The user becomes increasingly tolerant of a drug's effects, so that increased amounts of the drug are needed in order to prevent withdrawal symptoms.
- *Psychological dependence:* The user develops a craving for or compulsive need to use drugs because they provide him or her with a feeling of well-being and satisfaction.
- *Tolerance:* The user who continues regular use of a drug must administer progressively larger doses to attain the desired effect, thereby reinforcing the compulsive behavior known as drug dependence.

- *Withdrawal:* The user experiences a physical reaction when deprived of an addictive drug, characterized by increased excitability of the bodily functions that have been depressed by the drug's habitual use.

These outcomes suggest that drug abuse is maladaptive and thus potentially dangerous. Still, whether the U.S. government should wage a war on drug abuse is debatable, given that drug abuse is more likely to respond to medical treatment. It is clear, however, that our investment in stopping simple drug use is costing us far more than it is returning. Kappeler, Blumberg, and Potter (2000, p. 150) conclude that illicit drug-related deaths are infrequent and that they are actually more likely to occur because of the effects of drug laws.

TYPES OF DRUGS

Drugs can be categorized according to their principal effects on brain function and hence on human behavior. The major general categories of drugs include *stimulants*, *depressants*, *hallucinogens*, and *narcotics/opiates* (Inciardi and McElrath 1998; Liska 2000). Lyman and Potter (1998) also add *inhalants* (drugs that are drawn into the body by breathing in) as a separate category because of their use among young people in particular. Inciardi and McElrath (1998) add *analgesics* (painkillers), *sedatives* (which produce calm and relaxation), and *hypnotics* (depressants that produce sleep).

As defined by Inciardi and McElrath (1998, pp. xii–xiii), these substances are as follows.

- *Stimulants:* Drugs that stimulate the central nervous system (CNS) and increase the activity of the brain and spinal cord
- *Depressants:* Drugs that act to lessen the activity of the CNS, diminishing or stopping vital functions
- *Hallucinogens:* Drugs that act on the CNS to produce mood and perceptual changes varying from sensory illusions to hallucinations
- *Narcotics:* A category of illegal drugs including opium and opium derivatives, as well as their synthetic versions (Lyman and Potter 1998)

The following box gives some examples of drugs that fall into each category. Note that some of the substances within each category are legal; others, illegal. Thus, the nature of the drug does not determine its legal status.

Examples of major drugs

- *Stimulants:* Caffeine, nicotine, cocaine, amphetamines, methamphetamine, ecstasy
- *Depressants:* Alcohol, barbiturates, gamma-hydroxybutyrate (GHB), Rohypnol
- *Hallucinogens:* Marijuana, lysergic acid diethylamide (LSD), phencyclidine (PCP), psilocybin mushrooms, peyote cactus, ketamine
- *Narcotics:* Opium, heroin

As you might guess, stimulants stimulate brain activity. The most common stimulants in the United States are legal—caffeine (in coffee) and nicotine (in cigarettes). These drugs make people feel stronger, alert, decisive, and even exhilarated. Depressants, as you also might guess, depress brain activity. Users become sluggish, have impaired judgment and slurred speech, and suffer from loss of motor coordination. Hallucinogens distort perceptions of reality through the auditory (hearing), tactile (touch), and visual (sight) systems. Narcotics, which produce feelings of euphoria in users, can be accompanied by undesirable effects including nausea, vomiting, drowsiness, apathy, respiratory depression, loss of motor coordination, and slurred speech.

Another way of categorizing drugs is by the government classification system. The Controlled Substances Act (CSA), Title II of the Comprehensive Drug Abuse Prevention and Control Act of 1970, consolidated many laws regulating the manufacture and distribution of narcotics, stimulants, depressants, hallucinogens, steroids, and chemicals used in the illicit production of controlled substances. This law classified drugs into five categories:

- *Schedule I:* These drugs or other substances have a high potential for abuse and have no currently accepted medical use in treatment in the United States. There is a lack of acceptance of use of the drug or other substance under medical supervision. Examples include heroin, LSD, marijuana, and methaqualone.
- *Schedule II:* The drug or other substance has a high potential for abuse but has a currently accepted medical use in treatment in the United States or a currently accepted medical use with severe restrictions. Abuse of the drug or other substance may lead to severe psychological or physical dependence. Examples include morphine, PCP, cocaine, methadone, and methamphetamine.
- *Schedule III:* The drug has less potential for abuse than the substances in Schedules I and II and has a currently accepted medical use in treatment in the United States. Abuse of the drug or other substance may lead to moderate or low physical dependence or high psychological dependence. Examples include anabolic steroids, codeine and hydrocodone with aspirin or Tylenol, and some barbiturates.
- *Schedule IV:* The drug has a lower potential for abuse than the substances in Schedule III and has a currently accepted medical use in treatment in the United States. Abuse of the drug or other substance may lead to limited physical dependence or psychological dependence relative to the drugs or other substances in Schedule III. Examples include Darvon, Talwin, Equanil, Valium, and Xanax.
- *Schedule V:* The drug or other substance has a low potential for abuse relative to the drugs or other substances in Schedule IV and has a currently accepted medical use in treatment in the United States. Abuse of the drug or other substances may lead to limited physical dependence or psychological dependence relative to the drugs or other substances in Schedule IV. Over-the-counter cough medicines with codeine are classified as Schedule V.

This classification system is useful for reference later in the chapter when we examine which drugs are targeted by criminal justice agencies. The higher the level of a drug (Schedule I is the highest), the more vigorously it is pursued, regardless of whether it is being used for recreational purposes or is being abused.

EXTENT OF DRUG USE IN THE UNITED STATES

Table 11.2 lists several sources of drug use data available in the United States. The most important sources of drug use data include (1) the *National Household Survey on Drug Abuse (NHSDA)*, conducted by the Substance Abuse and Mental Health Services Administration (SAMHSA), which is a survey of people age 12 years and older; (2) the *Monitoring the Future Survey (MFS)*, conducted by the National Institute on Drug Abuse (NIDA), which is a survey of high school students in 8th, 10th, and 12th grades; and (3) the *Drug Abuse Warning Network (DAWN)*, conducted by the National Institute on Drug Abuse (NIDA), which collects total mentions of drug use by patients in emergency rooms. These sources of drug use data give us a pretty good picture of drug use in the United States.

Arrestee Drug Abuse Monitoring (ADAM), conducted by the National Institute on Justice (NIJ), is a survey and drug testing of arrestees in 34 cities. The *Survey of Inmates in State Correctional Facilities*, conducted by the Bureau of Justice Statistics (BJS) every 5 years, is a survey of inmates. The *Survey of Health Related Behavior among Military Personnel*, conducted by the Department of Defense every 3 years, is a survey of military personnel. These sources allow us to see drug use trends in the military and among our nation's arrestees and inmates.

Figure 11.3 shows how many people use each type of drug in the United States. The most commonly used drugs are legal substances such as caffeine, nicotine, and alcohol. More than 100 million Americans use caffeine (in the form of coffee) and consume alcohol, meaning that about half of the U.S. adult population consumes caffeine in coffee and drinks alcohol. Another 10 million

TABLE 11.2
Sources of Data on Drug Use

1. **National Household Survey on Drug Abuse (NHSDA)**
   By Substance Abuse and Mental Health Services Administration (SAMHSA)
   yearly since 1976
   Survey of people age 12 years and older
2. **Monitoring the Future Survey**
   By National Institute on Drug Abuse (NIDA) yearly since 1972
   Survey of high school students in 8th, 10th, and 12th grades
3. **Survey of Health Related Behavior among Military Personnel**
   By Department of Defense every 3 years since 1980
   Survey of military personnel
4. **Drug Abuse Warning Network (DAWN)**
   By NIDA yearly since 1972
   Mentions of drug use by patients in emergency rooms
5. **Survey of Inmates in State Correctional Facilities**
   By Bureau of Justice Statistics (BJS) every 5 years since 1974
   Survey of inmates
6. **Arrestee Drug Abuse Monitoring (ADAM)**
   By National Institute on Justice (NIJ) yearly since 1997
   Survey and drug testing of arrestees in 34 cities

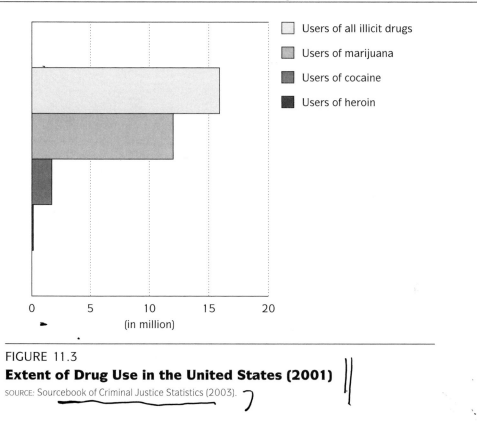

FIGURE 11.3

Extent of Drug Use in the United States (2001)

SOURCE: Sourcebook of Criminal Justice Statistics (2003).

people under the age of 21 years admits to drinking alcohol. There are 67 million users of nicotine (through some form of tobacco use).

The 2001 NHDSA survey found that nearly 40% of all Americans admit to trying an illegal drug at least once in their lifetime. Of these, 54% had tried an illegal drug by high school gradua-tion. Nearly 16 million (15.9 million) Americans 12 years of age or older had used an illegal drug within the previous month. The most commonly used illegal drug is marijuana: 12 million used it within the previous month. Fewer people use cocaine (1.7 million users), heroin (123,000), and other illegal drugs. Are legal drugs more widely used by Americans because they are less harmful than those that are currently illegal, such as marijuana, cocaine, and heroin? Actually, no. I return to this issue later in this chapter.

Figure 11.4 shows drug use trends in the United States according to the NHSDA. Figure 11.5 illustrates drug use trends among the nation's youth according to the MFS. Figure 11.6 depicts emergency-room mentions of drug use in the United States according to DAWN. Figure 11.7 shows deaths attributable to illicit drugs in the United States. Table 11.3 illustrates the percent-age of high school seniors who say that they can easily or very easily obtain drugs.

Examining these figures allows us to return to some of the key questions to assess the effective-ness of the drug war:

- First, is drug use down? No, according to NHSDA data, there has been virtually no change among adults in the percentage of previous-month drug users in the United States

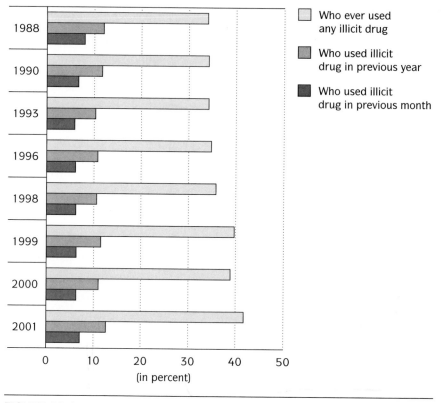

FIGURE 11.4
Trends in Drug Use (NHSDA)
SOURCE: Office of National Drug Control Policy (2003).

for more than 10 years. There has been virtually no change in the number of previous-month marijuana users in the United States for more than 10 years, virtually no change in the number of previous-month cocaine users in the United States for more than 10 years, and virtually no change in the number of previous-month heroin users in the United States for more than 10 years. According to MFS data, previous-month drug use among high school students increased for 10 years before declining over the previous two years. New drug initiates have increased for most drugs, including ecstasy, LSD, PCP, and marijuana.

- Second, are drug users more healthy? No, mentions of drug use in emergency rooms have increased in the United States over the previous 20 years. And drug-related deaths have increased in the United States for more than 10 years.
- Third, are drugs less available? Yes, the war on drugs has made illegal drugs slightly harder to obtain for young people in the United States but drugs are still easily accessible.

The answer to the other key questions are also No, as direct and indirect social costs of drug abuse have increased every year through the 1990s, treatment is no more available to drug abusers, and drugs still flow freely into our borders (see the Issue in Depth at the end of this chapter). Finally, crime is down, yet as you saw in Chapter Four, this is not due to the war on drugs. In fact, a recent study (Sphon and Halleran 2002) reports that drug offenders sentenced to prison have higher rates of recidivism than those sentenced to probation, and tend to re-offend more quickly.

HARMS ASSOCIATED WITH DRUGS

Every drug, legal or illegal, is at least potentially harmful. In this section I examine the relative harms of nicotine (found in tobacco) and tetrahydrocannabinol (THC; found in marijuana), two drugs that are consumed through smoking. The following box contains the U.S.

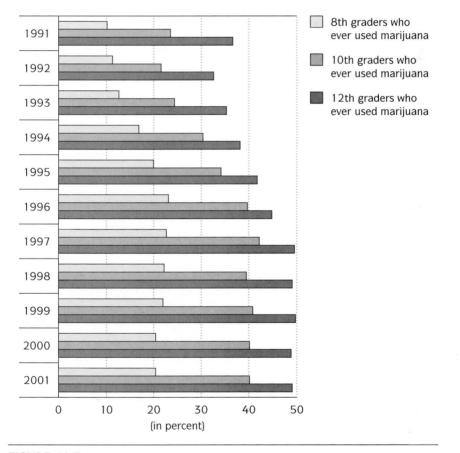

FIGURE 11.5
Trends in Youth Drug Use (MFS)
SOURCE: Sourcebook of Criminal Justice Statistics (2003).

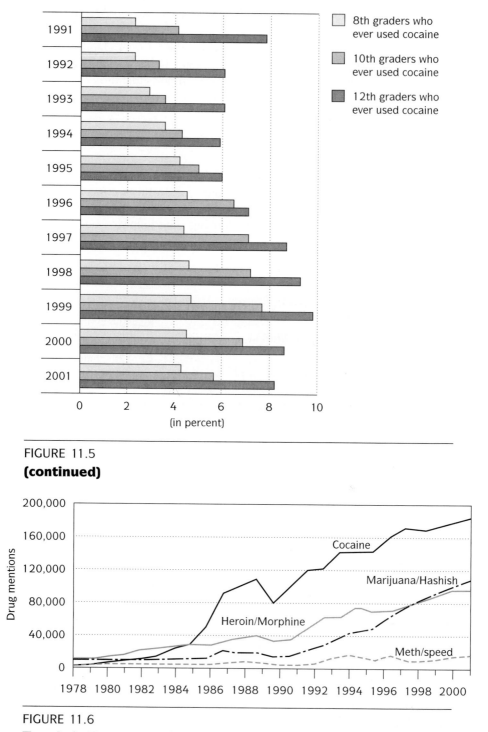

FIGURE 11.5

(continued)

FIGURE 11.6

Trends in Emergency-Room Mentions of Drugs (DAWN)

SOURCE: Office of National Drug Control Policy (2003).

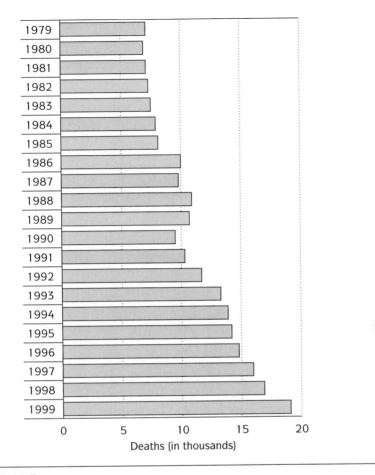

Year	Deaths (in thousands)

FIGURE 11.7

Trends in Deaths Attributed to Illicit Drugs

SOURCE: Sourcebook of Criminal Justice Statistics (2003).

TABLE 11.3

Availability of Drugs among High School Students

	Percentage Saying "Fairly Easy" or "Very Easy" to Obtain Drugs
Marijuana	88.5
Ecstasy	61.5
Amphetamines	57.1
Cocaine	46.2
LSD	44.7
Crack	40.2
Barbiturates	35.7
Tranquilizers	33.1
Heroin	32.3
Crystal methamphetamine	28.3
PCP	27.2

SOURCE: Sourcebook of Criminal Justice Statistics (2003).

government's "official line" on the dangers of marijuana versus those of cigarettes. Which sounds worse to you?

Marijuana versus cigarettes

Short-term effects of using marijuana

- Sleepiness
- Difficulty keeping track of time, impaired or reduced short-term memory
- Reduced ability to perform tasks requiring concentration and coordination, such as driving a car
- Increased heart rate
- Potential cardiac dangers for those with preexisting heart disease
- Bloodshot eyes
- Dry mouth and throat
- Decreased social inhibitions
- Paranoia, hallucinations

Long-term effects of using marijuana

- Enhanced cancer risk
- Decrease in testosterone levels for men; also, lower sperm counts and difficulty having children
- Increase in testosterone levels for women; also, increased risk of infertility
- Diminished or extinguished sexual pleasure
- Psychological dependence, requiring more of the drug to get the same effect

Risks associated with smoking cigarettes

- Diminished or extinguished sense of smell and taste
- Frequent colds
- Smoker's cough
- Gastric ulcers
- Chronic bronchitis
- Increase in heart rate and blood pressure
- Premature and more abundant face wrinkles
- Emphysema
- Heart disease
- Stroke
- Cancer of the mouth, larynx, pharynx, esophagus, lungs, pancreas, cervix, uterus, and bladder
- Cigarette smoking is perhaps the most devastating preventable cause of disease and premature death.
- Smoking is particularly dangerous for teens because their bodies are still developing and changing and the 4,000 chemicals (including 200 known poisons) in cigarette smoke can adversely affect this process.

SOURCE: Substance Abuse and Mental Health Services Administration, an agency of the U.S. Department of Health and Human Services (2000).

Nicotine is a drug. It is the substance in tobacco that keeps smokers smoking. Since nearly one-fourth of all Americans smoke, nicotine is the most prevalent psychoactive drug—that is, affecting the mind and mental processes—used in the United States. Nicotine is the second most abused drug in the United States, behind alcohol. This is attributable to many factors, including the legal status of the drug, the numerous social contexts in which smoking nicotine is acceptable and even expected, and the advertising campaigns of the tobacco industry. Given the highly addictive nature of nicotine, tobacco use is thus considered a legal form of substance abuse. According to the Boston University Medical Center, each cigarette delivers about 6 to 8 milligrams of nicotine.

The most likely future nicotine addicts are teens targeted by tobacco industry advertisers. Children are about twice as likely as adults to smoke the three most advertised brands. According to recent study, tobacco advertising has increased every year since 1998, the year big tobacco companies signed an agreement with Congress to stop targeting children. Nicotine addiction occurs when a person has a compulsive need for nicotine, as discussed earlier. Smokers thus feel a persistent craving for a cigarette, which is, in essence, what the Food and Drug Administration calls "a delivery system for an addictive drug" (Centers for Disease Control and Prevention 1994b).

The large majority of smokers begin smoking before the age of 18 (M. Robinson 1998). Every day, thousands of new young people begin to smoke. Teenagers see smoking as "cool" or "sexy," images created by the tobacco industry and reinforced by peers in social situations. The amount of nicotine used and the frequency of use start small but increase over time as the user becomes addicted to nicotine. People continue to use nicotine even after they learn of the health risks associated with smoking. Smokers claim that they cannot quit because they experience irritability, lowered concentration, weight gain, cravings for nicotine, and even tremors. These effects suggest that nicotine is being used to avoid physical withdrawal symptoms (Boston University Medical Center 2000).

Nicotine is smoked because it is most rapidly absorbed into the body in this way. About 90% is absorbed into the lungs, oral cavity, and gastrointestinal system. Nicotine particles act on every cell and thus on every organ of a user's body, including the heart, kidneys, skin, and brain. According to the Boston University Medical Center (2000), nicotine increases salivation, stomach acid and motility, heart rate, and blood pressure and reduces circulation in the blood. It also can lead to impotence in as little as 10 years of prolonged use.

Nicotine can be used more safely through alternative methods of ingestion, for example, through an inhaler. Tobacco companies developed such a mechanism, similar to that used by asthmatics, but ultimately rejected it because it was inconsistent with their portrayals of cigarettes as harmless and nonaddictive products (Glantz et al. 1996).

When inhaled by smoking, nicotine becomes a very dangerous drug. For example, cigarettes contain more than 40 known carcinogens as well as thousands of other harmful chemicals such as carbon monoxide, carbon dioxide, formaldehyde, and ammonia (M. Robinson 1998). Cigarettes include various amounts of metals such as aluminum, copper, lead, mercury, and zinc. Not surprisingly, then, smoking kills more than 30 times as many people as murder does each year, through lung diseases such as cancer, emphysema, chronic mucus secretion and air flow blocks, bronchitis, and respiratory and bacterial infections. It also causes heart disease because of cholesterol buildup, which restricts blood flow (the same thing that causes impotence). Smoking causes stiffness in the artery walls, high blood pressure, blood clots, and oxygen demand in muscles (Boston University Medical Center 2000).

Lung cancer is not the only type of cancer caused by smoking, which is also a major cause of cancer of the lips, tongue, salivary glands, mouth, larynx, esophagus, stomach, bladder, renal pelvis, uterine cervix, and pancreas. Secondhand smoke also kills thousands (M. Robinson 1998), mainly because it contains dozens of dangerous chemicals (Centers for Disease Control and Prevention 1997). Thus, nonsmokers (such as children of smokers) suffer chronic ear infections, coughing because of phlegm buildup, and acute respiratory illnesses such as bronchitis and pneumonia.

What about marijuana? Does this illegal substance cause the same problems as tobacco, which is legal? Virtually every expert who has studied this issue answers a resounding "no."

Let us start by dispelling some myths about marijuana, which come from Zimmer and Morgan's (1997) book, *Marijuana Myths, Marijuana Facts:*

- Marijuana is relatively harmless. The British medical journal *Lancet* concluded in 1995 that "the smoking of cannabis, even long term, is not harmful to health."
- Most people who smoke marijuana do not smoke it regularly. Only about 1% of users smoke the drug daily.
- Marijuana does not lead to physical dependence or addiction.
- Smoking marijuana does not lead to use of hard drugs (the so-called gateway drug hypothesis). Because marijuana is the most popular illegal drug in the United States, the majority of people who use other drugs have also used marijuana at one time. Most marijuana users, however, never use another illicit drug, and, in fact, virtually every illicit drug user started with tobacco and alcohol.
- Marijuana offenders are not dangerous. The effects of marijuana use are relatively mild. About 80% of those arrested for marijuana in any given year are arrested for mere possession of the drug, not for growing or selling it.

In 1988, Francis Young, a judge affiliated with the DEA, reached the following conclusions about marijuana (in Kappeler, Blumberg, and Potter 2000, p. 152):

- There has never been a single documented cannabis-related death.
- Among the 70 million Americans who have used marijuana, there has never been a reported overdose.
- Marijuana in its natural form is one of the safest therapeutically active substances known to humans.
- In strict medical terms, marijuana is far safer than many foods we commonly consume.

Still, the THC in marijuana is a drug and it is harmful. It is the substance in marijuana that is addictive. The use of marijuana as a psychoactive drug is far less prevalent than nicotine use, for many reasons: Marijuana is illegal, there are fewer social contexts in which smoking marijuana is acceptable compared to smoking cigarettes, and it is not advertised by any corporate industry.

Smoking marijuana is typically a behavior associated with young people. Whereas smoking tobacco increases over time as the user becomes addicted to nicotine, smoking marijuana is consistently limited to relatively small amounts. Effects of marijuana begin immediately upon ingesting the substance into the body, so there is no need to smoke greater and greater amounts over time. As explained by the National Institutes of Health (NIH) (1997):

> THC is quite potent when compared to most other psychoactive drugs. An intravenous (IV) dose of only a milligram or two can produce profound mental and phsyiologic effects (Agurell et al., 1984, 1986; Fehr and Kalant, 1983; Jones, 1987). Large doses of THC delivered by marijuana or administered in the pure form can produce mental and perceptual effects similar to drugs usually termed hallucinogens. . . . However, the way marijuana is used in the United States does not commonly lead to such profound mental effects.

THC is smoked because it is more rapidly absorbed into the body in this way, much like nicotine. THC particles are absorbed within seconds and delivered to the human brain immediately, and they also act on every cell and thus on every organ of a user's body, including the heart, kidneys, skin, and brain. Marijuana contains over 400 chemicals, including THC and other cannabinoids, which are the psychoactive chemicals in the plant. Yet it has a "remarkably low lethal toxicity" (NIH 1997). Whereas one in three cigarette smokers will die from a smoking-related illness, there has never been a recorded human death associated with marijuana use. The effects of marijuana on the user are numerous, including the following:

> a sense of well-being (often termed euphoria or high); feelings of relaxation; altered perception of time and distance; intensified sensory experiences; laughter; talkativeness; and increased sociability when taken in a social setting; impaired memory for recent events; difficulty concentrating; dreamlike states; impaired motor coordination; impaired driving and other psychomotor skills; slowed reaction time; impaired goal-directed mental activity; and altered peripheral vision are common associated effects. (Adams and Martin 1996; Fehr and Kalant 1983; Hollister 1988; cited in NIH 1997)

Other adverse effects can include anxiety, panic, depression, delusions, and hallucinations (Adams and Martin 1996; Fehr and Kalant 1983; Hollister 1988). Such effects usually present themselves rapidly and last for only 2 to 3 hours. Although marijuana use can heighten the effects of mental illnesses such as schizophrenia and bipolar affective disorder, it is not a significant cause of these illnesses, which are thought to be biologically based (Raine 1993). Use of the drug can, however, lead to temporary lessening of motivation and impaired educational performance (Pope and Yurgelun-Todd 1996).

The physical effects of smoking marijuana include temporary increases in heart rate and blood pressure, as well as lowered body temperature, which has not "presented any health problems for healthy and relatively young users" (NIH 1997). However, chronic use can lead to bronchitis, pharyngitis, and increased frequency of pulmonary and respiratory illnesses because of suppressed antibody formation and resistance to infection from bacterial and viral infections. Still, "[c]onclusive evidence for increased malignancy, or enhanced acquisition of HIV, or the development of AIDS, has not been associated with marijuana use" (NIH 1997).

From this comparison, we can confidently conclude the following:

- Cigarettes contain nicotine, a physically addictive drug that produces dependence and withdrawal symptoms when ceased.
- Smoking cigarettes is a highly deadly form of drug use.
- Marijuana contains THC and other cannabinoids, which are psychologically addictive drugs that do not cause dependence or physical withdrawal symptoms when ceased.

- Smoking marijuana is a potentially harmful form of drug use.
- Smoking cigarettes is far more dangerous than smoking marijuana.

Nevertheless, smoking cigarettes is generally legal, while smoking marijuana is generally illegal. Even though there are only one-sixth as many marijuana users as nicotine users, smoking kills about 440,000 people each year, and marijuana kills none. Alcohol kills approximately 110,000 people per year. The death rate for tobacco users in any given year (440,000 deaths per year divided by 67 million users) is 0.66%, meaning that in any given year, 1 in 152 tobacco users will die from the drug. The death rate for alcohol (110,000 deaths per year divided by 109 million users) is 0.1%, meaning that 1 in 990 alcohol users will die from the drug. The death rate for illicit drugs (19,000 deaths divided by 15.9 million users) is 0.12%, meaning that 1 in 837 illicit drug users will die from the drugs. This means that tobacco use is 4.5 times more deadly than illicit drug use, yet tobacco is legal. The death rates for illicit drugs and alcohol are nearly identical, yet alcohol is legal.

Government-funded studies in the 1970s, as summarized by Hamid (1998, pp. 47–51), were far more pessimistic and alarmist in their conclusions with regard to marijuana. These studies found evidence of what Hamid calls amotivational syndrome, cannabis psychosis, mental and physical deterioration, brain damage, and escalation to harder drugs. Evidence from more recent studies shows that these effects were, at best, grossly overstated.

Use and abuse of other illicit drugs include adverse health consequences (Jensen and Gerber 1998; Liska 2000). In 2000, for example, more than 1 million people visited emergency rooms and mentioned some form of drug use, including 175,000 for cocaine use and 97,000 for heroin use. Long-term health consequences of opiates include hypotension, allergies, and insomnia; overdose can cause fatal convulsions and seizures. Cocaine's adverse effects include death via seizures and strokes (Fishbein and Pease 1996). Most deaths from cocaine are caused by smoking the drug in the form of crack (Goode 1999); these deaths are not attributable to the dangers of cocaine itself, but rather to the fact that there are fewer quality controls on street-level crack than on powder cocaine.

Even relatively harmless drugs, such as marijuana, produce smoke that is carcinogenic, and chronic smokers of marijuana suffer from "toxic effects on several organs, including the brain, heart [and] lungs" (Fishbein and Pease 1996, p. 310). Of course, these outcomes are not as severe as those suffered by users of legal drugs such as tobacco and alcohol. Using the harmfulness of illegal drugs to justify their illegal status while simultaneously ignoring the harms of these legal drugs is hypocritical at best.

Glaser (1997, p. 117) describes the hypocrisy of the nation's drug war when he writes: "The law prohibits marijuana, cocaine, and the opiates but allows our intake of items that can be equally disabling, including whiskey, wine, and beer, as well as tranquilizers, sedatives, analgesics, stimulants, and antidepressants sold in drug stores, some without prescription." At the same time, "Relatively affluent users (and abusers) of illicit drugs are able to engage in their habits with impunity. They are likely to be able to insulate themselves from criminal justice activity. If they are in need of medical assistance, they are likely to arrange for private care and are likely to have health insurance that covers such treatment." In contrast, poor people who live in urban areas are the most likely to suffer from the horrible side effects of illegal drugs, are most likely to be discovered because of their limited access to medical care, and are most likely to suffer whatever violent crime does result from drug use and abuse (p. 199).

LEGAL STATUS OF EACH DRUG: WHY ARE THE MOST HARMFUL DRUGS LEGAL WHILE SOME RELATIVELY HARMLESS DRUGS ARE ILLEGAL?

Given that illegal drugs (such as marijuana) are typically less dangerous than legal drugs (such as tobacco), why are these drugs illegal? One primary reason is the fear that illegal drug use is associated with an increased risk for criminality.

According to Nuro, Kinlock, and Hanlon (1998, p. 221): "Evidence of criminal activity among narcotics users is longstanding and abundant; however, it is apparent that relationships among the important variables involved are much more complex than were initially believed." These authors suggest that prevalence and diversity of criminality among narcotics users are high, but that most crime committed by drug users is for the purpose of supporting drug use. Higher levels of drug use, then, tend to be associated with higher involvement in criminality. For heavy users of drugs and persistent criminals, initiation into both criminality and drug use begins at early ages (p. 225).

The smallest portion of criminality among drug users is violent crime (Nuro, Kinlock, and Hanlon 1998, p. 227), and most crime is petty, nonviolent crime (Goldstein 1998, p. 246), but amounts and types of crimes vary by individual (Nuro, Kinlock, and Hanlon 1998, p. 229). Drug research thus supports the claims of legalization proponents that alternative approaches to the drug war would reduce overall criminality in the United States (see the Issue in Depth at the end of this chapter).

The drugs most relevant for a psychopharmacological violence effect are alcohol, stimulants, barbiturates, and PCP (e.g., see Asnis and Smith 1978; d'Orban 1976; Ellingswood 1971; Feldman, Agar, and Beschner 1979; Gerson and Preston 1979; Glaser 1974; Tinklenberg 1973; Virkunnen 1974). The suspected and sometimes asserted link between opiates and marijuana and violence has been discredited (e.g., see Finestone 1967; Greenberg and Adler 1974; Inciardi and Chambers 1972; Kozel, Dupont, and Brown 1972; Kramer 1976; Schatzman 1975). In fact, these drugs may actually "ameliorate violent tendencies. In such cases, persons who are prone to acting violently may engage in self-medication, in order to control their violent tendencies" (Goldstein 1998, p. 245). Heroin users will refrain from committing violent crimes to acquire money to buy their drug if alternatives exist (e.g., see Cushman 1974; Goldstein 1979; Gould 1974; Johnson et al. 1985; Preble and Casey 1969; Swezey 1973).

There is obviously violence in the drug business, so what causes it? According to Reuter (1998, p. 315), "The violence, overdoses, and massive illegal incomes that are such a prominent part of our current concerns with psychoactive drugs are not consequences of the nature of the drugs themselves, but rather of the conditions of use that society has created." In other words, violence typically does not stem from drug use per se, but rather from the fact that drug use is illegal and violence is required to protect business interests of drug dealers. This is systemic violence rather than psychopharmalogical violence.

James Inciardi, a notable expert on the drug war, agrees. In his book *The War on Drugs III* (2002, p. 193), he writes, "The economic compulsive model or violence best fits the aggressive behavior of contemporary heroin, cocaine, and crack users." This means that many, if not most, violent crimes committed by users of these drugs are aimed at obtaining resources to buy their drugs, rather than caused by the influence of the drugs on their brains. In fact, Inciardi concludes that there is more evidence of a crime–drugs connection (drug use intensify criminal careers) than a drugs–crime relationship (drug use produces crime).

In numerous drug scares throughout U.S. history, this fact has escaped the public. Each drug scare has centered on some type of illicit drug use. Beckett (1997, pp. 45–46) briefly outlines several of these, including the antiopium movement in California in the late 1870s, the temperance (antialcohol) movement of the Women's Christian Temperance Union (WCTU) in the 1890s, the cocaine scare of the post-Reconstruction South, the "killer weed" antimarijuana movement in the southwestern United States in the 1930s, and the crack cocaine scare of the 1980s. Each of these drug scares blamed all sorts of societal evils on "outsiders" (Becker 1963) or on poor minority groups, from Chinese immigrants (opium smoking in the 1870s) to Mexicans (marijuana in the 1930s) to African Americans (cocaine and crack). As explained by Beckett and Sasson (1998, p. 37), crime and drug problems were typified as "'underclass' problems resulting from insufficient social control."

Traditionally, drug use becomes characterized as problematic only when it involves particular groups of people (Jensen and Gerber 1998, p. 3). In essence, this serves as a form of "institutional racism" (p. 21). Drug use by targeted groups is characterized as a source of other societal problems (Reinarman 1994), while institutional sources of poverty and crime are ignored. The nation's drug war meets the definition of *institutional discrimination* proposed by Walker, Spohn, and Delone (2000), because race and class are not explicitly stated as valid factors for utilizing criminal justice agencies selectively against drug offenders, yet racial and ethnic disparities appear in criminal justice outcomes that result from the application of racially neutral factors. In the drug war, the racially neutral factor is the fallacious notion that "their drugs" are more harmful than "our drugs." In the case of crack versus powder cocaine, this spurious belief is built directly into the written criminal law.

Because such drug scares are focused on relatively powerless groups such as minorities, immigrants, and lower-class people, you may be wondering whether the drug scares are actually aimed at lowering drug use and abuse rates or whether their legislative intent is aimed at other outcomes. Recall from Chapter Two the difference between intended goals and functions served by particular criminal justice policies (policies can serve functions without being intentional). By examining the role of the media in portraying drug scares, you may get a sense of the functions they serve for powerful members of society.

The Role of the Media in Drug Scares

As discussed in Chapter Five, the media, in what they portray and in what they choose not to portray, reinforce moral boundaries in society. At various times, the media have created *moral panics* focused on drug use. The crack cocaine scare is the most recent of those discussed earlier. As Potter and Kappeler (1998) write, "The media—particularly news magazines, televison, and newspapers—and the state engaged in a frenzied attempt to create a moral panic in the form of a drug scare as a means of continuing and extending the 'War on Drugs' begun in the Reagan administration" (p. 9). As noted by Merlo and Benekos (2000, p. 16), images and stories in the media (especially about crack cocaine) spread fear that drug use was a major source of the nation's problems, especially crime.

Claims by field sources from the Community Epidemiology Work Group (CEWG), established by the National Institute on Drug Abuse to provide community-level surveillance of drug abuse in 20 metropolitan areas, show the concern about crack cocaine in American inner cities. The following box contains some quotes from field sources in the early 1980s.

Community Epidemiology Work Group field quotes about crack cocaine

- Boston: "Cocaine is a massive problem."
- Miami: "Cocaine is more available than ever before."
- Newark: "Cocaine is gaining rapid popularity."
- New Orleans: "Cocaine appears to be dominating the drug scene."
- Philadelphia: "There is a significant increase in availability and use."
- Phoenix: "Large quantities are available through Miami; prices have dropped."
- Seattle: "Cocaine is the county's most important problem."
- Buffalo: "There has been a marked increase in cocaine use."
- Chicago: "Cocaine is the only drug to have shown consistently increasing patterns of abuse."
- Denver: "It's the major drug of abuse in the state."
- Detroit: "Cocaine use continues to increase."
- Los Angeles: "Cocaine use has reached epidemic levels."
- New York City: "Cocaine activity continues to increase."
- St. Louis: "Cocaine is readily available throughout the metropolitan area."
- Washington, DC: "Cocaine use continued to rise."
- Dallas: "Pushers were selling cocaine in capsules in African American lower income communities. Cuban cocaine traffickers were arrested."
- Newark: "African Americans were dealing large amounts of cocaine."

These quotes from field sources suggest that crack cocaine was becoming a significant problem for American cities. As a result, a war was launched to stop crack cocaine.

Public demand did not create this "war on drugs." Beckett (1997, pp. 55, 58) reports that in 1981 more Americans believed that reducing unemployment would be more effective in curbing drug use than cutting the drug supply. Only about 2% of Americans at that time felt that drug abuse was the nation's most important problem (also see J. Roberts 1992). In fact, public concern over drugs increased only after President George Bush (the first) made the nationally televised speech mentioned at the beginning of this chapter. After Bush said on national television, "All of us agree that the gravest domestic threat facing our nation today is drugs" (Bertram et al. 1996, pp. 113–114), media coverage of problematic drug use increased, as did concern about drugs among Americans. Thus, public concern did not start the drug war.

Reinarman and Levine (1989a) outline this 1980s drug scare, in which all sorts of societal problems were blamed on crack cocaine. These authors argue that media portrayals of crack cocaine were highly inaccurate. The scare began in late 1985, when the *New York Times* ran a cover story announcing the arrival of crack to the city. In 1986, *Time* and *Newsweek* magazines ran five cover stories each on crack cocaine. *Newsweek* and *Time* called crack the largest issue of the year (Beckett 1997). In the second half of 1986, NBC News featured 400 stories on the drug. In July 1986 alone, the three major networks ran 74 drug stories on their nightly newscasts (Potter and Kappeler 1998). Drug-related stories in the *New York Times* increased from 43 in the second half of 1985 to 92 and 220 in the first and second halves of 1986 (Beckett 1997), and thousands of stories about crack appeared in magazines and newspapers (Reinarman 1995).

After the *New York Times* coverage, CBS produced a 2-hour show called *48 Hours on Crack Street*, and NBC followed with *Cocaine Country*. In April 1986, the National Institute on Drug Abuse (NIDA) released a report called "Cocaine: The Big Lie," and 13 public service announcements that aired between 1,500 and 2,500 times on 75 local networks. This was followed by 74 stories on crack cocaine on ABC, CBS, and NBC in July 1986 alone. In November 1986, approximately 1,000 stories about crack appeared in national magazines, where crack was called "the biggest story since Vietnam," a "plague," and a "national epidemic."

As media coverage of drugs increased, people were paying attention. Consumers of media information are more likely to recognize issues as the "most important problems" when they receive a lot of notable attention in the national news (Bennett 1980; Iyengar and Kinder 1987; Leff, Protess, and Brooks 1986; McCombs and Shaw 1972). Drug coverage in the media was more extensive in the 1980s than at other times. The CBS program *48 Hours on Crack Street* obtained the highest rating of any news show of this type in the early 1980s (Reinarman and Levine 1989a, pp. 541–42).

Once the media and public were all stirred up, laws were passed aimed at toughening sentences for crack cocaine. For example, the *Anti-Drug Abuse Act of 1986* created the 100:1 disparity for crack and powder cocaine (5 grams of crack would mandate a 5-year prison sentence, versus 500 g of powder cocaine). Additionally, the *Anti-Drug Abuse Act of 1988* lengthened sentences for drug offenses and created the Office of National Drug Control Policy (ONDCP). The U.S. Sentencing Commission recommended to Congress that this disparity be eliminated, yet Congress rejected this (which was the first time Congress ever rejected the Commission).

The intense media coverage of crack cocaine is problematic because it was invented, inaccurate, and dishonest. News coverage did not reflect reality, as crack cocaine use was actually quite rare during this period (Beckett 1994; Orcutt and Turner 1993; Walker 1998) and, according to research from the NIDA, was in fact declining at this time. According to the NIDA, most drug use peaks occurred between 1979 and 1982, except for cocaine, which peaked between 1982 and 1985 (Jensen and Gerber 1998, p. 14). Media coverage of cocaine use increased in the late 1980s even after drug use had already begun to decline.

The crack war was dishonest and the media failed to report this. The war was aimed at getting tough on crime and maintaining the status quo approaches to fighting drugs. The public was not concerned about drugs until after the media coverage captured their attention. Jensen and Gerber (1998, p. 17) suggest that President Reagan's declaration of war against drugs in August 1986 created an "orgy" of media coverage of crack cocaine, and public opinion about the seriousness of the "drug problem" changed as a result. According to Clymer (1986), in mid-August 1986, drugs became the most important problem facing the nation in public opinion polls. By late August 1986, 86% of Americans said that "fighting the drug problem" was "extremely important" (*U.S. News & World Report* 1986).

This coverage of drugs in the media typified social problems as stemming from the pharmacological properties of drugs such as crack cocaine, when in reality most of the associated violence stemmed from volatile crack cocaine markets (Beckett and Sasson 2000, p. 28). News stories were also generally inaccurate and/or misleading in the way they characterized addiction to crack cocaine as "instantaneous," as if everyone who tried crack would become addicted immediately (Reinarman 1995). As a teenager in the 1980s, I recall, adults warned me that one-time use of crack cocaine would lead to inevitable addiction. Without personal experience to rely on, these adults were likely relying on information supplied by the media. In fact, the NIDA estimates that very few of those who use cocaine will become addicted: Fewer than 3% of users will ever become problem users (Kappeler, Blumberg, and Potter 2000). Cocaine does not produce physical dependence, as, say, tobacco does and, thus, is not considered a physically addictive drug.

The addictive nature of nicotine in tobacco received relatively little if any attention in the 1980s (Reeves and Campbell 1994), although, for every cocaine-related death in that decade, there were 300 tobacco-related deaths and 100 alcohol-related deaths (Potter and Kappeler 1998), facts that escaped widespread media coverage. Although there is much more media focus on tobacco these days, the negligent and reckless actions of tobacco companies were not discussed widely until the mid- and late 1990s.

Finally, the coverage of crack in the news did not accurately portray the racial composition of people involved in drugs. The Sentencing Project reports that about two of every three crack users are Caucasians, even though in 1994, 84.5% of people convicted in federal courts for crack possession and 88.3% of those convicted for crack trafficking were African Americans.

Even though half of all television news stories about drugs show African Americans using or selling drugs (Reed 1991), the majority of drug users are white; African Americans are not overrepresented among users (Walker 1998). This does not imply that the media are racist in their coverage of drug issues but, rather, that the media, like most Americans, were duped by the focus of criminal justice agencies on particular types of drugs and drug users. Harrigan (2000, pp. 137–38) suggests that most Americans

> lead lives that are far removed from the pictures of their lives portrayed on television. They go to work regularly, pay most of their taxes, try to raise their children as best they can, are faithful to their spouses for years on end, do not steal from their employers, have no connection with drug traffickers or organized crime, and live from paycheck to paycheck without margin for economic setbacks.

Because these facts do not make for "news," they are ignored. The stereotypical image of the poor person or the African American person as lazy or criminal results from such ignorance.

Beckett (1997) reviewed media depictions of drug-fighting strategies and found that two types of "frames" for drug issues were most often used. She calls these the "Get the Traffickers" and "Zero-Tolerance" frames. Criminal justice policies aimed at reducing drug use do not necessarily have to reflect a "law and order" perspective (see the Issue in Depth at the end of this chapter). Yet according to Beckett, stories that depict drug raids and tough sentences for drug runners dominate the media. These depictions create and reinforce public support for get-tough measures and hence a "war on drugs," despite the tremendous harms that result.

The influence of drug policies on people's perceptions of drugs, crime, and the proper role of government in intervening in lives of drug users is an example of how "[p]olicy-making is a form of reality construction" (Brownstein 1996, p. 59). Although criminal justice policy perhaps should be the primary source of information for policymakers (Barak 1988; Brownstein 1991; Burnstein and Goldstein 1990), criminal justice policy today is neither rational nor orderly. Instead, it is driven by "competition and collaboration of claimsmakers as they strive to advise and influence policymakers [where] . . . lobbyists, political constituents, and anyone else with a vested interest argues in this arena for their own favored position" (Brownstein 1996, p. 61).

Even when research clearly shows that crack-related homicides are mostly systemic (because they are related to volatile, illicit crack markets) rather than due to the pharmacological effects of the drug, laws tend to get tough on crack users for fear they will become violent (Brownstein 1996, p. 65). And even when disparities in sentencing for crack versus powder cocaine were demonstrated to Congress to be unjustified, given that crack cocaine is no more addictive or dangerous than powder cocaine (Lockwood, Pottieger, and Inciardi 1996; W. Moore 1995), lawmakers voted to reduce the disparities but, nevertheless, to maintain them. The National Criminal Justice Commission claims that "evidence of meaningful pharmacological differences between crack and powder cocaine is exceedingly thin" and that "violence associated with crack stems more from turf battles between police and crack dealers, and among crack dealers battling between themselves to control lucrative markets, than from the narcotic effect of crack itself" (Donziger 1996, p. 119). Perhaps this is why many judges in the United States do not agree with sentencing disparities between crack and powder cocaine (Gray 2001).

The drug war has been aimed at disrupting, dismantling, and destroying the illegal market for drugs (Brownstein 1996, p. 45). Of course, a war can be conducted only against people, as noted, not against an abstract target such as "drugs." A "declaration of war suggests an imminently threatening national crisis or open conflict requiring the use of extraordinary power and authority, and the mobilization of massive resources to curb the threat and vanquish the enemy" (Merlo and Benekos 2000, p. 17). The real enemy in this war has unquestionably been poor minorities, as indicated by the prison populations in the United States today (see Chapter Nine). In fact, more than half of prison admissions for drug offenses are African Americans and Hispanics (Donziger 1996), largely because of the focus of law enforcement in minority communities (Tonry 1995). Not surprisingly, the majority of people convicted and sentenced for crack cocaine offenses are African American (M. Robinson 2000).

Imagine if Presidents Nixon, Reagan, Bush, and Clinton had declared war directly on poor people or minorities. Such a thing would have alarmed the media and would have been rejected by Americans as unacceptable, intolerant, and downright bigoted, especially after the struggles of the civil rights movement. A more indirect war against the same people, however, apparently is acceptable.

Imagine also a president suggesting that we take away individual Constitutional rights of all Americans to stop some from using drugs. The media would have featured such a story on the front page of every magazine and newspaper in the United States. Americans of all political persuasions—from members of the National Rifle Association (NRA) to members of the American Civil Liberties Union (ACLU)—would join forces to fight such a move. Yet the declared war on drugs in the 1980s has led to increased use of law enforcement actions that infringe upon Second, Fourth, Fifth, and Sixth Amendment rights. "Taking away rights of criminals" is how such infringements are sold to Americans, even though all of us enjoy less freedom today. Apparently, we see such sacrifices as necessary to stop drug abuse (Treaster 1990). Each of these is a cost of the drug war, which I discuss below.

HARMS CAUSED BY THE DRUG WAR

The war on drugs not only fails to meet its own goals, but also creates or exacerbates significant harms. These include the following.

• *The drug war leads to overburdened criminal justice agencies.*

As you have seen in this chapter, our police, courts, and corrections spend a significant portion of their time and resources dealing with drug offenses. Every minute and every dollar spent fighting the war on drugs are a minute and a dollar not spent fighting those acts that most threaten us, including violent crime and white-collar deviance. Since many drug offenders are sentenced through mandatory sentences, when correctional facilities are overburdened, drug offenders cannot be released early. Instead, more serious offenders are released early, including violent criminals. Thus, the war on drugs can create crime.

• *The drug war leads to crime and violence.*

Since drugs are illegal, crimes such as theft, prostitution, and other secondary crimes are committed to support drug habits. Drug offenders are also involved in gangs, drive-by shootings, and murders for the right to sell drugs. Internationally, we see that the drug war creates money laundering, funds revolutionary groups, and provides money for the training of terrorists (Gray, 2001). Systemic violence caused by drugs is discussed earlier in the chapter.

Some drug users also commit crimes to support their habits. Hamid (1998, p. 106) claims, "The greater the police presence on the streets, the greater the resort to risky behaviors on the part of users." These risky behaviors include stealing, selling sex for money, breaking and entering, robbery, and even murder. Vigorous drug enforcement by police may actually lead to more rather than less "organized, professional and enduring forms of criminality" (p. 109, citing Dorn and Smith 1992).

Currently, "Because [drug] criminal entrepreneurs operate outside of the law in their drug transactions, they are not bound by business etiquette in their competition with each other. . . . Terror, violence, extortion, bribery, or any other expedient strategy is relied upon by these criminals" (Goldstein 1998, p. 249, citing Glaser 1974).

There is a positive relationship between a drug's perceived seriousness by government and the price at which it sells. That is, as a drug is made illegal, and especially as it is labeled a serious threat to the community, it becomes more expensive to buy, even though production costs for most illicit drugs are comparable to those for many legal drugs. As noted by Nadelmann (1991, p. 29), "Most of the price paid for illicit substances is in effect a value-added tax created by their criminalization which is enforced and supplemented by the law-enforcement establishment, but collected by the drug traffickers." This amounts to a subsidy by the government (i.e., taxpayers) paid to the black-market drug offenders. Herbert Packer (1968) called it a *crime tariff* paid to those individuals and groups who must be willing to take tremendous risks to succeed in the drug business. Essentially, as the risks associated with drug offenses increase, so too will the rewards that drug offenders will expect. The American drug war, aimed at deterrence through increased risk, seems simultaneously to achieve higher rewards for those willing to engage in the drug trade.

Wisotsky (1991, p. 107) claims that the war on drugs has made things worse by spinning a "spider's web of black market pathologies," including homicides and other street crimes and widespread governmental corruption. Wisotsky claims that these pathologies were foreseeable because of the laws of supply and demand inherent in the market for an illicit substance that is in high demand. The crime tariff is the result. It is "what the seller must charge the buyer to monetize the risk he takes in breaking the law, in short, a premium for taking risks" (p. 107).

• *The drug war erodes Constitutional protections and privacy.*

In addition to creating crime, the drug war erodes our freedoms. As explained by Wisotsky (1991, p. 108), the U.S. drug war has led to greater levels of pretrial detention resulting from a statutory bias in favor of such detention for those facing certain drug offense charges. Second, within the political framework of the war on drugs, the Supreme Court has eroded defendants' rights not to have illegally seized evidence used against them in a court of law (Gray 2001). Wisotsky (1991, p. 109) outlines some of these erosions:

- Establishing the authority of police officers to stop, detain, and question people who fit the "profile" of drug couriers in airports, even without probable cause
- Permitting travelers' luggage to be sniffed by dogs without probable cause
- Making searches of automobiles without a warrant
- Searching ships in inland waterways without probable cause
- Obtaining warrants based on informants' tips
- Establishing the "good-faith exception" for police who use flawed warrants
- Permitting warrantless searches of open fields and barns adjacent to residences
- Enlarging the authority of police to stop motorists on the road without probable cause
- Permitting warrantless aerial searches over private residences and of motor homes used as residences.
- Allowing warrantless searches of public high school students' purses

Police also can claim exigent circumstances to justify gathering and using unlawful evidence, including evidence that was in their plain view or within reach. Also, police can seize a person's property though asset forfeiture programs based on suspicion of drug activity. The burden of proof falls on the accused to prove that he or she is not involved in the drug trade; even when this is accomplished, the government can keep up to 30% of the property for administrative purposes. This is inconsistent with the presumption of innocence and due process, as defined in Chapter One.

• *The drug war is a significant source of corruption.*

Related to increased powers of police and prosecutors, the war on drugs is a significant source of corruption in agencies of criminal justice. The amount of money involved in the drug trade is a source of unbelievable temptation, leading to numerous highly publicized cases of corruption in law enforcement (Gray 2001). Recent cases include the Dallas Police Department (Texas) and the Tulia Police Department (Texas), where minorities were arrested after officers planted evidence and invented cases against innocent individuals (see Chapter Six).

• *The drug war leads to death and illness among drug users.*

Ironically, the drug war ends up causing death and illness among users (Gray 2001). Addicts are less likely to seek medical attention and treatment because of fear of criminal sanctions (Mac-Coun and Reuter 2001). Deaths are directly attributable to high prices of illegal drugs, and as you've seen in this chapter, emergency-room mentions of drugs and deaths due to illicit drugs are actually increasing.

The Food and Drug Administration (FDA) does not have the jurisdiction to regulate illicit drugs (or to regulate nicotine in tobacco, according to the Supreme Court in 2000). This means that the levels of active ingredients in drugs are typically not known and certainly not intentionally managed as is alcohol content. "Imagine that Americans could not tell whether a bottle of wine contained 6%, 30%, or 90% alcohol, or whether an aspirin tablet contained 5 grams or 500 grams of aspirin" (Nadelmann 1991, p. 33). Also, imagine that manufacturers of legal drugs like alcohol were permitted to add far more dangerous substances to their products, as in the case of cocaine and heroin. The drug war makes even relatively harmless recreational drug use much more dangerous than it would be if drugs were legal and regulated for quality control.

- ### *The drug war leads to financial cutbacks to other social services.*

Every dollar we spend fighting the war on drugs is a dollar not spent on other social services. This ultimately harms Americans. For example, since the 1970s, spending on the war on drugs has increased tremendously, as you've seen in this chapter. Now that state budgets are in crisis, it is nearly impossible to cut back funding for operations of police, courts, and corrections as they fight the war on drugs. Yet funding for social service functions has been cut, including education, mental health treatment, and welfare assistance, as have basic investments in vital infrastructures needed to run communities effectively.

- ### *The drug war heightens racial disparities.*

As discussed earlier in this chapter, minorities disproportionately suffer criminal justice processing when it comes to the war on drugs. According to Hamid (1998, p. 122), "Minority persons who have been arrested for drug offenses and other crimes far outnumber European Americans." The penalties they receive are frequently harsh and unfair. Figure 11.8 illustrates that even though Caucasians account for a higher percentage of drug users and people arrested for drugs, minorities account for the majority of inmates convicted of drug offenses and sentenced to the nation's prisons.

- ### *The drug war causes environmental damage.*

Many harms associated with the war on drugs are rarely considered because they tend to be felt most by those who reside in *producer countries* (e.g., Colombia, Afghanistan) and *transporter countries* (e.g., Mexico) rather than *consumer countries* (such as the United States). One of the harms is the destruction of crops, the soil in which it is grown, and the drinking water that surrounds it, by the use of pesticides and other means by the U.S. government (and foreign governments in cooperation with the U.S. government). Crop eradication is one means by which the war on drugs is fought. Yet according to our very own ONDCP, total cultivation of illicit drugs is unchanged: As one spot is eradicated, another pops up in its place, which is a form of displacement.

- ### *The drug war threatens the sovereignty of other countries.*

Another harm of our drug war is that we threaten the sovereignty of other nations. Countries such as Mexico and Colombia have had numerous disagreements with the U.S. government over our threats to *decertify* them if they do not cooperate with our war on drugs. This causes resentment among the people of these countries because it interferes with their ability to govern themselves as they see fit.

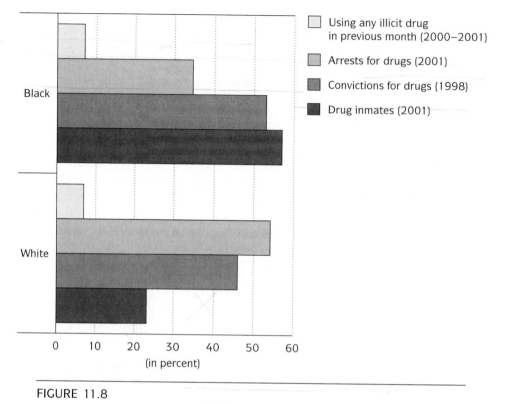

FIGURE 11.8
Race and Drugs
SOURCE: Sourcebook of Criminal Justice Statistics (2003).

ON LEGALIZATION

This chapter concludes with an examination of the relative merits of drug legalization as a policy alternative to America's drug war. Before I begin discussing legalization, consider the range of possible outcomes of the drug war.

When law enforcement agencies invade a neighborhood or community to interfere with drug activity, any combination of three outcomes may result. These outcomes are depicted in the three models shown in Figure 11.9. These models are ideals and are not necessarily mutually exclusive.

Model 1, which I call the *subterfuge model*, characterizes all neighborhoods where drug-related activity exists. Because selling drugs is illegal, drug dealers must hide their activity from the police. Police are at a distinct disadvantage in the war on drugs because they must identify, locate, and apprehend drug offenders, who are typically very good at concealing and disguising their activities. For example, street-level crack cocaine dealers utilize numerous strategies to avoid detection by the police. Two strategies involve moving transactions from street corners to apartment buildings and frisking potential buyers for wires (Gaines, Kaune, and Miller 2000, p. 611). In the subterfuge model, when police efforts are directed at a particular neighborhood,

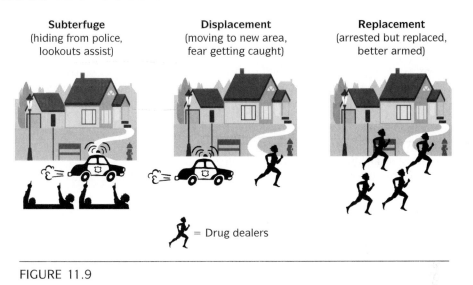

FIGURE 11.9
Possible Outcomes of Policing Drugs

drug dealers utilize lookouts to warn them of police presence. This makes preventing or controlling drug sales very difficult.

It is illogical to assume that police agencies can ever stem the flow of the tide of illicit drug dealing in the United States. There are currently only 2.86 police officers per 1,000 U.S. citizens. Given the amount of illicit drug use among these 1,000 people, it would be impossible for the police ever to be able to stop enough of it to make much of a difference. Additionally, given that drugs can be grown virtually anywhere, and given that growers of drugs "camouflage and protect" their operations from detection efforts (Nadelmann 1991, pp. 22–23), national and international efforts to stem the production of drugs in the United States and the flow of drugs into the United States are doomed to fail. Consider these facts:

- Thirteen truckloads per year can satisfy the entire national demand for cocaine.
- The United States has 88,633 miles of shoreline, 7,500 miles of international borders with Canada and Mexico, and 300 ports of entry (Frankel 1997).
- Most arrests for drug offenses are for small-time offenders such as people who simply possess drugs (Page 1999).

Nadelmann (1991, p. 22) makes an argument consistent with the evidence from the study of street-level crack dealers mentioned above. He writes: "In the final analysis, the principal accomplishment of most domestic drug-enforcement efforts is not to reduce the supply or availability of illegal drugs, or even to raise their price; it is to punish the drug dealers who are apprehended, and cause minor disruptions in established drug markets."

In Model 2, the *displacement model*, drug dealers are literally scared away by the police into other neighborhoods and communities. In the presence of zero-tolerance policing, police intervene in even the most minor of criminal infractions and attempt to eliminate "social incivilities" such as the presence of homeless and mentally ill people on the streets. Street sweeps of the homeless and mentally ill are merely means of "sweeping such problems under the rug," so to speak, rather than dealing with them more effectively and, some would say, more humanely. Likewise, efforts to capture and arrest street-level drug dealers, under the umbrella of zero-tolerance laws, is a very ineffective method of attempting to eliminate drug use and abuse in the United States.

Zero-tolerance laws are based on the following assumptions:

- If there were no drug abusers, there would be no drug problem.
- The market for drugs is created not only by availability, but also by demand.
- Drug abuse starts with a willful act.
- Drug users are not powerless to act against the influences of drug availability and peer pressure.
- Most illegal drug users can choose to stop their drug-taking behaviors and should be held accountable if they do not.
- Individual freedom does not include the right to self-destruction and societal destruction.
- public tolerance for drug abuse must be reduced to zero. (Inciardi 1991, p. 11)

With zero-tolerance laws, drug dealers are theoretically deterred from engaging in drug-related crimes in the presence of police. But rather than giving up their illegal and immensely profitable livelihoods, drug offenders simply move their criminal operations elsewhere.

In Model 3, the *replacement model*, law enforcement efforts are temporarily successful. In neighborhoods and communities where police efforts result in numerous arrests of drug offenders, drug dealers are temporarily put out of business. Yet, as suggested by the title of this model, when drug dealers are taken off of the street, others simply take their place in the illegal drug market. This is because of the "push-down/pop-up" nature of urban drug markets (Nadelmann 1991, p. 23)—when one market is shut down, another simply "pops up" in its place. Glaser (1997, p. 119) claims: "Arrest of any individual involved in drug production usually impairs the drug supply only briefly, because the trade consists of many independent entrepreneurs in diverse roles, in all types of illegal drug distribution, and most getting the highest income from it. Others hurry to replace anyone removed from the industry by arrest."

Because the new drug dealers will be aware of the increased risks of apprehension, they will be better prepared to avoid detection and arrest. They may also be better armed and more ruthless than the previous drug dealers so that they can better battle the police. Skolnick (1997, p. 412) calls this the "Darwinian trafficker dilemma," whereby only the "fittest" drug dealers survive.

So we are left with this result: When drug dealers are taken off the street, others simply step in and take their place. We are left with the same number of drug dealers on our streets but more inmates in our prisons. There are no fewer drugs available but we're spending more of our money. The National Criminal Justice Commission puts it this way:

> Somebody else almost always steps in to take the place of the dealer when he or she goes to prison. Incarcerating the second drug dealer costs just as much as incarcerating the first. By the time the criminal justice system has passed through several generations of drug dealers, billions of dollars have been spent and the corner is still scattered with empty vials of crack cocaine. (Donziger 1996, p. 61)

As noted, these models represent ideals, so any neighborhood or community with any amount of drug-related problems and any level of law enforcement presence will experience some of each outcome. That is, to some degree, subterfuge, displacement, and replacement will occur as police attempt to prevent and control illicit drugs. This means that the likely results of the American drug war are arrests, convictions, and punishment of some but not most drug dealers, entrenchment of new drug dealers to replace those who are removed from the market, and displacement of drug offending to areas where law enforcement presence is not as great. Do you consider this a success?

For these reasons, success in the war on drugs is not likely. In fact, I argue that because of the effects of subterfuge, displacement, and replacement, it is impossible to win the war on drugs. This is why American drug control efforts, though they may be well intended, are futile at best. Whether this provides a valid rationale for legalizing drugs is debatable, but it does suggest that the United States should abandon its war on drugs—unless, of course, you believe that the war really is successful at something else entirely. The following box briefly shows how the war on drugs could be considered a success.

How America's drug war is a success

Failure in the war on drugs may actually amount to success if, as pointed out in Chapter Two, the goal is really not to succeed. Erickson and Butters (1998, p. 177) assert that if we look at the war on drugs as a policy aimed at reducing harm, then prohibition is a failure. Yet if we look at it as an ideology (an orientation that characterizes the thinking of a group), then it is "one of the great success stories of the twentieth century." That is, as a means to shift control to the political right and lock people up for political gain, the war on drugs is working. It is pretty clear who benefits from the failing drug war and who is most harmed by it. While the incarceration boom may be beneficial for those with vested financial interests, it disproportionately affects poor people and minorities. Given the resulting disparities based on race and class, by definition the drug war is not just. This is why the war on drugs provides evidence that American criminal justice agencies are not blind. Instead, they seem to have poor people of color clearly in their sights. Tonry (1995, p. 105) writes, "Urban African-Americans have borne the brunt of the War on Drugs. They have been arrested, prosecuted, convicted, and imprisoned at increasing rates since the early 1980s, and grossly out of proportion to their numbers in the general population or among drug users." Now that we know this to be fact, how can we allow it to continue?

Results of the war on drugs have included "enormous profits for drug dealers and traffickers, overcrowded jails, police and other government corruption, a distorted foreign policy, predatory street crime carried on by users in search of the funds necessary to purchase black market drugs, and urban areas harassed by street-level drug dealers and terrorized by violent drug gangs." Astonishingly, efforts to prevent drugs from coming into the country stop only about 20–30% of illicit drugs such as marijuana and cocaine from entering the United States (ONDCP, 2004). Inciardi (1991), a staunch opponent of drug legalization, nonetheless admits that interdiction efforts aimed at reducing the passage of drugs into the United States have failed and that more drug abuse treatment is needed (p. 75). Finally, the nation's drug war is a major source of police and criminal justice corruption (Lyman and Potter 1998). This led Kappeler, Blumberg, and Potter (2000, p. 166) to call the drug war a "government-sponsored subsidy to organized crime."

Given these startling revelations, some alternatives to the American drug war may be justified. These include

- *decriminalization,*
- *legalization,* and
- *harm reduction.*

Decriminalization calls for eliminating or reducing the penalties for the recreational use of illicit substances. Canada and Britain have recently decriminalized marijuana possession. Another alternative includes outright *legalization* of all drugs, although, considering all the possible negative outcomes, I do not personally support this approach. Legalization calls for eliminating drug offenses from the criminal statutes and thus could lead to a complete government withdrawal from drug-related issues. In a commercialized, capitalistic society, advertisers would push substances and inevitably increase drug use (MacCoun and Reuter 2001). Decriminalization does not take the government out of drug prevention efforts. Instead, decriminalization involves limiting the use of drugs and taxing and limiting their production, promotion, sales, and use. Further, profits from drug use would be used to treat those who are involved in harmful drug abuse (Kleiman 1997). *Harm reduction* approaches are not necessarily aimed at reducing drug use. Based on the realization that some drug use is inevitable, harm reduction strategies are simply aimed at reducing harms associated with recreational drug use. They include *methadone maintenance, needle exchange programs,* and similar approaches to reduce overall harm. These are discussed in the Issue in Depth at the end of this chapter.

Will Americans embrace alternatives to the drug war? Americans do seem well aware that the drug war is not working. For example, 94% of respondents in a survey by the Harvard School of Public Health reported their belief that drug use was not under control, and 58% thought that drug use would get worse with time (Blendon and Young 1998). Despite the implications of these findings, Gallup polls still show that Americans want more of the same to stop drug use—more severe criminal penalties, more money for police, and increased military involvement in intervention efforts (Gaines, Kaune, and Miller 2000). In other words, Americans may think that the war on drugs is failing, but they still want more of it.

CONCLUSION

American history is dotted with wars on drugs. In these wars, which we seem to conduct every so often against drugs perceived to be used by problematic populations, we generally ignore the lessons of the past. The criminal justice network remains blind to its own illogical drug war. Even though the actual harms attributed to use of illicit drugs pale in comparison to the harms caused by legal drugs, we seem content to use law enforcement and military efforts to try to solve problems associated with the medical problem of drug abuse. Although our recent efforts have had no appreciable effect on drug use or abuse in the United States, our nation's prisons and jails are filling up with poor street criminals, many of whom are people of color, who have committed very minor drug crimes. The media continue to fall prey to politicians' efforts to wage war against the poor and people of color in the name of the war on drugs rather than independently asserting how the nation's drug war is a massive failure. More violence is attributable to the nation's drug war than to the actual use of drugs. Thus, decriminalization seems to be a legitimate alternative worth pursuing.

ISSUE IN DEPTH
Decriminalize It!

James Inciardi (1991, pp. 47–49), editor of *The Drug Legalization Debate*, lays out some of the key questions:

- What drugs should be legalized?
- What potency level of drugs should be allowed?
- Should there be age limits and other restrictions on drug use?
- How much drug use should be allowed?
- Where should drugs be sold?
- Who should manufacture drugs?
- What economic restrictions should be placed on the legal drug market, including rules for advertising and the like?
- Where will people be allowed to use drugs?
- Which government agency or agencies will be charged with regulating drug use?

Although answers to these questions must be developed before we allow legal drug use, I do not attempt to answer them directly here. This should be left to people with experience in policymaking (for an example of one model legalization proposal, see Karel 1991). Instead, I hope to lay out the main argument in favor of some level of drug decriminalization.

The main argument in favor of decriminalization is that the drug war fails so miserably in controlling drug use (which is mostly recreational in nature) and drug abuse (which is in essence a medical problem). The main argument against decriminalization is that drug use and abuse will increase and cause unimaginable harms. Most Americans may think that any form of legalization of drugs is "an invitation to drug infested anarchy" (Nadelmann 1991, p. 18), but this does not have to be the case. Even the staunchest drug legalization advocates acknowledge that use of certain substances might increase if they were legalized, not only because they would be more readily available but also because the deterrent effect of the criminal sanction would no longer apply. No one will argue that more drug use would actually be a good thing, but it might not be as bad a thing as you would imagine. The harms associated with increased use would depend on the specific drug legalization proposal. For example, if the government decided to legalize all drugs and then regulated their quality and availability and also restricted their use to competent, mature adults, increased recreational drug use might actually be a cost-effective alternative to the American drug war.

No, decriminalization is not sure to be a success (e.g., see J. Wilson 1998), for "no one knows for certain the extent to which it would increase the number of addicts. . . . Few would deny . . . that the greater availability of, and easier access to, drugs would increase drug use (and addiction) beyond current levels" (Nuro, Kinlock, and Hanlon 1998, p. 230). This seems a logical and fair conclusion.

Nadelmann (1998) does suggest that drug legalization would increase the availability of drugs, lower their prices, and remove whatever deterrent effect the law has currently, which might suggest increased drug use. Price is a function of supply and demand (Reuter 1998): When demand for drugs is high, prices are low, and when prices are low, demand may be high. As long as drugs are illegal, sellers can artificially inflate the price to whatever levels they see fit—whatever price warrants the inherent risks associated with being in the illicit drug business.

Could we at least consider decriminalization of illicit drugs as a policy possibility, especially given that current interdiction efforts "have shown little success in stemming the flow of cocaine and heroin into the United States" (Nadelmann 1998, pp. 289–90)? Law enforcement cannot ever possibly "go to the root of the problem" (Reuter 1998, p. 315). Making some drugs illegal "has proven highly costly and counterproductive in much the same way that the national prohibition of alcohol did" (Nadelmann 1998, p. 290).

Nadelmann writes that legalization is not a "get out of jail free card" for drug dealers. Rather, it is a way to put them out of the drug business and to remove much of the criminality surrounding drugs as well. It is also not an excuse for irresponsible use or abuse of drugs. What I propose, echoing the sentiments of Nadelmann, is that the government make currently illicit substances legally available to adults, while simultaneously regulating their production, distribution, and sale. In conjunction with these efforts, the government must provide drug-related education about the true harms associated with all drug use, including the use of currently legal drugs such as tobacco and alcohol (Jonas 1991, p. 172). It must also offer drug treatment programs for people who are addicted to or abuse any drugs.

I believe that criminal justice agencies should get out of the drug war business for a number of reasons. As shown in this chapter, the drug war fails to achieve its goals, including to reduce illicit drug use and abuse. Additionally, our drug control efforts are highly costly, both financially and socially. For example, as discussed, the criminalization of drugs creates crime through an illegal black market, which actually encourages people to get into the illicit drug business; our drug reduction efforts have led to an erosion of Constitutional protections; and because drugs are illegal, there are no quality controls in place to ensure safe use.

In addition, I suggest that

- the drug war is hypocritical
- drug abuse would not likely increase if illicit drugs were decriminalized
- drug abuse is a medical problem, not a criminal justice problem
- alternatives to the war would be much more effective at reducing drug use and abuse and would reduce overall harms.

Each of these is discussed below.

The Drug War Is Hypocritical

Without doubt, one primary purpose of the criminal law is to promote morality (see Chapter Three). Thus, a primary function of the government is "the promotion of moral behavior and good health practices among its citizens" (Rouse and Johnson 1991, p. 185). To focus on some drugs and characterize them as immoral, while virtually ignoring others that cause more harm, seems illogical at best.

As discussed earlier in this chapter, far more harms are associated with legal drugs like tobacco and alcohol than with illicit drugs such as marijuana, cocaine, and heroin. Even relative to their levels of use in the United States, some legal drugs are far more deadly and dangerous than many illicit drugs (Jonas 1991). So, Nadelmann (1991, p. 25) concludes:

> There is little question that we could reduce the health costs associated with use and abuse of alcohol and tobacco if we were to criminalize their production, sale, and possession. But no one believes that we could eliminate their use and abuse, that we could create an "alcohol-free" or "tobacco-free" country. Nor do most Americans believe that criminalizing the alcohol and tobacco markets would be a good idea.

As explained by Nadelmann (1991), criminalizing legal drugs is a bad idea because of two primary beliefs of Americans: "that adult Americans have the right to choose what substances they will consume and what risks they will take; and that the costs of trying to coerce so many Americans to abstain from those substances would be enormous."

Still, we have identified and isolated some drugs that, even when used recreationally or when merely possessed, are criminalized on the basis of their likelihood of causing harm. This focus seems hypocritical, given that a shift from casual alcohol use to the recreational use of marijuana would likely lead to a decrease in violence in the United States (Nadelmann 1991, p. 31). Yet Americans overwhelmingly support the drug war and draw a "moral line in the sand" between unlawful and lawful substances. However, just because "the American people simply do not want it" (Inciardi 1991, p. 66) does not mean that legalization of drugs is wrong. To the degree that Americans base their opinions about crime and justice on media information and public stances of politicians (see Chapter Five), it is not surprising that they tend to oppose decriminalization.

Drug Abuse Would Not Likely Increase If Drugs Were Decriminalized

As noted earlier in this chapter, most drug use in the United States is recreational. It is intimately linked to American culture as a whole and to particular subcultures within the larger society, and it is typically limited to certain social situations and social groups. Because most drug users do not become drug abusers, any increase in drug use resulting from decriminalization would not likely lead to very large levels of drug abuse. Experimentation with relatively minor drugs such as marijuana would also not likely lead to the use of "harder" drugs such as cocaine and heroin, as proponents of the "gateway hypothesis" suggest. In fact, most people who use marijuana recreationally do not use or abuse harder drugs; the gateway to illicit drugs is found in legal drugs such as tobacco and alcohol (Casement 1987; Schoenborn and Cohen 1986; Trebach 1987). Even the federal government and the ONDCP admit that the first steps in drug use are tobacco and alcohol, yet these drugs are not criminalized. Tobacco and alcohol users are far more likely, according to the ONDCP, to use illicit drugs.

As predispositions to drug abuse continue to be discovered, it is likely that we soon will be able to identify those individuals most susceptible to drug addiction and dependence and be able to focus our drug use education programs and drug abuse prevention programs directly at these individuals. Perhaps drug use would become more socially acceptable if all drugs were not criminalized. This could be counteracted with effective education programs that make drug use socially undesirable except in very specific circumstances.

Another reason to doubt that drug abuse would increase is that drugs are already widely available to most people (Inciardi 1991, p. 56). Legalization might make it easier to obtain drugs for use, but Americans can already easily obtain illicit substances as they wish. Inciardi cautions that once illicit drugs become legal, the market economy will take over or at least become heavily involved in maintaining drug use. This may be true, given corporate involvement in the U.S. alcohol and tobacco industries. But again, nothing mandates that the government has to permit this.

Interestingly, legalization opponents such as Inciardi argue against all forms of legalization, in part because they hold that drug legalization would be a "program of social management and control that would serve to legitimate the chemical destruction of an urban generation and culture" (Inciardi 1991, p. 65). Why? Because disenfranchised segments of the population might end up using more drugs, Inciardi posits that drug legalization would be a racist and elitist policy. I conclude the opposite: that the war on drugs currently results in alarming criminal justice disparities based on race and class, and that these disparities would be lessened if drug offenses were decriminalized. This would make criminal justice more just and thus more in line with its ideal goals.

Wisotsky (1991, pp. 108–9) concludes that the American drug war "makes a net negative contribution to the safety, well-being, and national security interests of the American people." If this is true, as I believe it is, then the criminal justice network, by waging a war against drugs, is not only failing to meet its goal of reducing crime but may in fact be exposing U.S. citizens to greater threats to their personal safety.

Drug Abuse Is a Medical Problem Rather than a Criminal Justice Problem

Decriminalization would also deemphasize the use of criminal justice resources to deal with the medical problem of drug abuse (Nadelmann 1998). Our money might be better spent dealing with tobacco and alcohol use and abuse, as well as serious violent crimes. As Nadelmann points out, "The standard refrain regarding the immorality of drug use (such as that in Nancy Reagan's 'Just Say No' campaign) crumbles in the face of most Americans' tolerance for alcohol and tobacco use" (p. 294).

Research shows that treatment works to reduce drug abuse and to alleviate the harms associated with it (Gray 2001; MacCoun and Reuter 2000). According to the RAND Corporation, drug treatment is 7 times more cost effective than law enforcement, 11 times more than interdiction, and 23 times more than drug eradication (Gray 2001). According to the National Institute of Drug Abuse (NIDA), "Most people don't believe treatment works, and they're wrong" (MacCoun and Reuter 2001). And according to the National Criminal Justice Reference Service (2003), rearrest rates are lower for people involved in special court drug programs than those handled in normal court processes.

The war on drugs has allowed American policing to get bigger and meaner, resulting in numerous tragic abuses of human rights. Growing use of undercover operations and electronic surveillance may infringe upon our freedoms, and the growing use of informants flies in the face of crime control goals. Says Nadelmann (1998, p. 195):

> Overzealous enforcement of the drug laws risks undermining (the ethic of tolerance toward those who are different but do no harm to others) and propagating in its place a society of informants. Indeed, enforcement of the drug laws makes a mockery of an essential principle of a free society, that those who do no harm to others should not be harmed by others, and particularly not by the state.

Decriminalization would allow people to engage in drug-using behaviors that are relatively harmless while simultaneously leading to the development of possible mechanisms to identify and treat drug abusers medically. Criminal justice responses to drug use and abuse do not allow for this.

Alternatives to the Drug War Would Be Much More Effective

According to MacCoun and Reuter, in their exhaustive book *Drug War Heresies* (2001), many alternative drug reduction and harm reduction programs have proven to be effective in European nations. These include needle exchange programs, which save lives by reducing HIV and AIDS infections but do not seem to lead to increased use. Needle exchange programs are endorsed by the Centers for Disease Control and Prevention, the National Academy of Sciences, and numerous health and medical organizations. Other successful programs include drug treatment programs (which have been proven more effective at reducing drug use and abuse than prisons), methadone maintenance programs (which allow drug users to lead functional lives with a much lower risk of overdose or death as a result of their use), and marijuana decriminalization (which has kept use rates lower in the Netherlands than the United States). The Dutch also have not seen increases in the use of harder drugs and have saved money by not incarcerating marijuana offenders—the United States currently incarcerates at least 50,000 marijuana offenders.

According to Nadelmann (1998, p. 299), decriminalization of drugs would accomplish the following:

- Shift control of drug manufacturing and distribution to the government
- Afford consumers opportunities to make more informed decisions about drug use
- Lessen the degree of harms associated with impure substances
- Correct the hypocritical and dangerous message that legal drugs are harmless
- Allow government to shape drug consumption patterns

The bottom line is that the U.S. war on drugs creates far more harm than it stops. MacCoun and Reuter (2001, p. 386) conclude, as I have in this chapter, that our policies "have failed to eliminate drug dependence, have at best only moderately reduced drug use, and have left its harms largely intact" and that our policies themselves are a source of many drug-related harms. They also point out that although the U.S. government claims that one of its goals is harm reduction, there is not one specific program aimed at achieving that goal.

An alternative to waging war on drugs would be a policy of harm reduction, which "is the emphasis on the reduction of adverse consequences rather than the elimination of drug use. Harm reduction is a framework from which policy and program strategies are conceptualized, developed, and implemented with the outcome goal being the reduction or minimization of harm (without requiring user abstinence or less consumption)" (Jensen and Gerber 1998, p. 179). It is aimed at reducing adverse physical, social, and economic consequences of drug use.

A more effective antidrug strategy would thus be characterized by the following (Jensen and Gerber 1998):

- A focus on harm reduction
- No mention of war or war-related rhetoric, which create enemies
- Less criminal justice spending
- Honesty and research-informed policy

For such an approach to be effective, it must be "accompanied by the view of users as mainstream or potentially functional members of society rather than marginal deviant misfits." Also, truths about drug use must emerge, meaning that myths of drug use must be overcome (p. 189). One example is that most of the population of virtually every nation never tries cocaine. Of those who do, most do not become addicted. In fact, only 5% to 10% of cocaine users use the drug frequently (Erickson 1993). Imagine politicians and the media trying to sell the war against cocaine to Americans in the face of these facts.

MacCoun and Reuter (2001, p. 409) challenge U.S. policymakers to at least consider the evidence. They say, "We earnestly believe that, ignoring specific proposals, the desirability of major reform has a reasonable empirical and ethical basis. To scorn discussion and analysis of such major change, in light of the extraordinary problems associated with current policies, is frivolous and uncaring."

I conclude by echoing the sentiment of Kappeler, Blumberg, and Potter (2000, p. 167), who I think speak for most within the disciplines of criminology and criminal justice when they write, "Drug control policy has not failed for lack of resources, funding, legal powers, or adequate personnel. It has failed because the problem is not amenable to a criminal justice solution." We know this. Failing to correct it produces outcomes inconsistent with the ideal goals of the U.S. criminal justice network.

Discussion Questions

1. What is the war on drugs?
2. Identify and discuss the main elements of the drug war in the United States.
3. Can a war really be fought against inanimate objects like drugs? Why or why not?
4. What are the main goals of our nation's drug wars?
5. Do you think we need a war on drugs? Why or why not?
6. Identify examples of how wars on drugs have been declared on powerless groups in the United States.
7. What is a drug?
8. Contrast drug use with drug abuse.
9. Discuss some of the potential outcomes of drug abuse.
10. Make a list of the major categories of drugs and discuss the effects they have on those who use them.
11. Differentiate the five schedules of drugs.
12. Do you think drug use would increase if drugs were not illegal? Why or why not?
13. Why do you think more people smoke cigarettes than marijuana?
14. According to the evidence discussed in the chapter, which is more harmful to smoke, cigarettes or marijuana? Why?
15. Is there a link between drugs and crime? If so, what are some of the relationships?
16. Discuss the role of the media in promoting drug scares.
17. Outline and compare the main arguments for and against legalization of drugs.
18. Identify and discuss three possible outcomes of drug intervention, including subterfuge, displacement, and replacement.
19. Do you think zero-tolerance laws are a logical approach to fighting drugs? Why or why not?
20. Identify the main arguments in favor of decriminalization.

CHAPTER TWELVE

THE WAR ON CRIME AS A THREAT TO EQUALITY: INNOCENT BIAS AGAINST THE POOR, PEOPLE OF COLOR, AND WOMEN

KEY CONCEPTS

Is the war on crime a war on the poor?
- *Box: Functions served by the war on crime*

Is the criminal justice network biased against people of color?
- *Box: Race and criminality according to sources of crime data*
- *Race, ethnicity, and social class*
- *Race, ethnicity, government policy, and criminal justice*
- *Box: Race and criminal justice in history*

Gender and criminal justice

Conclusion

Issue in Depth: The Greatest Threat to Civil Rights Is the Criminal Justice Network

Discussion Questions

INTRODUCTION

Consider the following facts established in previous chapters:

- The law is made by a group who are not representative of the general public.
- Lawmakers are voted for by a group who are not representative of the general public.
- Most people do not vote.
- Lawmaking is influenced by special interests.
- Whoever spends the most money in political campaigns is virtually guaranteed to win.
- Crime is not a label used to identify the most serious threats to our lives and property.
- Media coverage of crime is focused disproportionately on street crime, especially violent crimes committed by poor people and people of color.

- The police, because they are located predominantly in the inner cities of America and focused almost exclusively on street crime, are disproportionately likely to stop, question, arrest, and use force against the poor and minorities.
- The power among courtroom workgroups is imbalanced in favor of prosecutors, and both pretrial (bail and plea bargaining) and trial processes are inherently biased in favor of the wealthy and against the poor and members of minority groups.
- The poor and minorities are disproportionately likely to be sentenced to probation, jail, prison, and other criminal sanctions through mandatory sentences and make up the majority of people under correctional supervision in the United States.
- The administration of capital punishment is biased in favor of the wealthy and killers of Caucasians and against the poor.
- The war on drugs disproportionately affects the poor and minorities.

Given these facts, is it possible that the criminal justice network is biased against particular groups in society, such as the poor, people of color, and women? In this chapter, I examine the evidence that the criminal justice network as a whole is biased against these groups. I revisit some key findings from previous chapters and try to make sense of why agencies of criminal justice seem focused so squarely on some people and some acts but ignore others.

IS THE WAR ON CRIME A WAR ON THE POOR?

Recall from Chapter Two that Jeffrey Reiman (1998) argues that criminal justice operations are biased against the poor at every step of the process, beginning with the law. In his book *The Rich Get Richer and the Poor Get Prison*, Reiman demonstrates that the criminal law essentially ignores harmful acts committed by the powerful, such as those committed in white-collar jobs and by corporations. As discussed in Chapter Four, these acts either are not illegal (such as the manufacture and sale of tobacco) or are against the law but are not seen as "serious" and thus not widely pursued by law enforcement agencies (e.g., manufacturing and selling defective products).

The label *criminality* is almost always reserved for the poor, even though criminality is not a function of social class. After reviewing the alleged links between social class and crime, M. Robinson (2004) concludes that social class only predicts the types of crime that people are likely to commit. For example, poor people tend to acquire wealth through crimes such as theft and robbery. Middle-class and wealthy individuals tend not to rob people, stores, or banks. Instead, they steal through means such as embezzlement and fraud. This is not to say that everyone steals, but most people do (at least occasionally).

Yet we are filling up our prisons with poor street criminals and building more prisons to accommodate the growing number of convicted street criminals. So, is the war on crime a war on the poor?

In a convincing and moving analysis of antipoverty policies in the United States, Herbert Gans (1995) outlines the main components of what he calls *The War Against the Poor* throughout American history. Gans analyzes U.S. government policy generally, but his analysis speaks volumes about how the criminal justice network in the United States operates. Keep in mind that politics and criminal justice cannot be separated (see Chapter Two). Thus, some government attempts to reduce poverty may have implications for criminal justice, and vice versa.

Gans (1995) uses the term *underclass* to refer to a segment of the poor that supposedly refuses to "behave in the (1995) 'mainstream' ways of the numerically or culturally dominant middle class" (p. 2). William Julius Wilson (1987) used the same term to explain how a small segment of the United States has become socially isolated and "truly disadvantaged," although he has subsequently replaced this term with *ghetto poor*. Wilson writes that the poor become socially isolated when they are detached from middle-class role models who successfully moved out of poor areas. Singh (1991, p. 509) concurs, claiming, "Unemployment and growing isolation from the mainstream economy have led to unwed parenting, dependency, lawlessness, joblessness, and school failure."

Gans (1995) argues that the label of *underclass* is a term used to describe a culture supposedly unique to poor people. This historical view of the poor suggests that the underclass are to blame for their own problems because of their questionable morality and deteriorating values: "The labeling of the poor as moral inferiors . . . blames them falsely for the ills of the American society and economy, reinforces their mistreatment, increases their misery, and further discourages their moving out of poverty" (p. 1). In essence, application of the *underclass* label amounts to an accusation against people who are seen as undeserving of assistance because of their bad values and moral deficiencies. Lauer and Lauer (2000, p. xi) call such depictions of the poor as flawed individuals "simplistic." Simplistic understandings of complex problems—rooted in individuals' own assumptions about human nature and general perspectives about the world rather than in empirical evidence or scientific facts—lead to simplistic and ineffective solutions to social problems such as poverty and crime.

Numerous mainstream explanations of crime are at least based on cultural assumptions about the poor (Bohm 2001; M. Robinson 2004; Vold, Bernard, and Snipes 1998). Many actually state cultural assumptions explicitly. I would even suggest that conditions of poverty and criminality have traditionally been treated synonymously in criminological theory. W. Miller's (1958) *theory of focal concerns*, for example, posits that the lower class has its own unique value system. It is an allegiance to the lower-class focal concerns of trouble, toughness, fate, smartness, excitement, and autonomy, Miller contends, that accounts for their higher involvement in street-level criminality. Virtually all American theories of crime have their roots in the *Chicago School of Criminology*, which studied "delinquency areas" in Chicago, inhabited by waves of immigrants. Scholars such as Shaw and McKay explained criminality as a function of conditions of *social disorganization*, where citizens in the inner city were not equipped to mobilize community resources to fight criminogenic influences unique to certain areas of the city, typically inhabited by immigrant cultures (Bohm 2001; Vold, Bernard, and Snipes 1998).

Interestingly, this is one of the ways in which Gans (1995) claims that the label of the underclass is reified. He writes that "extreme poverty areas" of the U.S. Bureau of the Census and "underclass areas" of other researchers are chosen for stigmatization and a disproportionate withdrawal of poverty-ameliorating facilities and services (p. 64). These are the same areas in which police are disproportionately located because of the assumed higher criminality within these areas (see Chapter Six).

Gans explores how the United States has always been involved in a war against the poor, which, he argues, has worsened since the 1980s. Incidentally, this is the time during which the country's entrenchment in the crime control model of criminal justice became so evident, as discussed in Chapter Two. Given the increasingly punitive nature of U.S. criminal justice policy since the 1980s directed at street criminals, it becomes easy to see the war on crime as really a war on crimes committed by the poor. Gans argues that this is the result of how Americans have come to see the poor as "deserving" of their poverty and suffering and "undeserving" of assistance.

Gans (1995, pp. 6–7) lays out four aspects of the "undeserving" nature of the poor (and thus the criminal). He argues:

- If poor people do not behave according to the rules set by mainstream society, they must be undeserving . . . because they believe in and therefore practice bad values, suggesting that they do not want to be part of mainstream America culturally or socially. As a result of bad values and practices, undeservingness has become a major cause of contemporary poverty. If poor people gave up these values, their poverty would decline automatically, and mainstream Americans would be ready to help them, as they help other, "deserving" poor people.
- The men among the undeserving poor are lazy or unable to learn the cultural importance of work and its requirements; in some cases, their bad values turn them into street criminals. If they really wanted to work, jobs would be available for them, and they would be able to earn their own income like other Americans.
- The women among the undeserving poor have an unhealthy and immoral taste for early sexual activity and for having babies as adolescents. If they would wait until they were older, sufficiently mature, and ready to find work as well as husbands who wanted to work, they and their children would not need to be poor, and poverty might even end with the current generation.
- If the deserving poor do not alter their values and practices voluntarily, they must be forced to do so, for example, by ending welfare payments, placing illegitimate children in foster care or orphanages, and other forms of punishment.

The deserved forms of punishment include criminal sanctions such as imprisonment. Of course, as you saw in Chapter Three, criminal sanctions are specified by the criminal law, which is not made by or informed by poor people.

This is particularly true given that the umbrella label of underclass encompasses other labels such as criminal. I illustrate this in Figure 12.1. This visual is meant to depict that our war against the poor encompasses many forms, the most significant of which may be our war against crime. As you saw in Chapter Eleven, the war on drugs is a major component of our war on crime. These wars on the poor, the criminal, and those involved in the drug trade lead to massive increases in

Government Policies

The War on Crime

The War on Drugs

Incarceration

FIGURE 12.1
The Wars on Crime, Drugs, and the Poor

incarceration, in addition to scores of other destructive outcomes for the underclass. Americans seem to be unconcerned with these outcomes, perhaps because they perceive criminal justice as something that affects only "them"—the poor.

The American view of the poor suggests that they are different from the rest of us. This is similar to the conception of criminals versus noncriminals: They deserve what they get, including punishment, for their wrongdoings. The American notion of "just deserts" or vengeance for punishment is rooted in the assumption that criminals choose to commit crimes and, therefore, deserve whatever punishment they get (see Chapter Eight). When criminals are poor, our view of the poor is reinforced: "See, they are so lazy and immoral they would rather commit crimes than work!" Given that most people who are processed through the criminal justice network are poor, crime is seen as a problem of the poor. Both "underclass" and "criminality" are seen as deserved labels, oftentimes applied to the same people.

This is not to say that only the poor are "bad apples"; in fact, bad apples exist at all levels. As noted by Gans (1995, p. 4), "As one moves up the socioeconomic ladder, however, the bad apples and their questionable behavior become less visible." In Chapter Four, you saw that the crimes considered serious by the federal government are those that are committed primarily by the poor; in Chapter Five you saw that these are the same acts covered disproportionately in the media. As a result, these are the most visible crimes to Americans, meaning that we fear them the most and support measures that deal with these acts through any and all means possible. Not surprisingly, police, courts, and corrections are most focused on these acts.

As noted in Figure 12.1, one means of dealing with these people is through incarceration, often even for relatively minor offenses (see Chapter Nine). This raises the question, Does incarceration serve the function of population control, as suggested in Chapter Two? Gans (1995) writes, "In an economy in which there may no longer be enough decent jobs for all who want to work, the people who are labeled as undeserving can be forced out of the economy so as to preserve the jobs of the deserving citizens" (p. 8). If the underclass cannot find decent work, they may commit property and drug crimes for income. In these cases, the corresponding views of the poor as undeserving of government assistance and the criminal as deserving of punishment make criminal justice intervention certain.

But is all of this intended? As noted in Chapter Two, not necessarily. Functions of a war against the poor or the criminal may not be intended. Rather, they may be so beneficial to those in positions of power that there may exist little incentive to change the way things are so that the criminal justice network does not serve functions detrimental to a small segment of U.S. society or the United States as a whole. Gans outlines the functions served by the war on the poor. In the following box, I apply these same functions to the war on crime.

Functions served by the war on crime

- *Reducing risk:* If we can identify those who are dangerous and deserving of intervention, we can minimize the likelihood that we will have contact with them. In particular, if we lock them up in prison, we do not even have to think about them.
- *Supplying objects of revenge and repulsion:* By identifying them as wrongdoers, we gain the right to punish them, even in a system of justice

in which victims play little role in the criminal justice process. In essence, victims regain the right to be involved in the punishment of the guilty, even if their involvement is limited to an emotional one.

- *Creating jobs for the better-off population:* The behaviors of the lower class must be modified so that they will act in socially approved ways. This means that they must be policed and processed through the system. In Chapter Two, you saw how many jobs are provided by the existence of crime.

- *Staffing the reserve army of labor:* In the case of criminal justice, the government obtains a means of very cheap labor in offenders who work when they are locked away from society.

- *Forcing the poor out of the labor force:* What better way to lower the unemployment rate than to take a large portion of the unemployable off of the streets?

- *Value reinforcement:* How would we know what was wrong if people didn't show us by pushing the limits of acceptable behavior? Crime serves the function of demonstrating what is not acceptable behavior.

- *Legitimating values:* The same laws that determine what is illegal also define what is law-abiding. Numerous forms of harmful behaviors either are not considered criminal or are against the law but are not considered serious (see Chapter Four). This undeniably serves the interests of dangerous upper-class citizens and corporations.

- *Creating popular cultural villains:* The poor as undeserving and criminals in general are depicted as the enemy in the wars against the poor and against crime. Those who fight these wars are seen as important and even heroic.

- *Scapegoating institutions:* Focusing on the shortcomings of certain groups in society all but guarantees that no attention will be paid to the real problems of poverty and criminality, which are more complex in nature than depicted.

- *Reproducing stigma and the stigmatized:* As we fight our wars against poverty and crime, we virtually guarantee that we will continue to see an enemy to target. In the current era of U.S. crime control and drug reduction policies, for example, more resources have gone toward reactive law enforcement and corrections approaches than to preventive approaches, thereby ensuring failure and guaranteeing that a future segment of the population will commit crime and use drugs.

- *Shifting power to conservatives:* By focusing on crime and poverty through a law-and-order approach, conservative crime control economic campaigns can be launched and strengthened by public support. The result is a shift to a crime control model of justice and a diminishing of due process rights for all Americans.

To the degree that these functions are actually served by U.S. criminal justice processes, the criminal justice network is failing to do justice. How can it be, in the "land of the free and the home of the brave," that our criminal justice processes are biased against those who are least able to protect themselves? To understand this, it is important to recall an important lesson from Chapter Two.

Recall that politics is about who gets what economic benefits in society, when they get them, and how they get them (Lasswell 1936), and is concerned with deciding who gets to keep most of the income generated in the United States, and how that income will be used (Harrigan 2000). Similarly, Parenti (1983, p. 4) defines politics as

> the process of struggle over conflicting interests carried out in the public arena; it may also involve the process of muting and suppressing conflicting interests. Politics involves activation and mediation of conflict, the setting of public priorities, and goals and the denials of others . . . the bulk of public policy is concerned with economic matters.

Since the 1980s, the effects of politics on poor people and on U.S. crime control policy have been particularly startling. Harrigan (2000) demonstrates how the past 20 years have produced higher incomes for the top 40% of wage earners in the United States, while the bottom 60% actually earn a smaller share of the total national income today. Since 1974, the wealthy have captured more of the national income, while the rest of us have received less. In fact, the top 1% of the wealthy now own an astounding 40% of the nation's wealth. According to a study cited in *U.S. News & World Report* (2000), since 1970, the average living space has doubled to more than 800 square feet per person, over 60% of households own two or more automobiles, and air travel has increased by over 400%. These averages are skewed by those at the top of the economic ladder. The result is *income inequality*, whereby the top 20% of the population gets 83% of the national income and the other 80% gets 17% of the income (Kuttner 2003). The top 1% of the population owns 47% of all assets, and the bottom 90% owns only 20% of the assets. Now the ratio of top 5% of wage earners to bottom 20% of wage earners is nearly 20:1, the largest gap in the United States' recorded history. In fact, in 1997, the average income of the top 1% of households was $644,300, versus $8,700 for the lowest 20% of the population and $33,200 for the middle 20% of the population (Phillips 2003). What is most troubling about these figures is that the average income of the bottom and middle 20% of households has remain unchanged since 1979, while the average income of the top 1% has grown 150%.

Alan Greenspan, the Federal Reserve Board chairman, claims that this type of income inequality could pose a "major threat to national security" (*U.S. News & World Report* 2000). As the nation's poor are more and more likely to live together in conditions of "social isolation" (as discussed by Wilson 1987), they are more likely to be aware of their oppression and logically be less happy about it. They are also disproportionately exposed to increased rates of depression and other forms of mental illnesses, asthma, heart disease, and cancer, as well as joblessness, family disruption, and community instability (Pearson 2000). The nation's poorest are minorities, who also are exposed to more pollution and toxic waste, what Maher (2000, p. 147) calls *environmental racism* (also see Boer, Pastor, and Sadd 1997). Krahn, Hartnagel, and Gartrell (1986) suggest that countries with higher levels of inequality also have higher rates of murder (also see Land, McCall, and Cohen 1990; Messner and Tardiff 1986; Sampson 1987). This is one source of the incredibly high U.S. murder rate.

In general, people living in conditions of extreme and concentrated poverty are exposed to more violence. In fact, about half of all murders in the United States occur in large cities that are inhabited by less than one-fifth of the population. Within cities, rates of homicide are 20 times the national average in areas where poverty is highly concentrated (Sherman et al. 1997). Politicians are either unaware of these concentrated criminal victimizations or unable to understand their implications. Because of their lack of action, politicians appear unconcerned and unwilling to prevent them. This is one indication that the criminal justice network fails to reduce crime and do justice adequately.

One possible source of income inequality is corporate downsizing. Ranney (1999) illustrates how efforts such as downsizing aimed at cheapening labor have had the most devastating effects on those with the least political power. For example, in part because of downsizing, income distribution has shifted in favor of corporate chief executive officers (CEOs). In 1974, the average CEO of the 200 largest U.S. companies earned 35 times as much as their average worker; by 1990, the average CEO earned 150 times as much (R. Frank 1994). According to Mokhiber and Weissman (1999, p. 167), CEO salaries average $5.8 million. Their pay rose 54% between 1995 and 1996 and has increased almost 500% since 1980. Meanwhile, the average hourly earnings for working people have dropped since 1980, from $12.70 in 1980 (in 1996 dollars) to $11.81 in 1996. Corporations claim that downsizing is good for business because it allows them to maximize profits (which is good for the U.S. economy). Of course, it is not usually good for the downsized employee.

Levy (1988) documents the upward shift of income and suggests that the middle class is falling behind the well-off and that the poor are falling even farther behind. This supports at least part of Reiman's (1998) contention that "the rich get richer . . ." as discussed in Chapter Two. Harrigan (2000, p. 215) explains growing income inequality as a function of tax policies passed by Congress that benefit the wealthy, along with cuts in domestic programs that traditionally have benefited poorer people. Taxation has also shifted from corporations to individual citizens. In the 1940s, for example, corporations paid one-third of all taxes; today they pay only about 15%. D. Simon and Hagan (1999) illustrate that each year about 90,000 U.S. corporations pay no taxes! At the same time, the poorest of the poor have been left "surrounded by other poor people . . . physically removed from the suburban areas of dynamic job growth, and . . . out of personal contact for the most part with middle-class America." Hence, they "lack the skills, knowledge, and behavioral habits with which to improve their situations" (Harrigan 2000, p. 16). Yes, the poor are getting poorer and thus are more likely to end up in prison, supporting the other part of Reiman's argument.

In her book *Pigs at the Trough*, Arriana Huffington (2003) demonstrates how wealthy CEOs of corporations now indicted for widespread fraud and abuse made out like bandits while their employees lost unimaginable amounts of money. For example, she reports that the "CEOs of 23 large companies under investigation by the SEC and other agencies" (such as WorldCom and Enron) earned $1.4 billion between 1999 and 2001. Yet, since January 2001 "the market value of these 23 companies nosedived by over $500 billion, or roughly 73%, and they have laid off over 160,000 employees."

Harrigan (2000), in his book *Empty Dreams, Empty Pockets: Class and Bias in American Politics*, analyzes American political institutions and argues that the "main institutions of politics today have a significant bias against the economic interests of lower-status people" (p. xii). Harrigan argues that "American government and politics are not neutral. When government acts, or does not act, some groups of people get most of the benefits, while other groups get most of the costs" (p. 1). Although there are more jobs for the poor and the middle class, especially in the low-paying service sector, "there are still millions of people without health insurance, without secure jobs, and just as economically desperate today as they were at the beginning of the decade before the boom began" (p. xiii). At the same time, the move toward conservative politics and greater crime control efforts has diluted the influence of the nonwealthy. Is any of this consistent with the United States' supposed devotion to justice?

Political and criminal justice policy and practice can be biased and thus unjust both by what they do and by what they do not do. Currently, there are more than 40 million Americans without health insurance (U.S. Census 1998), meaning that at least 15% of Americans are not insured. The burden falls, not surprisingly, on the poor and people of color. Harrigan (2000) illustrates, for example, that one-third of families who earned more than twice the poverty level in 1991 had no medical insurance, whereas only 6% of those with incomes four times the poverty level lacked health insurance. Because the poor are disproportionately African American and Hispanic, it is not surprising to see that they also suffer from high rates of noncoverage. Simultaneously, politicians enjoy excellent health care benefits. And efforts to guarantee all Americans high-quality, affordable health care, spearheaded in the early 1990s by President Clinton and First Lady Hillary Clinton, were defeated after the health care industry lobbied Congress to vote against it and created the illusion through advertising that a national health care plan would not allow citizens to choose their own doctors. In other words, the efforts were defeated by politics (Hagan 1998). It is ironic that government policies that harm the poor and people of color simultaneously make it more likely that these groups will live in conditions conducive to criminal activity and thus in need of intervention by the criminal justice network.

IS THE CRIMINAL JUSTICE NETWORK BIASED AGAINST PEOPLE OF COLOR?

With all this focus on the poor, what is the role of race and ethnicity in criminal justice processes? Numerous scholars claim that the criminal justice network is in essence racist because of its built-in biases against people of color (Mann 1993). Consistent with this view is the claim by Gans (1995, p. 16) that "although most labels for the poor are literally neutral with respect to ethnicity and race, they have actually been meant mainly for immigrants and dark-skinned people in the United States." Figure 12.2 illustrates one's relative risk, based on race and class, of becoming involved in the criminal justice network.

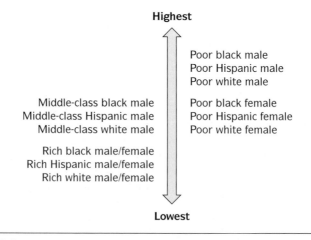

FIGURE 12.2

Risk of Criminal Justice Involvement, by Demographic Characteristics

- **Systematic:** Discrimination at all stages of the criminal justice network, at all times, and in all places
- **Institutionalized:** Racial and ethnic disparities in outcomes that are the result of the application of racially neutral factors such as prior criminal record, employment status, and demeanor
- **Contextual:** Discrimination found in particular contexts or circumstances
- **Individual:** Discrimination that results from the acts of particular individuals but is not characteristic of entire agencies or the criminal justice network as a whole
- **Pure justice:** No racial or ethnic discrimination at all

FIGURE 12.3
Degrees of Discrimination
SOURCE: Walker, Spohn, and Delone (2000).

As you can see, poor people and people of color are at the greatest risk for criminal justice involvement. The highest risk is for poor men of color. The criminal justice system disproportionately arrests, convicts, and punishes poor people and people of color. But does this mean that the criminal justice network is biased against these groups?

Walker, Spohn, and Delone (2000), in their book *The Color of Justice*, conclude that American criminal justice is characterized by what they refer to as *contextual discrimination*, defined in Figure 12.3. These authors write:

> We believe that the criminal justice system is characterized by obvious disparities based on race and ethnicity. It is impossible to ignore the disproportionate number of minorities arrested, imprisoned, and on death row. Some of the decisions that produce these results involve discrimination. . . . After considering all of the evidence, we conclude that the U.S. criminal justice system is characterized by *contextual discrimination*. (p. 287; emphasis in original)

Contextual discrimination implies that there is discrimination based on race and/or ethnicity at some places and at some times in certain circumstances in the United States. Walker, Spohn, and Delone (2000) explain that contextual discrimination is different from *systematic discrimination*, which they define as "discrimination at all stages of the criminal justice system, at all times, and all places," or *institutional discrimination*, defined as "racial and ethnic disparities in outcomes that are the result of the application of racially neutral factors such as prior criminal record, employment status, demeanor, etc." (p. 16). Note that the presence of contextual discrimination suggests that the problem is more complicated than discrimination resulting from behaviors of particular individuals and that pure justice does not exist in the United States. The authors argue that the "salience of race and ethnicity varies from jurisdiction to jurisdiction" in part because "the major racial and ethnic minority groups are not evenly distributed across the country" (p. 14). The important point for this book is that since race and ethnicity play some role in the criminal justice process across the United States, the criminal justice network by definition is failing to achieve its ideal goal of doing justice (which assumes that race and ethnicity play no role).

The racial disparities in American criminal justice are stunning. As you saw in Chapter Nine, black males between 20 and 39 years of age made up 34% of all state and federal prison inmates at the end of 2001. The war on crime is clearly having its greatest effects on young African American males. At mid-year 2002, 12.9% of all African American males between 25 and 29 years of age were in prison, versus only 4.3% of young Hispanic males and 1.6% of young Caucasian males, making young African American males seven times more likely than young Caucasian males and two times more likely than young Hispanic males to be in prison. At mid-year 2002, 12% of African American males in their 20s and 30s were in prison or jail, compared with 4% of Hispanic males in this age group and only 1.3% of Caucasian males. At mid-year 2002, African American males in their 20s and 30s made up an astounding 596,400 of all 2,021,223 inmates in the United States, or nearly 30% of all people locked up in America.

The U.S. network of justice agencies consistently catches, punishes, and convicts people who are both poor and of color, so it is difficult to establish whether social class or race and ethnicity are driving criminal justice activity (Weitzer 1996). Walker, Spohn, and Delone (2000, p. 60) claim that both "[r]ace discrimination and social and economic inequality have a direct impact on crime and criminal justice, accounting for many of the racial disparities in the criminal justice system."

Walker et al. also attribute some racial and ethnic disparities to legal factors such as offense seriousness and offender's prior record. This implies that African Americans and Hispanics commit more than their share of criminality. This issue is discussed in the following box.

Race and criminality according to sources of crime data

Some believe that the notion of a racist criminal justice network is a myth (Wilbanks 1987) and/or that skin color is declining in importance when it comes to criminal justice activity (DeLisi and Regoli 1999). For example, some claim that the criminal justice network is not focused on race, ethnicity, or class but that it processes the poor and people of color disproportionately because of their higher levels of involvement in criminality (DeLisi and Regoli 1999; Wilbanks 1987). The data suggest differently.

As discussed in Chapter Four, sources of crime data include the Uniform Crime Reports (UCR), the National Criminal Victimization Survey (NCVS), and self-report studies. Remember that the UCR is a measure of crimes known to the police, crimes cleared by arrests, and arrests. UCR data do not contain detailed information about ethnicity and crime and "therefore do not tell us anything about rates of offending" (Walker, Spohn, and Delone 2000, p. 13).

Official rates of offending based on the UCR are in fact higher in poor, minority communities and for African Americans generally (R. Kennedy 1997; Tonry 1995). Yet relying on the UCR and other such official statistics for discovering offender characteristics is flawed and can create misconceptions about who is dangerous and who should be feared.

J. Miller (1997, p. 29) writes, "Relying on 'experience' emanating from the justice system is dicey even in the best of circumstances. Its rituals and procedures distort social realities and feed stereotypes at virtually every step." The UCR is a more valid measure of police experience than of crime because it measures the behavior of police rather than that of criminal offenders; therefore, it is not surprising that over 40% of every 100 individuals who are arrested for felonies are never prosecuted or have their cases dismissed at first appearance (J. Miller, 1997).

UCR arrest statistics tend to create myths about who is dangerous and who is guilty. If we relied on arrest statistics to develop composites of "dangerous classes," we would not get an accurate picture of those who threaten us most (see Chapter Six for a lengthier discussion of arrest rates and their meaning). Walker, Spohn, and Delone (2000, p. 37) comment: "The picture of the typical offender that emerges from official arrest statistics may be racially distorted. If police target enforcement efforts in minority communities or concentrate on crime committed by racial minorities, then obviously racial minorities will be overrepresented in arrest statistics."

Russell (1998, p. 114) calls the stereotypical criminal in the United States the *criminal-blackman*. Consider the following quote from the Reverend Jesse Jackson, a long-time civil rights activist who also happens to be an African American: "There is nothing more painful for me at this stage in my life than to walk down the street and hear footsteps and start to think about robbery and then to look around and see if it's somebody white and feel relieved" (R. Kennedy 1997, p. 15). The truth is, people fear African Americans and other minorities and perceive them to pose significant threats to their personal safety (e.g., see Hurwitz and Peffley 1997; Miethe 1995; Peffley and Hurwitz 1997; Skogan 1995; St. John and Heald-Moore 1996).

"Blackness," in particular, is treated as a sign of increased risk of criminality (R. Kennedy 1997, p. 387). As illustrated by the Jesse Jackson example, this is a normal phenomenon, which results not from individual racism or bias but, rather, from deep-seated myths about race and crime that are created and reinforced by official sources of crime data such as the UCR, as well as media portrayals of crime and criminal justice.

Recall that the NCVS is a measure of self-reported victimizations, including both crimes reported to the police and those not reported to the police. The NCVS, generally thought to be a more valid measure of criminal behavior than the UCR, shows that households headed by African Americans and Hispanics have higher rates of victimization than Caucasian households. Also, African Americans and Hispanics are more likely than Caucasians to suffer personal criminal victimization. Finally, one's lifetime risk of being victimized by certain violent street crimes is highly correlated with one's race.

According to the Bureau of Justice Statistics, in 2002 African Americans were more likely to be victimized by violent crime (28 victimizations per 1,000 people) than Caucasians (23 victimizations per 1,000 people) and Hispanics (15 victimizations per 1,000 people). In 2001, according to the UCR, Caucasians accounted for 49% of homicides, versus 47% for African Americans. For African American males, the risk of homicide is about eight times the risk for Caucasian males. For young males, the risk is about 10 times higher for African Americans than for Caucasians. African American males, who make up only 6% of the population, account for about 18% of the nation's homicide victims (Walker, Spohn, and Delone 2000, p. 33). Because most street crimes are intraracial in nature, logic would dictate that African American and Hispanic people are disproportionately committing street crimes against their own households and persons. Yet, according to the Bureau of Justice Statistics (2003), higher victimization rates are partially a function of social class, also, because household victimization rates are highest in inner cities.

For the purpose of this examination, I assume that people of color commit more street crime (but not more crime generally) than one would logically expect given their proportion of the population. For example, the NCVS also shows that victims report a higher percentage of victimizations at the hands of African Americans than one would expect given their percentage of the population (R. Kennedy 1997, p. 23): "African Americans are overrepresented as offenders for all of the offenses" of the NCVS (Walker, Spohn, and Delone 2000, p. 42). Assuming that NCVS data are valid in this regard is questionable, because NCVS researchers must rely on victims' perceptions of their offenders. Whatever the case, the real question for the issue of whether disparities in the criminal justice network stem from higher involvement in criminality by minorities is whether the very small differences in offending suggested by the NCVS can account for the observed disparities in official arrest, conviction, and incarceration statistics. Virtually no one thinks that they can (e.g., see Akers 1996).

Why are African American males more likely to be incarcerated for crimes than other groups? According to the NCVS, the proportion of violent street crimes committed by African American males has remained steady since the 1980s, yet the disproportionate use of imprisonment has worsened since then (Tonry 1995, p. 4). Steffensmeir, Ulmer, and Kramer (1998, p. 789) call this the "high cost of being black, young, and male." Spohn and Hollerman (2000, p. 281) suggest that convicted criminals who happen to be young, male, and African American will pay an added "incarceration penalty" on top of the sentence given to other groups in America.

In support of the notion that observed disparities in official arrest, conviction, and incarceration statistics cannot be explained by differences in offending behaviors, Reiman (1998, p. 103) compares criminal victimization statistics of the NCVS and arrest statistics of the UCR. He concludes that "police are arresting blacks from 30 to 50 percent more frequently than the occurrence of their perceived criminality. Because arrest determines the pool from which charged, convicted, and imprisoned individuals are selected, this suggests that deep bias persists throughout the criminal justice system." This is why Kappeler, Blumberg, and Potter (2000, p. 223) write, "Comparisons of UCR and NCVS statistics offer clear evidence of racism." A similar conclusion is reached by Walker, Spohn, and Delone (2000, p. 42): "African Americans are represented in arrest figures in much higher proportions than the perception of offenders from victim interviews suggest."

Tonry (1995) argues that African American males are more involved in crimes that are punishable by imprisonment. To prove this, Tonry examines various sources of data (UCR arrest data, NCVS victim identification records, self-report studies) and concludes that arrests by police and sentences by prosecutors are not discriminatory or biased. For example, Tonry shows that crime victims are only slightly less likely to identify African Americans as their assailants in robbery and aggravated assault cases than one might expect given trends in black arrests for these crimes.

Unfortunately for Tonry's argument, he does not even address the question of whether the law is biased. If the law has disproportionately criminalized what poor people do and if African Americans tend to be poor, then the law is where one needs to look to see bias against African Americans. An example is seen in the case of robbery, a crime committed by the poor. NCVS data show that African Americans are perceived to be offenders in about half of robberies but in no more than 30% of any other violent offense. According to UCR data African Americans make up about 54% of people arrested for robbery crimes (Sourcebook of Criminal Justice Statistics 2003). Both data sets suggest that African Americans are disproportionately involved in robberies. Given that monetary gain is the primary motive for robbery, it is not a stretch to conclude that it is the offenders' social class that explains their involvement in the crime of robbery. Rich people do not have to stick a gun in your face to get your money, nor do they have to rob a bank to steal money from it. Instead, they can and do steal money through fraud and embezzlement, as in the case of the savings and loan (S&L) scandals, which produced more financial losses than all the bank robberies in the history of the United States. Yet such crimes have not been treated as "serious" throughout our country's history. Even now, when fraud and embezzlement are treated roughly as seriously as theft, law enforcement resources are not adequate to fight fraud and embezzlement. In fact, most American police officers, who work for city and county governments, are not involved in investigating and apprehending acts of white-collar deviance (see Chapter Six). Instead, they are on the streets, fighting the types of thefts committed primarily by the poor, such as robbery.

You might argue that robbery is more serious than similar acts of white-collar deviance because, technically, it is violent in nature (that is, it implies that some force or weapon was used to achieve the theft). But robbery is clearly aimed at property gain, just like fraud and embezzlement. The primary difference is that rich people do not have to resort to robbery to acquire wealth illegally—they have the luxury of illegitimate opportunities to engage in other, less risky forms of theft.

So, although Tonry (1995) suggests that African Americans actually commit proportionally more felonies than Caucasians, he does acknowledge a potential bias when he writes, "Whatever their race, most felony defendants are poor, badly educated, un- or underemployed, and not part of a stable household" (p. 101). These are America's enemies in the war on crime.

Self-report studies provide some unique insight into criminal behavior by assessing the degree to which respondents admit to engaging in criminal behaviors. Self-report studies question the disparities found in official criminal justice statistics such as the UCR (e.g., see Pope 1979). Whereas the UCR may suggest that African Americans commit a disproportionate amount of crime because they are more likely to get arrested by the police, self-report studies do not show such patterns. Instead, self-report studies show that rates of offending in middle-class minority communities are equivalent to those in the general population. Earlier self-report studies showed little or no differences in self-reported delinquent and criminal behavior between different groups.

Unlike early studies, which typically assessed minor acts of delinquency, more recent studies assess more serious criminal behaviors. According to Tittle and Meier (1990) studies assessing relationships between social class and crime show "mixed results"; according to Akers (1996, p. 127), "Self-report studies find class and race variations in criminal and delinquent behavior, but they are not as great as class and race differences in officially arrested, convicted, and/or imprisoned populations." So, when unemployed citizens are disproportionately found in incarcerated populations (Chiricos and Bales 1991), it is not likely due to their increased involvement with criminal behavior, nor can the overrepresentation of African Americans in the criminal justice network be explained by their higher involvement in criminal behavior. There is some evidence that African Americans tend to underreport their involvement in criminality (e.g., see Hindelang, Hirschi, and Weis 1981; O'Brien 1993), but no one knows for sure whether this is true.

It should also be reiterated that self-report studies typically assess involvement in street crimes. If studies examined racial, ethnic, and class differences in people who commit other harmful acts (including legal acts), huge differences would be found—the vast majority of offenders would not be African American, Hispanic, or poor. This fact seems to escape those who argue that people of color commit "more crime." The people we end up viewing as criminals depends on what is called crime, and that is a function of who makes the law. As pointed out in Chapter Three, "criminal" is a label generally reserved for people who look very different from lawmakers and voters.

Even if legal factors explain some racial and ethnic disparities in the criminal justice network, some disparities are explained by extralegal factors based on race, ethnicity, social class, and so forth. In other words, even if it were true that people of color committed disproportionately more crime than we might expect given their percentage in the population, their proportion of arrests, convictions, and correctional populations cannot be explained by their criminality alone. So, what then explains the overrepresentation of minorities in America's criminal justice network? A careful analysis of statistics relating to race, ethnicity, and social class and their relationships with crime and criminal justice may lead to some answers.

Race, Ethnicity, and Social Class

There is an intimate relationship among race, ethnicity, and social class in the United States. Specifically, racial and ethnic minorities are disproportionately likely to be poor and to be exposed to harmful environmental conditions. For example, in American slums, where there is far greater despair and deterioration than in the suburbs and rural areas, nearly seven of every eight people are minorities (Beckett and Sasson 2000, p. 37). Walker, Spohn, and Delone (2000, pp. 62–65) explain the differences in social class standing between racial and ethnic groups on the basis of income, wealth, employment, and poverty rates. *Income*—how much money a family earns in a year—for African Americans ($29,470) and Hispanics ($33,565) is lower than for Caucasians ($46,305) (U.S. Census 2003). *Wealth*—a measure of all assets accumulated—is nearly 11 times lower for African Americans than for Caucasians and about 8 times lower for Hispanics. Meanwhile, the *unemployment* rate is more than twice as high for African Americans and almost twice as high for Hispanics than for Caucasians. *Poverty* rates are also higher for African Americans (22.7%) and Hispanics (21.4%) than for Caucasians (9.9%). Finally, child poverty rates are more than two times higher for African Americans and Hispanics than for Caucasians.

Others discuss the role of *underemployment*, which is also higher for people of color than for Caucasians (Bluestone and Rose 2000). The so-called *poverty wage* (Jennings 1999, p. 25) is a major source of poverty. Earning a minimal amount of money for a full-time job leaves people poor and is thus a form of "inclusive exclusion"; that is, these workers are included in the workforce but excluded from enjoying the benefits of full-time, well-paying jobs (George 1999, p. 202). According to Kim (1999, p. 307), "the working poor constitute one of the fastest growing segments of the impoverished population." These "forgotten Americans" cannot make more money, cannot work more hours, and hence are still poor because of factors beyond their own control (Quan 2000).

Ehrenreich (2001), in her book *Nickel and Dimed*, clearly demonstrates how difficult it is to make it in the working world of American's service economy for many people. In 1998, Ehrenreich moved across three states, working as a waitress, a maid, a cleaning woman, an aide at a nursing home, and a sales clerk for Wal-Mart. She shows that it is impossible to have a residence earning only $6 to $7 per hour and that service-type jobs are not highly valued or rewarding jobs in our society. Yet these are the jobs that have grown the fastest in our economy.

Disparities in employment are greatest for young, male minorities, that segment of the population most likely to have encounters with the police (see Chapter Six). Regular wages are also lower for minorities and women than for Caucasians and men (Weinberger 2000). Why do people of color have lower average household incomes and lower levels of net worth than Caucasians (Beckett and Sasson 2000, p. 34)? There are two competing explanations. According to R. Smith (1995, p. 107), *cultural perspectives* "emphasize the values, beliefs, attitudes, and lifestyles" of the poor, whereas *structural perspectives* "emphasize enduring features of the economic and social systems." The cultural view "sees" the problem as coming from within the poor people themselves; the structural view "sees" the problem as originating outside the poor people. Murray and Herrnstein (1994), supporters of the cultural perspective, posit that the United States will be "dumbed down" as a result of illegitimate children being born to those with lower IQs.

Even if there is a culture unique to people of color or the poor, it may emerge from the U.S. capitalist economy. Such is the claim of Marxist and conflict criminologists, who hold that crime is a reaction by those at the bottom of the capitalist economy to oppression and domination (e.g., see Greenberg 1993; Lynch 1997). Unemployment is a key factor in accounting for this culture or way of life, and it has always been higher for African Americans and Hispanics than for Caucasians. Unemployment is associated with murder, suicide, mental illness, divorce, separation, child abuse, and drug abuse (R. Smith 1995, pp. 131–32).

The cultural explanation of poverty ignores poverty's structural correlates. Kushnick and Jennings (1999, p. 1) explain that poverty is produced by structural factors such as the "increasing imbalance in the distribution of wealth, with the rich continually becoming richer; the unbridled mobility of capital, both in finance and in production; and the prevalence of low wages coupled with levels of relatively high unemployment of certain groups." When "national policies . . . allow corporate leaders to pursue profits without consideration of the social costs incurred by their strategies," things only get worse.

Poverty is usually framed in politics as a "lack of work ethic" or a "failure of personal responsibility" among poor people. The media then "racialize" poverty by depicting poverty as a "minority thing," which then diverts attention from the real problems associated with the U.S. economic system. The role of the wealthy and the state in creating and reinforcing inequality is thus virtually ignored (Dill, Zinn, and Patton 1999, p. 263). Given the corporate ownership of the media (see Chapter Five), this is not surprising. One example is that African American criminals are depicted as "thoughtless, sadistic, and callous" individuals who commit random crimes (Franklin 1999, p. 128). Additionally, in the 1990s, the media "saturated the public with stories and pictures about African American teenager birth rates, African American illegitimate birth rates, and African American female AIDS rates" (Franklin 1999, p. 130, citing J. Jackson 1988). Typically, these images and stories feature members of the poor "African American underclass," who represent less than 1% of the population and who live in the nation's largest urban areas.

The media also "socialize the entire population, mainstream and minority, young and old, by the way they depict and discuss minorities" (Chaffee and German 1998, p. 311; also see Reed 1993). "The kind of coverage, positive or negative, may also impact the nature of treatment, beneficial or negative, accorded to minorities in the political system" (Chaffee and German 1998, p. 312). Overall, positive views of minorities are lacking in media portrayals, and African Americans receive most minority-related news coverage.

American politicians go on to depict poor individuals as being born with a unique "ethos" that reflects immorality, a lack of hard work, and low levels of intelligence (Banfield 1973), as well as being psychologically and programmatically dependent (Murray 1984). Since the 1980s, politicians have talked about a "lack of family values" as responsible for the "significant decline in living standards for African Americans" in the 1980s (George 1999, p. 198). High unemployment rates are thus blamed on lazy people.

Katz (1999, p. 63) argues that one reason that African Americans in particular experience such tremendous poverty is that they historically have lacked an ethnic niche in employment: "Every time African Americans gained a modest presence in a promising trade, discrimination undercut their efforts, and whites replaced them." *Strain theory* predicts that African Americans thus have been forced either into *retreatism* (unemployment and drug use) or into *innovation* (selling African American market goods, including drugs). Innovation involving illegitimate activity is a means to overcome strain (Merton 1938b) and *differential opportunity* (Cloward and Ohlin 1961). When African Americans turn to illegal activity to tilt the scales back in their favor, they become more likely to have run-ins with the law.

Another option for the poor is to seek government assistance in the form of welfare. Although the U.S. government has been willing to assist its own poor to varying degrees throughout its history, antipoverty programs have become anti–poor people efforts since the early 1970s. People who are in trouble are characterized as "people who make trouble" (Beckett and Sasson 2000, p. 155). Recently, the U.S. government passed laws that limit the total time a person can be on welfare over the course of his or her life to 5 years. This attack on welfare rights during the 1980s and 1990s "has served the interests of corporate capital and its political and media allies" (Kushnick 1999, p. 147). As the attack against the poor was stepped up, the code words for welfare dependency became "big government," and right-wing political leaders such as Ronald Reagan, Pat Buchanan, and Newt Gingrich began to call for "smaller government." In reality, the majority of Americans did not vote for the Congress that passed this type of reform: "The majority of Americans either voted for candidates who lost or, even more telling, did not bother to vote at all." Nevertheless, some of the harshest social policies we have seen in generations are being carried out in the name of the American people (Ransby 1999, p. 327). Ironically, these same leaders share responsibility for increasing the size and strength of criminal justice agencies in the United States, all of which are funded and operated by the government. That is, these self-styled opponents of big government are responsible for creating big government in the form of the U.S. criminal justice network.

Meanwhile, according to the Children's Defense Fund, in 2000, 11.6 million American children (16.2% of the total) lived in poverty. African American children (30.9%) and Hispanic children (28%) had higher rates of child poverty than Caucasian children (9.4%). Poor children have worse nutrition, are at a heightened risk of stunted growth, receive less education, and will earn lower incomes. Poor children are also disproportionately minorities and living in single-parent households. Obviously, criminal justice officials are not equipped to address these social facts. What is clear is that every dollar invested by the U.S. government in criminal justice is a dollar not invested in social programs that can assist in alleviating childhood poverty rates in the United States.

Even though most poor, single, childbearing women are not African American (Sidel 1996), "family breakdown is often a thinly veiled attack on the African American urban underclass" and "single mother" is often used as a code word to mean "African American single mother" (Dill, Zinn, and Patton 1999, p. 269). Given that 1996 welfare reform law all but eroded the notion that Americans are "entitled" to assistance from their own government, it is easy to imagine how Americans have come to see African Americans as unentitled, even though "they live in one of the richest countries in the world" and most of them have paid taxes to the federal government (Ransby 1999, p. 332).

Meanwhile, corporate perks are growing. Former secretary of labor Robert Reich spoke critically of benefits enjoyed by corporate elites because of government policies (Ransby 1999, p. 324). For example, corporate taxes accounted for about one-third of federal revenues in the 1950s but only about 10% in the 1990s. In essence, taxation became more of a burden on individual Americans and their families, while corporations pay virtually no taxes today. Corporate profits have increased as a result, but this has not stopped companies from downsizing and even moving overseas or south of the border for cheaper labor costs.

According to the Bermuda Project, corporations cheat taxpayers out of $70 billion per year by using overseas tax shelters. Major corporations set up a headquarters (typically a post office box only) overseas (such as in Bermuda) and, therefore, do not have to pay taxes in the United States.

Fortune 500 companies, such as Halliburton, not only have dodged their fair share of taxes, but also have continued to receive government contracts while doing it.

Race, Ethnicity, Government Policy, and Criminal Justice

From the previous review of the relationship among race, ethnicity, and social class, it is apparent that many of the criminal justice biases against minorities in the United States are at least partly attributable to social class. Of course, one's social class standing is affected by many other factors, including race, ethnicity, and historical and contemporary discrimination against people of color.

Walker, Spohn, and Delone (2000, p. 61) note three important facts that implicate economic factors as major sources of criminal justice bias against people of color: an economic gap between the rich and the poor, regardless of race or ethnicity; an economic gap between Caucasian Americans and people of color; and a growing segment of the population that is very poor. In addition to these factors, widespread patterns of residential segregation still exist. Those residents stuck in our nation's inner cities "find it extremely difficult both to learn about job opportunities and to travel to and from work. Public transportation systems are either weak or nonexistent in most cities" (p. 69). Inner-city residents are also less likely to have the necessary contacts to attain jobs. In case you think that anyone who wants to can move away from the inner cities, keep in mind that real estate agents and banking personnel play major roles in maintaining residential segregation by discriminating against poor people and people of color.

Criminologists and sociologists claim that being socially isolated in inner cities leads to an increased risk of criminality because these residents have less contact with good role models and less ability to participate in controlling institutions (Skogan 1990; W. J. Wilson 1987). Increased crime in inner-city neighborhoods lowers the quality of life as well. Thus, many government policies in the United States promote criminality among the nation's poor and people of color.

Simultaneously, race and ethnicity play significant roles in government policy and the criminal justice process. The result is discrimination in numerous government policies and overwhelming disparities throughout the criminal justice network. Mann (1993) calls this *Unequal Justice*. The result for young minority males has been *Lock 'Em Up and Throw Away the Key* (Mauer 1998) because of what some call a *Search and Destroy* mission by the criminal justice network (J. Miller 1998). Although racial disparity does not necessarily imply racial discrimination (Walker, Spohn, and Delone 2000), if the disparity is harmful, the intent is really not important, especially if we know about it but do nothing to stop it (R. Kennedy 1997).

Some studies do not find evidence of racial bias in the criminal justice network. For example, most studies examining sentencing severity find that length of sentence is typically determined by legal factors such as seriousness of offense and prior record (see Chapter Eight). However, if the law is biased, then the seriousness of offense is a function of the bias in the law rather than bias in the courts. An offender's prior record would also be affected by criminal justice factors such as the presence of police in one's neighborhood. This means that discrimination in criminal justice cannot be dismissed even in the face of findings that legal variables account for offenders' sentences. Other studies that do not appear at first glance to show evidence of bias may also show bias on closer examination. For example, as discussed in Chapter Ten, numerous studies of the death penalty process find that prosecutors are actually less likely overall to seek the death penalty against African Americans.

Some may use such studies to show that criminal justice activities are clearly not biased against African Americans. However, as you learned in Chapter Ten, careful analysis shows that the bias is still against African Americans and is most apparent in interracial crimes.

Racism today is less overt—no more fire hoses and police dogs being used to suppress minorities, as was common during the civil rights movement—and is intertwined with legitimate government activity. For example, crime control is a legitimate state goal, yet "law and order" and "tough on crime" are phrases that are used to conjure up images of dangerous people of color. They are thus "code words," words that refer indirectly to minorities but appear not to revolve around racial themes (Omi and Winant 1986). Do not be fooled, however. Punitiveness is partially "a manifestation of hostility toward African Americans" (Beckett and Sasson 2000, p. 135). Is it a coincidence that most American punitiveness is directed at minorities, particularly African Americans? At the very least, because African Americans are disproportionately poor and are socially isolated in poor communities, they become more susceptible to criminal justice focus. In essence, they live where the police are most likely to patrol, making it more likely that they will be arrested and become involved with the criminal justice network.

Most scholars agree that our nation has made great strides to become less biased since the civil rights movement of the 1960s. For example, Walker, Spohn, and Delone (2000) demonstrate that American schools are less segregated today than they were in the 1960s, that more voters and elected officials are minorities, and that minorities are more likely to work in the criminal justice network and serve on juries. These authors write, "The civil rights movement eliminated *de jure* segregation and other blatant forms of discrimination, but pervasive discrimination in society and the criminal justice system continues" (p. 77; emphasis in original). The evidence supports this statement. Changes in the law and in attitudes of individuals within the criminal justice network have made systematic discrimination against African Americans much less likely. Yet even though the civil rights movement led to rapid changes for people of color, economic inequality of racial and ethnic groups has not been widely addressed. The following box discusses how things have improved for African Americans since the civil rights movement.

Race and criminal justice in history

Clearly, the significance of race for criminal justice has declined (e.g., Sakamoto and Tzeng 1999; Thomas 1993). The careful analysis by Walker, Spohn, and Delone (2000) of bias in the American criminal justice process suggests that racism is not as prevalent as it once was. For example, consider these facts:

- Most police in the early American South were charged with catching runaway slaves.
- Until the 1960s, most police departments in the South refused to hire African American officers. Those African American officers who were hired usually were not permitted to arrest Caucasians.
- Northern police departments that hired African Americans would not assign these officers to patrol Caucasian neighborhoods.
- Calls for service by minorities were historically ignored by the police.
- African Americans were not permitted to serve on juries because they were not entitled to vote.

- African Americans were more likely to be arrested, detained in jail until trial, and tried by all-Caucasian juries and were more likely to be convicted and sentenced to more severe sentences than Caucasians.

According to Charles Silberman (1978, pp. 117–18):

> For most of their history in this country . . . African Americans were victims, not initiators, of violence. In the Old South, violence against African Americans was omnipresent—sanctioned by both customs and the law. Whites were free to use any method, up to and including murder, to control 'their Negroes. . . .' There was little African Americans could do to protect themselves. To strike back at whites, or merely to display anger or insufficient deference, was not just to risk one's own neck, but to place the whole community in danger. It was equally dangerous, or at best pointless, to appeal to the law.

You may have heard of recent cases in which people of color have experienced similar victimization, but this is not the norm for most people of color today.

In 1968, the same year that the Reverend Dr. Martin Luther King, Jr., was assassinated, the Kerner Commission (Africanaonline 2003, p. 1) wrote that "our Nation is moving toward two societies, one African American, one white—separate and unequal." Today, the United States is indeed highly segregated. Civil rights have allowed many African Americans to "make it"; yet, many, if not most, African Americans lag behind Caucasians in economic indicators of success and are vastly more likely to have run-ins with the criminal justice system. And although many middle-class African Americans enjoy successes similar to those of members of the Caucasian middle class, things are the worst for the poorest African Americans (Jaynes and Williams 1989; Thernstrom and Thernstrom 1997).

Robert Smith (1995), in *Racism in the Post–Civil Rights Era: Now You See It, Now You Don't*, convincingly argues that institutional racism is alive and well in the United States. Smith (citing Carmichael and Hamilton 1969), defines *institutional racism* as "the predication of decisions and policies on considerations of race for purpose of *subordinating* a racial group and maintaining control over that group" (p. 2; emphasis in original). Smith provides evidence of racism in several American institutions, including employment, education, housing, health, and consumer services. Disparities in such institutions produce injustice in the United States and may explain the greater criminal justice involvement of African Americans. Ironically, we don't see higher rates of street crime in minority neighborhoods as a product of racial and ethnic discrimination, but as indicators that the residents of those neighborhoods are simply different from (and inferior to) us.

Smith (1995) does not claim that institutional racism is necessarily intentional; rather, he suggests that "whenever one observes policies that have the intent or effect of subordinating a racial group, that phenomenon is properly identified as racism" (p. 29). Institutional racism occurs when the "normal, accepted, routine patterns and practices of society's institutions have the *effect or consequence* of subordinating an individual or group . . ." (p. 33; emphasis in original). Because African Americans are disproportionately affected by criminal justice processes, Smith might claim that the U.S. criminal justice network is involved in institutional racism.

Smith does not address this issue directly, although he does briefly mention the war on drugs as an example of racist U.S. policy. Rather, he examines how institutional racism has evolved from individual racism and become entrenched in the contemporary United States. Beckett and Sasson (2000, p. 39) claim that racial segregation of housing, for example, is a product of racial discrimination. Massey and Gross (1990) calls housing discrimination a form of "American apartheid" that undoubtedly leaves African Americans living in ghettos where jobs and legitimate opportunities for success are scarce. Criminological theories such as social disorganization, strain, and social bonding have historically attributed such environmental conditions to increased risks for criminality (Bohm 2001; Vold, Bernard, and Snipes 1998).

When people are not working and may be committing crimes, it becomes easy to characterize them as lazy, inferior, and bad, even though the real villain may be downsizing in corporations and the restructuring of the American workforce from manufacturing to service jobs. The myth of a free economy creates the illusion of equal opportunity for all Americans, which appears to prove that people who do not make it are to blame. Smith documents the historical notion of "black inferiority" among Americans, which has been used to justify both slavery and colonization of other countries. One need only look around to find "official" evidence of African American inferiority—in unemployment rates, relative housing conditions, and educational attainment of various groups and in rates of family dissolution, out-of-wedlock births, alcohol abuse, and crime. The fact that African Americans are disproportionately likely to be unemployed, live in poor housing conditions, lack formal education, be single parents, abuse some drugs, and commit street crime is used as proof of African Americans' inferiority to Caucasians.

Although Caucasians are less likely now to express openly beliefs in African American inferiority, public opinion polls such as the General Social Survey (GSS) still illustrate high levels of negative views of African Americans. Almost half of Americans believe that African Americans tend to be lazy. More than half think that African Americans are violence-prone, and nearly one-third think that African Americans are unintelligent (R. Smith 1995, p. 39).

According to Beckett (1997, p. 84), beliefs about crime and punishment are "highly correlated with race and racial attitudes." For example, those who most strongly believe in a law-and-order approach to crime fighting tend to be more racist and not to support equal rights for minorities. They believe that African Americans are inferior to Caucasians and thus are deserving of punitive sanctions when they violate the law. Further, people who have hostilities toward African Americans are more likely to support the death penalty (see Chapter Ten).

In reality, African Americans cannot be inferior to Caucasians simply because of their skin color or ethnicity, because race is a societal-level variable rather than an individual-level variable. Race cannot be used, for example, as evidence of inborn differences between Americans of African and Americans of European descent in terms of intelligence or will power. Genetic variation is higher within the races than between them (Jeffery 1990). R. Smith (1995) claims that anti–African American stereotypes are worse in the 1990s than in the 1970s. Smith blames this, as well as increased racist violence in the 1980s, on the political dogma generated by Presidents Reagan and Bush (the first), particularly with regard to crime control issues—for example, the use of the Willie Horton incident to make early prison release a campaign issue, as discussed in Chapter Two. Smith writes, "The use by the 1988 Bush campaign of the now infamous Willie Horton ad was an indirect, subtle appeal to this racist stereotype" of the libidinous, dangerous African American male. "For twenty-eight days during the 1988 fall campaign an ad [showed] a picture of Horton, a person very dark in skin color and in a photograph that he himself said pictured him as 'depraved and maniacal' and as the 'devil incarnate' (Horton says at the time the photograph was taken he had not been permitted a shave or haircut for six months or more)" (p. 21).

The fact that Horton was accused of raping a Caucasian woman allowed politicians to tap into deeply held fears that characterize African American males as sexually aggressive and dangerous. In reality, most rapists are Caucasian males, and most people out on temporary prison release do not commit crimes, although these facts are not reflected in public opinion polls (Anderson 1995).

But then, Willie Horton was also poor. Whether the ad campaign was intended to create fear of African Americans or of poor criminals is not entirely clear and perhaps not actually important. As noted, untangling the effects of race and social class is very difficult. As explained by R. Smith (1995, p. 34), "Any policy having an adverse impact on blacks should not be conceptualized as institutionalized racism because of the intersection of race and class in the United States. African Americans in the United States are disproportionately lower class, and in any class-stratified society most institutional arrangements have an adverse impact on the poor and dispossessed whatever their race." So, "much of what may appear to be institutional racism is simply the effects of routine class bias in a market economy" (p. 53).

An example of negative consequences suffered disproportionately by African Americans is poor health, which has "substantially deteriorated" in the post–civil rights era. R. Smith (1995) demonstrates that infant mortality rates are nearly twice as high for African Americans as for Caucasians and that the life expectancy is shorter. He writes: "Much of the data [*sic*] suggest that the vast differentials in African American and white health are to be explained on the basis of social class and public policy; in terms of the latter, primarily because of the absence of a comprehensive national health insurance program" (p. 69).

Nevertheless, Smith believes that class-related disparities in health have likely resulted from hundreds of years of individual racism and the institutions created by racists; thus, he includes them as a form of institutional racism. Figure 12.4 depicts five forms of institutional discrimination facing the poor and racial minorities, as well as the likely outcomes, in the areas of (1) employment, (2) education, (3) housing, (4) health, and (5) consumer services. This results in an increased likelihood of exposure by African Americans to criminogenic conditions such as unemployment, underemployment, lack of formal education, poverty, environmental pollution, and

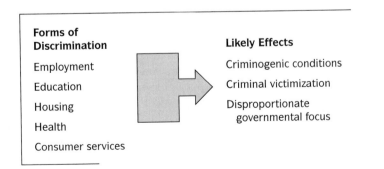

FIGURE 12.4
Forms of Institutional Discrimination

violence. Such conditions lead not only to increased physical and financial harms, but also to lower levels of self-esteem among African Americans living in conditions of severe poverty, expressed through the American polity, church, media, schools, and popular culture.

Smith argues that, because of the negative meanings of the word black—which has been "associated with discouragement, despair, depression, coldness, the unknown, the haunting shadow and nightmare" (C. Anderson and Cromwell 1977, p. 76)—some African Americans see themselves as violent, dependent on government assistance, and, to a lesser degree, lazy and unintelligent. He (R. Smith 1995) writes that "a significant minority of African Americans (ranging from 10 to 25 percent depending on the survey and the question) continue to tell survey researchers that they hold negative images of the race" (p. 95). It is not surprising that the militant "Black Power" movement of the mid- to late 1960s became the focus of criminal justice agencies. In essence, when African Americans began to rise up in an effort to assert their rights and be recognized as good people—reflected in the slogan "Black is beautiful," for example—their actions were criminalized by the dominant Caucasian power structures in Southern criminal justice agencies. If they were not jailed and/or threatened with bodily violence, they were beaten during riots initiated by the police, even though they are no more criminal than other groups in society.

GENDER AND CRIMINAL JUSTICE

Gender bias is also prevalent in the U.S. criminal justice network (Boritch 1992). Gottfredson and Jarjoura (1996, p. 49) state it this way, "Extreme racial (and gender) disproportionalities have existed in America's prison and jail populations for at least 175 years." Gender bias includes decisions that favor or harm individuals on the basis of gender. Overall, criminal justice activities seem to be less punitive toward women. We can call this a bias against men, who are responsible for a much larger portion of street crime and violence in general than women (Jeffery 1990). This may be due to what Belknap (1996, pp. 69–70) calls the *chivalry or paternalism hypothesis*. For example, you saw in Chapter Ten that although women commit more than 10% of all murders in any given year, they make up less than 2% of all people on death row and 1% of all executions.

Generally speaking, women are less likely to be victimized by crime, less likely to commit it, less likely to be arrested, less likely to be convicted, and less likely to be sentenced to prison or jail and generally are sentenced to less time than men. Table 12.1 shows that, in 2001, the rate of criminal victimization was lower for women than men for every crime except sex offenses. The

TABLE 12.1

Rates of Criminal Victimization, by Gender (2001)

	Men	Women
All personal offenses	28.0 per 1,000	23.9 per 1,000
Violent offenses	27.3 per 1,000	23.0 per 1,000
Murder/manslaughter	8.5 per 1,000	2.6 per 1,000
Sexual assault/rape	0.2 per 1,000	1.9 per 1,000
Robbery	3.8 per 1,000	1.7 per 1,000
Assault	23.2 per 1,000	19.4 per 1,000

SOURCE: Sourcebook of Criminal Justice Statistics (2003).

TABLE 12.2
Arrests, by Gender (2001)

	Men	Women
All offenses	77.8%	22.2%
Violent offenses	82.6%	17.4%
Murder/manslaughter	89.4%	10.6%
Forcible rape	98.9%	1.1%
Robbery	89.9%	10.1%
Aggravated assault	79.9%	20.1%
Property offenses	70.1%	29.9%
Forgery/counterfeiting	61%	39%
Fraud	55.1%	44.9%
Embezzlement	50%	50%
Prostitution/commericialized vice	37.9%	62.1%

SOURCE: Sourcebook of Criminal Justice Statistics (2003).

rate of female victimization was lower than the rate of male victimization for all personal crimes (23.9 per 1,000 people versus 28.0 per 1,000 people), for violent crimes (23.0 per 1,000 people versus 27.3 per 1,000 people), for robbery (1.7 per 1,000 people versus 3.8 per 1,000 people), and for assault (19.4 per 1,000 people versus 23.2 per 1,000 people).

Table 12.2 shows the percentage of arrests that were men and women in 2000 for various types of crimes. As you can see, women (who make up 51% of the U.S. population) are underrepresented among arrestees for every category of crime except for prostitution and commericialized vice offenses (62.1%) and embezzlement (50%). Women made up only 22.2% of all arrests in 2000, including 17.4% of violent crimes arrests and 29.9% of property crime arrests.

According to the Sourcebook of Criminal Justice Statistics (2003) and the Bureau of Justice Statistics (2003), women are underrepresented among court clients as well. Table 12.3 shows that, of all

TABLE 12.3
Convictions by State Courts, by Gender (2001)

	Men	Women
All offenses	83%	17%
Violent offenses	90%	10%
Murder/manslaughter	91%	9%
Sexual assault	98%	2%
Robbery	93%	7%
Aggravated assault	86%	14%
Property offenses	75%	25%
Burglary	92%	8%
Theft	75%	25%
Motor vehicle theft	90%	10%
Fraud	59%	41%
Drug offenses	83%	17%

SOURCE: Sourcebook of Criminal Justice Statistics (2003).

TABLE 12.4

Sentences Under Federal Sentencing Guidelines, by Gender (2001)

	Men	Women
All offenses	85.7%	14.3%
Murder	92.3%	7.7%
Manslaughter	85.7%	14.3%
Sexual abuse	99.6%	0.4%
Robbery	93.4%	6.6%
Assault	90%	10%
Burglary	94.3%	5.7%
Theft	64.9%	35.1%
Motor vehicle theft	94.6%	5.4%
Fraud	74.4%	25.6%
Embezzlement	42%	58%
Forgery/counterfeiting	77.6%	22.4%
Drug trafficking	86.9%	13.1%

SOURCE: Sourcebook of Criminal Justice Statistics (2003).

people convicted of felonies in state courts, only 17% were women, including 10% of convicted violent felons, 25% of convicted property felons, and 17% of convicted drug offenders. The crime for which their percentage of convictions is most similar to their representation in society is fraud (41%). Of all crime for which women were convicted of felonies in state courts, fraud accounted for 22% of their offenses, whereas for men it was only 6%. Nearly half (42%) of convictions for women come in the form of property offenses, whereas for men they account for only 26% of all convictions.

In federal courts, the picture is very similar. Table 12.4 shows that women made a minority of people sentenced under federal sentencing guidelines in 2000, including 14.3% of sentences for all offenses, 13.1% of sentences for drug trafficking, 10% of all sentences for assault, and 6.6% of all sentences for robbery. The only crime for which women made up more than half of all sentences was for embezzlement (58%).

Women are also underrepresented among sentences to prison and jail for most crime at the state level. As shown in Table 12.5, 72% of males were sentenced to incarceration in 2000 for felony convictions, versus only 57% of women. Males were more likely than women to be sentenced to incarceration for violent offenses (81% versus 65%), for property offenses (70% versus 525%), and for drug offenses (70% versus 61%). Simultaneously, women convicted of felonies in state courts were more likely than men to be sentenced to probation for all offenses (38% versus 24%), for violent offenses (31% versus 17%), for property offenses (42% versus 26%), and for drug offenses (34% versus 26%).

Convicted female felons at the state level also tend to receive shorter sentences than men. Table 12.6 illustrates that women receive shorter sentences than men for all offenses (23 months versus 28 months), for violent offenses (44 months versus 70 months), for property offenses (19 months versus 29 months), and for drug offenses (19 months versus 30 months). These patterns generally hold true for both incarceration sentences and probation sentences.

It is generally thought that courts are more lenient to convicted female felons than convicted male felons because of legal factors—that is, women generally cause less damage through their

TABLE 12.5
Rates of Incarceration of Convicted Felons, by Gender (2001)

	Percentage Incarcerated	
	Men	Women
All offenses	72	57
Violent offenses	81	65
Murder/manslaughter	96	90
Sexual assault	84	83
Robbery	89	83
Aggravated assault	75	58
Property offenses	70	52
Burglary	78	73
Theft	68	51
Fraud	61	49
Drug offenses	70	61

SOURCE: Sourcebook of Criminal Justice Statistics (2003).

criminality and typically have shorter criminal records. Yet when comparing sentences for certain types of crimes, women are sometimes sentenced at a rate closer to that of men. For example, in 2000, 39% of African American females convicted of drug offenses were sentenced to prison, versus 50% of African American men but only 34% of Caucasian men and 23% of Caucasian women. For the crime of drug possession, 40% of African American females convicted of drug offenses were sentenced to prison, versus 51% of African American men but only 29% of Caucasian men and 21% of Caucasian women. For the crime of drug trafficking, 38% of African American females convicted of drug offenses were sentenced to prison, versus 50% of African American

TABLE 12.6
Average Sentences Imposed on Convicted Felons, by Gender (2001)

	Number of Months	
	Men	Women
All offenses	38	23
Violent offenses	70	44
Murder/manslaughter	258	166
Sexual assault	89	43
Robbery	84	56
Aggravated assault	39	31
Property offenses	29	19
Burglary	39	26
Theft	22	16
Fraud	21	19
Drug offenses	30	21

SOURCE: Sourcebook of Criminal Justice Statistics (2003).

men but only 36% of Caucasian men and 25% of Caucasian women. Given the biases in policing (see Chapter Six) and the biases of the drug war (see Chapter Eleven), it is highly likely that some of these disparities are attributable to biases in the law rather than actual behavior differences. This is discussed further in the Issue in Depth at the end of the chapter.

As of 2000, men made up 93.7% of all inmates in state and federal prisons, for a rate of 896 inmates per 100,000 people. This is 14.4 times higher than the female rate of imprisonment at 58 per 100,000 people. Men also made up 88.3% of jail inmates in 2000. Yet the number of female inmates in both jails and prisons has increased at a much faster rate for females than males since the 1970s. As you have seen throughout this book, this is attributable to the explosion of get tough policies, including the war on drugs, that regularly catch small-time and nonviolent offenders who increasingly tend to be women.

There is some evidence of what Belknap (1996) calls the *evil woman hypothesis*, which posits that women will be treated more harshly for similar crimes than men. Morgan-Sharp (1999, p. 384) suggests that the criminal justice network is tougher on women when they "do not adhere to prescribed gender roles." According to the National Criminal Justice Commission, even though the vast majority of people punished in the United States are men, "women are the fastest-growing category of prisoners nationwide" (Donziger 1996, p. 146). For example, in the 1980s the rate of female incarcerations increased more than the rate of male incarcerations in every year except one. The commission attributes this fact to changes in sentencing policy that have overcome traditionally lenient sentences for women compared to men (Daly 1994; Steffensmeir, Ulmer, and Kramer 1998) and to the war on drugs, which is discussed in depth in Chapter Eleven. From 1990 to 1996, the number of female prisoners per 100,000 people in Florida increased by 65%; for male inmates, the increase was only 45% (Crawford 2000, p. 263). Crawford writes, "Although the Florida system is extremely reluctant to classify women as habitual offenders, there is a notable and disturbing exception based on offenders' race and drug-related crimes" (p. 277). Crawford found evidence of a sentencing bias against minority women in Florida. His research suggests that the state's habitual offender statute was being used disproportionately against African American women, even after controlling for legal factors such as prior criminal record and crime seriousness.

American sentencing practices and the war on drugs have most dramatically affected women of color (Crawford 2000). In 1990, for example, The Sentencing Project found that only 1 in 100 Caucasian women ages 18 to 29 years was under some form of criminal justice supervision, versus 1 in 56 Hispanic women and 1 in 37 African American women in this age group (Mauer 1990, p. 3). As you saw in Chapter Eleven, the war on drugs tends to net low-level drug offenders, many of whom are women with little to offer to prosecutors in exchange for lesser sentences.

The increasingly punitive response of our criminal justice agencies to female offenders does not owe itself to a female crime wave. Instead, women are simply more likely to be sent to prison for offenses that typically did not receive imprisonment in the past. According to Bureau of Justice Statistics figures cited by the National Criminal Justice Commission, increases in female arrests and incarcerations were mostly due to relatively minor, nonviolent charges such as shoplifting, check forgery, welfare fraud, and drug crimes (Donziger 1996, p. 149). Some female incarcerations for drug offenses stemmed from mandatory sentences, which give judges no discretion in setting punishment. Thus, judges cannot consider factors such as the subordinate role women may have played in criminal offenses, the fact that women are less likely to commit additional crimes after release, or women's child care needs (Raeder 1993). For these reasons, women are hurt more than men by mandatory sentencing.

Most women in prison, like their male counterparts, can be considered "truly disadvantaged." For example, in the 1990s: "Two-thirds of women in prison are minorities, about half ran away from home as youths, a quarter had attempted suicide, and a sizable number had serious drug problems. Over half had been victimized by physical abuse and over a third reported sexual abuse. Most had never earned more than $6.50 an hour" (Donziger 1996, p. 150). Perhaps the saddest aspect of female incarceration is that almost three of every four female inmates are mothers (Bureau of Justice Statistics 2003).

When we punish mothers for relatively minor crimes, it increases the harms associated with the mothers' criminality. Children of incarcerated mothers are more likely to be incarcerated later in their lives (Dressel and Porterfield 1998). These children suffer from "traumatic stress, loneliness, developmental regression, loss of self-confidence, aggression, withdrawal, depression, interpersonal violence, substance abuse, and teenage pregnancy" (Donziger 1996, p. 153). The vast majority of incarcerated mothers are not permitted to see their children. About three of four of the children end up living with relatives other than the natural father, or even in foster care (Bureau of Justice Statistics 1994). All of this may be considered punishment for the mothers, but it is also harmful to the children. Why would Americans want to separate mothers from their children and increase the likelihood that the children also will come under the supervision of criminal justice agencies in the future?

Simultaneously, women are not protected by the criminal justice network from the crimes that most threaten them—domestic violence and sexual assault. According to the Centers for Disease Control and Prevention, more women seek hospital treatment from domestic violence incidents than from all muggings, car accidents, and rapes combined (Donziger 1996, p. 146). No one knows how many women are abused in their own homes at the hands of domestic or "intimate" violence, but it is estimated that somewhere between 2 and 27 million women are beaten every year (p. 156). In fact, in 1992, the U.S. surgeon general ranked abuse by intimates as the leading cause of injuries to women ages 15 to 44 years (Feder 2000; Gosselin 2000; S. Miller 2000). The National Criminal Justice Commission claims, "All things considered, women in this country are nine times more likely to be a victim of crime in the home than out on the streets" (Donziger 1996, p. 156).

The criminal justice network does very little to assist women with leaving their abusive husbands and partners, even though women are more likely to be murdered when attempting to leave than at any other time (Browne 1993). And it does very little to prevent domestic violence, even though reducing crime is one of its ideal goals. Given that domestic violence occurs in a cycle—since rationalization for and techniques of behavior are learned—when we fail to prevent it in one generation, we are guaranteeing that it will occur again in the next. Children from violent homes are more likely to become violent and abusive, to commit crimes, and to commit suicide than children from nonabusive homes (M. Robinson 2004).

In terms of sexual assault, there is evidence that law enforcement officers and prosecutors are less likely to pursue cases where the victim knows the attacker and where the victim has had an active sex life or was dressed in a way thought to provoke the attack. Additionally, judges may set lower bail for alleged rapes where the offender is known to the victim.

These are a few ways in which the American criminal justice network operates based on gender. It is evident that most of the "clients" of the U.S. criminal justice network are men, even above and beyond their representation in the criminal population. Yet with the war on drugs and the advent of mandatory sentences for some types of drug offenders, more and more women, who are usually poor and of color, are being processed through criminal justice agencies.

CONCLUSION

In this chapter, I have demonstrated how the criminal justice network is biased against the poor and people of color, as well as against women, to a lesser degree. It is difficult to say why discrimination against people of color persists in the United States, but one thing is certain: It does persist. The findings of this chapter suggest that the U.S. criminal justice network is failing to meet its goal of doing justice, because it is inherently unfair in its treatment of some groups. Thus, the reality of justice in the United States is that it is not blind, as it is ideally thought to be. Although it is not clear that the criminal justice network is intentionally biased against any group, it is obvious that various functions are served for people in positions of power by the fact that the criminal justice network fails to live up to its ideal goal of being just.

ISSUE IN DEPTH

The Greatest Threat to Civil Rights Is the Criminal Justice Network

An organization formed by the Leadership Conference on Civil Rights and the Leadership Conference Education Fund (LCCR/LCEF)(2000) published a study called *"Justice on Trial: Racial Disparities in the American Criminal Justice System."* The major claim of this chilling report is that "racial disparity in the criminal justice system is the most profound civil rights crisis facing America in the new century. It undermines the progress we have made over the past five decades in ensuring equal treatment under the law, and calls into doubt our national faith in the rule of law."

As the authors of this report explain:

In the half century since a tired seamstress named Rosa Parks refused to give up her seat on the bus, the United States has made significant progress toward the objective of ensuring equal treatment under law for all citizens. The right to vote and the right to be free from discrimination in employment, housing and public accommodations are enshrined in statute. The number of minorities in positions of authority in public and private life continues to grow. America's minorities now enjoy greater economic and educational opportunities than at any time in our history. While it certainly cannot be said that the United States has achieved complete equality in these areas, we continue to make slow but steady progress on the path toward that goal. But in one critical arena—criminal justice—racial inequality is growing, not receding. Our criminal laws, while facially neutral, are enforced in a manner that is massively and pervasively biased. The injustices of the criminal justice system threaten to render irrelevant fifty years of hard-fought civil rights progress.

When Martin Luther King, Jr., was assassinated in 1968, many major achievements had been realized by the civil rights movement. Yet since then, these gains have being rescinded through criminal justice processes. For example, according to the report at www.civilrights.org (LCCR/LCEF 2000):

- In 1964 Congress passed the Civil Rights Act prohibiting discrimination in employment. Yet today, 3 of every 10 African American males born in the United

States will serve time in prison, a status that renders their prospects for legitimate employment bleak and often bars them from obtaining professional licenses.

- In 1965 Congress passed the Voting Rights Act. Yet today, 31% of all black men in Alabama and Florida are permanently disenfranchised as a result of felony convictions. Nationally, 1.4 million black men have lost the right to vote under these laws.
- In 1965 Congress passed the Immigration and Nationality Act, which sought to eliminate the vestiges of racial discrimination in the nation's immigration laws. Yet today, Hispanic and Asian Americans are routinely and sometimes explicitly singled out for immigration enforcement.
- In 1968 Congress passed the Fair Housing Act. Yet today, the current housing for approximately 2 million Americans—two-thirds of them African American or Hispanic—is a prison or jail cell.
- Our civil rights laws abolished Jim Crow laws and other vestiges of segregation and guaranteed minority citizens the right to travel and utilize public accommodations freely. Yet today, racial profiling and police brutality make such travel hazardous to the dignity and health of law-abiding black and Hispanic citizens.

The main argument of this report (LCCR/LCEF 2000) is that the U.S. Constitution's guarantees of equal treatment under the law have been eroded because of criminal justice:

> Unequal treatment of minorities characterizes every stage of the process. Black and Hispanic Americans, and other minority groups as well, are victimized by disproportionate targeting and unfair treatment by police and other front-line law enforcement officials; by racially skewed charging and plea bargaining decisions of prosecutors; by discriminatory sentencing practices; and by the failure of judges, elected officials and other criminal justice policy makers to redress the inequities that become more glaring every day.

The report claims that the biases begin with police: "The disparate treatment of minorities in the American criminal justice system begins at the very stage of that system: the investigation of suspected criminal activity by law enforcement agents." In fact, the problem clearly starts with the law (see Chapter Three). This report discusses several examples of biased laws, including the disparate treatment of crack versus powdered cocaine (see Chapter Eleven) and the various rulings, including the decision in *McCleskey v. Kemp* (1987), in which the Supreme Court refused to overturn capital punishment in the face of overwhelming evidence of racial disparities that could not be explained away by legal factors (see Chapter Ten).

The main problems with policing, according to this report (LCCR/LCEF 2000), include the following:

- The use and abuse of discretion by police, which allows and even encourages under legal techniques (such as pretextual traffic stops and stop-and-frisk searches), to use racial profiling to disproportionately stop African Americans with little evidence of wrongdoing
- Immigration practices that disproportionately detain and deport Hispanics

- Department policies and laws that permit and encourage police to respond to flight by citizens as suspicious behavior, which increases the risk of use of force and use of lethal force by police against people not involved in criminal activity
- Police brutality and corruption, each of which disproportionately affects minorities
- The disparate enforcement of open-air drug markets (which occur disproportionately in inner cities, where minority residence is high) rather than markets that are better hidden and tend to involve the people who are most likely to deal drugs—Caucasians

I discussed most of these issues in Chapters Six and Eleven of this book. With the exception of brutality and corruption, these are forms of *innocent bias*, and their occurrence does not require "bad cops." In fact, this organization (LCCR/LCEF 2000) concurs that police brutality and corruption are made more likely in an environment characterized by a "get tough on crime" approach where police officers find ways to justify behaviors that they normally would not condone or commit because of the fact that most police officers are "good cops."

The main problems with courts, according to this report (LCCR/LCEF 2000), include the following.

- Prosecutors have unchecked discretion in deciding who to prosecute, what charges to press, and what sentences to pursue, which generally benefits Caucasian defendants (except in death penalty cases).
- Federal prosecutors have the discretion to decide to pursue some cases (especially drug cases) in federal courts rather than state courts, where sentences are generally harsher. With drug cases, this occurs disproportionately when cases involve minority defendants.
- Preventive detention, rather than granting of bail, is used disproportionately for African Americans and the poor, as well as inflated bail amounts to deny the poor freedom while awaiting the disposal of their cases.
- Mandatory sentencing laws (such as three-strikes laws) are disproportionately used to harm minorities, especially when it comes to drug laws, by tying the hands of judges and not allowing them to use their own discretion to impose more rational sentences for relatively minor offenders.
- Death sentences are more routinely handed down for cases involving Caucasian murder victims, especially Caucasian victims murdered by minorities.

Most of these issues are discussed in Chapters Seven, Eight, Ten, and Eleven of this book. I have shown that the pretrial phase of courts, including charging, bail, and plea decisions, is inherently biased against people of color and the poor. The authors of this report (LCCR/LCEF 2000) do not discuss trial procedures but do point out some of the same sentencing biases that I have discussed. The authors of the report write: "As an empirical matter, it is undeniable that prosecutors exercise their discretion in ways that have racially disproportionate impacts, even if their intent is race neutral. Such unfairness may ultimately be more dangerous than explicitly racist behavior, since it is harder to detect . . . and harder to eradicate. . . ." In other words, the authors of this report identify the same types of *innocent bias* that I conclude characterize American courts and agree that race has effects on sentencing.

The main problems with corrections, according to this report, include

- the abolition of parole at the federal level and in some states, which lengthens the time served in prison and worsens correctional overpopulation
- the massive increase in minority incarceration above and beyond their actual involvement in crime
- the generally longer sentences for minority males and females for drug offenses
- the increased imprisonment of nonviolent offenders, who are disproportionately likely to be minority males and, increasingly, minority females.

I discuss most of these issues in Chapters Nine, Eleven, and Twelve. Each of these outcomes is the result of America's "get tough on crime" attitude. The report (LCCR/LCEF 2000) shows how this general approach to crime most directly affects minorities and the poor.

According to the authors of the report, the following are consequences of America's "get tough on crime and minorities" approach:

- Disenfranchising minorities convicted of criminal offenses (e.g., the loss of voting rights)
- Destabilizing communities by routinely removing large numbers of African Americans males and females from certain neighborhoods over decades
- Compromising the entire criminal justice apparatus by reducing respect for the law generally
- Reducing the willingness of minorities to assist police with investigations, and crime prevention through community policing, because of perceived racial bias
- Reducing the willingness of minorities to serve on juries, because of perceived racial bias
- Reducing funding for education and other social services, which also disproportionately affects the poor and people of color
- Increasing exposure to harmful conditions, including illnesses and violence, in overcrowded prisons
- Increasing economic strain on American society by reducing the size of the American workforce and tax base
- Lowering America's standing in the world by harming our human rights image

The authors of the report conclude, "If the American criminal justice system were a corporation, it would be found to violate the civil rights laws so extensively that it might well be shut down. But for several reasons, racial inequality in the criminal justice system cannot be eradicated easily." This is because of the fact that there is truly no "criminal justice system" (see Chapter One), so changing the conditions that produce these problems requires changing laws and practices within thousands of agencies at various levels of governments. Also, "racial disparities emerge from deeply rooted, self-fulfilling stereotypes and assumptions" that are hard to root out. Finally, the political nature of crime and criminal justice in America is not conducive to honesty (see Chapter Two).

Overall, the authors of the study (LCCR/LCEF 2000) conclude that the U.S. criminal justice network is one of the greatest threats to civil rights in our country: "The criminal justice arena is an especially critical battleground in the continued struggle for civil rights. Current disparities in criminal justice threaten fifty years of progress toward equality." Because "criminal justice reform is a civil rights challenge that can no longer be ignored," the authors of the report put forth several recommendations for overcoming the problems they outline. Many of these correspond nicely to the 50 recommendations I put forth in Chapter Thirteen.

Discussion Questions

1. Who are the underclass?
2. In what ways is the war on crime a war on the poor?
3. What functions are served for U.S. society by the war on crime?
4. List some major sources of income inequality in the United States.
5. How do you think income inequality produces crime?
6. Do you think it is "right" that more than 40 million Americans do not have health insurance? Why or why not?
7. What is the difference between race and ethnicity?
8. Which groups in the United States have the greatest risks of involvement with the criminal justice system? Why do you think this is true?
9. Define contextual discrimination.
10. Discuss the apparent relationships among race, ethnicity, and social class.
11. Identify some possible reasons that people of color are more likely to be poor.
12. How have minorities made progress since the civil rights movement?
13. In what ways do you think the criminal justice system is biased against people of color?
14. Do people of color commit more crime than Caucasians? Why or why not?
15. Should the crime of robbery (a Part I offense of the UCR) be considered more serious than crimes such as fraud and embezzlement (Part II offenses of the UCR)? Why or why not?
16. How are the responses of the criminal justice system affected by gender?
17. Discuss the "chivalry or paternalism" hypothesis.
18. Discuss the "evil woman" hypothesis.
19. How is American criminal justice a threat to civil rights?

CHAPTER THIRTEEN

SUMMARY, CONCLUSIONS, AND RECOMMENDATIONS FOR THE FUTURE

KEY CONCEPTS

Summary: The criminal justice network fails to achieve justice and reduce crime

Where to go from here: Alternatives to current criminal justice practice
- *General recommendations about government and informing citizens*
- *Box: Planned change*
- *Recommendations about reforming the law and crime*
- *Recommendations about the media*
- *Recommendations about the police*
- *Box: Victims of white-collar deviance and the criminal justice network*
- *Recommendations about the courts and about sentencing*
- *Recommendations about corrections*

Likelihood of success

Conclusion

Issue in Depth: Toward Social Justice: Groups Doing the Work Now

Discussion Questions

INTRODUCTION

This final chapter summarizes the main arguments made throughout the book. I illustrate precisely how agencies of criminal justice fail to achieve their goals of doing justice and reducing crime. I then provide recommendations to overcome the factors that produce injustice in American criminal justice. My hope is that the reality of criminal justice in America can move closer to the ideals of criminal justice if these recommendations are adopted and implemented. I end the chapter with a discussion of how likely it is that the recommendations will be adopted.

SUMMARY: THE CRIMINAL JUSTICE NETWORK FAILS TO ACHIEVE JUSTICE AND REDUCE CRIME

In Chapter One, I showed that there is no such thing as a criminal justice system, because the numerous agencies of criminal justice do not work together in an efficient, coordinated, harmonious way to fight crime or assure justice. Yet I showed that the U.S. criminal justice network (the collective of thousands of criminal justice agencies) is ideally aimed at doing justice and reducing crime. Our agencies of criminal justice fight crime in a mostly reactive way, to control crime rather than to prevent it. I illustrated clearly that politicians in the United States have allocated resources and employees disproportionately to law enforcement and corrections, at the expense of American courts. I argued in that chapter that the United States has shifted toward a crime control model of justice since the 1970s at the expense of due process rights of citizens. Ironically, this shift has not made Americans safer from the harms that most threaten them.

In Chapter Two, I suggested some alternative goals of criminal justice, including controlling certain segments of the population to serve limited interests. I suggested that, most likely, these functions are not intended but rather are inevitable because of the role that politics and ideology play in American criminal justice. In our system of government, politics equals power, and politicians define acts as crimes and especially serious crimes when they are committed by the relatively powerless groups in our society. The policies that result from our get-tough-on-street-crime mentality are unplanned and thus unlikely to reduce crime before they are even implemented. Part of the problem, as our culture has been greatly influenced by large corporations, is that our agencies of criminal justice have become McDonaldized, as I showed in Chapter Two. Thus, much of our crime-fighting effort is aimed at efficiency, calculability (more for less), predictability, and control rather than justice.

Law	Media	Police	Courts	Corrections	Other
Legislators not representative	Owned by large corporations	Discretion	Demographics of courtroom workgroups	Probation	War on drugs
Most people do not vote	Run for profit	Profiling	Power of prosecutor	Incarceration	Poverty
Voters not representative	Inaccurate reporting	Location by place	Charging	Death penalty	Income inequality
Money drives politics (PACS, wealthy donors)	Focus on street crime	Focus on street crime	Bail & preventive detention		Unemployment
	Focus on violent, bizarre crimes		Plea bargaining		
	No context provided		Voir dire		
	Rely on police, prosecutors for info.		Private attorneys		
			Expert witnesses		
			Mandatory sentencing		
			Drug crimes		

FIGURE 13.1

Sources of Bias in American Criminal Justice

Injustice in American criminal justice most profoundly affects poor people and people of color. In recent years, the groups most likely to suffer at the hands of criminal justice processes are poor women of color. Figure 13.1 summarizes criminal justice bias in the United States. The diagram is organized around the areas discussed in the book: the law, the media, the police, the courts, and corrections.

All criminal justice activity stems from the law, so bias in the criminal justice process begins with the law. As I showed in Chapter Three, the law in the United States does not represent all Americans. Specifically, legislators at the federal and state levels are not representative of Americans in demographic terms, voters are not representative of Americans in demographic terms, and most people do not vote. Additionally, I illustrated how monied interests assert their influence on lawmakers through lobbying and donations to elections and political parties in the form of hard money and soft money from wealthy donors and political action committees (PACs). These facts lead to the possibility that the criminal law does not label the most dangerous acts as the most serious crimes.

Chapter Four illustrated that crimes do not exist until they are invented by human beings who write down the law. Perhaps because U.S. lawmakers and others are not demographically representative, American criminal law does not define as crimes those acts that are most threatening to the safety and well-being of Americans—acts of white-collar deviance. Instead, it labels as the most serious crimes those acts that are committed primarily by the poor and by people of color. Our criminal justice focus is squarely on those acts, while we virtually ignore other acts that are more dangerous and costly. This is not consistent either with doing justice or with reducing crime.

As I showed in Chapter Five, the media promote stereotypes about crime and criminal justice by focusing on the most violent, bizarre, and random types of crime in the United States, which ultimately increases fear of crime and support for crime control values rather than due process values. The media, which are largely for-profit institutions owned by large corporations, serve the interests of wealthy and powerful members of society by providing inaccurate reports about crime and criminal justice that lack critical context. The media also misrepresent crime trends and promote moral panics, mostly for ratings. Most troublesome, the media give relatively little attention to acts of white-collar deviance, even though these acts are much more damaging to society as a whole than common street crimes. They also focus little on misguided criminal justice policies that are not only costing us now but will continue to do so in the future. The inner ring of the media has the greatest impact on the news, and recent rule changes to media ownership (if approved by Congress) will ultimately lead to further monopolization of the media by larger and larger corporations. As illustrated in Chapter Five, the causes of media inaccuracies include the way in which mainstream media institutions are organized for profit, the peer culture of journalism, the lack of basic criminological education, and the politics of crime and criminal justice.

The police, as gatekeepers of the criminal justice network and soldiers on the front lines of the American wars on crime and drugs, are biased against poor people and people of color. This is not because of bad police officers (although they clearly exist) but because of what I term *innocent bias* in Chapter Six. This innocent bias—a function of enforcing bad law—comes in many forms. Because police are able to use discretion—to act according to their own personal judgments— stereotypes about groups of people are allowed to seep into policing. Police profiling based on fallacious stereotypes of dangerous groups, the concentration of police in the United States' inner cities, and the focus on street crimes all explain why poor people and people of color are disproportionately likely to be stopped, questioned, and arrested by law enforcement officers. They are also more likely to be victims of excessive force by the police. The criminal law and the organization of policing in the United States combine to create unjust outcomes. In their daily jobs, police do not spend most of their time fighting crime and drugs. When they do, the opportunities for financial gain are too great for some to ignore, leading to corruption and abuses unimaginable to most Americans.

Courts are also biased against the poor and against people of color. The bias occurs in all three phases of the court process, the pretrial, trial, and posttrial phases. Most of the criminal justice bias occurs in the pretrial phase behind closed doors, where decisions about bail and charging are made. The bail process, by definition, is biased against people without money. Poor people and people of color are less likely to be offered bail and thus are more likely to be detained in jail awaiting their trial dates. As I illustrated in Chapter Seven, more than 90% of felony court cases are disposed of through plea bargaining, so most people charged with crimes do not have a reasonable expectation of a criminal trial. When cases go to trial, poor people and people of color are less likely to receive justice as an outcome because of biases in the voir dire process, such as the use of peremptory challenges to exclude minorities and the use of jury consultants by those with money. Poor people also are less able to afford private attorneys and hire expert witnesses; thus, they receive less competent defenses when charged with crimes.

Sentencing, the subject of Chapter Eight, is biased in some places against poor people, people of color, and women, meaning that it is characterized by contextual discrimination. Overall, minorities in the United States receive no more severe sanctions than Caucasians do for most crimes, but they are disproportionately sentenced to imprisonment for drug felonies. African Americans also are sentenced to longer jail terms than Caucasians. I tied these findings to false conceptions of dangerousness created in the criminal law and media coverage of crime and criminal justice. Examples of biased sentencing practices include mandatory sentences such as the three-strikes laws that are almost universally condemned by criminologists and criminal justice experts. Clearly, American punishment is driven mostly by the desire for retribution (getting even with offenders), incapacitation (warehousing offenders), and deterrence (creating fear in people to prevent future crime). Yet a majority of Americans report that they support rehabilitation (eliminating the factors that produce crime), which is now largely absent in American criminal justice. Our criminal justice network practices punishments that have been shown by research to be ineffective on the very offenders we try to catch—more evidence that the network fails to meet its ideal goals. Currently, the U.S. courts are overloaded, with more than 2 million felony cases per year, a significant portion of which is drug crimes. Almost all of these cases are pursued against the poor and a significant portion is against minorities, the very people who are least represented in courtroom workgroups. Meanwhile, prosecutors now enjoy the most power in the court process, thereby assuring wrongful convictions in our crime control model of criminal justice.

Corrections, the last phase of the criminal justice process, was addressed in Chapter Nine (imprisonment) and Chapter Ten (the death penalty). The U.S. incarceration rate has exploded since the early 1970s, at a tremendous cost to American taxpayers and to the residents of our inner cities. The United States now leads the world in its rate of imprisonment. The incarceration binge did not result from increased crime rates, was not called for by Americans, and has not resulted in proportionate declines in crime. Surprisingly, most offenders in our nation's prisons are not repeat violent offenders as one might expect given the tough talk by politicians and media coverage of crime and criminal justice. In fact, a large share of our nation's prisoners are nonviolent property and drug offenders who are suffering the tremendous pains of imprisonment discussed in Chapter Nine. In essence, we seem intent on making prisoners suffer enormous hardships in hopes that they will somehow be turned into law-abiding citizens. Yet most offenders enter prison uneducated, unskilled, and underemployed (and thus poor) and leave prison the same way, yet also with the stigma of being ex-convicts. Offenders return to the same criminogenic environments that produced them, and police and parole officers harass parolees, increasing the likelihood that they will end up back in prison. Indeed, prison is a massive failure, yet politicians have sworn an allegiance to it. We now spend more money building prisons than on higher education. In Chapter Nine, I also showed that clear evidence of disparities in all forms of American punishment.

In Chapter Ten, I discussed the use of capital punishment, the rarest of all criminal sanctions. In essence, the death penalty is a punishment that is applied so arbitrarily that it is freakish and clearly ineffective. I illustrated how and why the death penalty is disproportionately used against the nation's poor and people of color and why we are likely to execute even the innocent, with the apparent acceptance of Americans. Given the irrefutable evidence that the death penalty is biased against particular groups in the United States and that executions do not deter crime, its practice is the clearest proof that the criminal justice network does not meet its ideal goals of doing justice and reducing crime. The main problems with capital punishment, as applied in the United States, include its political nature, numerous flaws with capital juries, and enormous financial costs. The error rate is so high in capital cases that it is outrageous that we still practice this punishment.

Drug crimes, a major focus of criminal justice in the past few decades, have led to major increases in the incarcerated populations in the United States. In Chapter Eleven, I demonstrated that our criminal justice network punishes people for being involved in the illicit drug trade—mostly for simple possession—even though the illegal drugs involved are relatively less harmful than such legal drugs as alcohol and tobacco. On the basis of this evidence, the nation's drug war cannot be considered a valid means of either doing justice or reducing crime. Furthermore, my assessment of the nation's war on drugs demonstrates that we fail to meet our stated goals of reducing drug use, crime, and harms associated with drugs and interrupting the flow of drugs into the country. Instead, drug use is unchanged or increasing (depending on the data source and type of drug), more drug users are dying, and drugs are still easily and very easily obtainable by young people. Additionally, the war on drugs causes far more harm than it prevents, especially to the poor and people of color and to the freedoms that we as Americans supposedly enjoy.

I illustrated in Chapter Twelve that the criminal justice network as a whole is focused almost exclusively on crimes perceived to be the acts of the poor and people of color. Thus, the criminal justice network is characterized by discrimination against these groups. Although this discrimination is not typically intentional, criminal justice processes are nevertheless biased against poor people, people of color, and, in some cases, women. Most of this bias is "innocent"; that is, it comes from the criminal law rather than from the intentional actions of "bad apples" working in criminal justice. But because the biases are functional for powerful segments of society, efforts aimed at overcoming them are typically resisted. As you saw in Chapter Twelve, some of the biases result from class-related issues such as poverty, income inequality, and unemployment, and some are institutionalized or rooted in legitimate government policies such as our criminal laws.

WHERE TO GO FROM HERE: ALTERNATIVES TO CURRENT CRIMINAL JUSTICE PRACTICE

This book has shown you that the U.S. criminal justice network fails to achieve its goals of doing justice and reducing crime. Of course, it is easy to criticize people, institutions, and policies without attempting to suggest alternatives. This seems to be the American way: We know how to criticize but are less well equipped to offer alternatives for our own failed policies.

To counter this, in this chapter I provide 50 recommendations for creating positive change within the U.S. criminal justice network. Each recommendation suggests an alternative to the current direction of criminal justice policy in the United States. Because the recommendations stem directly from the literature reviewed in this book, I arrange them in a manner consistent with the overall organization of the book. Thus, I offer recommendations in the following areas: general recommendations about government and informing citizens, recommendations about law and crime, recommendations about the media, recommendations about police, recommendations about the courts and sentencing, and recommendations about corrections.

I firmly believe that we can change the direction of American criminal justice to make it more just and more effective at reducing crime. These recommendations are a step in that direction (for other ideas, see Currie's [1998] *Crime and Punishment in America*).

Before I move to the specific recommendations, I offer a few words about predicting the future. There are many texts that essentially guess at the future of American criminal justice. One, *Visions for Change: Crime and Justice in the Twenty-First Century* by Muraskin and Roberts (1999), is particularly helpful because of its breadth of scope. In the final chapter, Muraskin (1999, p. 435) asks, "Can we predict the future with any precision?" She answers, "Probably not." She notes, however—consistent with the great majority of criminologists and criminal justice scholars—that crime problems will be solved "not by the building of bigger and better cells, but through education, alternative programs, and [by] stopping problems before they begin. . . . Violence is a symptom of other problems and we must deal with those problems" (p. 436).

In the next section, I offer suggestions for preventing crime and promoting justice in the United States. I believe that our only hope lies in the careful creation of criminal justice policies that strive to move away from the reactive, carelessly constructed criminal justice policies of the late 20th century. As Muraskin (1999) explains, "Policies are needed that attack the root of the problem. 'Band-aid' programs do not work. Without strong policies, the next millennium will see crime as a growing and larger problem than in prior centuries" (p. 436).

General Recommendations about Government and Informing Citizens

1. Our government should write clear statements reflecting the goals of American criminal justice.

Given the importance of justice as a process, due process values should be emphasized over crime control values. At each step of the criminal justice process, we must ensure that every individual's Constitutional rights are protected and that innocent people are not wrongfully subjected to criminal justice processes. In other words, we must act in ways consistent with the ideal of "innocent until proven guilty." The first step is to reorganize the thousands of criminal justice agencies into something more like a system.

2. Our government should develop clearly stated policies of government aimed at not discriminating on the basis of race, ethnicity, social class, and gender.

If justice is to be blind, and thus fair, we must first state clearly that we will not, in any circumstances, tolerate discrimination based on factors such as race, ethnicity, class, and gender. These values should be codified and exhibited by government for all to see.

3. **The government should also make a commitment to evaluate the performance of our criminal justice agencies at regular periods of time, to assess how well we are achieving our stated goals.**

How can we know how well we are doing unless we assess our performance carefully? Evaluation can be relatively inexpensive. Given the importance of the goal of providing justice, evaluation of the criminal justice network's performance on a regular basis is warranted. Criminologists and criminal justice experts should be involved in this regular evaluation.

4. **To be more effective at reducing crime, our government must encourage a fundamental shift away from punitiveness toward prevention, treatment, and restoration.**

Conditions in communities and society that produce criminality must be eliminated, sick people who commit crimes must be treated, and both victims of crime and criminal offenders must work together toward restoration of each to noncriminal and nonvictim status. For this to happen, we must commit ourselves to forgiveness rather than vengeance. Forgiveness is the only mechanism proven to produce peace for victims of crime. Thinking outside the box allows us to imagine forms of community and restorative justice, staffed by normal people trained in conflict and dispute resolution and mediation of common problems.

5. **Our government must shift its focus from criminal justice responses to violence toward medical, public-health models to treat violence as an epidemic in the United States.**

As I have explained in this book, violence is the main problem in the United States when it comes to crime. Crime rates are not exceedingly high relative to those of other similar countries. Yet we suffer from alarmingly high rates of violent victimization, especially murder. We must shift our focus away from criminal justice approaches toward public-health approaches to reducing violence by treating violence as the epidemic that it is.

6. **Our government should also stop "shooting itself in the foot" by hurting its own citizens. For example, we need to reinvest in American labor—to stop engaging in practices such as downsizing to increase profits and to cap CEO/CFO earnings to limit conditions of income inequality.**

Government should regulate businesses by requiring victim impact statements when decisions affecting a company's workers will be made. Politicians who talk about the importance of families should not tolerate the practice of maximizing profits by moving jobs overseas and south of the border at the expense of American workers and families. Sudden unemployment has been related to many adverse consequences, including depression, family instability, and domestic violence. When corporations plan to make decisions that will affect American workers and their families, criminal justice implications should be considered.

7. **Other legitimate opportunities must be developed for citizens who find themselves living in conditions of poverty.**

On the basis of a review of evidence, street crimes are not the most harmful types of crime committed. Yet street crime is tremendously harmful and disproportionately affects poor people. Politicians claim that poor people choose to commit criminal acts to maximize pleasure, gain rewards, earn money, and so forth. Our response, based on this premise, has been to increase the punishments and other pains associated with choosing crime. An alternative to this futile approach would be to increase the benefits associated with choosing noncriminal acts. People should be rewarded for abiding by the law, going to work, and raising their families.

8. Overall, Americans must insist that politics be taken out of crime and criminal justice issues.

Politicians have created cynicism in Americans by using partial facts and distorted truths about crime that have made developing sensible policy impossible. Recall the Willie Horton example discussed in the book. Horton had been out on furlough in Massachusetts eight times without committing any apparent criminal acts. On his ninth release, he committed a rape and aggravated assault. The 1988 presidential candidate, George Bush (the first), used the image of Horton as evidence that his opponent, Michael Dukakis (who was then governor of Massachusetts), was soft on crime. This was, at the least, dishonest of the Bush campaign; at worst, it was deceitful and racist. Politicians promote criminal justice policies that they should know do not and cannot work, and Americans and our media should call them on it rather than giving politicians a free pass to say whatever they want.

9. A rational system of planned change should be used to reduce crime in the United States.

Currently, criminal justice policy seems to be made based on subjective decisions, characterized by unreliability, low validity, bias, and variability among decision makers (Gottfredson 1999, p. 443). According to Walker (1998, p. xxi), most American crime control policies simply do not work: "They are nonsense." Walker critically assesses U.S. criminal justice policies, including both conservative "get tough" approaches and liberal efforts at "rehabilitation," and concludes that almost none of them is effective. Neither conservative nor liberal approaches are carefully planned. The conservative approach has traditionally involved more police, more prisons, and swifter, harsher punishment, whereas the liberal approach has focused more on rehabilitation and treatment. As noted in Chapter Two, both conservatives and liberals now support more police, more prisons, and the death penalty as effective means of fighting crime.

The following box highlights an alternative approach to reducing crime. *Planned change* (see Walsh and Harris 1999) is an alternative to quick-fix, feel-good, short-term approaches to reducing crime in the United States.

Planned change

Planned change is an alternative way to reduce crime. Crime, despite its many functions and the interests it serves, has always been viewed as a problem, and problems require solutions. To be effective, solutions require time, thought, and planning. Criminal justice policy driven by short-term thinking and unplanned change results in inefficiency, wasted resources, and failure.

Planned change is spearheaded by change agents who have specifically thought about a problem and investigated it thoroughly. *Unplanned change,* in contrast, involves little explicit or proactive planning and "comes about as a reaction to a crisis, a dramatic incident publicized by the media, a political opportunity, a lawsuit against criminal justice officials or an untested set of assumptions about a specific problem" (Walsh and Harris 1999, p. 3).

In today's heated political environment, where U.S. crime problems are typically created and/or used at election time as political issues, criminal justice policy is often shortsighted and poorly planned (and at times reactive and altogether unplanned). Not surprisingly, current criminal justice policy fails to produce significant declines in crime-related problems. Such failure stems from poorly planned criminal justice policy.

To overcome our current path of injustice and ineffectiveness, we must dedicate ourselves to planned change and must insist that our policymakers use strategies of planned change to reduce crime. Planned change can be achieved through policies, programs, and projects. Policies are a "set of rules or guidelines for how to make a decision" (p. 5); programs are a "set of services aimed at achieving specific goals and objectives within specified individuals, groups, organizations or communities"; and projects are essentially time-limited programs (p. 6). Policies are more general than programs and projects and often motivate the development of specific programs and projects aimed at reducing some problem.

To solve problems related to crime, a step-by-step approach to problem analysis and criminal justice planning must be utilized. This includes analyzing the problem, setting goals and objectives, designing programs and policies, developing action plans, developing monitoring plans, designing evaluation plans, initiating the program or policy, and then fully evaluating the program or policy so that it can be altered and continued.

The first step in policy or program design is analyzing the problem, including the need for change, the history of the problem, and potential causes of the problem. A systems approach to addressing casual factors based on the belief that crime problems stem from factors at various levels of analysis—individual, group, organizational, community, and social–structural—will likely lead to the most fruitful policy changes. Policy and program designers or "change agents" should look for all causes of a problem and carefully document such causes with scientific evidence. Previous interventions that have been used to change the problem should be examined, and opponents and supporters of change should be identified. Once it is determined what works, what is promising, and what does not work, and once vital supporters are brought onboard and opponents are appeased or defeated, effective crime reduction policies can be successful.

The next stage in policy and program development is setting goals and objectives. Goals lay out the general aims of the policy or program, and objectives more specifically restate the goals in measurable form. Clear goals and objectives are vital to success, for one cannot know if a policy has succeeded or failed unless one clearly specifies what one wants to achieve and sets forth a means of measuring the degree of effectiveness.

Effective action plans, the "blueprint" of policies or programs, must specify "all the necessary materials, supplies and tools required" to achieve successful planned change (p. 135). Action planning involves specifying the entire sequence of activities and completion dates required to carry out the program or policy design.

Monitoring must assess how well a planned policy or program is being implemented (i.e., how well the ideal matches the reality). Evaluation of the policy or program—assessing how well the policy or program achieved its goals and objectives—is also important. Data must be collected to monitor the implementation of the policy or program, to evaluate its degree of success, and to decide how to manage potential problems and confounding factors. How much longer can we afford to continue with our massive and failing American criminal justice experiments?

> Nothing less than a dramatic transformation in the formulation of criminal justice policy, from unplanned change to planned change, is necessary if criminal justice in the United States is to turn its direction from one of disastrous failure to one of success.
>
> SOURCE: Adapted from Walsh and Harris (1999).

10. The nation's crime experts must strive to educate citizens about injustice in American criminal justice and about their true risks of victimization.

It is highly unlikely that many Americans are aware of how the criminal law is biased against particular groups of people in the United States. Given our devotion to justice, it is likely that when Americans become aware of injustice, they will revolt against it and demand change, as they did during the civil rights movement. Victims of other forms of culpable harmful acts, such as victims of white-collar deviance, "are often much more confused than are victims of conventional crime about where to turn for help, and a much larger group of such victims are not even conscious about having been victimized" (Friedrichs 1995, p. 277). If we truly want to stop victimization, we must make sure that people know they are being victimized and then increase and clarify their options for law enforcement assistance.

Recommendations about Reforming the Law and Crime

11. As the criminal law currently is not made by people who are representative of the population, it should not be a surprise that the criminal law does not serve the interests of most Americans. Thus, we need to make the law more representative by increasing the representativeness of lawmakers.

This would entail increasing informed voting behavior by educating citizens about crime and criminal justice, as well as minimizing and equalizing the funding of elections, candidates, and parties by special interests and lobbying groups.

12. We must shift our focus from criminalization to harm reduction.

Americans and their leaders apparently think that we can stop people from engaging in harmful behaviors by criminalizing them. In fact, the most effective controls may very well be informal in nature—that is, instilled by families, peers, churches, and schools rather than by police, courts, and corrections. Instead of criminalizing behaviors to reduce harms, we ought to encourage policies of harm reduction, aimed at preventing harms associated with behaviors such as drug use and abuse. Rather than punishing drug users and sellers, for example, treatment options ought to be available for addicts, and alternative means of employment ought to be made available for sellers, especially once we put them out of business.

13. The government must define crimes based on the degree of harm caused.

To the degree that the criminal law is necessary, acts ought to be as serious as the harms they cause. This entails careful study (much of which has already been done and is discussed in this book) about which behaviors are really most likely to kill, injure, or result in property loss for Americans. Those behaviors that are most harmful ought to be called the most "serious" and should be the focus of law enforcement, courts, and corrections.

14. "Victimless" crimes such as drug use and possession ought to be decriminalized.

American police spend a disproportionate amount of time and resources on some "victimless" street crimes, called this not because they are truly harmless but because they are engaged in by consenting adults so that no one involved feels victimized. The best example is the war on drugs. As explained in this book, law enforcement focus on drug crimes and mandatory sentencing laws that call for longer minimum sentences for drug offenders explain the United States' unprecedented overreliance on imprisonment. Many of those we are incarcerating are first-time, low-level drug dealers or people who simply were found in possession of marijuana. Meanwhile, victims of other forms of harm are virtually ignored. Drug use can be a normal behavior that occurs in various recreational contexts, and government can decriminalize drug use while simultaneously discouraging people from using drugs. Criminalizing drug use will not deter our children from experimenting. In fact, the illegal status of drugs likely leads to much drug use, as well as a lot of crime and violence, in the United States.

15. Create and administer a national source of data on white-collar deviance.

To discover more accurately how much damage is caused by these types of acts, our government must create a measure to gather valid data on acts of white-collar deviance, much as it does on street crime. If we are to shift our focus toward the acts that cause the most harm in society, we must first commit ourselves to collecting data on the acts.

Recommendations about the Media

16. Educate the media about crime and criminal justice through planned workshops.

The nation's crime experts can no longer afford to sit on the sidelines, watching the media continue to get it wrong. We seem to know how and why the media are misinforming citizens about the true nature of crime and criminal justice in the United States. It is our responsibility to ensure that this misinformation stops, especially given that most Americans get their crime information from media outlets.

17. Insist that the media get it right by reducing consumer demand for sleazy news.

We must encourage citizens to pursue alternative forms of education and news rather than crime shows and sensational news. Research clearly shows that crime entertainment and news promote a "siege mentality" among some viewers, who become more likely to stay inside and to fear the poor and people of color rather than wanting to help them achieve legitimate success. The news media should develop and broadcast clear statements reflecting their intention to cease broadcasting sleazy, sensationalized crime stories.

18. Develop a network of contacts between criminal justice scholars and the media.

All criminologists and criminal justice experts owe it to the nation to insert themselves into the media when stories about crime and criminal justice are discussed. We cannot afford to allow politicians and the police to be the primary sources of information about crime and criminal justice in the United States, given their clear biases in favor of the status quo, and because we study crime and criminal justice for a living.

19. Utilize, advertise, and celebrate independent media outlets.

One thing we can all do, including criminologists and their students, is use independent media outlets that are not privately owned and that operate with the interests of the people in mind. We ought to tell our colleagues and students and everyday people to turn off the television unless they are watching public television or, at least, to boycott television shows and networks that sell us crime and more criminal justice and harm the nation in so doing.

Recommendations about the Police

20. Reorganize police resources (including the numbers of law enforcement officers allocated to each level of government, the types of behaviors they focus on, and the ways in which they use their time) so that victims of all culpable harmful acts, whether legal or illegal, will be served by law enforcement.

Policing in the United States is organized in a manner that mandates that officers focus almost exclusively on street crime victimization. Simultaneously, U.S. police officers spend most of their time doing work not related to crime or victimization. This must change so that police can serve all victims of culpable harms.

To correct this, we must do the following.

21. Reallocate policing resources away from local government to the states and, to a lesser degree, to the federal government.

22. Increase training of local, state, and federal police on matters related to white-collar deviance.

23. Reallocate policing resources to better assist victims of all culpable, harmful acts.

We must reeducate police officers about forms of victimization other than street crimes because state and federal officers are currently best equipped, given their special training, to provide assistance to victims of other forms of harm. To ensure that victims of such acts receive sufficient attention, police agencies at the state and federal levels must be granted more resources, including both employees and funding, than local police. Local police must be educated about forms of culpable harm other than street crime, particularly to the degree that they will likely be called on to assist with victims of such harms. City and county law enforcement assistance will not be possible unless allocation of local police personnel by location and time is systematically changed from urban areas, where street crime is perceived to occur, to areas where other forms of culpable harms occur. That is, for local police to provide their traditional services to a more diverse set of victims, the times and places they patrol must also change. Since police "tend to respond most emphatically to . . . events that they perceive as conforming to legal definitions of serious crimes" (Sacco and Kennedy 1996, p. 65), they will be unlikely to sympathize with victims of culpable behaviors other than street crimes, unless such acts are recognized as serious crimes by society and treated as such by criminal justice agencies.

Police should devote free time to forms of victimization other than street crimes committed by individuals against individuals. We might also decide as a society to let police exclusively fight victimization and leave service functions to other agencies. Perhaps we can also redesign our social service agencies to operate on a 24-hour basis, so that police can devote themselves exclusively to fighting victimization and/or crime through their law enforcement function. Given the amount of time that police at all levels of government spend on service functions, it is apparent that this time is not being allocated to victim assistance, although it is difficult to ascertain how much police service time is spent on precisely this function. Additionally, many criminal victimizations are never discovered, and virtually all noncriminal victimizations are ignored. From these facts, we can confidently conclude that police are not very effectively serving victims of culpable harms.

The following box illustrates how the criminal justice network generally deals with victims of white-collar deviance. Typically, such victims receive very little justice.

Victims of white-collar deviance and the criminal justice network

Many victims, including those who are physically maimed or injured at work, receive little attention from law enforcement agencies. As noted by Friedrichs (1995, p. 271), "The proportion of apparent white collar crimes that are officially investigated and lead to enforcement actions is lower than is the case for conventional crime. In the simplest and most colloquial terms, what occurs in the street is more visible and more easily investigated than what occurs 'in the suite,' behind closed doors." Just because it is hidden, however, does this mean its victims are not worthy of both compensation for their suffering and justice for the harms committed against them?

Such victims are typically left to seek assistance from state and federal law enforcement agencies, or from regulatory agencies, because of the "complex, often interjurisdictional character" of the harmful acts that produce the victimizations (Friedrichs 1995, p. 272). Law enforcement agencies involved include "over two dozen separate federal agencies" including "the Federal Bureau of Investigation (FBI), the Inspector Generals, the U.S. Postal Inspection Service, the U.S. Secret Service, the U.S. Customs Service, and the Internal Revenue Service Criminal Investigative Division" (Friedrichs 1995, p. 273). Recall how few officers work for these agencies relative to city and county police forces in the United States.

Regulatory agencies include the Occupational Safety and Health Administration (OSHA) for negligent workplace injuries and deaths, the Food and Drug Administration (FDA) for adulterated food products, the Consumer Product Safety Commission (CPSC) for unsafe products, and the Environmental Protection Agency (EPA) for acts against the environment. According to Friedrichs (1995, p. 285), "Regulatory agencies are greatly understaffed and underfunded. . . . Public pressure for agency action is small relative to that for conventional crime, and business interests have traditionally lobbied for various limitations on agency powers and budgets." For example, OSHA has only hundreds of inspectors, who must investigate millions of businesses. Although victims of culpable harms committed by entities such as groups of people or corporations can also turn to the civil law for redress, it is clear that their victimizations are not treated as seriously as street crimes. Lynch and Stretesky (1999, p. 24) add that "administrative agencies rarely use the criminal penalties that some of them can access to control corporate criminality. Many are staffed by people who were once top executives in the industries they police and oppose regulation of corporate activities" (also see Burkholz 1994; Claybrook 1984; Glantz et al. 1996). We can easily understand why most policing in the United States is focused exclusively on street crimes instead of other harmful acts committed intentionally, recklessly, negligently, or knowingly. Friedrichs (1995, p. 271) claims that this is due to a lack of jurisdiction, expertise, and resources. To facilitate police involvement in victimizations caused by other culpable harmful acts, changes in police jurisdiction, expertise, and resources must be made.

24. Increase the educational qualifications for American police officers to a minimum of a bachelor's degree.

The Police Executive Research Forum claims that education benefits the police and the community. Through education, police gain greater maturity and increase their knowledge base about criminal justice and American government, as well as an increased understanding and appreciation of people of different cultures (Carter and Sapp 1993). These factors, along with high intelligence, flexibility, and honesty, have been shown to be related to better policing.

25. Increase police officer pay to reduce police corruption.

It is understandable that some good cops will "go bad" when they are paid very little and see huge amounts of money exchanged regularly in criminal enterprises. To reduce the likelihood that police will steal cash from offenders, we must pay our police officers more and create other mechanisms by which to show our appreciation for the valuable services they provide to Americans.

26. Develop mandatory multicultural educational efforts within police academies.

As evidence shows that police disproportionately hassle ethnic minorities and people of color, police should be exposed to more educational materials about other cultures to increase their understanding of, and appreciation for, people unlike themselves, especially given that most police are Caucasians.

27. Outlaw the use of police profiling based on race and ethnicity.

There is no valid justification for this practice. Even if profiling results in more arrests, more seizures of evidence related to criminal activity, and so on, the ends cannot be justified by the means. Recall that justice as a process is what criminal justice agencies in America ideally value. Police profiling is an ugly practice that should never be tolerated. We should require police to gather statistics about interactions with citizens and then evaluate each jurisdiction for evidence of racial profiling. When racial profiling is found, departments must be punished accordingly.

28. Develop police–community partnerships where they are needed most.

Community policing, the buzzword in policing for the past three decades or so, has not been beneficial to the communities where it is needed most. Inner cities and high-crime areas have witnessed the greatest lack of respect for police and the least police involvement in community policing. These are the areas where community policing strategies must be stepped up.

Recommendations about the Courts and about Sentencing

29. Reallocate criminal justice resources so that they are more equitable, particularly to "courthouse regular" defense attorneys.

This book has shown that most money spent on criminal justice is allocated to law enforcement and then to corrections. In essence, we spend more money trying to catch criminals and punish them than making sure that we have caught the right ones. Is it any wonder, given the presumption of guilt inherent in plea bargaining, that sometimes we end up punishing innocent people for crimes they did not commit? If we truly believe in due process and "innocent until proven guilty," we must give defense attorneys the resources necessary to defend their clients adequately. Ideally, each side must be assured of the resources necessary to take cases to trial.

30. Increase representation by racial and ethnic minorities in courtroom workgroups.

As was shown, people of color are underrepresented as members of the courtroom workgroup. Here, the government could assist by providing people of color targeted scholarships to attend law school, with the stipulation that they will serve a minimum number of years working for the government as officers of the court.

31. Reassign sentencing discretion to judges, instead of prosecutors.

The current move to allow prosecutors to decide sentences through the charging process has resulted in an imbalance in the court. Sentencing discretion must reside in the hands of judges, not prosecutors. Judges tell researchers that they do not support mandatory sentences such as three-strikes laws because of their inability to consider mitigating factors when sentencing some of the nation's truly disadvantaged. Prosecutors, as elected officials, are more likely to be concerned about their image as being "tough on crime" and to maintain high conviction rates at virtually any cost. Their discretion must be reduced if we want to ensure that justice is done. This can be accomplished by abolishing mandatory sentences, at least for relatively harmless acts.

32. Prohibit preventive detention based on the criterion of "to protect the community," and permit it only when a significant flight risk exists.

Stated plainly, there is no justification for locking up people who have yet to be convicted of criminal offenses. Only in rare circumstances, such as when officers witness a person in the act of committing violence or when a person is found to be mentally unstable because of a severe brain disorder, can we justify locking up a person who is supposedly "innocent until proven guilty." Yet approximately half of the people now in our nation's jails have not been convicted of any crime. These people are being punished without conviction. When preventive detention is used, all efforts must be made to speed up the criminal justice process for these cases in particular and to provide treatment to those with mental illness.

33. Create a system of structured bail based on how much the accused can afford to pay and assess bail outcomes regularly to ensure that bail is not being used to discriminate against any group of persons.

If bail is simply to be used to ensure the presence of the defendant at trial, and not as punishment, unreasonably high bails for the poor cannot be tolerated. Many poor citizens are forced to sit in jail even for accusations of relatively minor criminality because they cannot afford bail. Given the evidence showing biases in bail against the poor and people of color, something must be done to correct these biases. At regular intervals, bail outcomes should be evaluated to ensure that unreasonably high bail is not being used disproportionately against any group. If bail is found to be differentially applied, mandatory bail amounts should be established by independent assessors of the courts.

34. Prohibit plea bargaining and resolve to give citizens their right to trial.

The plea bargaining process does not address the guilt or innocence of the accused. Rather, the issue addressed by plea bargaining is what to do about the defendant, who is assumed to be guilty by everyone involved in the criminal justice process. Neither justice as an outcome nor justice as a process is achieved through this process. Decriminalization initiatives would aid in the effort to ensure that court caseloads do not grow to the point where it would be impossible to hold a trial for each criminal case.

35. Insist that indigent clients be given quality counsel by creating incentives to represent poor clients zealously.

Part of this incentive should be financial. Courthouse regulars who make their living defending the poor need to be able to afford to investigate the charges against their clients thoroughly and to mount an adequate defense. Nothing less than justice depends on fair court processes.

36. Jurors ought to be selected from sources other than voter lists, for the majority of people in the United States do not vote.

Voters tend not to be representative of the nation's population, so biases in the law will result against those who do not vote. Alternative jury lists must be created from other sources such as lists of people with driver's licenses.

37. Prohibit the use of peremptory challenges in jury selection.

There is no valid reason to allow any challenge to a juror without adequate cause being stated to (and supported by) a judge. Because peremptory challenges are used to disqualify people of color and people who "look suspicious," the jury process has been corrupted by the use of these challenges.

38. Encourage citizens to participate in jury duty by providing adequate financial compensation.

Jurors provide a valuable service to the country. They are supposed to be the backbone of the criminal justice network, ensuring that arbitrary and overzealous governments do not unnecessarily interfere in the lives of American citizens. Thus, they should be paid a reasonable amount to compensate for their lost wages and service to the government and people of the United States. Jury duty should not be something Americans dread.

39. Prohibit the use of jury consultants during voir dire.

The use of jury consultants clearly biases the trial phase in favor of those clients who can hire individuals to hand-pick a jury sympathetic to their case. The poor and, often, people of color do not enjoy this privilege.

40. Allow jurors to ask questions and take notes during the trial phase.

Currently, jurors must listen to long trials and complex testimony and other forms of evidence without being able to write anything down or ask questions for clarification. This likely gives more credence to opening and closing arguments than to the actual evidence presented during trial.

41. Make jury instructions understandable.

Research clearly shows that jury instructions cannot be understood by many Americans. They should be written with the lay person in mind, and examples of major terms should be provided to help the jury make just decisions. Sample jury instructions can be tested on everyday Americans to make sure that they are understandable.

42. Require monitoring of jury deliberations.

To be sure that juries are considering only the evidence allowed by judges when making their decisions, jury deliberations should be subjected to judicial review to identify and correct unjust jury decisions. This does not mean that jury verdicts should be overturned upon review; it means that when juries use invalid criteria in their decisions, verdicts should be reconsidered by a panel of judges and perhaps adjusted on the basis of legal precedents.

43. Acknowledge that deterrence is a myth, and not a likely outcome of criminal sentencing.

Very few criminal sanctions provide a deterrent effect, especially for those most likely to commit street crimes. Those with little legitimate opportunity for success—a "stake in conformity"—are far less likely to be scared into crime-free lifestyles when legal means of earning income are so restricted and unavailable to them.

44. Eliminate three-strikes laws unless it is assured that they will be used only against repeat violent felons (that is, who actually hurt people).

We will inevitably need to lock some criminals away from society for our own protection, but many relatively minor offenders do not warrant such severe sentences. Mandatory sentences are not a cost-effective way to punish these offenders. These sanctions also contribute to the "get tough" approach that permeates much of U.S. society, a major impediment to effective change within the criminal justice network. These laws should only be used against offenders who have committed more than one violent offense, at least one of which led to some actual injury.

Recommendations about Corrections

45. Increase the use of intermediate sanctions as cost-effective alternatives to prison.

These sanctions are not necessarily any more effective than prison, but they are certainly less expensive. Many such sanctions are at least considered promising by criminologists and criminal justice experts, but they are not used widely enough to demonstrate how well they work. For relatively minor offenders likely to end up in prison, these sanctions seem to be a better investment.

46. Humanize prisons—minimize the pains of imprisonment.

Those criminals who simply must be kept away from society for our protection should not be subjected to unnecessary forms of punishment while incarcerated. Instead, they should be humanely incapacitated and treated as human beings, not as wild animals. Remember, virtually all of them will be released one day.

47. Insist on educational and vocational skill development in prison as a criterion for release.

Prisoners should be required to demonstrate that they will likely make it in the free world before they are released. This means that correctional facilities must do more than simply warehouse offenders. Imprisoned offenders ought to be encouraged, indeed required, to work, study, make decisions for themselves, and be prepared to live in the free world. This may be unpopular with Americans who want to see the guilty suffer, but it likely will be more effective in preventing future crimes than brutal punishment.

48. Shift the role of probation and parole officers to social service functions rather than supervisory, law enforcement functions.

Probationers and parolees are currently sent to prison for violating rules not imposed on free people. This must stop. Those who are charged with supervising the progress of such offenders ought to be rewarded for successes and urged to help offenders make it in the free world by assisting their clients with necessary vocational, educational, and medical rehabilitation.

49. Provide more resources for probation and parole officers.

Currently, it is impossible for probation and parole officers to supervise their large caseloads. A society as wealthy as the United States ought to be able to afford to pay for enough officers to ensure successful integration of offenders into society during and after punishment.

50. Abolish the death penalty.

The United States is the only industrialized Western nation that still practices capital punishment, a shameful practice that is applied so rarely and arbitrarily that its use is clearly ineffective. It is so evidently biased against the poor and minorities that one wonders how it can possibly be legal. There is no valid evidence showing that the death penalty deters crime, and there is some evidence that an opposite effect may occur. Given that we cannot administer the death penalty enough to make it effective, capital punishment should be replaced by an ultimate sanction of life imprisonment without possibility of parole, plus restitution for victims (LWOP+R). An alternative, which most Americans already support, is an immediate moratorium on executions while we determine whether our administration of capital punishment can be fixed.

LIKELIHOOD OF SUCCESS

I do not pretend that these reforms will be rapidly accepted and implemented in the United States. In fact, considering past efforts by criminologists and criminal justice scholars to make criminal justice processes more just, it may be unwise to expect many of these reforms to be adopted in the immediate future. Yet change is possible, and, based on the evidence presented in this book, change is necessary. American criminal justice policy is misconceived and dangerous. We must invest in prevention rather than more prisons (Greenwood 1998).

Most change is gradual, but gradualism can lull us all to sleep. As Americans, we must insist that the criminal justice network achieve justice as both an outcome and a process. The debate over the death penalty is now raging across the country, so it is possible that capital punishment will soon be stopped (probably through a temporary moratorium, but perhaps through a permanent abolition). Some discussion has occurred with regard to America's responses to the attacks of September 11, 2001, but less debate is occurring with regard to many of the other issues addressed in this book. I hope that this book serves as a starting point for such debate.

Vila (1997) has pointed out how ironic it is that as knowledge about what works to reduce crime becomes clearer, we live in a time when effective or promising efforts are less likely to be implemented. His research, like that presented here, suggests that the media, politicians, and public impatience will be significant barriers to effective change. I advocate a team approach, based on consensus building among the media, politicians, and the public, to bring about effective change. And you, the reader of this book, have a tremendous opportunity to work from within agencies of criminal justice to bring about positive change.

CONCLUSION

This chapter has summarized the main findings of *Justice Blind?* and put forth recommendations for overcoming injustice in the United States. Our criminal justice network is supposed to do justice and reduce crime, yet, according to the findings reported in this book, we fail miserably at both. Since the 1970s, we have chosen a crime control model of justice at the expense of due process rights of citizens. Ironically, this shift has not made Americans safer from the harms that most threaten them. As I have demonstrated in this book, injustice in American criminal justice most greatly affects poor people and people of color, and it has begun to affect poor, minority women at a rate higher than that for men. The late Martin Luther King, Jr., would be saddened to know that injustice in America is more prevalent now than at any time during his life. For example, the percentage of African American males in our nation's prisons and jails has increased consistently since King's death. In effect, the war on crime is one of the nation's leading causes of segregation. The Issue in Depth that follows considers an alternative approach to justice, called social justice, that we should pursue if we are ever to realize the goals of Dr. King.

ISSUE IN DEPTH
Toward Social Justice: Groups Doing the Work Now

Is justice blind? The obvious answer is No. In this book, I have outlined numerous ways in which police, courts, and corrections fail to produce justice as a process. I hope that this troubles you as much as it does me. After all, the United States is supposed to be devoted to the notion of blind justice, based on the U.S. Constitution, the American Declaration of Independence, and the figure of a blindfolded woman holding scales that adorns many of our courthouses and legislative buildings.

Supposedly, Americans will not support criminal justice processes that fail to punish those who deserve it. Ideally, they will not support criminal justice processes that wrongfully convict the innocent or are biased against any group. Why, then, do we tolerate the shortcomings of our criminal justice agencies?

In this last chapter, I have outlined numerous recommendations to make our criminal justice network more just. I hope that these recommendations are taken into account as criminal justice reforms are debated now and in the future. I want to conclude by drawing your attention to an important point about justice: that injustice in criminal justice is a threat to social justice.

Social justice is perhaps the broadest conception of justice. It is bigger than the criminal justice network and exists when all forms of culpable harmful behaviors are abhorred, opposed, denounced, combated, and abolished (Barak and Henry 1999, p. 152). It exists when all people are treated equally under the law. Criminal justice is not necessarily aimed at achieving social justice, nor must it be. According to Arrigo (1999, pp. 9, 253), the goals of criminal justice (to do justice and to reduce crime) may be completely separate and distinct from the goal of achieving social justice. In fact, the way our agencies of criminal justice are organized may actually make it harder to achieve social justice (Barak and Henry 1999).

I believe that one goal of the criminal justice network should be to achieve social justice—that is, "to advance principles of fairness, equity, reasonableness, and so forth, through police, court, and correctional practices" (Arrigo 1999, p. 253). In other words, I believe that the criminal justice network not only must seek to achieve justice as an outcome and justice as a process, but also must never be allowed to interfere with the realization of social justice. Our criminal justice agencies must, in their operations, remain anchored in "fairness, equity, proprietorship, due process, and so forth" (p. 9). Otherwise, social justice will not be possible.

Many of the impediments to realizing social justice exist outside of criminal justice. Achieving social justice may not be possible simply by adopting the recommendations made in this chapter. It may require making changes to the basic structure of the United States' governments. One example is suggested by Reiman (1998), who, in *The Rich Get Richer and the Poor Get Prison*, advocates a redistribution of wealth as a means of reducing the conditions of poverty that produce much of the street crime in the United States. He does not suggest handouts to the poor but, rather, writes that our government needs to give the poor more of a helping hand to achieve the so-called American Dream. Reiman does not specifically lay out how this would be achieved, leading many to wonder how this can be achieved without socializing our government.

I do not seriously believe that the fundamental structure of American government will soon, if ever, be changed in such a way. Instead of advocating such structural changes, I advocate an approach that seeks change from within. That is, you, who may one day work within some agency of criminal justice in the United States (or, at least, most likely will live in this country as an American), will be called upon to put into practice the changes required to make the criminal justice network more just. It will be up to you to achieve social justice in America.

Crime victims must be involved in achieving the goal of social justice. Consider, for example, SAFES (Survivors Advocating for an Effective System; http://crimevictims.net/SAFES/message.html). This organization, located in Oregon but relevant for every state in the United States, is based on this premise:

> Our vision is a safer and more humane Oregon. Oregon's justice system is based on vengeance. We believe it should be based on what works:
>
> - Prevention;
> - Rehabilitation;
> - Restitution.

SAFES was founded by Arwen Bird, who, in February 1993 (at age 18), was hit by a drunken driver in Oregon. Twenty-five-year-old Kevin Nielsen, the drunken driver, had spent the night drinking at a bar and was speeding when his vehicle collided with Bird's car from behind, sending it into an embankment, where it rolled 360 degrees.

Arwen Bird's cervical spine was dislocated, and the accident left her paralyzed below the waist. Her sister, who was also in the car, suffered permanent brain damage. Nielsen, who was uninjured, was convicted of assault and of driving under the influence of alcohol (DUI). Part of his sentence was to pay $115,000 to Arwen for her medical bills, but she has not received much of that money.

You might think that Arwen Bird, as a crime victim, would favor victims' rights measures aimed at getting tougher on criminals. Instead, Arwen, has formed the alternative group, SAFES. According to Bird, many so-called victims' rights measures will not benefit crime victims.

Arwen was quoted in a July 4, 1999, article in *The Oregonian*: "I feel [the legislature has] lost sight of what victims' rights are. It reflects a vengeful attitude and an unproductive one." Arwen believes that priority should be placed on strengthening victims' assistance programs and restitution collection. Her efforts have included testifying against some "victims' rights" measures being debated by her state legislature.

According to Arwen, she has little time to be angry: "It does not serve me well to be angry. That's energy I can use to heal and be productive and go fight the Legislature." Consider the irony of a crime victim having to fight the legislature to stop passing crime bills that are supposedly in her best interests.

Of course, Arwen does not speak for all or even most crime victims. But her message is one that cautions us about being too quick to jump on the bandwagon of efforts by politicians to erode Constitutional protections that all Americans, including those accused of committing crimes, enjoy.

A special message from Arwen appears on her organization's Web page (http://crimevictims.net/SAFES/message.html). It states:

Dear Friends—

My life changed forever on a cold and clear February evening six years ago when my sister and I were hit by a drunk driver. I never could have imagined the philosophic and lifestyle changes that have resulted from my paralysis. I'm grateful for this new perspective, though I could do without the wheelchair.

As we've worked to heal from that fateful day, we've learned something important. Nobody out there truly speaks for survivors of crime who believe as we do. Plenty of "victims rights" groups are vying for attention, but we don't consider ourselves victims. We're survivors.

We've learned something else that's important. Most of the people spouting "get tough on crime" rhetoric claim to speak for us. They don't!

We disagree with the death penalty, mandatory minimum sentences, rampant prison construction and all the other planks of a criminal justice philosophy motivated by revenge and profit.

We favor prevention, rehabilitation and restitution. We favor positive action over emotional and political action.

We founded this organization because the voice of survivors has not yet been heard in Oregon. Some of us have been assaulted or robbed. Some of us have had family members murdered. The events that altered our lives may have differed, but we now share a common goal: to shift the debate in Oregon from what gets people elected (get tough rhetoric) to what works to reduce crime.

We will work wherever we can be most effective. With the media, in the legislature, at the ballot box. Please consider adding your voice to this movement toward a safer and more human Oregon by joining us. Together we can make a difference.

Sincerely,
Arwen Bird
SAFES founder

In case you think that Arwen Bird is alone, or that her vision is unusual for a crime victim, consider the growing list of organizations that feel the same way. For example, visit the following Web sites:

- Campaign for Effective Crime Policy: http://www.crimepolicy.org/
- Center for Justice and Reconciliation: http://www.restorativejustice.org/
- Center for Restorative Justice and Peacemaking: http://ssw.che.umn.edu/rjp/
- Centre for Social Justice: http://www.socialjustice.org/
- Coalition for Federal Sentencing Reform: http://www.sentencing.org/
- Crime Victims for a Just Society: http://www.crimevictims.net/index.html
- Criminal Justice Policy Foundation: http://www.cjpf.org/
- Families Against Mandatory Minimums: http://www.famm.org/index2.htm
- Journey of Hope: http://www.journeyofhope.org/
- Murder Victims Families for Reconciliation: www.mvfr.org
- National Center on Institutions and Alternatives: http://www.ncianet.org/
- Restitution Incorporated: http://www.restitutioninc.org/
- Stopviolence.com: http://stopviolence.com/
- Tolerance.org: http://www.tolerance.org/index.jsp
- Victim Offender Mediation Association: http://www.voma.org/

Each of these organizations, along with so many others, is currently doing work to achieve social justice. Thus, there is hope. And there is something you can do.

This book has demonstrated that the U.S. criminal justice network fails to achieve any of these conceptions of justice. And so we've come full circle, returning to the first words in the Preface:

Injustice anywhere is a threat to justice everywhere.
—MARTIN LUTHER KING, "A Letter from the Birmingham Jail"

As I wrote there, injustice anywhere in the United States is a threat to all persons living in the United States. And injustice in America is every American's business. Now that you understand the many ways in which the American criminal justice is unjust, let's get down to the business of making it more just.

Discussion Questions

1. Do you agree with the overall assessment of the U.S. criminal justice network as it is summarized in this chapter? Explain.
2. Explain each step of planned change.
3. Are the U.S. criminal justice network's efforts to reduce crime consistent with planned change? If so, how? If not, why not?
4. Which of the recommendations discussed in this chapter do you think is most likely to be implemented in the near-future? Which are the least likely to be put into place? Explain.
5. What is social justice? How is it related to criminal justice?

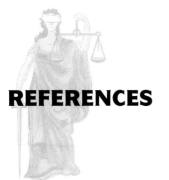

REFERENCES

Acker, J., and C. Lanier. (1998). Death penalty legislation: Past, present, and future. In J. Acker, R. Bohm, and C. Lanier, eds., *America's experiment with capital punishment: Reflections on the past, present and future of the ultimate penal sanction*. Durham, NC: Carolina Academic.

Adams, I., and B. Martin. (1996). Cannabis: pharmacology and toxicology in animals and humans. *Addiction* 91(11): 1585–1614.

Adler, F., G. Mueller, and W. Laufer. (1995). *Criminology*. New York: McGraw–Hill.

Africanaonline. (2003). Kerner report. Online: www.africanaonline.com/reports_kerner.htm.

Agnew, R. (1993). An empirical test of general strain theory. *Criminology* 30: 475–99.

Akers, R. (1996). *Criminological theory: Introduction and evaluation*. Los Angeles: Roxbury.

Albonetti, C. (1987). Prosecutorial discretion: The effects of uncertainty. *Law and Society Review* 21: 291–313.

Albonetti, C. (1997). Sentencing under the federal sentencing guidelines: Effects of defendant characteristics, guilty pleas, and departures on sentencing outcomes for drug offenses, 1991–1992. *Law and Society Review* 31: 789–822.

Alexander, E. (2000). The care and feeding of the correctional-industrial complex. In J. May, ed., *Building violence: How America's rush to incarcerate creates more violence*. Thousand Oaks, CA: Sage.

Altheide, D. (1984). TV news and the social construction of justice: Research issues and policy. In R. Surette, ed., *Justice and the media*. Springfield, IL: Charles C Thomas.

Alvarado, M., and O. Boyd-Barrett. (1992). *Media education: An introduction*. London: Milton Keynes.

Ambrosio, T., and V. Schiraldi. (1997). *From classrooms to cell blocks: A national perspective*. Washington, DC: Justice Policy Institute.

American Academy of Pediatrics. (2000). Online: www.aap.org.

American Bar Association. (1991). Standards for criminal justice. Online: www.abanet.org/crimjust/standards/home.html.

American Bar Association. (1993). Online: www.abanet.org/crimjust/standards/home.html.

American Bar Association. (1997). Online: www.abanet.org/crimjust/standards/home.html.

Amsterdam, A. (1982). Capital punishment. In H. Bedau, ed., *The death penalty in America*. New York: Oxford University Press.

Anderson, C., and R. Cromwell. (1997). Black is beautiful and the color preferences of Afro-American youth. *Journal of Negro Education* 46: 76.

Anderson, E. (1995). *Streetwise: Race, class and change in an urban community*. Chicago: University of Chicago Press.

Anderson, K. (1983). An eye for an eye. *Time,* January 24: 28–39.

Angolabahere, S., R. Behr, and S. Iyengar. (1993). *The media game: American politics in the television age*. New York: Macmillan.

Arrigo, B., ed. (1999). *Social justice/criminal justice: The maturation of critical theory in law, crime, and deviance*. Belmont, CA: Wadsworth.

Asnis, S., and R. Smith. (1978). Amphetamine abuse and violence. *Journal of Psychedelic Drugs* 10: 317–77.

Ayers, I., and J. Waldfogel. (1994). A market test for race discrimination in bail setting. *Stanford Law Review* 46 (May): 987.

Bagdikian, B. (2000). *The media monopoly,* 6th ed. Boston: Beacon Press.

Bailey, W. (1998). Deterrence, brutalization, and the death penalty: Another examination of Oklahoma's return to capital punishment. *Criminology* 36: 711–33.

Bailey, W., and R. Peterson (1997). Murder, capital punishment, and deterrence: A review of the literature. In H. Bedau, ed., *The death penalty in America: Current controversies*. New York: Oxford University Press.

Baker, R., and F. Meyer. (1980). *The criminal justice game: Politics and players*. Lexington, MA: D. C. Heath.

Banfield, E. (1973). *Unheavenly city*. Boston: Little, Brown.

Barak, G. (1988). Newsmaking criminology: Reflections on the media, intellectuals, and crime. *Justice Quarterly* 5: 565–87.

Barak, G. (1994). *Media, process, and the social construction of crime*. New York: Garland.

Barak, G. (1995). Between the waves: Mass-mediated themes of crime and justice. *Social Justice* 21(3): 133–47.

Barak, G., and S. Henry. (1999). An integrative-constitutive theory of crime, law, and social justice. In B. Arrigo, ed., *Social justice/criminal justice: The maturation of critical theory in law, crime, and deviance*. Belmont, CA: Wadsworth.

Barber, J. (1994). The jury is still out. *American Criminal Law Review* 31: 1225–52.

Barclay, G., and C. Tavares (2002). *International comparisons of criminal justice statistics 2000*. London: Home Office.

Barkan, S. (1997). *Criminology: A sociological understanding*. Upper Saddle River, NJ: Prentice Hall.

Barkan, S., and S. Cohn. (1994). Racial prejudice and support for the death penalty by whites. *Journal of Research in Crime and Delinquency* 31: 202–29.

Barlett, D., and J. Steele. (1992). *America: What went wrong?* Olympia, WA: Democratic Media Services, House of Representatives.

Barnett, C. (2003). The measurement of white-collar crime using Uniform Crime Reporting (UCR) data. Online: www.fbi.gov/whitecollarforweb.pdf.

Bayley, D. (1994). *Police for the future*. New York: Oxford University Press.

Beard, C. (1913). *An economic interpretation of the Constitution of the United States*. New York: Macmillan.

Beccaria, C. (1776). *Dei delitti e della pena* [An essay on crime and punishments], 6th ed.

Beck, A. (1998). Trends in United States corrections population. In K. Haus and G. Alpert, eds., *The dilemmas of corrections*. Prospect Heights, IL: Waveland Press.

Becker, H. (1963). *Outsiders*. New York: Free Press.

Beckett, K. (1994). Setting the public agenda: "Street crime" and drug use in American politics. *Social Problems* 41: 425–47.

Beckett, K. (1997). *Making crime pay: Law and order in contemporary American politics*. New York: Oxford University Press.

Beckett, K., and T. Sasson. (1998). *The politics of injustice*. Thousand Oaks, CA: Sage.

Beckett, K., and T. Sasson. (2000). *The politics of injustice: Crime and punishment in America*. Thousand Oaks, CA: Pine Forge Press.

Bedau, H., ed. (1982). *The death penalty in America*, 3rd ed. New York: Oxford University Press.

Bedau, H. (1997). *Capital punishment in America: Current controversies*. New York: Oxford University Press.

Belenko, S. (1993). *Crack and the evolution of the anti-drug policy*. Westport, CT: Greenwood Press.

Belknap, J. (1996). *The invisible woman*. Belmont, CA: Wadsworth.

Benjamin, D., and R. Miller. (1991). *Undoing drugs: Beyond legalization*. New York: Basic Books.

Bennett, L. (1980). *Public opinion in American politics*. New York: Harcourt Brace Jovanovich.

Berry, J. (1984). *The interest group society*. Boston: Little, Brown.

Bertram, E., M. Blachman, K. Sharpe, and P. Andreas. (1996). *Drug war politics: The price of denial*. Berkeley: University of California Press.

Best, J., ed. (1989). *Images of issues*. Hawthorne, NY: Aldine de Gruyter.

Best, J. (1999). *Random violence*. Berkeley: University of California Press.

Biskupic, J. (1991). Letter writing and campaigns. *Congressional Quarterly Weekly Report* 49: 171–74.

Bittner, E. (1970). The police and the "war on crime." In *The functions of police in modern society*. Washington DC: U.S. Government Printing Office.

Black, C. (1974). *Capital punishment: The inevitability of caprice and mistake*. New York: Norton.

Black's law dictionary, 6th ed. (1991). St. Paul, MN: West.

Blakemore, E. (1998). The effect of mandatory minimum sentencing on black males and black communities. Online: www.udayton.edu/~race/annotate/s98blake.htm.

Blendon, R. J., and J. T. Young. (1998). The public and the war on illicit drugs. *Journal of the American Medical Association* 279 (March 18): 827–32.

Bluestone, B., and S. Rose. (2000). Overworked and underemployed. In R. Lauer and J. Lauer, eds., *Troubled times: Readings in social problems*. Los Angeles: Roxbury.

Blumberg, A. (1967). The practice of law as confidence game: Organizational cooption of a profession. *Law and Society Review* 4: 115–39.

Blumstein, A. (1995). Prisons. In J. Wilson and J. Petersilia, eds., *Crime*. San Francisco: San Francisco Institute for Contemporary Studies.

Blumstein, A. (2000). The connection between crime and incarceration. In J. May, ed., *Building violence: How America's rush to incarcerate creates more violence*. Thousand Oaks, CA: Sage Publications.

Blumstein, A., and J. Cohen. (1973). A theory of the stability of punishment. *Journal of Criminal Law and Criminology* 35(1): 133–75.

Blumstein, A., and J. Wallman, eds. (2000). *The crime drop in America*. New York: Cambridge University Press.

Blumstein, A., J. Cohen, S. Martin, and M. Tonry, eds. (1983). *Research on sentencing: The search for reform*. Washington, DC: National Academy Press.

Boer, J., M. Pastor, and J. Sadd. (1993). Is there environmental racism? The demographics of hazardous waste in Los Angeles County. *Social Science Quarterly* 78(4): 793–810.

Bohm, R. (1999). *Deathquest: An introduction to the theory and practice of capital punishment in the United States*. Cincinnati, OH: Anderson.

Bohm, R. (2001). *A primer on crime and delinquency*, 2nd ed. Belmont, CA: Wadsworth.

Bohm, R. (2002). *Deathquest II: An introduction to the theory and practice of capital punishment in the United States*. Cincinnati, OH: Anderson.

Bohm, R., and R. Vogel. (1994). A comparison of factors associated with uninformed and informed death penalty opinions. *Journal of Criminal Justice* 22(2): 125–43.

Bonnie, R., and C. Whitebread. (1974). *Marihuana conviction: A history of marihuana prohibition in the United States*. Charlottesville: University of Virginia.

Bonsignore, J., E. Katsh, P. D'Errico, R. Pipkin, S. Arons, and J. Rifkin. (1998). *Before the law: An introduction to the legal process,* 6th ed. Boston: Houghton Mifflin.

Boritch, H. (1992). Gender and criminal court outcome: An historical analysis. *Criminology* 30: 293–325.

Boston University Medical Center. (2000). Online: www.bmc.org.

Bowers, W., G. Pierce, and J. McDevitt. (1984). *Legal homicide.* Boston: Northeastern University Press.

Bradley C. (2000). Reforming the criminal trial. In G. Mays and P. Gregware, eds., *Courts and justice: A reader,* 2nd ed. Prospect Heights, IL: Waveland Press.

Bridges, C., and R. Crutchfield. (1988). Law, social standing, and racial disparity in imprisonment. *Social Forces* 66: 699–724.

Brown, E., K. Defenbacker, and W. Sturgill. (1977). Memory for faces and the circumstance of encounters. *Journal of Applied Psychology* 62: 311–18.

Browne, A. (1993). Family violence and homelessness: The relevance of trauma histories in the lives of homeless women. *American Journal of Orthopsychiatry* 63: 370–84.

Browning, S., F. Cullen, L. Cao, R. Kopache, and T. Stevenson. (1994). Race and getting hassled by the police: A research note. *Police Studies* 17: 1–11.

Brownstein, H. (1991). The social construction of public policy: A case for participation by researchers. *Sociological Practice Review* 2: 132–40.

Brownstein, H. (1996). *The rise and fall of a violent crime wave: Crack cocaine and the social construction of a crime problem.* Albany, NY: Harrow and Heston.

Brunk, G., and L. Wilson. (1991). Interest groups and criminal behavior. *Journal of Research in Crime and Delinquency* 28: 157–73.

Buckhout, R. (1974). Eyewitness testimony. *Scientific American* 231: 23–31.

Bureau of Justice Assistance. (1993). Online: www.ojp.usdoj.gov/bja.

Bureau of Justice Statistics. (1994, 1995, 1996, 1997, 1998, 1999, 2002, 2003). Online: www.ojp.usdoj.gov/bjs.

Burkholz, H. (1994). *The FDA follies.* New York: Basic Books.

Burnstein, H., and P. Goldstein. (1990). Research and the development of public policy. *Journal of Applied Psychology* 7: 77–92.

Bushway, S. (2000). The stigma of a criminal history record in the labor market. In J. May, ed., *Building violence: How America's rush to incarcerate creates more violence.* Thousand Oaks, CA: Sage.

Caffrey, A. (2003). FBI takes up heavy load of corporate fraud probes. Online: www.truthout.org.

Cahalan, M. (1986). *Historical corrections statistics in the United States, 1850–1984.* Washington, DC: U.S. Department of Justice, Bureau of Justice Statistics.

Carlson, J., and T. Williams. (1993). Perspectives on the seriousness of crimes. *Social Science Research* 22: 190–207.

Carmichael, S., and C. Hamilton. (1969). *Black power.* New York: Vintage Books.

Carter, D., and A. Sapp. (1993). Police response to street people: A survey of perspectives and practices. *FBI Law Enforcement Bulletin* 62: 5–10.

Casement, M. (1987). Alcohol and cocaine. *Alcohol and Health Research World II* 4: 18–25.

Casper, J. (1972). *American criminal justice: The defendant's perspective.* Upper Saddle River, NJ: Prentice Hall.

Caulkins, J., C. Rydell, W. Schwabe, and J. Chiesa. (1997). *Mandatory minimum drug sentences.* Santa Monica, CA: Rand Corp.

Center for Media and Public Affairs. (1997). *Media monitor.* Washington, DC: Center for Media and Public Affairs.

Center for Media and Public Affairs. (2000). Online: www.cmpa.com/factoid/agenda.htm.

Center for Media Education. (2000). Online: www.cme.org.

Center for Public Integrity (2003). Online: www.publicintegrity.org.

Center for Responsive Politics (2003). Online: www.opensecrets.org.

Center for Voting and Democracy (2003). Online: www.fairvote.org.

Centers for Disease Control and Prevention. (1994). Cigarette smoking among adults in the United States, 1994. *Morbidity and Mortality Weekly Report* 45: 588–90.

Centers for Disease Control and Prevention. (1997). *CDC's tobacco use prevention program: Working toward a healthier future*. Atlanta, GA: Centers for Disease Control and Prevention.

Chaffee, R., and D. German. (1998). New frontiers in political socialization research. In K. Hufer and B. Wellie, eds., *Sozialwissenschaftliche und bildungstheoretische Reflexionen: Fachliche und didaktische Perspektiven zur politisch-gesellschaftlichen Aufklarung*. Cambridge, MA: Galda and Wilch Verlag.

Chambliss, W. (2000). *Power, politics, and crime*. Boulder, CO: Westview Press.

Champion, D. (1997). *The Roxbury dictionary of criminal justice*. Los Angeles: Roxbury.

Chapper, J. A., and R. A. Hanson. (1990). *Intermediate appellate courts: Improving case processing*. Williamsburg, VA: National Center for State Courts.

Chermak, S. (1994). Crime in the news media: A refined understanding of how crime becomes news. In G. Barak, ed., *Media, process, and social construction of crime: Studies in news making criminology*. New York: Garland.

Children's Defense Fund. (1992). *The state of America's children*. Washington, DC: Children's Defense Fund.

Children's Defense Fund. (2003). Poverty status of persons younger then 18: 1959–2000. Online: www.childrensdefense.org/fs_cptb_young18.php.

Chiricos, T. (1995). The moral panic of the drug war. In M. Lynch, ed., *Race and criminal justice*. Albany, NY: Harrow and Heston.

Chiricos, T., and W. Bales. (1991). Unemployment and punishment: An empirical assessment. *Criminology* 29: 701–24.

Chiricos, T., and M. Delone. (1992). Labor surplus and punishment: A review and assessment of theory and evidence. *Social Problems* 39: 421–46.

Chiricos, T., and S. Eschholtz (2002). The racial and ethnic typification of crime and the criminal typification of race and ethnicity in local television news. *Journal of Research in Crime and Delinquency* 39(4): 400–420.

Chiricos, T., S. Eschholtz, and M. Gertz. (1997). Crime, news and fear of crime: Toward an identification of audience effects. *Social Problems* 44: 342–57.

Christie, N. (1994). *Crime control as an industry*. New York: Routledge.

Christopher, W. (1991). *Report of the Independent Commission on the Los Angeles Police Department*. Los Angeles: The Commission.

Clark, C. (1994). Prison overcrowding. *Congressional Quarterly Researcher* 4 (February): 100.

Claybrook, J. (1984). *Retreat from health and safety*. New York: Patterson.

Clear, T., and G. Cole. (1994). *American corrections*. Belmont, CA: Wadsworth.

Clemmer, D. (1940). *The prison community*. Boston: Christopher.

Cline, A. (2002). Agnosticism/atheism. Online: www.about.com.

Cloward, R., and L. Ohlin. (1961). *Delinquency and opportunity: A theory of delinquent gangs*. London: Routledge.

Clymer, A. (1986). Public found ready to sacrifice in drug fight. *New York Times,* September 2: A1, D16.

Coalition for Federal Sentencing Reform. (1997, 1999). Online: www.sentencing.org.

Cochran, J., M. Chamlin, and M. Seth. (1994). Deterrence or brutalization? An impact assessment of Oklahoma's return to capital punishment. *Criminology* 32: 107–34.

Cohen, J. (2003). Bush and Iraq: Mass media, mass ignorance. Online: www.commondreams.org/views03/1201–13.htm.

Cohen, M. (1991). Some new evidence on the seriousness of crime. *Criminology* 26: 343–53.

Cohen, S. (1972). *Folk devils and moral panics: The creation of the mods and the rockers*. London: Macgibbon and Kee.

Cohen, S., and S. Solomon. (1995). How *Time* magazine promoted a cyberhoax. Online: www.fair.org/media.beat.

Cohen, S., and J. Young, eds. (1981). *The manufacture of news.* Newbury Park, CA: Sage.

Cole, D. (1999). Conditional sentencing: Recent developments. In J. Roberts and D. Cole, eds., *Making sense of sentencing.* Toronto: University of Toronto Press.

Cole, G., and C. Smith. (1998). *The American system of criminal justice,* 8th ed. Belmont, CA: Wadsworth.

Cole, G., and C. Smith. (2000). *The American system of criminal justice,* 9th ed. Belmont, CA: Wadsworth.

Coleman, J. (1990). *The criminal elite,* 2nd ed. New York: St. Martin's Press.

Coleman, J. (1998). *The criminal elite,* 4th ed. New York: St. Martin's Press.

Committee on the Judiciary. (1994). Racial disparities in federal death penalty prosecutions 1988–1994. Online: www.deathpenaltyinfo.org/article.php?scid=45&did=528.

Common Cause. (1999). Online: www.commoncause.org/laundromat/results.html.

Common Cause (2003). Online: www.commoncause.org

Common Dreams. (2003). A richer Congress: Nearly half of incoming freshmen are millionaires. Online: www.commondreams.org/headlines02/1225-02.htm.

Community Epidemiology Work Group. (1999). *Identifying and monitoring emerging drug use problems: A retrospective analysis of drug abuse data/information.* Bethesda, MD: National Institute on Drug Abuse.

Congress Link. (2003). Online: www.congresslink.org.

Congressional Quarterly. (1999). New Congress is older, more politically seasoned. *Congressional Quarterly,* January 9: 60–63.

Conklin (2002). *Why crime rates fell.* Boston: Allyn & Bacon.

Cook, P., D. Slawson, and L. Gries. (1993). *The cost of processing murder cases in North Carolina.* Raleigh: North Carolina Administrative Office of the Courts.

Costanzo, M. (1997). *Just revenge: Costs and consequences of the death penalty.* New York: St. Martin's Press.

Cox, S., and J. Wade. (1998). *The criminal justice network: An introduction.* New York: McGraw–Hill.

Coyne, R., and L. Entzeroth. (1994). *Capital punishment and the judicial process.* Durham, NC: Carolina Academic Press.

Crawford, C. (2000). Gender, race, and habitual offender sentencing in Florida. *Criminology* 38(1): 263–80.

Cromwell, P. (1995). *In their own words.* Los Angeles: Roxbury.

Cromwell, P., J. Olson, and D. Avary. (1991). *Breaking and entering.* London: Sage.

Cronin, F., T. Cronin, and M. Milakovich. (1981). *The U.S. versus crime in the streets.* Bloomington: Indiana University Press.

Cullen, F., B. Link, and L. Travis. (1985). Consensus in crime seriousness: Empirical reality or methodological artifact? *Criminology* 23: 99–118.

Culver, J., and K. Knight. (1979). Evaluative TV impressions of law enforcement roles. In R. Baker and F. Mayer, eds., *Evaluating alternative law enforcement policies.* Lexington, MA: Lexington Books.

Culverson, D. (1998). Stereotyping by politicians: The welfare queen and Willie Horton. In C. Mann and M. Zatz, eds., *Images of color, images of crime.* Los Angeles: Roxbury.

Currie, E. (1998). *Crime and punishment in America.* New York: Holt.

Curtis, D., and J. Resnick. (1987). Images of justice. *Yale Law Journal* 96: 1727–72.

Cushman, P. (1974). Relationship between narcotic addiction and crime. *Federal Probation* 38: 38–43.

Daly, K. (1994). *Gender, crime, and punishment.* New Haven, CT: Yale University Press.

Dattu, F. (1998). Illustrated jury instructions. *Judicature* 82 (September–October): 79.

Davis, J., and T. Smith. (1996). *General Social Surveys, 1972–1996.* Chicago: National Opinion Research Center.

Davis, M., and K. Davis. (1995). Star rising for Simpson jury consultant. *ABA Journal* 81: 14.

Davis, R., and S. Meddis. (1994). Random killing hit a high. *USA Today,* December 5: 1a.

Death Penalty Information Center. Online: www.deathpenaltyinfo.org.

Death Penalty Information Center. (2003). *A broken system II. Questions and answers.* Online: www.deathpenaltyinfo.org/article.php?scid=19&did=244.

DeFrances, C., and G. Steadman. (1998). Prosecutors in state courts, 1996. *Bureau of Justice Statistics Bulletin,* July: 1–10.

del Carmen, A., and M. Robinson. (2000). Crime prevention through environmental design and consumption control in the United States. *Howard Journal of Criminal Justice* 39(3): 267–89.

DeLisi, M., and B. Regoli. (1999). Race, conventional crime, and criminal justice: The declining importance of skin color. *Journal of Criminal Justice* 26(6): 549–57.

Democracy North Carolina. (2003). Online: www.democracy-nc.org.

Denno, D. (1994). Is electrocution an unconstitutional method of execution? The engineering of death over the century. *William and Mary Law Review* 35: 551–692.

Devine, F. (1988). Inside the jury room: Deliberations of a mock jury. *Trial* 24: 74–78.

Devlin, P. (1959). *The enforcement of morals*. London: Oxford University Press.

Dill, B., M. Zinn, and S. Patton. (1999). Race, family values, and welfare reform. In L. Kushnick and J. Jennings, eds., *A new introduction to poverty: The role of race, power, and politics*. New York: New York University Press.

Dillehay, R., and M. Sandys. (1996). Life under Wainwright v. Witt: Juror dispositions and death qualification. *Law and Human Behavior* 20: 147–65.

Dinitz, S. (1996). Foreword. In R. Huff, A., Rattner, and E. Sagarin, eds. *Convicted but innocent: Wrongful conviction and public policy*. Thousand Oaks, CA: Sage.

Dodge, M., and Harris, J. (2000). Calling a strike a ball: Jury nullification and three strikes cases. In L. May and P. Gregware, eds., *Courts and justice: A reader*. Prospect Heights, IL: Waveland Press.

Dominick, J. (1978). Crime, law enforcement, and the mass media. In C. Winick, ed., *Deviance and the mass media*. Beverly Hills, CA: Sage.

Dominick, J. (1997). Dumb kid: Petty crimes: A life term? *Los Angeles Times,* July 24: B9.

Donaldson, S. (1995). *Rape of incarcerated prisoners: A preliminary statistical look*. New York: Stop Prison Rape.

Donziger, S., ed. (1996). *The real war on crime: The report of the National Criminal Justice Commission*. New York: HarperPerennial.

d'Orban, P. (1976). Barbiturate abuse. *Journal of Medical Ethics* 2: 63–67.

Dorn, N., and N. Smith. (1992). *Traffickers*. London: Routledge.

Douglas, J., and J. Johnson. (1977). *Official deviance—Readings in malfeasance, misfeasance, and other forms of corruption*. Philadelphia: Lippincott.

Douglas, S. (1996). Pooh-poohing populist discontent: Mass media and corporate responsibility. *The Progressive* 60(5): 17.

Downs, A. (1995). *Corporate executions: The ugly truth about layoffs—How corporate greed is shattering lives, companies, and communities*. New York: American Management Association.

Dreschel, R. (1983). *News making in the trial court*. New York: Longman.

Dressel, P., and J. Porterfield. (1998). Mothers behind bars: Incarcerating increasing numbers of mothers has serious implications for families and society. *Corrections Today* 60(7): 90–94.

Durham, A. 1992. Observations on the future of criminal justice education: Legitimating the discipline and serving the general university population. *Journal of Criminal Justice Education* 3(1): 35-52.

Early America Review. (1999). The Alien and Sedition Acts of 1798. Online: www.animus.net/~earlya/review/index.html.

Easton, D. (1953). *The political system*. New York: Knopf.

The Economist. (1998a). A social profile. *The Economist* 346(8061): 27–28.

The Economist. (1998b). Too poor to be defended. *The Economist* 346(8063): 36–37.

Eddings, J. (2000). The covert war: Stealth racism in America. In R. Lauer and J. Lauer, eds., *Troubled times: Readings in social problems*. Los Angeles: Roxbury.

Edelman, M. (1988). *Constructing the political spectacle*. Chicago: University of Chicago Press.

Edsall, T., and M. Edsall. (1991). *Chain reaction: The impact of race, rights, and taxes on American politics*. New York: Norton.

Ehrenreich, B. (2001). *Nickel and dimed*. New York: Owl Books.

Elikann, P. (1996). *The tough on crime myth*. New York: Insight.

Ellingswood, E. (1971). Assault and homicide associated with amphetamine use. *American Journal of Psychiatry* 127: 90–95.

Ellsworth, P. (1991). To tell what we know or wait for Godot? *Law and Human Behavior* 15: 77–90.

Epperlein, T., and B. Nienstedt. (1989). Reexamining the use of seriousness weights in an index of crime. *Journal of Criminal Justice* 17(5): 343–60.

Erez, E. (1981). Thou shalt not execute: Hebrew law perspective on capital punishment. *Criminology* 19: 25–43.

Erickson, P. (1993). Prospects of harm reduction for psychostimulants. In N. Heather, A. Wodak, A. Nadelmann, and P. O'Hare, eds., *Psychoactive drugs and harm reduction*. London: Whurr.

Erickson, P., and J. Butters. (1998). The emerging harm reduction movement: The de-escalation of the war on drugs? In E. Jensen and J. Gerber, eds., *The new war on drugs: Symbolic politics and criminal justice policy*. Cincinnati, OH: Anderson.

Ericson, R., P. Baranek, and J. Chan. (1989). *Negotiating control: A study of news sources*. Toronto: University of Toronto Press.

Erving, J., and B. Houston. (1991). Some judges punish people without benefit of a trial. *Hartford Courant*, June 17: A1.

Eschholtz, S. (1997). The media and fear of crime: A survey of the research. *University of Florida Journal of Law and Public Policy* 9(1): 37–59.

Espy, M., and J. Smykla. (1987). Executions in the United States, 1608–1987: The Espy file. Machine-readable data file. Ann Arbor, MI: Inter-University Consortium for Political and Social Research.

Evans, D. (1997). Exploring police–probation partnerships. *Corrections Today* 59: 86.

Evans, S., and R. Lundman. (1987). Newspaper coverage of corporate crimes. In M. Erdman and R. Lundman, eds., *Corporate and government deviance: Problems of organizational behavior in contemporary society*. New York: Oxford University Press.

Fagan, J., and M. Guggenheim. (1996). Preventive detention and the judicial prediction of dangerousness for juveniles: A natural experiment. *Journal of Criminal Law and Criminology* 86(2): 415–48.

Faust, F. (1995). Personal communication, August 14.

Feagin, J. (2000). *Racist America*. New York: Routledge.

Feder, L. (2000). Likelihood of an arrest decision for domestic and nondomestic assault calls: Do police underenforce the law when responding to domestic violence? In R. Muraskin, ed., *It's a crime: Women and criminal justice*, 2nd ed. Upper Saddle River, NJ: Prentice Hall.

Federal Bureau of Investigation. (1994, 2003). Online: www.fbi.gov.

Federal Bureau of Investigation. (2002). *Uniform crime reports*. Online: www.fbi.gov/ucr/ucr.htm.

Federal Bureau of Prisons. (1996, 1998). Online: www.bop.gov.

Feeley, M. (1979). *The process is the punishment*. New York: Russell Sage Foundation.

Fehr, A., and H. Kalant. (1983). Behavioral effects of prolonged administration of delta 9-tetrahydrocannabinol in the rat. *Psychopharmacology* 80(4): 325–30.

Feldman, H., M. Agar, and G. Beschner, eds. (1979). *Angel dust: An ethnographic study of PCP users*. Lexington, MA: Lexington Books.

Fields, C., and B. Jerin (1999). The media and the criminal justice system. In R. Muraskin and A. Roberts, eds, *Visions for change: Justice and the twenty-first century*. Upper Saddle River, NJ: Prentice Hall.

Finestone, H. (1967). Narcotics and criminality. *Law and Contemporary Problems* 22: 60–85.

Fishbein, D., and S. Pease. (1996). *The dynamics of drug abuse*. Boston: Allyn and Bacon.

Fishman, M. (1978). Crime waves as ideology. *Social Programs* 25: 531–43.

Flemming, R., P. Nardulli, and J. Eisenstein. (1992). *The craft of justice: Politics and work in criminal court community*. Philadelphia: University of Pennsyslvania Press.

Frank, N., and M. Lynch. (1992). *Corporate crime, corporate violence*. Albany, NY: Harrow and Heston.

Frank, R. (1994). Talent and the winner-take-all society. *American Prospect* 17: 99.

Frankel, G. (1997). Federal agencies duplicate efforts, wage costly turf battles. *Washington Post,* June 8: A1.

Franklin, R. (1999). White uses of the black underclass. In L. Kushnick and J. Jennings, eds., *A new introduction to poverty: The role of race, power, and politics.* New York: New York University Press.

Free, M., Jr. (2000). The impact of federal sentencing reforms on African Americans. In R. Lauer and J. Lauer, eds., *Troubled times: Readings in social problems.* Los Angeles: Roxbury.

Freedman, E. (1998). Federal habeas corpus in capital cases. In J. Acker and C. Lanier, eds., *America's experiment with capital punishment: Reflections on the past, present and future of the ultimate penal sanction.* Durham, NC: Carolina Academic Press.

Friedman, L. (1993). *Crime and punishment in American history.* New York: Basic Books.

Friedman, W., and M. Hott. (1995). *Young people and the police: Respect, fear and the future of community policing in Chicago.* Chicago: Chicago Alliance for Neighborhood Safety.

Friedrichs, D. (1983). Victimology: A consideration of the radical critique. *Crime and Delinquency* 29(2): 283–94.

Friedrichs, D. (1995). *Trusted criminals: White collar crime in contemporary society.* Belmont, CA: Wadsworth.

Friedrichs, D. (1999). *Trusted criminals: White collar crime in contemporary society.* Beverly Hills, CA: Wadsworth.

Fyfe, J. (1983). The NIJ study of the exclusionary rule. *Criminal Law Bulletin* 19: 253–60.

Fyfe, J., and J. Skolnick. (1993). Above the law: Police and excessive use of force. New York: Free Press.

Fyfe, J., J. Greene, W. Walsh, O. Wilson, and R. McLaren. (1997). *Police administration,* 5th ed. New York: McGraw–Hill.

Gaines, L., and P. Kraska, eds. (1997). *Drugs, crime, and justice.* Prospect Heights, IL: Waveland Press.

Gaines, L., M. Kaune, and R. Miller. (2000). *Criminal justice in action.* Belmont, CA: Wadsworth.

Gallup Organization. (2003). News media get good marks for terrorism coverage. Online: www.gallup.com/subscription/?m=f&c_id=13168.

Gans, H. (1979). *Deciding what's news.* New York: Vintage Books.

Gans, H. (1995). *The war against the poor.* New York: Basic Books.

Gaynes, E. (1993). The urban criminal justice system: Where young + black + male = probable cause. *Fordham Urban Law Journal* 20: 621.

Gebotys, R., and B. Dasgupta. (1987). Attribution of responsibility and crime seriousness. *Journal of Psychology* 121: 607–13.

Gebotys, R., J. Roberts, and B. Dasgupta. (1988). News media use and public perceptions of crime. *Canadian Journal of Criminology* 30: 3–16.

Geller, W., and M. Scott. (1992). *Deadly force: What we know.* Washington, DC: Police Executive Research Forum.

Geller, W., and H. Toch, eds. (1995). *And justice for all.* Washington, DC: Police Executive Research Forum.

George, H., Jr. (1999). Black America, the underclass, and the subordination process. In L. Kushnick and J. Jennings, eds., *A new introduction to poverty: The role of race, power, and politics.* New York: New York University Press.

Gerbner, G. (1994). Television voice: The art of asking the wrong question. *Currents in Modern Thought* July: 385–97.

Gerbner, G., et al. (1980). The mainstreaming of America: Violence profile No. 11. *Journal of Communications* 30: 10–29.

Gershman, B. (2000). Why prosecutors misbehave. In G. Mays and P. Gregware, eds., *Courts and justice: A reader,* 2nd ed. Prospect Heights, IL: Waveland Press.

Gerson, L., and D. Preston. (1979). Alcohol consumption and the incidence of violent crime. *Journal of Studies on Alcohol* 40: 307–12.

Gest, T. (2001). *Crime and politics.* New York: Oxford University Press.

Gilliard, D. (1999). *Prison and jail inmates at midyear 1998.* Washington, DC: U.S. Department of Justice, Bureau of Justice Statistics.

Gilmer, W., Jr. (1986). *The law dictionary*, 6th ed. Cincinnati, OH: Anderson.

Glantz, S., J. Slade, L. Bero, P. Hanauer, and D. Barnes. (1996). *The cigarette papers*. Berkeley: University of California Press.

Glaser, D. (1974). Interlocking dualities in drug use, drug control, and crime. In J. Inciardi and C. Chambers, eds., *Drugs and the criminal justice system*. Beverly Hills, CA: Sage.

Glaser, D. (1997). *Profitable penalties: How to cut both crime rates and costs*. Thousand Oaks, CA: Pine Forge Press.

Glassner, B., and J. Loughlin. (1987). *Drugs in adolescent worlds: Burnouts to straights*. New York: St. Martin's Press.

Goetz, E. (1996). The U.S. war on drugs as urban policy. *International Journal of Urban and Regional Research* 20: 539–49.

Gold, S. (1990). *The state fiscal agenda for the 1990s*. Denver, CO: National Conference of State Legislatures.

Goldstein, H. (1975). *Police corruption: A perspective on its nature and control*. Washington, DC: Police Foundation.

Goldstein, H. (1990). *Problem-oriented policing*. New York: McGraw–Hill.

Goldstein, P. (1979). *Prostitution and drugs*. Lexington, MA: D. C. Heath.

Goldstein, P. (1998). The drugs/violence nexus: A tripartite conceptual framework. In J. Inciardi and K. McElrath, eds., *The American drug scene: An anthology*, 2nd ed. Los Angeles: Roxbury.

Goode, E. (1999). *Drugs in American society*, 5th ed. New York: Knopf.

Goode, E., and N. Ben-Yehuda. (1994a). Moral panics: Culture, politics, and social construction. *Annual Review of Sociology* 20: 149–71.

Goode, E., and N. Ben-Yehuda. (1994b). *Moral panics: The social construction of deviance*. Cambridge, MA: Blackwell.

Gorr, M. (2000). The morality of plea bargaining. *Social Theory and Practice* 26(1): 129–51.

Gosselin, D. (2000). *Heavy hands: An introduction to the crime of domestic violence*. Upper Saddle River, NJ: Prentice Hall.

Gottfredson, D. (1999). *Exploring criminal justice: An introduction*. Los Angeles: Roxbury.

Gottfredson, S., and D. Gottfredson. (1994). Behavioral prediction and the problem of incapacitation. *Criminology* 32(3): 441–74.

Gottfredson, S., and G. Jarjoura. (1996). Race, gender, and guidelines-based decision making. *Journal of Research in Crime and Delinquency* 33: 49–69.

Gould, L. (1974). Crime and the addict: Beyond common sense. In J. Inciardi and C. Chambers, eds., *Drugs and the criminal justice system*. Beverly Hills, CA: Sage.

Gove, W., M. Hughes, and M. Geerken. (1985). Are uniform crime reports a valid indicator of the index crimes? An affirmative answer with minor qualifications. *Criminology* 23: 451–501.

Gow, H. (1986). Religious views support the death penalty. In B. Szumski, L. Hall, and S. Bursell, eds., *The death penalty: Opposing viewpoints*. St. Paul, MN: Greenhaven.

Graber, D. (1980). *Crime news and the public*. Westport, CT: Praeger.

Graber, D. (1996). The new media and politics: What does the future hold? *Political Science and Politics* March: 33–36.

Graham, B. (2000). Judicial recruitment and racial diversity on state courts: An overview. In G. Mays and P. Gregware, eds., *Courts and justice: A reader*, 2nd ed. Prospect Heights, IL: Waveland Press.

Gray, J. (2001). *Why our drug laws have failed and what we can do about it*. Philadelphia: University of Temple Press.

Gray, M. (1998). *Drug crazy*. New York: Random House.

Greenberg, E. (1993). *The American political system: A radical approach*, 5th ed. Glenville, IL: Scott, Foresman.

Greenberg, S., and F. Adler. (1974). Crime and addiction: An empirical analysis of the literature, 1920–1973. *Contemporary Drug Problems* 3: 221–70.

Greenwood, P. (1998). *Diverting children from a life of crime: Measuring costs and benefits.* Santa Monica, CA: Rand Corp.

Greenwood, P., C. Rydell, A. Abrahamse, J. Cavlkins, J. Chiesa, K. Model, and S. Klein. (1994). *Three strikes and you're out—Estimated benefits and costs of California's new mandatory sentencing law.* Santa Monica, CA: Rand Corp.

Greenwood, P., and S. Turner. (1987). *Selective incapacitation revisited: Why the high rate offenders are hard to predict.* Santa Monica, CA: Rand Corp.

Gurevitch, M. (1982). *Culture, society, and the media.* London: Methuen.

Gusfield, J. (1967). Moral passage: The symbolic process in public designations of deviance. *Social Problems* 15: 175–88.

Haas, K., and G. Alpert, eds. (1999). *The dilemma of corrections,* 4th ed. Prospect Heights, IL: Waveland Press.

Hagan, J. (1989). Why is there so little criminal justice theory? Neglected macro- and micro-level links between organization and power. *Journal of Research on Crime and Delinquency* 26(2): 116–35.

Hagan, J. (1998). *Political crime, ideology, and criminality.* Boston: Allyn & Bacon.

Hall, J. (1992). *Deadly force: The common law and the Constitution.* Washington, DC: U.S. Department of Justice, Federal Bureau of Investigation.

Haltom, W. (1998). *Reporting on the courts: How the mass media cover judicial elections.* Chicago: Nelson–Hall.

Hamid, A. (1998). *Drugs in America: Sociology, economics, and politics.* Newbury Park, CA: Sage.

Hansen, D. (1999). Answer to question about origin of lady of justice. Online: www.commonlaw.com/Justice.html.

Hansom, R., and B. Ostrom. (1993). Litigation and the courts: Myths and misconceptions. *Trial* 29: 40–44.

Harmsworth, E. (1996). Bail and detention: An assessment and critique of the federal and Massachusetts systems. *New England Journal on Criminology and Civil Confinement* 22: 213.

Harrigan, J. (2000). *Empty dreams, empty pockets: Class and bias in American politics.* New York: Addison–Wesley Longman.

Harris, D. (1999). *Driving while black: Racial profiling on our nation's highways.* New York: American Civil Liberties Union.

Harriston, K., and M. P. Flaherty. (1994). Law and disorder—The District's troubled police. *Washington Post,* August 28–31: 20–32.

Hart, H. (1968). *Punishment and responsibility.* New York: Oxford University Press.

Harvard Law Review. (1988). Developments in the law—Race and the criminal process. *Harvard Law Review* 101: 1496.

Heath, L., and K. Gilbert. (1996). Mass media and fear of crime. *American Behavioral Scientist* 39: 379–86.

Henderson, J., and D. Simon. (1994). *Crimes of the criminal justice system.* Cincinnati, OH: Anderson.

Herbert, B. (1998). Cheap justice. *New York Times,* March 1: 15.

Herman, E., and N. Chomsky. (1988). *Manufacturing consent.* New York: Pantheon.

Hess, S. (1981). *The Washington reporters.* Washington, DC: Brookings Institution.

Hilgartner, S., and C. Bosk. (1988). The rise and fall of social problems: A public arenas model. *American Journal of Sociology* 94: 53–78.

Hindelang, M., T. Hirschi, and J. Weis. (1980). *Measuring delinquency.* Beverly Hills, CA: Sage.

Hirschi, T. (1969). *Causes of delinquency.* Berkeley: University of California Press.

Hollinger, R., and L. Lanza-Kaduce. (1988). The process of criminalization. *Criminology* 26: 101–26.

Hollister, L. (1988). Cannabis—1988. *Acta Psychiatrica Scandinavica Supplementum* 345: 108–18.

Holten, G., and M. Jones. (1982). *The system of criminal justice,* 2nd ed. Boston: Little, Brown.

Hoppe, C. (1992). Life in jail, or death? Life term is cheaper. *Charlotte Observer,* March 22: 12A.

Huff, C., A. Rattner, and E. Sagarin. (1996). *Convicted but innocent: Wrongful conviction and public policy.* Thousand Oaks, CA: Sage.

Huffington, A. (2003). *Pigs at the trough*. New York: Random House.

Hurwitz, J., and M. Peffley. (1997). Public perceptions of race and crime: The role of racial stereotypes. *American Journal of Political Science* 41(2): 375–401.

Ian, J., and S. Richards (2003). *Convict criminology*. Belmont, CA: Wadsworth.

Inbau, F., and J. Reid. (1967). *Criminal interrogation and confessions*. Baltimore, MD: Williams and Wilkins.

Inciardi, J., ed. (1991). *The drug legalization debate: Studies in crime, law, and justice*. Newbury Park, CA: Sage.

Inciardi, J. (2002). *The war on drugs III*. Boston: Pearson Education.

Inciardi, J., and C. Chambers. (1972). Unreported criminal involvement of narcotic addicts. *Journal of Drug Issues* 2(2): 57–64.

Inciardi, J., and K. McElrath, eds. (1998). *The American drug scene: An anthology*, 2nd ed. Los Angeles: Roxbury.

Ingley, S. (2000). Corrections without corrections. In J. May, ed., *Building violence: How America's rush to incarcerate creates more violence*. Thousand Oaks, CA: Sage.

Ingraham, B. (1994). The right of silence, the presumption of innocence, the burden of proof, and a modest proposal. *Journal of Criminal Law and Criminology* 85: 59–95.

Irwin, J. (1985). *The jail: Managing the underclass in American society*. Berkeley: University of California Press.

Irwin, J. (2003). Preface. In J. Ian and S. Edwards, eds., *Convict criminology*. Belmont, CA: Wadsworth.

Irwin, J., and J. Austin. (1997). *It's about time: America's imprisonment binge*. Belmont, CA: Wadsworth.

Iyengar, S., and D. Kinder. (1987). *News that matters: Television and American opinion*. Chicago: University of Chicago Press.

Jackson, D. (1994). Politician crime rhetoric. *Boston Globe*, October 21: 15.

Jackson, J. (1988). Aging black women and public policies. *Black Scholar* (May–June): 33.

Jaynes, G., and R. Williams. (1989). *A common destiny: Blacks and American society*. Washington, DC: National Academy Press.

Jeffery, C. (1990). *Criminology: An interdisciplinary approach*. Beverly Hills, CA: Prentice Hall.

Jennings, J. (1999). Persistent poverty in the United States: A review of theories and explanations. In L. Kushnick and J. Jennings, eds., *A new introduction to poverty: The role of race, power, and politics*. New York: New York University Press.

Jensen, E., and J. Gerber, eds. (1998). *The new war on drugs: Symbolic politics and criminal justice policy*. Cincinnati, OH: Anderson.

Johnson, B., P. Goldstein, E. Preble, J. Schmeidler, D. Lipton, B. Sprunt, and T. Miller. (1985). *Taking care of business: The economics of crime by heroin abusers*. Lexington, MA: Lexington Books.

Johnson, S. (2000). The Bible and the death penalty: Implications for criminal justice education. *Journal of Criminal Justice Education* 11(1): 15–33.

Jonas, S. (1991). The United States drug problem and the United States drug culture. In J. Inciardi, ed., *The drug legalization debate: Studies in crime, law, and justice*. Newbury Park, CA: Sage.

Jones, D. (1987). *History of criminology: A philosophical perspective*. New York: Greenwood.

Kaminer, W. (1999). Games prosecutors play. *American Prospect* 46: 20–26.

Kappeler, V., M. Blumberg, and G. Potter. (1996). *The mythology of crime and criminal justice*. Prospect Heights, IL: Waveland Press.

Kappeler, V., M. Blumberg, and G. Potter. (2000). *The mythology of crime and criminal justice*, 3rd ed. Prospect Heights, IL: Waveland Press.

Karel, R. (1991). A model legalization proposal. In J. Inciardi, ed., *The drug legalization debate: Studies in crime, law, and justice*. Newbury Park, CA: Sage.

Karmen, A. (1996). *Crime victims: An introduction to victimology*, 3rd ed. Belmont, CA: Wadsworth.

Kassin, S. (2000). The American jury: Handicapped in the pursuit of justice. In G. Mays and P. Gregware, eds., *Courts and justice: A reader*, 2nd ed. Prospect Heights, IL: Waveland Press.

Katz, M. (1999). Reframing the underclass debate. In L. Kushnick and J. Jennings, eds., *A new introduction to poverty: The role of race, power, and politics*. New York: New York University Press.

Kelling, G., T. Pate, D. Dieckman, and C. Brown. (1974). *The Kansas City preventive patrol experiment: A summary report*. Washington, DC: The Police Foundation.

Kellner, L. (1988). Narcotics-related corruption. In *Prosecution of public corruption cases* (pp. 39–53). Washington, DC: U.S. Department of Justice.

Kennedy, D. (1997). Pulling levers: Chronic offenders, high crime settings, and a theory of prevention. *Valparaiso University Law Review* 31(2): 449.

Kennedy, R. (1997). *Race, crime and the law*. New York: Vintage.

Kim, M. (1999). The working poor: Lousy jobs or lazy workers? In L. Kushnick and J. Jennings, eds., *A new introduction to poverty: The role of race, power, and politics*. New York: New York University Press.

Kitsuse, S., and M. Spector. (1973). Toward a sociology of social problems: Social condition, value judgments, and social problems. *Social Problems* 20: 407–19.

Kittel, N. (1986). Police perjury: Criminal defense attorneys' perspectives. *American Journal of Criminal Justice* 11: 1.

Klain, J. (1989). *International television and video almanac*. New York: Quarterly.

Kleiman, M. (1997). Neither probation nor legalization: Grudging toleration in drug control policy. In M. McShane and F. Williams, eds., *Drug use and drug policy*. New York: Garland.

Klockars, C. (1991). The rhetoric of community policing. In J. Greene and S. Mastrofski, eds., *Community policing: Rhetoric and reality*. New York: Praeger.

Kohn, L., J. Corrigan, M. Donaldson, and W. Richardson. (2000). *To err is human: Building a safer health system*. Washington, DC: National Academy Press.

Koning, H. (1993). *The conquest of America: How the Indian nations lost their continent*. New York: Monthly Review Press.

Kooistra, P., J. Mahoney, and S. Westervelt. (1999). The world of crime according to "COPS." In G. Cavender and M. Fishman, eds., *Entertaining crime: Television reality programs*. Hawthorne, NY: Aldine de Gruyter.

Kozel, N., R. Dupont, and B. Brown. (1972). A study of narcotic involvement in an offender population. *International Journal of the Addictions* 7: 443–50.

Krahn, H., T. Hartnagel, and J. Gartnell. (1986). Income inequality and homicide rates: Cross-national data and criminological theories. *Criminology* 24: 269–93.

Krajicek, D. (1998). *Scooped! Media miss real story on crime while chasing sex, sleaze, and celebrities*. New York: Columbia University Press.

Kramer, J. (1976). From demon to ally—How mythology has and may yet alter national drug policy. *Journal of Drug Issues* 6: 390–406.

Kraska, P. B. (1990). The unmentionable alternative: The need for, and the argument against the decriminalization of drug laws. In R. Weisheit, ed., *Drugs, crime, and the criminal justice system*. Cincinnati, OH: Anderson.

Kraska, P., and V. Kappeler. (1997). Militarizing American police: The rise and normalization of paramilitary units. *Social Problems* 44(1): 1–17. VSE .

Kull, S., C. Ramsay, S. Subias, E. Lewis, and P. Warf. (2003). Misperceptions, the media, and the war on Iraq. Online: http://www.pipa.org/OnlineReports/Iraq/Media_10_02_03_Report.pdf.

Kushnick, L. (1999). Responding to urban crisis: Functions of white racism. In L. Kushnick and J. Jennings, eds., *A new introduction to poverty: The role of race, power, and politics*. New York: New York University Press.

Kushnick, L., and J. Jennings, eds. (1999). *A new introduction to poverty: The role of race, power, and politics*. New York: New York University Press.

Kuttner, R. (2003). Sharing America's wealth. *American Prospect* Summer: A3–A5.

Lacayo, R. (1994). Lock 'em up! *Time*, February 7.

Ladinsky, J. (1984). The impact of social background of lawyers in legal practice and the law. In J. Bonsignore, E. Katsh, D'Errico, R. Pipkin, S. Arons, and J. Rifkin, eds., *Before the law: An introduction to the legal process*, 1st ed. Boston: Houghton Mifflin.

Land, K., P. McCall, and L. Cohen. (1990). Structural co-variates of homicide rates: Are there any invariances across time and space? *American Journal of Sociology* 95: 922–63.

Langan, P. (1994). No racism in the criminal justice system. *Public Interest* 117: 48–51.

Langbein, J. (2000). On the myth of written constitutions: The disappearance of criminal jury trial. In G. Mays and P. Gregware, eds., *Courts and justice: A reader*, 2nd ed. Prospect Heights, IL: Waveland Press.

Lapley, R., and M. Westlake. (1988). *Film theory: An introduction.* Manchester, UK: Manchester University Press.

Lasswell, H. (1936). *Politics: Who gets what, when, how.* New York: McGraw–Hill.

Lauer, R., and J. Lauer, eds. (2000). *Troubled times: Readings in social problems.* Los Angeles: Roxbury.

Lazarus, E. (2000). How Miranda really works and why it matters. Online: http://writ.news.findlaw.com/lazarus/20000605.html.

Leadership Conference on Civil Rights and the Leadership Conference Education Fund. (2000). Justice on trial: Racial disparities in the American criminal justice system. Online: www.civilrights.org.

Leff, D., D. Protess, and S. Brooks. (1986). Crusading journalism: Changing public attitudes and policy-making agendas. *Public Opinion Quarterly* 50: 300–315.

LEMAS. (2003). LEMAS statistics, 2000. Online: www.ojp.usdoj.gov/bjs/abstract/lemas00htm.

Leo, R. (1996). Miranda's revenge: Police interrogation as a confidence game. *Law and Society Review* 30(2): 259–88.

Levy, F. (1988). *Dollars and dreams: The changing American income distribution.* New York: Norton.

Lewis, D. (1981). Crime in the media: Introduction. In D. Lewis, ed., *Reactions to crime.* Beverly Hills, CA: Sage.

Lichter, R., and E. Edmundson. (1992). *A day in the life of television violence.* Washington, DC: Center for Media and Public Affairs.

Lichter, S. (1988). Media power: The influence of media on politics and business. *Florida Policy Review* 4: 35–41.

Lichter, S., L. Lichter, and S. Rothman. (1994). *Prime time: How TV portrays American culture.* Washington, DC: Regnery.

Liebman, J., J. Fagan, and V. West. (2000). *A broken system: Error rates in capital cases, 1973–1995.* New York: Columbia University Law School.

Liebman, J., J. Fagan, A. Gelman, V. West, G. Davies, and A. Kiss. (2002). *A broken system, Part II: Why there is so much error in capital cases, and what can be done about it.* Online: www2.law.columbia.edu/brokensystem2.pdf.

Lilly, J., and P. Knepper. (1993). The corrections-commercial complex. *Crime and Delinquency* 39: 150–66.

Lindsell-Roberts, S. (1994). *Loony laws and silly statutes.* New York: Sterling Publications.

Liska, K. (2000). *Drugs and the human body*, 6th ed. New York: Macmillan.

Livingston, J. (1996). *Crime and criminology*, 2nd ed. Upper Saddle River, NJ: Prentice Hall.

Lockwood, D., A. Pottieger, and J. Inciardi. (1996). Crack use, crime by crack users, and ethnicity. In D. Hawkins, ed., *Ethnicity, race, and crime.* Albany: State University of New York Press.

Loftus, E. F. (1979). *Eyewitness testimony.* Cambridge, MA: Harvard University Press.

Lowi, T., and B. Ginsburg. (1990). *American government: Freedom and power.* New York: Norton.

Luginbuhl, J., and M. Burkhead. (1994). Sources of bias and arbitrariness in the capital trial. *Journal of Social Issues* 103–124.

Lule, J. (2002). *Daily news, eternal stories: The mythological role of journalism.* New York: Guilford.

Lyman, M., and G. Potter. (1998). *Drugs in society.* Cincinnati, OH: Anderson.

Lynch, M. (1997). *Radical criminology.* Brookfield, VT: Aldershot.

Lynch, M., and P. Stretesky. (1999). Marxism and social justice: Thinking about social justice, eclipsing criminal justice. In B. Arrigo, ed., *Social justice, criminal justice.* Belmont, CA: Wadsworth.

MacCoun, R. (1990). The emergence of extralegal bias during jury deliberation. *Criminal Justice and Behavior* 17: 303–14.

MacCoun, R., and Reuter, P. (2001). *Drug war heresies*. New York: Cambridge University Press.

Magagnini, S. (1988). Closing death row would save state $90 million a year. *Sacramento Bee*, March 28: 1.

Maguire, M., and T. Bennett. (1982). *Burglary in a dwelling*. London: Heinemann.

Maguire, K., and T. Flanagan. (1997). *Sourcebook of criminal justice statistics—1996*. Albany, NY: Hindelang Criminal Justice Research Center.

Maguire, K., and A. Pastore. (1995). *Sourcebook of criminal justice statistics, 1994*. Washington, DC: Bureau of Justice Statistics.

Maguire, K., and A. Pastore, eds. (1997). *Sourcebook of criminal justice statistics, 1996*. Washington, DC: U.S. Department of Justice, Bureau of Justice Statistics.

Maguire, K., and A. Pastore, eds. (1999). *Sourcebook of criminal justice statistics, 1998*. Washington, DC: U.S. Department of Justice, Bureau of Justice Statistics.

Maher, T. (2000). Environmental racism. In R. Lauer and J. Lauer, eds., *Troubled times: Readings in social problems*. Los Angeles: Roxbury.

Mann, C. (1993). *Unequal justice*. Bloomington: Indiana University Press.

Manning, P. (1997). *Police work: The social organization of policing*, 2nd ed. Prospect Heights, IL: Waveland Press.

Marion, N. (1995). *A primer in the politics of criminal justice*. Albany, NY: Harrow and Heston.

Marongiu, P., and G. Newman. (1987). *Vengeance: The fight against injustice*. Totowa, NJ: Rowman and Littlefield.

Marsh, H. (1991). A comparative analysis of crime coverage in newspapers in the United States and other countries from 1960–1989: A review of the literature. *Journal of Criminal Justice* 19: 67–80.

Martin, S. (2000). Sanctioned violence in American prisons. In J. May, ed., *Building violence: How America's rush to incarcerate creates more violence*. Thousand Oaks, CA: Sage.

Martinson, R. (2000). What works? Questions and answers in prison reform. *Public Interest* 35: 22–55.

Marx, G. (1981). Ironies of social control: Authorities as contributors to deviance through escalation, nonenforcement, and covert facilitation. *Social Problems* 28: 221–46.

Masci, D. (1994a). The modified crime bill. *Congressional Quarterly Weekly Report* 52: 2488–93.

Masci, D. (1994b). $30 billion anti-crime bill heads to Clinton's desk. *Congressional Quarterly* 27 (August): 2488–93.

Massey, D., and A. Gross. (1990). *A pessimistic interpretation of recent declines in black residential segregation*. Chicago: Ogburn–Stouffer Center.

Mauer, M. (1997). *Americans behind bars: United States and the international use of incarceration*. Washington, DC: The Sentencing Project.

Mauer, M. (1998). "Lock 'em up and throw away the key": African Americans and meals and the criminal justice system. In K. Haas and G. Alpert, eds., *The dilemma of corrections*. Prospect Heights, IL: Waveland Press.

Mauer, M., and T. Huling. (1995a). One in three young black men ensnared in justice system. *Overcrowded Times* 6: 1–10.

Mauer, M., and T. Huling. (1995b). *Young black Americans and the criminal justice system: Five years later*. Washington DC: The Sentencing Project.

May, J., ed. (2000). Building violence: How America's rush to incarcerate creates more violence. Thousand Oaks, CA: Sage.

Mayhew, P., and J. Van Dijk. (1997). *Criminal victimization in eleven industrialized countries: Key findings from the 1996 International Crime Victims Survey*. The Hague: Dutch Ministry of Justice.

McAdams, J. (1998). Racial disparity and the death penalty. *Law and Contemporary Problems* 61(4): 153–70.

McAnamy, P. (1992). Asset forfeiture as drug control strategy. Paper presented at the annual meeting of the American Society of Criminology, New Orleans, LA, November.

McCaghy, C., T. Capron, and J. Jamieson. (2000). *Deviant behavior*, 5th ed. Boston: Allyn & Bacon.

McCleary, R., B. Nienstedt, and J. Erven. (1982). Uniform crime reports as organizational outcomes: Three time series quasi-experiments. *Social Problems* 29: 361–72.

McCombs, M., and D. Shaw. (1972). The agenda setting function of the mass media. *Public Opinion Quarterly* 36: 176–87.

McElhaney, J. W. (1998). The jury consultant bazaar. *ABA Journal* 84: 78–79.

McEwen, T., and F. Leahy. (1994). *Less than lethal force technologies in law enforcement and correctional agencies.* Alexandria, VA: Institute for Law and Justice.

McGarrell, E. (1993). Institutional theory and the stability of a conflict model of the incarceration rate. *Justice Quarterly* 10(1): 7–28.

McGinnis, K. (2000). Make 'em break rocks. In J. May, ed., *Building violence: How America's rush to incarcerate creates more violence.* Thousand Oaks, CA: Sage.

McGucken, E. (1987). *Crime news reporting in the New York Times, 1900 to 1950: A content analysis.* Ph.D. dissertation, University of Akron.

McLaughlin, C. (2000). Prisoner rehabilitation: Feeling better but getting worse. In J. May, ed., *Building violence: How America's rush to incarcerate creates more violence.* Thousand Oaks, CA: Sage.

McQuail, D. (1994). *Mass communication theory,* 3rd ed. London: Sage.

McShane, M., and F. Williams. (1992). Radical victimology: A critique of victim in traditional victimology. *Crime and Delinquency* 38(2): 258–71.

Meddis, S. (1993). In twin cities, a tale of two standards. *USA Today,* July 26: 6A.

Meeker, J. (1984). Criminal appeals over the last 100 years: Are the odds of winning increasing? *Criminology* 22: 551–71.

Meier, R., and J. Short. (1985). Crime as hazard: Perceptions of risk and seriousness. *Criminology* 23: 389–99.

Merlo, A., and P. Benekos. (2000). *What's wrong with the criminal justice system: Ideology, politics and the media.* Cincinnati, OH: Anderson.

Merriam-Webster's Collegiate Dictionary, 10th ed. (1998). Springfield, MA: Merriam-Webster.

Merton, R. (1938a). *Science, technology and society in seventeenth century England.* Bruges, Belgium: Saint Catherine Press.

Merton, R. (1938b). *Social structure and anomie.* Indianapolis, IN: Bobbs–Merrill.

Messner, S., and K. Tardiff. (1986). Economic inequality and levels of homicide: An analysis of urban neighborhoods. *Criminology* 24: 297–316.

Miethe, T. (1982). Public consensus on crime seriousness: Normative structure or methodological artifact? *Criminology* 20: 515–26.

Miethe, T. D. (1995). Fear and withdrawal from urban life. *Annals of the American Academy of Political and Social Science* 539: 14–27.

Mill, John Stuart. (1859). *On liberty.* Tokyo: Kenkyusha.

Miller, J. (1994). *African American males in the criminal justice system.* Alexandria, VA: National Center on Institutions and Alternatives.

Miller, J. (1997). African American males in the criminal justice system. *Phi Delta Kappan* (June): 22–30.

Miller, J. (1998). *Search and destroy: African-American males in the criminal justice system.* New York: Cambridge University Press.

Miller, M. (1995). The road to Panama City. *Newsweek* 126(18): 84.

Miller, R. (1997). Symposium on coercion: An interdisciplinary examination of coercion, exploitation, and the Law: III. Coerced confinement and treatment: The continuum of coercion: constitutional and clinical considerations in the treatment of mentally disordered persons. *Denver Law Review* 74: 1169–1214.

Miller, S. (2000). Arrest policies for domestic violence and their implications for battered women. In R. Muraskin, ed., *It's a crime: Women and criminal justice,* 2nd ed. Upper Saddle River, NJ: Prentice Hall.

Miller, T., M. Cohen, and B. Wiersma. (1997). *Victim costs and consequences: A new look.* Washington, DC: U.S. Department of Justice, Office of Justice Programs, National Institute of Justice.

Miller, W. (1958). Lower class culture as a generating milieu of gang delinquency. *Journal of Social Issues* 14: 5–19.

Milovanovich, Z. (2000). Prosecutorial discretion: A comparative perspective. In G. Mays and P. Gregware, eds., *Courts and justice: A reader,* 2nd ed. Prospect Heights, IL: Waveland Press.

Minow, M. (2000). Stripped down like a runner or enriched by experience? Bias and impartiality of judges and jurors. In G. Mays and P. Gregware, eds., *Courts and justice: A reader,* 2nd ed. Prospect Heights, IL: Waveland Press.

Mintz, M. (1992). Why the media cover up corporate crime: A reporter looks back in anger. *Trial* 28: 72–77.

Mokhiber, R., and R. Weissman. (1999). *Corporate predators: The hunt for mega-profits and the attack on democracy.* Monroe, ME: Common Courage Press.

The Mollen Commission. (1994). *Police brutality and excessive force in the New York City Police Department.* New York: The Mollen Commission.

Moore, W. (1995). Targeting Harlem, not Hollywood. *National Journal,* February 11: 388.

Morgan, M., and N. Signorielli, eds. (1990). *Cultivation analysis: New directions in media effects research.* Newbury Park, CA: Sage.

Morgan-Sharp, E. (1999). The administration of justice based on gender and race. In R. Muraskin and A. Roberts, eds., *Visions for change: Crime and justice in the 21st century,* 2nd ed. Upper Saddle River, NJ: Prentice Hall.

Morris, E. (1988). *The thin blue line* [film]. New York: Miramax Films.

Move On. (2002). Online: www.moveon.org.

Muraskin, R. (1999). The future. In R. Muraskin and A. Roberts, eds., *Visions for change: Crime and justice in the twenty-first century,* 2nd ed. Upper Saddle River, NJ: Prentice Hall.

Muraskin, R., and A. Roberts. (1999). *Visions for change: Crime and justice in the twenty-first century,* 2nd ed. Upper Saddle River, NJ: Prentice Hall.

Murray, C. (1984). *Losing ground—American social policy, 1950–1980.* New York: Basic Books.

Murray, C., and R. Herrnstein. (1994). *The bell curve: Intelligence and class structure in American life.* New York: Free Press.

Myers, S. (1987). Introduction. Special issue on race and crime. *Review of Black Political Economy* 16: 5–15.

NAACP Legal Defense and Educational Fund. (1998, 2003). Death Row, U.S.A., 99 Hudson, Street, Suite 1600, New York, NY 10013–2897.

Nacos, B. (2002). *Mass-mediated terrorism: The central role of the media in terrorism and counterterrorism.* Lanham, MD: Rowman & Littlefield.

Nadelmann, E. (1991). The case for legalization. In J. Inciardi, ed., *The drug legalization debate: Studies in crime, law, and justice.* Newbury Park, CA: Sage.

Nadelmann, E. (1998). Experimenting with drugs. *Foreign Affairs* 1: 111–26.

Nader, Ralph. (1999). Introduction. In R. Mokhiber and R. Weissman, eds. *Corporate predators: The hunt for mega-profits and the attack on democracy.* Monroe, ME: Common Courage Press.

Nakell, B., and K. Hardy. (1987). *The arbitrariness of the death penalty.* Philadelphia: Temple University Press.

Nardulli, P., J. Eisenstein, and R. Flemming. (1988). *The tenor of justice: Criminal courts and the guilty plea process.* Urbana: University of Illinois Press.

National Association for the Advancement of Colored People (NAACP). (1993). Online: www.naacp.org.

National Association of Criminal Defense Lawyers. (1996). *Racism in the criminal justice system.* Washington, DC: National Association of Criminal Defense Lawyers.

National Association of State Budget Officers. (1996). *Capital budgeting in the states.* Washington DC: National Association of State Budget Officers.

National Center on Addiction and Substance Abuse. (1998). *Behind bars: Substance abuse and America's prison population.* New York: National Center on Addiction and Substance Abuse.

National Center on Institutions and Alternatives. (1999). What every American should know about the criminal justice system. Online: www.ncianet.org/ncia/facts.html.

National Criminal Justice Reference Service. (2003). In the spotlight. Drug courts—Summary. Online: www.ncjrs.org/drug_courts/summary.html.

National Institutes of Health. (1997). *SAMHSA's National Clearinghouse for Alcohol and Drug Information: A service of the Substance Abuse and Mental Health Services Administration*. Bethesda, MD: NIH.

National Institute of Justice. (1997). *A study of homicide in eight U.S cities: An NIJ intramural research project*. Washington, DC: National Institute of Justice, U.S. Department of Justice.

National Institute on Money in State Politics. Online: www.followthemoney.org.

Nazario, S. (1993). Odds grim for black men in California. *Washington Post,* December 12: A9.

Nelson, L., and B. Foster. (2001). *Death watch*. Upper Saddle River, NJ: Prentice Hall.

Nettler, G. (1984). *Explaining crime*, 3rd ed. New York: McGraw–Hill.

Neubauer, R. (1998). The future of women in policing. *Police Chief* 6 (December): 53–57.

Newman, G. (1990). Popular culture and criminal justice: A preliminary analysis. *Journal of Criminal Justice* 18: 261–74.

The New York Times. (1997). *Special reports on downsizing*. New York: The New York Times.

Nisbet, M. (2001). Media coverage after the attack: Reason and deliberative democracy put to the test. Online: www.csicop.org/genx/terrorattack/.

Nobling, T., C. Spohn, and M. Delone. (1998). A tale of two cities: Unemployment and sentencing severity. *Justice Quarterly* 15: 459–85.

Norris, P., M. Korn, and M. Just. (2003). *Framing terrorism: The news media, the government, and the public*. London: Routledge.

Nuro, D., T. Kinlock, and T. Hanlen. (1998). The drugs-crime connection. In J. Inciardi and K. McElrath, eds., *The American drug scene: An anthology,* 2nd ed. Los Angeles: Roxbury.

O'Brien, D. M. (1993). *Storm center*. New York: Norton.

O'Connell, M., and A. Whelan. (1996). Taking wrongs seriously: Public perceptions of crime seriousness. *British Journal of Criminology* 36: 299–318.

Office of National Drug Control Policy. (2002). Online: www.whitehousedrugpolicy.gov.

Omi, M. (1987). We shall overturn: Race and the contemporary American right. Dissertation, University of California at Santa Cruz.

Omi, M., and H. Winant. (1986). *Racial formation in the United States*. New York: Routledge and Kegan Paul.

Orcutt, J., and J. Turner. (1993). Shocking numbers and graphic accounts: Quantified images of drug problems in the print media. *Social Problems* 6: 217–32.

Packer, H. (1968). *The limits of the criminal sanction*. Palo Alto, CA: Stanford University Press.

Page, C. (1999). Hasta la vista, baby. *Chicago Tribune,* January 13: 17.

Page, J. (2000). Violence and incarceration: A personal observation. In J. May, ed., *Building violence: How America's rush to incarcerate creates more violence*. Thousand Oaks, CA: Sage.

Palermo, G., M. White, and L. Wasserman. 1998. Plea bargaining: Injustice for all? *International Journal of Offender Therapy and Comparative Criminology* 42(2): 111–23.

Parenti, M. (1983). *Democracy for the few,* 4th ed. New York: St. Martin's Press.

Parton, D., M. Hansel, and J. Stratton. (1991). Measuring crime seriousness: Lessons from the National Survey of Crime Severity. *British Journal of Criminology* 31: 72–85.

Pate, T., and L. Fridell. (1994). *Police use of force: Official reports, citizen complaints, and legal consequences, 1991–1992*. Ann Arbor, MI: Interuniversity Consortium for Political and Social Research

Paulsen, D. (2000). Murder in black and white: The newspaper coverage of homicide in Houston, 1986–1994. Ph.D. dissertation, Sam Houston State University.

Pearson, D. (2000). Minority health. In R. Lauer and J. Lauer, eds., *Troubled times: Readings in social problems*. Los Angeles: Roxbury.

Peffley, M., and J. Hurwitz. (1997). Racial stereotypes and whites' political views of blacks in the context of welfare and crime. *American Journal of Political Science* 41(1): 30–60.

Peoples, E. (2000). *Basic criminal procedures*. Upper Saddle River, NJ: Prentice Hall.

Perlmutter, D. (2001). Before rushing to judge cops for their actions. *Law Enforcement News* 27(557): 11.

Petersilia, J. (1995). Racial disparities in the criminal justice system: A summary. *Crime and Delinquency* 31: 15–34.

Petersilia, J. (1998). Probation in the United States. *Perspectives* 37: 30–49.

Petersilia, J., and S. Turner. (1986). *Prison versus probation in California: Implications for crime and offender recidivism*. Santa Monica, CA: Rand Corp.

Pew Research Center for the People and the Press. (1998). Online: www.people-press.org.

Phillips, K. (1991). *The politics of rich and poor*. New York: Random House.

Phillips, K. (2003). How wealth defines power. *American Prospect* Summer: A8–A10.

Phipps, A. (1986). Radical criminology and criminal victimization: Proposals for the development of theory and intervention. In R. Matthews and J. Young, eds., *Confronting crime*. Beverly Hills, CA: Sage.

Pizzi, W. (1999). *Trials without truth: Why our system of criminal trials has become an expensive failure and what we need to do to rebuild it*. New York: New York University Press.

Platt, L. (1999). Armageddon—Live at 6! In R. Hiebert, ed., *Impact of mass media: Current issues*, 4th ed. New York: Longman.

Podgor, E., and J. Israel. (1997). *White collar crime*. St. Paul, MN: West.

Pojman, L. (1998). *The death penalty: For and against*. New York: Rowman and Littlefield.

Police Foundation. (1981). *The Newark foot patrol experiment*. Washington DC: Police Foundation.

Pontell, H., K. Calavita, and R. Tillman. (1994). *Fraud in the savings and loan industry: White collar crime and government response*. Washington, DC: National Institute of Justice.

Pope, C. (1979). Race and crime revisited. *Crime and Delinquency* 25(3): 347–57.

Pope, H., and D. Yurgelun-Todd. (1996). The residual cognitive effects of heavy marijuana use in college students. *Journal of the American Medical Association* 275: 7.

Poporino, F. (1986). Managing violent individuals in correctional settings. *Journal of Interpersonal Violence* 1: 213–37.

Potter, G., and V. Kappeler. (1998). *Constructing crime: Perspectives on making news and social problems*. Prospect Heights, IL: Waveland Press.

Pound, R. (1912). *The scope and purpose of sociological jurisprudence*. Cambridge, MA: Harvard Law Review Association.

Pratt, C. (1992). Police discretion. *Law and Order* March: 99–100.

Pratt, T. (1998). Race and sentencing: A meta-analysis of conflicting empirical research results. *Journal of Criminal Justice* 26(6): 513–23.

Preble, E., and J. Casey, Jr. (1969). Taking care of business: The heroin user's life in the streets. *International Journal of Addictions* 4: 1–24.

Prejean, H. (1993). *Dead man walking*. New York: Random House.

Quan, S. (2000). A profile of the working poor. In R. Lauer and J. Lauer, eds., *Troubled times: Readings in social problems*. Los Angeles: Roxbury.

Quinney, R. (1970). *The social reality of crime*. New Brunswick, NJ: Transaction.

Quinney, R. (1977). *Class, state, and crime: On the theory and practice of criminal justice*. New York: D. McKay.

Radelet, M., H. Bedau, and C. Putnam. (1992). *In spite of innocence: The ordeal of 400 Americans wrongly convicted of crimes punishable by death*. Boston: Northeastern University Press.

Raeder, M. (1993). Gender and sentencing: Single moms, battered women, and other sex-based anomalies in the gender-free world of the federal sentencing guidelines. *Pepperdine Law Review* 20: 948.

Raine, A. (1993). *The psychopathology of crime*. New York: Academic Press.

Randell, D. (1995). The portrayal of business malfeasance in the elite and general media. In G. Geis, R. Meier, and L. Salinger, eds., *White-collar crime: Classic and contemporary views*. New York: Free Press.

Ranney, D. (1999). Class, race, gender, and poverty: A critique of some contemporary theories. In L. Kushnick and J. Jennings, eds., *A new introduction to poverty: The role of race, power, and politics*. New York: New York University Press.

Ransby, B. (1999). The black poor and the politics of expendability. In L. Kushnick and J. Jennings, eds., *A new introduction to poverty: The role of race, power, and politics*. New York: New York University Press.

Rasmussen, D., and B. Benson. (1994). *The economic anatomy of a drug war*. Lanham, MD: Rowman and Littlefield.

Rauma, D. (1991). The context of normative consensus: An expansion of the Rossi/Berk model, with an application to crime seriousness. *Social Science Research* 20: 1–28.

Reed, I. (1991). Tuning out network bias. *New York Times*, April 9: A11.

Reed, I. (1993). It's racist. *American Journalism Review* 15(7): 22–23.

Reeves, J., and R. Campbell. (1994). *Cracked coverage: Television news, the anti-cocaine crusade, and the Reagan legacy*. Durham, NC: Duke University Press.

Reiman, J. (1998). *The rich get richer and the poor get prison: Ideology, class, and criminal justice,* 5th ed. Boston: Allyn & Bacon.

Reiman, J., and P. Leighton (2003). Getting tough on corporate crime? Enron and a year of corporate financial scandals. Online: www.stopviolence.com.

Reinarman, C. (1994). Unanticipated consequences of criminilization: Hypotheses on how drug laws exacerbate drug problems. *Perspectives on Social Problems* 6: 217–32.

Reinarman, C. (1995). Crack attack: America's latest drug scare, 1986–1992. In J. Best, ed., *Images of issues: Typifying contemporary social problems*. New York: Aldine de Gruyter

Reinarman, C., and H. Levine. (1989a). The crack attack: Politics and media in America's latest drug scare. In J. Best, ed., *Images of issues: Typifying contemporary social problems*. New York: Aldine de Gruyter.

Rendell, S., and T. Broughel. (2003). *Extra!* May/June. FAIR. Online: www.fair.org.

Rengert, G., and J. Wasilchick. (1985). *Suburban burglary: A time and place for everything*. Springfield, IL: Charles C. Thomas.

Reppetto, R. (1974). *Residential crime*. Cambridge, MA: Ballinger.

Reuter, P. (1998). Hawks ascendant: The punitive trend of American drug policy. In J. Inciardi and K. McElrath, eds., *The American drug scene: An anthology*, 2nd ed. Los Angeles: Roxbury.

Roberts, D. (1993). Crime, race and reproduction. *Tulane Law Review* 1945: 1.

Roberts, J. (1992). Public opinion, crime, and criminal justice. In M. Tonry, ed., *Crime and justice: A review of research,* Vol. 16. Chicago: University of Chicago Press.

Roberts, J., and A. Doob. (1990). News media influences on public views of sentencing. *Law and Human Behavior* 14: 451–68.

Roberts, J., and L. Stalans. (2000). *Public opinion, crime, and criminal justice*. Boulder, CO: Westview Press.

Robinson, M. (1998). Tobacco: The greatest crime in world history? *Critical Criminologist* 8(3): 20–22.

Robinson, M. (1999). The historical development of CPTED: 25 years of responses to C. Ray Jeffery's work. *Advances in Criminological Theory* 8: 427–62.

Robinson, M. (2000). The construction and reinforcement of myths of race and crime. *Journal of Contemporary Criminal Justice* 16(2): 133–56.

Robinson, M. (2002). The case for a "new victimology": Implications for policing. In L. Moriarty, ed., *Police and victims*. Upper Saddle River, NJ: Prentice Hall.

Robinson, M. (2004). *Why crime? An integrated systems theory of antisocial behavior*. Upper Saddle River, NJ: Prentice Hall.

Robinson, M., and B. Zaitzow. (1999a). Criminologists: Are we what we study? A national study of crime experts. *Criminologist* 24(2): 1, 4, 17–19.

Robinson, M., and B. Zaitzow. (1999b). Like the pot calling the kettle black: Criminologists who engage in criminal, deviant, and unethical behavior. Paper presented to the American Society of Criminology, November.

Robinson, R. (1993). What does "unwilling" to impose the death penalty mean anyway? *Law and Human Behavior* 17: 471–77.

Rold, W. (2000). Legislating barriers to effective solutions: An indelicate tool for a complex problem. In J. May, ed., *Building violence: How America's rush to incarcerate creates more violence*. Thousand Oaks, CA: Sage.

Rome, D. (1998). Stereotyping by the media: Murderers, rapists, and drug addicts. In C. Mann and M. Zatz, eds., *Images of color, images of crime*. Los Angeles: Roxbury.

Rosch, J. (1985). Crime as an issue in American politics. In E. Fairchild and V. Webb, eds., *The politics of crime and criminal justice*. Beverly Hills, CA: Sage.

Rosenbaum, D., and G. Hanson. (1998). Assessing the effects of school-based drug education: A six-year multilevel analysis of project D.A.R.E. *Journal of Research in Crime and Delinquency* 35(4): 381–412.

Rosenbaum, D., A. Lurigio, and R. Davis. (1998). *The prevention of crime: Social and situational strategies*. Belmont, CA: Wadsworth.

Rosoff, S., H. Pontell, and R. Tillman. (1998). *Profit without honor: White-collar crime and the looting of America*. Upper Saddle River, NJ: Prentice Hall.

Ross, D. (1999). Assessing the patterns of citizen resistance during arrests. *FBI Law Enforcement Bulletin* 68(6): 5–11.

Ross, J., and S. Richards. (2003). *Convict criminology*. Belmont, CA: Wadsworth.

Rothman, D. (1971). *The discovery of the asylum*. Boston: Little, Brown.

Rouse, J., and B. Johnson. (1991). Hidden paradigms of morality in debates about drugs: Historical and policy shifts in British and American drug policies. In J. Inciardi, ed., *The drug legalization debate: Studies in crime, law, and justice*. Newbury Park, CA: Sage Publications.

Ruprecht, C. (1997). Are verdicts, too, like sausages? Lifting the cloak of jury secrecy. *University of Pennsylvania Law Review* 146(1): 217–68.

Rusche, G., and O. Kirchheimer. (1939). *Punishment and social structure*. New York: Columbia University Press.

Rush, G. E. (2000). *The dictionary of criminal justice*, 4th ed. Boston: Dushkin/McGraw–Hill.

Russell, K. (1998). *The color of crime*. New York: New York University Press.

Sabato, L. (1993). *Feeding frenzy*. New York: Free Press.

Sacco, V. (1995). Media constructions of crime. *Annals of the American Academy of Political and Social Science* 539: 141–54.

Sakamoto, A., and J. Tzeng. (1999). A fifty-year perspective on the declining significance of race in the occupational attainment of white and black men. *Sociological Perspectives* 42(2): 157–79.

Salant, J. (1999). Tobacco giant Philip Morris tops list of political contributors. Online: www.nandonet.com.

Sampson, R. (1987). Urban black violence: The effect of male joblessness and family disruption. *American Journal of Sociology* 93: 348–82.

Sampson R., and J. Laub. (1997). A life-course theory of cumulative disadvantage and the stability of delinquency. In T. Thornberry, ed., *Developmental theories of crime and delinquency*. New Brunswick, NJ: Transaction.

Sandor, R. (1995). Legalizing/decriminalizing drug use. In R. Coombs and D. Ziedonis, eds., *Handbook on drug abuse prevention: A contemporary strategy to prevent the abuse of alcohol and other drugs*. Boston: Allyn & Bacon.

Sandys, M., and E. McGarrell. (1995). Attitudes toward capital punishment: Preferences for the penalty or mere acceptance? *Journal of Research in Crime and Delinquency* 32: 191–213.

Sasson, T. (1995). *Crime talk: How citizens construct a social problem*. New York: Aldine de Gruyter.

Scarr, H. (1973). *Patterns of burglary*. Washington, DC: National Institute of Law Enforcement and Criminal Justice.

Schatzman, M. (1975). Cocaine and the drug problem. *Journal of Psychedelic Drugs* 7(1): 7–17.

Schecter, D. (2003). *Embedded: Weapons of mass deception: How the media failed to cover the war on Iraq*. Amherst, NY: Prometheus Books.

Scheingold, S. A. (1984). *The politics of law and order: Street crime and public policy*. New York: Longman.

Schlesinger, P., and H. Tumber. (1994). *Reporting crime: The media politics of criminal justice*. Oxford: Clarendon.

Schlosser, E. (1998). The prison industrial complex. *Atlantic Monthly* December: 51–77.

Schmalleger, F. (1999). *Criminal law today.* Upper Saddle River, NJ: Prentice Hall.

Schmalleger, F. (2001). *Criminal justice today,* 6th ed. Upper Saddle River, NJ: Prentice Hall.

Schneider, V., and J. Smykla. (1991). A summary analysis of executions in the United States, 1608–1987: The Espy file. In R. Bohm, ed., *The death penalty in America: Current research.* Cincinnati, OH: Anderson.

Schoenborn, C. A., and B. H. Cohen. (1986). Trends in smoking, alcohol consumption, and other health practices among U.S. adults, 1977 and 1983. Hyattsville, MD: National Center for Health Statistics, U.S. Department of Health and Human Services, No. 118: 1–16.

Sebba, L. (1984). Crime seriousness and criminal intent. *Crime and Delinquency* 30: 227–44.

Seidman, D., and M. Couzens. (1974). Getting the crime rate down: Political pressure and crime reporting. *Law and Society Review* 8: 457–93.

Sennott, C. (2000). The $150 billion "welfare" recipients: U.S. corporations. In R. Lauer and J. Lauer, eds., *Troubled times: Readings in social problems.* Los Angeles: Roxbury.

The Sentencing Project. (1997, 1998). *Facts about prisons and prisoners.* Washington, DC: The Sentencing Project.

The Sentencing Project. (2003). Briefing sheets. Online: www.sentencingproject.org/pubs_02.cfm.

Shapiro, B. (1997). Victims and vengeance: Why the victim's rights amendment is a bad idea. *The Nation* 264: 11–19.

Shapiro, S. (1995). Collaring the crime, not the criminal: Reconsidering the concept of white-collar crime. *American Sociological Review* 55: 346–65.

Shelden, R. (2001). *Controlling the dangerous classes.* Boston: Allyn & Bacon.

Sherizen, S. (1978). Social creation of crime news: All the news that's fitted to print. In C. Winick, ed., *Deviance and the mass media.* Beverly Hills, CA: Sage.

Sherman, L., D. Gottfredson, D. MacKenzie, J. Eck, P. Reuter, and S. Bushway. (1997). *Preventing crime: What works, what doesn't, what's promising.* Washington, DC: U.S. Department of Justice, Office of Justice Programs, National Institute of Justice.

Sherrill, R. (1997). A year in corporate crime. *The Nation,* April 7: 16–17.

Sidel, R. (1996). *Keeping women and children last.* New York: Penguin.

Siegel, L. (1998). *Criminology,* 6th ed. Belmont, CA: Wadsworth.

Sigal, L. (1973). *Reporters and officials: The organization and politics of newsmaking.* London: D. C. Heath.

Signorielli, N. (1990). Television's mean and dangerous world: A continuation of the cultural indicators perspective. In M. Morgan and N. Signorielli, eds., *Cultivation analysis: New directions in media effects research.* Newbury Park, CA: Sage.

Silberman, C. (1978). *Criminal violence, criminal justice.* New York: Random House.

Sileo, C. (1993). Sentencing rules that shackle justice. *Insight* 11.

Simon, D., and D. Eitzen. (1993). *Elite deviance,* 4th ed. Boston: Allyn & Bacon.

Simon, D., and F. Hagan. (1999). *White-collar deviance.* Boston: Allyn & Bacon.

Simon, J. (1994). *Poor discipline: Parole and the social control of the underclass, 1890–1990.* Chicago: University of Chicago Press.

Simpson, D., K. Knight, and C. Pevoto. (1996). *Research summary: Focus on drug treatment in criminal justice settings.* Fort Worth: Texas Christian University Institute of Behavioral Research.

Singh, V. (1991). The underclass in the United States: Some correlates of economic change. *Sociological Inquiry* 61: 505–21.

Skogan, W. (1990). *Disorder and decline.* Berkeley: University of California Press.

Skogan, W. (1995). Crime and the racial fears of white Americans. *Annals of the American Academy of Political and Social Science* 539: 59–71.

Skolnick, J. (1967). Social control in the adversary system. *Journal of Conflict Resolution* 11: 52–70.

Skolnick, J. (1994). Wild pitch. *American Prospect* 17: 31–37.

Smith, D. (1986). The plea bargaining controversy. *Journal of Criminal Law and Criminology* 77: 949.

Smith, P. (1990). *Felony defendants in large urban counties, 1990.* Washington, DC: Bureau of Justice Statistics.

Smith, P. (1993). Private prisons: Profits of crime. *Covert Action Quarterly* 4: 1–6.

Smith, R. (1995). *Racism in the post–civil rights era: Now you see it, now you don't.* Albany: State University of New York Press.

Snell, T. (1997). *Capital punishment 1996. Bureau of Justice Statistics Bulletin* (December). Washington, DC: U.S. Department of Justice.

Son, I., M. Davis, and D. Rome. (1998). Race and its effect on police officers' perceptions of misconduct. *Journal of Criminal Justice* 26(1): 21–28.

Sourcebook of Criminal Justice Statistics (2003). Online: www.albany.edu/sourcebook.

Spelman, W. (2000). The limited importance of prison expansion. In A. Blumstein and J. Wallman, eds., *The crime drop in America.* New York: Cambridge University Press.

Spire, R. (1990). Breaking up the old boy network. *Trial* 26(2): 57–58.

Spitzer, S. (1975). Toward a Marxian theory of deviance. *Social Problems* 22: 638–51.

Spohn, C., and M. Delone. (2001). When does race matter? An analysis of the conditions under which race affects sentence severity. Unpublished paper.

Spohn, C., and D. Halleran, (2002). The effect of imprisonment on recidivism rates of felony offenders: A focus on drug offenders. *Criminology* 40(2): 329–57.

Spohn, C., and D. Hollerman. (2000). The imprisonment penalty paid by young, unemployed, black and Hispanic male offenders. *Criminology* 38(1): 281–306.

Steel, B. S., and M. Steger. (1988). Crime: Due process liberalism versus law and order conservatism. In R. Tantalovich and B. W. Daynes, eds., *Social regulatory policy.* Boulder, CO: Westview Press.

Steele, W. Jr., and E. Thornburg. (1991). Jury instructions: A persistent failure to communicate. *Judicature* 74: 249–54.

Steele, W. Jr., and E. Thornburg. (2000). Jury instructions: A persistent failure to communicate. In G. Mays and P. Gregware, eds., *Courts and justice: A reader,* 2nd ed. Prospect Heights, IL: Waveland Press.

Steffensmeir, D., J. Ulmer, and J. Kramer. (1998). The interaction of race, gender, and age in criminal sentencing: The cost of being young, black, and male. *Criminology* 36: 763–98.

Steiker, C., and J. Steiker. (1998). Judicial developments in capital punishment law. In J. Acker, and C. Lanier, eds., *America's experiment with capital punishment: Reflections on the past, present, and future of the ultimate penal sanction.* Durham, NC: Carolina Academic Press.

Stephen, J. (1883). *Liberty, equality, fraternity.* New York: H. Holt.

Sterling, J. (1983). Retained counsel versus the public defender: The impact of type of counsel on charge bargaining. In W. McDonald, ed., *The defense counsel.* Beverly Hills, CA: Sage.

Stevens, J., and H. Garcia. (1980). *Communicating history.* Newbury Park, CA: Sage.

Stevenson, N. (1995). *Understanding media culture: Social theory and mass communication.* London: Sage.

Stossel, S. (1997). The man who counts the killings. *Atlantic Monthly* 279(5): 86–105.

Streib, G. (2001). Foreword. In L. Nelson and B. Foster, eds., *Death watch.* Upper Saddle River, NJ: Prentice Hall.

Streisand, B. (1994). Can he get a fair trial? *U.S. News & World Report,* October 3: 61–63.

Strinati, D. (1995). *An introduction to theories of popular culture.* London: Routledge.

Stuckey, G., C. Robertson, and H. Wallace. (2001). *Procedures in the justice system,* 6th ed. Upp— River, NJ: Prentice Hall.

Surette, R. (1992). *Media, crime, and criminal justice: Images and realities.* Pacifi—

Surette, R. (1998). *Media, crime, and criminal justice: Images and realitie.* Wadsworth.

Sutherland, E. (1977a). Is "white-collar crime" crime? In G. Geis and R. Meier, — *Offenses in business, politics, and the professions.* New York: Free Press.

Sutherland, E. (1977b). White-collar criminality. In G. Geis and R. Meier, eds., *White-collar crime: Offenses in business, politics, and the professions*. New York: Free Press.

Swezey, R. (1973). Estimating drug crime relationships. *International Journal of the Addictions* 8: 701–21.

Sykes, G. (1958). *The society of captives: A study of a maximum-security prison*. Princeton, NJ: Princeton University Press.

Thernstrom, S., and A. Thernstrom. (1997). *America in black and white: One nation, indivisible*. New York: Simon and Schuster.

Thomas, C. (1993). *Sex discrimination*. St. Paul, MN: West.

Tillman, R. (1987). The size of the "criminal population": The prevalence and incidence of adult arrest. *Criminology* 25: 561–79.

Tillman, R., and H. Pontell. (1992). Is justice "collar-blind"? Punishing Medicaid provider fraud. *Criminology* 30: 547–73.

Tinklenberg, J. R. (1973). Alcohol and violence. In P. G. Bourne, ed., *Alcoholism: Progress in research and treatment*. New York: Academic Press.

Tittle, C., and R. Meier. (1990). Specifying the SES/delinquency relationship. *Criminology* 28: 271–99.

Tonry, M. (1992). Mandatory penalties. In M. Tonry, ed., *Crime and justice: A review of research* (p. 16). Chicago: University of Chicago Press.

Tonry, M. (1995). *Malign neglect: Race, crime and punishment in America*. Oxford: Oxford University Press.

Torrey, E., J. Steiber, J. Ezekiel, S. Wolfe, J. Sharftein, J. Noble, and L. Flynn. (1992). *Criminalizing the seriously mental ill: The abuse of jails as mental hospitals*. Washington, DC: National Alliance for the Mentally Ill and Public Citizens Health Research Group.

Treaster, J. (1990). Is the fight on drugs eroding civil rights? *New York Times*, May 6: A1, A9.

Trebach, A. (1997). *The great drug war*. New York: Macmillan.

Tuchman, G. (1978). *Making news: A study in the social construction of reality*. New York: Free Press.

Tunnell, K. (1992). Film at eleven: Recent developments in the commodification of crime. *Sociological Spectrum* 12: 293–313.

Tuohy, L. (1995). CCLU suit lays bare a public defense system in crisis. *Hartford Courant*, January 8: A1.

Uchida, C., and T. Bynum. (1991). Search warrants, motions to suppress, and "lost cases": The effects of the exclusionary rule in seven jurisdictions. *Journal of Criminal Law and Criminology* 81: 1034.

UCR Handbook. (1999). Online: www.fbi.gov/ucr.htm.

Unah, I., and J. Boger (2001). Race and the death penalty in North Carolina. Online: www.deathpenalty-info.org/article.php?scid=19&did=246.

Unnever, J., and L. Hembroff. (1988). The prediction of racial/ethnic sentencing disparities: An expectation states approach. *Journal of Research in Crime and Delinquency* 25: 53–82.

Uphoff, R. (2000). The criminal defense lawyer: Zealous advocate, double agent, or beleaguered dealer? In G. Mays and P. Gregware, eds., *Courts and justice: A reader*, 2nd ed. Prospect Heights, IL: Waveland Press.

USA Today. (1999). Tragedy in Colorado. Online: www.usatoday.com/news/index/colo/colo000.htm.

U.S. Census Bureau. (2003). Income. Online: www.census.gov/hhes/www/income.html.

U.S. Census. (1998). *Statistical abstract of the United States: 1998*. Washington, DC: U.S. Government Printing Office.

U.S. Census. (1999). Poverty in the United States: 1997. Online: www.census.gov/.

U.S. Department of Education. (1998). *Early warning, timely response: A guide to safe schools*. Washington, DC: U.S. Department of Education.

U.S. Department of Education and U.S. Department of Justice. (1999). Annual report on school safety. Online: www.ed.gov/pubs/edpubs.html.

Department of Health and Human Services. (2000). Drugs. Online: www.samhsa.gov/oas/drugs.cfm.

Department of Justice. (1994, 1997, 1998). Online: www.usdoj.gov.

U.S. Department of Justice. (1996). *National data collection on police use of force*. Washington, DC: U.S. Government Printing Office.

U.S. Department of Justice. (1997, 1998). *Sourcebook of criminal justice statistics*. Washington, DC: U.S. Government Printing Office.

U.S. Department of Justice. (2001). The federal death penalty system: A statistical survey, 1988–2000. Online: www.usdoj.gov/dag/pubdoc/_dp_survey_final.pdf.

U.S. Department of Justice. (2003). Survey of inmates in local jails. Online: www.ojp.usdoj.gov/bjs/correct.htm.

U.S. News & World Report. (2000). The rich get richer: What happens to American society when the gap in wealth and income grows larger? *U.S. News & World Report*, February 21: 40.

Van den Hagg, E. (1997). The death penalty once more. In H. Bedau, ed., *The death penalty in America: Current controversies*. New York: Oxford University Press.

Vandiver, M. (1998). The impact of the death penalty on the families of homicide victims and of condemned prisoners. In J. Acker, R. Bohm, and C. Lanier, eds., *America's experiment with capital punishment: Reflections on the past, present, and future of the ultimate penal sanction*. Durham, NC: Carolina Academic Press.

Van Horn, C., D. Baumer, and W. Gormley, Jr. (1992). *Politics and public policy*. Washington, DC: CQ Press.

van Kesteren, J., Mayhew, P., and P. Nieuwbeerta (2001). Criminal victimisation in seventeen industrialized countries: Key findings from the 2000 International Crime Victims Survey. Online: www.minjust.nl.

Varinsky, H. (1993). Trial consulting: The art and science of selling a case to a jury. *Washington State Bar News* 47: 47–50.

Vila, B. (1997). Motivating and marketing nurturant crime control strategies: Reply to comments. *Politics and the Life Sciences* 16: 48–55.

Virkunnen, M. (1974). Alcohol as a factor precipitating aggression and conflict behavior leading to homicide. *British Journal of the Addictions* 69: 149–54.

Vold, G. (1958). *Theoretical criminology*. New York: Oxford University Press.

Vold, G., T. Bernard, and J. Snipes. (1998). *Theoretical criminology*, 4th ed. Beverly Hills, CA: Sage.

Von Drehle, D. (1988). Bottom line: Life in prison one sixth as expensive. *Miami Herald*, July 10: 12A.

Walker, S. (1998). *Sense and nonsense about crime and drugs: A policy guide*, 4th ed. Belmont, CA: West/Wadsworth.

Walker, S., C. Spohn, and M. Delone. (1996). *The color of justice: Race, ethnicity, and crime in America*. Belmont, CA: Wadsworth.

Walker, S., C. Spohn, and M. Delone. (2000). *The color of justice: Race, ethnicity and crime in America*, 2nd ed. Belmont, CA: Wadsworth.

Waller, I., and N. Okihiro. (1978). *Burglary: The victim and the public*. Toronto: Centre of Criminology, University of Toronto.

Walsh, D. (1980). *Break-ins: Burglary from private houses*. London: Constable.

Walsh, W., and P. Harris. (1999). *Criminal justice policy and planning*. Cincinnati, OH: Anderson.

Warr, M. (1991). What is the perceived seriousness of crime? *Criminology* 27: 795–821.

Washington Post. (1983). January 11: C10.

Weaver, D., and G. Wilhoit. (1986). *The American journalist: A portrait of U.S. news people and their work*. Bloomington: Indiana University Press.

Webb, G., and M. Brown. (1998). United States drug laws and institutionalized discrimination. In E. Jensen and J. Gerber, eds., *The new war on drugs: Symbolic politics and criminal justice policy*. Cincinnati, OH: Anderson.

Weil, A. (1998). Why people take drugs. In J. Inciardi and K. McElrath, eds., *The American drug scene: An anthology*, 2nd ed. Los Angeles: Roxbury.

Weinberger, C. (2000). Race and gender wage gaps. In R. Lauer and J. Lauer, eds., *Troubled times: Readings in social problems*. Los Angeles: Roxbury.

Weinstein, C. (2000). Even dogs confined to cages for long periods of time go berserk. In J. May, ed., *Building violence: How America's rush to incarcerate creates more violence*. Thousand Oaks, CA: Sage.

Weisburd, D., E. Chayet, and E. Waring. (1990). White-collar crime and criminal careers: Some preliminary findings. *Crime and Delinquency* 36: 342–55.

Weisburd, D., and K. Schlegel. (1992). Returning to the mainstream: Reflections on past and future white-collar crime study. In K. Schlegel and D. Weisburd, eds., *White-collar crime reconsidered*. Boston: Northeastern University Press.

Weisman, A. (2000). Mental illness behind bars. In J. May, ed., *Building violence: How America's rush to incarcerate creates more violence*. Thousand Oaks, CA: Sage.

Weitzer, R. (1996). Racial discrimination in the criminal justice system: Findings and problems in the literature. *Journal of Criminal Justice* 24: 313.

Weitzer, R., and S. Tuch. (1999). Race, class, and perceptions of discrimination by the police. *Crime and Delinquency* 45(4): 494–507.

Welch, M. (1999). *Punishment in America: Social control and the ironies of imprisonment*. Thousand Oaks, CA: Sage.

Welch, M., M. Fenwick, and M. Roberts. (1998). State managers, intellectuals, and the media: A content analysis of ideology in experts' quotes in feature newspaper articles on crime. *Justice Quarterly* 15(2): 219–41.

Welsh, W., and P. Harris. (1999). *Criminal justice policy and planning*. Cincinnati, OH: Anderson.

Whitehead, T. (1997). Urban low income African American men, HIV/AIDS, and gender identity. *Medical Anthropologist Quarterly* 11(4): 411–47.

Whitehead, T. (2000). The "epidemic" and "cultural legends" of black male incarceration: The socialization of African American children to a life of incarceration. In J. May, ed., *Building violence: How America's rush to incarcerate creates more violence*. Thousand Oaks, CA: Sage.

Wice, P. (1985). *Chaos in the courthouse: The inner workings of the urban criminal courts*. New York: Praeger.

Wilbanks, W. (1987). *The myth of a racist criminal justice system*. Monterey, CA: Brooks/Cole.

Williams, C. (1991). The federal death penalty for drug-related killings. *Criminal Law Bulletin* 27(5): 387–415.

Williams, J. (2000). The politics of jailing. In J. May, ed., *Building violence: How America's rush to incarcerate creates more violence*. Thousand Oaks, CA: Sage.

Wilson, J. (1975). *Thinking about crime*. New York: Basic Books.

Wilson, J. (1998). Foreword: Never too early. In F. Loeber and D. Farrington, eds., *Serious and violent juvenile offenders*. Thousand Oaks, CA: Sage.

Wilson, W. J. (1987). *The truly disadvantaged: The inner city, the underclass, and public policy*. Chicago: University of Chicago Press.

Winchester, S., and H. Jackson. (1982). *Residential burglary: The limits of prevention*. Home Office Research Study No. 74. London: Her Majesty's Stationery Office.

Wisotsky, S. (1991). Beyond the war on drugs. In J. Inciardi, ed., *The drug legalization debate: Studies in crime, law, and justice*. Newbury Park, CA: Sage.

Wolfgang, M., R. Figlio, and T. Sellin. (1972). *Delinquency in a birth cohort*. Chicago: University of Chicago Press.

Wright, R. (1993). A socially sensitive criminal justice system. In J. Murphy and D. Peck, eds., *Open institutions: The hope for democracy*. Westport, CT: Praeger.

Wright, R., and S. Decker. (1994). *Burglars on the job: Streetlife and residential break-ins*. Boston: Northeastern University Press.

Wrobleski, H., and K. Hess. (2000). *An introduction: Law enforcement and criminal justice*. Belmont, CA: Wadsworth.

Zehr, H., and M. Umbreit. (1982). Victim offender reconciliation: An incarceration substitute. *Federal Probation* 46(1): 3–68.

Zerbisias, A. (2003). Hawks turned media into parrots. Online: www.globalpolicy.org/security/issues/iraq/media/2003/0612censorship.htm.

Zimmer, L., and J. Morgan. (1997). *Marijuana myths, marijuana facts: A review of the scientific evidence.* New York: Lindesmith Center.

Zimring, F., and G. Hawkins. (1986). *Capital punishment and the American agenda.* New York: Cambridge University Press.

Zimring, F., and G. Hawkins. (1997). *Crime is not the problem: Lethal violence in America.* New York: Oxford University Press.

Zuckerman, M. (1994). The limits of the TV lens. *U.S. News & World Report,* July 25: 64.

INDEX

References to figures are indicated by f, tables by t.